Campaigns and Elections

FOURTH EDITION

Campaigns and Elections
Rules, Reality, Strategy, Choice

FOURTH EDITION

John Sides
VANDERBILT UNIVERSITY

Daron Shaw
UNIVERSITY OF TEXAS, AUSTIN

Matt Grossmann
MICHIGAN STATE UNIVERSITY

Keena Lipsitz
QUEENS COLLEGE, CITY UNIVERSITY OF NEW YORK

W. W. NORTON & COMPANY

Independent Publishers Since 1923

Editor: Peter Lesser
Associate Editor: Anna Olcott
Project Editor: Kurt Wildermuth
Editorial Assistant: Tichina Sewell-Richards
Managing Editor, College: Marian Johnson
Managing Editor, College Digital Media: Kim Yi
Senior Production Manager, College: Sean Mintus
Media Editor: Spencer Richardson-Jones
Media Associate Editor: Lexi Malakhoff
Media Editorial Assistant: Quinn Campbell
Marketing Manager, Political Science: Ashley Sherwood
Design Director: Rubina Yeh
Designer: Lissi Sigillo
Photo Editor: Stephanie Romeo
Director of College Permissions: Megan Schindel
Permissions Associate: Patricia Wong
Composition: Westchester Publishing Services
Manufacturing: Lakeside Book Company

Permission to use copyrighted material is included on page C-1.

ISBN 978-0-393-44168-0 (pbk.)

W. W. Norton & Company, Inc., 500 Fifth Avenue, New York, NY 10110
www.wwnorton.com
W. W. Norton & Company, Ltd., Castle House, 15 Carlisle Street, London W1D 3BS

1 2 3 4 5 6 7 8 9 0

Contents

4
Financing Campaigns 94

5
Modern Campaign Strategies 128

6
Political Parties 162

7

Interest Groups

8

Media

9

Presidential Campaigns

10

Congressional Campaigns   278

11

State and Local Campaigns   302

12

Voter Participation   328

13

Voter Choice   360

Preface

This book aims to present a comprehensive treatment of campaigns and elections in the United States. It is structured around four key components: the *rules* that govern the electoral process; the *reality* that candidates confront when a campaign begins; the *strategies* employed by important campaign actors, including candidates, parties, interest groups, and the media; and the *choices* made by voters, which are themselves a response to the rules, reality, and strategies.

The rules that govern the electoral process include institutions such as the electoral college as well as the laws that govern redistricting, voter registration, and campaign finance. The reality that parties and candidates confront consists, in part, of current events, the state of the economy, the presence of an incumbent in the race, and the partisan leaning of constituents. The importance of rules and reality is augmented by the fact that candidates cannot easily change them. Instead, these factors structure candidate strategy in important ways. The strategic choices made by candidates include familiar elements of modern campaigns, such as message development, television advertising, fundraising, and voter mobilization. These choices combine with rules and reality to create the "outputs" of campaigns that are manifest to voters. The response of voters to these outputs helps answer the broader question, Do campaigns affect voters? We contend that any good answer to that question is a version of "it depends," and we devote significant attention to what magnifies or diminishes the effects of campaigns.

Throughout the book, we also draw attention to the *democratic functions* of campaigns. We discuss debates about the roles that campaigns should play in our democracy and consider how well contemporary campaigns achieve democratic goals. We focus on four standards. The first, free choice, means that citizens can participate free of coercion or manipulation. The second, political equality, means that laws cannot disadvantage certain groups of citizens—as, for example, Jim Crow laws disadvantaged southern Black people before the civil rights era. The third, deliberation, refers to the quality of the information that citizens receive from the candidates, the media, and other political actors. Is it sufficient to ensure that citizens can make an informed choice? The fourth standard, free speech, refers to the constitutional protections that affect whether and how the government might regulate political campaigns. Could the government require, for example, that opposing candidates spend identical amounts of money so that neither candidate dominates the airwaves? In discussing such debates, we do not promote any one viewpoint but instead seek to describe how these values can inform both why campaigns are the way they are and whether we should attempt to reform them. We emphasize the difficulty of meeting all of these standards simultaneously. Making campaigns "better" by one standard may make them "worse" by another.

This book aims to be comprehensive. We discuss national and state electoral rules and realities and cover campaigns at all levels of office, including presidential, congressional, state, and local. Doing so illuminates both similarities and differences. Although candidates at all levels of office have the same basic goal—to craft a compelling message and thereby win elections—they do so with vastly different levels of resources and thus with different kinds of campaign strategies. A presidential campaign spends more on catering in a week than many local campaigns spend in total.

This book builds on the work of political scientists, who use systematic data and careful research to study the factors that influence campaigns and elections. We also draw on the work of political theorists, who debate the democratic functions of political campaigns. Ultimately, we hope to provide a thorough and rigorous account of the origins and impact of electoral rules, political realities, and campaign strategies as well as the merits and demerits of the American electoral system.

Finally, we hope that the book engages readers as citizens. Most Americans experience political campaigns primarily as spectators and profess to dislike what they see. Thus, we want to help readers think critically about two things: what campaigns actually do and what campaigns should do. The former entails identifying when, how, and for whom campaigns matter. With this knowledge, readers will have a more sophisticated view of campaign effects—one that does not attribute great significance to every twist and turn but does not rule out influence entirely. The question of what campaigns should do is meant to engage readers in a broader conversation about the ideals that underpin the electoral process and whether the process can be reformed to better approximate those ideals.

Revisions to the Fourth Edition

Highlights of the new edition:

- All chapters cover and contextualize the 2020 campaigns and election results, particularly Chapters 2 (The American Electoral Process), 5 (Modern Campaign Strategies), 6 (Political Parties), 7 (Interest Groups), 8 (Media), 9 (Presidential Campaigns) and 10 (Congressional Campaigns).

- Revisions to Chapters 2 (The American Electoral Process) and 4 (Financing Campaigns) capture important debates about the rules of American elections, including issues that came to the fore in 2020, such as mail balloting.

- Chapters 8 (Media), 10 (Congressional Campaigns), and 11 (State and Local Campaigns) have been revised to emphasize the increasing nationalization of American campaigns.

- Chapters 5 (Modern Campaign Strategies) and 8 (Media) analyze how technology and news media—particularly social media—affect voters' consumption of information about candidates and their eventual decisions at the ballot box.

- Numerous chapters have been reoriented to place more emphasis on how affective polarization and negative partisanship affect candidate strategies, including Chapter 6 (Political Parties), Chapter 12 (Voter Participation), and Chapter 13 (Voter Choice).

- New and timely anecdotes introduce chapters throughout the book, including the campaign strategies used by both presidential candidates in 2020 in Chapter 5 (Modern Campaign Strategies), the 2018 midterm elections in Chapter 10 (Congressional Campaigns), and the state and local races of 2019 and 2020 in Chapter 11 (State and Local Campaigns).

Resources to Accompany this Book

The following resources, developed specifically to accompany this book, are available to students and instructors:

- **Chapter outlines** provide an overview of each chapter.
- **Flashcards** help students review the key terms from each chapter.

- **PowerPoint slides** of all figures and tables from the text. These are also provided in JPEG format.
- A comprehensive **test bank**, with multiple choice and short answer questions for every chapter. Test bank questions are searchable by topic, difficulty, and Bloom's taxonomy level.
- **Activity modules**, with detailed instructions for in-class and out-of-class assignments, as well as materials for these activities. These modules allow students to apply what they have learned in the text as they work through hands-on simulations of several aspects of campaigns.

Acknowledgments

We are grateful to those who have assisted us in writing this book. Many scholars read portions of the book at various stages: Scott Adler, Brian Arbour, Suzanne Chod, David Dulio, Philip Habel, Danny Hayes, Valerie Hyman, Phil Jones, Ray LaRaja, Mingus Mapps, Seth Masket, Jennifer Merolla, Nate Persily, Andrew Reeves, Travis Ridout, Joe Romance, Wayne Steger, Jessica Trounstine, Chris Warshaw, and Jonathan Winburn. Special thanks to Ken Moffett, who authors the test bank that accompanies *Campaigns and Elections*.

For their thoughtful feedback, we thank:

Jennifer Anderson, University of Louisville

Jeffrey L. Bernstein, Eastern Michigan University

Jamie L. Carson, University of Georgia

Anthony Corrado, Colby College

Bernard Fraga, Emory University

Peter L. Francia, East Carolina University

Michael Franz, Bowdoin College

John Gastil, Pennsylvania State University

Howard Gold, Smith College

Craig Goodman, University of Houston-Victoria

Susan Grogan, St. Mary's College of Maryland

Matt Guardino, Providence College

Michael G. Hagen, Temple University

Eitan Hersh, Tufts University

Marc Hetherington, Vanderbilt University

Benjamin Highton, University of California, Davis

Sunshine Hillygus, Duke University

Jack Johannes, Villanova University

Tyler Johnson, University of Oklahoma

Cindy D. Kam, Vanderbilt University

Yanna Krupnikov, Stony Brook University

Christina Ladam, University of Nevada, Reno

Danielle Martin, California State University, Sacramento

Seth Masket, University of Denver

Seth McKee, Texas Tech University

Kenneth M. Miller, University of Nevada, Las Vegas

Hans Noel, Georgetown University

Christopher Ojeda, University of Tennessee

Kathryn Pearson, University of Minnesota

Markus Prior, Princeton University

Priscilla Southwell, University of Oregon

Michael Tesler, University of California, Irvine

Emily Thorson, Syracuse University

Nicholas Valentino, University of Michigan

Bertha G. Vitela, University of Louisiana at Lafayette

Kenneth F. Warren, Saint Louis University

Jennifer Wolak, University of Colorado

We thank W. W. Norton for supporting and nurturing this project—including our editor, Pete Lesser, for his expert guidance and feedback; associate editor Anna Olcott; editorial assistant Tichina Sewell-Richards; media editor Spencer Richardson-Jones; project editor Kurt Wildermuth; copy editor Samantha Held; and production manager Sean Mintus.

John Sides

Daron Shaw

Matt Grossmann

Keena Lipsitz

1

—

Introduction

On January 21, 2020, the Centers for Disease Control announced the first confirmed case of the 2019 novel coronavirus in the United States. As the outbreak became a global pandemic, the world saw millions of infections and deaths from COVID-19, the respiratory disease caused by the virus. The pandemic upended many aspects of life in the United States—overwhelming hospitals, closing schools and businesses, and keeping people isolated from friends and family.

The pandemic also upended the campaigns and elections scheduled for 2020. For one, it changed how and how much candidates campaigned. Typically, candidates for all levels of office would have been out giving speeches, holding rallies, and talking to voters throughout the year. Their staff and volunteers would have been knocking on doors to persuade voters or remind them to vote. Much of this activity was canceled. The Democratic presidential nominee, Joe Biden, largely stayed in his home for months, holding meetings via teleconference and recording remarks and speeches. His public activity, when it did occur, was highly circumscribed. Biden's opponent, President Donald Trump, scaled back his own campaign activity, although by June he had resumed holding rallies despite the risks associated with large gatherings. The pandemic affected the presidential campaign even more directly when Trump contracted the virus in October as part of a larger outbreak among White House staff and officials. On October 2, Trump was even hospitalized after he had trouble breathing. Ultimately, about 10 days passed before Trump returned to public events—a long interlude at a time when candidates are usually campaigning nonstop.

The pandemic also altered the election-year agenda and thus the messages of the candidates. Trump had planned to campaign on the economic growth that had occurred during his first three years as president, but the pandemic led to a sharp recession in the spring of 2020 and only a partial recovery thereafter. Biden thus gained a new angle of attack, zeroing in on Trump's handling of the pandemic and its consequences for Americans' lives and livelihoods.

Meanwhile, state and local officials faced the challenge of administering elections during the pandemic. A typical Election Day—where most voters line up at local polling places—was seen as risky given the threat of infection, but there was no consensus on an alternative. Voting in 2020 thus became another chapter in the ongoing partisan battle over how Americans vote. Democrats pushed to expand voting options, particularly by enabling voters to request mail ballots that they could fill in at home and then mail back or drop off. Many Republican leaders, including Trump, opposed such

Core of the Analysis

Focusing on four aspects of campaigns—rules, reality, strategy, and citizens' choices—helps us understand American elections and to what extent they reflect democratic values:

- The *rules* refer to laws and constitutional doctrines that govern the electoral system and affect how campaigns are carried out and ultimately who wins elections.

- Broader economic and political *realities* shape the tenor of public opinion and often place limits on how much campaigns can affect opinion.

- The *strategies* employed by candidates, political parties, interest groups, and the media reflect their unique interests and agendas. They affect one another and the campaigns that voters see.

- The *choices made by citizens*—whether and how to vote—depend on a mix of long-standing habits, current realities, and new information from campaigns.

- The *democratic values* of free choice, political equality, deliberation, and free speech help us determine how well campaigns meet important standards.

measures. As a result, Republican voters were more likely than Democrats to vote in person on Election Day, and Democrats were more likely than Republicans to vote early or vote by mail.

In turn, this system complicated the process of quickly counting votes and declaring a winner. In some key battleground states, ballots cast on Election Day could be counted before mail ballots because state rules did not allow the additional certification process for mail ballots to begin until Election Day. Because mail ballots were disproportionately cast by Democratic voters, the initial vote count overstated the Republican advantage. In the presidential race, this meant that the count increasingly favored Biden as mail ballots were counted. But this took time. Biden's victory in Pennsylvania, and with it his victory in the presidential race, was not declared until four days after Election Day.

Once it became clear that Biden had won, this complicated vote-counting process only fueled the objections of Trump and his allies. Trump had long claimed that he would lose the election only if it were "rigged," and his team filed dozens of unsuccessful legal actions in an attempt to contest various election procedures. Trump personally pressured state election officials to "find" votes for him as well. This effort culminated in a rally in Washington, D.C., on January 6, 2021—the day that Congress was set to officially certify the election results—where Trump told supporters that his election victory was being stolen. Afterward, some 800 attendees illegally entered the U.S. Capitol, forcing a stop to the certification process. One protester was shot and killed inside the Capitol. After the building was finally cleared that afternoon, Congress reconvened that evening. Ultimately, eight Republican senators and 139 Republican representatives voted to object to the certification of some states' election results. But that was not enough, and the election was over. Joe Biden was inaugurated on January 20, 2021.

The pandemic and tragic aftermath of the 2020 election were extraordinary in many ways. The United States certainly fell well short of a peaceful transfer of power, which is a traditional standard for any functioning democracy. But in other respects, the events of 2020 fit with preexisting trends and patterns. Partisanship shaped the campaign and election results. Presidential vote tallies in states and counties were strongly correlated with the outcome of the previous presidential election in 2016. Partisanship also meant that states or districts that voted for one party's candidate for president tended to elect candidates of that same party in other races, like those for seats in the U.S. Senate or House of Representatives. The partisan divisions over election procedures also reflected long-standing battles about who should be eligible to vote, how people should be able to vote, how to

Why was Joe Biden able to accomplish the relatively rare defeat of an incumbent president? Did smart campaigning give him the edge? Or were factors like the COVID-19 pandemic more important than campaign strategy?

count votes fairly, and how to determine a winner. These battles have long intersected with some of the country's biggest challenges, particularly the struggle to ensure voting rights for racial and ethnic groups.

Despite important progress, conflicts over voting rules have intensified as the power divide between Democrats and Republicans has narrowed. The outcomes of presidential elections hinge on voters in a handful of closely contested states. In Congress, both political parties have what political scientist Frances Lee has called "insecure majorities." As a result, federal elections often change the party that controls the White House, House, Senate, or some combination.[1]

Indeed, in recent years elections have routinely produced dramatic shifts in party power and upended the ambitions of the incumbent party. In 2004, Republican George W. Bush was elected to a second term as president, and the Republican Party retained control of both the Senate and House. Republican euphoria, however, proved short-lived. Two years later, Democrats took back control of the House and Senate in the 2006 midterm elections. This was not unusual: unless the president is especially popular, the president's party typically loses congressional seats in midterm years. In 2002, for example, Bush enjoyed high approval ratings because so many Americans rallied to his side after the terrorist attacks of September 11, 2001, and Republicans actually picked up seats in the House and Senate. But by 2006, with the Iraq War dragging on, Bush's sliding popularity helped the Democrats win control of both chambers for the first time since 1994.

In 2008, Democrat Barack Obama won the presidency amid a painful economic recession—a victory all the more noteworthy because he became the first African American to hold the office. Obama and congressional Democrats moved swiftly despite nearly unanimous Republican opposition to pass an economic stimulus package, a climate change bill in the House, and, most notably, health care reform in March 2010. But in the 2010 midterm elections, the Democrats lost six seats in the Senate and a whopping 63 seats in the House—the largest loss in the House for the president's party since 1938.

In the 2012 presidential election, Obama beat Republican presidential challenger Mitt Romney, but Republicans retained control of the House, thereby complicating Obama's ability to pursue his second-term agenda. In 2014, Republicans expanded their House majority and won a Senate majority as well.

In 2016, Democrat Hillary Clinton seemed destined to succeed Obama as president and to carry on his legacy. But ultimately, Democrats experienced bitter disappointment when Donald Trump won a narrow electoral college majority (even as he lost the national popular vote), and Republicans retained control of the House and Senate. In 2018, however, it was Republicans' turn to discover how hard it is to build a permanent majority. Although Republicans expanded their narrow Senate majority by two seats, Democrats picked up 40 seats in the U.S. House, giving them the power to stymie Trump's agenda, investigate his administration, and impeach him twice.

Finally, in 2020, Biden's victory brought yet another change in power to the White House. Although the Senate seats were split 50-50 between Democrats and Republicans, the Democrats gained a very narrow majority, with Vice President Kamala Harris able to break ties in their favor. Democrats lost seats in the House, however, making their majority even more insecure.

These frequent transfers of power between the Democratic and Republican parties have been the norm in presidential elections for the past 70 years and in congressional elections for about 30 years. These shifts might seem to suggest that most voters regularly swing back and forth between the two political parties, but the party in power can change even if only a small group of voters switches sides or if a different subset of citizens decides to vote in each election. This points toward one of the central questions of this book: *What explains the outcomes of American elections—presidential, congressional, and state and local?* To address this question, we must consider others: Why do some candidates choose to run and others do not? Why do some candidates win and others lose? How do electoral rules and the broader political and economic context shape the decisions of both candidates and voters? There are many ways to interpret elections, but political science research builds evidence for firmer answers.

An obvious explanation for election outcomes could be campaigns themselves. A political campaign combines elements of two other, nonpolitical types of campaigns. In some ways, it is like a military campaign, with the goal of winning a contest and vanquishing an opponent. It is also like an advertising campaign, with the goal of persuading citizens to buy a product. One might think that political campaigns are always consequential, with millions of dollars being spent, professional strategists scheming, advertisements blanketing the airwaves, and armies of volunteers pounding the pavement. But this is not necessarily so. Democratic and Republican voters have become increasingly polarized, with differing views on political figures and public policies. It is difficult to persuade much of the electorate to support a side they do not already favor. Hence the second central question of this book: *How much does the campaign itself matter?*

Answering that question means examining campaigns alongside broader trends that may also affect voter decision-making. For example, when voters do change their minds in an election, they are often responding to the overall state of the country, which even brilliant campaigning cannot change. Thus, any campaign's impact, however meaningful, could prove secondary to that of other events. For example, what was more important for Obama's victory in 2008: the $730 million that he spent campaigning or the fact that the economy was in a recession? And what was more important for Obama in 2012: the $1.1 billion that he and his allies spent or the fact that the economy had actually turned around on his watch? Moreover, in both 2016 and 2020, Trump was outspent by his opponents, but one of them won (Biden) and one did not (Clinton). Why? One possibility is that in 2020 Trump was the **incumbent** (the candidate currently holding office) seeking reelection amid a pandemic and economic downturn.

In addressing what explains the outcomes of campaigns and how much campaigns actually matter, we draw on the important research done by political scientists and other scholars who study campaigns and elections. This research seeks to go beyond anecdote and personal experience to estimate the impact of various factors on election outcomes as well as the impact of political campaigns on voters. To do this research, political scientists draw on different types of data, such as historical data on election outcomes, voter registration and turnout data maintained by states, surveys of voters, information about electoral laws, and reports of campaign donations and spending. They use various research strategies to identify, to the best of their ability, actual causes and effects. This helps provide concrete and reliable answers to the many questions that flow from the central questions of this book. For example, if a state tries to make voting more convenient, how much does that increase turnout? If states use taxpayer dollars to help candidates run for office and reduce the demands of fundraising, does that actually diminish the traditional advantages of incumbent officeholders? To what degree do local election outcomes depend on unique features of local communities as opposed to the broader features of national politics? And at the end of the day, how much does the money spent on U.S. elections really "buy"? How many voters are influenced?

Finally, we will offer an answer to the third central question of this book: *How should we evaluate the American electoral process?* One complaint is that American campaigns are just too expensive and that incessant fundraising distracts and possibly corrupts politicians. People wonder whether the system allows the best candidates to emerge. They question whether campaigns are fair, informative, truthful, and engaging. They worry that citizens fail to learn what they need to know in order to make political decisions or that constant mudslinging alienates citizens and leads them to stay home on Election Day. Others are concerned that the rules governing both campaigns and elections are adopted by parties to benefit themselves. It is important to think through these complaints analytically—to ask, for example, whether negative campaigning really turns citizens off or whether requiring photo identification really prevents some people from voting. But it is also important to think critically about what elections and campaigns *should* be like. Evaluating this question will help us understand not only how much campaigns affect citizens but also how much they help or hurt our democracy.

A Framework for Understanding Campaigns and Elections

In this book, we use a simple framework to understand American **campaigns** and **elections** that emphasizes four things. First, we consider the *rules* that govern elections, which influence who runs, how campaigns operate, who votes, and who wins. Second is the broader *reality*—economic, political, and historical—that parties and candidates confront, which profoundly affects whether they decide to run and how they campaign. Third are the *strategic choices* that various actors—including candidates, the media, political parties, and interest groups—make; these actors constrain one another and shape the campaigns that voters see. Finally, the *choices of citizens* ultimately decide the outcomes.

The goal of this framework is to identify the major features of the American electoral system that influence the actual outcomes of elections—who wins and who loses. We will also see how the elements of the framework depend on each other. For example, the strategic choices of candidates depend on both the electoral rules and the broader reality that candidates must face. Similarly, the choices of citizens, especially in the voting booth, may depend on rules and reality but also on the strategies of candidates, parties, the media, and others, all of whom broadcast information that may influence citizens' feelings about the candidates.

Rules

The prolonged debate about how to conduct the 2020 election during the COVID-19 pandemic touched a variety of electoral rules. Many of these rules were the kind of arcane stuff that rarely makes the headlines. As part of the broader discussion about how to facilitate early voting or voting by mail, there were arguments about whether voters should be able to deposit ballots at designated drop boxes, and, if so, how many drop boxes there should be. There were debates about whether election authorities should be able to begin processing mail ballots ahead of Election Day in order to mitigate potential delays in vote counting. There were debates about which mail ballots to count that involved the postmarked dates on ballots, voters' signatures on ballots, and a host of other details.

The 2020 election showed how rules affect every aspect of American elections: who is qualified to run for office, when elections are held and thus when campaigns begin, the size and characteristics of constituencies, how much money can be donated and spent, who is eligible to vote, and, ultimately, who wins. All of the actors involved in elections—citizens, candidates, parties, interest groups, the media—find themselves subject to rules. For example, 16-year-olds cannot vote, and 30-year-olds cannot be president. Candidates and parties cannot accept unlimited amounts of money from any one wealthy donor. Interest groups cannot coordinate their campaign spending with the candidates it would benefit. Television stations cannot sell advertising time to one candidate but refuse to sell time to that candidate's opponent.

The rules of elections are important because, in many cases, they cannot be changed easily. Changing a rule may require legislation, a U.S. Supreme Court decision, or even a constitutional amendment. Moreover, except in unusual circumstances like the pandemic, rule changes typically do not occur in the middle of the campaign itself. Thus, as the campaign gets underway, the rules constitute a hand that all the candidates are dealt and thereby constrain candidate strategy in important ways. Consider some of the basic rules about campaign finance. Existing laws limit the amount of money that any individual can donate but do not limit the amount a candidate can spend of their own money. The former means that candidates must devote a lot of time to fundraising as they try to amass campaign funds from many individual donors. The latter means that some wealthy people will be tempted to run for office and finance their own campaigns. For instance, about 20 percent of the money spent by Trump's 2016 campaign came from Trump himself. The challenges of financing a campaign under the existing rules also seem to discourage potential female candidates. In a survey of women and men in professions that frequently lead to political careers, such as law and business, women were less likely than men to say that they had contemplated running for office, and many women cited the challenges of raising money as a dissuading factor.[2]

Reality

The context in which an election occurs—what we call "reality"—also strongly affects a candidate's success or failure. In 2020, for example, as the pandemic dragged on and the death toll mounted, most Americans came to disapprove of how Trump was handling the crisis. This may have hurt Trump's chances because voters tend to blame the incumbent president when things in the country are not going well.

Trump's experience illustrates the importance of the broader reality that candidates face. Here, "reality" refers to several factors in particular: the candidates' biographies, the records of the political parties, and recent and current political and economic events, such as a war, pandemic, or recession. These elements of the broader context are similar in one crucial respect: they are not fully under the control of the candidates themselves. Although critics accused the Trump administration of mismanaging the government's response to the pandemic, the sheer emergence of COVID-19 was not Trump's or any other politician's fault. Moreover, in the American political system, which divides authority among national, state, and local governments, responding to the pandemic was not just the responsibility of the president. It also required coordination and decision-making among many different political leaders. Ultimately, the things that candidates can control, such as their campaign strategy, may not overcome the effects of events that conspire against them.

Reality also involves the backgrounds of the candidates themselves: their identities, such as their gender or race; their personal lives; and their professional lives, including prior service in elected office. Candidates cannot easily change certain identities or rewrite their biographies from scratch. What they have done or said in the past, both good and bad, will follow them. Candidates try to capitalize on the best aspects of their biography, such as a happy family, service to their community or country, and support for popular policies. Opponents will emphasize the worst aspects, such as lies, unpopular actions, and scandals.

Another component of reality is current or recent events that are connected to government policies and the formal powers of political office. For example, foreign policy crises and wars are particularly important for the electoral prospects of presidents and presidential candidates. The long, costly Vietnam War certainly affected Lyndon Johnson, who decided not to run for reelection in 1968. The terrorist attacks of September 11, 2001, produced a surge of support for President George W. Bush and helped the Republican Party pick up seats in the 2002 midterms. Both the attacks and the Iraq War also loomed large in the 2004 election, both Bush and his opponent, Senator John Kerry, focused on war and national security issues. To be sure, foreign affairs and war may not be completely outside politicians' control, but elected leaders often confront the unexpected abroad. The same is true for other elected officials in other policy areas.

The economy is another important component of reality. Just as the public tends to prefer peace to war, it prefers prosperity to poverty. The public holds incumbent officeholders, particularly the president, at least somewhat responsible for economic conditions, and incumbents presiding over a robust economy will typically win a larger share of the vote than will those presiding over a weak economy. As with foreign affairs and war, elected officials often have some influence on the economy. In March 2020, for example, as the pandemic began to spread and schools and businesses were forced to close en masse, Congress passed and President Trump signed a large bill intended to stimulate the economy and provide government support to unemployed Americans. These types of measures can be important, but they can be less effective than politicians and the public would like. In general, the ups and downs of the economy depend on many factors outside any politician's control.

A final component of reality involves political parties. Their identities have deep historical roots and thus matter for any candidate affiliated with a party. For example, Democratic and Republican parties have each developed reputations for giving attention to specific key issues as well as for holding particular positions on those issues.[3] The Democratic Party has traditionally favored government action to help people. The Republican Party has favored lowering taxes, partly in an effort to shrink the size of government. Over time, differences on policy have increased as the parties have polarized, making it difficult for a conservative Democrat or a liberal Republican to find a comfortable home in either party. It also means that citizens often have firm views of the parties and interpret events through their partisan perspective. Democrats tend to judge the economy more negatively than Republicans do when a Republican is president, for example. And many elections are held in places that overwhelmingly support one party, so even a highly qualified candidate from the other party cannot overcome their party's reputation in the area.

The parties have also developed coalitions of supporters from different groups in society. The Democratic Party's early commitment to civil rights, despite the resistance of southern Democrats, earned it the lasting loyalty of most African Americans. The Republican Party's conservative positions on social issues, such as abortion and equal rights for gay people, have earned it the support of most evangelical Christians. Candidates must appeal to the core groups within their party's coalition and may find it difficult to make inroads with groups that have not traditionally supported their party.

Moreover, as the two parties' platforms and coalitions have grown more different, candidates within a party find that their electoral fortunes increasingly depend on the party's standing or "brand." In particular, candidates of the president's party find that their fortunes are tied to the president's, making it harder for candidates to use their own individual biographies or connections to their district or state to appeal to voters. Today's partisan elections are less about local politics and more about national issues and debates. In other words, elections are becoming "nationalized."

Taken together, these elements of reality affect candidate strategies, the decisions of citizens, and, ultimately, election outcomes. It is therefore difficult to credit candidates or campaign strategy for every victory and blame them for every defeat. Incumbent candidates running during a time of peace and prosperity may win easily even if their campaigns are full of strategic miscalculations. These same candidates running in the face of an unpopular war and a weak economy may lose, no matter the brilliance of their campaign strategy.

Strategy

Although the impacts of rules and reality can constrain the effects of campaign strategy, campaign strategies can and do matter. As we will discuss in later chapters, rigorous studies have shown that campaigns can use certain tactics to increase voter turnout and persuade voters to support a candidate. These tactics do not always create sea changes in voter behavior or necessarily affect the overall outcome of the election, especially in lopsided races. But parties and interest groups know that, and they concentrate resources in races expected to be close. Tactics can make the difference in these closely contested races—and party control of the government may depend on the outcomes.

Campaigns involve a variety of actors. Most visible are the candidates themselves. Their strategic choices involve every facet of a campaign: whether to run in the first place, what issues to emphasize, what specific messages or themes to discuss, which kinds of media to use, and which citizens to target. Candidates' personal campaign organizations, sometimes with paid

Most campaigns aim to mobilize voters as part of their strategy. In 2020, the pandemic restricted many in-person campaign activities, though both the Trump and Biden campaigns used canvassing to gin up votes in key states like Pennslyvania in the final days before the election.

professionals on board, create much of the visible campaign activity, from yard signs and bumper stickers to television ads and YouTube videos. Political parties also make decisions about messages and targeting as they deploy resources on behalf of their candidates, including ads, voter registration drives, and get-out-the-vote operations on Election Day. The same is true of interest groups, which raise and spend money in support of favored candidates. The news media are also crucial throughout the campaign. Although candidates can communicate directly with citizens through advertising, social media, email, and postal mail, many citizens receive information from news media outlets. Thus, the news media's coverage constitutes the campaign that many voters see.

All of these actors are in part following their own strategies and in part responding to the strategies of others. Candidates routinely try to "stay on message" but can be sidetracked by responding to their opponents' claims. Parties and interest groups often structure their campaign activity to complement that of their favored candidates, but at times the strategies of candidates, parties, and interest groups diverge. Interest groups, for example, are more likely than candidates to air negative advertisements.[4] The media depend on political parties, interest groups, and especially candidates to make news, but they impose their own definitions of newsworthiness. And these actors have goals beyond just influencing elections: the media want viewers, interest groups want to focus on the issues they care most about, and parties want to keep their broad coalition together. The media's agenda, for instance, often clashes with candidates' agendas, as news media frequently talk about issues that neither candidate wants to highlight.[5] This is one reason candidates criticize the media coverage they receive.

Campaign strategy is the element of elections that candidates and other actors can control. They may not be able to end a war or boost the economy, but they can craft a slogan, produce a television advertisement, give a speech, and kiss a lot of babies at campaign rallies. Much money is spent doing these things. The ultimate question is how much difference it makes.

Citizens' Choices

In any democratic political system, an election's outcome depends on the people. Eligible American citizens have two choices to make in an election: *whether* to vote and *how* to vote. Rules and reality affect these choices. Campaign strategists aim to influence these choices as well by convincing people to support a particular candidate and encouraging supporters to vote on

Election Day. The central question is, How much are citizens affected by all of these things?

Citizens are not blank slates. They have preexisting political habits that affect how likely they are to turn out and vote. Habits may put limits on the effects of electoral rules, for example. Not every rule change that is intended to facilitate voter turnout may actually increase turnout very much, especially if there are not many voters whose decision to vote depends on the particular rule that changed. For example, early research suggests that states that tried to facilitate absentee voting during the COVID-19 pandemic did not actually see higher rates of turnout in the 2020 election than states who did not try to facilitate absentee voting.[6] Many more people turned out overall, but that was true in both groups of states.

Citizens also have preexisting political identities and values that affect whether they vote for Democratic or Republican candidates. Indeed, as the parties have become more polarized, those identities and values have become more important, and party loyalty has increased. This limits what a campaign can accomplish, no matter how much money candidates spend or how catchy and engaging their advertisements are. Moreover, at a time when citizens have many entertainment media choices to consume in lieu of political news, campaigns can struggle simply to command the public's attention. Some people do not follow politics closely and are not interested in watching the news, candidate debates, or political advertisements. Simply put, many votes are not up for grabs, and those that are may not easily be won with the tools of modern campaigns. Indeed, undecided citizens may respond more to "reality" than to campaign messages.

Evaluating Campaigns and Elections

Thinking about rules, reality, strategy, and citizen choice helps illuminate what actually happens in campaigns and elections. The next question is, What *should* happen? Here, "should happen" does not mean "my candidate should win." Rather, the question is, What is good for the democratic political system in which we live?

In democratic systems, campaigns and elections are crucial processes. During election season, citizens typically pay the most attention to politics, and leaders are able to achieve a level of interaction with citizens that they can rarely attain at other times. Thus, a lot is at stake in getting this process "right." Yet changes to the electoral system are too often enacted to benefit one party over the other. Elected officials who make the rules that govern their own elections are usually motivated by self-interest rather than democratic values. Moreover, they often make these changes without a full understanding of their consequences.

Thinking about the consequences of electoral reform means answering questions like: Should the United States continue to use the electoral college? Should voters be able to cast mail ballots? Should independent commissions oversee the process of drawing district boundaries for the U.S. House and state legislatures? To answer these questions, people need to understand the potential effects of reforms—this is where political science research comes in—and they need to think hard about whether such reforms bolster or undermine the key political values that undergird the U.S. political system.

In this section, we introduce four values that can guide analysis of election reform proposals, and we will refer to these values in later chapters (see Table 1.1). Together these four values may not capture every conceivable value that is important to campaigns and elections, but they do represent a starting point. What they require of campaigns and elections sometimes conflicts, however. Thus, improving these political processes may require making difficult trade-offs among values.

Free Choice

In a representative democracy, such as the United States, elections allow citizens to choose who will represent them in government. By definition, a choice involves selecting one of a number of alternatives. This means that voters must be allowed to choose between at least two parties or candidates for any given elected office. If an election is uncontested, voters have no real choice. This scenario may seem far-fetched, but it is actually quite common in the United States. For example, **primary elections**—in which voters choose the nominees in each party who will go on to compete in the general election—are often uncompetitive. In the 2020 election, only 58 percent of U.S. House primary elections featured at least two candidates.[7] Even if this minimal requirement of contestation has been met, free choice is not guaranteed. Political scientists have long recognized the power of agenda-setting—that is, the ability to manipulate outcomes by constraining political choices.[8] The ability to influence nominations is an example of this power. As we discuss in Chapter 3, prior to the modern era, party leaders could strongly influence or even choose the candidates who would represent their party in the general

TABLE 1.1 What Free Choice, Political Equality, Deliberation, and Free Speech Require of Campaigns and Elections

Free choice	• Citizens must have a choice between at least two candidates. • Citizens must play a role in determining the final set of candidate choices. • Citizens must not be intimidated, manipulated, or coerced into making certain vote choices.
Political equality	• Each citizen's vote should have an equal impact on election outcomes. • To the extent it is possible, the burdens associated with voting should be equal for all people. • All candidates should be able to disseminate similar amounts of information to voters. • The rules governing campaigns and elections must apply equally to all voters and candidates.
Deliberation	• Candidates and citizens must have opportunities to deliberate before an election. • Citizens must have a high volume of campaign information from a diverse range of sources. • Candidates must offer reasons for the positions they take. • Candidates should not be required to refrain from criticizing one another.
Free speech	• The government cannot enact laws that infringe on political speech. • Political parties, candidates, and interest groups should be able to express what they believe. They should also hear from voters, even those who disagree.

election. In the modern era, the widespread use of primary elections gives voters that power.

Free choice is also undermined when voters are coerced or manipulated into voting a particular way. Elections that involve violent intimidation of opposition-party supporters do not meet this standard, nor do campaigns in which the incumbent regime controls all major news outlets.

Widespread false or misleading information can also work to undermine free choice. For example, Trump continues to claim that he won the 2020 presidential election, and polls show that a majority of Republicans believe him.[9] This false assertion has already affected the political behavior of many Americans: it encouraged some to protest the counting of electoral votes in early January 2021 and has driven others to donate to Trump and other Republicans, enabling them to raise millions of dollars for future elections. In the primary elections ahead of the 2022 midterms, Trump and his allies may use false claims about the 2020 election to encourage their supporters to vote against Republican incumbents who refused to back Trump's "victory." If Trump's claims about the 2020 election encouraged his supporters to vote against Republican incumbents in the 2022 primaries, it is fair to say that they were manipulated and that their vote was less free.

Political Equality

Political equality has always been a central value of the American political system. The principle of "one person, one vote" is a natural extension of the belief that "all men are created equal." Yet throughout American history, many citizens—people of color, women, immigrants, and poor Americans—were not recognized as persons worthy of the right to vote. Thus, our electoral system long upheld the value of political equality for some while denying it to others. Today, most U.S. adult citizens can vote in elections. As we discuss in Chapter 2, only citizens under the age of 18, nonresidents, and (in most states) people serving prison time for felony convictions lack the right to vote.

Yet political equality applies not only to the question of who can vote but also to the question of how easy or hard it is to exercise that right—what we might call equality of access. If certain people must exert considerably more effort to vote than others do, then one can ask if they are being treated equally by the law. For example, at points in American history, some voters have been required to pay a poll tax or pass a literacy test to cast a ballot. The former requirement was deemed unconstitutional by the Supreme Court, and Congress prohibited the latter when it passed the Voting Rights Act of 1965. Today, debates about political equality revolve around voting rules that are less burdensome but are hurdles nonetheless. For example, in some states voters are required to present government-issued photo identification in order to vote. Opponents of these voter identification laws argue that they unfairly burden people who are unlikely to have such identification.

The 2020 election raised other questions about equality of access as rules changed to accommodate voting during the pandemic. For example, Texas governor Greg Abbott attracted criticism when he issued an order stipulating that each county could provide no more than one drop-off location for voters to hand deliver (rather than mail in) their absentee ballots—even though Texas counties range dramatically in population from less than 100 people in Loving County to 4.7 million people in Harris County. Although a state court judge rejected Abbott's proclamation, arguing that "the limitation to a single drop-off location . . . needlessly and unreasonably substantially burden[s] voters' constitutionally protected right to vote,"[10] the Texas Supreme Court ultimately upheld Abbott's order. It is hard to know what effect the order may have had on election outcomes, especially because turnout in Texas increased compared to 2016, as it did across the country. Nevertheless, the limits that Texas placed on drop-off locations show how electoral rules can be evaluated in terms of equality.

At the same time, equality of access must be balanced against the need to ensure that every voter has equal political influence. If a person can easily cast more than one ballot without being caught—a form of voter fraud—then their opinion has more weight than someone else's, and the principle of "one person, one vote" is violated. Thus, those trying to restrict access often make political equality arguments in the name of "election security." For example, Abbott justified his drop box order by saying, "As we work to preserve Texans' ability to vote during the COVID-19 pandemic, we must take extra care to strengthen ballot security protocols throughout the state."[11]

When balancing equality of access against equality of influence, it is important to consider both the burden a law places on voters and the likelihood that it will prevent fraud. For example, most states require people to register to vote before they can cast a ballot, but 21 states and the District of Columbia allow people to register and vote on the same day. Research has found that "same-day registration" increases turnout by about 3 percentage points, suggesting that preelection registration requirements are a burden for some.[12] Opponents of same-day registration argue that it increases the likelihood of fraudulent votes being cast because election officials do not have time to verify voters' information before they cast their ballots. However, numerous studies have found that voter fraud in general is exceedingly rare, as is fraud related specifically to Election Day registration.[13] Thus, from the standpoint of political equality, it is difficult to justify preelection registration requirements.

The value of political equality can be applied to other aspects of campaigns and elections. In *A Preface to Democratic Theory*, the political scientist Robert Dahl argues that preserving equal political influence requires that voters possess identical information about the choices available to them on Election Day.[14] Here, *identical* means that candidates should be able to disseminate similar amounts of information to voters so that no one candidate or party can monopolize the avenues of communication in a campaign. The constitutional scholar Ronald Dworkin arrives at the same conclusion by arguing that citizens are equals not only as voters but also as candidates for office.[15] In fact, he argues that the equality of candidates for office is just as important as the equality of voters. He argues that all citizens—including elected officials, candidates for office, and organized groups—should have a fair and equal opportunity to publish, broadcast, or otherwise command attention for their views. A candidate who controls the flow of political communication has a disproportionate influence over citizen opinion.

Others argue that political equality also requires citizens to vote on the same day; otherwise, they are voting with different information.[16] In 2020, for example, voters in California could cast ballots in the state's Democratic Party presidential primary between February 3 and Super Tuesday, which took place on March 3. Some who voted early for South Bend, Indiana, mayor Pete Buttigieg after he won the Iowa caucuses held on February 3 regretted that decision after he dropped out of the race just before Super Tuesday. "[I] voted two weeks ago for Pete and I wish I waited later to vote for Biden," said one voter who was concerned that Democratic candidate Bernie Sanders would win the state. He concluded, "It's my fault for voting early during a close primary."[17] This example not only drives home how much can happen in just a few weeks during a campaign but also shows why early voting may be problematic from the standpoint of political equality.

Deliberation

Like political equality, deliberation has long been associated with democracy. In his eulogy of democratic Athens, the Greek statesman Pericles called the period of discussion preceding a political decision "an indispensable preliminary to any wise action at all." But political decisions, and even elections, are not inherently deliberative. The side with the most votes wins whether or not there has been discussion. The possibility that political decisions are made without such discussion is particularly bothersome to those in the minority; they would prefer a more deliberative campaign to give them an opportunity to persuade the majority. And even if they lose, such a campaign would leave them with the sense that they had a fair hearing.

How can we evaluate the deliberative quality of a campaign? First, a large volume of information must be available to ensure that citizens receive at least a portion of it. Second, voters must be exposed to information from diverse sources, including candidates, parties, and interest groups, so that their views are not biased by information from only one side. Third, campaigns should provide reasons for supporting or opposing a particular candidate. If a candidate for office says, "I oppose abortion," citizens may know where the candidate stands but not know the candidate's reasoning. When candidates offer reasons for their beliefs—for example, "I oppose abortion because I believe life begins at conception and that it is immoral to end a life"—it helps citizens understand candidates' views and encourages more discussion. Finally, deliberation demands accountability. Earnest and honest discussion requires that candidates identify themselves and take responsibility for their words.

Deliberation does *not* require that candidates refrain from criticizing one another. Because deliberation requires candidates to be honest and substantive, attacks become a concern when they are misleading or irrelevant. For example, in the 2020 election, Trump said that Biden was in favor of "defunding" the police, even though Biden opposed doing so. The Biden campaign misleadingly edited a video of one of Trump's speeches to suggest that Trump said COVID-19 was a "hoax."[18] These kinds of false statements undermine deliberation because they may discourage citizens from paying attention to politics at all. Who can blame people for tuning out when candidates are so disrespectful to one another? However, attacks must be distinguished from valid criticisms. Politics inevitably involves disagreement, and it is important to clarify areas of disagreement among opposing candidates. A useful distinction, for instance, came during a 2020 presidential debate when Trump advocated for eliminating the Obama-era health care law known as "Obamacare," while Biden pledged to uphold and expand it.[19] Voters can weigh such meaningful differences when they decide how to vote.

Media coverage of campaigns can be evaluated by the standard of deliberation as well. Do the news media give citizens adequate information on the similarities and differences between the candidates? Critics often complain that campaign reporting is more focused on the latest polls—what is often called "horse race" coverage—than it is on candidates' policy proposals. The 2020 election provides but one of many examples. A study by the Shorenstein Center on Media, Politics, and Public Policy found that "horserace reports easily outnumbered reports on other topics, including the candidates' policy positions and their leadership ability."[20] Is the public learning enough about the real differences between the candidates when their views on issues are so rarely discussed? Before we are too quick to criticize the media, we must also ask, Does the focus on who is "winning" merely reflect the desires of news consumers, who are happy to read about polls but not so interested in long articles about the candidates' views on complicated aspects of policy? One study that presented participants with a collection of campaign news from which they could read anything they wanted found that people gravitated toward horse race coverage, not coverage of policy.[21]

What role do citizens play in a deliberative campaign? Ideally, they would reflect on their own values and interests, spend time learning about the candidates and their issue positions, and vote for the candidate who best represents their views. A key part of a deliberative campaign is exposure to disagreeable viewpoints: prospective voters should inform themselves about *all* of the candidates and discuss the election with people who are supporting different camps. Of course, citizens rarely behave this way in elections, but it is important to recognize that, for a campaign to truly fulfill deliberative ideals, citizens must take advantage of opportunities to engage with different perspectives.

Freedom of Speech

The First Amendment of the U.S. Constitution, which says that "Congress shall make no law . . . abridging the freedom of speech," is normally interpreted as giving American citizens the legal right to speak freely and openly without government regulation. Because free speech is a fundamental American right, it is difficult to regulate campaigns in ways that might promote some of the values just discussed because these regulations would limit speech and expression. For example, to support the value of political equality, Congress could establish campaign spending limits to prevent one candidate from spending more and thus providing more information to citizens than the other candidates. It could also prevent political candidates from supporting their campaigns with their own money to ensure that a wealthy candidate would not have an advantage over a less wealthy competitor. In fact, as we discuss in Chapter 4, Congress passed a law that did both of these things: the Federal Election Campaign Act of 1971. However, in *Buckley v. Valeo*,[22] the Supreme Court ruled that these provisions were unconstitutional because they violated the free speech protections of the First Amendment.

Because of this commitment to free speech, the United States has one of the least regulated campaign systems in the world.[23] In fact, many of the laws and regulations that other countries have adopted to improve campaign discourse would very likely be overturned by the Supreme Court if they were implemented in the United States. For instance, political parties in Japan can use television advertising only to discuss policy positions and must refrain from mentioning the name or record of any other individual candidate. Some other countries prohibit the publication of public opinion polls during a certain period of time before an election so that their results do not discourage people from voting. Still other countries limit the duration of campaigns entirely. Even if Americans wanted to adopt such restrictions, any governmental attempt to do so would likely violate the principle of free speech, at least as it is interpreted by contemporary U.S. courts.

The First Amendment does not apply to the actions of private corporations, however. This is why Twitter, Facebook, Instagram, and other social media companies did not run afoul of the First Amendment when they banned Trump from posting after the January 6 attack on the Capitol. But those decisions drew complaints. Some believe the principle of free speech means that candidates, political parties, interest groups, and voters should be able to express themselves on any platform, publicly or privately owned, even in ways that many find odious.

Designing the ideal campaign or election is difficult, especially because the four values discussed here are not always compatible. But they are still useful for evaluating the rules and institutions that govern the electoral process—such as the electoral college, voter identification laws, and campaign finance rules—as well as the strategies pursued by candidates. For example, Americans commonly complain when candidates attack their opponents, but are such attacks always a bad thing? These standards can help us address that question. They can also help us evaluate the behavior of citizens. Do Americans pay enough attention to campaigns and know enough about the candidates to live up to democratic ideals?

Conclusion

In the wake of the 2020 presidential contest, Democratic and Republican leaders moved quickly—and in sharply different ways—to change certain rules governing U.S. elections. Democrats in Congress, for example, pushed legislation that would reverse state laws requiring voter identification and require states to automatically register eligible Americans to vote—measures that they believed would help Democratic-leaning voters get to the polls. In many state legislatures, Republicans advocated for new restrictions on voting, particularly on procedures that were disproportionately used by Democratic voters during the pandemic, such as absentee or mail voting. The bitter election between Trump and Biden and its aftermath produced no truce in the ongoing partisan battle over how this country conducts its elections.

Thus, it is all the more important to understand and analyze how campaigns and elections work. In the chapters that follow, we seek to explain the relevant laws, history, and features of U.S. elections at all levels of office. We will also bring to bear both classic and contemporary political science research to better understand the causes and consequences of electoral laws, news coverage, campaign strategy, and voter behavior, among other things. This research will identify how, and how much, electoral changes like those being debated in Congress and state legislatures may matter for ordinary voters.

The next chapter outlines the basic rules of the electoral process in the United States. Chapter 3 describes how American political campaigns have evolved throughout history and the important long-term trends that continue to shape today's elections. Chapter 4 describes how contemporary campaigns are financed—another aspect of the rules that has important consequences for strategy. Chapter 5 discusses the major elements of modern campaign strategy, drawing on political science as well as the thinking of political consultants; much of this chapter focuses on the behavior of candidates. Chapters 6 to 8 consider the specific roles played by other actors: political parties, interest groups, and the media.

Chapters 9 to 11 delve into three categories of campaigns: presidential, congressional, and state and local. An important theme throughout the book is that the rules, realities, and strategies inherent to campaigns may differ across levels of office. Thus, it is important to examine how each type of campaign typically unfolds. Chapters 12 and 13 focus on citizens, including how they decide to participate in elections (or not) and how they decide to support particular candidates. These two chapters devote particular attention to how campaigns may affect each decision. Chapter 13 also considers, in the wake of the 2020 presidential election and the questions surrounding its outcome, whether the American electoral process is "broken."

KEY TERMS

incumbent (p. 7)   elections (p. 8)

campaigns (p. 8)   primary elections (p. 16)

FOR DISCUSSION

1. What are the implications of party polarization for how candidates campaign and how voters make decisions?

2. Why do the rules constrain candidates when they are campaigning? Why don't candidates simply change the rules to their benefit?

3. What are several dimensions of "reality" that might affect campaign strategies and election outcomes?

4. Why would the standards of deliberation and equality potentially come into conflict with the standard of free speech?

2

The American Electoral Process

In the spring of 2001, Barack Obama, a state senator in Illinois, was a year removed from his most stunning political defeat. In the 2000 Democratic primary for a U.S. House seat, he had challenged another Black Democrat, the incumbent congressman Bobby Rush, and lost by 31 points. Obama struggled to win votes in some parts of Rush's district, particularly Black neighborhoods where professors at the University of Chicago—even African American professors like Obama—were viewed with suspicion. Obama had more appeal in South Side neighborhoods around the university and North Side neighborhoods closer to downtown, including the so-called Gold Coast along Lake Michigan. The Gold Coast is home to many wealthy (and mostly White) Chicagoans, an ideal group from which to raise money for a political campaign. The problem was that as a state senator, Obama did not represent the North Side and its Gold Coast; his district was on the South Side.

One day that spring, Obama went to a room guarded with fingerprint scanners and coded keypads in a building in downtown Springfield. Inside the room were computers on which a select few employees of the Illinois Democratic Party worked. Their job was to draw legislative districts. The Democrats had won control of the Illinois House and now, the year after the 2000 census, were drawing up a new set of state legislative districts—as was the Republican majority in the Illinois Senate. Obama sat with Democratic consultant John Corrigan and drew himself a new state senate district, one that started in the South Side and then stretched north to the Gold Coast.

After a protracted battle, the Democrats succeeded in implementing their districts. This gave Obama a new district well suited to funding his political ambitions, and it also helped the Democrats win a majority in the Illinois Senate in the 2002 elections. This majority helped Obama by allowing him to establish a record of legislative accomplishments more easily. With this newfound potential for raising money and promoting legislation, Obama was poised to run for the U.S. Senate in 2004.[1]

This chapter is about the rules of campaigns and elections, the first part of the framework introduced in Chapter 1. All democracies depend on rules to govern political life. This anecdote from early in Obama's political career illustrates their importance. It also illustrates how politicians will do their best to make the rules work in their favor. In Obama's case, this meant leveraging the existing rules to determine who his constituents would be. In other cases, this could mean trying to change the rules. This cannot always be accomplished easily, especially when the rules are defined in the U.S. Constitution itself. But many kinds of election laws can be changed if one political party or faction is powerful enough.

The rules of the American electoral process can help us answer many crucial questions pertaining to campaigns. This chapter explores six of them: who can vote, how people vote and how votes are counted, who can run for

Core of the Analysis

- Elections are conducted according to rules that determine who can vote, how people vote and how votes are counted, who can run for office, when elections are held, where to run, and who wins.

- The rules often vary across states and levels of office because they are designed by multiple decision makers, including the framers of the Constitution, Congress, state legislatures, local officials, and political parties.

- The rules reflect values about what constitutes a "good" election, but they often further certain values at the expense of others.

- Candidates and political parties strive to shape the rules in a way that favors them, especially when and where elections are close.

- The rules strongly affect the decisions of every relevant actor during a campaign, including candidates, parties, interest groups, the media, and voters.

When Barack Obama was a member of the Illinois legislature, the rules for redistricting determined who his constituents were. New district boundaries gave him a set of wealthier constituents, and their support helped Obama run a successful U.S. Senate campaign in 2004.

office, when elections are held, where to run, and who wins. For each, we first explore what the rules are. The answers are not always straightforward, due in part to a second consideration: who makes the rules. The Constitution, Congress, state legislatures, and political parties all have some say. The rules are not the same for every level of office or in every state, but even general answers are informative.

Knowing what the rules are and who makes them leads to the question, Why these rules and not others? Electoral rules reflect ideals or values—that is, conceptions of what makes a good or fair election. For example, a good election might feature a vigorous competition between two candidates that provides information to citizens and motivates them to vote. But competitive elections are also more expensive, as candidates have an incentive to raise more money so that they can effectively communicate with potential voters. Many people fear that soliciting campaign contributions corrupts candidates. Whether one favors increased competition might depend on what one considers more important: informing voters or mitigating the potential for corruption. Inevitably, electoral rules reflect compromises and trade-offs among competing values, and they almost never fully codify any particular value.

From a candidate or political party's point of view, however, the most important question about electoral rules is not necessarily whether they uphold any philosophical value but whether they help that person or party win elections. Partisan contestation over rules has only grown more frequent and more fractious as the American electorate has become more narrowly divided, with control of the White House, Congress, and many state and local offices at stake in almost every election. Perhaps Obama had philosophical objections to a system in which his party got to redraw the Illinois political map to help both him and his party, but he made it work in his favor.

However, electoral rules can also serve to check self-interested politicians. After the 2020 presidential election, Donald Trump's long campaign to overturn the results eventually foundered because a range of political actors—from local and state election officials, including many Republicans, to federal judges and the Supreme Court—sought to ensure that the votes were counted according to the rules and refused to change the rules or the vote count to help Trump. Ultimately, electoral systems need rules not only to organize political competition but also to ensure that election outcomes cannot be changed simply because the loser is unhappy. Electoral rules both affect the quality of our democracy and protect the sheer existence of democracy in the first place.

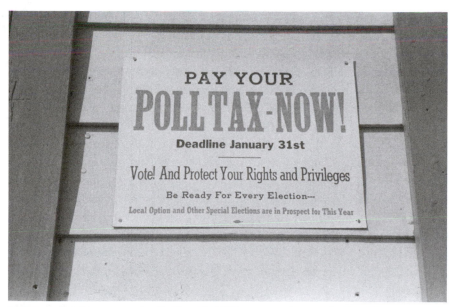

Poll taxes, like this one required in Texas in 1939, were used to restrict Black Americans and other groups from voting. Laws that require the payment of poll taxes were invalidated by the Voting Rights Act of 1965 and declared unconstitutional in *Harper v. Virginia* in 1966.

Who Can Vote

Electoral rules determine a crucial aspect of any democracy: who is eligible to vote. Today, most adults in the United States can vote as long as they register to do so, but the qualifications for voting have changed a great deal throughout American history. The Nineteenth Amendment (1920) invalidated restrictions based on sex. The Twenty-Sixth Amendment (1971) relaxed restrictions based on age by lowering the voting age from 21 to 18. But the fight to invalidate restrictions based on race followed a particularly tortuous path.

Although the Fifteenth Amendment (1870) stated that the right to vote could not be denied on the basis of race or color, political leaders in southern states used various tactics to keep Black Americans from voting. One such strategy was **poll taxes**, or fees that one had to pay in order to vote, which disenfranchised not only Black Americans but many Native Americans, Asian Americans, and poor White Americans as well. Another was **literacy tests**, which required prospective voters to prove they could read and understand English. These were administered and interpreted by local elections officials who could exercise their discretion to "fail" test takers and thus ensure that certain types of people could not vote. A third strategy was the **White primary**, which allowed only White voters to vote in primary elections. Because the South was dominated by the Democratic Party, the Democratic primary essentially chose who the eventual general election winner would be.

It took decades for this racist system to be dismantled. The Supreme Court struck down the White primary in 1944.[2] The Twenty-Fourth Amendment (1964) invalidated restrictions based on wealth, such as poll taxes. Most consequentially, the **Voting Rights Act of 1965 (VRA)** invalidated other discriminatory measures, such as literacy tests, and established federal oversight of elections to prevent discrimination against African Americans. The VRA singled out "covered" jurisdictions, which were specific states and counties with a history of persistent discrimination, including virtually the entire South. The law forbade these jurisdictions from instituting changes that would restrict the political power of African American voters. To ensure that these jurisdictions adhered to the law, they had to submit any changes in voting procedures or electoral laws to the U.S. Department of Justice for "preclearance." Only after the Department of Justice signed off on these changes could they be implemented.

After 1965, the VRA was expanded in several ways. In 1975, the number of covered areas was expanded and the VRA's protections were extended to Native Americans, Asian Americans, and Latino Americans. One study of the 1975 expansion of preclearance found that it led to an increase in turn-out of 4–8 percentage points in covered areas in elections between 1980 and 2016, driven almost entirely by the increasing turnout of people of color.[3] In 1982, amendments to the VRA established an even stricter stan-dard: the voting power of people of color could not be weakened even as an unintentional by-product of some other action. It was no longer necessary to prove that discrimination was the intentional goal.

Taken together, these reforms dramatically expanded the size of the American electorate, making it more inclusive in terms of gender, race and ethnicity, and education level. Two remaining restrictions are in place nation-wide: the requirement that eligible voters be native or naturalized citizens and the minimum voting age of 18—with the exception of a few communi-ties that allow 16- and 17-year-olds to vote in local elections.

Other restrictions vary across states. For example, state laws about the vot-ing rights of people with mental illnesses are wide-ranging, although it is not clear how often these restrictions are actually enforced. And while nearly every state bans people convicted of felonies from voting while in prison (only the District of Columbia, Maine, and Vermont permit incarcerated people to vote), states differ widely in whether they allow people convicted of felonies to vote while on parole or probation or after their sentences are served. States also require these individuals to jump through different hoops to regain their right to vote.[4] For example, Floridians convicted of felonies were banned from voting for life until 2018, when voters passed a constitutional amendment that restored their voting rights upon completion of their sentences. In response, Republicans in the Florida State Legislature passed a law in 2019 restricting voting eligibility to only those people who had served their sen-tences *and* paid all outstanding fines or fees related to their court cases. These sums can be substantial: one study in the neighboring state of Alabama found that the average amount owed was $4,000.[5] Critics have likened the Florida law to a poll tax. Such laws have become increasingly consequential as the number of people convicted of felonies has grown over time.

States also differ in whether they require citizens to declare themselves as a member of a political party in order to participate in primary elections. In a **closed primary**, only party members can vote in that party's primary. In a **semi-closed primary**, both unaffiliated voters and members of the party can vote in that party's primary. In an **open primary**, all voters can vote in either party's primary, but not in both primaries. In a **blanket primary** (sometimes called a **jungle primary**), voters receive a single ballot with the candidates for each party listed, and citizens can mix and match, voting for a Democratic nominee for senator, a Republican candidate for governor, and so on. This form of primary was invalidated by the Supreme Court in 2000 on the grounds that it violated the parties' First Amendment right of association: a party's nominee could be chosen in part by people who do not affiliate with that party and who even actively oppose it.[6] The blanket primary survives only in a nonpartisan form. For example, in Louisiana, all candidates are listed on the primary ballot, and a candidate that wins 50 percent of the vote for a given office is elected directly to that position after the primary. If no candidate wins 50 percent of the vote for a given office, the top two vote-getters go on to the general election regardless of their party affiliation. In Washington state and California, the same ballot structure is used, but there is no possibility of winning the election outright at the primary stage. The top two vote-getters go on to the general election no matter what percentage of the vote the front-runner received. Alaska has a similar system in which the top four vote-getters advance to the general election.

Voter Registration and Identification

Restrictions on who may vote are enforced via a system of voter registration. In every state except North Dakota, citizens must register to vote and provide evidence that they meet certain criteria. Among the states that require registration, laws differ in two respects: how citizens are registered and when they must register in order to be eligible to vote. In many states, citizens are registered only when they take the initiative to register themselves. But 20 states and the District of Columbia have implemented a form of **automatic voter registration**.[7] In this system, citizens who interact with a government agency, such as a state's department of motor vehicles, will automatically be registered to vote unless they opt out. The specific details of these programs vary state by state, but the common goals are to make it easier for eligible voters to register as well as to help states update their voter databases more efficiently.

States also vary in their registration deadlines—ranging from 30 days prior to the election to the day of the election itself. Twenty states as well as the District of Columbia have approved or implemented **same-day registration** (also called **Election Day registration**), in which citizens can both register and vote on Election Day. Same-day registrants must supply proof of residency as well as a valid form of identification.[8]

Thirty-six states have passed **voter identification laws** that request or require citizens to present some form of identification before voting.[9] These laws differ in what forms of identification are acceptable and in the procedures that voters must follow if they show up to vote but do not have one of the required forms of identification. The strictest voter identification laws typically require voters to present photo identification, such as a driver's license or passport.

All these requirements can affect the number of citizens who actually vote. The less onerous the requirements are, the more likely it is that some eligible citizens will register to vote or turn out on Election Day who might not have done so otherwise. For example, automatic voter registration is estimated to increase the percentage of eligible voters who are registered by 2 points, and in Oregon, the first state to implement the policy, it appeared to increase overall turnout by 2–3 points in the 2016 election.[10] Studies of Election Day registration suggest that it increases turnout by about 3 points when it is implemented in a state that previously required voters to register at least 15 days before the election.[11] Of course, as more states experiment with these kinds of reforms, and as we have more elections to evaluate their impact, estimates of their effects may change. But for now, the literature suggests that helping people register to vote increases turnout.

Less clear, however, is whether voter identification laws reduce turnout. They do reduce turnout among those who lack identification: one study of North Carolina's voter identification law found that it decreased turnout by 1 point among this group in the 2016 primary election and by almost 3 points in the 2016 general election—even though in between the two elections the law was suspended.[12] These figures suggest that the law created a lasting perception among people without identification that they were ineligible to vote. In addition, other research has found that people may not vote when they are required to show identification because they cannot find or access their identification or because they lack information about what forms of identification are valid.[13] But because these groups of people are typically small, voter identification laws do not appear to affect the *overall* turnout rate, as a variety of studies have shown.[14]

One reason why voter identification laws have not depressed turnout rates is that political parties and voters actively seek to counter their potential effects. Just reminding Democratic voters that these laws could reduce turnout elicits anger and a greater willingness to participate in politics.[15] Political parties can also work to mobilize voters to help maintain turnout in places where these laws are in effect.[16] However, incorporating specific messages about the effects of voter identification laws into mobilization efforts may not directly increase turnout, according to experiments conducted among African American voters in Virginia in 2013, 2016, and 2017, when the state required identification in order to vote.[17] More effective in Virginia may have been notices sent by the state to remind registered voters without records at the Department of Motor Vehicles that identification would be required at the polls.[18] The general point is that the effects of voter identification laws are not necessarily automatic. They depend on the actions of governments and political actors.

Indeed, the American system provides both opportunities for and burdens on candidates and parties. Because voting in the United States is not compulsory, as it is in countries like Brazil and Australia, many eligible citizens choose not to vote. It is thus particularly important for campaigns to mobilize their supporters, and to this end, many campaigns have dedicated programs for registering and turning out voters. During the 2012 campaign, for example, the Obama campaign reported registering 1.8 million voters (Obama won by about 5 million votes).[19] Successful mobilization can help a candidate win, but mobilization efforts demand time, energy, and money that could also be spent elsewhere.

Rules about voter registration also matter because they affect which types of citizens are eligible to vote or can vote. For example, automatic voter registration appears to have a particularly large impact on the registration rates of Latinos, young people, and people who live in poorer neighborhoods.[20] Election Day registration also seems to encourage the participation of people of color and young people.[21] All these groups tend to have a lower propensity for voting relative to White Americans and older people, suggesting that facilitating voter registration may increase turnout most among those who are not already habitual voters.

Candidates and parties naturally tend to resist reforms that they fear will increase voter turnout among members of the opposite party. Voters are no different: two studies found that people were less likely to support policies like same-day registration when they were told that those policies would benefit the other party.[22] Thus we should expect parties to fight for any law or rule that they believe will give them a small advantage. Both parties typically assume that making voting easier helps Democratic candidates, while restrictions on voting—like voter identification laws—help Republican candidates. The reality is often more complicated because electoral laws can have unexpected or simply very small effects. For example, the introduction of Election Day registration in Wisconsin appeared to help Republicans more than it helped Democrats.[23]

Another notable example concerns felon disenfranchisement. The usual presumption is that making it easier for people convicted of felonies to vote could help Democratic candidates—in part because such people are disproportionately African American. But one study found that the effects of enfranchising this group might be muted. The study examined the voting habits of 150,000 Floridians convicted of felonies who were granted the right to vote by Florida's governor between 2007 and 2011. Based on whether they registered to vote (most did not) and which party they registered with (if any), the researchers estimated that if *every* person with a felony record in Florida had voted in the 2016 election—a big if, to be sure—Democrats would have gained about 102,000 votes, Republicans would have gained 54,000, and 40,000 votes could have gone to either party.[24] If these 40,000 votes were then split evenly between the parties, Democrats would have won 122,000 votes and Republicans would have won 74,000—an advantage for Democrats of about 48,000 votes. That is not nothing, but it would not have been enough to alter the outcome of the 2016 presidential election in Florida, which Trump won by about 113,000 votes, or that year's Senate election, which Republican Marco Rubio won by over 700,000 votes.

Thus, electoral reforms would not necessarily lead to a vastly different political landscape. They may increase or decrease turnout by only a few percentage points at most, and, as the Rubio race illustrates, many elections are won by such large margins that small changes in turnout would probably not change many outcomes.[25] Moreover, the voting patterns of new voters who take advantage of laws that make voting easier may not differ dramatically from those of habitual voters who tend to vote no matter what.[26] Finally, the new laws enacted by one party can lead to a backlash among voters or to counteractions by the opposing party, as we have seen in response to voter identification laws. If these counteractions are successful, then the initial laws may have little or no effect—or even the opposite of their predicted effect.

Political Values and the Right to Vote

Perhaps the most important value considered throughout the history of voting rights has been political equality. Much of the battle for voting rights, particularly for women and African Americans, was about changing laws that denied these rights to particular groups. Those conflicts continue to this day. For example, debates over voter identification laws center on political equality because certain groups—particularly people of color as well as the youngest and oldest eligible voters—are less likely to have the forms of identification that these laws typically require.[27]

Conflicts over equality and voting rights have grown even more fraught as the power of the VRA has eroded.[28] In *Shelby County v. Holder* (2013), a narrowly divided Supreme Court struck down the part of the VRA that defined which states and counties were "covered" and subject to the law's preclearance requirements.[29] A majority of the Court argued that the law's formula for determining coverage, which was based on data from the 1960s and early

1970s, was no longer valid because it was "based on 40-year-old facts having no logical relation to the present day." Although the Court left intact the law's provision that some states and counties must seek preclearance, there is currently no way to enforce preclearance if there is no formula to define which states and counties must seek it. The Democratic majority in the U.S. House passed legislation to reestablish preclearance in December 2019, but it has not won sufficient support to overcome Republican opposition in the Senate.

Because the VRA still prohibits discriminatory voting laws, it is possible to challenge a law by suing to block it after it is passed. For example, courts have suspended voter identification laws in Texas and North Carolina that they deemed to be intentionally discriminatory against people of color—a direct violation of the VRA. Texas amended its law as a result, and North Carolina's law remains enjoined by a court order and has not taken effect. The challenge, however, is that lawsuits may not be as effective as preclearance at preventing discriminatory laws or actions.[30] One reason is that the burden of proof shifts from the government that is seeking to enact a new law to the plaintiffs who are challenging that law. There may also be situations where potential plaintiffs do not know enough or cannot act quickly enough to successfully block or overturn a new law or administrative decision by local election officials.

One such administrative decision involves local election officials removing voters who they believe ineligible from the list of registered voters. One study found that after the *Shelby County* decision and before the 2014 election, counties that were previously "covered" under the VRA removed more names from their lists of registered voters than did counties that had not been covered.[31] This is exactly the kind of move that preclearance may have prevented, especially given evidence that updating and maintaining voter lists can inadvertently burden voters of color.[32] At the same time, a study of voter turnout since *Shelby County* found that the decision has not adversely affected the overall turnout of African American voters relative to White voters.[33] This could also reflect the efforts of candidates, parties, and other political actors to counter the effects of laws that might otherwise disproportionately affect African Americans.

A second relevant value is participation. For many people, "good" elections are ones in which large percentages of eligible citizens vote. In their view, turnout in the United States is too low, and rules about voter qualifications should be structured to ensure that as many people as possible can and will participate. From this perspective, even compulsory voting would be a reasonable requirement.

But maximizing equality and participation may not be the only relevant goals. Some limits on participation may be justifiable, even if those limits fall disproportionately on certain groups. Restrictions with regard to age and mental illness imply a concern about competence; very young people or people who are mentally ill are assumed, correctly or incorrectly, unable or unready to vote. Requiring citizenship implies a concern about loyalty; the people choosing a country's leaders should be "members" of that country themselves. Disenfranchising people convicted of felonies reflects the belief that the right to vote depends on a willingness to obey the law. Requiring party registration for a primary election reflects a belief that a party's candidates should be chosen by voters loyal to that party. Requiring voters to register ahead of the election or to provide identification on Election Day is intended to prevent fraud, such as impersonating another voter or attempting to vote more than once. While these rationales can be critiqued—for example, cases of voter fraud are exceedingly rare[34]—the broader point is that electoral rules are geared not simply toward promoting strict equality before the law or encouraging citizens to participate; they are also intended to further other goals.

How to Vote

Closely related to the question of who can vote is the question of how people vote. This question became even more salient during the 2020 election, which was conducted during the COVID-19 pandemic and necessitated consideration of how people could vote with less risk of infection.

Traditionally, the norm has been in-person voting on Election Day. That is, most people voted by traveling to their assigned polling place and voting there. As of 2020, 43 states and the District of Columbia allowed in-person voting before Election Day—what is known as **early voting**. States vary a great deal in how they implement early voting. For example, the early voting period varies from four to 45 days before Election Day. Whether the early voting period includes weekends and how many early voting locations there are also vary from state to state.[35]

The main alternative to in-person voting is to vote using the postal system. This happens in two primary ways. One is **absentee voting**. In this system, citizens request that a ballot be mailed to them, which they then fill out and either mail in or drop off at a designated place. People who vote this way are "absentee" only in the sense that they are absent from the polling place. Like early voting, this process typically takes place before Election Day, as citizens need to request a ballot ahead of time. Once again, the details vary state by state. One important issue is whether states require citizens to provide a reason or "excuse" for voting absentee. Most states require no reason, but others do—typically things like being out of the county on Election Day, having an illness or disability, or a religious belief or practice. (Americans living overseas, including military personnel, are exempted from having to provide an excuse.)

A second alternative to in-person voting is sometimes called **vote-by-mail** or postal voting. In this system, voters automatically receive a ballot by mail. They do not have to request it. They then mail it back or drop it off. In theory, the entire election could be conducted by mail, although in practice states with vote-by-mail typically provide some opportunities for in-person voting as well. Five states have vote-by-mail systems: Colorado, Hawaii, Oregon, Utah, and Washington state. California, Nebraska, and North Dakota allow counties to decide if an election will be held entirely by mail. Many other states allow certain elections to be conducted by mail, typically local elections or special elections.

Systems like early voting, absentee voting, and vote-by-mail are sometimes grouped under the heading of **convenience voting**. For many advocates, the hope is that making voting more convenient will also increase voter turnout. Although there is some evidence for this, the effects of convenience voting depend on the details of the laws. A comprehensive study of the 1972–2008 elections found that no-excuse absentee voting was associated with a 3-point increase in turnout.[36] There is less evidence that early in-person voting increases turnout, however, unless there is a long 45-day period of early voting, which most states do not have.[37] The limited effect of early voting matches research from other democracies showing that having Election Day on a weekend or making it a holiday does not appear to increase turnout.[38]

The effects of vote-by-mail are not straightforward either. Vote-by-mail was associated with a 3–4 point increase in turnout in Oregon and Washington state when it was first introduced, but later research suggested that some of this initial effect wore off over time and was limited to special elections, which typically see very low turnout compared to regular primary and general elections.[39] A recent study that examined the rollout of vote-by-mail systems in Washington state, California, and Utah found a smaller increase in turnout—about 2 points.[40]

Convenience voting may affect not only overall turnout but also the strategies employed by campaigns. This is because convenience voting replaces a single Election Day with a longer "election period" that may last days or weeks. As we noted in Chapter 1, this means that some people may cast their votes without seeing all the information that the candidates had hoped to present, such as in debates or television advertisements that occur late in the campaign. Convenience voting may therefore incentivize candidates to advertise heavily for a longer period of time.

Convenience voting also means that candidates and parties have to employ different tactics to ensure that their supporters vote. For example, some voters who are sent a ballot in the mail may forget or fail to return it, so campaigns must engage in "ballot chasing" to follow up with voters and make sure they have filled out and mailed in their ballots. Other voters may fill out their ballots incorrectly, invalidating their votes. States typically offer voters a chance to correct any mistakes—a process known as "ballot cure"—and campaigns may seek to help supporters with this process. Altogether, this additional work makes campaigns more expensive, adding perhaps as much as 25 percent to their cost.[41]

Convenience voting is also thought to influence the types of voters who vote. However, just as with reforms such as same-day registration, there is little historical evidence that convenience voting changes the composition of the electorate in a way that helps Democratic or Republican candidates. Vote-by-mail systems do not appear to generate additional vote share for either party, and the same is true for early voting and absentee voting. Indeed, some evidence suggests that the voters who vote early may simply be more interested in politics and stronger partisans generally.[42] These, of course, are the types of people most likely to vote, period. For this reason, convenience voting does not necessarily remedy or counteract the traditional socioeconomic biases in voting, whereby habitual voters tend to have higher levels of formal education and income than the average American.

The 2020 election thrust convenience voting systems to the forefront of American politics. Although the percentage of people using these systems had already been increasing over time, it skyrocketed during the COVID-19 pandemic. According to the 2020 Current Population Survey, only 30 percent of voters voted in person on Election Day, while 26 percent voted in person before Election Day, and 43 percent voted by mail. By contrast, in 2016 about 60 percent of voters voted in person on Election Day.[43] These shifts reflected both voters' concerns about the risks of gathering indoors to vote in person and the degree to which states expanded convenience voting during the pandemic. States took such steps as suspending eligibility requirements to vote absentee, deeming concerns about COVID-19 as a valid "excuse" to vote absentee, and even mailing ballots to all registered voters—creating temporary vote-by-mail systems in states that did not otherwise have them.[44]

But unlike in earlier elections, there were clearer partisan differences in who used which mode of voting. As we discussed in Chapter 1, Trump criticized mail balloting and suggested that it would lead to fraudulent votes. This led to a sharp drop in support for vote-by-mail among Republicans.[45] As a result, only 33 percent of Republican voters voted by mail compared to

57 percent of Democrats, according to one postelection survey.[46] And because in a few key states it took longer to count mail ballots, which by state law could not be examined or certified before Election Day, the election results appeared to "shift" in Democratic candidates' favor as the counting progressed. This trend fueled even more claims that the election results were fraudulent.

Again, there is vanishingly little evidence of fraud that involves convenience voting. For example, one concern is that vote-by-mail systems encourage people to fill out ballots and vote on behalf of deceased individuals. When Trump called Georgia's secretary of state after the election to pressure him to change the outcome, he made this claim, saying, "So dead people voted. And I think the number is . . . close to 5,000 people."[47] But in fact, very few ballots cast in the name of deceased individuals are improperly counted as valid votes. One study of Washington state's vote-by-mail system examined 4.5 million voters and identified only 14 deceased individuals whose ballots could have been counted—and some of these 14 people may have been lawful voters, perhaps because they happened to have the same name and birth date as a different voter who was alive.[48]

But the mere possibility of a dead person "voting" highlights a central challenge of convenience voting and especially absentee or mail balloting: ensuring the security and validity of votes. This need for security creates new political debates over what security measures are necessary. For example, in Pennsylvania in 2020, voters using a mail ballot had to first insert it in an unmarked "secrecy envelope" before inserting that envelope into the return envelope, where they would then write their address and sign their name. Election administrators could then verify that the vote was valid using the information on the return envelope without seeing the ballot itself.[49] But what if a voter forgot the secrecy envelope, thereby creating a "naked ballot"? Should an otherwise valid vote be thrown out? The Pennsylvania Supreme Court said that it should, and some analyses found that about 1 percent of mail ballots in some parts of Pennsylvania were invalidated for this reason.[50] Debates about how to ensure ballot security without making convenience voting, well, inconvenient are only likely to continue. This is especially true for internet voting, which has been employed only in a few states and only for small populations, such as voters living overseas. Voting via the internet or even a cell phone app would be very convenient, but so far, no system has been developed that would be secure enough to ensure voting integrity.[51]

Debates about how people vote, like debates about who can vote, frequently involve the value of equality. Decisions about modes of voting will not affect all groups equally. For example, if absentee or mail voting were to be eliminated, the groups most affected would include older people, people with disabilities, or others who cannot easily travel to a polling place. Similarly, in the midst of the COVID-19 pandemic, the health risks of in-person voting also fell disproportionately on older people as well as those with pre-existing medical conditions.

Even outside of a pandemic, in-person voting raises questions of equality. The number and location of polling places can dramatically affect how long people must stand in line to vote. Research has shown that waiting an hour to vote reduces one's chance of voting in the next election by 1 percentage point.[52] And the burden of waiting does not fall equally on all voters: people of color are likely to wait longer.[53] In 2020, for example, 31 percent of Black Americans reported waiting at least half an hour to vote, but only 18 percent of White Americans reported waiting that long.[54]

The potential for voting systems to affect groups differently only fuels political debates, as political parties will continue to push for systems that they believe will advantage their voters. In the wake of the 2020 election, for example, Republican leaders in a number of states sought to limit mail balloting or absentee voting—even though scholars who studied the implementation of no-excuse absentee voting in 2020 did not find that it increased turnout or helped Democratic candidates.[55] This and other research suggests that making voting more convenient typically does not create a partisan advantage. Nevertheless, it seems likely that politicians will continue to assume otherwise.

Who Can Run

Who is eligible to run for office? In the American political system, the qualifications usually involve a minimum age, American citizenship, and a minimum time living in the community one seeks to represent. For federal office, the Constitution spells out these requirements. A candidate for the House of Representatives must be at least 25 years old, a citizen for seven years, and an "inhabitant" of the state the district is in. The qualifications for senator are similar, except that the candidate must be at least 30 years old and a citizen for nine years.

The requirements for president are even more restrictive. Candidates must be at least 35 years old and U.S. residents for at least 14 years (although the Constitution does not specify when that period of residency must have occurred). Moreover, they must be native-born citizens of the United States. Naturalized citizens may run for the House and Senate.

Candidates for state and local offices typically must meet requirements for minimum age and residency, although different localities have different rules. For example, in Louisiana, candidates for governor need to be at least 25 years old and citizens of the United States and residents of Louisiana for at least five years immediately before the election. In Minnesota, candidates for governor must also be at least 25, but they need only have lived in the state for the year before the election. Candidates for the Louisiana State Legislature must be at least 18 years old, state residents for the preceding two years, and residents of their legislative district for at least the preceding year. Candidates for the Minnesota Legislature must be at least 21 years old and must be residents of the state for one year and of their district for at least six months immediately preceding the election. Other states have their own stipulations about age and residency.

Despite specific differences, federal, state, and local qualifications for office reflect a common set of values. One is competence. Age requirements help ensure that candidates have the intellectual and emotional maturity to handle the job. To be sure, age is an imperfect measure of competence. There have been cases where older politicians, due to age or infirmity, lost a significant degree of competence but still held office. In 1919, for example, President Woodrow Wilson suffered a debilitating stroke. His wife, Edith, took over and saw to it that important tasks were delegated to the proper cabinet secretaries—all of whom were kept in the dark about the president's condition.[56] But although any age threshold is somewhat arbitrary, it would be foolish to have no thresholds whatsoever. Whatever their talents, 13-year-olds are probably not ready to be leaders of the free world.

A second value reflected in these qualifications is loyalty. Requiring candidates to be citizens of the United States helps to ensure that they will work for its interests and not those of another country. Residency requirements for state offices reflect a similar concern: the desire to have representatives who will work for their constituents' interests and not the interests of people in some other district or state. Residency requirements also imply a third value: familiarity with the people candidates seek to represent. Having lived among their constituents could help candidates better understand their needs. Of course, citizenship does not ensure loyalty, and residency does not ensure good representation. But both kinds of requirements may foster a candidate's commitment to these ideals.

Outside of age, citizenship, and residency, there are relatively few requirements in widespread use. Two more deserve brief mention, however. First, although it is not codified in the U.S. Constitution or state constitutions, the dominance of political parties in American elections virtually requires candidates to be party members in order to seek office. Party membership does not necessarily imply years of loyal service, and often parties will accept defectors from a competing party with open arms. That said, candidates cannot credibly hopscotch back and forth among parties, and this leads most of them to commit to a single party. This commitment is valuable to parties, who want to ensure that candidates represent the views of party members.

A major-party affiliation is helpful for a prospective candidate because of rules that can make it difficult for **independent candidates**—those unaffiliated with a party—and candidates from smaller political parties simply to get on the ballot. States typically require candidates to collect a certain number of signatures from voters to get on the ballot. In some cases, this requirement is not too onerous; for a potential candidate for the U.S. House of Representatives, Tennessee requires only 25 signatures from registered voters who reside in that House district—a tiny fraction of the 700,000 or so residents in each district. But in Texas, a potential candidate for governor who seeks to run in a party that does not already have ballot access must get a number of signatures equal to 1 percent of all voters in the previous gubernatorial election. One percent may not sound like a lot, but for a candidate in the 2018 gubernatorial election, that entailed over 47,000 signatures.[57] This requirement, which does not apply to candidates in established political parties, is one way that ballot access laws can make it harder for new or smaller parties to field candidates.

Second, politicians can sometimes be disqualified from seeking reelection if they have already served in an office for a specified length of time. The shorthand for such a rule is **term limits**: limits on the number of terms politicians can serve in a particular elected office. For example, because of the Twenty-Second Amendment (1951), the president can be elected to the office only twice, or only once if the president has served more than half of the previous president's term (that is, after something caused it to be cut short). Members of Congress have no term limits; laws passed by some state legislatures to impose term limits on members of Congress were overturned by the Supreme Court in 1995.[58] However, term limits on governors and state legislators are not prohibited. Thirty-six states limit the number of terms a governor may serve, typically to two.[59] Fifteen states limit the number of terms a state legislator may serve.[60] Term limits imply a certain vision of representation: good representatives are closer to the people, and this can best be achieved with frequent turnover. Otherwise, representatives may go to their respective capitals, spend years in office, and lose perspective on what their constituents want. Critics of term limits tend to emphasize a different ideal: good representatives are more experienced and more knowledgeable about public policy. Research does show that term-limited legislators have less incentive to develop expertise because they know that they will soon be out of a job.[61]

Note the tension between the values underlying minimum age and residency requirements, on the one hand, and term limits, on the other. Minimum age requirements are intended to ensure basic competence, and residency requirements are meant to ensure a better connection with constituents. But to the extent that a longer tenure in office builds representatives' competence and their connection to their constituents, term limits will harm both.

In some respects, the rules regarding age, citizenship, and residency rarely constrain candidates. Most potential candidates are not motivated to run for office until they are older. Nearly all meet the necessary requirement for U.S. citizenship, with the exception of naturalized citizens, who are not eligible to run for president. Residency is only occasionally an issue, and this is usually not because candidates fail to meet the letter of the law but because opponents claim that although they maintain a home in the state or district, they really live elsewhere (for instance, in Washington, D.C.), or that they arrived too recently in a state to represent it well (as some said when Hillary Clinton moved to New York the year before she mounted a Senate campaign there in 2002). In fact, party membership and term limits probably have a larger impact on who can run. The advantages that come with party membership discourage candidates who do not identify with either major party. Term limits regularly force elected leaders to leave office or run for a different office, even when they would prefer to run for reelection to the same office.

The natural criticism of eligibility requirements hinges on the standard of free choice that we discussed in Chapter 1. One might argue that such requirements restrict the choices that citizens have by eliminating candidates who might otherwise be qualified but for one characteristic. Some critics of term limits make precisely this argument: it should not be a law but the will of the voters that requires politicians to leave office, as demonstrated by the election of another candidate. The same might be said of other requirements. For example, citizens may be able to evaluate whether a candidate is mature enough to hold office even without a law that sets a minimum age. The implication is not that eligibility requirements are inherently unnecessary but that imposing them tends to prioritize certain values (such as competence or loyalty) over free choice.

The standard of deliberation is relevant here as well: any requirement that restricts the candidates who can run for office might degrade the quality of deliberation. This is easiest to see when considering the plight of many independent candidates, particularly those not affiliated with the Democratic or Republican parties, who can face an uphill battle even to be listed on the ballot. Critics argue that ballot access laws deny voters the ability to consider these alternative candidates. Of course, some hurdle for ballot access may be necessary to prevent unserious candidates from appearing on the ballot. The question is how high that hurdle should be.

When Elections Are Held

At the federal level, the timing of elections is set by the Constitution. Elections for the House of Representatives are held every two years; for the Senate, every six years; for president, every four years. These terms in office vary in part because the framers of the Constitution envisioned a different kind of representation from each type of office. House members were meant to be in closer contact with the people, and shorter terms were meant to help ensure more frequent interaction. By contrast, senators were expected to be more insulated from public opinion and thus better able to deliberate about public policy. George Washington said that "we pour legislation into the senatorial saucer to cool it [the legislation]."[62] For all federal offices, the date of the general election is, by law, the first Tuesday after the first Monday in November.

States typically follow the same practices, with similar terms in office for legislators (typically two or four years) and governors (typically four years). They use the same November election date that was established by federal law in 1845. States vary in what year they elect governors—some hold gubernatorial elections during years with a presidential election, others during even-numbered years without a presidential election, or, in Virginia and New Jersey, in every other odd-numbered year. Many local elections are not held concurrently with federal elections.

General elections are actually the second stage of the electoral process: most candidates must first secure the support of their party. This is typically determined in a primary election, where candidates compete with others for their party's nomination for a particular office. States have a great deal of leeway in setting the date of their primary, although for the presidential nomination process (which we discuss further in Chapter 9), the parties pressure states to adhere to a particular calendar. Candidates in some states thus face an earlier primary than candidates in other states do. Only after a primary election victory do candidates then compete in the general election.

The timing of American elections powerfully affects candidate strategy, including when candidates can start campaigning for office. Because politicians and potential candidates at every level of office know when the next election is scheduled, they can begin preparing for it well in advance. This creates campaigns that are longer than campaigns in many other countries and that require extraordinary effort from candidates. Presidential candidates often begin campaigning for the nomination years before the November general election. In preparation for the 2020 presidential primary, two candidates, Representative John Delaney and entrepreneur Andrew Yang, actually announced their campaigns in 2017. Even better-known candidates, like Senators Bernie Sanders and Elizabeth Warren, announced their campaigns in February 2019. Joe Biden was relatively late in announcing his campaign on April 25, 2019, but even then there were months to go before any votes were cast.

Because campaigns are so long and politicians are always eyeing the next election, campaigning essentially never stops. Politicians raise money and do other things to improve their chance of winning on an almost daily basis—even though they routinely express their dislike for this life. In 2016, then representative David Jolly (R-Fla.) told CBS News that the emphasis placed on fundraising is "beneath the dignity of the office that our voters in our communities entrust us to serve."[63] But most politicians appear unwilling to take chances on letting opponents get a jump on them, and they raise money constantly. They travel to their states or districts nearly every week to interact

Andrew Yang announced that he was running for president in November 2017—about three years before the 2020 election.

with constituents, and they conjure up creative ways to appear in the news media whenever possible.

What is good and bad about this **permanent campaign**? On the one hand, it may help improve the quality of deliberation in the campaign. The longer the candidates campaign, the more information citizens receive, as news coverage and advertising persist for weeks if not months before an election.[64] A permanent campaign can also improve the quality of representation because such a campaign keeps politicians in constant contact with citizens and perhaps better aware of their needs and interests. On the other hand, critics respond that much of this effort is for naught. Citizens often do not pay much attention until the election is close at hand, and thus at least some early campaigning may be less effective. There is, for example, little evidence that televised advertisements in the summer before the November election actually produce additional votes.[65]

A permanent campaign may also hurt the ideal of free choice by dissuading good candidates from running. Some talented people, faced with the prospect of endless fundraising and nights away from home, will simply opt out. And for those who do run, campaigning takes time away from learning about policy or writing legislation. The permanent campaign may therefore detract from good governance. This is all the more true if the permanent campaign keeps politicians focused only on short-term electoral benefits at the expense of long-term solutions to the country's problems.

Where to Run

Where do candidates run for office? For some offices, such as president, senator, and governor, the boundaries of the constituency are easily determined and do not change. The president represents the country as a whole—although, as we discuss in Chapter 9, candidates often focus their campaigns on "battleground states." Senators, governors, and other statewide officeholders represent their states. But for others, notably members of the House of Representatives and state legislatures, the answer to this question is more complicated.

Single-Member Districts

With a few exceptions, federal and state legislators are elected in **single-member districts**. That is, each state is subdivided into districts and each district is represented by one legislator. In a handful of states with small populations, such as Alaska and Wyoming, there are no subdivisions, and the state is represented by one member of the U.S. House of Representatives. A system of single-member districts contrasts with a system in which each district is represented by multiple representatives. This is the case in **at-large elections**. For example, for elections to Maryland's House of Delegates, many of its 47 districts elect three representatives. Vermont's House of Representatives is composed of some districts represented by one state legislator and some represented by two legislators. Nevertheless, single-member districts are the norm.

Reapportionment

The number of U.S. House districts in each state is proportional to the state's population, and the actual number of districts is determined by the process of **reapportionment**. After the decennial census, the total number of House seats stays the same, but the number of representatives in each state may be adjusted depending on changes in state populations.[66] For example, after the 2020 census, Colorado, Florida, Montana, North Carolina, and Oregon each gained a seat in the House, and Texas gained two seats. A number of states lost a seat—including California, Illinois, Michigan, New York, Ohio, Pennsylvania, and West Virginia.

Redistricting

Far more controversial than deciding the number of seats in each state is the process of drawing district boundaries, known as **redistricting**. Redistricting affects both state legislative and U.S. House district boundaries. As a state senator, Obama was involved in redistricting his state legislative seat. The fights over U.S. House district boundaries are usually more visible in the news media. In most states, both state and congressional district boundaries are drawn by the state legislature, often with the governor's approval required. Less frequently, states use independent commissions to redraw districts, although in some states the legislature picks the members of the commission, which can make it somewhat less neutral.

There are two major requirements for U.S. House and state legislative districts: fulfilling the "one person, one vote" criterion and avoiding discrimination against people of color.

Malapportionment and "One Person, One Vote" Legislative districts must have nearly equal numbers of residents. This prevents **malapportionment** and ensures that representatives each have essentially the same number of constituents. It was not always this way. Prior to a series of Supreme Court decisions in the 1960s, malapportionment was widespread in both congressional and state legislative districts. While urban areas had typically grown in population relative to rural areas, influential rural legislators prevented the districts from being redrawn, leaving rural districts with far fewer constituents per representative. In the mid-twentieth century, rural areas held the majority of seats in state legislatures even though more than two-thirds of Americans lived in urban areas.[67]

The Supreme Court dismantled this system in two key cases. In *Baker v. Carr*, the Court established that questions related to reapportionment and redistricting were justiciable—meaning that the courts could intervene even though these issues had historically been the domain of legislatures.[68] In *Gray v. Sanders* (1963), the Court invalidated Georgia's "county unit" system, in which the candidate who won the majority of votes in each county unit was awarded that unit, and the candidate who won the most units was declared the victor.[69] The problem with this arrangement was that the units were not equal in size, which sometimes meant that the candidates who won the most county units actually received fewer votes than their opponent. In rejecting this system, the Court established the important principle of "**one person, one vote**." Because the Fourteenth Amendment (1868) guarantees equal protection under the law, states must have electoral systems in which each person's vote counts equally.

The Court noted, however, that the Constitution allows deviations from this principle in two important institutions. One is the U.S. Senate, which is famously malapportioned. As of 2020, California was estimated to have 39.5 million residents, or almost 20 million people for each of its two senators, while Wyoming had about 577,000 residents, or only about 283,500 people for each senator. The other institution is the electoral college, which formally elects the president. Each state is assigned a number of electors equal to its number of representatives and senators combined. The inclusion of senators in this tabulation makes the votes of the residents of less populous states count more.

The establishment of the "one person, one vote" rule had two main implications for drawing district boundaries. First, these Court decisions made redistricting actually happen. Previously, many state legislatures simply failed to redistrict after the census even when their state constitution required it, especially when the party in power was advantaged by the existing districts.

Second, the Court's decisions mandated that districts had to be roughly equivalent in population. In two 1964 cases, *Wesberry v. Sanders* and *Reynolds v. Sims*, the Court invalidated Georgia's congressional districts and

Alabama's state legislative districts, respectively, because both states' districts were drawn so that they had dramatically different populations.[70] Subsequent Court decisions have established a strict standard of equivalence: today, even small deviations among U.S. House districts might be held unconstitutional, while greater leeway is given to differences in state legislative districts.[71] A 2016 Court decision held that states could use total population, not just the total number of eligible voters, to calculate population sizes.[72] Using only eligible voters would tend to disadvantage districts with larger ineligible populations, such as immigrants who are not naturalized citizens. This would weaken the voting power of Latinos, for example.[73]

The "one person, one vote" rule transformed American elections, legislatures, and public policy. As Stephen Ansolabehere and James Snyder write in their history of this rule, "The American states began in the 1960s as the most unequal representative bodies in the world, and they finished the decade adhering to one of the strictest standards of equal representation." Although it did not eliminate the ability of self-interested politicians to influence legislative district boundaries—see the discussion of gerrymandering later in this chapter—the application of the rule did produce state legislatures that were much more representative of state populations in their partisan and ideological complexion. It also led to a more equitable distribution of government spending within states.[74] Equal votes really did result in more equal power.

The Voting Rights of People of Color The second requirement for congressional districts is to avoid discrimination against people of color. After Reconstruction, southern states took various steps to weaken the voting power of African Americans. One way was to draw political boundaries in such a way that excluded Black voters. In 1960, the Supreme Court took a step toward prohibiting this practice, arguing that a redrawing of the Tuskegee, Alabama, city boundaries to exclude most Black voters violated the Fifteenth Amendment.[75] Another strategy was to dilute the power of Black voters by placing a small number of Black residents into each legislative district, thereby limiting their ability to elect a candidate who reflected their background and preferences.

Over time, however, the VRA's protections for the voting power of people of color have been interpreted to apply to the redistricting process. In *Thornburg v. Gingles* (1986), the Supreme Court ruled that a state legislative redistricting plan in North Carolina discriminated against African American voters, and in so doing, it established three preconditions for demonstrating that district boundaries dilute the voting power of groups of people of color.[76] First, the group must be both sufficiently large and geographically concentrated to comprise a majority in a single district. Second, the group must be politically cohesive, meaning that members tend to have similar political preferences. Third, racially polarized voting, wherein the majority typically votes as a bloc for a candidate other than the one the group prefers, must be present. Plaintiffs challenging a districting plan must demonstrate that those preconditions hold and then provide persuasive evidence that the plan would hurt the ability of the group to elect the representatives of its choosing. The decision was interpreted as a broad endorsement of the VRA as amended in 1982.[77]

The Supreme Court's decision in *Shelby County* now means that states do not have to submit redistricting plans to the federal government before they take effect. Instead, any concerns about the consequences of these plans for voters of color must be pursued in court. In 2017, for example, one such suit led federal judges to rule that the Texas congressional map drawn in 2011 was discriminatory.[78]

Besides "one person, one vote" and the constraints on diluting the voting power of people of color, there is little else in federal law that formally constrains the drawing of district boundaries. Districts are often drawn to be relatively compact and also contiguous. *Contiguity* means that a district is not composed of "islands" of territory within a state, as would be the case for a district made up of a couple neighborhoods in San Francisco, a couple in Los Angeles, and nothing in between. Districts are also often drawn to correspond to **communities of interest**, such as existing towns or cities. These guidelines are not codified as formal rules at the federal level, but some states require that districts respect community boundaries.

Gerrymandering Without more explicit rules, the people in charge of drawing district boundaries can engage in **gerrymandering** (with the resulting set of districts constituting a "gerrymander"). Gerrymandering is the deliberate manipulation of district boundaries for some political purpose, and it can result in oddly shaped districts. (The term was coined in response to a redistricting plan implemented under Massachusetts governor Elbridge Gerry in 1812 that included a district thought by some to resemble a salamander. "Elbridge Gerry's salamander" begat "gerrymander.")

Gerrymandering can serve multiple aims. It can protect incumbents by ensuring that their districts are populated with voters likely to support them. Alternatively, the party in control of the redistricting can engage in **partisan gerrymandering** by trying to maximize the number of seats it can win. To do so, the gerrymandering party needs to spread its voters across districts so that it has a margin large enough to win in as many districts as possible—but not too large a margin in any one district, or otherwise it is just wasting votes. As part of its redistricting plan, the gerrymandering party may "pack" voters from the opposite party into as few districts as possible so that the opposite party wastes most of its votes electing only a few representatives. It may "crack" apart an existing district where the opposite party has been dominant, forcing that district's incumbent into a new district with many unfamiliar constituents. "Hijacking" forces two incumbents from the opposite party to compete against each other. If partisan gerrymanders are successful, then the gerrymandering party will typically win a percentage of legislative seats that is larger than its share of the votes cast.

Partisan gerrymanders are less severe now than they were before 1960, in part because there are limits on redistricting like "one person, one vote." But having control of the redistricting process still benefits the party in power. One analysis of congressional elections from 2002–18 found that in states where one party drew the district map, that party gained at most 10 additional U.S. House seats, compared to states in which maps were drawn by a bipartisan process.[79] Another analysis compared actual legislative maps to hypothetical nonpartisan maps drawn by a computer algorithm that relied only on traditional criteria like contiguity and compactness. It also found that partisan control of redistricting for the U.S. House tended to produce more seats for the party that drew the map than did the simulated nonpartisan maps.[80] Whether this adds up to a partisan advantage in the House depends on how many states are controlled by each party and how effective the gerrymanders are. For many years, redistricting tended to advantage the Democratic Party. But in recent years, the Republican Party has controlled the redistricting process in more states and has drawn more severe, successful gerrymanders, thereby allowing Republicans to win more seats than votes.[81] In 2012, for example, Republican candidates won about 49 percent of all votes cast for the U.S. House but 54 percent of the seats (234 of 435), giving them control of the chamber.

Gerrymandering can also create districts that maximize the number of voters of color, thereby helping to ensure the election of representatives who are people of color themselves. Districts in which the majority of voters are people of color are sometimes called **majority-minority districts**, and these districts can help ensure that the voting power of these communities is adequately protected.

However, the Court has raised objections to some redistricting plans geared toward empowering African Americans under the auspices of the VRA. The most famous case was a North Carolina plan that included a district (the 12th District) some 160 miles long, which was drawn to include

FIGURE 2.1 North Carolina's 12th Congressional District, 1992–98

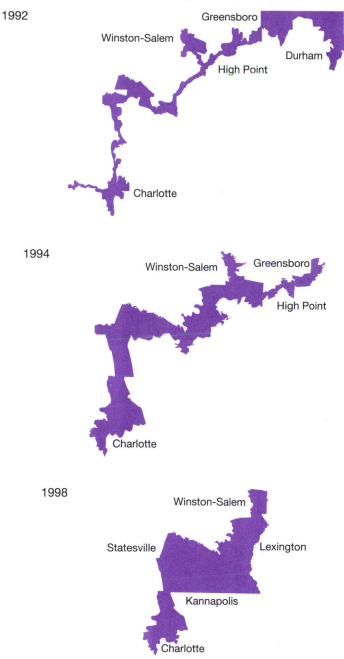

1992

Greensboro
Winston-Salem
Durham
High Point
Charlotte

1994

Winston-Salem   Greensboro
High Point
Charlotte

1998

Winston-Salem
Statesville   Lexington
Kannapolis
Charlotte

Source: "North Carolina Redistricting Cases: The 1990s," National Conference of State Legislatures, www .senate.leg.state.mn.us/departments/scr/redist/redsum/NCSUM.HTM (accessed 9/20/17).

Black communities in several different cities and was sometimes scarcely any wider than the interstate highway that connected them (see Figure 2.1). In *Shaw v. Reno* (1993),[82] the Court's majority described this district as "highly irregular" and expressed discomfort with racial gerrymanders in general. This district was then subject to years of court battles, including three further Supreme Court cases, as well as much tinkering with its boundaries.[83] Ultimately, the Court upheld the district only after North Carolina successfully argued that its boundaries reflected a political goal—to create a safe Democratic seat—rather than a racial goal.

More recently, Court majorities have raised similar concerns about state legislative and congressional district maps drawn by Republicans in North Carolina (again), Alabama, and Virginia.[84] Plaintiffs in these cases argued that Republicans had diluted the voting power of people of color not by spreading them out across districts but by packing them into a small number of districts.

Taken together, these many cases do not mean that states cannot take race into account when drawing districts. But the Court's rulings have forced states that take race into account when drawing districts to justify them on different and more demanding terms. It is also worth noting that in many of these cases, the Court's rulings were narrowly divided, signaling that the justices sharply disagreed on the validity of racial gerrymandering.

The Court's concern about racial gerrymandering has not extended to other forms of gerrymandering. In 1973, the Court upheld a Connecticut plan that created separate Democratic and Republican strongholds and thereby provided considerable protection for incumbents.[85] The Court saw benefits in the plan because it provided a legislative body that mirrored the partisan composition of Connecticut voters. Subsequent decisions confirmed that incumbent protection is not necessarily problematic in the view of the Court.[86]

The Court has not declared partisan gerrymanders unconstitutional, no matter how extreme they may sometimes be. It has not been able to agree on a standard by which to judge these types of gerrymanders or even on whether they are justifiably the domain of the courts, as opposed to political bodies like state legislatures.[87] In 2019, a slim majority of justices ruled that partisan gerrymanders were not justiciable.[88] This likely forecloses challenges to partisan maps at the federal level, at least until the composition of the Court changes. Instead, battles over districts will take place mainly at the level of state legislatures and state courts.

How does redistricting affect candidate strategy? In some cases it may forestall a candidate's political career: in a district strongly skewed toward one party, a candidate of the opposite party is unlikely to win or, perhaps, to run for office in the first place. At the same time, a particular redistricting cycle may endanger or even end the career of someone already in office, particularly if district boundaries change dramatically and the incumbent must confront large numbers of new, unsupportive constituents. Campaign messages also reflect the realities of district boundaries and constituent demographics. The issues that candidates emphasize, the groups they target, and actions they take if elected to office all reflect the nature of their constituency.

Redistricting and gerrymandering raise philosophical questions as well. For many people, the mere existence of abnormally shaped districts is objectionable. But a weird shape alone does not mean a district is "bad." Judging a district or map of districts requires making hard decisions about what types of districts produce "good" representation. Consider the following criteria:

- Good representation happens when representatives are beholden to specific geographical communities that are believed to have common interests. This is a reason to draw districts that correspond to existing cities, towns, and the like.

- Good representation happens when the largest possible majority of people gets to elect the representative of its choice. This is a reason to draw lopsided districts with large partisan majorities.

- Good representation happens when groups who have been historically excluded from the electoral process—like people of color—get to elect the representative of their choice. This is a reason to draw majority-minority districts.

- Good representation happens when a district is politically competitive, which means that representatives work harder to represent "the people" because there is always a good chance they could be voted out of office. This is a reason to draw districts with a 50-50 partisan balance.

- Good representation happens when each party wins a percentage of legislative seats roughly equal to its percentage of the vote. This ensures that the partisan composition of the legislature matches the electorate as a whole.

There are extensive debates about the merits of these different concepts of representation. For example, consider the question of whether districts should be more or less competitive. One view is that *less* competitive districts could be better because they help a larger majority of voters feel well represented by their representative—whether in terms of race or ethnicity (as in majority-minority districts) or in terms of party.[89] In a very competitive district where voters are divided 51 to 49 percent between the two major parties, a large fraction of voters—possibly even 49 percent—will feel poorly represented if the majority wins.

On the other hand, gerrymanders that limit the competitiveness of legislative elections and favor an incumbent legislator or a particular party make it difficult for opposing candidates to raise money and effectively advertise their candidacy (that is, if they run at all).[90] The resulting election may fall short of the ideals of both free choice and deliberation because citizens will receive less information than they would if the election were competitive; thus, they may find it harder to deliberate about the candidates' relative merits.[91] Critics also argue that in districts that are deliberately gerrymandered to let one party dominate, the favored party's candidates will cater only to that party's base once elected, becoming more ideologically extreme and further polarizing the parties in the state legislature or Congress.

Concerns about redistricting's effects on competition and polarization have led a number of states to reform their redistricting processes—for example, by placing the responsibility with an independent commission rather than the state legislature and by instituting more detailed rules about how districts can be drawn. Fourteen states now have independent redistricting commissions.[92] Washington state, for instance, requires that its commission exercise its powers "to provide fair and effective representation and to encourage electoral competition." In 2015, the Supreme Court strengthened the institution of independent redistricting commissions by ruling that citizens could take away redistricting power from legislators and give it to a commission (as had happened in Arizona via initiative).[93]

How successful have these commissions been? There is evidence that compared to maps drawn by state legislatures, maps drawn by courts and commissions produce a larger number of competitive districts as well as districts that are more compact and better respect existing community boundaries.[94] Redistricting commissions may thus help satisfy certain criteria for good representation.

At the same time, we should be cautious in assuming that reforms to the redistricting process will ameliorate problems in our politics. For example, gerrymandering does not appear to increase political polarization.[95] Furthermore, redistricting reforms can only increase competition to a certain degree. In some areas of the country, preexisting residential segregation naturally produces politically homogeneous communities and makes it hard to draw competitive districts unless mapmakers are willing to ignore existing community boundaries.[96] More generally, the growing urban–rural gap in American party politics—with urban areas increasingly Democratic and rural areas increasingly Republican—may create a natural disadvantage for Democrats who are concentrated in urban areas.[97] Respecting urban political boundaries may mean "packing" Democrats into districts and reducing their voting power. In sum, designing "good" maps of districts inevitably means making trade-offs among different criteria and different philosophies of representation.

Who Wins

Once candidates have campaigned and citizens have voted, a crucial question arises: How are votes counted to determine a winner (or winners)? In the United States, most elections adhere to a simple winner-take-all or "first past the post" principle. Typically, the person with the most votes (a plurality of votes) wins the election. For example, in order for a presidential candidate to win a state and therefore receive all of that state's electoral college votes, the candidate need only win more votes than any other candidate in that state. (We discuss the implications and consequences of the electoral college in Chapter 9.) A plurality is not necessarily a majority, or more than half of, the votes. **Plurality rule** is more common than majority rule in American elections, although some states do have rules in place for certain offices to ensure that the winning candidate is elected by a majority. This often entails a runoff election between the top two vote-getters, as in the Louisiana system discussed earlier. Georgia also has runoff elections for statewide offices if no candidate gets a majority in the November election. This happened most recently in 2020, when races for both of Georgia's U.S. Senate seats advanced to the runoff stage.

A few states and localities have begun to experiment with another alternative to plurality rule: **ranked-choice voting**, which is sometimes called the "alternative vote" or "instant runoff voting." Instead of selecting a single candidate, voters rank their top candidates in order of preference. If a candidate is the top choice of a majority of voters, then that candidate wins. But if no candidate wins a majority, then the candidate with the fewest first-choice votes is eliminated. The votes of people who put that candidate first are then reallocated based on those voters' second choices. This process of eliminating candidates and reallocating votes continues until a candidate wins a majority. To date, ranked-choice voting has been adopted statewide in Maine and Alaska as well as for local elections in a number of cities, including New York City, Minneapolis, Oakland, and San Francisco.

The prevalence of plurality rule in single-member districts makes the United States different from many other democracies. A helpful contrast involves those countries whose legislatures are chosen by **proportional repre-sentation**, such as the Netherlands, Denmark, Sweden, Israel, and Switzer-land. In these systems, seats are allocated to parties in proportion to the percentage of the vote they received overall. A party that wins 20 percent of the vote can expect to receive close to 20 percent of the seats, although many countries have a threshold such that a party must win some minimum percentage of the vote to gain any seats. To achieve proportionality, these systems often do not have single-member districts but either nationwide elections or districts with multiple winners. Voters vote for a slate of candi-dates chosen by the party rather than for an individual candidate nominated via a primary election. To be sure, proportional systems differ from each other in their specific rules, and some countries combine features of both kinds of systems. But this general description highlights the major points of contrast between these systems and the American system.

One consequence of the American system was spelled out by the French social scientist Maurice Duverger in what became known as **Duverger's Law**: in a system with single-member districts and plurality voting, there is a strong tendency for only two parties to emerge, and candidates not affiliated with either of those parties face serious obstacles. This is because in an election with more than two candidates, voters in a plurality system often engage in **strategic voting**—voting for a candidate who is not their first choice but has a better chance of winning. Some supporters of independent candidates or can-didates from minor parties do not want to "waste" their votes on candidates who have little chance of winning a seat, so they end up defecting to which-ever of the two major-party candidates they like better (or dislike less). Third-party or independent candidates typically fare poorly. Duverger's Law helps explain why the American party system is characterized by long periods of two-party dominance. By contrast, in a system that uses proportional repre-sentation, candidates from smaller parties may still win some seats, even if they have no chance of winning the most votes, so their supporters are less likely to defect.

The use of plurality rather than proportional rules in the United States gives candidates a strong incentive to affiliate with a major party. For exam-ple, in the past 60 years there have been only six members of the U.S. House or Senate who identified as an independent at any point in their con-gressional career, and only one—Senator Bernie Sanders—has been an inde-pendent for his entire career.

The U.S. system also incentivizes parties and candidates to invest signifi-cant effort only in competitive races. For example, political parties raise money that they can then spend on behalf of any of their candidates. Where is that money best spent? In an uncompetitive district where it might help the party's candidate win, say, 30 percent of the vote instead of 15 percent? Probably not. In a winner-take-all election, 30 percent of the vote earns nothing more than 15 percent does. Instead, parties will target more competitive districts where this money might make the difference between winning and losing. The same logic applies to presidential candidates, given the winner-take-all nature of the electoral college. It makes little sense for candidates to campaign in states where they are virtually guaranteed to win or to lose. They go instead to the "battleground" states where the outcome is in doubt and additional campaign dollars may make a difference.

The dominance of the two major parties is one criticism of the American system and is frequently cited by reformers as a reason for favoring ranked-choice voting or proportional representation. Ranked-choice voting means that independent and minor-party candidates will not be "spoilers"—that is, candidates who siphon so many votes from a major-party candidate that the other major-party candidate wins, even though most voters do not prefer that candidate. Proportional representation also tends to lead to multiparty systems that provide more options for voters. In either system, increased options may enhance free choice as well as the deliberative potential of elections, as more issues and policy proposals are likely to be discussed by candidates from different parties. Fewer votes are "wasted" because more citizens are encouraged to select their first choice. In particular, minority groups—whether political, racial, ethnic, or otherwise—may find it easier to elect representatives of their choice under a proportional system. Some supporters also argue that citizens may be more likely to vote if more options are available that truly represent their preferences, although there is not much evidence that turnout is higher in proportional systems.[98]

Ranked-choice voting advocates often emphasize that it can produce clear majority winners when plurality voting rules would not. But ranked-choice voting introduces complexities for voters in terms of how they fill out their ballots. Ranking candidates typically requires more effort than choosing a single candidate, and voters in cities that use ranked-choice voting do say that it is not as easy to understand, compared to voters in cities that use plurality voting.[99] If voters do not rank all of the candidates they are asked to rank, their ballot may not ultimately count toward the final outcome. One study of ranked-choice elections in California in which voters were asked to rank their top three candidates found that between 25 and 50 percent of voters failed to do so and that between 10 and 27 percent of ballots did not actually count toward the outcome—thereby calling into question whether ranked-choice voting can really produce the winner favored by a majority.[100] However, some of these challenges may reflect the novelty of ranked-choice voting. The longer this system is employed, the more adept voters may become.

This brief discussion hardly captures the full range of debate about the different rules for counting votes and determining winners. The larger point remains: any set of rules will promote certain values over others.

Conclusion

This chapter has discussed the basic rules of the American electoral system—rules that govern nearly every aspect of the electoral process. Even in this brief overview, it is clear that the American system reflects no grand logic. It is the result of many compromises that are guided by multiple decision makers, including the framers of the Constitution, the Supreme Court, and federal, state, and local lawmakers. As such, the rules can change over time and vary across states and localities. The rules often depend on which party is in power, since parties will seek to change the rules in their favor. The rules are also products of contending values about what a "good" election looks like. Whether rules strike observers as fair or unfair will depend in part on which party they belong to and which values they hold dear. Moreover, it is challenging to construct electoral rules that uphold all these values simultaneously. Trade-offs are inevitable.

The rules that govern elections affect all of the actors whose roles we describe in later chapters. The rules provide the framework for the decisions of candidates, parties, and citizens alike. Electoral rules that cannot be changed quickly or easily—the use of single-member districts, the need to redistrict after reapportionment—become part of the hand that candidates are dealt.

Even seemingly arcane rules can be consequential. In the 2020 presidential election, for example, this would include rules about secrecy envelopes and "naked ballots" or, as we noted in Chapter 1, how many drop boxes would be available for voters to deposit mail ballots. In Illinois in 2001, the adoption of the new district that Obama helped draw literally came down to a piece of paper that was picked out of a hat. The Democrats, who controlled the Illinois House, had drawn up one set of districts. The Republicans, who controlled the Illinois Senate, had drawn up another. A commission composed of four Democrats and four Republicans was appointed to choose a map, but they failed to agree. In accordance with Illinois law, the Illinois Supreme Court submitted the names of one Democrat and one Republican. Those names were put in a hat—a hat made to resemble Abraham Lincoln's stovepipe hat, no less—and one name was drawn: the Democrat's. This person became the tie-breaking vote on the commission, and his vote enacted the Democrats' map and thus Obama's new district. The rest, as they say, is history.

KEY TERMS

poll taxes (p. 30)

literacy tests (p. 30)

White primary (p. 30)

Voting Rights Act of 1965 (VRA) (p. 30)

closed primary (p. 31)

semi-closed primary (p. 31)

open primary (p. 31)

blanket (or jungle) primary (p. 31)

automatic voter registration (p. 32)

same-day (or Election Day) registration (p. 32)

voter identification laws (p. 32)

early voting (p. 37)

absentee voting (p. 37)

vote-by-mail (p. 38)

convenience voting (p. 38)

independent candidates (p. 43)

term limits (p. 43)

permanent campaign (p. 47)

single-member districts (p. 47)

at-large elections (p. 48)

reapportionment (p. 48)

redistricting (p. 48)

malapportionment (p. 48)

one person, one vote (p. 49)

communities of interest (p. 51)

gerrymandering (p. 51)

partisan gerrymandering (p. 51)

majority-minority districts (p. 52)

plurality rule (p. 57)

ranked-choice voting (p. 57)

proportional representation (p. 58)

Duverger's Law (p. 58)

strategic voting (p. 58)

FOR DISCUSSION

1. What are arguments for and against term limits?

2. How have different electoral rules affected the ability of Black Americans to vote and to elect representatives of their choosing?

3. How might different rules about who can vote affect how candidates campaign?

4. How does the American system's combination of single-member districts and plurality rule disadvantage minor political parties and independent candidates?

3

The Transformation of American Campaigns

On May 23, 2016, the online political newsletter *Morning Consult* published an article titled "Why 2016 Will Be the Most Negative Campaign in History."[1] Relying on an analysis of public opinion polls and television advertisements, the article painted a bleak picture of what to expect from a presidential campaign between Donald Trump and Hillary Clinton:

> The 2012 campaign between President Obama and former Massachusetts Gov. Mitt Romney devolved into the most negative presidential contest in modern American history. The 2016 race could make that battle look tame by comparison . . . And while voters maintain they don't like seeing negative advertising, both Democrats and Republicans have signaled that the tone of the general election battle is likely to spiral into a morass of attacks that will use fear to motivate voters who are unenthusiastic about either candidate. Campaigning to persuade undecideds is out; campaigning to motivate the partisan base is in.

There is some truth to *Morning Consult*'s characterization of 2016, especially the idea that the polarized politics of today provides incentives for mobilizing the base rather than competing for persuadable voters. During the 2016 campaign, Trump repeatedly referred to Clinton as "crooked Hillary,"[2] said she was a "dangerous" and "pathological" liar who was "unbalanced" and "unstable," and warned voters that a Clinton presidency would lead to the "destruction of this country from within."[3] Clinton referred to Trump's supporters as a "basket of deplorables."[4] She criticized his ideas as "dangerously incoherent. They're not even really ideas, just a series of bizarre rants, personal feuds, and outright lies," and she went on to say that Trump was "not just unprepared, he's temperamentally unfit to hold an office."[5] In a polarized era, these attacks played particularly well to hard-core Republican and Democratic voters, respectively. If nothing else, the 2016 campaign showed that Republicans loved to hate Hillary Clinton and Democrats loved to hate Donald Trump.

But was 2016 "the most negative campaign in history"? An analysis of television advertising by the Wesleyan Media Project suggests that 2016 was not even as negative as 2012: in 2016, slightly more than half of the ads aired by all sponsors (including outside groups) from early April through Election Day were "attack" ads, compared to over 60 percent in 2012.[6] In 2020, the percentage of attack ads declined to about one-third, probably because the 2020 contest was distinguished both by a mostly civil nominating contest on the Democratic side and by a global pandemic that made personal attacks seem out of place. Still, Trump and Joe Biden traded sharp words and even sharper accusations by the end of the 2020 campaign, providing evidence for the argument that negativity is almost always a central feature of American political campaigns.

In fact, the negativity of recent campaigns is of a piece with—and perhaps pales in comparison to—that seen in some previous campaigns. For example, in the election of 1828, a local newspaper printed this attack

Core of the Analysis

- Many aspects of modern campaigns can be seen in campaigns throughout American history.

- Changes in the conduct and content of campaigns have been produced by changes in rules, reality, strategy, and the electorate.

- Campaigns can be sorted into five eras, each of which is distinguished by distinct forms of campaigning.

- The increasingly competitive and polarized party system, driven by coalitional shifts in the Republican and Democratic parties and accentuated by sophisticated targeting and digital communication, signifies a new era for campaigns.

- There are commonalities across these eras, particularly in the length, expense, and content of American campaigns.

against Democratic candidate Andrew Jackson: "Gen. Jackson's mother was a common prostitute brought to this country by the British soldiers. She afterwards married a mulatto man, with whom she had several children, of whom Gen. Jackson was one." In 1860, Abraham Lincoln was attacked as "a fourth-rate lecturer, who cannot speak good grammar and who, to raise the wind, delivers his hackneyed, illiterate compositions at $200 a piece." As if that were not enough, Lincoln was also characterized as "a horrid looking wretch. . . . Sooty and scoundrelly in aspect, a cross between the nutmeg dealer, the horse swapper, and the night man, a creature fit evidently for petty treason, small stratagems, and all sorts of spoils."[7]

This chapter focuses on the lessons that past campaigns can teach us about contemporary American campaigns. Are there certain patterns and characteristics that appear repeatedly? Or is the essential nature of campaigns dynamic, shifting as the American electorate and its candidates evolve? In this chapter we argue that although the rules and reality that drive election campaigns are frequently a source of intense contestation, there has tended to be a fair amount of continuity within defined eras. When the rules and realities do change, however, they tend to do so abruptly, producing periods in which campaigns innovate and campaign strategies adapt. We propose that there are five major eras of American political campaigns: 1788–1824 ("Pre-Democratic Campaigns"), 1828–92 ("Mass Mobilization Campaigns"), 1896–1948 ("Progressive Era Campaigns"), 1952 to 2012 ("Candidate Campaigns"), and 2016 to the present ("Contemporary Campaigns"). Each is distinct enough from the others to warrant its own category, but each also contains elements common to the other eras.

The First Campaign Era: Pre-Democratic Campaigns, 1788–1824

In some ways, the earliest era of campaigning, which we refer to as the **era of pre-democratic campaigns**, is unique. The first two presidential contests, which resulted in unanimous elections of George Washington, were like no others in American history. Washington was considered the logical choice for the job—indeed, there are some who believe the Constitution would not have been ratified had lawmakers not assumed Washington would serve as the first president—and there was no serious campaign against him. Unsurprisingly, the sum total of Washington's campaign expenditures in 1788 was two casks of Virginia spirits provided for electors.[8] Similarly, the election of John Adams as Washington's successor in 1796, though contested, involved only trace elements of the partisan effort, conflict, and machinations that emerged just four years later.

The 1800 election between John Adams and Thomas Jefferson marked a turning point within the first era in American campaigns. Adams's first term as president saw the unraveling of the uneasy truce that had held during Washington's tenure. In its place, two camps emerged. On one side was the **Federalist Party**. The Federalists, who were especially numerous in New England and the mid-Atlantic states, believed in a strong federal government, preferred to ally with Great Britain, and were suspicious of the radical ethos of the French Revolution. They were led by many of the architects of the Constitution, including John Adams and Alexander Hamilton. On the other side was the **Democratic-Republican Party**. The Democratic-Republicans distrusted the expanding federal government and suspected that it only served the commercial interests of the northeastern states. They preferred an alliance with France, even in the face of the French Revolution, to an alliance with Great Britain and its monarchy. Democratic-Republicans, who were numerous in the southern states, were led by Thomas Jefferson and his trusted ally James Madison.

The actions of these two camps as the presidential election of 1800 approached illustrate one of our major themes: the importance of the rules that govern campaigns and elections. At this point in time, presidential electors were chosen by state legislators and not by ordinary citizens. Furthermore, only a narrow sliver of property-owning White males had the right to vote. In fact, citizens did not come to dominate the presidential election process until the 1820s, which is why we characterize this era as one of "pre-democratic campaigns." Because state legislators were so consequential, presidential candidates sought their support and attempted to influence the composition of state legislatures. Candidates also tried to get legislatures to adopt rules that would give them more votes in the electoral college. In early 1800, for example, Jefferson's Democratic-Republicans worked hard to win a majority of seats in Pennsylvania's lower house and then attempted to change Pennsylvania's rules so that all of the state's electors would go to the candidate whose party commanded a legislative majority. The Pennsylvania Senate, where Adams's Federalists had a majority, blocked

FIGURE 3.1 Five Major Eras of Political Campaigns

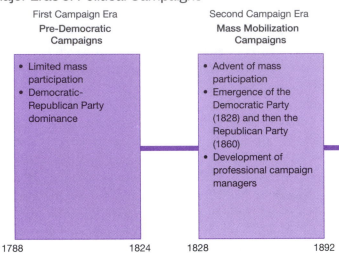

the move. This state-by-state effort to design favorable electoral rules offers the earliest glimpse of the strategic emphasis on "battleground states" that dominates presidential campaigns today.

The importance of state legislators also led to another innovation in strategy: the first organized attempts to get eligible citizens to the polls, what we would refer to today as **get-out-the-vote (GOTV) efforts**. These operations encompass a wide range of activities and outreach undertaken by candidates, campaigns, political parties, and interest groups to contact eligible voters and get them to cast ballots in an election. In New York, Aaron Burr built a political network that helped the Democratic-Republicans win crucial seats in the state legislative elections of 1798—seats that would prove important in 1800 when Burr became Jefferson's running mate. In building this network, Burr employed several strategies that later became staples of political campaigns, including identifying sympathetic citizens and turning them out to vote on Election Day.

The 1800 election also featured the kind of negative campaigning that pundits today sometimes bemoan. There were attack ads, many of which centered on Jefferson's sympathies with the French Revolution as well as his religious faith (or lack thereof). One such passage from a Federalist newspaper attacked Jefferson and other members of the "anti-federal junto":

> Citizens choose your sides. You who are for French notions of government; for the tempestuous sea of anarchy and misrule; for arming the poor against

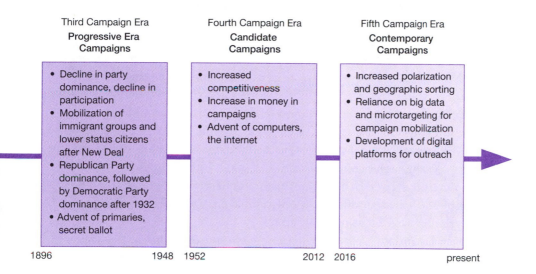

the rich; for fraternizing with the foes of God and man; go to the left and support the leaders, or the dupes, of the anti-federal junto. But you that are sober, industrious, thriving, and happy, give your votes for those men who mean to *preserve the union* of the states, the purity and vigor of our excellent Constitution, the sacred majesty of the laws, and the holy ordinances of religion.[9]

The central difference between the 1800 election and contemporary presidential elections is how little campaigning the candidates themselves actually did in the earliest presidential contests. For the most part, surrogates carried out the organizational activity and the negative campaigning. Although Adams did some campaigning during a trip from Massachusetts to Washington, D.C., in the spring of 1800, it was mainly Hamilton and other Federalists who worked on his behalf to influence legislative elections and wrote letters and articles excoriating Jefferson and his Democratic-Republican allies on every issue of the day. Jefferson stayed mainly in his Virginia home, Monticello, communicating by letter with Madison, Burr, and other Democratic-Republican leaders.

The election of 1800 culminated in Jefferson's victory. Popular discontent over the prospect of higher taxes and more intrusive government worked against Federalist arguments. Moreover, the Federalists made several key mistakes, such as supporting the Alien and Sedition Acts, which had been passed in 1798 under the Adams administration and which made it illegal for the press to publish "false, scandalous, and malicious writing" about the government or its officials.

The next 25 years brought relative stasis to American political parties and campaigns. Federalist presidential candidates attempted to hold electors in their New England base while winning over electors in the mid-Atlantic and southern states by emphasizing the need for greater national government support for commercial development and infrastructure. Meanwhile, Madison and James Monroe maintained—and in some ways expanded on—the coalition established by Jefferson. Candidates and their surrogates continued to campaign behind the scenes, writing letters, encouraging supporters, dictating strategy, and suggesting lines of argument and attack. The brutality of 1800 abated somewhat, but campaigns were marked by differences over policy as well as personal attacks.

However, conditions were changing even as Jefferson assumed the presidency in the spring of 1801. Most notably, states began changing their rules so that presidential electors would be chosen by statewide popular vote. Moreover, they also began changing their voting laws in ways that significantly expanded the eligible electorate. This set the stage for a more democratic mode of campaigning.

The Second Campaign Era: Mass Mobilization Campaigns, 1828–92

The two decades between 1820 and 1840 saw the development of the first mass democratic electorate. Politicians began to campaign with the goal of winning over this electorate rather than state legislatures, thus changing the nature and meaning of campaigning. The 1828 presidential campaign was particularly important in setting the tone for all subsequent American campaigns. Although the level and sophistication of campaigning varied over time and from place to place after 1828, the innovations of this election became increasingly widespread.

The 1828 campaign arguably began four years earlier, when a political slight against Andrew Jackson produced a personal vendetta. In the presidential election of 1824, Jackson was the most popular candidate running. He received 41 percent of the national vote and won seven states worth 99 electoral votes in total. Unfortunately for Jackson, there were 261 total electoral votes at the time, and 131 votes were needed to win the presidency. His competitors John

Quincy Adams (84 electoral votes), William Harris Crawford (41 electoral votes), and Henry Clay (37 electoral votes) had more than enough electoral votes among them to prevent the race from being decided in the electoral college. Because no candidate won an electoral college majority, the election was decided in the U.S. House of Representatives, where, as stipulated in the Constitution, each statewide delegation was to cast a single vote. In this case, a reputed deal between Speaker of the House Henry Clay and supporters of John Quincy Adams resulted in the election of Adams. Jackson was outraged. Perhaps more significantly, so were his supporters.

Jackson and a handful of confidants, stung by the "stolen" election of 1824, began to lay plans to avoid what they felt would be another "theft" in 1828. As in modern presidential campaigns, all of this commenced well in advance of the election itself.

Jackson's campaign operation provided the template for all subsequent American campaigns, especially presidential campaigns. The first element of that template was its structure. Jackson's campaign was led by a small group of friends and supporters who were motivated by their personal loyalty to Jackson. These individuals recruited political operatives in important counties. The operatives were not paid, but Jackson's promise to "clean house" led them to (reasonably) expect that they would receive jobs in a Jackson administration in return for their work. This expectation—that working on a campaign may lead to a government job—remains to this day.

The second element of the template was its emphasis on organizing voters. This may seem like an obvious strategy, but in fact it was an important innovation made possible by changes in state voting laws—such as abolishing the requirement that citizens own property in order to vote—that enfranchised a larger segment of the electorate and thus created more eligible citizens to target. Jackson's operatives were in charge of mobilizing eligible voters in their counties.

The third element of the template concerns how these voters were organized. As in previous campaigns, Jackson's followers promoted his candidacy with a sustained public relations campaign in local newspapers, writing letters and enlisting the aid of sympathetic editors. However, the need to appeal to a mass electorate necessitated a new tactic: entertainment. Jackson's and subsequent campaigns featured rallies, public speeches, picnics, torchlit parades, songs, slogans, and bombastic rhetoric. Policy issues took a back seat to partisan allegiances and personalities. Thus, even though many people criticize modern campaigns for their superficiality, the 1828 election shows that American campaigns have long emphasized style over substance.

In the nineteenth century, candidates were more likely to engage personally in campaigning when the election was expected to be close. When Stephen Douglas ran for the U.S. Senate in 1858, he campaigned vigorously against Abraham Lincoln in a closely fought race, as this cartoon depicts.

This emphasis on reaching out to the masses gave rise to a further innovation: candidates increasingly campaigned for office themselves. To be sure, many candidates were still reticent about campaigning, but as early as the 1840s, it was no longer unheard-of. For example, when Stephen Douglas ran for the U.S. Senate in 1858, he campaigned tirelessly on his own behalf, making dozens of speeches across the state of Illinois. During the course of this campaign, Douglas participated in seven public debates with his opponent, a state legislator named Abraham Lincoln. As was often the case for candidates in this era, Douglas's actions were influenced by his expectation that the election would be close. Candidates appeared more likely to embrace electioneering when facing tough competition.

Many subsequent campaigns during this era adopted the strategies pioneered in 1828. After Jackson's victory, his supporters formed the core of what was to become the **Democratic Party**. Beginning in 1832, the Democrats faced stiff competition from the newly formed **Whig Party**, which favored congressional authority over presidential authority and supported a program of modernization and economic protectionism. This competition came to a head

This Log Cabin was the first building erected on the North Bend of the beautiful Ohio River, with the barrel of Cider outside and the door always open to the traveller. The wounded Soldier is one of Gen. Harrison's comrades, meeting him after his celebrated Victory at Tippecanoe and not only does the brave old Hero give his comrade a hearty welcome, but his dog recognises him, as an old acquaintance, and repeats the welcome by a cordial and significant shake of his tail. If the lookeron will only watch close enough he can see the tail absolutely shake in the picture, particularly in a clear day; and if it is held due East and West, so as to feel the power of the magnetic attraction from the Great West.

Lith.& Published by T.Sinclair N? 79 S. Third St. Phil?

When the Democrats claimed that William Henry Harrison was the type of man who would live off his pension, sitting on his porch drinking hard cider, Harrison's supporters turned the charge around to portray Harrison as a man of the people. In this 1840 engraving, Harrison is depicted welcoming a veteran with his "hard cider hospitality."

in 1840, when Whig candidate William Henry Harrison attempted to unseat Jackson's successor, incumbent Democratic president Martin Van Buren.

Just as Jackson's campaign did in 1828, Harrison's campaign emphasized his war record, particularly his role in the battle of Tippecanoe, a famous victory for U.S. forces against an American Indian confederation in the Indiana Territory in 1811. The Democrats charged that Harrison was the sort of fellow who would just as soon live off his pension, sipping hard cider on the porch of his log cabin. Harrison's campaign countered by turning this into a virtue, presenting Harrison as a man of the people—a strategy that Jackson had used 12 years earlier. Meanwhile, the emphasis on mobilizing eligible voters continued. More citizens voted in 1840 than in any previous presidential contest—80 percent of those eligible—thanks in part to campaign rallies, parades, and other hoopla. The strategies of 1828 proved successful again, and Harrison won relatively easily.

The 1876 presidential race, between Republican Rutherford Hayes and Democrat Samuel Tilden, brought up bitter rivalries from the Civil War. The election was so close that it was decided (controversially) by an election commission. This 1877 cartoon calls for an end to the rancor surrounding the election.

Even growing disagreements over slavery and the Civil War itself did not create significant changes in political campaigns. As the Whig Party split up over the issue of slavery, a series of antislavery parties emerged: the Free Soil Party, the Liberty Party, and (finally) the **Republican Party**. Although the Republicans were a party dedicated to the preservation of the Union and were hostile to slavery, they adopted the campaign tactics and strategies of the Whigs. In the 1860 election, held on the eve of the Civil War, the Republicans chose not to emphasize the policies of their nominee, Abraham Lincoln. Instead, in almost every broadside and campaign missive they spoke of Lincoln's honesty and his connection with the common man.[10] After the Civil War, campaigns continued to focus on pageantry, personality, and symbolic (rather than substantive) issues. In the presidential elections of 1868 and 1872, for example, the newly dominant Republicans nominated General Ulysses S. Grant, and they focused their campaigns on reminding Americans who had been on the winning side of the war.

The 1876 presidential election provides a striking example of campaigning from this period. By then, the Republicans were faltering after the scandal-plagued second term of President Grant. In the election for his successor, Rutherford Hayes, a Republican, faced off against Samuel Tilden, a Democrat. Hayes and Tilden agreed on almost all of the major issues of the day, but, once again, the campaign was rancorous. Republicans continued to link the Democrats with the South's secession during the Civil War. One supporter of Hayes claimed, "Every man that endeavored to tear the old flag from the heavens that it enriches was a Democrat. Every man that tried to destroy this nation was a Democrat. . . . The man that assassinated Abraham Lincoln was a Democrat. . . . Soldiers, every scar you have on your heroic bodies was given you by a Democrat!"[11] For their part, Democrats thought up some bold lies, too. Hayes was said to have stolen the pay of dead Civil War soldiers in his regiment, cheated Ohio out of vast sums of money as governor, and shot his own mother.

Perhaps more important, the resolution to the 1876 presidential election brought about the end of **Reconstruction** efforts to enfranchise African Americans in the South, one of the major changes that would contribute to a new era of political campaigns. After the Civil War, new state constitutions had granted Black voters the franchise, and with this came unprecedented political power. During the 1870s, more than half a million Black men voted for the first time in their lives. According to one recent study, "By the time the new voter registration process was completed, Blacks were a majority of the registered voters in Mississippi, Alabama, Florida, Louisiana, and Georgia. In South Carolina, there were nearly two Blacks registered for every white person."[12] In every former Confederate state, African Americans were elected to public office. Shortly after North Carolina's constitutional convention, Abraham Galloway—a formerly enslaved person from the eastern part of the state—was elected to the state senate. Jonathan Clarkson Gibbs served as Florida's first—and to date, only—Black secretary of state. In total, about 2,000 Black men held public office during Reconstruction.[13] The newly won voting power of African Americans was thus a major feature of national and statewide elections in the South in the late 1860s and early 1870s. This came to an end after 1876.

In the aftermath of the 1876 election, four states—Oregon, South Carolina, Louisiana, and Florida—had disputed presidential vote results; Hayes needed all four states to win, while Tilden needed only one. An election commission was appointed that comprised five senators, five representatives, and five Supreme Court justices. Seven of the members were Republicans, seven were Democrats, and one was an independent. But the independent—Justice David Davis—was elected to the Senate by the Illinois legislature before the commission completed its work, and he had to be replaced by Justice Joseph Bradley, a Republican. Bradley voted with the Republicans on all disputes, and Hayes ended up winning the election. As part of their efforts to appease outraged Democrats, Hayes and the Republicans agreed to pull federal troops out of Louisiana and South Carolina, hastening the end of Reconstruction. The end of Reconstruction coincided with former Confederate states adopting a wide range of electoral practices that made it virtually impossible for Black people to vote, including literacy tests, poll taxes, and White primaries (see Chapter 2 for more on these rules).

Although these practices prevented some poor, uneducated Whites from voting, together they quickly hastened the end of widespread Black participation in southern politics.[14] Furthermore, they were prevalent until the passage of federal civil and voting rights legislation in the 1960s. From a purely partisan political perspective, because almost all White southerners identified with the Democratic Party, these practices essentially delivered the South to the Democrats for close to a century.

Another significant change that affected campaigning in the latter half of the 1800s was the gradual weakening of the partisan press. During the American Revolution and in the years after the ratification of the U.S. Constitution, most newspapers were essentially party organs, sometimes created and funded by candidates and parties, that ran stories promoting a particular political agenda. By the 1830s, some East Coast cities—with their burgeoning middle- and working-class populations—began to see the development of the "penny press": for one cent (more traditional newspapers cost six cents), people could get information on crime, gossip, and adventure. By the late 1800s, many newspapers had become more financially independent, thanks in part to sensationalized coverage of people and events that attracted readers. The newspapers of publishing moguls William Randolph Hearst and Joseph Pulitzer were prime examples of this kind of coverage, which was commonly referred to as "yellow journalism" (due to the yellow parchment that Pulitzer's newspapers were printed on). Newspapers no longer needed the funds provided by political parties, and so their connections to those parties began to weaken. At the same time, journalism was becoming increasingly professionalized, with an emphasis on objectivity and impartiality; this was the approach taken by elite metropolitan newspapers such as the *New York Times*. The norm of impartiality began to crowd out the openly partisan journalism of earlier periods.

A final change was that political party organizations, which had grown stronger throughout the nineteenth century, were about to face challenges.

Their growth was particularly notable in such cities as New York and Boston, where waves of immigrants became the loyal foot soldiers of local party organizations and were often rewarded with government jobs and services. The parties functioned as **political machines**—a uniquely American combination of mass politics and government programs, with more than a whiff of money and corruption. In the local urban campaigns of the 1800s, issues were almost incidental, particularly when compared with party performance and loyalty. Similarly, candidates were often irrelevant; their personal background and qualifications were less important than their party membership. Political power was wielded by party bosses, who never stood for election.

Although political machines were never as pervasive as is sometimes assumed, they were still controversial. The crushing economic depression of the 1890s helped usher in a new era, one that would hamstring the parties, elevate the importance of individual candidates, and demobilize segments of the American electorate.

The Third Campaign Era: Progressive Era Campaigns, 1896–1948

In addition to the continued suppression of Black voting in the South, the third era of campaigns, which began with the 1896 presidential election, had three important features: the continued trend toward more personal campaigning, with candidates increasingly involved in day-to-day electioneering; reforms that weakened political parties and their ability to mobilize potential voters, resulting in a dramatic decline in voter participation; and, with the Nineteenth Amendment enfranchising women and effectively doubling the number of eligible voters, a need for parties and candidates to appeal to a massive new group of people.

In the 1896 election, the Democratic nominee for president, William Jennings Bryan, ran a campaign that was especially aggressive in its appeal to Americans. He traveled over 18,000 miles by train, made more than 600 speeches (sometimes 10 or 20 in a day), and addressed 5 million people over the course of the campaign. His campaign speeches were filled with religious imagery, and his entire effort took on the aura of an evangelical crusade.

Bryan's Republican opponent, William McKinley, ran a much quieter but no less energetic campaign. After Bryan delivered his famous "Cross of Gold" speech at the Democratic National Convention, in which he appealed to farmers and factory workers by proclaiming support for easing the money supply and rejecting close adherence to the gold standard, Republican strategists were worried. But McKinley refused to mimic Bryan's efforts.

> I cannot take the stump against that man. . . . I can't outdo him and I am not going to try. . . . If I should go now, it would be an acknowledgment of weakness. Moreover, I might just as well put up a trapeze on my front lawn and compete with some professional athlete as go out speaking against Bryan.[15]

Instead, McKinley emulated Benjamin Harrison's 1888 **front-porch campaign** and conducted business from his home in Canton, Ohio. His manager, Mark Hanna, arranged for hundreds of delegations representing various interest groups and demographic groups to visit McKinley, whereupon the candidate would deliver a short speech that was often reprinted in the newspapers. McKinley also raised and spent $3.35 million (the equivalent of about $106.5 million today) and enlisted 14,000 speakers across the country on his behalf. Bryan spent only $300,000 (the equivalent of about $9.5 million today) and, lacking the support of many influential Democrats, largely spoke on his own behalf.[16] These differences between McKinley and Bryan illustrate how reality—in this case, the backgrounds, connections, and abilities of the candidates—influenced their campaign strategies. Despite Bryan's efforts, McKinley beat him by five points.

While the 1896 presidential campaign was distinct from those that came before and immediately after it, in several ways it foreshadowed modern campaigns. As we hinted at in Chapter 1—and discuss in detail in Chapters 6 and 9—it was the first presidential election in which a major-party nominee (McKinley) used the primary elections to help him win the nomination. It also provided a blueprint for the candidate-centered campaigning that dominated the twentieth century. Beyond campaign strategies and tactics, the 1896 election reshuffled the parties' coalitions to the Republicans' advantage by strengthening their hold on businessmen, professionals, skilled factory workers, and prosperous farmers. Meanwhile, it crushed the Democrats' dream of a national majority of poorer farmers, unskilled industrial laborers, and White southerners.

In the 1912 presidential election, the candidates were also quite involved in their campaigns. This election featured an unusual three-way race among the incumbent president, Republican William Howard Taft; his Democratic opponent, Woodrow Wilson; and former president Theodore Roosevelt, who ran as the nominee of the **Progressive (or "Bull Moose") Party** after being denied the Republican nomination by Taft's forces.

Taft mostly sat on the sidelines, giving few speeches and almost no interviews. But for the first time, two major presidential candidates—Wilson and Roosevelt—campaigned vigorously and personally. Roosevelt toured the country by rail, made hundreds of speeches, and worked the press with intensity and candor. Wilson also spent extensive time on the campaign trail. The passion of the campaign was embodied in the events of October 14, when Roosevelt was shot at close range before a speech in Milwaukee. Refusing to be driven to the hospital, Roosevelt insisted on giving his speech, which lasted for well over an hour. Later, doctors found that the bullet had fractured his fourth rib and lodged near his lung. He took two weeks off from the campaign, and Wilson and Taft halted their own activities out of a sense of fairness and respect. But Roosevelt was soon back on the trail, and by Election Day he had utterly exhausted his voice. Although Wilson ultimately won the election, this new style won the day. With increasingly few exceptions, this was to be the new style of presidential campaigns: personal, aggressive, and relentless.

The second major development of this era was the suite of reforms that weakened political parties. Until the turn of the century, the Republican and Democratic parties had been extremely effective at mobilizing citizens to vote. But the Progressive movement—a loose association of activists dedicated to reforming government—believed that strong party organizations were often corrupt and empowered party bosses at the expense of ordinary citizens. The Progressives helped institute or advance three significant strands of reform.

One important reform built on the creation of the federal **civil service** in 1872. The term "civil service" has two distinct meanings: (1) a branch of governmental service in which individuals are employed on the basis of professional merit as proven by competitive examinations, or (2) the body of employees in any government agency other than the military. We are referring to the first of these definitions. The civil service gave federal government jobs to individuals on the basis of their professional qualifications and not party loyalty, which was naturally the most important criterion when party organizations controlled government jobs. At the turn of the century, the number of civil service positions in the federal government expanded considerably. This undermined the parties' abilities to incentivize and compensate campaign workers.

Two other strands of reform concerned elections. One was ballot reform: in particular, the adoption of the **Australian ballot**. Australian ballots presented all candidates for all offices in a standardized fashion. Counties or states prepared these ballots, replacing ballots prepared and printed by the parties themselves. This reform enabled voters to split their tickets (that is, to vote for one party's candidate for one office and other parties' candidates for other offices), secured the secrecy of voter preferences, and prevented parties from monitoring voters and rewarding or punishing them accordingly. The second election-related reform was the advent of primary elections to determine nominees. Primaries, which a small number of states adopted during this era, took power out of the hands of party leaders, who had typically been responsible for selecting candidates for office, and gave it to voters. The widespread adoption of primaries by states and localities did not come until much later, but one sees their origins here.

These reforms once again show how rules affect campaign strategy and the subsequent behavior of voters themselves. In this case, the reforms reduced parties' control over candidates and voters. Individual candidates could then tailor messages to fit specific constituencies rather than simply adopting the positions of their party. Voters, now more anonymous because of the secret ballot, were freer to defect from the party line.[17]

Perhaps most important, these reforms had an unintended chilling effect on voter participation and turnout. In major cities such as New York, Boston, and Philadelphia, reforms that limited the benefits that parties could offer to encourage campaign workers crippled the parties' mobilization and outreach efforts. At the same time, in the South, selective enforcement of ballot reforms was used as a means to disenfranchise eligible Black voters. For example, the secret ballot served as a de facto literacy test: many Black people could not read, and because their vote was now to be secret, no person could assist them in the voting booth (these rules were not so rigorously enforced for southern White voters who could not read). Consequently, turnout plummeted. Even in the highly contentious election of 1912, turnout was 20 points lower than turnout in the 1896 election. Subsequent national events like the Great Depression and World War II also failed to increase turnout to its previous levels. Turnout in the presidential elections between 1932 and 1948 averaged 58 percent—compared with 74 percent in the second era of campaigns (1828–92).

Finally, women gained the right to vote in 1920 with passage of the Nineteenth Amendment. Never before had the number of eligible voters expanded so dramatically in the United States. At first, women voted at lower rates than men and tended to vote in a similar fashion to their husbands, which led some to suggest that suffrage for women was a failure.[18] Even so, both the Democratic and Republican parties began to court female voters through the establishment of women's clubs and by emphasizing issues that they believed were important to them: Republicans emphasized women's traditional, domestic roles while Democrats began to court them as workers.[19] These strategies for pursuing women voters that emerged in the 1920s and 1930s would continue for decades.

This third era of campaigning ended amid more important transformations in the nature of news media. The continued movement away from the partisan press toward a more professional style of reportage created the need for candidates and parties not only to counter the negative stories in the outlets of the partisan opposition but also to shape how journalists reported on their own campaigns.

In addition, important technological innovations began to change campaign strategy. The days of torchlit parades and four-hour speeches were passing into history. A more complete continental rail system, soon to be followed by air travel and a national network of interstate highways, gave candidates a greater ability to travel. Campaigns could adjust their strategies more quickly as the telephone replaced telegrams and letters. Even something as simple as the microphone allowed candidates and their surrogates to address larger crowds. Finally, the radio emerged as a revolutionary way for people to reach mass audiences, although its campaign potential would not be realized until the 1940s and 1950s. However, these changes taken together were not as transformational as the technology that would inaugurate the fourth era of campaigns: television.

The Fourth Campaign Era: Candidate Campaigns, 1952–2012

From the 1950s through the early 2000s, American political campaigns were defined by television. The development of broadcasting technology and the proliferation of television sets across the United States in the 1950s ushered in a new age of political communication. Although campaigns continued to revolve around **retail politics**—door-to-door canvassing, speeches to crowds by the candidates and their supporters, and other in-person interactions— well into the 1960s, presidential and Senate candidates of the 1950s began to focus on **wholesale politics**, which mostly consisted of producing and airing television and radio advertisements to reach mass audiences. Dwight Eisenhower's 1952 and 1956 presidential election campaigns purchased advertising in specific time slots in selected media markets in battleground states. The New York advertising agency Doyle Dane Bernbach devised similar strategies for both John F. Kennedy in 1960 and Lyndon Johnson in 1964.

The rise of television had four important consequences for campaign strategy: it elevated the role of fundraising, shifted power from parties to individual candidates, altered the content of political messaging, and changed the geographic unit for targeting and measuring the effects of the campaign.

First, the allure of reaching millions of potential voters through television ads was something few campaigns could resist. But the cost of television advertising dwarfed the expenses of candidate travel, campaign literature, and wages for staff and workers. As a result, parties and candidates had to spend more time and effort on fundraising. Indeed, the need to raise money in order to produce and air television ads has become one of the most prominent features of American politics today. As we note in Chapter 4, about a quarter of U.S. House candidates report spending as much as half of their days raising money during election years. These fundraising demands increased the pressure on officeholders and candidates to recruit and train more staffers, and to do so early in the campaign cycle. The demands also meant that accountants and lawyers became commonplace in campaigns.

Second, the rise of television shifted the focus away from political parties and onto individual candidates. We have noted that American campaigns have always tended to focus on personalities rather than policies. But this tendency was magnified with the advent of a medium that put candidates into the living rooms of American voters. Television made politicians stars in a more personal and immediate way than ever before.

Third, television changed the content of political communication, further emphasizing the sloganeering that had dominated American campaigns since the 1830s. The restricted length of television commercials—political ads usually last no more than 30 seconds—makes it imperative to communicate a message quickly and memorably. Moreover, political ads compete not only against other campaign ads but also against expensively produced, and often very entertaining, commercial product ads.

Finally, the rise of television shifted the strategic focus of consultants away from precincts, cities, and counties and onto media markets. The fundamental unit of analysis in campaigns had long been the county. But television advertisements are bounded by signal reach and are measured at the level of the media market.[20] These media markets thus became the fundamental units of political and campaign analysis.

More generally, the logic and sequencing of candidates' television advertising campaigns came to dominate the strategy of most high-level political campaigns. The itinerary and talking points of any candidate on a given day often reflected the television advertising strategy, as candidates visited the markets in which their advertisements were running and repeated the messages contained in those advertisements. Campaigns thus looked to reinforce their TV advertisements with other sorts of campaign activity.

A separate development of the fourth campaign era rivaled the rise of television in its effect on campaigns: the rise of primary elections as the dominant means for selecting candidates. The statewide nominating conventions that marked the 1800s and the first half of the 1900s were still the preferred method for choosing candidates well into the 1960s. But the exclusion of Black voters from selection processes throughout the South and dramatic protests at the Democratic National Convention in 1968 by voters who felt excluded from the nomination system resulted in reforms that led states to opt for primary elections. As we describe in detail in Chapter 9, the McGovern–Fraser Commission significantly revamped the Democratic Party's method for selecting presidential candidates, emphasizing delegates selected through statewide primary elections rather than state party conventions. As states modified their nominating procedures after McGovern–Fraser, primaries also became the standard method by which candidates for nonpresidential offices were selected. The Republican Party, not wanting to appear less open or less democratic, similarly adopted primaries for its nominating contests. By the mid-1970s, over 40 states were using primary elections of some sort to select candidates.

The move to primary elections reinforced some of the effects of television's rise. Candidates often needed to raise and spend money to compete in both the primary and the general elections. This required raising money earlier, which in turn necessitated building an effective campaign organization as much as 18 months before Election Day. Primary elections also changed how candidates approached campaign messaging; for the first time, candidates needed to develop messages that distinguished them from other contenders in their party. Some observers argue that this has influenced candidates to take more ideologically extreme positions in order to appeal to presumably more partisan and ideological primary voters. Candidates who veer too far to the left or the right to win primary elections, in turn, may face difficulties in repositioning themselves as more centrist for the general election (see Chapter 9). Others argue that primary elections encourage campaigns to focus more on biography and personality because candidates have no other way to distinguish themselves from competitors within their party, most of whom share their views on issues. For example, in the 2008 Democratic presidential primary, Hillary Clinton and Barack Obama differentiated themselves from each other mainly in terms of who had the most experience (Clinton's argument) or who could best bring about change (Obama's argument).

While not as significant as television or primary elections, the proliferation of polling is another noteworthy development of the fourth campaign era. Campaigns have always attempted to craft popular messages and present their candidates in the most appealing light possible. But the application of probability theory and statistical inference—two branches of mathematics—to the whims of the public at large turned what had once been guesswork into a science. George Gallup, among others, pioneered the field of **survey research** in the 1930s and 1940s, in which representative samples were drawn from the broader population in order to produce more accurate estimates of public opinion. The commercial applications of survey research were obvious, but political practitioners soon discovered its utility for campaigns.

Campaigns did not begin to conduct extensive polling until the 1960s and especially the 1970s, when telephones became sufficiently widespread to ensure that survey samples could be both representative and cost-effective. Since that time, polling has become a staple of campaigns, and top pollsters have become famous and sought-after individuals. Polls have also increased our understanding of what citizens think and how they will react to issue positions and messages.

Throughout this fourth era and into the contemporary era of political campaigns, pollsters and campaign managers have worked closely together, using poll data to fine-tune campaign strategy regarding positions on issues, to play up candidates' strengths and play down their weaknesses, to exploit the vulnerabilities of the opposition, and to target various groups of voters.

Some claim that polls and pollsters have effectively cheapened political discourse because candidates today simply advocate whatever message appears popular with citizens. Regardless of whether that is true, polling was particularly useful in television advertising. Polls helped candidates formulate and test messages before spending millions of dollars to broadcast them.

A final change in this fourth era speaks to an important reality that candidates must confront: the balance of partisanship in the electorate as a whole. This era began with the Democratic Party somewhat dominant in national politics, in no small part due to its strong hold on elections in the South. More broadly, Democrats' advantage stemmed from the simple fact that since President Franklin Delano Roosevelt's New Deal, more people had identified as Democrats than as Republicans. The allegiance of many to the

Democratic Party was an apparent result of the perceived success of Roosevelt's administration.

This pro-Democratic competitive balance changed in the mid-1960s. Democratic support for the Civil Rights Act of 1964 and (especially) the Voting Rights Act of 1965 caused Black voters—along with other voters of color—to shift from the Republicans (the party of Abraham Lincoln) to the Democrats (the party of Lyndon Johnson). This swing won the Democrats many votes, not only because support for the party increased among Black voters but also because many more Black voters were allowed to participate. After all, the Voting Rights Act ended a wide range of discriminatory practices, particularly in the southern states, and thereby re-enfranchised citizens who used their newly won votes to reward Democratic candidates. But by taking a more progressive stance on race and civil rights, the Democrats also cost themselves support among conservative White voters, especially in these same southern states. As a net result, the Republicans became much more competitive in the South and slightly more competitive nationally.

By the late 1980s and early 1990s, the Democrats' advantage was eroding. Electoral coalitions continued to shift, and not only over the parties' evolving positions on race. The Democratic and Republican parties had become more consistently liberal and conservative, respectively, on social issues such as abortion and gay rights. This caused more socially progressive voters, especially on the Atlantic and Pacific coasts, to move toward the Democrats, while more socially conservative voters, especially White southerners and Catholics, moved toward the Republicans (Figure 3.2). Again, while both parties added new voters, the net shift was marginally favorable for the Republicans. For example, in 1952, much more of the public identified with or leaned toward the Democratic Party (59 percent) than the Republican Party (36 percent). But by the 1990s, the Democrats' 23-point edge had shrunk by half—to an average of 12 points over the period between 1990 and 2008. And by the 2010s, the Democrats' edge had decreased even further—to an average of 7 points between 2012 and 2020.[21] This slimmer margin, combined with the wholesale transformation of the South from solidly Democratic to largely Republican, produced a series of very competitive elections and ultimately allowed the Republicans to take control of the U.S. House in 1994 for the first time in 40 years.

It is not surprising that a more competitive electoral environment created even greater incentives for candidates to raise and spend money. Moreover, with the presidency and control of Congress regularly in play, candidates and parties focused even more on a handful of competitive districts and battleground states.

FIGURE 3.2 Average Percent Democratic Margin in Presidential Elections among Key Social Groups

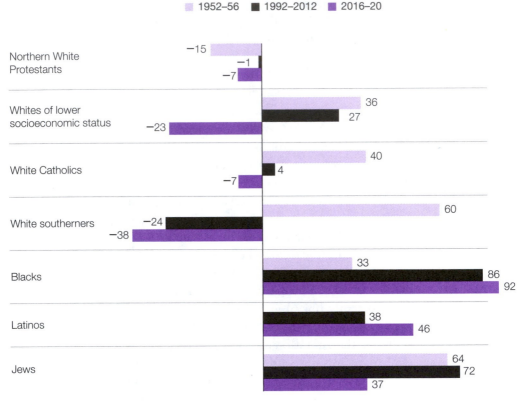

■ 1952–56   ■ 1992–2012   ■ 2016–20

Source: American National Election Studies, 1952–2020.

The innovations of technology and polling, combined with the shift to primary elections and increasingly competitive national elections, made campaigns in the fourth era qualitatively different from their forebears. At the same time, there was continuity with the past. The need to raise money to run a campaign was nothing new; this fourth era simply made it a much more significant task. Similarly, the personalized campaigns of the modern era—where candidates took to the airwaves to present themselves to potential voters—merely magnified a tendency that has always been present in American campaigns. Indeed, despite the many dim opinions of modern campaigns, it is not clear that those of the fourth era were less substantive or any more negative than campaigns were in the past.

The Fifth Campaign Era: Contemporary Campaigns, 2016–Present

As the 2010s proceeded, the coalitional changes that marked the era of candidate campaigns continued. Younger voters and college-educated voters swung to the Democrats, while Republicans mobilized less-educated White voters.[22] These shifts coincided with changing issue positions and emphases, as Republicans embraced populist positions on trade and foreign policy while Democrats aligned themselves with more progressive stances on race, income inequality, and the environment. Beyond these shifts, the pace of technological innovation has continued to accelerate, and cutting-edge technologies increasingly define contemporary campaigning. Social media, including YouTube, Facebook, Twitter, Instagram, Parler, Snapchat, and TikTok, has superseded television as the most important mode of campaigning. Though some may argue that these new forms of media represent merely a continuation of earlier campaign dynamics, our view is that we have moved into a new era of electioneering—one marked by new electoral coalitions and a combination of broadcast advertising, personalized voter targeting, and digital voter outreach. Let us consider the ways in which campaigns today both differ from and resemble previous campaigns.

Data Collection and Analysis

Technological innovations have influenced campaign strategy. Campaigns no longer have to rely on the information they can collect via polls, small focus groups of voters, or other indirect means. Both parties have information on the vast majority of Americans in the form of enormous databases that combine data from state voter files—including individuals' addresses, records of which elections individuals have voted in, and, sometimes, party registration—with data from census reports and private marketing firms.[23] A typical profile for any individual might include name, age, address, phone number, voting history, political donations, estimated income, race, family structure, mortgage data, magazine subscriptions, and other indicators. Campaigns use this information to engage in more sophisticated targeting strategies, such as estimating people's political views and the likelihood that they will turn out to vote. Campaigns can even target special interest groups—say, subscribers to *Guns & Ammo* magazine.

Beginning in 2012 and certainly by 2016, practitioners and pundits noted the emergence of "big data" and campaign "analytics" and pondered their impact on the conduct and quality of campaigns. In the context of American elections, **big data** refers to large data sets containing extensive information on individual voters. **Analytics** refers to the use of sophisticated statistical models to identify politically meaningful patterns in these voter data.

Big data and analytics allow campaigns to identify specific groups of voters for particular forms of outreach with greater precision. Campaigns might use big data and analytics to identify voters who are particularly open to persuasion if contacted and presented with information about a candidate's views on gun rights. In 2016 and 2020, some of the more analytically minded campaigns—including Hillary Clinton's—used the results of their analytics instead of traditional polling to estimate the vote, especially as Election Day drew near. Though these efforts are novel, it is unclear whether analytics have improved the accuracy of election day vote estimates.[24]

In addition to the proliferation of data and statistical modeling, the late 2000s saw the rise of **field experiments** as an important new way for campaigns to test outreach and persuasion tactics. Field experiments randomize subjects—in this case, voters—into **treatment groups** (those who are exposed to particular forms of outreach) and **control groups** (those who are not) and then compare outcomes. For example, a campaign might test the effectiveness of different subject lines on a fundraising email to potential contributors by conducting the following field experiment: identify a group of 900 potential donors; randomly assign 300 of them an email with the subject line "Give now"; randomly assign another 300 an email with the subject line "We need you"; randomly assign another 300 to a control group that received no email. Then see whether the amount of money raised is different across the three groups. Both Democratic and Republican campaigns have conducted field experiments, although the systematic and rigorous commitment of the Obama team in 2012 to scientific testing was (at the time) unprecedented.[25]

Media Platforms

New developments in the media have multiplied the ways candidates can disseminate their message and target particular audiences. The rise of cable television, talk radio, and podcasting is one such development. Each platform offers opportunities for candidates to target advertisements at relatively small but demographically distinct audiences. For example, Republicans can reach a large and like-minded audience through talk radio shows and podcasts hosted by conservative personalities like Sean Hannity and Joe Rogan. Cable news networks such as CNN, Fox News, MSNBC, and HLN (formerly Headline News) also present opportunities (or possibly burdens) for candidates. Because these networks broadcast news virtually 24 hours a day, candidates can put out a new message and see it picked up and rebroadcasted almost instantly. At the same time, continuous news can distract candidates, who may feel compelled to respond to stories that circulate on these networks even though they would prefer to talk about other issues entirely.

The digital revolution, marked by the emergence of political and candidate websites, social media platforms, and the rise of email and text-messaging technologies, has facilitated the widespread and instantaneous transmission of information. According to the Wesleyan Media Project, the Trump campaign spent $201 million on digital campaigning and $175 million on television ads in 2020. The Biden campaign spent $166 million and $250 million, respectively. Although large numbers of people still consume traditional media like television and newspapers, consumption of information online is growing quickly—a trend we discuss in Chapter 8.

Rather than simply air television advertisements and send out generic mail pieces, campaigns today engage in a variety of more targeted, personal campaign activities. They provide apps that allow supporters to access campaign-sanctioned information, goals, talking points, and volunteer opportunities all in one place. They post videos on their YouTube channels. They send small-batch fundraising emails carefully tailored to appeal to groups of people with specific issue interests. They direct community volunteers to visit potential voters in specific households, make specific appeals driven by polling information, and send their responses back to the campaign using smartphones.

Misinformation and Propaganda

Rumors and innuendo have long been a part of American election campaigns. But since the development of the "professional" press in the aftermath of the First World War, numerous mainstream news media organizations have served to check the assertions of candidates and campaigns and thus limit the spread of false or misleading information. In the 2010s, however, the confluence of several circumstances facilitated the rise of inaccurate news. First, the credibility of the mainstream news media—television networks ABC, CBS, and NBC; cable network CNN; news organizations like NPR, the Associated Press, Reuters, and Bloomberg; and newspapers such as the *New York Times* and *Washington Post*—collapsed among conservatives.[26] Meanwhile, conservative news media outlets—such as *National Review* and (especially) Fox News—came to be viewed by liberals as almost completely illegitimate.[27] Many media outlets are therefore no longer perceived as unbiased judges of political claims.[28] Second, comprehending the potential within this vacuum, strategic politicians made use of contentious or even outright false information to appeal to partisan audiences. These audiences appeared quite willing to accept this information, as it fit with their predispositions and was not contested by their preferred news outlets. Third and finally, digital and online platforms allowed false information to be precisely targeted to and widely spread among those most likely to believe it. In short, the old-school guardians today control neither the dissemination nor the content of political information.

Partisan Polarization and Demographic Change

The narrowing gap between the numbers of self-identified Democratic and Republican voters has been accompanied by another trend: the ideological sorting and polarization of the parties. **Sorting** means that people's partisan preferences have become more closely aligned with their political views. While parties in the past were not ideologically homogeneous, today, liberals have gathered in the Democratic Party, while conservatives have moved to the Republican Party. This trend has reshaped campaign strategy.[29] It has become harder for candidates to persuade voters who identify with the opposing party to support them; after all, it is unlikely that they will have enough common political ground. Instead, candidates focus even more on mobilizing their own party's base, as we saw in the example offered at the beginning of this chapter.[30] The parties' expansive databases of information about individual citizens help make this possible, as candidates can more accurately locate and communicate with people who are already likely to support them.

Other demographic changes are afoot in the American electorate. As noted in Chapter 2, the electorate expanded in the mid-twentieth century as a result of the enfranchising of 18- to 20-year-olds and the removal of impediments that made it difficult for Black people to vote. But an even more significant transformation may be at work thanks to the nation's growing racial and ethnic diversity. Immigration and high fertility rates have greatly increased the share of the American population that identifies as Asian or Latino. The U.S. Census Bureau projects that by 2060, non-Hispanic White people will make up less than 50 percent of the population (44 percent). The Latino share of the population is projected to grow to 27.5 percent by 2060, up from 18 percent in 2018.[31]

Campaign strategists are already seeking ways to reach these potential voters. Spanish-language political ads have become commonplace. In 2020, Trump's campaign aggressively targeted Mexican American voters in south Texas with campaign messages asserting that the Democrats would take away their right to own guns. Meanwhile, Biden's campaign targeted Puerto Rican voters in central Florida with ads highlighting Trump's tepid response to Hurricane Maria, which ravaged the island in 2017.

It will be even more interesting to see whether the agendas and opinions of these populations lead candidates to develop different messages. For example, a candidate who seeks to appeal to Latinos may need to talk about immigration differently than a candidate who seeks to appeal to White people. The fact that Latinos and Asian Americans have tended to vote Democratic has raised concerns among some Republicans, who believe that their party needs to broaden its appeal in this diversifying electorate.

In addition to racial and ethnic changes, other coalitional shifts merit mention. Since 2000, younger voters have been entering the electorate with stronger Democratic leanings than older voters, reflecting the fact that younger voters are more liberal on social issues.[32] In addition, the percentage of religiously observant Americans has declined, a phenomenon known as the "rise of the religious 'nones'" (a reference to the survey question in which people who do not identify with a particular religious denomination are classified as "none").[33] Less-religious voters, like young voters, are more likely to identify and vote with the Democrats. On the other side of the ledger, the percentage of White citizens with less than a high school education who registered to vote and voted increased substantially in 2016 and 2020. These voters were receptive to Trump's arguments about the pernicious effects of illegal immigration and unfair trade agreements, and they tended to identify and vote Republican.[34] All told, long-term population trends seem to favor the Democrats, although the notion that either politics or the underlying demographic trends will adhere to a predictable pattern seems fanciful.

The Case for Continuity

Although there are good reasons to think that we have entered into a new and distinct era for political campaigns, a skeptic might observe that these changes in technology, the media, and demographics do not necessarily make campaigns today significantly different from the campaigns of the fourth era. In fact, some apparent innovations are modern-day versions of campaign strategies from centuries past. For example, the rebirth of partisan or ideological media on talk radio and cable news hearkens back to the partisan press of the 1800s. Similarly, sending volunteers door to door to mobilize potential voters, even if they are carrying smartphones or iPads, is fundamentally similar to the campaigning of old-school party organizations. Indeed, these recent trends make today's campaigns look like updated versions of nineteenth-century campaigns rather than the slick, mass media–focused campaigns of the 1980s.

Contemporary campaigns have not changed much in other respects. For example, the proliferation of primary elections in the 1960s and 1970s was most responsible for lengthening campaigns, and today's campaigns are not significantly longer than campaigns were in the 1980s.[35] On December 12, 1974—691 days before the general election—Jimmy Carter announced his presidential campaign.[36] In the four most recent elections without an incumbent (2016, 2008, 2000, and 1992), the nominees announced their candidacies an average of 531 days before the general election.[37]

If campaigns have not gotten significantly longer of late, have they gotten more expensive? As we show in Chapter 4, the presidential elections of 2008, 2012, 2016, and 2020 set all-time records for candidate fundraising and expenditures. In fact, 2020 federal election campaigns in the United States cost about $14.4 billion. But from a historical perspective, it is unclear whether increased spending in recent elections makes them relatively more expensive.

Other frequent complaints about recent campaigns concern their content: they do not focus enough on policy, they lack substance, they are too negative, and so on. As we have suggested throughout this chapter, American political campaigns have always focused on personality more than policy. Even now, with the political parties taking increasingly distinct positions on the issues, this polarization is not always reflected in how candidates campaign. Candidates are often reluctant to sacrifice their broader electoral appeal in favor of party loyalty or ideological purity. In recent presidential elections, at various times John McCain, Barack Obama, Mitt Romney,

Hillary Clinton, and Joe Biden were each accused of "playing it safe" by focusing on personalities over issues. Political science research shows this may be smart politics, though, as voters often fixate on personality characteristics.[38] Candidates do care about policies, of course, but you cannot implement a policy if you do not win the election.

Thus, in American campaigns issue positions are often ambiguous.[39] Instead, candidates say they want to "make America great again" or "build back better." The logic here is straightforward: candidates know that specific issue positions involve costs and trade-offs that may alienate some voters, so they tend to endorse broadly popular goals rather than any specific means of achieving those goals. Of course, present and past campaigns have involved clear and specific policy differences. Nevertheless, there is a venerable tradition of policy ambiguity in American campaigns.

Similarly, negative campaigning is hardly a recent invention. American political campaigns have been negative ever since Federalists were calling Thomas Jefferson an infidel. This does not mean that negative campaigning is necessarily more common or more important to vote choice than positive campaigning, now or then. It means that American campaigns have always involved contrasting the relative merits of the candidates, which typically necessitates providing unflattering information about one's opponent. But are contemporary campaigns any more negative than those of earlier campaign eras? It is difficult to say. One well-known study examined negativity in presidential elections since 1960 and showed little systematic change in the negativity of campaigns. Rather, variables like the competitiveness of the race are better predictors of how negative the campaign will be.[40] No one, however, has conducted a study comparing the information received by typical Americans in 1840 and in 2020, for example. Such a study would likely reveal that today's voters get substantially more information and a similar ratio of positive to negative information.

Conclusion

In this chapter, we have made the case that the United States has seen substantively different campaign eras. These differences have arisen for a variety of reasons, but chief among them is the transformation in information and communications technology, particularly the development of broadcast media (radio and television) and then digital technology (the internet and mobile devices). At the same time, campaigns throughout U.S. history have shared common qualities, including a focus on the candidates' biographies and personalities and a willingness to attack opponents. Thus, although most Americans believe that campaigns have gotten "worse," it is difficult to prove that this is true. As we noted in Chapter 1, the quantity and quality of information provided to citizens are important criteria by which to judge campaigns. We are quite certain that more information is available to Americans today than 200 years ago, and it is far from clear whether that information is less useful or more superficial. This does not make contemporary campaigns "good" in any absolute sense, and there are reasonable arguments about how they might become better. Still, a historical perspective can be important in making such assessments.

KEY TERMS

era of pre-democratic campaigns
(p. 64)

Federalist Party (p. 65)

Democratic-Republican Party
(p. 65)

get-out-the-vote (GOTV) efforts
(p. 66)

Democratic Party (p. 70)

Whig Party (p. 70)

Republican Party (p. 72)

Reconstruction (p. 73)

political machines (p. 75)

front-porch campaign (p. 76)

Progressive (or "Bull Moose") Party
(p. 77)

civil service (p. 77)

Australian ballot (p. 77)

retail politics (p. 79)

wholesale politics (p. 79)

survey research (p. 82)

big data (p. 86)

analytics (p. 86)

field experiments (p. 86)

treatment groups (p. 86)

control groups (p. 86)

sorting (p. 88)

FOR DISCUSSION

1. In what ways are today's campaigns similar to those of the second campaign era (1828–92)?

2. Thinking back to the second and third campaign eras, under what circumstances were candidates more likely to campaign personally for elected office? Why would this have been the case?

3. How did the rise of television and primary elections influence campaigns?

4. Some have argued that the internet, especially social media, has reinvigorated the more personal approach to campaigning that characterized earlier campaign eras. Do you agree or disagree with this argument?

4

Financing Campaigns

Every election year, commentators and citizens bemoan the amount of money spent in American elections. The 2020 election was no different. Together, the Democratic and Republican presidential candidates spent almost $4 billion in the primary elections and general election combined. This total more than doubled the $1.5 billion spent in 2016, when there were competitive primaries in both major parties. Spending on the 2020 House and Senate races also far outpaced spending in 2016. The average House candidate spent about $1.7 million in 2020, almost four times what the average candidate spent in 1980 (Figure 4.1). Although the trend in Senate races is more variable, in part because campaign expenditures depend on which states have Senate races in any given year, spending has still increased over time. The average Senate candidate in the 2020 general election spent $16.7 million, while the average candidate in 1980 spent just $3.4 million.[1] Part of the reason for this hike in spending is the increasingly nationalized political environment. People across the country are asked to donate to competitive congressional races in certain states, making it easier for those candidates to raise large sums of money from donors outside their state or district. In the 2020 race for South Carolina's contested U.S. Senate seat, for example, Democrat Jaime Harrison raised over $130 million, 90 percent of which came from out-of-state donors.[2] He eventually lost the race by a 54-44 margin.

What does all this money buy? More than half of the average campaign's expenditures go to efforts to persuade and mobilize voters. For example, in the 2020 election cycle, 55 percent of candidates' spending went to media, predominantly advertisements on television and other outlets. The next largest category of spending (10 percent) was fundraising itself. A chunk of the rest was spent on salaries (8 percent) and administrative expenses (8 percent), such as travel, hotels, and rent for campaign offices.[3]

Candidates are not the only ones raising and spending more money. Political parties are also raising much more money in elections, which they donate to candidates, spend on behalf of candidates, and use to mobilize voters, among other things. In the 1992 electoral cycle, the Republican and Democratic parties combined raised roughly $650 million. In the 2020 cycle, they raised almost $2.7 billion (Figure 4.2).[4]

The other major actors spending money in elections are outside groups that work independently of the candidates and parties but can raise and spend money to support candidates. Their spending in presidential elections increased from about $14 million in 1992 to $393 million in 2008, then climbed dramatically to $1.1 billion in 2012 and $1.5 billion in 2016 (Figure 4.3). But 2020 saw an even more dramatic increase to $2.8 billion.

Despite these increasing costs and the public's concern about out-of-control spending, it is not obvious whether American political campaigns are "too" expensive. By some metrics, in fact, they are cheap. For example, Americans spent almost as much on pizza delivery in 2020 ($14 billion) as was spent in that year's election.[5] Some even wonder why American campaigns are not more expensive. Given the value of government policies to interest groups and corporations, these actors contribute remarkably little money to political candidates and parties.[6] Ultimately, it may not be necessary to determine whether

Core of the Analysis

- The rules governing campaign finance place caps on donations but not on spending, which has allowed the cost of American campaigns to increase.

- These rules have an important implication for strategy: candidates and parties must raise the money necessary to fund their campaigns. Private donations are more important than any public funding provided by the government.

- Campaign finance rules also allow independent groups, corporations, and labor unions to raise and spend money to try to elect or defeat candidates of their choice.

- These rules reflect a fundamental philosophical trade-off between two competing values: the right of donors and candidates to free speech and the need to guard against the potentially corrupting influence of money.

FIGURE 4.1 Congressional Candidate Spending, 1980–2020

Average spending in millions (2018 dollars)

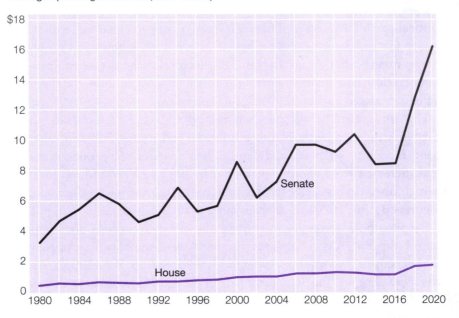

Sources: Campaign Finance Institute; OpenSecrets.org.

American political campaigns are too costly. The more important questions are *why* American elections cost what they do and what consequences this money has for elections and the political system. Much of the answer lies in the rules of American campaign finance.

As we discussed in Chapter 2, electoral rules govern crucial aspects of political campaigns. Campaign finance rules affect both donors, including individuals and interest groups, and spenders, including political candidates, parties, and interest groups. Regarding donors, the rules determine who can give, to whom they can give, and how much they can give. Regarding recipients, the rules determine whether, how much, and when they can spend. As with electoral rules, federal law governs federal elections, but state and local laws govern state and local elections. Any state's campaign finance laws may differ from federal law and from the laws of other states.

Campaign finance rules affect candidate strategies, most notably by allowing (or forcing) candidates to raise money for their campaigns. Although systems of public financing exist, American campaigns largely depend on private donations. Campaign finance rules also empower parties and interest groups, each of which can raise and spend money on behalf of the candidates they favor

FIGURE 4.2 Political Party Spending in All Federal Races, 1992–2020

Total spending in millions (2018 dollars)

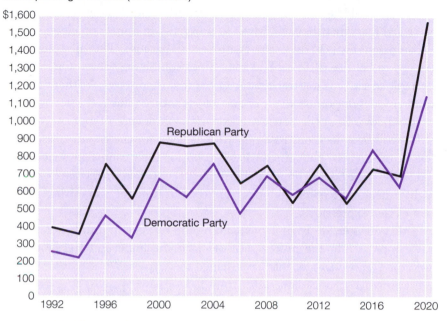

Source: Campaign Finance Institute.

FIGURE 4.3 Spending by Independent Groups, 1990–2020

Total spending in millions (2018 dollars)

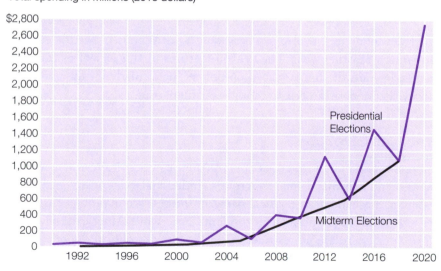

Note: These data are the totals spent by independent groups (excluding party committees) in 2018 dollars.
Source: OpenSecrets.org.

or against candidates they oppose. The increasing role of these outside groups has raised fears that they will have too powerful an impact on elections.

Campaign finance rules are controversial because, like all rules, they attempt to balance different and sometimes conflicting values. One value is the right of citizens and candidates to express themselves. Without money, certain modes of expression are impossible. Another value is the need to insulate candidates from the potentially corrupting influence of money. We want leaders to make decisions based on what is good for the country, or at least their constituents—not simply what is good for their campaign donors. The trade-offs are evident: limiting the money raised and spent on campaigns might mitigate the potential for corruption, but it might also infringe on the right to free expression.

In this chapter, we begin by explaining the rules central to financing federal campaigns. In the process, we describe the important legislation and Supreme Court decisions that have shaped these rules. We also describe how state campaign finance laws differ from federal law. We will once again see that the central consequences of these laws, from the perspectives of candidates, parties, and interest groups, concern campaign strategy and each candidate's chances of winning. It is usually not possible for candidates to change the rules, but they can make them work to their advantage.

Rules for Donors

The rules for donors involve two basic questions: Who is allowed to give, and how much can they give? The central features of this aspect of campaign finance law are the limits placed on donors, particularly on the amount of money that donors can give to candidates and parties.

Who Can Give?

There are two main types of donors in American political campaigns: individuals and organized interest groups. Individual Americans are free to donate to any candidate, political party, or interest group provided that they are either citizens or permanent residents. And while Americans have to be 18 to vote, there are no restrictions on the age of political donors. Minors can give as long as they give their own money and do so voluntarily.

Organized interest groups can also donate as long as they are not themselves tax-exempt groups. (Otherwise, the federal government would be indirectly subsidizing political campaigns by allowing groups to give money they would have paid in taxes to particular candidates.) Potential donors therefore include corporations and labor unions, but not charities and churches. Neither corporations nor unions, however, can donate simply by giving some of their revenue directly to candidates or parties. Direct corporate donations were banned in 1907 with the passage of the **Tillman Act**, and direct labor union donations were banned in 1947 with the passage of the Taft-Hartley Act. Instead, corporations and labor unions must establish separate **political action committees (PACs)**, which are groups that directly work toward the election of candidates, to pass or defeat legislation, or to advance a political agenda on the corporation or union's behalf. A small amount of corporate revenue can be spent to set up the PAC, but thereafter the PAC must raise money on its own. The PACs that give the largest amounts to political campaigns typically represent labor unions or industry associations (for example, the National Association of Realtors or the National Beer Wholesalers Association).

Membership organizations (groups with members who pay dues) must also establish PACs in order to give to candidates. Thus, there are PACs that represent groups with issue-oriented or ideological agendas, such as the National Rifle Association and Planned Parenthood. Political parties and political leaders can establish their own PACs as well. Political party organizations with PACs include the Democratic Senatorial Campaign Committee and the National Republican Congressional Committee. Political leaders' PACs, sometimes called "leadership PACs," raise money and donate to candidates whom those politicians favor. For example, House Speaker Nancy Pelosi (D-Calif.), showing an affection for terrible puns, has her "PAC to the Future."

Campaign donations by PACs have increased sharply over time. For instance, PAC donations to federal candidates and national party candidates grew from $333 million in 1990 to $541 million in 2020 (Figure 4.4). But this increase conceals an important fact: individuals donate more money to campaigns than PACs do. This is somewhat counter to the impression fostered by media coverage, which exaggerates PAC contributions.[7] In 2020, PAC contributions constituted only about 30 percent of the money raised by House candidates and 8 percent of the money raised by Senate candidates.[8]

Campaign finance law also requires the disclosure of donors. In 1971, the **Federal Election Campaign Act (FECA)** established rules for disclosure. Candidates, parties, and PACs must each maintain a central committee that receives all donations. Candidates, parties, and PACs are then required to file regular reports with the **Federal Election Commission (FEC)** identifying anyone who has contributed at least $200, with additional reports filed immediately before and after the election. In the final days of a campaign, any

FIGURE 4.4 PAC Contributions to Federal Candidates
                and National Party Committees, 1990–2020

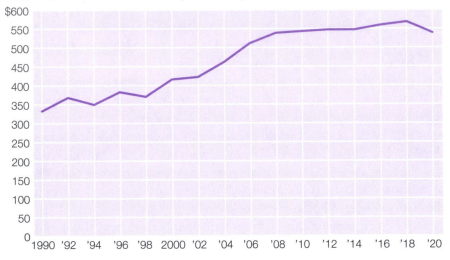

Total PAC contributions in millions (2018 dollars)

Source: OpenSecrets.

donation of $1,000 or more must be reported within 48 hours. In turn, the FEC maintains a searchable database of campaign donors. One can see that, for example, Ben Affleck, identified in the database as an actor and director living in Santa Monica, California, has given money to many different Democratic candidates, including the 2020 presidential campaigns of Joe Biden and Kamala Harris.

How Much Can Donors Give, and to Whom?

Federal campaign finance law sets limits on campaign donations. These limits were established by the 1974 amendments to the FECA and remained unchanged until 2002, when the **Bipartisan Campaign Reform Act (BCRA)** adjusted the limits upward and indexed them to inflation, meaning that the limits will continue to increase in the future. Limits are imposed on individuals, political party committees, and PACs and affect what they can give to candidates, parties, and PACs. Table 4.1 summarizes the limits in effect for the 2021–22 election cycle. Individuals can donate $2,900 to any given candidate per election, for a maximum of $5,800 to each candidate for the primary and general elections combined. There was previously an overall limit on how much individuals could give to all federal candidates combined, but this limit

TABLE 4.1 Contribution Limits in the 2021–22 Election Cycle

	To Candidate	To National Party Committee	To State, District, and Local Party Committees	To Other Committees (e.g., PAC)	Overall Limits
Individual	$2,900 per election	$36,500 per year	$10,000 combined per year	$5,000	No limit
National party committee	$5,000*	No limit	No limit	$5,000	No limit
State, district, and local party committees	$5,000	No limit	No limit	$5,000	No limit
PAC	$5,000	$15,000	$5,000 combined per year	$5,000	No limit

* A national party committee and its senatorial campaign committee may also contribute up to $51,200 combined per campaign to each Senate candidate.
Source: "Contribution Limits," Federal Election Commission, www.fec.gov/help-candidates-and-committees /candidate-taking-receipts/contribution-limits (accessed 7/21/21).

was struck down by the Supreme Court in 2014.[9] PACs can give no more than $5,000 per election to any candidate, with no overall limit. (See Table 4.2 for more on contribution limits as they apply to candidate committees and PACs.)

Most states follow federal law in imposing limits on individual and PAC contributions for gubernatorial and other state-level races. The actual limits, however, vary widely. As of the 2020–21 election cycle, 11 states—Alabama, Indiana, Iowa, Mississippi, Nebraska, North Dakota, Oregon, Pennsylvania, Texas, Utah, and Virginia—had no such limits. Individual donors could give a candidate for the Massachusetts state legislature no more than $2,000 over these two years, while donors in Ohio could give state legislature candidates up to $13,704.41 in the same time frame.[10] State restrictions on donations by PACs and parties are similarly diverse.

Political Parties and Soft Money

Current federal restrictions on contributions are now more far-reaching than they were before the BCRA passed in 2002. Before 2002, political party organizations, such as the Democratic National Committee (DNC) and

TABLE 4.2 Groups with Contribution Limits

	Candidate Committee	Political Party (PAC)	Federal PAC
Example	McConnell Senate Committee	Democratic Congressional Campaign Committee	American Meat Institute PAC
Description	Committee formed by the candidate to raise and spend money during the campaign	PACs formed by the parties that donate money to the candidates or spend it for other purposes, such as get-out-the-vote efforts	PACs organized by interest groups that collect contributions from members or employees and then donate to candidates, parties, or other PACs
Limits on contributions to the group	Individuals: $2,900 per election PACs: $5,000 per election Corporations: Cannot give except via a PAC	Individuals: $36,500 per year to a national party committee PACs: $15,000 Corporations: Cannot give except via a PAC	Individuals: $5,000 per year PACs: $5,000 per year Corporations: Cannot give except to their own PAC
Limits on how the group can use its money	A candidate committee cannot contribute more than $2,000 to another candidate committee or $5,000 to a PAC.	A political party PAC can give no more than $5,000 a year to a candidate committee or another PAC.	A federal PAC can give $5,000 per election to a candidate, $5,000 per year to another PAC, and $15,000 per year to a party PAC.
Are donors disclosed?	Yes, to the FEC	Yes, to the FEC	Yes, to the FEC

Republican National Committee (RNC), could raise **soft money**, or donations that were not subject to contribution limits or disclosure provisions. **Hard money** donations, by contrast, are subject to these rules. During the 1990s, the parties became increasingly successful at raising soft money: in 2000, the Democratic and Republican parties raised a combined $718 million.[11]

Soft money contributions could be spent on registering and mobilizing voters and on some kinds of political advertisements, but they could not pay for **express advocacy**—that is, directly advocating for a particular candidate.

Spending on ads that stopped short of express advocacy was permitted; the key was whether an ad used **magic words**, such as "vote for." Parties found ways to craft ads that conveyed a clear partisan message anyway, often by merging criticisms of a candidate from the opposite party with **issue advocacy**, or arguments for positions on a particular issue. Consider this ad from a 1998 Wisconsin congressional race, in which a party organization, the Democratic Congressional Campaign Committee (DCCC), targeted Mark Green, the Republican candidate:

> Mark Green has taken over $22,000 from the health care industry's lobbyists. It's no wonder that he voted against keeping our medical records private, allowing HMOs and insurance companies to make our records public. It's no wonder he wanted to let negligent health care providers off the hook, even when they operated under the influence of drugs or alcohol. Tell Mark Green our health care isn't for sale. Support HMO reform.

This ad avoids the magic words and is ostensibly about an issue—namely, reform of health maintenance organizations (HMOs) and insurance companies. Nevertheless, the partisan intent is clear. Citizens are not fooled, either. In a 2000 study, participants watched several party-sponsored ads that were nominally issue advocacy but included critical statements about the opposing presidential candidates. The vast majority of participants, about 80 percent, said that the primary objective of the ad was to "persuade you to vote against a candidate," not to "present an issue."[12]

The ability of parties to raise soft money was a big loophole in the rules: even though a labor union or corporation could not give a million dollars directly to a candidate, the loophole allowed these groups to give this kind of money to party committees. Critics argued that this created the appearance of, and perhaps the reality of, corruption, and so the BCRA banned soft money. Now, national parties can only raise hard money, which is subject to contribution limits. Although critics of the BCRA feared that it would impoverish the parties, this has not come to pass. In recent years, the DNC and RNC have raised significantly more than they raised before the BCRA was passed.[13]

Independent Groups

The BCRA did not close a second loophole, however. Independent groups, which are groups unaffiliated with political parties or candidates, are able to raise soft money without contribution limits (see Table 4.3). As we discuss later, independent groups may not give this money directly to candidates as traditional PACs do. Rather, they spend it independently of candidates on

TABLE 4.3 Independent Groups

	Independent Expenditure-Only Committee	527 Organization	Nonprofits: 501(c)4, 501(c)5, 501(c)6
Example	American Crossroads	NEA Fund for Children and Public Education	Crossroads Grassroots Policy Strategies, U.S. Chamber of Commerce
Description	A PAC that pays for communications that can support or oppose a candidate by name	A tax-exempt group that raises money for political activities, including voter mobilization, issue advocacy, and the election of a candidate	Tax-exempt groups that can engage in political activity, including the support of a candidate, as long as political activity is not their primary purpose
Limits on contributions to the group	Unlimited	Unlimited	Unlimited
Limits on how the group can use its money	These groups cannot donate to a candidate or PAC or coordinate their spending with parties or candidates.	These groups cannot donate to a candidate or PAC or coordinate their spending with parties or candidates.	These groups cannot donate to a candidate or PAC or coordinate their spending with parties or candidates.
Are donors disclosed?	Yes, to the FEC	Yes, to the IRS	No, unless the contributor gives money for a specific political advertisement

Source: Adapted from "A Donor Taxonomy," *New York Times*, September 21, 2010, www.nytimes.com /imagepages/2010/09/21/us/politics/21money-graphic.html (accessed 3/16/15).

things such as political advertising, although their goal is still to help elect or defeat particular candidates. Spending by independent groups increased dramatically after passage of the BCRA and then again after the 2010 *Citizens United v. Federal Election Commission* decision, which we will discuss in greater detail later in this chapter (also see Figure 4.3 on p. 97).

There are three main legal categories of independent groups, some identified by a confusing array of numbers and letters that correspond to designations under the federal tax code as administered by the Internal Revenue Service (IRS). The crucial differences among them involve federal laws about whether they must disclose their donors and whether and how they can be involved in campaign activity.

The first category of groups is **independent expenditure committees**, which first came into existence during the 2010 campaign. These are PACs that pool donations from various sources and then use the funds to advocate explicitly for or against candidates. Because these PACs are not associated with a specific political party, corporation, or interest group and instead gather contributions from multiple sources—individual donors, corporations, unions, and so on—they have been termed **super PACs**. Unlike traditional PACs, they can collect donations of unlimited amounts as a consequence of *Citizens United*. However, like traditional PACs, they are required to disclose their donors. Super PACs were initially created to influence national elections, but over time they have become involved in state elections as well.[14] For example, super PACs may raise money from wealthy donors and then give that money to other organizations working to influence gubernatorial or state legislative elections.

The second category of independent groups is **527 organizations**. (The number 527 refers to a specific section of the tax code.) 527s are officially designated as political organizations under the tax code and are also required to disclose their contributors to the IRS. These organizations came to the fore during the 2004 election, which was the first election to occur after the BCRA banned soft money contributions to parties. Because donations to 527s are not subject to contribution limits, wealthy Americans can give them large amounts of money. Although super PACs have become more prominent in federal races, 527s are increasingly active in state-level races, in part because organizations like the Republican State Leadership Committee and the Democratic Governors Association are organized as 527s.[15]

The third category of independent groups is known as **501(c) organizations**. These groups are designated as nonprofit organizations, are not required to pay taxes, and are not required to disclose their donors. There are various kinds of 501(c) organizations that are further designated with an additional number. For example, 501(c)3 organizations include charities, churches, and educational institutions. An example would be the March of Dimes. 501(c)4 organizations, such as the League of Women Voters, are designated as "social welfare" organizations under the tax code, meaning that their goal is to "operate primarily to further the common good and general welfare of the people of the community (such as by bringing about civic betterment and social improvements)."[16] 501(c)5 organizations include agricultural, horticultural, and labor organizations. In the context of U.S. campaigns, the most important 501(c)5 organizations are labor unions. 501(c)6 organizations include business leagues and chambers of commerce—the most important being the U.S. Chamber of Commerce.

Tax laws restrict the campaign activities of 501(c)3 and 501(c)4 organizations. Organizations with 501(c)3 status are prohibited from participating in political campaigns, although some occasionally attempt to bend or skirt the law. For example, a 501(c)3 organization might post a sign on its property endorsing a candidate. By contrast, 501(c)4 organizations are allowed to participate in campaign activity as long as that activity is not their "primary purpose." 501(c)4 organizations, particularly those working to support Republican candidates, have become prominent since the 2010 election. Like many 527s, these organizations use nondescript names such as "Crossroads Grassroots Policy Strategies," and they attract some donors, particularly corporations, that do not want their identities revealed. Some have questioned whether groups like Crossroads flout the law by making campaign activity their primary purpose, although it appears unlikely that the government will investigate these groups. For one, the IRS has limited staffing and funding that it can direct toward this end.[17] Moreover, the IRS's previous attempts to determine whether groups applying to become 501(c)4 organizations were likely to be primarily political organizations ended in controversy, as Republicans in 2013 questioned whether the IRS was subjecting conservative groups in particular to extra scrutiny. The controversy has arguably made it less likely that the IRS will begin to regulate these groups more stringently. Even if the IRS did increase regulation of 501(c)4s, this would not address critics' other concern, which is that these groups can legally raise and spend money without disclosing their donors.

Rules for Spenders

The spenders in American political campaigns include candidates, parties, PACs, and independent groups. The rules for spenders involve three basic questions: how much they can spend, when they can campaign, and how they can campaign. These rules, particularly those regulating independent groups, are among the most controversial aspects of campaign finance law.

How Much Can They Spend?

Central to American campaign finance law is this principle: contributions are limited, but spending is not. The federal government cannot limit how much candidate campaign committees, party committees, PACs, or independent groups such as 527s spend on campaign activity. And candidates can spend an unlimited amount of their own money on their campaign—that is, they can "self-finance."

Originally, the FECA limited both campaign spending and contributions. But when these FECA provisions were challenged in the Supreme Court in the 1976 case **Buckley v. Valeo**,[18] the Supreme Court upheld only the contribution limits. The Court reasoned that although donating to candidates was an act of speech subject to First Amendment protections, the federal government had a compelling interest in preventing the possibility of corruption, which might arise if a candidate could raise large amounts of money from only a few donors. Thus, contribution limits were declared constitutional. However, the Court ruled that there was no compelling interest in limiting spending, and thus the spending limits violated the free speech clause of the First Amendment.

At the federal level, spending can be limited only in presidential races, and then only if the candidates agree to it. The FECA set up a system of public financing for presidential elections, which was upheld by the Court in *Buckley* and remains in place today. Public financing comes from tax dollars; there is, in fact, a box on federal tax forms that taxpayers can check if they want to give a small amount of money to help finance federal campaigns. Candidates who accept public financing then agree to a spending limit—although, of course, party committees and independent groups may also spend money in ways that help the candidate. For many years, most presidential candidates accepted public financing for the nomination phase, the general-election phase, or both. Every major-party presidential candidate accepted public funds for the general election and almost all accepted in the primaries until 2008, when then candidate Barack Obama refused public funding, allowing him to spend more than his opponent, John McCain. After that, it became increasingly uncommon for presidential candidates to accept **public funding**—funds provided to candidates by the federal government in exchange for their agreeing to restrictions on spending and fundraising from other sources. In 2020, no one did.

Public financing systems also exist in some states and localities. All are optional and come with strings attached, such as minimum fundraising requirements, pledges to limit or refuse private donations, and spending limits. For example, for the New Jersey gubernatorial election in 2021, candidates needed to raise $490,000 to be eligible for public financing. The state then matched every $4,900 in private contributions with $9,800 in public money—up to $4.6 million for the primary-election campaign and $10.5 million for the general-election campaign. However, participating candidates could not spend more than $7.3 million in the primary campaign and $15.6 million in the general campaign. In 2021, both the incumbent Democratic candidate, Governor Phil Murphy, and his Republican opponent participated in the public financing program.[19]

Three states have gone further and established full public funding, also known as **clean elections systems**, for statewide elections, legislative elections, or both.[20] In Arizona, to be eligible for public funding, candidates for governor must gather at least 4,000 contributions from individuals of $5 or more, with the total not to exceed $63,450. Once candidates decide to accept public financing, they receive a grant from the state and may not receive any further private donations from citizens or PACs. Gubernatorial candidates in Arizona are thus limited to about $855,000 in the primary and $1.3 million in the general election.[21] These amounts reflect the goal of limiting the amount of money spent on campaigns.

Another example of public funding at the local level is Seattle's Democracy Vouchers program. In this system, public funding for campaigns is raised via taxes, just as in the presidential public financing system. The city then issues $100 in "vouchers" to eligible residents, who can choose how they want to distribute those funds among their preferred candidates. In essence, this allows citizens to donate to candidates with public funds rather than private funds.[22] Ultimately, the central goals of public financing are to reduce the potential for corruption, whereby donors have undue influence over candidates, and to reduce the amount of spending in elections.

When and How Can Independent Groups Campaign?

A final set of rules applies to when and how campaigning can take place. In line with the lack of limits on campaign spending, the American system also imposes few restrictions on when and how candidates may campaign. In contrast, some other democratic countries restrict televised political advertising. For example, in Belgium, France, the United Kingdom, and Spain, candidates and parties cannot buy broadcasting time on either commercial or public television. In lieu of purchased time, these countries provide free air time either on commercial or public television, albeit with substantial restrictions on when and how much advertising can be aired.[23] The lack of such restrictions in the American system is one reason why campaigns are so expensive: the largest category of candidate spending is for television advertising, and that advertising can be aired at any point in any amount. It is not surprising that this makes for long campaigns with seemingly endless advertisements.

The American system places more restrictions on independent groups than on the candidates or parties. A first rule is that if these groups want to spend their resources to support a candidate or the candidates of a party, they cannot consult with, coordinate with, or receive help from the candidates or the party. If a labor union PAC wants to help Democratic candidates, neither those candidates nor their staff can help the PAC with fundraising, producing television advertisements, or deciding when and where to air the ads. However, candidates and their supporting groups have found ways to bend this rule despite the renewed vigilance of the U.S. Department of Justice. In 2016, for example, several politicians established super PACs and began working with them closely before they officially declared their presidential candidacies—in essence, delaying their "official" presidential campaigns to give them more time to fundraise for their super PACs. Candidates have done other things that skirt the no-coordination rule, such as independently placing footage of themselves campaigning on YouTube that super PACs can then use in their campaign advertisements.[24]

Second, federal restrictions limit the content of advertising by independent groups. When the BCRA was passed in 2002, its proponents were worried that the law's ban on soft money contributions to political parties would drive even more soft money to independent groups, who would use these contributions to produce advertisements that paraded as issue advocacy but essentially endorsed or attacked specific candidates. So, the BCRA established new rules. First, it defined a new and expanded category of *electioneering communication*: ads that referred to a clearly identified candidate for federal office (whether the magic words were mentioned or not) and that were publicly distributed via radio or television to an electorate of at least 50,000 people up to 60 days before a general election or 30 days before a primary election. The BCRA then stated that electioneering communication could not be funded with corporate or union treasury funds—that is, the revenue that corporations or unions raise as part of their regular operations. In order to engage in electioneering communication, these groups would have to establish PACs and raise hard money subject to contribution limits and disclosure provisions. Of course, the BCRA's rules on electioneering communication contained exceptions. They did not regulate ads that aired outside the 30- or 60-day windows or other forms of campaigning such as direct mail, online ads, and telephone calls.

Subsequent Supreme Court decisions weakened these BCRA provisions substantially. The most important decision, **Citizens United v. Federal Election Commission**, was handed down in 2010.[25] Citizens United is a nonprofit organization that received corporate funding to produce *Hillary: The Movie*, a documentary film that was critical of Hillary Clinton. The group wanted to run commercials advertising the film and to air it on cable television during the 2008 presidential primaries. The FEC considered this to be an electioneering communication—essentially, an argument that Clinton should not be elected—that could not be aired 30 days before a presidential primary. Citizens United asserted that the documentary was factual and politically neutral.

During oral arguments, the more conservative justices on the Court took the unusual step of going beyond the narrow questions surrounding the documentary to consider a more fundamental issue: whether corporations and unions could be banned from spending their general treasury funds for electioneering communication. Commentators assumed that this signaled the conservatives' willingness to overturn the ban, and, indeed, that hunch was correct. In a 5–4 decision, the Court ruled that the ban was unconstitutional. While corporations and unions are not literally people, the majority argued that "associations of persons" also have a right to free speech. The Court's decision has opened the door to advertising by corporations and labor unions—not simply their PACs—that both targets specific candidates (express advocacy) and is aired within the 30- and 60-day windows. The decision called into question laws in 24 states that had imposed similar restrictions or bans on independent expenditures by corporations or unions. It also provoked criticism by President Obama in his 2010 State of the Union address, a speech made in front of members of both houses of Congress and the Supreme Court. We discuss the debate over *Citizens United* in more detail later in the chapter.

Since the *Citizens United* decision, there has been a sharp increase in spending by outside groups, peaking in 2020 at $2.8 billion (see Figure 4.3, p. 97). Party and candidate spending has also increased dramatically in recent elections, but not as much as outside group spending has. As a result, the percentage of all televised campaign advertisements that were sponsored by outside groups increased from about 7 percent in 2008 to between 25 and 30 percent from 2012 to 2020.[26]

Commentators have therefore speculated about whether independent spending decides elections, but the answer is unclear. Outside groups typically target competitive races in which candidates and parties are also campaigning heavily. This means that advertisements sponsored by independent groups must compete with the more numerous advertisements from candidates and parties. Indeed, in 2010, Democratic candidates' disadvantage in terms of independent group spending was largely compensated for by their advantage in spending by candidates and party organizations. Similarly, in the 2012 presidential election, Barack Obama compensated for Mitt Romney's three-to-one advantage in outside group spending by raising significantly more than his opponent in individual contributions. Moreover, there is simply no guarantee that the balance of outside spending will determine who wins. In the 2016 presidential election, Hillary Clinton spent far more than Donald Trump—both in terms of what she raised herself and what outside groups spent on her behalf—and still lost.

Does this mean that spending by outside groups does not matter? Absolutely not. In 2012, if one excludes ads sponsored by interest groups, for every 53 ads that Romney aired in a media market, Obama aired 100 ads in the same media market. When one includes ads by independent groups, for every 82 ads favoring Romney in a media market, there were 100 Obama ads.[27] In other words, it can be argued that outside group spending kept Romney in the race and enabled him to mount a strong challenge against an incumbent president. Thus, an advantage in independent spending does not guarantee that a candidate will win an election, but it can improve their chances.

Campaign Finance Rules and Political Strategy

As we discussed in Chapter 2, understanding electoral rules is important because they profoundly influence the actions of citizens, candidates, parties, and interest groups. This is true for campaign finance law as well. Here, we identify some of the implications of the campaign finance system for each category of actors.

Citizens

By making private donations central to campaign fundraising, the American system gives private citizens another way to express their political voice, one distinct from voting or writing to a member of Congress, for example. As with other forms of political participation, donating allows citizens to establish ties with candidates and hold elected leaders accountable for their performance in office. Donations are a particularly powerful way to encourage accountability: any candidate's central goal is to be elected, and it is virtually impossible to win an election without the resources provided by donations.

How do citizens decide which candidates to support with donations? Most of the time, the decision is straightforward: donors give to candidates who share their values and goals.[28] But the decision can be strategic as well. Consider, for example, primary elections, in which there are often few differences between the candidates. How might donors decide then? One important factor is whether donors expect one candidate to win. If two candidates have similar platforms, donors often prefer to support the likely winner rather than "waste" their money on the likely loser. Potential donors will thus look to various indicators of candidates' viability, including polls, news coverage, and donations made by other individuals and interest groups.[29]

Candidates

Campaign finance rules profoundly affect political candidates. Because the American system does not limit spending, it gives candidates an incentive to raise and spend as much as possible. Limits on the amount of each donation, however, make it particularly onerous to raise money because candidates must reach a larger number of donors. If there were no limits on the size of donations, candidates could conceivably fund their campaigns with money from a small number of rich donors. Instead, candidates ask for contributions from thousands of donors via phone calls, at receptions and dinners, and so on. One study of House candidates in the 1996 and 1998 elections found that a substantial fraction (42 percent) reported spending at least a quarter of their time engaged in fundraising. Almost a quarter of these candidates (24 percent) reported spending at least half their time fundraising.[30] More recently, an orientation hosted by the DCCC for newly elected Democratic members of Congress recommended that they spend four hours each day making phone calls to raise funds.[31]

Given this reality, candidates must seek out efficient ways to raise money. The internet is helpful, as fundraising online does not require receptions or dinners. Campaigns increasingly rely on online donations, particularly from donors who give in smaller amounts, to help fund campaigns. Indeed, candidates and parties sometimes experiment with campaign email blasts to determine which features of the messages most motivate people to give. For example, in 2012 the Obama fundraising team tested different subject lines, different text, different colors, and so on to see which emails elicited the most donations. For example, in one experiment, the Obama team determined that the subject line

"I will be outspent" raised more money than "If you believe in what we're doing" or "Do this for Michelle."

Some organizations are dedicated to helping candidates raise money online, and these groups often help out smaller campaigns that may not have the resources of a presidential campaign. The Democratic Party uses ActBlue, a very prominent and successful purveyor of software that helps candidates raise money online. In fact, it has been successful enough that both Hillary Clinton and Joe Biden relied on it in their presidential campaigns alongside their other fundraising efforts. In an effort to play catch-up, Republicans established a parallel organization called WinRed.

Online fundraising from small donors has perhaps been most visible in the presidential campaigns of Vermont senator Bernie Sanders, who has mounted two well-funded efforts in Democratic presidential primaries. Sanders' campaigns have been supported in large part by small donors, many of whom donated online. But Sanders is unusual in this regard. Most candidates continue to rely on a mixture of small donations and larger donations raised from wealthier individuals. Candidates also seek out "bundlers," wealthy donors who can enlist a set of friends and acquaintances to donate.

Fundraising takes considerable time and energy, but not every candidate faces the same burden. The American system of campaign finance advantages incumbents to a significant degree. As we discuss further in Chapter 10, incumbent members of Congress are typically much more successful than challengers in raising money. Incumbents are better known, they already have the status and power that make them valuable to donors and interest groups, and they are usually perceived as the likely victors. All of this stacks the deck against challengers.

The campaign finance system may also benefit wealthy candidates. The lack of spending limits means that candidates can fund their own campaigns, potentially giving wealthy individuals a significant advantage over candidates who are less wealthy. Thus, American elections often feature candidates who spend large amounts of their personal wealth to get elected. For example, in the 1992 presidential campaign, Ross Perot spent $63 million of his own money running as an independent candidate. Similarly, in 2016, about 20 percent of Trump's campaign funds came from his own bank accounts, while less than 1 percent of Hillary Clinton's campaign funds came from hers.[32] Potential opponents may be discouraged from running against a wealthy, self-financed candidate.

However, the experiences of self-financed candidates also suggest that personal wealth does not guarantee victory. In 2020, for example, the billionaires

The limits on how much individual donors can contribute mean that candidates have to spend much time and effort amassing enough contributions to fund their campaigns by attending fundraisers, wooing potential donors, and soliciting contributions. Here, Congressman Steve Watkins (R-Kans.) meets with supporters at a fundraiser for his reelection campaign in 2020.

Michael Bloomberg and Tom Steyer spent a combined $1.4 billion in their campaigns for the Democratic presidential nomination. Steyer won no primaries and Bloomberg only won the primary in American Samoa. Although the two candidates gained some support in the polls from spending money on television ads, it clearly was not enough.[33] Why might self-financed candidates lose? First, the candidates who spend their own money are often the ones who are struggling the most to begin with. Perhaps they are facing strong opposition and could easily be defeated if they only use what they raise from other donors, or perhaps they are languishing in the polls and desperately need to give their campaign a jolt. In the 2004 presidential primaries, Senator John Kerry mortgaged his house so that he could loan $6.4 million to his campaign, which was struggling at that time (although he did go on to win the Democratic nomination). Second, dollars raised from other donors appear to produce more votes than dollars provided by the candidate. This may reflect the additional benefits of cultivating a network of supportive donors. Private donations signal the strength of the candidate to the media and political elites. It will surprise no one that a candidate would give their own campaign $3 million—after all, it is the candidate's money, and the candidate wants to win.

But if 3,000 people give the candidate $1,000 each, it may convince others that the candidate is a serious contender. Moreover, the act of fundraising may generate local media coverage of fundraising events and may strengthen a candidate's ties to crucial interest groups and blocs of voters. Thus the possibility of self-financing entails a complex series of strategic calculations.[34]

By accepting private donations, candidates face another strategic imperative: keeping donors happy. Donors can withhold their money to ensure accountability, and it is up to candidates to make sure that their donors are not disappointed. The problem, however, is that what donors want may not match up with what voters want. Studies of campaign donors have found that that they are unrepresentative of voters in several respects; for example, both men and White Americans are overrepresented among donors, and women of color are especially underrepresented.[35] Campaign donors also have different views on political issues. For example, Republican donors are more conservative than Republican voters on economic issues, while Democratic donors are more liberal than Democratic voters on social issues.[36] And given that donors to a candidate may not even reside in the candidate's state or district—as was true for Jaime Harrison in South Carolina—candidates may find themselves responding to people who do not share the interests of voters in the communities the candidate actually seeks to represent.[37] Thus, candidates may find themselves forced to take one position to please donors but another position to please voters—a difficult balancing act and one that often attracts criticism if contradictory positions become public knowledge.

Political Parties and Interest Groups

Under the current rules, political parties and interest groups, including corporations and unions, can raise and spend their own money on campaign activities. The BCRA's ban on soft money has not hindered the parties in this regard, and the Supreme Court's decision in *Citizens United* gave interest groups even freer rein to spend independently. This poses both an opportunity and a challenge for candidates. On the one hand, they may benefit from the campaign activities of their party and of interest groups that support them. On the other hand, they may find that their party and ostensibly supportive interest groups are not actually interested in helping them. They may also be attacked by the opposing party and its aligned groups. Thus, the presence of parties and interest groups can both facilitate and complicate candidates' efforts.

A dispute within the Democratic Party during the 2006 election illustrates the complex ways in which the strategies of candidates and parties interact. The chair of the DNC, former Vermont governor and 2004 presidential candidate Howard Dean, advocated a "50-state strategy" that would invest the DNC's money in building up the Democratic Party organizations in every state, even in states where the party rarely won elections. This was a boon to many Democrats in such states, who typically did not attract much support from the party. At the same time, the chair of the DCCC, Rahm Emanuel, had a very different strategy: he sought to use DCCC money to bolster Democratic House candidates in competitive races only, and he thought it was wasteful to spend party money in states where the party had little chance of winning. This was a boon to Democrats in hard-fought campaigns, but not to Democrats in Republican-dominated states. No matter which strategy the party pursued, some Democratic candidates would benefit more than others.

Like political parties, interest groups must make strategic decisions about which candidates to support through donations or independent expenditures. Their choices will depend on their agendas. Groups that find their interests well served by current officeholders will pursue an "access" strategy: they support incumbents of both parties and use their campaign contributions to guarantee access and opportunities to press their agenda if the incumbents are reelected. This creates an incentive for incumbents to be responsive to groups while in office to ensure their support during reelection campaigns. Groups that have more ideological agendas further from the views of the average officeholder will pursue a "replacement" strategy, seeking to replace incumbents with new representatives who share their goals. These new representatives will typically come from one party or even one ideological faction within a party.[38] The Club for Growth, a group that promotes conservative economic policies, is famous for targeting incumbent "RINOs"—Republicans in Name Only—that it considers too moderate. Of course, incumbent candidates will not sit idly by if they are threatened with such a challenge. They may take new steps to placate the interest groups and attempt to convince them not to support their more ideological challengers. If that is unsuccessful, incumbents may adjust their own positions on issues to be more in line with those of their challengers, thereby negating some of the rationale for replacing them.

The agendas of candidates and their interest group supporters may not be well aligned—a very plausible scenario, given that under current campaign finance law, candidates and interest groups are not permitted to coordinate their campaign activities. Supportive interest groups often emphasize the same issues or themes as the candidates they support, but groups with a single-issue agenda—such as abortion rights or gun rights—often do not, creating potential problems for candidates who want to downplay that issue.[39] For example, the ads aired by parties and interest groups are generally more negative than the ads aired by candidates. This may not bother candidates, who can take the high road and let others do the dirty work.[40] But sometimes, candidates may have to disavow a particularly aggressive ad aired by a supporter. In the 1988 presidential election, the National Security Political Action Committee (NSPAC) aired an ad attacking the Democratic candidate, Michael Dukakis, for a Massachusetts program that allowed prisoners to leave jail temporarily for furloughs as part of a rehabilitation effort. The ad focused on one prisoner, William Horton (the ad called him "Willie"), who had raped a woman and assaulted her fiancé while on furlough. The ad featured a photograph of Horton, who was Black, and it became controversial after critics argued that it played on racial fears. The campaign of Dukakis's opponent, George H. W. Bush, ultimately requested that NSPAC withdraw the ad, although some have argued that the Bush campaign knew about the ad in advance and delayed their request for withdrawal to give the ad time to have an impact. The FEC investigated whether there was illicit cooperation between the Bush campaign and NSPAC, but it deadlocked 3–3 on the question (not surprising, given the presence of three Republicans and three Democrats on the commission) and thus did not produce a conclusive ruling.[41]

Ultimately, candidates may find that much of the campaigning that takes place, even on their behalf, is out of their control. As such, campaign spending may both help and hurt their campaign, at least as they see it. By expanding the number of actors eligible to raise and spend money, the American system of campaign finance creates loose alliances among candidates, parties, and interest groups that contain significant tensions even as these players seek a common goal.

The Debate over Campaign Finance Reform

The American system of campaign finance is perennially controversial, as the debate over the *Citizens United* decision illustrates. To understand this controversy, it is worth considering the values that underlie the campaign finance system, discussing the tensions among these values, and evaluating proposed reforms to the system. As noted earlier, two important values underlying campaign finance law are freedom of speech, as discussed in Chapter 1 and as enumerated in the First Amendment, and a desire to guard against the corrupting influence of money. The Supreme Court has defined

Two protesters mark the anniversary of the Supreme Court's *Citizens United* decision in 2015. The ongoing consequences of that decision continue to provoke debates about the role of money in politics.

"corruption" fairly narrowly as a form of bribery whereby a campaign contribution essentially "pays" a politician to do favors for the donor. That is, money buys a politician's vote or some other action. But some legal authorities have argued for a broader definition of corruption, and, indeed, many voters consider actions besides outright bribery to be corrupt—such as promoting the overall interests of donors at the expense of the public interest or having more meetings with donors than with nondonors.[42] Debates about campaign finance also engage other values discussed in Chapter 1, especially free choice and political equality.

The Supreme Court has weighed those values in different ways when considering the rules imposed on donors and spenders. In *Buckley v. Valeo*, the Court argued that while donations to a candidate pose a significant threat of corruption, spending on behalf of a candidate (for example, by an interest group) does not. It also argued that donations are not as meaningful as spending in terms of their communicative content. Donations serve to convey general support but not the reasons for that support. Spending, on the other hand, is central to communicating one's ideas during a campaign. Both of these arguments buttressed the Court's decision in *Buckley* to limit donations but not spending. Concerns about free speech also led to the

Court's decision in *Citizens United*, which struck down laws that restricted the spending of independent groups.

The Case against the Status Quo

Critics object that these legal decisions (and the American system in general) have given money too much influence on politics, and they point to a number of possible negative consequences. First, the system is hard on candidates, who must fundraise incessantly to stay competitive—even to the detriment of other, possibly more beneficial activities, such as policy making. Even candidates with valuable prior political experience and qualifications are likely to drop out of their race if their fundraising lags.[43] Fundraising demands may also discourage some talented individuals from running in the first place, especially ones who have no ability to self-finance as an alternative to raising private donations. In a 2011 survey of potential political candidates, 19 percent of women and 16 percent of men said that the prospect of soliciting campaign contributions would "deter them from running for office."[44]

Second, critics fear that money simply buys elections, meaning that whoever can spend the most wins. They point to the fundraising disparities between incumbents and challengers and to the extraordinarily high rate at which incumbents win. This criticism is based on the values of free choice and political equality. Voters do not really have a choice, the argument goes, when a well-funded incumbent can scare off many potential challengers and then easily defeat the poorly funded challenger who decides to run. Is it fair that campaign finance rules create such inequality, whereby some candidates have vastly more resources to spend than others?

Third, critics argue, the campaign finance system favors those wealthy enough to donate to campaigns, giving them a greater voice in politics than those who cannot donate. In this way, it violates the value of political equality.[45] Wealthy individuals are far more likely than other people to donate to candidates. Indeed, campaign contributions have become increasingly concentrated among the wealthiest individuals as their wealth has grown and they have become more interested in politics.[46] One analysis of early fundraising in the 2016 presidential campaign found that fewer than 400 families had donated almost half the money raised.[47] Moreover, critics claim, interest groups that represent wealthy Americans and business or corporate interests are more powerful than groups that represent the poor and working classes. In the 2019–20 election cycle, business PACs contributed about $6 billion to congressional and presidential candidates, while labor PACs contributed just $244 million.[48]

Fourth, critics point to the fact that some outside groups can raise and spend money without disclosing their donors. This prevents observers and voters from knowing the identities or agendas of the people trying to influence election outcomes. This is made all the more problematic, critics argue, by the fact that these outside groups can raise donations in unlimited amounts. For example, of the $180 million raised by the 501(c)4 organization Crossroads GPS during the 2012 election cycle, $22.5 million came from a single donor, whose identity is unknown.[49]

Fifth, and perhaps most important, critics argue that the current system does not do enough to combat corruption, or at least the appearance of corruption. They note that candidates and political parties still find ways to raise large amounts of money that violate the spirit of campaign finance law. For example, in recent elections presidential candidates and their parties have established "joint fundraising committees." A donor can write a single check to one of these committees, and the funds are then distributed among the candidate, national party committees, and perhaps state parties. These joint fundraising committees raise a lot of money—$2.6 billion in 2020, up from $1.2 billion in 2016.[50] Although donations from joint committees to individual campaigns or party committees cannot exceed contribution limits, critics argue that the overall impact of a single large check gives wealthy donors added clout. Furthermore, the committees established to fund the presidential nominating conventions can accept large individual donations; any single donor can contribute up to $106,500 per year.[51]

Fundamentally, critics are concerned that the money that donors and organized interests give and spend can influence elected leaders. Stories about the possible influence of money are common. After the mass shooting in Parkland, Florida, in February 2018, some were quick to blame campaign donations by the National Rifle Association for the unwillingness of many politicians to support new gun control measures.[52] A 2002 survey of state legislators also found that many believed that campaign contributions had at least some influence on the content and passage of bills in their state's legislature.[53] In critics' minds, campaign contributions may lead to policies favored by donors rather than policies that would serve other important goals and perhaps even the general good of the country.

A proposed solution to many of these potential problems is public financing, especially a clean elections system like the one in Arizona. Clean elections systems can help equalize resources by providing the same amount of public funding to all candidates and by forbidding any other fundraising by the recipients of public funding (although outside groups could continue to spend money on behalf of candidates). With equal amounts of funding, campaigns might then be more competitive, improving the quality of information provided to voters and giving them a more meaningful choice. In addition, with almost all campaign financing coming from the government, there would be little to no chance that wealthy donors or interest groups could have a disproportionate or corrupting influence. For example, when North Carolina instituted a voluntary public financing system for its state supreme court elections, justices who opted for public financing were less likely to rule in favor of the side whose attorney was a donor to a supreme court justice's campaign.[54] Advocates of clean elections have proposed a similar system for federal elections, the Fair Elections Now Act, which could, in the words of one of its proponents, make "elected officials beholden to the people they're supposed to represent instead of the wealthy special interests."[55]

Complicating the Case for Reform

How well do the arguments for campaign finance reform withstand empirical scrutiny? And are there good arguments in support of the system as it stands? Answers to these questions suggest that the American system of campaign finance, however imperfect, may have its merits.

Arguments for reform include two primary claims about the current system: simply stated, money buys elections and money buys legislators' votes. But can we verify that these statements are true? If the first claim means that the candidate who spends the most money will win the election, then it is clearly false. In 2016, Hillary Clinton raised and spent more than Trump, but she lost the Electoral College and thus the presidency. A similar point can be made about House elections. House incumbents typically raise much more money than challengers do, but is this why incumbents tend to win? Or do incumbents raise so much because they are already expected to win, and donors often prefer to give to the likely winner? And how do we separate the effects of incumbents' fundraising advantage from the other advantages they have as incumbents, including their work on behalf of constituents and consequent visibility? These sorts of advantages may help explain why incumbents were reelected at such high rates even *before* they were so dominant in fundraising. For example, in the early 1980s, House incumbents typically spent about 1.5 times as much as their challengers; in the 2000s, they typically spent about 2.5 or three times as much. Even though their fundraising advantage increased in the 2000s, incumbents' reelection rates in the early 1980s were above 90 percent—slightly higher than they were in the 2000s. To be sure, there is evidence of a correlation between a candidate's spending—particularly spending on direct communication with voters—and voters' support for that candidate.[56] But, incumbents' high reelection rates are not necessarily due *only* to their fundraising advantage.

Incumbents' other advantages may also explain why more stringent campaign finance rules do not necessarily make elections more competitive or make incumbents more vulnerable. For example, neither bans on corporate campaign spending nor different levels of limits on individual donations are associated with incumbent defeats.[57]

The evidence on the effects of clean elections is also somewhat equivocal. Public financing programs appear to reduce the amount of time that candidates spend fundraising for themselves and thereby increase the time they spend interacting with voters, but they may also increase the time candidates spend fundraising for their party.[58] Public financing programs do not appear to consistently reduce incumbents' advantages and make elections more competitive, although there is some evidence that more ambitious clean elections programs do increase competition.[59]

The claim that money buys legislators' votes also needs examination. There is relatively little evidence that this actually occurs. First, because of contribution limits, the amount that any donor or interest group can give is small relative to the large amounts of money that many candidates routinely raise and spend. Candidates who raise millions of dollars are not likely to "sell" their votes to a PAC for a measly $5,000.

Second, many donations to campaigns are strategic: donors do not want to waste their money on someone who will never support their agenda. Instead, they give to legislators who already share their goals or beliefs or who are working on behalf of constituents who share their goals or beliefs. Consider this hypothetical example. The National Farmers Union PAC gives an incumbent member of Congress $5,000 for his reelection campaign. The member represents a rural district in Iowa whose economy revolves around growing corn. After the election, he votes to give additional government subsidies to corn farmers. Did he vote this way because he simply believes that government subsidies are necessary, because many of his constituents are farmers and others who benefit from subsidies, or because he got that PAC contribution?

None of this is to say that campaign donations are ineffectual. Some research suggests that donations are more likely to buy the involvement of elected officials on an issue, if not their votes. This is particularly true when that involvement is not necessarily easily visible to the broader public. Donations appear to motivate representatives to be more active in promoting a given issue on congressional committees, for example. However, this is true only for representatives who already share the donors' positions.[60]

Donors may also get more "access" to elected officials—that is, a greater opportunity to advocate for their views in front of a representative or their staff.[61] Of course, this does not imply that the representative will always agree with these views—only that the representative will agree to hear them. Ultimately, campaign donations may not be quite as powerful an influence as reformers claim and as media coverage often suggests. Indeed, surveys of campaign finance experts have found that they are much less likely than voters to believe that "elective offices are for sale to the highest bidder" or "campaign contributions are the equivalent of bribes."[62]

The American system of campaign finance can also be defended on phil-osophical grounds. Two of the features that reformers routinely target—private donations and unlimited spending by candidates—could in fact be considered valuable. By allowing private donations to candidates, the Amer-ican system gives citizens and interest groups an opportunity to have a voice and to help elect candidates they believe can best represent them. By allow-ing unlimited spending, the American system allows for more campaign activity, including advertising that communicates information about the candidates, activities that mobilize citizens to vote, and so on. This point was made in the *Buckley v. Valeo* decision: "A restriction on the amount of money a person or group can spend on political communication during a campaign necessarily reduces the quantity of expression by restricting the number of issues discussed, the depth of their exploration, and the size of the audience reached." And, indeed, there is evidence that campaign spend-ing helps voters learn about political candidates.[63] Given that Americans still do not always know much about the candidates or vote in large num-bers, it could be counterproductive to limit campaign spending.

Leaving aside arguments about the merits of the current campaign finance system, critics face one further challenge: incumbent leaders have little incen-tive to reform the system. Despite the public's complaints about money in elections, polls reveal a limited appetite for reform. Majorities of Americans do favor limits on campaign contributions (which do exist) and limits on campaign spending (which do not exist). But they are ambivalent at best about more dramatic reforms, such as public financing. For example, a 2010 poll conducted by Common Cause, a group advocating for public funding, found that 63 percent of respondents supported public financing when described this way:

> Under this plan, candidates for Congress could run for office without rais-
> ing large campaign contributions. Instead they would collect a large num-
> ber of small contributions from their home state in order to qualify for a

limited amount of public funding for their campaign. They would be prohibited from taking any contributions over 100 dollars or any contributions from lobbyists. Contributions of 100 dollars or less would be matched with public funds on a four to one basis, up to a strict limit.[64]

However, a 2013 Gallup poll found that only 50 percent would vote for a "law that would establish a new campaign finance system where federal campaigns are funded by the government and all contributions from individual and private groups are banned." A November 2015 poll found that 56 percent of Americans believed that candidates should rely on donations, while only 26 percent supported full public funding and 17 percent supported a system in which the federal government would match private donations.[65] And a March 2021 poll found that 67 percent opposed a "proposal to use government dollars to match donations to political campaigns."[66] Americans' reluctance to embrace public financing wholeheartedly reflects their ambivalence about using government money—in other words, their taxes—to fund campaigns.

Despite their apparent concern about money in elections, Americans also know relatively little about the campaign finance system. Surveys in 2015–16 found that, on average, Americans could correctly answer only five out of 17 questions about the rules pertaining to donor disclosure, contribution limits, and spending limits. Nor do Americans appear to pay much attention to how individual candidates finance their campaigns. In an October 2008 Gallup poll, about 70 percent of voters either did not know whether Obama and McCain had accepted public financing or were mistaken in their view—even though Obama's decision to refuse public funding made headlines.[67] More generally, the public typically considers campaign finance reform to be far less important than the economy, foreign affairs, war, health care, education, and a host of other issues. In a December 2020 poll conducted by the Associated Press and the National Opinion Research Center, only 1 percent of respondents mentioned anything related to campaign finance or money in politics when asked what problems the government should work on in the year 2021. Indeed, the legislation that became the BCRA languished for years until a major scandal involving the energy company Enron—which had developed a close relationship with many elected politicians even as it was covering up financial problems that would eventually lead to bankruptcy—prompted action.

Without a significant push from the public, incumbent leaders are often reluctant to embrace reform. This is entirely rational: they were elected under the status quo, and changing the rules would introduce uncertainty into their bids for reelection. Incumbent leaders are especially nervous about public financing because they often believe it will make their opponents more competitive—and, of course, this is precisely what some proponents of public financing want. The point is not who is wrong or right. The point is that the implications of campaign finance rules for elected leaders often mean that their best strategy is to not change the rules.

Campaign Finance and the Political System

Debates about campaign finance often revolve around their effects on elections themselves or on the behavior of individual legislators. But we should also think about the implications of campaign finance reform for the political system as a whole. For example, people frequently bemoan how few Americans say that they trust the government, and they wonder if campaign finance reform could help restore some of that trust. Alas, the evidence suggests otherwise: research has found that respondents are no more likely to trust their state government in states with more stringent campaign finance laws than they are in states with less stringent laws.[68]

Campaign finance laws also have implications for the partisan polarization endemic in American politics—but those implications complicate common beliefs about what types of campaign finance laws are "good" or "bad." For example, it is often perceived as "better" when candidates and parties rely on the support of individual donors, especially donors who only give small amounts, than when they rely on PAC contributions. But individual donors—including small donors—tend to have more ideologically extreme opinions on issues.[69] The influence of individual donors may therefore exacerbate polarization.[70] By contrast, ordinary PACs and political parties often appear to prefer more moderate candidates, and so rules that empower them to give—such as those that relax the limits on PAC and party contributions to candidates—may actually reduce polarization.[71] Public financing may also make legislatures more polarized by reducing the influence of interest groups that tend to support moderate candidates.[72] Even more ambitious forms of public financing, like the clean elections programs in Arizona and Maine, do not appear to reduce polarization, although they have not exacerbated it.[73]

"Let's reduce polarization by empowering PACs!" is not a rallying cry you hear in politics very much. And the point is not that changes to campaign finance law would definitely lead to the election of enough moderate candidates to facilitate a new era of bipartisan compromise in Congress. There is always uncertainty about the impact of political reform. Instead, the point is that choices about campaign finance law involve trade-offs among competing values and goals for both U.S. elections and the broader political system.

Conclusion

Debates about campaign finance laws in the United States reinforce the important connections among rules, reality, strategy, and citizen choices. Recent changes in campaign finance law have increased the amount of money in federal election campaigns, mostly by allowing interest groups to solicit and spend funds more freely. Some observers have gone so far as to suggest that trying to keep money out of politics is like trying to keep ants out of a kitchen: plugging one hole will only lead the ants to find another as long as there is any sugar around. Although proponents of campaign finance reform continue to try to plug as many holes as possible, the American system will likely remain unusual among democracies in that it gives candidates and other actors considerable latitude in terms of what they can say, when they can say it, and how they pay for it.

KEY TERMS

Tillman Act (p. 99)

political action committees (PACs) (p. 99)

Federal Election Campaign Act (FECA) (p. 99)

Federal Election Commission (FEC) (p. 99)

Bipartisan Campaign Reform Act (BCRA) (p. 100)

soft money (p. 102)

hard money (p. 102)

express advocacy (p. 102)

magic words (p. 103)

issue advocacy (p. 103)

independent expenditure committees (p. 105)

super PACs (p. 105)

527 organizations (p. 105)

501(c) organizations (p. 105)

Buckley v. Valeo (p. 107)

public funding (p. 107)

clean elections systems (p. 108)

Citizens United v. Federal Election Commission (p. 110)

FOR DISCUSSION

1. According to Supreme Court decisions about campaign finance, why are contributions to candidates limited while spending by candidates is unlimited?

2. What are the costs and benefits to a candidate of funding their campaign via (a) money raised from private donors, (b) public funding, and (c) their own money?

3. How did the BCRA and the *Citizens United* decision affect the ways in which political parties and interest groups can raise and spend money in elections?

4. What are arguments for and against the belief that money corrupts politicians?

5

Modern Campaign Strategies

One day early in 2019, Joe Biden called a meeting of his advisers in the basement of his home in McLean, Virginia. Longtime Biden operative Mike Donilon opened the meeting by laying out the "three pillars" of Biden's presidential campaign. The first pillar was Biden's battle for "the soul of America." The second was fighting for the "backbone" of America—the middle class. The third was bringing the country together.[1] Biden's team formed these three pillars in reaction to the perceived deficiencies of Donald Trump's presidency; together, they suggested a pendulum swing away from the roller-coaster ride of the Trump administration and back toward "normalcy."

A year later, in early 2020, Biden's strategy was called into question as he languished in the early Democratic primaries. But after a decided win in South Carolina, the party coalesced around Biden (see Chapter 6). At almost the same time, the COVID-19 pandemic caused a national public health crisis and halted the country's robust economic growth. As the Trump administration desperately attempted to grapple with the virus and its economic and political fallout, the Trump campaign's plan to run for reelection on a strong economy was compromised. The political environment of the pandemic also compromised Trump's plans to paint Biden as old, out of touch, and beholden to the far left; though his campaign made this case, the charges fell mostly flat. Attacking a political opponent as tens of thousands of people died from the virus proved somewhat problematic. Meanwhile, Biden's emphasis on empathy, unity, and normalcy took on a new resonance. His ultimate campaign theme, "Build Back Better," combined the initial messages into one designed to acknowledge the challenges of the pandemic. Whether by steadfastness or luck, the Democratic challenger was on his way.

The issues and policy positions that animated Biden's campaign reflected two core beliefs. First, that the Trump administration had benefited the wealthy and done little for the middle or working classes. Second, that voters were exhausted by the tumult of Trump's first term. For example, Biden's economic plan was largely defined by increased spending on health care, infrastructure, and climate change programs, and he committed to rolling back the Trump tax breaks, closing tax "loopholes," and imposing additional taxes on the top 1 percent of all earners. Taken as a whole, the plans allowed the campaign to tap into voters' anxieties about health care costs and inequities in the American economy. They also allowed Biden to burnish his credentials as someone in touch with blue-collar voters, and they highlighted his empathy in contrast to Trump's callousness toward the people he purportedly championed. The Biden campaign's issues and positions rarely changed after the team tweaked them to account for the pandemic, and Biden's limits as a speaker—including his propensity for gaffes and misstatements—were played down by a pandemic-friendly strategy of few public appearances and almost no press conferences. This "no campaign"

Core of the Analysis

- A campaign must develop a strategy in order to compete effectively in a competitive district or state.
- Campaigns try to mobilize supporters and persuade undecided voters.
- Campaign strategy involves decisions about whether to run, which issues to emphasize, what positions to take on issues, whether to attack the opposition, and how to allocate resources to different constituencies and media.
- These strategic decisions depend strongly on the broader rules and realities that candidates confront.
- Campaign organizations have general features in common but vary considerably depending on the size and scope of the campaign.
- Modern political campaigns rely on professionals to devise and execute their strategies and to organize their campaigns.

campaign perfectly complemented the Biden team's desire to contrast their candidate's low-key, stable, safe approach to that of Trump.

Meanwhile, Trump's campaign struggled to deal with a reality dramatically altered by the pandemic. Instead of running for reelection on the back of a booming economy and a promise to "Keep America Great," the campaign had to argue that Trump was uniquely qualified to rebuild the post-pandemic economy. And instead of using their campaign war chest to launch a spring 2020 offensive defining Biden as "yesterday's news," Trump and his team had to content themselves with jabs at Biden's "basement campaign," implying that he was too scared to engage politically, or comments on his occasional gaffes, implying that he was suffering from mental decline. Could the Trump campaign have successfully changed its focus from the economy to Trump's leadership through the public health challenge of our lifetime? Could he have become something like a "wartime president" and rallied the country with informative fireside chats, messages from the Oval Office, or a rousing speech in front of a joint session of Congress in the days following the pandemic's arrival on U.S. shores? Given the closeness of the results, it is tempting to conclude that even a nod in this direction might have swung the election in favor of the incumbent.

But how important—and influential—are campaign strategies, really? Did Biden really have a coherent and consistent strategy that guided his campaign's activities? And, if so, how "good" of a strategy was it? Was it really a major factor in his successful run to capture the White House? On the other side of the coin, how "bad" was Trump's campaign strategy? Did it cost him the presidency? Or was he simply done in by his own ambivalent approach toward a global pandemic and by an electorate that was worn out by four years of relentless and incendiary back-and-forth between Trump and his detractors? More generally, how do political scientists define and evaluate campaign strategies as they interpret the results of voting and elections?

The goal of this chapter is to describe and consider the role of strategy (and strategists) in American political campaigns. We begin by defining strategy and discussing how a modern campaign develops a strategy. Next, we outline the important strategic decisions of a campaign, examining both professional practice and academic research. Among other things, we argue that campaigns are selective with respect to what they say and to whom they say it. Some voters are critical to victory, and they receive most of the campaign's attention. The skill with which a campaign identifies and convinces these voters can be important for the election's outcome. We then examine what a campaign looks like, how it is organized, and the role of political consultants. Finally, we discuss the normative implications of the rise of more professionalized, strategic campaigns.

How Are Campaign Strategies Constructed?

Assuming a candidate has decided to run—a decision we will consider in greater detail later in this chapter—there are many tasks the campaign must address immediately. The campaign needs a physical space for a headquarters so that people have a place to work. The candidate has to announce their candidacy. There are people who must be contacted, including past candidates and party leaders, whose expertise, advice, and endorsement are all potentially valuable. The campaign needs to identify the main issues the candidate intends to run on and prepare position papers. Finally, the campaign must purchase some of the staples of the modern campaign: computers, servers, Wi-Fi and internet connections, smartphones, and materials for brochures, bumper stickers, buttons, and pamphlets.

But perhaps more than anything else, a campaign needs to quickly develop a **campaign strategy**. Put simply, a strategy is a proposed pathway to victory. It is a plan for how to win, and it is driven by an understanding of who will vote for the candidate and why they will do so. The political scientist Joel Bradshaw posits four key propositions for developing a successful campaign strategy.[2] First, in any election, the electorate can be divided into three groups: the candidate's base, the opponent's base, and the undecided. Second, past election results, data from lists of registered voters, and survey research make it possible to estimate which people fall into each of these three groups. Third, it is neither possible nor necessary to get the support of all people everywhere to win the election. Research should allow a campaign to determine how best to mobilize the candidate's base and persuade the undecideds. Both mobilization and persuasion are central to a campaign's efforts, although the relative balance between the two depends on the characteristics of the electorate and the race.[3] Fourth, and last, once a campaign has identified how to win, it can act to create the circumstances to bring about this victory. In order to succeed, campaigns should direct campaign resources—money, time, and message—to key groups of potential voters and nowhere else. Resource allocation is therefore defined by strategy.

Vote Targets

Implicit in these propositions is the need to develop specific **vote targets** (or vote goals). These targets are based on estimates of what the upcoming election will look like: how many total votes the campaign believes will be cast in the election, how many it will need to win, how many votes its candidate can expect no matter what, and how many **persuadable (or swing) votes** are out there.

Campaigns typically come up with vote targets by examining data from recent comparable elections. For example, let us say that a hypothetical candidate is running for governor in the 2022 general election in Ohio. The simplest way to estimate how many total votes will be cast in the upcoming election is to look across the most recent gubernatorial elections (see Table 5.1).

Notice that we are not looking at turnout in presidential years, which is invariably higher than turnout in midterm elections; we only want to look at data from other gubernatorial elections. Notice also that the Ohio turnout rate varies a bit from year to year, from a low of about 41 percent in 2014 to a high of about 54 percent in 2018. The number of registered voters bumps around as well, increasing by 177,754 from 2006 to 2010, declining by 289,605 from 2010 to 2014, and then increasing by 322,716 from 2014 to 2018. Based on this information, for the 2022 election it is reasonable to assume that (1) turnout will be about 50 percent of registered voters, and

TABLE 5.1 Turnout in Ohio Gubernatorial Elections, 2006–18

Year	Registered Voters	Total Votes	Turnout Rate
2006	7,860,052	4,185,597	53%
2010	8,037,806	3,956,045	49%
2014	7,748,201	3,149,876	41%
2018	8,070,917	4,318,408	54%
Average	7,929,244	3,902,482	49%

Source: Ohio Secretary of State, "Voter Turnout: Election Results and Data," www.sos.state.oh.us/elections/election-results-and-data (accessed 12/3/18).

(2) the number of registered voters will be between 7.7 and 8.3 million. In a real election campaign, we would be able to access updated registration numbers from the Ohio secretary of state. For illustrative purposes, though, let us assume that there will be 8 million registered voters for the next election. If we assume that 50 percent of those who are registered will vote in the governor's race, the total number of votes cast will be about 4 million.

How many votes do we need to win? This depends, of course, on the number of candidates in the race. If it is simply a contest between two major-party candidates—a Republican versus a Democrat—our candidate will need slightly more than 50 percent of the votes. If there are minor-party or independent candidates, a candidate could conceivably win with less than 50 percent (a plurality, but not a majority). But let us assume that we have a two-party election on our hands. A bare majority (50.1 percent) of our expected electorate would be 2,004,000. Most campaigns round up when estimating a vote target because they want to avoid a situation in which they meet their target number of votes but lose the election because of unexpectedly high turnout. As a case in point, analysts of Hillary Clinton's 2016 presidential campaign said that she met her vote targets in the critical battleground state of Pennsylvania—including the key Philadelphia collar counties of Bucks and Montgomery—but ultimately lost because of unexpectedly high turnout in the heavily Republican rural counties of central and northern Pennsylvania (the Pennsylvania "T"). So let us be very cautious and set a vote target of 54 percent, or 2.16 million votes.

Next, our campaign should have an expectation about how large our candidate's base vote is. In other words, how many votes would a "bad" candidate from the party get in an election in which conditions favored the other side? Again, most campaign strategists turn to past results to estimate this (Table 5.2).

Consider things from the perspective of the Republican candidate. The election results vary a great deal—from a Republican high of 64 percent in 2014 to a low of just under 37 percent in 2006. In many ways, 2006 was a low-water mark for the Republican Party, both in Ohio and across the nation. Republican president George W. Bush was deeply unpopular, a controversial war was dragging on in Iraq, and the economy was beginning to show signs of recession. Moreover, in Ohio, the Republican gubernatorial candidate, Ken Blackwell, was widely regarded as having run an especially inept campaign. Thus, we can take the 2006 result as an estimate of

TABLE 5.2 Votes Won in Ohio Gubernatorial Elections, 2006–18

Year	Votes for Republican Candidate	Votes for Democratic Candidate	Votes for Other Candidates	Republican Candidate's Percentage
2006	1,474,331	2,435,505	113,019	37%
2010	1,889,186	1,812,059	151,224	49%
2014	1,944,848	1,009,359	101,706	64%
2018	2,187,619	2,005,627	124,848	51%

Source: Ohio Secretary of State, "Voter Turnout: Election Results and Data," www.sos.state.oh.us/elections/election-results-and-data (accessed 12/3/18).

the Republican base vote: the minimum that a Republican candidate can expect to win. If we use the figure of 37 percent of the expected 2022 turnout (4 million votes), our estimate of the Republican base vote in 2022 is 1,480,000.

To generate an estimate of the persuadable vote, we need an upper estimate of what a candidate from our party can achieve. In other words, how many votes would a "good" Republican candidate get in an election in which conditions favored the Republican Party? The 2014 election provides just such an example. The public was angry about the troubled rollout of the Affordable Care Act ("Obamacare") and the slow, uneven economic recovery, and people blamed the Democrats in power. Furthermore, the Republican gubernatorial candidate, John Kasich, was a popular figure who appealed to Democrats and independents as well as Republicans. Let us therefore take his 64 percent result as an estimate of the high potential for a Republican candidate. The difference between these extremes is 64 minus 37 percent, or 27 percent. So our estimate of the persuadable vote for our upcoming Ohio governor's race is 27 percent of the total expected vote of 4 million, or approximately 1,080,000 voters.

This last estimate is critical. To recap, we assume that approximately 4 million voters will cast ballots in the Ohio governor's election in 2022. We have a vote target of 2.16 million, and we estimate that our base vote is slightly under 1.5 million voters. The swing vote in the state is about 1.1 million voters. To get from our base (1.5 million) to our target

TABLE 5.3 Election Results and Vote Targets for Selected Ohio Counties (Republican Candidates)

County	2018: DeWine Votes	2014: Kasich Votes	2010: Kasich Votes	2006: Blackwell Votes	Average Contribution to Republican Vote Total	Vote Target for 2022 Election (Based on a Statewide Target of 2.16 Million)
Cuyahoga	148,045	172,319	148,611	107,258	7.70%	166,212
Franklin	162,328	161,747	169,487	122,601	8.22%	177,552
Hamilton	145,164	142,066	143,222	141,374	7.63%	164,808
Montgomery	97,677	90,683	89,218	76,189	4.72%	101,952
Statewide	2,187,619	1,944,848	1,889,186	1,474,331	—	2,160,000

Source: Ohio Secretary of State, "Voter Turnout: Election Results and Data," www.sos.state.oh.us/elections/election-results-and-data (accessed 12/3/18).

(2.16 million), we need to win 660,000 of the 1,080,000 swing votes (61 percent).

It is important to note that while many campaigns estimate the number of swing voters using this method, it does not translate into individual "targets"—that is, we have an idea of how many voters can be swayed, but we do not know from these data which individuals are most likely to be persuaded to vote for our candidate. Contemporary campaigns use data from registered voter lists to identify specific individuals to whom directed persuasive communication may be effective (more on this later).

We can also generate vote targets for each county in the state based on previous election results—for example, we might use the four most recent elections to calculate the average contribution of each county to the total statewide party vote (Table 5.3). Consider Cuyahoga County, where the city of Cleveland is located: it contributed, on average, 7.7 percent of the total Republican vote in Ohio in the past four elections. For the 2022 election, we would multiply this percentage by the total statewide vote target (2.16 million) to generate a target for Cuyahoga of 164,808 Republican votes. This can be done for every county and even the precincts within a county.

Profiling Vote Targets

How can the campaign hope to win over the swing voters it needs to meet its target? First and foremost, the campaign must identify who these voters are. Campaigns typically use surveys and, to a lesser degree, focus groups to do this. Initially, the campaign will conduct surveys to ascertain what sorts of people are persuadable. Most campaign surveys are **probability samples**, in which some number of individuals from a registered voter population are randomly selected and asked a set of questions. The key to a probability sample is that every individual in the population of interest has a known probability of being selected. Because selection is random, a small number of completed interviews (usually between 400 and 1,000) reveal the general opinions held throughout the population, with a known and relatively small (or at least acceptable) margin of error. In much the same way that a doctor can make inferences about your health based on a small sample of your blood, we can make inferences about public opinion based on a small sample of randomly chosen citizens. Over time, the willingness of people to take polls has declined, causing pollsters to "weight" their surveys by demographic characteristics such as gender, race, age, and education to increase the likelihood of an accurate representation of the electorate. Despite these challenges, campaigns still rely heavily on polls to identify persuadable voters and to develop appropriate strategies.

Thinking back to our governor's race, a survey (or poll) can thus be used to ask registered voters in Ohio whom they intend to vote for in the upcoming election. For those people with a preference, we can also ask how strongly they prefer their candidate. A survey allows us not only to identify how many people are currently undecided or might be moved from their current preference but also to see if persuadable voters are more common among certain groups, such as women, young people, or Latinos. In addition, we can examine the issue preferences of persuadable voters to develop a plan for winning them over.

Once surveys have been analyzed, many campaigns conduct in-depth interviews with small groups of persuadable voters to gather additional data and test specific issue positions. These are called **focus groups**. They have been a part of political campaigns since the mid-1980s, when campaign consultants noticed that businesses were using them to enhance their understanding of client preferences. They range in size from around eight to 20 participants, and they are led by a "facilitator" whose job is to pose questions and encourage full participation from all participants. Focus groups differ from polls in that participants are not selected randomly. In fact, they are intentionally recruited on the basis of certain characteristics that the campaign associates with persuadable voters (e.g., gender, age, or ethnicity). Because of this, focus group participants do not necessarily represent what the larger population thinks; they are simply suggestive of how certain sub-groups think about politics and the election. And while focus groups do not provide statistically generalizable information, they provide a depth of information that campaigns often find valuable.

Together, polls and focus groups give campaigns a strong sense of what sorts of voters they need to win over and the kinds of appeals that will most effectively accomplish this. This knowledge can be used to craft stump speeches, position papers, press releases, television and radio advertisements, and social media strategies.

The second step to identifying swing voters involves rating the persuadabil-ity of all registered voters in the district. This step involves two major tasks, both of which are large and expensive undertakings. Thus, campaigns typi-cally undertake this step only in presidential, gubernatorial, U.S. Senate, and hotly contested U.S. House races. Smaller state and local campaigns, as we discuss in Chapter 11, may rely on cheaper and less sophisticated strategies.

The first task is to acquire a list of registered voters and augment it with demographic information on each voter. As we discussed in Chapter 3, the major political parties have compiled extensive databases on voters that include their names, addresses, phone numbers, previous voting history, party affinity, demographic attributes such as gender or race, and financial and consumer data such as home values.[4] From these voter files, campaigns can estimate (1) a turnout propensity score, which models the likelihood of a voter casting a ballot based on past turnout and a series of known predic-tors such as residential stability, age, and education, and (2) a candidate support score, which models the likelihood of someone voting for a candi-date based on party affinity and a series of known predictors such as race, ethnicity, age, and geographic location.[5]

The second task is to use voter file information along with polling infor-mation to estimate a persuadability score, which predicts how open each voter on the list will be to appeals from the campaign's candidate. The cam-paign can then isolate specific voters—presumably those who are relatively less likely to currently favor its candidate—for digital outreach, mailings, phone calls, or in-person visits, all based on a combination of data from the poll and the voter list.[6] For example, the poll may show that suburban stay-at-home moms are persuadable and sympathetic to your candidate's position on education. The campaign might then target stay-at-home moms with phone calls to emphasize this issue. This process, called **microtargeting**, was developed in the 2000 and 2002 elections. Microtargeting avoids the need to make **voter identification (or voter ID) calls**, in which all voters on the voter list are contacted and asked about their preferences for the upcoming race. More broadly, the availability of microtargeting data, along with increased partisan polarization, means that general-election candidates are chasing similar (shrinking) pools of persuadable voters.

It is difficult to microtarget based on a standard campaign poll. A poll of 500 people, for example, will not have a sufficient number of respondents in certain groups—such as college students—to make reliable inferences about what these groups think. Nor will a standard poll ask enough questions about a respondent's background to take advantage of the information available in voter databases. Thus, microtargeting typically requires a very large poll—say, of 6,000 or more respondents—that includes additional questions about the respondents' backgrounds and habits. Microtargeting is expensive, but it is much less expensive than a round of statewide voter ID contacts.

The Context of Voter Targeting

Targeting voters effectively requires not only polling data and an accurate voter list but also an understanding of the reality associated with the particular election. Perhaps the most important aspect of this reality is whether the candidate is an incumbent or a challenger. For the incumbent, the election is to some degree a referendum on how things have gone on their watch. Citizens will associate prevailing conditions—the state of the economy, crime rates, traffic flow, and so on—with the incumbent candidate, and they will reward or punish the candidate accordingly. Many people viewed the 2020 presidential election, for instance, as a referendum on how the incumbent, Trump, handled the pandemic and all of its attendant issues. In this context, it is more difficult to persuade voters; people have seen the incumbent in action and have already formed opinions. Conversely, if the candidate is a challenger running against an incumbent, they will try to convince people that the incumbent has done a poor job and that it is time for a change. In addition, the challenger will be less familiar to constituents in the district. People prefer someone they know, and they are more likely to recognize the name of the incumbent than that of the challenger. In sum, when an incumbent is running for reelection, most of the campaign is about defending their record. Targeting is thus constrained by real-life conditions.

If there is no incumbent in the race, the central question for voters is simply: Who will do a better job? Candidates, however, do not necessarily have recent and relevant experience that voters can assess as they decide which

Maine U.S. Senate Debate

≈ C·SPAN ★ 2020

In the 2020 race for one of Maine's U.S. Senate seats, Republican Susan Collins (center) defeated Democrat Sara Gideon (left). In addition to turning out Republicans, Collins targeted independents and moderate Democrats by focusing on her independent streak and her advocacy for Maine's interests in the national conversation.

candidate to vote for. Perhaps more to the point, in an **open-seat** race, it is much easier to craft a strategy to persuade people to support your candidate.

Another important reality that campaigns must consider is the partisan makeup of the district in which the candidate is running. As we discussed in Chapter 2, the characteristics of a candidate's constituency affect nearly every dimension of campaign strategy. If 50 percent of voters in the district are Democratic, 20 percent are Republican, and 30 percent describe themselves as independent, the Democratic candidate will likely emphasize traditionally partisan appeals (and will usually win). The Republican candidate will need to win over some independents and Democrats, and is therefore likely to emphasize candidate-related appeals—experience and background—rather than party. This was the case in the 2020 U.S. Senate race in Maine between Sara Gideon, a Democrat, and Susan Collins, the incumbent Republican. Collins pulled off a surprising 51-to-42 percent victory in a state that typically leans Democratic. (Maine has gone for the Democratic presidential candidate in every election since 1988 and went for Biden over Trump by a 53-to-42 percent margin.) In her campaign, Collins focused on her record as an independent voice in the Senate and a strong advocate for Maine's economic and social interests, and she convinced a sufficient number of Democrats that the race was about something besides traditional party labels.

Now, consider another district in which 30 percent of voters are Republican, 30 percent are Democratic, and 40 percent describe themselves as independent. Here, campaigns will likely target the broad swath of independents. This was the case in the 2020 U.S. Senate race in Arizona, in which the Democratic challenger, Mark Kelly, defeated the Republican incumbent, Martha McSally. McSally, who lost Arizona's 2018 U.S. Senate election to Democrat Kyrsten Sinema, was appointed to Arizona's second Senate seat in 2019 to fill a vacancy. In her brief tenure as senator, McSally voted with the Trump administration 97 percent of the time and adopted the populist rhetoric that defined Trump's most ardent supporters. This helped Kelly paint her as an unpopular extremist. McSally won only 45 percent of independents, and Kelly won the seat with a narrow 2-point victory.

Although both state and national factors matter, they are not all-powerful. For example, Collins (a Republican) won in a state that had voted Democratic for president in eight straight elections. Kelly (a Democrat) won in a year when the partisan winds were mixed (Democrats narrowly won the White House and Senate, while Republicans gained seats in the House). The prevalence of the Democratic Party in Maine and the exhausted national mood in 2020 (both of which contributed to the political reality of the election) shaped Collins's and Kelly's respective campaign strategies, but both campaigns were able to target and mobilize electoral majorities. While these cases are illustrative and important, they are also somewhat unusual these days: very few candidates substantially outperform their party's presidential candidate anymore.

Strategic Campaign Decisions

Thus far, we have emphasized the broad outlines of strategy but have said little about how it influences the specific decisions that face every political campaign. Much of what we discuss below—especially regarding "what to say" to voters—can be understood as "messaging." Messaging includes the issues that candidates prioritize, the positions they take on them, and the broader theme or rationale for the campaign. We consider messaging content to be perhaps the foremost example of the strategic decisions that face most campaigns. We now turn to these decisions, paying particular mind to the similarities and differences in how campaign professionals and political scientists approach them.

The Decision to Run

We are so used to thinking about who wins and loses elections that sometimes we forget an important prior question: Who decides to run for office in the first place? Elections are significantly shaped not only by who chooses to run but also by who sits things out. In the run-up to the 2020 election, 30 Democrats decided to run for president, jumbling the field and making it difficult for any of the presumed front-runners to break through. Many have argued that the large Democratic field advantaged Biden, the eventual Democratic nominee, by spreading the far-left vote among progressive candidates such as Vermont senator Bernie Sanders and Massachusetts senator Elizabeth Warren. Might Sanders have been the nominee if he had been the only far-left candidate? Perhaps. But Biden's dominance was by no means assured at the outset of the early contests, as a number of moderate candidates—former South Bend mayor Pete Buttigieg, Minnesota senator Amy Klobuchar, and former New York City mayor Michael Bloomberg—initially complicated the former vice president's ascendancy. Then there is the fact that several "dream" candidates—most notably, former first lady Michelle Obama and billionaire talk show host and entrepreneur Oprah Winfrey—chose not to run in 2020. Indeed, for a time it was unclear whether Biden himself would run in 2020 after skipping the 2016 contest. And all this is simply a look at one party for one election: the effects of decisions whether or not to run—while most obvious at the presidential level—are felt in races at all levels of government.

Political consultants and political scientists largely agree that there are several important factors for candidates and their advisers to consider when thinking about whether to run for office. One is *motivation*. Do the candidates want to run for office, or are they being dragged reluctantly into the fray? While we tend to think of politicians as uniformly ambitious, many are ambivalent about moving up the political ladder. For example, incumbents might prefer their current positions to running for higher office and potentially losing.[7] Representative Ron Paul, who ran for the Republican nomination for president in 2008, provides a concrete example of such ambivalence. After the election was over, Paul's campaign manager said of his candidate, "We couldn't get him for six months to say that he wanted to be president."[8] For candidates who do want to run, it is also important to understand why they want to run. Their motivations—duty to country, particular policy goals, and so on—will help inform strategic decisions later on in the campaign.

In gauging motivation, it is also important to know how the candidate's family feels about their candidacy. For example, do they have a spouse who is willing to assist and endure the campaign? Do they have children? Are they willing to move the family around and use them in the campaign? Maybe more to the point, is the candidate willing to endure the potentially embarrassing scrutiny of their immediate and extended family? And do they have secrets that they would like to keep from their family? A concern about separation from his children was one thing that made Barack Obama hesitate before declaring his candidacy for president in 2008. One of his advisers, David Plouffe, told an audience after the campaign, "He's got young kids and he's very close to them. That was really the biggest hurdle—could he reconcile his desire to see his family a lot?"[9]

A second factor to consider is *resources*. Perhaps the most important question here is whether a candidate can raise money. As we discussed in Chapter 4, the American system of campaign finance puts the burden of fundraising on the candidate, and little can be accomplished without money on hand.[10] Besides money, other resources that affect a candidate's decision to run include credentials (has the potential candidate held an office that gives them relevant experience?) and time (can they take time off work and away from their family to campaign effectively?).

A third factor is whether a candidate can assemble a campaign organization. Do they have an experienced, enthusiastic staff? Is there adequate outside help available, or have the best pollsters, consultants, media people, and field organizers already committed to other campaigns? Modern-day campaign organizations often look like small armies, and it is ideal to put an organization in place at the beginning of the campaign. In the 2020 presidential election, Democratic candidates such as Kamala Harris, Michael Bennet, and Amy Klobuchar reportedly had difficulty locking down top-end talent to staff their campaigns, which not only hampered their ability to compete for early momentum but also caused negative news stories that hurt their fundraising efforts.

A final factor for a candidate and advisers to consider as they decide whether to run is the *opportunity* (or lack thereof) presented in the election. Opportunities derive from the realities that candidates face at a particular time and place, and they are crucial because they often determine *when* a candidate will run, as opposed to whether the candidate has a general inclination to run. Smart candidates will wait until the odds, and the realities of the election, are in their favor. What is the makeup of the electorate? Would the candidate be willing to run when the electorate is primarily composed of members of the opposite party? And what is the nature of the competition?

Will the candidate face a competitive primary challenger?[11] Will they face a competitive general-election opponent? What resources do opponents have? What about conditions in the country? How is the economy doing? How popular is the incumbent president? All of these things may influence whether the candidate feels it is possible to win.

The role of opportunity suggests that candidates can be thought of as "strategic politicians."[12] In some ways, potential candidates are rational actors looking to maximize the chances that they will win. Given the costs of running, and the potential damage to their reputation if they run and lose, they are unlikely to run unless they believe there is a significant chance they will win. Thus, strategic politicians rarely challenge dominant incumbents, rarely run in districts where they are outnumbered by partisans from the other side, and rarely run if the prevailing national mood is against their party. Conversely, they look for races in which the incumbent is retiring or weak. They tend to run in districts where most voters share their party affiliation. They tend to run if there is a national tide favoring their party. This mentality creates something of a self-fulfilling prophecy: strategic politicians rarely run unless they calculate favorable odds, so incumbents almost never face tough competition unless other factors are decidedly against them.[13]

To be sure, not every candidate will appear rational. Plenty of quixotic campaigns are waged every election year. Sometimes these candidates run because the upsides of victory are persuasive enough to offset the downsides of a loss. Long-shot presidential candidates fall into this category. At other times, candidates run in order to lay the groundwork for a later run for office. For example, then up-and-coming Texas Republican Ted Cruz (the former solicitor general) challenged the much better-known and well-financed lieutenant governor David Dewhurst for the 2012 GOP Senate nomination, possibly calculating that even a losing effort could enhance his status with the public and wealthy donors. While his candidacy was a gamble, Cruz won the primary and general elections and became the junior senator from Texas. He then ran for president in 2016, despite having served only three years in the Senate and despite the crowded Republican field. Apropos of this example, there is some evidence that Republicans are more likely than Democrats to run for office despite strategic reasons *not* to run.[14] But candidacies like these still seem exceptional, and there remain strong incentives for politicians to think strategically about the decision to run.

Political science research on the decision to run suggests that three of these four factors—motivation, resources, and opportunity—matter simultaneously. A good example comes from the research of Jennifer Lawless and Richard Fox on why so few women hold elective office relative to their share of the population. Their research has shown that although women candidates are just as likely as male candidates to win elections, they are less likely than men to run in the first place. In part, this is a question of motivation. Women report less enthusiasm for the rigors of campaigning, such as fundraising. They also seem to perceive themselves as lacking in resources. One such resource is their credentials: women are less likely than men to see themselves as qualified. Another resource is time. Even women who are employed full-time in high-status professions, such as law or business, report spending more time on household tasks and child care than do men in similar professions. Finally, they see fewer opportunities. Relative to men, they are more likely to believe that elections in their community are competitive, that raising money will be difficult, and that female candidates are less likely to win.[15] There is some evidence that more women ran for elected office in 2018 and 2020 than in previous election cycles and that outside groups may have been successful in recruiting and supporting female candidates, but the fundamental findings of Lawless and Fox undoubtedly remain true.[16]

Historically, people of color have also been relatively less likely to run for political office. One recent analysis of nearly 10,000 statehouse elections from 2000 to 2010 found that this was the main reason why Latinos were underrepresented in elected positions.[17] This is not to say that voters are color-blind; a wealth of research suggests that many voters are biased against candidates of different races and ethnicities.[18] But factors other than race and ethnicity (most notably, party affiliation) are even more important to voters, such that one can point to numerous examples of successful candidates of color: Barack Obama, Tim Scott (R-S.C.), Cory Booker (D-N.J.), Marco Rubio (R-Fla.), and Ted Cruz (R-Tex.), to name just a few. The problem of underrepresentation thus remains largely one of candidate recruitment, as Black and Latino candidates are relatively less likely to have held office previously, to have access to readily available money and donor lists, or to seek and obtain support from formal party organizations.[19]

Messaging: Issue Priorities

Perhaps the most obvious strategic question of a campaign involves issues and how to talk about them. Which issues should a candidate emphasize? Candidates select issues for their campaign agenda with care and then seek to emphasize only those issues—"staying on **message**," as the saying goes. Choosing issue priorities is a critical strategic decision because candidates want to control the campaign agenda whenever possible. Some issues will work to a candidate's advantage, and some will not. A candidate who keeps the focus on issues on which the public favors their policy positions may win over persuadable voters and perhaps win the election. For example, in the 2020 presidential election, Trump wanted to focus attention on the economy, trade, and immigration, while Biden wanted to focus on the pandemic, inequality, jobs, the environment, and social justice. In some ways, the main fight in the campaign was more about the agenda than specific proposals. Once most Americans decided that the election was a referendum on the pandemic and the contentious state of American politics, Biden (arguably) had won.

Like the candidates themselves, campaign consultants also believe strongly in the importance of agenda control. Many consultants assume that citizens do not care much about politics and only pay attention to the "loudest" moments of the campaign. Thus, while citizens' perceptions are malleable, candidates only have a couple of chances to tell them what the election is about. As a result, consultants structure campaigns so that they focus on one or two issues, **framing** (or presenting) them in simple, easy-to-understand terms. Each side attempts to define what matters.

Why might candidates choose some issues and not others? Here, the reality that candidates confront is crucial. Events outside of their control put certain issues on the agenda, leading the public to prioritize those issues and leaving candidates little choice but to address them. In the 2020 presidential election, both Biden and Trump talked a great deal about the COVID-19 pandemic. The issue was nettlesome for both sides: Trump tried to show that his administration was being responsive and making progress in fighting the virus as the death toll mounted, while Biden criticized the incumbent—but not so much that he might be seen as an opportunist intent on exploiting a public health crisis for political gain. Still, when certain issues become national priorities, as the pandemic did in 2020, it is common to see opposing candidates with similar agendas.

Candidates also base their agendas on the traditional strengths of their parties. In Chapter 1, we noted that the reputations political parties have for paying attention to particular issues give them greater credibility on these issues. This reality of campaigns and elections is known as **issue ownership**, a term that suggests that parties come to "own" issues because of their reputations.[20] Observers would typically say that the Republican Party owns the issues of national security, taxes, and crime, while the Democratic Party owns health care, education, and entitlement programs like Social Security and Medicare.[21]

If candidates emphasized only the issues their party owns, then we would expect to see them talking past each other rather than engaging one another on the issues. In reality, although candidates sometimes put greater emphasis on their party's "owned" issues, they often talk about all sorts of other issues, even those that "belong to" the other party.[22] Sometimes candidates do so deliberately in an effort to expand their electoral coalition. In the 1996 election, for example, President Bill Clinton emphasized his "crime bill" and additional funding for police to burnish his credentials as a centrist and broaden his appeal to socially conservative voters. Other times, national events demand discussion of issues "owned" by the other party. For example, in the summer of 2020, both Trump and Biden were forced to address the protests, social unrest, and issues of police misconduct in the wake of the death of George Floyd, a Black man who was killed by a White police officer during an arrest in Minneapolis, Minnesota. The incident and the subsequent protests called attention to weaknesses of both Trump and Biden. For Trump, they highlighted his seeming lack of regard for the civil rights and criminal justice issues facing communities of color. For Biden, the violence of some of the protests and the demands by some activists to "defund the police" recalled his past support for a stringent crime bill, which caused some progressives to distrust him on the issue of criminal justice. The summer's events also rekindled suspicions that Biden's party was "weak" on crime and unwilling to support law enforcement officials, which caused some conservatives to distrust Democrats generally on the issue. The immediacy and power of the events, however, demanded a response. Predictably, Trump's response emphasized the need for law and order, while Biden focused on racism, civil rights, and the need to reform the criminal justice system.

Campaign agendas are also influenced by the candidates' own personal experiences and reputations.[23] Regardless of the reputation of their party, candidates often develop areas of policy interest, expertise, and accomplishments, and they can talk credibly about these issues by highlighting their own achievements. For example, in the 2000 presidential election, George W. Bush emphasized education a great deal, even though the Democratic Party usually "owns" this issue. As governor of Texas, he had worked to improve primary and secondary education, and he believed that the state's progress gave him the credibility he needed to "trespass" on the Democrats' territory and to thereby broaden his electoral appeal to voters who might have otherwise preferred his opponent, Al Gore. Although personal experience can matter, candidates do discuss many issues with which they have limited expertise or experience. This again suggests that candidates are confident that they can frame issues in favorable ways, no matter what the reality is.

Before moving on from issue priorities, it is worth observing that sometimes the *candidate* is the main issue in an election. That is, the election is largely a referendum on the performance and character of one or more of the people running for office. Most political scientists and consultants believe that Trump was the main issue in the 2020 presidential election. The Biden campaign team worked assiduously to weave and reinforce criticisms of Trump into their presentation of any and all issues.

Messaging: Issue Positions

While formulating their agendas, candidates also must determine what positions they should take on the issues that they prioritize. In reality, they are not totally free to take any position. Candidates have ideologies that constrain them. Liberals, for instance, are unlikely to take a pro-life position on abortion just to win votes. Candidates also have histories that constrain them. Someone who has been conservative for their whole life is going to look like a panderer if they suddenly embrace moderate or liberal positions when heading into a tough campaign. Still, even with these limits, candidates for election face a choice: Should they simply take positions that are popular with citizens, or should they seek to persuade citizens to adopt their own point of view?

The logic of taking popular positions can be explained using the **median voter theorem**.[24] This theorem assumes that voters can be arrayed on a spectrum that captures the range of positions on a particular issue—from, say, liberal to conservative. Candidates seek to position themselves on that spectrum nearest to the hypothetical voter who would provide the winning vote for them: the median voter. The median voter is the person who falls in the exact middle of the spectrum. That is, half of all voters are more liberal than this hypothetical person, and half are more conservative. The candidate who wins the median voter, as well as all of those voters who are on the same side of the issue as the candidate, wins the election.

A diagram may help to illustrate. The bell-shaped curve in Figure 5.1 represents how many voters are positioned at each point along this spectrum, arrayed from left ("L") to right ("R"). The median voter is labeled "M." The two candidates are labeled "A" and "B." Currently, Candidate A appeals to more voters than Candidate B because Candidate A is closer to the median voter M. Both candidates could improve their support by adopting policy positions that move them closer to M.

The median voter theorem may seem too abstract to guide campaign strategy. After all, campaigns want to appeal to real voters, not some hypothetical median voter. However, the basic logic of the median voter theorem is quite evident in how campaign professionals and political commentators think about campaigns. For example, we often hear about candidates who are "moving to the center," with the presumption that this enables them to

FIGURE 5.1 The Median Voter Theorem

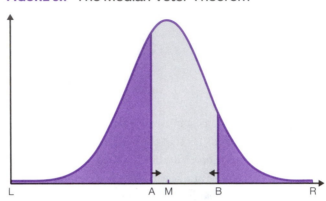

appeal to more "moderate," "independent," or "swing" voters whose support would allow them to win the election. Furthermore, the lion's share of empirical research from political science indicates that there is an electoral advantage in general elections for candidates who are seen as more moderate, although this advantage may be diminishing over time.[25]

Candidates can't always follow the median voter theorem's advice for several reasons. For one, as noted earlier, candidates are constrained in the positions they can take. If moving toward the median voter means contradicting some previous position, then the candidate may damage their credibility and risk earning a label like "flip-flopper." For example, when John Kerry ran for president in 2004, he repeatedly stated that he opposed the Iraq War. But as a U.S. senator, Kerry voted for a congressional resolution authorizing the use of force against Saddam Hussein and his regime in Iraq. His opponent, George W. Bush, pointed this out in a television ad in which Kerry's "flip-flop" was reinforced with images of Kerry windsurfing back and forth. The tagline— "John Kerry . . . whichever way the wind blows"—resonated strongly with voters.

Candidates also must appeal to various constituencies with views that often differ from those of the hypothetical median voter. Donors, activists, and interest groups—all three critical in providing funding, volunteers, and endorsements—tend to have opinions on political issues that are more ideologically extreme than those of the average citizen.[26] Taking moderate positions on issues may have more costs than benefits if it alienates ideologically driven supporters. During the 2020 campaign, for example, Biden faced criticism from progressive activists when he refused to make defunding the police part of his criminal justice reform platform.

The challenge of appealing to multiple constituencies with different opinions may lead candidates to avoid specific positions on some issues altogether. In Chapter 3, we noted that American campaigns have often centered on biography and personality, offering only vague platitudes about political issues. There may be advantages for candidates in this strategy, even though it seems counter to the conventional wisdom that candidates must take clear stands on the issues. Keeping their positions vague allows candidates to say things that are unobjectionable and popular—"I want to save Social Security" or "Our children need a good education." Various constituencies may interpret such statements as endorsing their particular positions, even when candidates have not done so explicitly. Candidates who take vague positions also provide less for the media and opposing candidates to pick apart. Studies of campaigns find that ambiguity is common and that, consequently, citizens often do not know candidates' positions on specific issues.[27]

This lack of knowledge among citizens points to one final problem with the median voter theorem: it assumes that citizens know where they stand on issues, know where the candidates stand, and vote accordingly. But as we noted earlier, there is reason to suppose that the average citizen is not that attentive to campaigns or to politics generally. Certainly, many campaign professionals believe this, and much political science research supports this view. In Chapter 13, we will discuss the assumptions of the median voter theorem and the strategies by which voters choose candidates in more detail.

If average citizens do not assess the candidates in relation to their own issue positions (which may not actually exist), then candidates may be empowered to pursue another strategy: attempting to persuade voters to support their positions on issues. Whether candidates can persuade voters speaks to a more general question: Can campaigns affect what citizens think? Just as candidates attempt to frame elections around particular issues, they would also like to persuade citizens to adopt their positions on those issues. In Chapter 13, we will discuss at greater length how successful candidates are in this enterprise. As we will see, campaign consultants and political scientists come to somewhat different conclusions on this question, with political scientists more skeptical than campaign consultants about the degree to which candidates can change public opinion.

Whether to Attack

Few things attract more attention during campaigns than attacks, which may come from candidates, parties, interest groups, and others. Despite the apparent proliferation of attacks, whether to campaign negatively—or "go negative"—is a complex decision that is largely contingent on the reality of the race.

Negative campaigning can be defined simply as any criticism leveled by supporters of one candidate against the opposing candidate.[28] By contrast, **positive campaigning** (sometimes called *advocacy*) focuses only on the background, record, and views of the sponsored candidate. Of course, campaigns are not limited to one type of campaigning or the other. A campaign message or advertisement may mix positive and negative information. Such advertisements, sometimes called **contrast advertisements**, focus on the differences—in character, qualifications, record, or issue positions—of the main candidates in the race.

Campaigns make decisions about other specific aspects of a negative message. One aspect is content: Should the negative ads criticize a candidate for their stand on issues that concern voters, or for their personal qualities? Another aspect is civility: Should a negative campaign be critical but respectful, or is it useful to be ugly or mean-spirited? In the discussion that follows, we simply focus on the general question of whether to campaign negatively or not, and not on specific questions about how to do so.

According to some political scientists and many campaign practitioners, several factors guide the decision of whether or not to attack. Most of these considerations reflect the political reality surrounding the race—in particular, which candidate is the front-runner and which is the underdog. The candidate who is ahead in the polls is less likely to attack than the candidate who is behind. This finding emerges in both academic research and in a survey of campaign consultants.[29] A related fact is that incumbents are less likely to attack than challengers because the latter tend to be more poorly funded and less well-known (see Chapter 9 for more on negative campaigning in presidential elections). Only if support for the challenger appears to be increasing would an incumbent seek to define them via negative campaigning. Another important factor is timing; attacks are more likely to occur early in campaigns because voters' impressions are more malleable at that point. Thus, in a scenario that we have seen often in recent cycles, an incumbent with a lot of political baggage will attack their well-financed, impressive challenger just as the campaign begins in earnest.[30] For example, in one of the 2020 U.S. Senate races in Georgia, incumbent senator David Perdue aired **attack ads** against his challenger, Jon Ossoff, claiming that Ossoff was "too radical" and had a "socialist agenda." Ossoff quickly responded with ads claiming that Perdue was "corrupt" and "out for himself." Ossoff ultimately won the race in a runoff.

Although it seems like common sense to advise front-runners to stay positive and underdogs to go negative, large-scale studies of campaign messages

In 2020, Joe Biden based much of his campaign on attacking Donald Trump's fitness to serve as president. Was Biden's emphasis on a negative message a brilliant strategic move?

and advertisements in American presidential elections suggest that front-runners and underdogs do not always follow this advice.[31] Sometimes incumbents run more-negative campaigns than their challengers do. Indeed, it is not uncommon for candidates well ahead in the polls to pound away on the underdog. In the 1964 presidential election, for example, Democrat Lyndon Johnson had a commanding lead throughout the campaign, but he still relentlessly attacked the Republican candidate, Barry Goldwater.

A final point should be made with respect to the decision to attack: negative communication may come not only from a candidate's campaign but also from independent groups and party organizations that support the candidate. Such was the case in August 2004, when the outside group Swift Boat Veterans for Truth aired controversial—but widely noted and exhaustively covered—attack ads against Democratic presidential candidate Kerry.[32] Although coordination between and among campaigns and outside groups in federal elections is regulated by law, a strategic campaign might refrain from attacking its opponent while signaling to affiliated groups that it would welcome such attacks from outsiders. Some research even suggests that attacks coming from outside groups are more credible—and thus potentially more effective—than those coming from opposing candidates.[33]

The effectiveness of these attacks is a critical variable here, as it is unclear whether negative campaigning actually wins votes. As we will see in Chapters 12 and 13, it is far from certain that negative advertising affects whether citizens vote or for whom they vote.[34] Ultimately, there is enough uncertainty to produce a wide range of professional opinions regarding who should go negative and to what extent negative campaigning influences voters.

Where to Campaign

Whether a candidate is running for president or for city council, decisions about where to deploy precious campaign resources are always hotly debated. Should the presidential candidate go to Florida or Ohio for that last-minute campaign stop? Should the city council candidate have greeted voters entering the polls in Precinct 1 or Precinct 4? The assumption shared by consultants and scholars is that a campaign's resources must be allocated strategically to achieve maximum effect.

Generally speaking, there are two models for where to campaign. The first model focuses on mobilizing partisans: a campaign locates and appeals to people who will probably vote for the candidate if they can be persuaded to turn out. Much of the campaign therefore targets supportive areas where turnout and enthusiasm might lag.

The second model focuses on persuading independent and weakly partisan voters. The campaign team develops issue positions that are aimed at the sensibilities of these voters; in fact, these issues and positions may be very narrowly tailored for specific, persuadable constituencies. The campaign is therefore multifaceted but tends to focus on areas with large numbers of independent voters.

The relative efficacy of these two models may depend on context. A political newcomer, like Trump in 2016, has a chance to reach out to independents and weakly partisan voters and convince them to support their candidacy.[35] A more established candidate, conversely, might have a record that limits their "flexibility" when it comes to winning over independent voters but may be better able to target and mobilize core supporters. Incumbent candidates, especially those in the more polarized context of today's politics, are therefore more likely to embrace the first model, as we saw with the reelection campaigns of Trump in 2020, Obama in 2012, and George W. Bush in 2004.

There are, of course, combinations of these models. Most campaigns seek to mobilize partisans *and* persuade independents. To do so, they rely on detailed plans for allocating resources. As discussed earlier, most major campaigns use polling and voter identification data to estimate the number of persuadable voters in their state or county. They can then price out the cost of a visit or television ad in that state or county and calculate the price per persuadable voter. Campaigns are thus able to rank-order all states or counties (or precincts) in terms of cost-effectiveness, and they can allocate dollars based on this ranking. Other factors may induce a campaign to visit a certain county or advertise in a certain market, but professional campaigns tend to adhere closely to their analytical rankings. Political science research confirms this, and it also supports the more general notion that television advertising seeks to persuade and mobilize (although persuasion is the higher priority).[36] For example, research on presidential campaigns from 1992 through 2008 shows that television advertising expenditures were mostly based on price-per-persuadable-voter estimates.[37] Campaigns below the presidential level are not as exacting in their deployment of resources. This is partly because the consulting talent, available data, and options of how and where to campaign decrease with more localized elections, making it more difficult to develop and execute a rigorous plan for resource allocation.

How to Campaign

Should the campaign use its funds to run television advertisements on the broadcast networks? Or should it purchase cable television advertisements instead? Would radio advertisements be better? Or maybe advertisements on social media platforms? What about billboards, lawn signs, bumper stickers, and buttons? And how much time and effort should be spent on the ground game—face-to-face campaigning by the candidate, staff, and volunteers? These are all nuts-and-bolts decisions that a campaign strategist must make. In some respects, they are questions of tactics—the means by which strategic goals are accomplished—as opposed to strategy.

Tactics are most affected by available resources. Candidates would prefer to draw on as many tactics as possible—saturating every form of mass media with advertisements, for example—but often they cannot afford to do so. If candidates have enough money to run advertisements on broadcast television, which is not only the most expensive medium but also the medium likely to reach the largest audience, then they will. If they do not, then the question becomes whether other mass media, such as cable television or radio, are affordable. Campaigns with even fewer resources often rely more on the ground game, which consists of personal campaigning by the candidate and outreach by volunteers, both door-to-door and over the phone, than on media buys. Well-funded campaigns will combine a ground game with the "air war" of advertising on radio, television, and the internet.

In the past decade, there has been renewed investment in the ground game.[38] Both political consultants and political scientists believe that strategies that prioritize personal contact with potential voters, like old-fashioned door knocking, are often more effective than direct mail or phone banking, especially if the contact is from familiar and credible sources of information, such as friends and neighbors. Political science studies have confirmed this: personalized contact is much more effective than mail or telephone calls in mobilizing citizens to vote, although phone calls made by professional telemarketers can be effective, especially compared to phone calls with a prerecorded voice.[39]

In recent elections, both parties have invested significant resources in developing field organizations that can carry out personalized mobilizations. Union organizations arguably started this trend in the 1998 and 2000 campaigns, and Democrats built a get-out-the-vote machine on top of the unions' initial efforts. Republican Party organizations, spooked by the Democrats, countered with their own volunteer efforts in 2002 and 2004. In 2008 and 2012, the Obama campaign created an extensive field organization of trained volunteers. Even in 2020, with a pandemic that made in-person outreach problematic during the summer and fall, the Trump campaign invested heavily in its ground game. The effort was run jointly by the Republican National Committee (RNC) and the Trump campaign, and it relied on 2.6 million volunteers, according to figures provided by the RNC. The field effort made over 182 million voter contacts—more than five times what the Republicans accomplished in 2016—and volunteers registered nearly 174,000 new GOP voters. The effort was particularly impressive in battleground states: voter registration figures in Florida, North Carolina, and other states show that Republicans were able to "essentially neutralize what had been a Democrat advantage" by mobilizing new voters.[40]

By contrast, Biden and the Democrats significantly curtailed their in-person contacting efforts due to the virus. Instead, they shifted their contacting activities to digital platforms. It is important to note that while old-fashioned door-to-door contacting still matters, online forms of social networking—candidate websites, Facebook, Twitter, Instagram, TikTok, and Reddit—are now being used to drive the sorts of in-person outreach that, after the advent of television, had seemed like a thing of the past. In fact, one could plausibly argue that online contacting is now the dominant form of campaign outreach. Today, most campaigns routinely integrate online volunteer outreach with field operations. Michelle Kleppe, national organizing director for Hillary Clinton's 2016 campaign, explained:

> [We are] really pushing our organizers to not only recruit and engage with
> volunteers on the phones and in their offices and offline, but also organizing
> online. . . . So an organizer is working with volunteers in their offices and in
> homes and around kitchen tables, but they are also engaging with volun-
> teers and supporters on Facebook and Twitter. Both in terms of getting
> them to come offline and actually help build our capacity and talk to addi-
> tional voters and supporters but also in helping a group of people online
> engage with their networks. It gives us a broader reach and more opportu-
> nities for volunteers to engage in the types of activities that [they] are best
> suited [for] and that they're most comfortable with.[41]

Offline forms of personal contact will likely continue to be significant
alongside online organizing and, in the case of advertising, on-air messages.
For the moment, however, television advertising continues to be the linch-
pin of contemporary campaigns, especially in statewide and federal races.

Campaign Strategists

The various strategic and tactical decisions we have discussed do not get made
by themselves. When a candidate decides to run for office, they need to identify knowledgeable people to help them design a strategy, set up a campaign
organization, answer important questions, and implement plans. But the
fact that campaigns face common dilemmas in determining and implementing their strategies does not mean that there is one common solution—in fact,
there is no such thing as a "typical" campaign. Campaigns vary in their
resources: some have huge budgets and target millions of citizens, and some
have tiny budgets and target hundreds or only dozens. Naturally, they will
have diverse organizations as well. Moreover, although many campaign organizations include similar positions of authority, these positions do not always
have the same job description or the same place in the organization's hierarchy. Campaign managers, who are in charge of organizing the campaign
and implementing the strategic plan, are not necessarily at the top of the
organization. Chief strategists, who (no surprise) are in charge of developing strategy, usually—but not always—hold centrally important positions.
Political directors are typically in charge of organizing the field staff, but
some engage in overall messaging strategy as well. Personal relationships can
drive the structure of the organization, with positions created to accommodate specific people that the candidate wants for specific purposes. So, who

are these campaign strategists? Where do they come from? As described in Chapter 3, since the 1950s American campaigns have been candidate-centered. This means that candidates recruit and develop their own advisers. From the 1970s onward, many of these advisers had backgrounds in public opinion research or television advertising. Since the 2000s, however, a class of campaign consultants with backgrounds in digital outreach or high-level statistical analysis has emerged. These consultants offer expertise in identifying and mobilizing partisan voters and have become perhaps the main purveyors of strategic advice in American elections.

The Backgrounds of Campaign Strategists

Although the development of professional campaign consultants is relatively new, there have always been strategists in American campaigns. Alexander Hamilton may have been the most famous political consultant in the early days of the new republic, as he constantly schemed and plotted how to win elections for those who shared his Federalist views. James Madison was only slightly less aggressive as Thomas Jefferson's top political strategist, although Jefferson himself was also an active strategist. Indeed, we could put together quite a catalog of campaign strategists from before the modern campaign era.

In today's campaigns, how does someone become a campaign consultant or strategist? First, there are those who become proficient at a specific campaign endeavor and parlay this into a broader role crafting and overseeing strategy. For example, in the 1960s and 1970s, people with a background in public relations or consumer advertising were much sought after by campaigns, as candidates attempted to develop personal loyalty among constituents through persuasive self-promotion. Public relations and advertising professionals naturally favored using market research to drive messaging and using mass media (especially television) to deliver these messages. The late Roger Ailes, who worked for Richard Nixon, Ronald Reagan, and George H. W. Bush and was the longtime president of Fox News, is a good example.

People with a background in journalism or speechwriting have also become successful strategists. Some have moved up by serving as the liaison between the candidates and the news media, while others have served as speechwriters before taking on the broader role of strategist. Democrats Bill Moyers (who served Lyndon Johnson), Bob Shrum (who worked for eight Democratic presidential candidates, including Edward Kennedy and John Kerry), and Ben Rhodes (who served Obama), along with Republican Bill Shine (who served Trump), are prime examples.

Pollsters, who are trained in the art and science of ascertaining what the public is thinking, have also become campaign strategists. Kellyanne Conway, Trump's campaign manager in 2016, ran her own polling and political consulting firm during the 1990s and 2000s. John Anzalone, Biden's messaging strategist, served as a pollster for Obama in 2008 and 2012 and for Hillary Clinton in 2016. Bob Teeter, a legendary Republican pollster, served as George H. W. Bush's presidential campaign strategist and manager in 1992.

More recently, people who are skilled with direct mail or telemarketing campaigns have used this success as a way to become general strategists. Both of these activities require a strong sense of which voters the candidate should address and what messages move them. Republican strategist Karl Rove dominated direct mail campaigning in Texas before taking up much broader responsibilities for George W. Bush.

Then there are those with backgrounds in "new" campaign technologies: statistics and voter data analytics, which give someone familiarity and experience with targeting, messaging, budgets, and resource allocation, and digital and social media strategy, which have become linchpins of modern campaign targeting. These are perhaps the newest routes to power in a campaign. On the data side, notable examples include Robby Mook, campaign manager for Hillary Clinton in 2016, and David Plouffe, campaign manager for Obama in 2008, each of whom had extensive backgrounds in data analytics and targeting prior to leading their respective presidential campaigns. On the digital and social media side, there is Brad Parscale, who parlayed a background as a digital consultant into a position as the senior adviser for data and digital operations for Trump's 2020 presidential campaign.

Finally, the emergence of campaign management schools has provided another route by which aspiring strategists can hone their craft. As yet, there are few examples of campaign school graduates becoming superstars, but the ranks of congressional and even presidential campaigns are now populated with people who cut their teeth at these academies.

A different path to becoming a campaign strategist consists of developing relationships with particular candidates and marshaling them through their political careers. These individuals may have only a few clients throughout their own careers, but they play a major role for those clients. James A. Baker, III, built his career in law but entered politics at the urging of his friend George H. W. Bush. He served in the Ford, Reagan, and Bush administrations but only in a handful of campaigns, the most prominent of which involved Bush. Baker's particular value to Bush was as someone who had his best interests at heart, someone who could tell him the unvarnished truth, and someone who knew his strengths and weaknesses inside out.

The star strategists of recent years have included Kellyanne Conway (left) and Mike Donilon (right). Conway is credited with helping Trump win in 2016 and served in the Trump administration, while Donilon devised Biden's strategies in 2020 and also went on to work in the White House.

Regardless of their path into the business, professional campaign strategists have attained much greater visibility in recent decades. Their lionization can be traced to a classic work of campaign journalism, Theodore White's *The Making of the President*.[42] White's narrative of the 1960 campaign details the machinations of Robert Kennedy and other advisers to John F. Kennedy, noting their disciplined targeting of states and voting groups and aggressive voter registration strategy, among other things. White also discusses the opposing side, particularly Richard Nixon's disastrous pledge to campaign in all 50 states and the challenge of attacking the elusive and charismatic Kennedy. The implication was clear—JFK's victory was due, at least in part, to the cool, methodical, professional campaign strategy developed by his team. The elevation of the strategist had begun, and soon many would become well-known: Hamilton Jordan (for Jimmy Carter), Ed Rollins (for Ronald Reagan), James Baker and Lee Atwater (for George H. W. Bush), James Carville and Dick Morris (for Bill Clinton in 1992 and 1996, respectively), Karl Rove (for George W. Bush), David Axelrod (for Obama in 2008 and 2012), Kellyanne Conway (for Trump in 2016), and Mike Donilon (for Biden in 2020).

Despite the visibility of superstar strategists, we know very little about their actual impact on contemporary elections. Commentaries like Joe McGinniss's *The Selling of the President* have criticized the mass marketing techniques so often employed in contemporary campaigns on the advice of consultants.[43] But little has been written about the degree to which campaign consultants actually help candidates win. What evidence exists suggests that hiring consultants is no panacea.[44] In part, this may reflect how much both campaign strategy and election outcomes are constrained by the rules governing elections and the reality that candidates face. Political scientists are therefore less likely than campaign professionals to attribute the success of candidates to the strategic genius of their advisers. This skepticism is at the heart of the more general disagreement between campaign consultants and political scientists with respect to whether campaigns "matter."

Conclusion

In this chapter, we have delineated what a campaign strategy is, discussed several key strategic decisions that campaigns make, and considered the perspectives of both campaign consultants and political scientists. We have also discussed how campaigns organize to make strategic decisions and examined who campaign strategists are. The central notion is straightforward: campaign strategists want to win elections, and everything they do can be understood as part of a rational, if sometimes imperfect, effort to achieve this goal. Practitioners and academics tend to agree on many of the factors that candidates can and should consider when deciding whether they should seek higher office, emphasize a particular issue, run an attack ad, or focus resources on a particular constituency. The central question, however, is how much these strategic decisions matter—a topic we will return to in subsequent chapters.

How should we view campaign strategy in light of the democratic values and ideals spelled out in Chapter 1? With respect to free choice, American campaigns attempt to frame electoral choices in a way that maximizes their prospects for victory. There is no systematic effort to explore the entire range of potential candidates, issues, or policy options. Indeed, campaigns strive to simplify the electoral decision for voters in a way that advantages their candidate. It isn't that most campaigns seek to dupe voters; rather, they attempt to take the current political reality and set of choices and present them in a way that makes the election of their preferred candidate desirable.

Do campaigns, by way of strategic choices, encourage thoughtful and appropriate deliberation? Certainly campaigns provide information, much of it relevant to vote choice. But it would be a stretch to claim that they seek to promote serious deliberation among voters. Campaign strategies are developed to win elections, and the cognitive route carved out for voters is unlikely to encourage deep and substantive thinking.

The influence of modern campaign strategies on free speech is, in our view, more encouraging. Historically, American campaigns have relied on volunteers and "ordinary citizens" to disseminate messages and to contact voters on behalf of candidates. However, the role of person-to-person contact and interpersonal discussion took a back seat to television and other broadcast media advertising in the latter half of the twentieth and early in the twenty-first centuries. But digital and social media platforms have re-empowered individual voters in the last decade or so. Opportunities for citizens to voice their opinions—and the potential audience for their opinions—have increased dramatically. One might question the efficacy of the new "public square" or the autonomy that campaigns actually grant to their supporters when it comes to voicing their opinions. Be that as it may, one could reasonably argue that there is now more speech than ever in American electoral campaigns.

When it comes to the implications of campaign strategy in American elections, perhaps the most intriguing value is that of equality. Intrinsic to campaign strategy is this notion: some citizens are more valuable than others. That is, campaigns routinely identify subsets of citizens to target—such as swing voters or voters in a certain geographic area—and ignore many others. This approach may run counter to several ideals. The laser-like focus of campaigns on partisan supporters, swing voters, or any other groups may violate the ideal of political equality. Of course, we are most concerned with citizens being equal in the eyes of the law, not in the eyes of campaign consultants. Nevertheless, this decision involves a trade-off of values. Similarly, targeted voters inevitably receive much more information about the campaign than other voters do, challenging the ideal of deliberation. The information that voters receive clearly differs depending on whether they are the targets of a campaign's strategy. That campaign strategy may fail to live up to these ideals reflects this simple fact: campaign strategy is fundamentally about winning elections, not about upholding civic standards.

KEY TERMS

campaign strategy (p. 131)

vote targets (p. 132)

persuadable (or swing) votes
  (p. 132)

probability samples (p. 136)

focus groups (p. 136)

microtargeting (p. 137)

voter identification (or voter ID)
  calls (p. 138)

open seat (p. 139)

message (p. 144)

framing (p. 145)

issue ownership (p. 145)

median voter theorem (p. 147)

negative campaigning (p. 150)

positive campaigning (p. 150)

contrast advertisements (p. 150)

attack ads (p. 150)

FOR DISCUSSION

1. Do campaigns attempt to convince all voters to support their candidate? Why or why not?

2. What factors influence whether or not a candidate chooses to run for an office?

3. Why are challengers more likely than incumbents to run negative advertisements?

4. How has the development of microtargeting influenced campaigns?

6

Political Parties

Despite leading by a large margin in national polls for most of 2019 and being widely favored to represent Democrats in the 2020 presidential race against Donald Trump, Joe Biden placed fourth in the first official contest of the nomination process: the Iowa caucuses on February 3, 2020. On February 11, he placed fifth in the New Hampshire primary. By that time, his cash was running dry, and in February, six other candidates spent more than Biden did. Frequently the target of attacks and without a clear base of enthusiastic supporters, the former vice president seemed unlikely to mount a comeback.

The biggest spender in the campaign up to that point was former New York City mayor Michael Bloomberg, who burned through more money on a daily basis than Biden did in all of February. That made Bloomberg, rather than Biden, the target at the February 19 debate among the Democratic candidates in Las Vegas, Nevada. Senators Elizabeth Warren and Bernie Sanders (the winner of the New Hampshire primary) attacked Bloomberg for trying to buy the election, while Senator Amy Klobuchar and former mayor Pete Buttigieg repeatedly sparred with one another. Biden, meanwhile, receded from the spotlight. A viewer would never have expected Biden to emerge triumphant less than two weeks later—on his way to victory after 14 states held primaries on Super Tuesday.

Biden's comeback happened in a matter of days. After Sanders won the Nevada caucuses on February 22 with more than double the support that Biden received in the state, Sanders looked like the frontrunner in polls and betting markets. But four days later, Biden won a key endorsement from the "dean" of South Carolina Democratic politics, House Majority Whip Jim Clyburn. Clyburn's endorsement and Biden's strong support among African American voters, who constituted a majority of the Democratic electorate in South Carolina, propelled him to victory in the state's primary—just three days before Super Tuesday.

On the Monday before the vote, the Democratic Party appeared to consolidate behind Biden. Both Klobuchar and Buttigieg dropped out, endorsed Biden, and appeared with him at campaign events. Biden also picked up endorsements from 23 other important party figures and dominated media coverage. Sanders, who was then leading in national polls, called it "a massive effort trying to stop Bernie Sanders. The corporate establishment is coming together, the political establishment is coming together."[1] Indeed, the consolidation was too much for Sanders, who ended up receiving about half as many votes and pledged delegates as Biden during the nomination process and withdrew from the race in April.

Biden's surprise turnaround was also a comeback of sorts for political scientists. During the 2016 campaign, journalists had regularly cited a prominent political science book, *The Party Decides*, as evidence that Donald Trump faced nearly insurmountable odds in his path to winning the Republican nomination for president.[2] The book argues that party leaders influence the process of choosing their party's presidential nominee by coordinating on a candidate acceptable to all party factions. The central evidence is that pre-primary endorsements from party leaders help predict who is ultimately nominated for president. Before voting in the 2016 primaries began, Trump

Core of the Analysis

- Political parties strategically participate in elections by recruiting candidates, airing advertisements, and mobilizing voters.

- Political parties still play a central role in elections, despite attempts by some reformers to weaken them.

- The two major political parties have adapted to new issues and slowly changed their voting coalitions, in the process becoming more ideologically polarized.

- Political parties fall short of achieving some democratic values, but it is unlikely that democracy could function without them.

received no endorsements from members of Congress or governors. That seemed like a clear signal that the party had rejected Trump. But Trump went on to win the nomination anyway.

The theory was pronounced disproven, with even the authors of *The Party Decides* issuing a mea culpa arguing that new media, outside money, and factional conflict had challenged party control of nominations.[3] But party elites seemed to regain control in 2020, preventing the nomination of Sanders in favor of the insider favorite Biden. And beyond some high-profile losses, party favorites continued to dominate primary elections for other offices.[4]

Despite the challenges that party leaders have faced in recent presidential nomination processes, they played important roles in the 2016 and 2020 general elections. The vast majority of Democrats, including Sanders' supporters, ultimately came around to support Biden in 2020. And after Trump's unexpected victory in 2016, Trump retained the support of Republicans throughout his presidency and afterward; most Republicans voted for him in both 2016 and 2020.

These recent events show that political parties have a permanent place in American politics, helping to structure and order the competition between candidates in American elections. Party organizations have diverse roles in campaigns. They recruit candidates, run advertisements, and mobilize voters. For most voters, decisions about whom to support in any general election follow from the more basic political decision of selecting a party, one of the two major sides of American political competition. Despite lacking full control of their presidential nominations, America's two major parties are remarkably stable and resilient.

In this chapter, we address several questions about the role of political parties in campaigns. What are political parties, and why do we have them? Why only the Democrats and the Republicans? How is their role in campaigns evolving? We also consider broader questions about how parties fit into American politics. How do electoral rules and political and economic realities constrain parties? Are parties contributing to ideological polarization or just adapting to a changing society and policy agenda? Each of these questions raises key philosophical concerns. Do parties serve or undermine democratic values in campaigns? Even if Americans are dissatisfied with parties, do viable alternatives exist? To evaluate parties, we first have to understand why they behave as they do.

What Are Political Parties?

Political parties are groups of people with a shared interest in electing public officials under a common label. Supporters of the two major political parties in the United States, the Democrats and the Republicans, each share the goal of winning elections. Each party has policy goals as well, but it is their electoral goals that unite parties and distinguish them from other kinds of groups.

The political scientist V. O. Key suggested three manifestations of political parties: the **party-in-the-electorate**, the **party-as-organization**, and the **party-in-government**.[5] The party-in-the-electorate includes all citizens who identify with the party, including those who participate in primaries and vote for the party in general elections. The party-as-organization comprises the institutions that administer party affairs, including the official bodies that raise funds and create the rules for the party. The party-in-government consists of the elected leaders and appointed government officials who shape party policy goals. Each is somewhat independent from the others. Partisans in the electorate do not directly decide how party leaders operate. Organizational leaders cannot tell a party's senators how to vote.

The party-as-organization is often the face of the party in a campaign and is sometimes seen as its home. Some scholars, however, consider parties to be "multilayered coalitions" of diverse actors that share mutual goals and collaborate regularly, including the political action committees and interest groups that usually support one party (we separately cover interest groups in Chapter 7).[6] For example, the parties share mailing lists across an "extended party network" of individual candidates, allied interest groups, and ideological news outlets.[7]

The extent of these networks means that American political parties can be seen as amorphous groups. Even basic questions, like who is in charge of the Democratic and Republican parties, often do not have straightforward answers. The president is usually the most prominent spokesperson for their party; during presidential campaigns, the presidential nominees generally take on this role. Following Trump's loss in 2020, the closest thing left to an official head of the Republican Party was the chair of the Republican National Committee, Ronna McDaniel. But McDaniel relies on Trump's support to maintain her position. She even stopped using her maiden name—Romney—to placate Trump, who has often viewed McDaniel's uncle, Senator Mitt Romney, as a political opponent. Like most party leaders, McDaniel does not run any government departments, vote in Congress, or appear on voter ballots. Senate Minority Leader Mitch McConnell and House

Who speaks for the Republican Party? a. Fox News Channel hosts Sean Hannity and Tucker Carlson; b. former president Donald Trump; c. House Minority Leader Kevin McCarthy and Senate Minority Leader Mitch McConnell; d. Republican National Committee Chair Ronna McDaniel; or someone else?

Minority Leader Kevin McCarthy, as of this writing, are the heads of the Republican party-in-government. Still, reporters often look to Trump to represent the party's views. And these actors all rely on well-known television talk show hosts on Fox News Channel as spokespeople for the party's views and to reach the Republican base.

Party membership, like party hierarchy, is not always clear. If your friend says that she is a Republican, this does not necessarily mean that she is officially registered with the party. In many states, individuals do not need to register with a political party in order to vote in that party's primary; in some states, there is no official party registration at all. Political scientists have found that even people who view themselves as independents—meaning that they are unaffiliated with either party—often vote consistently for one party's candidates. The same is true of elected officials who call themselves independents. Sanders, for instance, identifies as an independent, despite the fact that he ran for the Democratic nomination for president and is now a member of the Democratic leadership team in the Senate.

Why Do We Have Parties?

Most of the American Founders feared parties, even as they later participated in them. As he left office, George Washington warned of "the baneful effects of the spirit of party." Nevertheless, political parties quickly developed and took on important roles in American government. The first political parties, the Federalists and the Democratic-Republicans, coalesced around different views on the strength of the federal government and regional economic interests (see Chapter 3). Early parties almost immediately structured voting in Congress and created electoral coalitions for presidential candidates. But these parties developed even before they had clear public identities; politicians organized themselves into competing coalitions before voters started calling themselves partisans. In fact, parties have developed in all democracies across the world because politicians find them useful in legislative and electoral politics.

Political parties serve the needs of politicians who want durable legislative majorities in order to pass legislation.[8] Politicians also benefit from a reputation or "brand" that citizens recognize and can rely on when voting, and they need an infrastructure that helps persuade and mobilize voters during elections. Parties serve all of these functions. Political parties also promote the policy goals of various interest groups, which often affiliate with parties in order to advance their agendas.[9] Working through parties allows interest groups to help choose candidates and to assist these candidates in elections—efforts that they hope will ultimately give them influence over policy. The alternative to aligning with a party—negotiating with individual candidates and legislators to convince them to support a group's agenda—is more uncertain.

Political parties can also make democratic government work better. First, they aggregate and articulate interests. Every citizen and politician has their own interests and ideas, but democracy requires that they work with others to achieve their goals. With the help of parties, individuals can decide which of their goals are most important and find like-minded people. Second, parties organize coalitions. If every ethnic, religious, and economic group nominated its own candidates, it would be difficult for any one group to obtain a majority of the vote. Parties enable groups to unite under broader umbrellas. Third, parties coordinate elections and mobilize voters. Without them, candidates would have to work independently to convince voters that they share their views, and they would have to mobilize their own constituencies. Party labels make it easier for voters to form opinions about the candidates. Fourth, parties coordinate the legislative process. This role gives voters an idea of how their votes are likely to translate into public policy. Finally, parties facilitate collective political action. Both electing candidates and governing require individuals to work together, and parties provide a crucial channel through which people can join together in pursuit of shared goals.

The Democratic and Republican Parties

Two major political parties have long dominated the U.S. political system. The Democratic Party traces its history to the 1828 election of Andrew Jackson. The Republicans emerged as the Democrats' major challenger with the 1860 election of Abraham Lincoln. Since the 1920s, the two major parties combined have always controlled at least 95 percent of House and Senate seats and won at least 90 percent of electoral college votes for the presidency.

Ideologically, the Republican Party is more conservative, and the Democratic Party is more liberal. Internationally, political competition is usually organized on an ideological spectrum from left (liberal) to right (conservative), although other countries use different ideological labels. These ideologies can be generally defined by their views on the size and scope of government responsibility: the Democratic Party favors a greater degree of government intervention in the economy, often in an attempt to ameliorate inequality, than the Republican Party does. But American parties are also divided on social and moral issues, with Republicans generally favoring social traditions and Democrats generally favoring social diversity, and international issues, with Republicans prioritizing American military strength and Democrats prioritizing international cooperation. Republicans more uniformly share an ideological self-identification: 71 percent of Republicans identify as conservatives, but only 53 percent of Democrats identify as liberals (see Figure 6.1). In both parties, activists (those who volunteer or work on campaigns) and donors (those who provide money to a party or its candidates) are more ideologically consistent with their party than are people who merely identify with the party.

The Democratic voting coalition is largely made up of minority groups that vote for Democrats by large margins, such as African Americans, Jews, advanced degree holders, and union members. The Republican Party usually wins by smaller margins among larger groups, such as White people and married people. The largest change in the party coalitions has been the

FIGURE 6.1 Ideologies of Party Members, Activists, and Donors

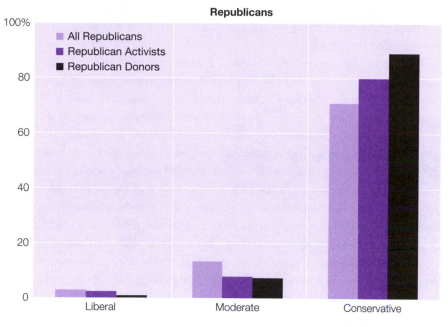

Republicans

Legend:
- All Republicans
- Republican Activists
- Republican Donors

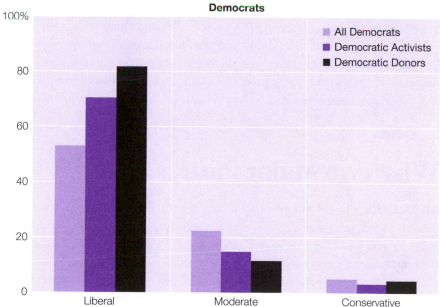

Democrats

Legend:
- All Democrats
- Democratic Activists
- Democratic Donors

Source: American National Election Studies.

move of the southern states from solidly Democratic in the early and mid-twentieth century to Republican in recent elections, but the parties are also increasingly divided along racial, educational, and gender lines (as we discuss in Chapters 3 and 13).

The American electorate as a whole contains more self-identified Democrats than Republicans, but the electorate also contains more self-identified conservatives than liberals. Neither party nor ideological label has maintained a consistent majority. The Democrats have the advantage in party identification, but the Republicans have the advantage in ideology. Republicans also tend to explain party competition as an ideological battle between the left and the right, whereas Democrats are more likely to see politics as a group competition between the rich on one side and the vulnerable on the other.[10] Republicans usually need to win a greater share of independents than Democrats do, whereas Democrats have to win more votes than Republicans among moderates because they have a smaller liberal ideological base.

On the whole, the United States has had strong two-party competition throughout its history, though different historical eras have favored one party or the other. The Democratic Party controlled a majority in the House of Representatives from 1955 to 1994, but the Republicans had a majority for all but four years from 1995 to 2018. The Senate has switched control more often, but it has usually been closely divided; since 1955, the Democrats have always held at least 44 U.S. Senate seats, and the Republicans have always held at least 32 seats. There have also been many party transitions in the presidency; since the 1930s, neither party has had more than two consecutive presidents, and the parties have alternated back and forth for the last six presidencies.

Why Two Major Parties?

It is rare for any candidate not affiliated with either major party to get elected to federal office. At the presidential level, the most successful third-party or independent candidates have won at best a handful of states and thus have always come up short in the electoral college. Theodore Roosevelt ran as the Progressive Party nominee in 1912 but won only six states. Strom Thurmond ran as the States' Rights Democratic Party (or Dixiecrat) nominee in 1948, and George Wallace ran as the American Independent Party's nominee in 1968; neither won any states outside the Deep South. In 1992, an independent candidate, Ross Perot, won 19 percent of the popular vote but no electoral votes. Consumer advocate Ralph Nader received 2.7 percent of the popular vote as the Green Party candidate in 2000. Libertarian Party nominee Gary Johnson won 3.3 percent of the popular vote in 2016. And in 2020, the Libertarian nominee only won 1.2 percent of the popular vote.

The largest obstacles that third parties face in U.S. elections are the rules of the electoral system. As discussed in Chapter 2, the use of single-member districts and plurality elections favors congressional candidates from the two major parties. Plurality voting within the electoral college—whereby the candidate who wins the most votes in each state wins all of that state's electoral votes—hurts the chances of national third parties or independent candidates at the presidential level. These electoral rules tend to make voters, activists, and candidates wary that encouraging third-party support will "waste" potential votes or "spoil" the efforts of a major-party candidate by diverting votes from that candidate. For example, if most Nader voters in 2000 had voted for their second choice instead, Al Gore would likely have been elected instead of George W. Bush.[11] Other legal hurdles for third parties, including requirements for getting on the ballot, make it difficult for third-party candidates to emerge (see Chapter 2). With the playing field tilted so strongly against them, third parties routinely find it difficult to attract media coverage, raise money, recruit experienced candidates, or earn a place in candidate debates. Despite these difficulties, third parties and independent candidates are sometimes successful. The Green Party and the Libertarian Party have elected more than 300 officeholders between them, mostly in local elections. Third parties and independent candidates can also influence the issues discussed in campaigns. For example, both the Democrats and the Republicans felt compelled to respond to Perot's concerns about the federal budget deficit in 1992. But this small amount of policy influence also makes third parties short-lived. One or both of the two major parties can adopt their issue positions and lure third-party supporters away.

What Roles Do Parties Play in Campaigns?

Political parties play central roles in contemporary campaigns. The party-in-the-electorate, the party-as-organization, and the party-in-government all affect the electoral process.

The Role of the Party-in-the-Electorate

The vast majority of Americans identify with or lean toward either the Democratic Party or the Republican Party and vote loyally for candidates from their preferred party. This makes the partisan complexion of a district or state a central feature of the reality that candidates confront. Candidates and campaign consultants carefully count partisans of both camps as well as independent and undecided voters when planning their campaign strategy (see Chapter 5). The party-in-the-electorate is also important as the volunteer base and cheering section for each party. Party supporters contact their friends, family members, and neighbors—both formally, in partnership with the candidates or party organizations, and informally, through their online and offline social networks—to try to convince them to support their party's candidates and to encourage participation. In local elections for city council, school board, or county commission, volunteer networks and party activists are often the only visible form of party involvement.

Because the United States is becoming more geographically polarized, many areas no longer support viable two-party competition or enable Americans to hear from both partisan sides. The contours of residential segregation, in which Democrats are mostly concentrated in dense areas, mean that Republicans and (especially) Democrats are now likely to be surrounded by others who share and reinforce their partisanship. Only about three in 10 of the average American's interactions are expected to be with a member of the opposite party, and 10 percent of Democrats rarely encounter a nearby Republican.[12]

The Role of the Party-as-Organization

The party-as-organization plays a central role in political campaigns. Party organizations such as the national committees, state committees, and legislative campaign committees recruit candidates and raise money for them. Recruiting candidates is harder than it might seem. In the average state legislative election in 2020, 27 percent of candidates faced no opposing candidate at all. Parties try to recruit quality candidates who are well-known to the electorate and have relevant experience for the office they seek. Candidates who have previously held elected office are much more likely to win future elections, so they are often the first people that party organizations try to draft. For instance, the Republican-affiliated organization GOPAC recruits and trains candidates to run for state and local offices. Under the leadership of Newt Gingrich, it was credited with helping to build the team of candidates that enabled the 1994 Republican takeover of Congress. In addition to recruiting candidates, parties also work to minimize retirements within their ranks because incumbents are more likely to win elections than newcomers.

Traditionally, the party organization also selected the party's general-election nominees. Before 1972, unpledged party delegates selected presidential nominees at the national conventions. That means candidates not endorsed by party leaders, such as Trump in 2016 or Sanders in 2020, could not have been competitive because the party leaders directly selected the nominees. Following the 1968 election, the Democrats assembled the McGovern–Fraser Commission to reform the presidential nomination system. As a result, first the Democrats and then the Republicans started tying their national convention delegate selection more to the winner of primary elections and caucuses, with less role for party leaders at the convention.

Primary elections became more important in nominations for lower-level offices as well, although party nominees for some statewide and local offices are still selected at party conventions or by party leaders. In many states, party organizations can also replace candidates who are no longer able to run and can select nominees for special elections. Even in races where party organizations no longer officially nominate their own candidates, party officials can influence primary results with their money or endorsements, as they did with Biden in 2020. They often discourage primary challengers at all, leaving only one well-known candidate.

The other main task of party organizations is to raise money for their candidates. As we discussed in Chapter 4, parties are quite successful at raising money. They contribute some of this money directly to individual campaigns. They sometimes pay campaign consultants, pollsters, and other vendors of campaign goods and services. Parties also spend money to produce and broadcast television advertisements, build local party organizations, and pay for get-out-the-vote drives.

Parties are now spending considerable sums on candidates' behalf, much of it on television advertisements. During the 2004 election cycle, party expenditures increased dramatically and shifted away from **coordinated expenditures**, which allow parties to cooperate with candidates in developing messages and communicating them to voters, toward independent expenditures (Figure 6.2). As we discussed in Chapter 4, court rulings on campaign finance cleared the way for unlimited independent expenditures, and both parties now use this option extensively.

Party organizations also play an important role in mobilizing voters to participate in elections. People who are contacted by a political party during a campaign are more likely to vote, more likely to persuade others how to vote,

FIGURE 6.2 Party Committee Coordinated and Independent Expenditures

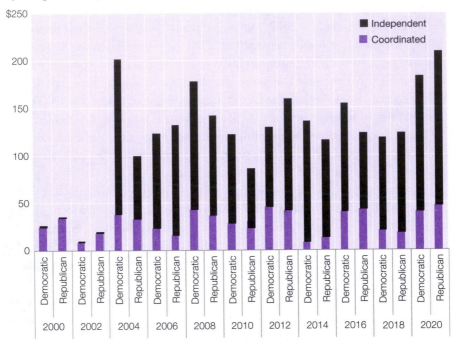

Spending in millions (2020 dollars)

Source: Data from Federal Election Commission, summarized by the Congressional Research Service and the Center for Responsive Politics.

more likely to work on behalf of their candidate, and more likely to contribute money.[13] Yet the parties consistently fail to contact most citizens. According to the American National Election Studies, the percentage of citizens who reported contact from either of the political parties decreased from 31 percent in 1982 to a low of 19 percent in 1990. From 2002 to 2012, at least 40 percent of citizens were contacted by one of the parties, but only 32 percent were contacted in 2016 (with the Republicans contacting fewer citizens than the Democrats). The COVID-19 pandemic made in-person party contact even more difficult in 2020. Political science experiments consistently show that knocking on voters' doors or calling them on the phones increases their likelihood of participation; these experiments have encouraged political consultants to recommend more mobilization activities and seem to have had some effect on the parties' allocation of resources.[14]

One reason parties do not contact all citizens is that party organizations tend to concentrate their resources on races that are closely contested and most likely to tip the balance of power in legislatures. They want to use their resources in a way that maximizes the number of their representatives who get elected, so they help candidates who have a good opportunity to win. This means that many candidates with minimal resources and little chance of winning do not receive help from the parties. How a party distributes its resources also sends important signals to other actors. Politicians who have leadership PACs, which they may establish to help fund other candidates' campaigns, usually donate to the same candidates that the parties invest in. Interest groups affiliated with the parties also usually follow the parties' lead. Party organizations make their priorities explicit by distributing lists of targeted districts or winnable elections to guide other actors.

Parties can also direct resources to where their needs are greatest. For example, in 2008, Democratic presidential candidate Barack Obama had a substantial fundraising advantage over his Republican opponent, John McCain, and so did not need to take money from the party; as a result, the Democrats could direct more resources to their congressional candidates. In 2016, presidential candidate Hillary Clinton and the Democrats had a fundraising advantage in the presidential race, and fewer super PAC resources were available to help Donald Trump close the gap. In 2020, both parties and candidates were well funded in the general election.

Of course, parties are not necessarily unified when developing a campaign strategy. Former Democratic Party leaders Howard Dean and Rahm Emanuel regularly battled over whether the party should devote resources to all of the states or only to competitive races. Another traditional conflict within party organizations is the trade-off between ideological purity and electability. Parties want elected officials who support their party's agenda. Yet sometimes candidates who are more ideologically moderate and less consistently partisan are more likely to win elections, especially in swing districts where voters are evenly divided along partisan lines.[15]

Nebraska's 2nd congressional district, home of metropolitan Omaha, has hosted repeated party battles. Because Nebraska allocates its electoral college votes partially by congressional district, it is the site of a quadrennial struggle over one electoral vote in the presidential election as well as a regularly competitive House seat. Democrat Brad Ashford won the traditionally Republican seat in 2014—only to lose by 1 percentage point in 2016. (Hillary Clinton also lost to Trump in 2016 by 2 points in the district.) In 2018, a better year for Democrats, social worker Kara Eastman defeated Ashford in the Democratic primary with the support of liberal activists and EMILY's List (which supports women candidates) but over the opposition of many party leaders. She went on to lose to incumbent Republican Don Bacon by 1 point. In 2020,

Eastman defeated Ann Ashford (Brad's wife) in the Democratic primary, again with the support of most liberals. But partially because Eastman was more liberal than most swing voters in this swing district, she lost again to Bacon (this time by 3 points), even though Biden defeated Trump in that same district by 6 points. Both split-ticket voting and internal party battles are relatively rare: party favorites usually win primaries, and U.S. House elections usually go the same way as the presidential vote. But when conflicts do arise, party organizations usually support experienced and moderate candidates for competitive seats because they are more likely to win.

Even party leaders, however, may not know which candidates are most likely to be successful. Their own prejudices—or prejudices they expect from the voters—may guide their decisions. County party chairs, for example, view candidates of color as less likely to win general elections and therefore may recruit them less often.[16] Interest groups may be willing to oppose leaders within their own party if they believe increased representation of racial and ethnic groups is worth any electoral risk.

The Role of the Party-in-Government

The party-in-government also influences campaigns and election outcomes. For better or worse, candidates with a party label are tied to the party's elected leaders. With a Democratic president, other Democratic politicians are seen as favoring the president's agenda, and Republican politicians are imagined to oppose it. If the president's approval rating is low, it may hurt all Democratic candidates. If the party leadership in Congress advances a legislative program, it will also reflect on that party's candidates. The same dynamics play out in state races, where candidates are seen as favoring or opposing the current governor's agenda. In legislative races, candidates are also affected by the balance of power between the parties. The party with a majority in the legislature gets to set the agenda, typically earns more donations from access-oriented contributors, and can time legislation to maximize its impact on elections.

Legislators must work through their party to pass bills that benefit their districts, such as legislation to support local road projects. Bringing federal money or other benefits to their districts can help increase an incumbent's popularity and prospects for reelection. Legislative party leaders know of this power and often decide which incumbents to favor with local goods or legislative achievements based on the importance of their districts in the next election.

How Rules and Reality Constrain Parties

Like candidates, political parties are strategic actors that must make decisions within the context of both the reality on the ground and the rules set by government. The major rules that affect the parties are election laws (Chapter 2) and campaign finance laws (Chapter 4). The most relevant election laws for parties are those that affect primary elections. There are long-running legal disputes about the extent to which parties can control their own nomination processes. Some states mandate open primaries that allow independents to vote in either party's election, but many party organizations prefer closed primaries in which only party members can vote. Parties have also attempted to set their own dates for primary elections and to administer the voting, but most states demand that party rules conform to state laws and procedures (often meaning that the two parties have to hold their elections on the same day). Parties still set many of their own rules, and changes to their nomination processes are closely contested by potential candidates and their supporters.

California has implemented a series of reforms intended to weaken the influence of party organizations in primary elections. In 1996, voters enacted a "blanket primary": all of the candidates from both parties were listed on the ballot, allowing voters to vote in the Democratic primary for one office and in the Republican primary for another (see Chapter 2). The Supreme Court struck down this practice in 2000, finding that it violated a political party's First Amendment right to freedom of association. In 2010, California voters passed another initiative that created a new "top-two primary" system: candidates from all parties run together in the first round of voting, and the two candidates with the most votes advance to the general election. This means that two Democrats (or two Republicans) might be the only candidates on the final ballot. Under this system, party organizations that convince fewer of their candidates to run for each office have an advantage.

Campaign finance rules affect how parties can raise and spend money. As discussed in Chapter 4, before the Bipartisan Campaign Reform Act (BCRA) of 2002, political parties could accept unlimited contributions—or "soft money"—to spend on party-building activities and issue advertising. The BCRA made soft money contributions illegal, but donors reacted by creating other organizations to channel the money that they had previously directed to parties. The BCRA's ban on soft money has not yet been overturned, despite several rulings weakening its restrictions on independent groups and corporations.

Federal campaign finance law does benefit political parties in one sense: unlike other organizations, such as super PACs, parties are allowed to coordinate their campaign expenditures with the candidates they support. Party organizations also make independent expenditures that are not coordinated with candidates (see Figure 6.2 on p. TK). A party can thus intervene in a federal election by donating money to its candidate, donating money to state party organizations, coordinating expenditures with the candidate, and running its own advertisements.

Parties are not only affected by rules but also constrained by the same realities that candidates face. For example, **party identification** is one reality: the party identification of voters is relatively stable (see Chapter 13), and parties cannot easily convince citizens to change their identification and "join" another party. Similarly, parties cannot easily change how the public perceives them and their leaders. Issue ownership, discussed in Chapter 5, means that the public trusts one party more than the other to deal with certain problems. For example, voters have traditionally trusted Democrats more than Republicans to handle education, while Republicans have typically been trusted to handle taxes.

Parties are also constrained by the reality of the prevailing economy. Many citizens come to disapprove of the party that presides over an economic recession and support the party that presides over an economic boom. Parties will often find it harder to recruit quality candidates and prevent incumbents from retiring when economic or political conditions are unfavorable.[17]

A party's ability to gain seats in an election can also depend on its recent success or failure. A party that has won recent elections and developed a large majority may find that there are few remaining seats it can gain because its candidates have already won so many of the competitive seats. Meanwhile, a minority that performed poorly in the most recent elections can sometimes win back a lot of seats with only a small swing in the national electorate. In 2010, one of the reasons Republicans were able to win 63 additional seats in the House of Representatives was that they had lost so many seats in competitive districts in the 2006 and 2008 elections.

Finally, parties may find themselves constrained by the decisions of other actors, including candidates and interest groups. At times, these actors may work at cross-purposes with the party they support. Candidates who are fearful of losing independent voters may renounce aspects of their party's accomplishments and agenda. Interest groups that are otherwise allied with the party may even work against that party's incumbents. But parties and their allied interest groups, consultants, and candidates typically strive to develop similar agendas and to target a similar set of competitive races.

Are Political Parties in Decline?

Although some observers have suggested that political parties are in decline, political scientists are skeptical of these claims. Political parties are certainly not in decline in government: research shows that they have become more, not less, unified in the last 40 years and are able to exert better control over the legislative process. Partisan voting has become increasingly common in state legislatures and even in the courts.

Most arguments for party decline emphasize the apparent disregard for parties within the electorate. Substantial percentages of the public identify as "independent," profess to dislike the major parties and their leaders, and favor a system with competitive third parties or independent candidacies. But reading too much into these sentiments is a mistake. Most citizens who claim to be "independent" still favor one of the major parties and tend to vote for that party. These voters are "closet partisans" who may seek to avoid public acknowledgment of their party and might be less likely to publicly promote candidates, but their votes are usually not up for grabs.[18] Independents that implicitly associate with one party, even if they are unwilling to acknowledge it, tend to favor that party and its proposals.[19] Only one in 10 voters is a pure independent with no preference for either party. Moreover, party identification is actually becoming *more* important in congressional and presidential elections.[20] This does not mean that most citizens are familiar with the platforms of the political parties or have political opinions that are always closely aligned with their preferred party. Party identification, however, is a useful shortcut that voters use to reach judgments on candidates with or without detailed information.

Perhaps the best evidence for party decline comes from the decreasing role of party organizations in elections. In Chapter 3, we discussed how a certain kind of strong party organization known as a "party machine" gradually declined after the nineteenth century because of reforms such as the secret ballot. The rise of candidate-centered elections in the latter half of the twentieth century created a relationship whereby parties serve rather than control candidates.[21] There is indeed some evidence that candidates position themselves as independent of parties and create their own constituencies, donors, and volunteer networks—though parties still provide important resources that help with fundraising, polling, and get-out-the-vote operations, including shared and integrated voter data operations.[22]

Today's party organizations also have less control over the selection of general-election nominees than they did several decades ago. Party leaders used to use the national party conventions to select the presidential nominees, largely ignoring the will of rank-and-file voters. State parties once performed similar roles. With the rise of direct primaries for presidential and legislative elections, party organization leaders no longer have complete control over their party's nominees. After all, Trump was the least preferred party nominee of most Republican elected officials.

Party leaders can try to coordinate their support for a candidate during the "invisible primary"—the period of time before the actual presidential primaries begin when party leaders can observe and interact with potential candidates and each other. As we noted at the beginning of this chapter, according to *The Party Decides*, party leader endorsements normally predict which candidate will win the nomination, irrespective of the candidates' support in polls, the amount of money they raise, and the amount of media coverage they receive.[23] But Trump's case, though dramatic, is not the only instance of party consensus failure. Neither Obama nor McCain won the support of enough party leaders to make the results of the 2008 presidential primary elections a foregone conclusion. In both 2008 and 2016, both parties experienced lengthy and intensely competitive primary seasons. But in many other presidential election years, the nominee with the most support from party leaders has quickly emerged as the winner.

Debates over the rise and decline of parties often return to definitional controversies. Who constitutes the party? If it is anyone who endorses candidates, the party includes affiliated interest groups, celebrities, and others with access to money or organizations. If it is anyone who gives money, the party includes PACs, business leaders, professionals, and activists. The more narrowly the party organization is defined—for instance, as only including official party committees—the more evidence there is for its decline. By contrast, the more broadly parties are defined, the more it becomes clear that two broad, competing coalitions still strive for power under the Democratic and Republican umbrellas.

Party Evolution and Polarization

Although there is little evidence of partisan decline, the issue positions and social coalitions of the Democrats and the Republicans have changed over time. The most important geographic change, the transformation of the South from solidly Democratic to a mostly Republican region, coincided with a sorting of voters into partisan camps based on their ideologies. Conservative

Democrats, concentrated in but not exclusively from the South, slowly left the party. Liberal Republicans, largely from the northern states, changed parties or became more conservative. Ideological sorting was also helped by religious coalition change. Catholic voters, once a part of the Democratic coalition, became more evenly divided, while White evangelicals gravitated toward Republicans.[24] The growing population of nonreligious voters is mostly Democratic. Less-educated White voters have become less tied to the Democratic Party over time, and white-collar professionals and single women have become more Democratic. As the nation has diversified, Latinos and Asian Americans have become larger components of the Democratic Party coalition. (We will discuss party identification further in Chapter 13.)

Some political scientists have argued that many of these changes were brought about by the rising salience of racial issues in American politics.[25] The civil rights movement of the 1960s split the parties' electoral coalitions, especially the Democratic Party's uneasy alliance of White segregationists and African Americans. As a result, voters' positions on civil rights policies, such as school integration and affirmative action, became more important to their overall partisan identification—leading some to switch parties and others to align their racial and economic policy views with those of their party. Some observers suggest that politicians' campaign messages now include "coded racial appeals"—that is, they discuss immigration, crime, and welfare in a way that taps into underlying White racial resentment.[26] Trump's 2016 campaign, which was openly negative toward Muslim and Latino immigrants, only accelerated these concerns.

Other scholars argue that the parties have extended their liberal-conservative ideological conflicts on economic issues to an array of new issues, including race, gender, and moral issues such as abortion.[27] When the Supreme Court struck down antiabortion laws in the 1973 *Roe v. Wade* decision, Republicans and Democrats (in both Congress and the electorate) were almost evenly divided between pro-choice and pro-life positions. Today, pro-choice Republicans and pro-life Democrats are rare. The same is true of other issues that formerly divided each party. As a result, citizens now learn a lot more about candidates based on their party affiliation alone, and partisans of either stripe find it harder to admire any candidates in the other party.

Increasing party-line voting in Congress (with most Democrats on one side and most Republicans on the other) demonstrates elite polarization: the two parties are moving further apart from one another on an underlying ideological spectrum. As legislators have sorted into two parties with diametrically opposed views on most issues, Democrats and Republicans in the American public also seem to be lining up against one another on more issues. Within each issue area, fewer members of each party now agree with the other party. This hardly means that the United States is a nation of extremists: many voters still express moderation, and relatively few have consistently conservative or liberal views on every topic or have moved toward more extreme positions. Consistent divisions across the issue spectrum, however, have made it more difficult for politicians to campaign on issue positions likely to draw in voters from the other camp. And since Republicans and Democrats are now more segregated geographically, many legislative districts are uncompetitive.

Voters in today's polarized environment also tend to dislike their rival party, and the groups associated with it, more intensely than voters did in the past. **Negative partisanship** is on the rise: people increasingly dislike the other party, even if they feel no more favorable toward their own.[28] Some citizens even fear their children marrying members of the other party or believe that the other party is a threat to the nation's well-being. This may be one reason why partisans now accept nearly anything that their side does. In 2016, most Republican voters who said they disliked Trump's views and behaviors still voted for him over the even-more-dreaded Hillary Clinton. By 2020, Republicans were more enthusiastic about Trump. Partisans see nearly everything in light of their positive attitude toward one party and negative attitude toward the other, with sometimes comical results. Directly before the 2020 election (with Trump still presiding), Republicans thought the economy was in good shape while Democrats feared the worst. But one week later, once Biden had been declared the winner, the pattern reversed: Democrats were more excited about the economy after Biden's victory, and Republicans saw the economy more gloomily, despite no underlying economic changes.[29]

Polarized parties also affect which candidates run for office; more moderate candidates are often afraid to put their names forward.[30] As the parties move apart, they tend to stimulate candidates who are consistent supporters of their agendas, making each generation of politicians even more polarized than the one before.

Evaluating Political Parties

To evaluate whether parties are helpful or harmful for democracy, we can use the standards for evaluating campaigns that we set out in Chapter 1. First, do parties help voters make informed choices, or do they manipulate voters? On the one hand, parties and their platforms provide voters with clear

Party polarization across the spectrum of social, economic, and political issues has contributed to the rise of negative partisanship in recent elections. Research has shown that voters hold increasingly negative opinions of members and candidates of the opposing party.

choices and information about those choices, which help voters select the candidates whom they agree with on most issues. In fact, simply voting on the basis of party affiliation can be an effective way for some people to identify the candidates whose views accord with their own.[31] Voters with different priorities than those of the major parties may find the information that parties provide less helpful. Yet there is evidence that when citizens hold a policy preference different from that of a trusted party leader, they change their own preferences rather than oppose their party.[32]

Second, do parties contribute to free choice? Here, too, the picture is mixed. The two major political parties provide for competitive elections in many places, especially at the national level. They are roughly equal in their resources, the quality of their candidates (as judged by experience), and the support they command from voters. Clearly this is better than the one-party systems in some authoritarian regimes. At the same time, the Democratic and Republican parties help entrench the American system's bias against third parties and independent candidates who might represent other preferences among the public; indeed, the major parties sometimes collude to exclude third-party competition.

Third, do parties contribute to deliberation? In one sense, they do. Competition between the major parties helps to clarify similarities and differences in what candidates and parties believe. But in other ways, parties do not contribute to healthy deliberation. Much like candidates, parties try to persuade voters, not promote conversation. They also tend to focus on the narrow range of issues that will appeal to swing voters. Multiparty systems encourage a much broader range of issue discussion.

Even if we are dissatisfied with the current role of parties, we may find that there is no viable alternative to them. Our criticisms of political parties do not always recognize the downsides that any alternatives might entail. In the 1950s, many political scientists and activists criticized the parties for not offering clear alternatives to voters; now that they do, we complain of polarization.

Because most major democracies feature parties, it is hard to know what elections would look like without them. It is true that many local elections are nonpartisan (see Chapter 11), but this does not necessarily stop parties from forming—even without official parties, candidates tend to develop stable alliances. One could argue that this is helpful in that identifiable "teams" of candidates are easier for voters to evaluate than a mass of lone rangers. A multiparty system would give voters more diverse options and better represent the range of views in the public. But multiparty systems may also make it more difficult for elected leaders to coordinate after elections in order to govern.[33]

Conclusion

Political parties are key features of American campaigns. Candidates and voters usually have preexisting ties to the Democrats or Republicans, and campaigns usually replicate partisan divisions on public policy issues. Party organizations often recruit and determine the viability of candidates, and they direct resources to those most likely to win. Primary elections are usually internal party battles in which partisan leaders and activists help to determine the nominees. General elections are largely fought along partisan lines, with each party's candidate presenting the party's issue positions and philosophy to voters already predisposed to choose one side in the battle.

In the abstract, most citizens disdain parties. But despite persistent claims of decline, America's two major political parties are here to stay. As groups of citizens, officeholders, and organizations, parties guide voters, train and organize candidates, and govern. Attempts to regulate their influence typi-cally succeed only in redirecting it. Whatever burdens parties create, it is difficult to imagine that democracy could work without them.

KEY TERMS

political parties (p. 165)

party-in-the-electorate (p. 165)

party-as-organization (p. 165)

party-in-government (p. 165)

coordinated expenditures (p. 173)

party identification (p. 178)

negative partisanship (p. 182)

FOR DISCUSSION

1. Would American elections improve if party organizations were more involved in selecting party nominees and informing voters about the differences between candidates, or would it be better to leave cam-paigning to the candidates? How would elections change with more or less party involvement?

2. Democratic and Republican candidates (and voters) now take distinct positions on most issues. Is this a positive trend because voters can now more easily tell the parties apart and elect candidates who share their views? Or is it a negative trend because the two parties are too extreme and rigid to compete for moderate voters?

3. Should political parties seek to maximize the seats that they control in Congress by running less loyal and less ideologically consistent candi-dates in the districts where they have fewer identifiers, or should they support only those candidates who adhere to the party's platform? Why?

4. How have the roles of the parties in American elections changed since the 1960s? Have parties gained or lost influence? How have their coalitions and issue positions evolved?

7

Interest Groups

As Election Day approached in 2020, Democrats were focused on the U.S. Senate and presidential races in North Carolina and Georgia. Although most pundits gave the party slightly better odds in North Carolina, Democrats lost both the Senate race in that state and its electoral college votes. Meanwhile, in Georgia, Democratic presidential candidate Joe Biden carried the state, and the Democratic candidates for Georgia's two Senate seats advanced to runoff elections. With subsequent victories in those runoffs, Democrats gained control of the Senate for the start of Biden's presidency. Many Democrats credited the Georgia performance to someone who was not even a candidate: Stacey Abrams.

A former Georgia House minority leader and gubernatorial candidate, Abrams had helped found eight organizations that offered major funding for 16 other groups predominantly focused on increasing voter participation among Georgians of color. It is unclear whether Abrams's focus made a difference, though some scholars argue that Black voter turnout increased in areas where her network had offices, including in the runoff elections.[1]

North Carolina also had an active campaign, led by Reverend William Barber, to advance the interests of Black voters. A former state president of the National Association for the Advancement of Colored People (NAACP), Barber worked with his organizations through that interest group's infrastructure rather than through Democratic Party organizations. He focused his energies on stimulating a protest movement, anchored by "Moral Mondays" protests against actions in state government, rather than influencing elections. These events generated a lot of attention in metropolitan area news coverage, but they may not have mobilized many voters.

Abrams's and Barber's efforts both involved interest groups—organizations that seek to influence policy—but Abrams's network was more directly linked to party organizations and an election campaign. Some interest groups are involved in social movements, others in lobbying, others in campaigns, and others in a mix of strategies. Elections can be central to their efforts or secondary. Their approaches to elections vary considerably, as do their levels of campaign involvement. When they do enter campaigns, interest groups have to compete alongside parties and candidates to influence elections. Because Abrams was a former candidate and party leader, she pursued a strategy that aligned with that of the Democratic Party—and even got some credit for the party's victory.

Interest groups play important roles in American campaigns, but neither Abrams's nor Barber's organizations exemplify the most common types of interest groups or their most common activities. The groups most involved in contemporary campaigns are often creations of rich patrons or shell organizations used to funnel money to one political party's efforts. In contrast, the most well-represented interest groups in Washington, businesses and trade associations, often stay out of campaigns or just donate small amounts of money to their favored candidates. This chapter explores interest groups' varied roles, focusing both on the traditional role of interest groups in mobilizing segments of the electorate, such as Black voters, and their contemporary role as vehicles for campaign spending independent of candidates and parties.

Core of the Analysis

- Interest groups are varied actors, only some of which get involved in campaigns. They have proliferated while changing form in response to changes in law.

- Interest groups donate money, run advertisements, and help mobilize voters, but their motives are distinct from those of the candidates and parties they support.

- Interest group spending can affect voters' choices, but evidence is limited that they redirect campaign agendas or deliver specific constituency votes.

- Interest group activity is at odds with some of our hopes for campaigns, although it can increase the diversity of voices in campaigns beyond those of the candidates.

Stacey Abrams's mobilization efforts in Georgia may have contributed to the Democrats' successes in the 2020 elections and the Georgia Senate runoff elections. Here, Abrams (right) campaigns with Raphael Warnock (left), one of the Democrats to win a Senate seat in Georgia.

We first discuss types of interest groups and why they have proliferated. The chapter then examines their involvement in campaigns and how it has coevolved with changes in campaign finance law. We also focus on their unique roles in initiative campaigns and note that most interest groups still avoid campaigns in favor of lobbying. The chapter then addresses interest group campaign strategy in the context of the rules and realities they face and assesses whether interest groups succeed in changing campaign debates or delivering constituency votes. Finally, we evaluate their role: Do interest groups add important voices to American campaigns? Or are they meddling, unaccountable groups that divert candidates from their messages and mislead voters? Their true role may be more pedestrian: motivated by liberal ideas and concern for Black citizens, Abrams and Barber helped create interest groups to advance those causes, only some of which were focused on helping Democrats win elections.

Types of Interest Groups

An **interest group** is a collection of people acting toward the shared goal of influencing public policy. Although political parties also have policy goals, interest groups differ from parties in key respects. Most important, interest groups do not run their own candidates for office. Interest groups usually seek more particular policy goals than parties do, often to the direct benefit of the group's supporters. Interest groups are not always aligned with a party, and many groups attempt to influence members of both parties. Even in campaigns, some groups will support candidates from both parties. Other interest groups do not participate in elections at all and focus instead on lobbying policy makers after they are elected. But election results influence policy outcomes, so many interest groups do participate in campaigns and can be important actors in elections.

There are several major types of interest groups. The largest sector of groups represents businesses. More than 3,000 individual corporations and trade associations have political offices in or near Washington, D.C., including large groups such as the National Association of Manufacturers and the American Farm Bureau Federation. Through affiliates, these groups regularly give money to and participate in campaigns. Yet most corporations do not have political action committees (PACs), make campaign contributions, or air their own campaign advertisements. Another large sector of interest groups comprises professional associations, which represent occupations; examples include the American Medical Association and the American Bar Association. The largest of these groups participate in elections, but most are small and do not participate in campaigns. Labor unions, a third sector of interest groups, regularly participate in campaigns. Most labor unions—for example, the American Federation of State, County, and Municipal Employees (AFSCME) and the Service Employees International Union (SEIU)—usually support Democratic candidates.

Some interest groups seek to represent broader social groups or ideological perspectives rather than the direct economic concerns of corporations, unions, and professionals. For example, the NAACP, which works on behalf of African Americans, represents a specific social group. Some groups, such as the American Conservative Union, speak on behalf of an ideological viewpoint. These groups usually refer to themselves as *public interest groups*. Other groups advocate for a single issue. The National Rifle Association (NRA), for example, promotes the rights of gun owners. Public interest and single-issue groups are more likely to participate in elections than economic groups are, but they are less numerous and have fewer resources.[2]

Interest groups differ in the extent of their ties to political parties. Some unions, such as the National Education Association, have endorsed the Democratic Party candidate in every presidential election of the past few decades; other unions, such as the Fraternal Order of Police, lean toward the Republicans. Many interest groups share close ties to a party and may exchange mailing lists and voter targets with that party even if they officially claim to be nonpartisan. Even these party-aligned groups, however, may have some incentive to maintain allies in the opposing party; the NRA, for instance, still gives money to some Democrats, even though the Republican National Committee was a top recipient of its largesse.

Why Does the United States Have So Many Interest Groups?

The United States has a large and growing number of interest groups. Citizens tend to bemoan groups as narrow "special interests," but the large number of groups also reflects the country's increasing diversity of ideas and backgrounds. The proliferation of interest groups has been particularly dramatic since the 1960s—a trend driven by four important factors. The first is the expansion of government. As all levels of government in the United States, particularly the federal government, have taken on more responsibilities, they have come to regulate more entities and provide resources to more people. This creates an incentive for groups to organize to lobby for more favorable regulations and additional resources.

Second, strategies for organizational maintenance have improved. A key innovation in this realm was direct mail fundraising, by which an organization could regularly solicit contributions from an expanding list of like-minded Americans. Today, organizations maintain email lists, social media accounts, and websites to further facilitate fundraising appeals.

Third, prominent social movements have served as models for other groups to mobilize. After the success of the African American civil rights movement, for example, other underrepresented groups organized into movements of their own. The increasing ethnic and religious diversity of the United States has furthered this trend. Successful mobilization by a group on one side of an issue can also stimulate mobilization by its counterpart on the other side. For example, a conservative group called the American Action Network was founded in 2010 in response to the liberal Center for American Progress, which was originally founded to counter conservative think tanks like the Heritage Foundation. The Heritage Foundation was itself founded to counter the liberal Brookings Institution. This pattern of response and counter-response is common.

Fourth, federal tax and campaign finance rules encourage organizations to create separate affiliated groups for distinct purposes. As noted in Chapter 4, many interest groups are registered with the Internal Revenue Service (IRS) as 501(c) nonprofit corporations. Interest groups also create PACs to accept contributions and donate them directly to political candidates. Some have 527 groups or super PACs (see Chapter 4) or some other combination of groups. For example, EMILY's List, a supporter of female Democratic candidates, is a PAC with affiliated 527s. Progress for America is a conservative 501(c)4 organization with a 527 affiliate. The Center for American Progress is a 501(c)3 with a 501(c)4 affiliate. The NRA is a 501(c)4 with a PAC aligned with a super PAC. State and local laws differ in how they treat these organizations and whether they allow the organizations to participate in state and local elections. As a result, groups with state or local affiliates can have even more complicated structures.

Campaign finance rules drive the formation of new groups in another way: because laws require political advertisements to publicly disclose the names of some sponsors, some groups create new organizations with names designed specifically to appeal to the electorate. For example, in a California ballot initiative campaign dealing with auto insurance, the side funded by insurance companies called itself "Californians for Fair Auto Insurance Rates" and created the "California Senior Advocates League" to promote its cause. Campaign finance laws thus encourage the same groups of people to create multiple organizations for legal and public relations purposes.

An increase in interest group campaign activity has accompanied the general increase in the number of groups. Yet these trends have not always followed the same trajectory. The largest increase in PACs occurred in the late 1970s and early 1980s. The number of lobbyists and PACs has changed only slightly in recent years, but they have been joined by new types of groups: 527s and super PACs. Expenditures by 527s were concentrated in the 2004 election cycle. Independent spending has increased most dramatically since 2006, with notable spending by super PACs in 2012. 501(c) organizations also began spending considerable sums on election-related activities in the last few election cycles.

FIGURE 7.1   Total Interest Group Campaign Contributions and
Direct Campaign Spending, 1998–2020

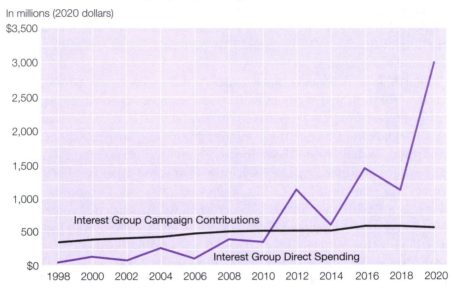

In millions (2020 dollars)

Source: OpenSecrets.org, based on data from the Federal Election Commission. Campaign contributions
include only PAC contributions. Direct spending includes independent expenditures, electioneering
communications, and communication costs.

Figure 7.1 compares how much interest groups have contributed to federal campaigns with how much they have directly spent in campaigns (including several types of expenditures) since 1998. Since PAC contributions go disproportionately to incumbents, who often lack competition, direct spending can be more influential than campaign contributions in close elections. It also has some disadvantages for interest groups, since independent spenders cannot coordinate with candidates and often have to pay higher rates for television advertising. In 2012, independent expenditures in federal elections eclipsed total PAC contributions for the first time, tripling the totals from the previous campaign. These trends were caused more by changes in campaign finance law than by changes in the number of groups trying to influence campaigns. As we discussed in Chapter 4, Supreme Court rulings and Federal Election Commission (FEC) interpretations enabled new super PACs to accept unlimited contributions and spend unlimited amounts to influence elections. Outside groups also outspent the candidates themselves in 26 congressional races in 2016 and 41 in 2018. This means that candidates now have less control over their messages in the most competitive congressional races.

How Are Interest Groups Involved in Campaigns?

Although the majority of interest groups do not get involved in campaigns, many groups contribute money and endorse candidates. Organizations commonly attempt to mobilize their members to volunteer and turn out to vote for their preferred candidates. A few interest groups engage in their own advertising, including an increasing number of groups that are founded exclusively for this purpose. But groups that form for the express purpose of spending unlimited sums in an election sometimes overwhelm the messaging coming from candidates and parties.

Because of donor disclosure requirements, campaign contributions are the easiest type of interest group electioneering to track. Interest groups often donate money to candidates and parties through their affiliated PACs. Total PAC contributions have been increasing since the 1970s (rising from $126 million in 1978 to $441 million in 2016).[3] Most PACs are associated with professional associations, unions, or corporations. Corporate, union, and association executives also make individual contributions to candidates. To track total giving by different industries over time, OpenSecrets combines PAC giving with donations from individuals associated with particular organizations. In 2016, according to their data, total giving by business entities accounted for 59.9 percent of large federal campaign contributions, labor unions contributed 4.6 percent, and ideological interest groups contributed 13.4 percent. Ideological and single-issue PACs are becoming more numerous, but their contributions still account for a small portion of total PAC giving.

Within the corporate sphere, the financial industry donates more money than any other sector, with companies in law, energy, health, and communications also accounting for a large portion of contributions (see Figure 7.2). Corporate sectors differ not only in how much they donate but also in who receives their donations. The building materials and oil and gas industries consistently favor Republicans, while the entertainment and publishing industries consistently favor Democrats. Unions are bigger supporters of Democratic candidates than any industry sector. Despite their different party preferences, most corporate and labor PACs donate overwhelmingly to incumbents. Although PACs are clearly important donors, their contributions must be put in context: as we discussed in Chapter 4, PACs donate less money to American political campaigns than individuals do, although many of these individuals are employees of corporations with political interests.

FIGURE 7.2 Total Political Contributions by Industry Sector

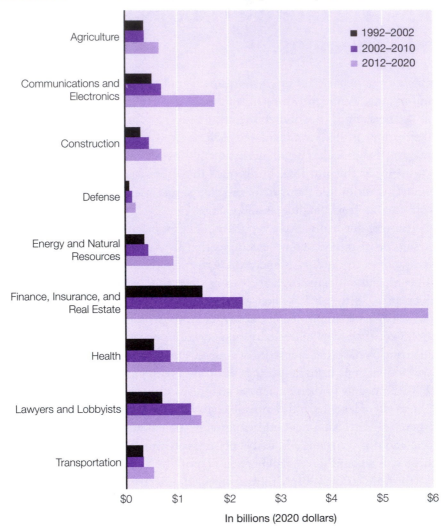

Source: OpenSecrets.org. Included are individual contributions, PAC contributions, and soft money.

Interest groups can also participate in elections by running their own advertising campaigns. Interest groups are less concerned than candidates or parties with protecting their reputation and are willing to risk any backlash from negative advertising—so they go negative far more often.[4] Interest group ads are less obviously tied to the candidates they are supporting, but voters may not necessarily distinguish interest group ads from candidate ads. Interest group ads are also more likely to focus on policy issues than candidate advertisements are. Candidates are more concerned with sharing their biographies, whereas interest groups often want to make their issues of concern more central to the campaign.

Examining contributions and independent expenditures may be the easiest way to measure interest group involvement in campaigns, but interest groups try to influence elections in other ways. Interest groups use direct communication and news media to get their campaign messages out and support specific candidates: many have large email lists and groups of supporters on social networking sites like Facebook and Twitter that they can use to mobilize donations or activism on behalf of causes or candidates.

Interest groups may also pursue independent efforts to mobilize and persuade voters. Unions, for example, have long engaged in grassroots voter mobilization among their members. Many interest groups produce voter guides or endorse slates of candidates. For instance, the Christian Coalition distributed millions of voter guides outside churches in 1994, making it clear that they believed Republican candidates were pro-life and pro-family whereas Democratic candidates were not. In 2020, during the COVID-19 pandemic, evangelicals instead reached out to their followers through church leaders and targeted Facebook ads.

Interest groups that undertake these campaign activities often claim to speak for broader **constituencies**, such as all voters from a particular ethnic or religious group. Organizations and leaders that represent a particular group can help to reinforce group members' allegiance to a party or set of candidates. Arguably, African American voters' loyalty to the Democratic Party has arisen in part because most Black leaders are allied with the party.[5] However, new social movements, such as Black Lives Matter, have come to challenge traditional interest groups as grassroots representatives of the Black community, and these newer groups sometimes question traditional groups' close ties to party politicians. Candidates may also sign on to an interest group's policy agenda, such as Americans for Tax Reform's "Taxpayer Protection Pledge," which entails a promise not to raise taxes. Candidates who sign the pledge expect not only to gain the support of individuals affiliated with the interest group but also to signal to all voters opposed to taxes that they share their views.

Interest Groups in Ballot Initiative Campaigns

In **ballot initiative campaigns**, which give voters a choice of whether to support or oppose specific policy changes, interest groups replace the candidates as the main actors. In states and localities that allow initiatives and referenda, coalitions of individuals and interest groups often form to pay firms to gather the required signatures from registered voters to get an issue on the ballot. In California, proponents of initiatives routinely pay millions of dollars just for the signature-gathering effort before the real campaign begins. Legislatures can also directly put questions on the ballot, and local governing authorities are sometimes required to put measures like tax increases to the voters. No matter how issues make their way onto the ballot, committees often form to support or oppose them. Statewide initiatives, especially those that will affect businesses' bottom lines, are most likely to generate active campaigns.

Interest group endorsements and advertising can provide clues to voters who might not otherwise understand the complex legislative language of initiatives. A study of California voters deciding on five complicated insurance initiatives found that knowing whether the insurance industry, trial lawyers, and consumer activists supported the measures was enough to help voters who could not understand the initiatives emulate the votes of those who did have full information.[6] Voters just had to know whether they favored the position of the insurance industry or the trial lawyers, not which particular law they preferred.

With enough money, even obscure interest groups can put their issues to the voters. In 2014, a wealthy technology businessman tried to qualify an initiative to divide California into six separate states, including one named "Silicon Valley," even though polls showed little support for the proposal and legal experts said that voters lacked the authority to break up the state. Because too many signatures were invalid, the initiative was kept off the ballot. Interestingly, interest group spending may have more of an impact when it is directed toward defeating initiatives than when it aims to support them. Interest group arguments are more effective at generating opposition to ballot measures than they are at generating support.[7]

Why Do Some Interest Groups Avoid Campaigns?

Many traditional interest groups avoid spending money on political campaigns. Most businesses that hire lobbyists fail to start PACs. Even some huge firms like Apple and Berkshire Hathaway lack PACs. All of the major industries that donate to candidates still spend considerably more on lobbying and charitable contributions than they do on campaigns.[8] Few interest groups give the maximum amounts allowed by law to candidates, and even fewer spend their own money directly in campaigns.

This points to a key difference between the goals of interest groups and the goals of political parties and candidates. Interest groups' primary concerns are policy outcomes, not who holds power. They care about elections because the party that controls government influences whether legislatures pass the laws they favor or oppose and how administrations implement those laws. Groups may also be able to identify the particular candidates most likely to support their policy goals. But elections are not interest groups' only opportunities to influence policy: they can also lobby whoever is elected or appointed. If a group plans to talk to members of both parties to advance its goals, it may be disadvantageous to have a firm tie to either the Democrats or the Republicans.

As judged by their spending habits, most interest groups view spending money on lobbying as a better strategy than spending on campaigns. The policy issues important to many corporations, such as specific tax exemptions or small appropriations, never come up in campaigns. Interest groups seeking government contracts or tax benefits also like to present an apolitical image of expertise and a willingness to work with anyone to achieve shared goals. Appearing to stay above the fray, rather than intervening in elections, may better serve that image.

Because some interest groups are campaign averse while others are invented for the sole purpose of running ads in campaigns, the groups most involved in elections are not representative of all the groups trying to influence policy. The campaigning groups are much more likely to take a clear partisan side and to be motivated by ideology than those who sit on the sidelines.

Rules, Reality, and Interest Group Strategies

Interest groups decide what role they want to play in campaigns (if any) in the context of the rules set by government. As we have seen, campaign finance law limits how much any group can donate and encourages groups to establish multiple subsidiaries in order to stay within the law. Groups are also prohibited from coordinating their advertising or mobilization efforts with candidates. Candidates cannot use interest groups' resources, even office space or printed materials, without counting those resources as in-kind contributions subject to disclosure and contribution limits. Furthermore, tax law limits the activities of interest groups organized as tax-exempt nonprofit organizations. Depending on their tax status, interest groups may be prohibited from publicly endorsing candidates or engaging in campaign activity.

They usually find a way around these rules by establishing multiple organizations of different types or by disbanding before the rules are enforced.

Interest group strategies are also constrained by certain realities that may be out of their control during any particular campaign. Some interest groups represent more popular issue positions than others. Some groups represent issues that are already of great concern to voters, but others need to stimulate interest in their issue areas. Some groups find it easier to raise money and thus have more resources to use in elections than others. Candidates inevitably cater to the wealthiest groups and those most able to deliver large numbers of votes.

Interest groups' strategies also depend on how their agendas and issue positions correspond to those of incumbent politicians.[9] Groups whose agendas are well served by incumbents will typically support them, regardless of party, and they will seek to maintain their access to these politicians to ensure that government policy continues to match their preferences. For example, the defense and aerospace industry—which has earned many billions of dollars in government contracts—routinely gives considerable sums to both parties. In 2020, the top donors in the industry, Lockheed Martin and Raytheon, gave $5.9 million to Democrats and $5.7 million to Republicans. By contrast, ideological and single-issue groups may seek to replace these incumbents, often with representatives who are more liberal or conservative than the average legislator. The actions of the Club for Growth exemplify this strategy, as the group often seeks to replace incumbents from both parties with more conservative alternatives. But most ideological groups still support incumbent candidates of their preferred party.

Substantial interest group resources—particularly in the form of independent expenditures—are often targeted at a few competitive races. Interest group involvement can complicate life for the candidates in these races, as groups' messages may center on their narrow agendas rather than the concerns of the average voter and may be more controversial than the messages of the candidates they support.

Interest Group Campaign Influence

Interest groups largely engage in the same activities as candidates and parties, meaning that their ultimate influence is tied to the same kinds of factors that affect how influential candidates and parties can be. If voters know little about the candidates, one side spends considerably more than the other, and a close race is projected, then interest group activities can help tip the balance. In races with well-known contenders or balanced levels of spending, interest group activities—just like candidate and party campaigns—will have a hard time affecting election outcomes. If ads or get-out-the-vote efforts are successful in the hands of parties or candidates, interest groups can use the same strategies to achieve similar effects. But interest groups face the same environment as their candidate and party allies: most group spending favored Mitt Romney over Barack Obama in the 2012 presidential election and Hillary Clinton over Donald Trump in 2016, but Romney and Clinton went on to lose their respective elections despite their financial advantages.

Recent increases in interest group campaign activity have stimulated some research on its impact. In the 2012 Republican presidential primary race, during which super PACs outspent candidates in many states, research has shown that super PACs extended the viability of poorly funded candidate Rick Santorum and reduced the influence of early-state primary wins on the later contests.[10] An experiment in which researchers showed 2012 super PAC ads to voters found that the ads reduced voters' evaluations of Romney, indirectly helping Obama and directly helping Romney's primary opponents.[11] Interest group expenditures may also be less valuable at the beginning of a candidate's primary campaign, when the actual campaign organization would benefit most from direct donations to build a competent organization and enable regular travel.

Since 2012, interest groups have aired more campaign ads in each election cycle than political parties have—including one out of every four ads in 2020. But many of the biggest spenders, such as those listed in Table 7.1, are closely connected to party actors.[12] Most interest groups do not fully disclose their donors in advertising, but there has been a decline in "dark money" groups that disclose little information at all. The 2020 cycle saw an increase in hybrid PACs (sometimes called Carey Committees), which both spend unlimited amounts (similar to super PACs) and donate limited amounts to candidates.

Many reformers are concerned that interest group influence will grow with unlimited spending. In 2011, comedian Stephen Colbert started a super PAC to dramatize the potential for unlimited and hidden political spending. He raised $1 million, but he seemed only to increase awareness of campaign finance laws among his television viewers without influencing many votes. In 2014, Harvard professor Lawrence Lessig started the Mayday PAC with an odd purpose: to support candidates who want to eliminate super PACs. He recommends that citizens "embrace the irony" of using super PACs to fight super PACs, but his effort has faced the uphill battle of

TABLE 7.1 Top Interest Group Spenders in 2020 Elections

	Amount spent	Partisan tilt
Senate Leadership Fund	$293,731,548	Republican
Senate Majority PAC	$250,180,567	Democratic
Congressional Leadership Fund	$142,783,829	Republican
Future Forward USA	$141,585,894	Democratic
House Majority PAC	$139,930,082	Democratic
America First Action	$133,819,980	Republican
Priorities USA Action	$127,513,342	Democratic
Preserve America PAC	$102,983,479	Republican
American Crossroads	$79,476,030	Republican
Club for Growth	$66,334,260	Republican
American Bridge 21st Century	$59,719,576	Democratic
Independence USA PAC	$56,530,420	Democratic
The Lincoln Project	$49,633,016	Democratic
Americans for Prosperity	$47,732,979	Republican
League of Conservation Voters	$42,272,125	Democratic

Source: OpenSecrets.org.

making the issue matter to electable candidates without stimulating over-whelming opposition spending.[13] Thus far, Lessig's operation has spent considerable sums (often on long-shot candidacies) to little apparent effect.

Interest groups may be especially likely to influence outcomes when other campaigning is limited, such as in ballot initiative campaigns, simply because they face fewer competitors in the battle to influence voters. In one field experiment, researchers worked with an advocacy group supporting and opposing statewide initiatives in Oregon to send persuasive mailers to randomly selected households; they found that precincts that received the materials were more likely to support initiatives favored by the group and oppose those that the group sought to defeat.[14]

Can Interest Groups Deliver Constituency Votes?

Interest groups often claim to represent constituencies like gun owners, union members, and African Americans. They offer candidates a deal: support our group's goals, and you will win the votes of our members and sympathetic fans in the electorate. But can interest groups actually deliver the votes they promise? An interest group's support is likely to translate into votes for a given candidate only if group members perceive a common fate, believe that an organization represents their interests well, and tend to vote together consistently. Securing a Farm Bureau organizational endorsement, for example, matters more if farmers see themselves as a group that will rise and fall based on support for particular agricultural policies. The endorsements of interest groups and their leaders may be especially important for candidates in local elections, where voters might know more about their neighborhood association, union, or business association than they know about many of the candidates. In local elections, candidates and local group leaders often negotiate directly over which candidates will receive group members' votes. For example, in a mayoral election, all of the local African American neighborhood leaders may endorse one of the candidates; these endorsements both send a message to potential voters that the candidate supports African American interests and signal to the candidate that they will mobilize local African Americans through churches and community associations on their behalf.

Yet candidates cannot be certain that earning the endorsement of groups or their leaders will influence group members to vote for them. For instance, former Florida governor and Republican presidential hopeful Jeb Bush gained the support of many group leaders as the 2016 campaign approached, but he never caught fire with voters. More generally, interest groups sometimes exaggerate their ability to "deliver" votes for a candidate. The views of group leaders are often more consistently ideological or strongly partisan than the views of group members. Members may also be more divided than leaders in their loyalties to parties or candidates. Ultimately, although candidates typically seek the support of sympathetic interest groups, the number of voters any group can deliver is uncertain.

For example, Democratic candidates often seek the support of unions, which have traditionally been a major force in Democratic Party politics. Much of the campaigning in Democratic primaries consists of traveling from union hall to union hall and gathering endorsements by talking at open meetings or negotiating with leadership. National labor groups like the AFL-CIO and the SEIU are still among the top Democratic Party donors and spend considerably on their own advertising and get-out-the-vote strategies.

Joe Biden, like most Democratic candidates, gained the support of major unions in 2020. Biden, who spoke at an AFL-CIO convention during the primary season in 2019, won the union's endorsement.

They also serve as national volunteer networks for Democratic campaigns. But Republican politicians regularly complain that union leaders fail to represent the views of unions' significant, but minority, Republican membership. Unions have also found it harder in recent years to reach out to the broader working class that they hope to mobilize on behalf of Democrats; union membership in general is declining, and unions increasingly represent government employees rather than private sector workers. In the 2016 presidential campaign, union efforts to spread Democrat Hillary Clinton's message faltered even among many union members; some trusted her opponent, Donald Trump, more than they trusted their own union leaders.

When a constituency is easily identifiable, motivated, and ascendant, interest groups can help channel members' energies toward candidates who share their views. Conservative organizations often support the same candidates in Republican Party primaries, stamping them with the moniker of "consistent conservative" and helping to direct conservative voters to the candidates they support. Although not many Americans are official members of these interest groups, many more are sympathetic to their broader aims. Interest group endorsements help codify one candidate as the favorite of the right, a notion often amplified by talk radio hosts and reported in media coverage.

Can Interest Groups Change the Campaign Agenda?

Some interest groups have goals beyond electing a particular candidate; they hope to change the **campaign agenda**: the issues at the heart of a campaign. Environmental organizations, for example, usually support Democratic candidates, but they also want issues like pollution and climate change to play a more prominent role in campaigns. They may advertise directly about the issues that most concern them, hoping to stimulate candidate and voter discussion on these issues. The League of Conservation Voters targets 12 candidates—the "dirty dozen"—that it says oppose clean energy. It funds television ads, voter contact operations, and online videos focused on these candidates' environmental records.

As interest group activity in campaigns has come to be dominated less by single-issue groups and more by ideological and partisan organizations established to funnel money toward advertising, group advertising has become less distinctive. If interest groups use the same political consulting firms, run similar focus groups, and use similar survey data to design their advertising, the output is likely to look the same as candidates' own advertisements. There is also little evidence that candidates follow interest groups' lead when they choose to advertise on different issues. Candidates choose their own issue focus and often respond to the issues raised by their opponents, but they do not necessarily shift their advertising on the basis of issues raised only by interest groups.

New multi-issue campaign groups more often follow the agendas of parties and their candidates, whereas traditional single-issue groups may not. Republican groups and candidates also appear to match their messaging more closely than their Democratic counterparts do.[15] Few interest groups are acting at cross-purposes with the parties and candidates they support, though some have different ideas about what is important to voters.

But even with limited resources for advertising, interest groups may draw their supporters' attention to candidates' records on the groups' main issues of concern. Many interest groups issue scorecards for elected officials that outline their votes for and against the groups' positions. Abortion rights groups regularly declare that Republicans have waged a "war on women" and highlight candidate statements that oppose legal abortion even in cases of rape or incest. Candidates are sometimes forced to respond to these interest group efforts, with reporters asking why they have a poor voting record according to a particular group or asking them to clarify a statement highlighted by a group.

Where Do Campaigns Fit in Broader Interest Group Strategies?

From the perspectives of candidates and parties, winning elections is the main goal. But interest groups are focused on winning policy victories however they can obtain them, which might entail a longer strategy that integrates selected electoral interventions with other tactics. Battles between education policy groups help illustrate how specific elections might fit into broader group strategies. Education interest groups seek to change policies through whatever venues are available. That sometimes means lobbying a school board or state legislature, but it can also mean running an initiative campaign, endorsing candidates in a local or state race, or backing a national effort to influence Congress or a presidential administration.

A 2017 election for the Los Angeles School Board, for example, attracted more than $15 million in spending, with donors like former New York mayor Michael Bloomberg, Netflix CEO Reed Hastings, and heirs to the Walmart, Gap, and Apple fortunes facing off against national unions. The races served as a national proxy fight between education interest groups: proponents of district-level reform and charter schools (including Bloomberg and Hastings) supported one set of candidates, and their opponents (especially teachers' unions) supported an alternative slate. The charter-supporting candidates won their first majority on the board, defeating the incumbent school board president.

The battle over education reform often plays out within the Democratic Party, the primary home for both teachers' unions and many charter school enthusiasts, but the combatants have not limited themselves to (largely nonpartisan) school board elections. Mayors guide education policy in their cities, meaning that mayoral elections can sometimes determine the fate of school reform efforts.

Neither side restricts its fight to the local level, either. At the state level, interest groups in Washington state helped legalize charter schools via a 2012 ballot initiative campaign that gathered bipartisan support. And at the federal level, Betsy DeVos was nominated to serve as secretary of education by President Trump on the basis of her philanthropic and political donations on behalf of charter schools in Michigan and other states.

Two national-level interest groups exemplify the divide over education within the Democratic Party: Democrats for Education Reform, which often supports pro-charter candidates, and the Network for Public Education, which was founded by Diane Ravitch, an education historian who has become a leading charter school skeptic. The partisan politics of education became even stranger with the fight over the Common Core, a set of national education standards promoted by business groups, unions, and the Obama administration and adopted by nearly all states before becoming a lightning rod that attracted opposition from Tea Party Republicans, Ravitch, and those on the ideological left.

According to Ravitch and other critics, recent education reforms are the pet projects of billionaire philanthropists like DeVos and Bill Gates: they are using their resources to disrupt public education and impose their untested ideas. The reformers, in turn, say that teachers' unions have controlled local education policy making for too long, blocking competition and protecting bad teachers. In other words, both sets of interest groups claim to be fighting the special interests—they are willing to intervene in many types of election campaigns to change policies in their favor while decrying their opponents' efforts to do the same.

Evaluating Interest Groups

Interest groups are often labeled "special interests" by politicians and even citizens—suggesting that these groups are opposed to the broader public interest. Some interest group advertising is notoriously misleading, and interest groups cannot be held as accountable as candidates can for their deceptions. Interest groups do represent a diversity of perspectives, which helps to ensure that Americans from a variety of backgrounds have a voice. But they are most likely to represent constituencies that are wealthier and have more to gain from government policy, which tends to heighten inequalities in political influence.[16]

The independent role of interest groups can be especially important. Interest groups advance the democratic ideal of free speech, empowering individuals and organizations other than the candidates to express their opinions. They highlight some concerns from voters and advocate views other than those articulated by the candidates themselves. Interest groups help serve the standards of free choice, but they do not always contribute to the ideal of equality. They add voices to campaign deliberation, but they intend to persuade rather than inform voters.

Would we be better off without interest groups? There have been numerous attempts to limit interest group involvement in American campaigns, most prominently via campaign finance law. However, courts have invalidated some of these laws, arguing that interest groups deserve free speech protection because they advocate for the concerns of their supporters. Even if the courts had not ruled in this way, it seems unlikely that interest groups could be significantly weakened. There will always be incentives for advocates of a cause to band together and attempt to influence parties and candidates. In fact, this may benefit democracy: citizens have political views that they want to share with politicians, and interest groups help citizens get politicians' attention. Hillary Clinton was roundly booed in 2007 when she told an audience of liberal bloggers that "lobbyists, whether you like it or not, represent real Americans," citing associations of nurses and teachers.[17] But sometimes, that is true.

Interest group involvement in campaigns also raises some unique concerns. Candidates may feel beholden to interest groups that donate to them or advertise on their behalf. Regardless of whether these groups change election outcomes, politicians may exchange favors or moderate their positions to stay on the groups' good side. If candidates believe that one person is likely to donate millions in support of a single presidential campaign, for example, they may look for ways to impress that person. At a 2014 gathering in Las Vegas led by the late casino magnate Sheldon Adelson, potential 2016 presidential contenders were careful to emphasize their favorable views of military support for Israel and trade with China, two issues about which Adelson cared deeply. Perhaps the downsides of interest group campaigning will not show up in campaigns at all but in one-sided policies advanced by parties or candidates trying to curry interest groups' favor.

Conclusion

Citizens complain about the "special interests" they believe are corrupting campaigns. Candidates encourage their condemnation by christening their opponents as supporters of nefarious groups. But one person's special interest is another person's professional association, advocacy group, workplace, or church. Interest groups can help shift campaigns away from vacuous assessments of personality toward policy debates designed to solve people's problems.

Interest groups regularly donate to candidates, air advertisements, and mobilize their followers, and they are likely to play increasingly important roles in driving campaigns. Voters in competitive districts may see more ads from interest groups than from the candidates. Although many groups that lobby still steer clear of campaigns, changes in campaign finance law and regulation are enabling more groups to play in campaigns—including many groups created for that express purpose.

Some interest groups are extensions of the political parties: they not only raise similar concerns but also play similar roles in voter mobilization and education. Other groups play unique roles in driving ballot initiative campaigns, representing ethnic or religious constituencies, or making sure that the candidates address the issues they care about most. They all see elections as an important method, but not always the only method, of advancing their policy goals.

As interest groups continue to spend considerable sums on campaigns, some fear that candidates may lose control of their own messages. The experience so far suggests that interest group campaigning looks a lot like candidate campaigning. Where candidate and interest group goals diverge, we should expect some different emphases. However, because winning elections still requires convincing the same voters, no matter who is running the campaign, interest groups are subject to the same constraints as candidates in convincing voters to support their side.

KEY TERMS

interest group (p. 189)

constituencies (p. 195)

ballot initiative campaigns (p. 195)

campaign agenda (p. 203)

FOR DISCUSSION

1. Would American elections improve if interest groups left campaigning to the candidates? How would elections change if groups donated less to candidates or spent less directly in campaigns?

2. If you were working for an interest group, how would you suggest attempting to influence elections in your state? Would you provide money to candidate campaigns, work to mobilize your own membership, or seek to influence voters directly through an advertising campaign? What are the advantages and disadvantages of each approach?

3. Should interest groups act as adjuncts to the campaign, funding the same types of advertisements and voter contact efforts as candidates, or should they focus more on the issues that most concern them and target their resources on the voters most sympathetic to their specific positions? How would each strategy help advance interest group goals?

4. Is it best for voters to hear only directly from the candidates about their positions on the issues? Or do interest groups compel candidates to take clear positions and better inform voters about their views?

8

Media

In an outtake from a 2005 appearance on the entertainment news show *Access Hollywood*, Donald Trump was caught on tape bragging about his aggressive pursuit of sexual contact with women. While approaching the actress Arianne Zucker with cohost Billy Bush, Trump said:

> I better use some Tic Tacs just in case I start kissing her. You know, I'm automatically attracted to beautiful—I just start kissing them. It's like a magnet. Just kiss. I don't even wait. And when you're a star, they let you do it. You can do anything. . . . Grab 'em by the pussy. You can do anything.[1]

The video had not been widely seen until the *Washington Post* released it online on October 7, 2016—two days before Trump's second presidential debate with Hillary Clinton and one month before his Election Day victory.

Trump's comments garnered immediate condemnation from across the political spectrum. Many Republican governors and members of Congress called on Trump to withdraw from the campaign, and dozens publicly rescinded their support for him. The story dominated headlines, and the video aired thousands of times on television news. While Trump at first dismissed the comments as "locker room talk," claiming that Bill Clinton had "said far worse to [him] on the golf course," he released a video later that night, and acknowledged, "I said it. I was wrong. And I apologize."

The tape fit a common media narrative suggesting that Trump was lewd, sexist, and disrespectful. In a series of prior campaign events, Trump's comments had helped advance this story line: he accused Mexican immigrants of being "rapists," then senator John McCain of not being a war hero, journalist Megyn Kelly of having "blood coming out of her wherever," Senator Ted

Cruz's father of consulting with John F. Kennedy's assassin, and a federal judge of being unfair due to his Mexican ancestry. During the 2016 campaign, he also mocked a disabled reporter, asked Russia to hack Hillary Clinton's email account, and told his crowds to "knock the crap out of" protesters.[2] All of these incidents were widely believed to undermine Trump's presidential stature. And all were replayed over and over again as media sound bites.

Yet the coverage of these comments—even the *Access Hollywood* video— did not override most voters' initial views of Trump. Even though many women came forward to report sexual assault allegations against him, most Trump supporters dismissed the claims. Voters who already opposed Trump only found additional reasons to oppose him. By Election Day, many normally Republican voters who said they personally disliked Trump still voted for him, reporting that they disliked Clinton even more.

The media's coverage of the *Access Hollywood* video highlights important features of the news media's role in contemporary American campaigns. First, the media's interest illustrates their news values, or the criteria by which they judge stories to be newsworthy. In this case, this story had video of the candidate—an inside look at an unguarded moment—and fit with a preexisting narrative about Trump's debauchery. In 2008, reporters were similarly attracted to a video that many observers believed would be detrimental to then candidate Barack Obama: television stations played a series

---

Core of the Analysis

- The news media, regular communicators of information on current events designed to reach large audiences, typically seek to be objective but also work to generate stories that will interest their audience.

- Candidates seek to persuade the public by influencing news and social media content.

- The incentives of candidates and the news media often diverge, creating conflict between them, but candidates can take advantage of the news media's need for compelling stories.

- Media coverage can affect citizens, but its impact is often limited because those who pay the most attention are the least likely to change their minds.

- The news media do not always live up to democratic ideals, but citizens share some of the responsibility for the shortcomings in media coverage of campaigns and in their own online interactions with media content.

of remarks made by Obama's retired pastor Jeremiah Wright—which included the words "God damn America"—on a nearly nonstop loop. Most of the news media do not champion one candidate or party; instead, they seek out stories that they deem newsworthy.

Second, the media's coverage diverged sharply from what the implicated candidate, Donald Trump, wanted to discuss. Although candidates attempt to shape media coverage to benefit themselves, media outlets often pursue a different agenda. Reporters view their job as sharing useful information rather than passing along unfiltered campaign messages.

Third, candidates often feel forced to respond to media coverage no matter how much they would rather repeat their preferred message. Rather than ignore the media, candidates attempt to reshape media coverage. In the case of the *Access Hollywood* tapes, the Trump campaign first minimized the incident, then apologized, and then went on offense. Immediately before the presidential debate on October 9, Trump's team held a surprise press conference with four women who had accused Bill Clinton of sexual harassment or assault (and Hillary Clinton of silencing their accusations) and invited them to attend the debate. Since the media were going to be discussing Trump's attitudes and actions toward women, the Trump campaign wanted to elevate a similar negative story about the Clintons.

Fourth, despite the media's extensive coverage of the *Access Hollywood* episode, it is unclear whether the video or the accusations changed many votes. This lack of major impact reflects two key facts: many citizens do not pay close attention to politics in the news, and it is difficult to sway those who do pay attention, as they have already made up their minds. That's especially true in presidential elections in our nationalized and polarized era, when most voters have decided that one of the parties is better than the other and can find reasons to support that partisan side no matter who is running.

Fifth, the episode raises questions about whether the news media's role is conducive to democratic values. Aren't there more important issues than what Trump said over a decade ago before an entertainment program? Is showing dramatic video, which makes Americans watch more news, the best way to inform them?

In this chapter, we discuss the types of news media outlets and their audiences. We then describe how the economics of the news business shape the content of the news. We next consider how the news media, voters, and candidates interact, given their distinct motives. We then evaluate the degree to which news coverage affects public opinion, considering that the media's impact is constrained by people's interest in the news and their willingness to believe what they read, see, or hear. Finally, we examine how well the news media help campaigns meet democratic values.

Who Are the News Media?

Most people learn about political campaigns from the news media rather than from direct interaction with candidates. The **news media** include any regular communicators of information about current events to mass audiences. Most news media outlets communicate through text, video, websites, or social media channels. For people who consume news primarily online, news outlets appear mainly as brands—such as the *New York Times*, the Fox News Channel, or HuffPost—that publish stories that can be read on smartphones and shared on social media. But the historical distinctions between these news outlets—as a newspaper, a cable television channel, and an online-only outlet, for example—help drive and explain their current behavior and influence. Outlets also differ in their resources for news production and original reporting and the incentives they have to provide neutral coverage versus coverage that supports a particular political side.

Historically, the daily print newspaper was the primary source of news for most Americans. Newspaper stories today, whether online or in print, still provide regular and in-depth coverage of candidates, issues, and campaign events. Newspapers are still a popular source of information, especially for older Americans, but the audience for the printed product has been shrinking. In 2020, 24.3 million copies of print newspapers were distributed daily, compared with a peak of 63.3 million in 1984.[3] Newspapers' websites are among the most popular online news sources. The top American newspapers, the *Wall Street Journal*, the *New York Times*, and the *Washington Post*, each have more than 2 million paid online subscribers and generate more attention online than they do for their printed products.

With the predominance of online readers, the audience is ever more concentrated in those few national providers. Although monthly unique users of the top 50 newspaper websites were up to 13.9 million per month in 2020, online audiences still do not compensate economically for print subscription losses—especially at regional and local papers. Even if newspapers no longer dominate campaign news coverage, they are still a source of information for citizens, politicians, and journalists (especially at the local level) and often shape the coverage of other media outlets. But with fewer reporters, newspapers now cover less political news and offer less substantive reporting, leading to reduced political knowledge and participation as smaller audiences receive less information.[4]

The most popular source of news today remains television. Sixty-nine percent of Americans report sometimes watching local television news, and 40 percent report watching often. There are 393 stations carrying local news, and each runs 10 hours per week of live news coverage on average.[5] Although local news offers only limited campaign coverage—with sports and weather accounting for a large share of local broadcasts—it is still an important news source for older Americans. In most geographic areas, local television stations and newspapers are also the most common sources of local news online, including on social media, and are still the most trusted sources of news.[6]

National network television news audiences are also relatively large, though not as large as they once were. In 2020, the nightly news programs on ABC, CBS, and NBC together averaged 19.1 million live viewers—down from more than 40 million viewers in 1980. Morning news shows, such as NBC's *Today* and ABC's *Good Morning America*, averaged a total of 10.7 million daily viewers in 2020.[7] Network news coverage differs from written news content in its preference for stories with better visuals and less depth. The average **sound bite** from presidential candidates broadcast on television news is only nine seconds long.[8] Sunday news interview shows, such as *Meet the Press* and *Face the Nation*, total 8.2 million viewers per week; television newsmagazines, such as *60 Minutes* and *Dateline*, total 11.2 million. These shows also help drive coverage by other reporters.

Cable news offers hours of continuous coverage for people who are politically engaged. The average prime-time cable news audience reached nearly 6.5 million in 2020, with daytime audiences exceeding 4 million. Fox News Channel viewership dominates CNN and MSNBC viewership in each time period throughout the day. All three networks' ratings spiked dramatically in 2020 as viewers were drawn to coverage of the COVID-19 pandemic and the presidential election. In the evenings, cable news channels are dominated by commentary, with Fox News featuring conservative pundits and MSNBC featuring liberal pundits. Since viewers can watch endlessly, the cable audience is larger than the broadcast audience in terms of total minutes watched, but cable networks reach fewer people overall than network broadcasts do.

Radio news also serves a niche audience. The United States has nearly 1,500 commercial news or talk radio stations and 900 National Public Radio (NPR) member stations, the latter of which are partially funded by listeners. NPR's programming, including *Morning Edition* and *All Things Considered*, averages more than 26 million listeners per week.[9] (Because these numbers are weekly rather than daily and include people who listen only sporadically, they cannot be compared directly with the television audience estimates.) In 2021, the top political talk radio hosts—Sean Hannity, Mark Levin, and Glenn Beck—were all conservatives. NPR, by contrast, is known for in-depth coverage and longer interviews, and its audience is more liberal. Although radio listenership is down, podcast listening is up (especially among young people); 28 percent of Americans report that they listen to a podcast each week, with both traditional radio brands and online-only outlets competing for audience share.[10]

Shared videos, of course, are also popular online. In this arena, legacy media outlets compete with campaign-produced content and amateur videos for attention. Most shared videos are not news stories at all, but traditional news providers will both slice up their newscasts into shareable segments and produce content designed for online sharing.

Although online-only news outlets have become an important source of news, most campaign stories still originate from traditional news providers. Judging the impact of news outlets requires understanding how they affect other news outlets, including their role in the production of original news as it flows across media. The most popular news websites include those of NBC, CBS, CNN, the *Washington Post,* the *New York Times,* Fox News, and NPR, along with aggregators of traditional news stories like Yahoo News and MSN. A few online-only outlets, such as HuffPost and Buzzfeed, are as prominent online and on social media as the legacy outlets are. Across both types of outlets, the largest news sites collectively average 32.1 million unique visitors monthly, but the average visit only lasts two minutes.[11] Increasing shares of the online audience for both legacy media and online-only outlets are accessing news through smartphones and social media apps. Although most people access some news online, the time they spend consuming news can be fleeting compared to the time spent by television viewers.

Facebook, YouTube, and Twitter have become major sources of traffic for news sites. Most original political news stories that circulate on these platforms, especially about state or local campaigns, come from newspapers,[12] but the share of social media content that comes from other avowedly conservative and liberal sources is increasing. Candidates, of course, also use social media to directly communicate with supporters and to drive mainstream media coverage of their campaigns.

Because stories are usually shared on social media by one's friends, some online content can generate audiences even without a familiar branded provider. Sites designed to support particular candidates or parties can thus gain a broader audience. In 2016, misinformation websites—mostly supporting Donald Trump—constantly churned out false content made for sharing on Facebook, spreading conspiracy theories, and gaining audiences toward the end of the campaign. Indeed, social media sharing of conservative news content, only a minority of which was misinformation, was concentrated in a segregated network that was more cut off from mainstream sources than sharing on the liberal side.[13] But all that sharing may not have had much of an influence: visits to misinformation websites were highly concentrated among the most conservative audiences, who did not need to be persuaded to support Trump.[14] In fact, most of the negative news that voters heard about both presidential candidates that year came from traditional news coverage.

Americans under 30 are only half as likely as those over 60 to report that they generally follow the news, but they are much likelier to prefer reading online news to watching news on television.[15] Younger people are also more likely to share and receive news via social media. This does not mean that online news consumers are ignoring newspapers or television: they are often seeing the same stories in a redistributed format.[16] In 2021, 31 percent of Americans reported regularly getting news from Facebook, 22 percent from YouTube, 13 percent from Twitter, 11 percent from Instagram, 7 percent from Reddit, 6 percent from TikTok, and 4 percent from LinkedIn and Snapchat. These platforms' news audiences are mostly under 50 years old and more likely to be Democratic than Republican.[17]

When users see information on social media, they may not know where it originated or whether it was produced by a news outlet. Users do not always remember the sources of their news, including whether it was original reporting, repackaged commentary, or a stray rumor. And users may learn some political information without clicking on news at all. Americans make assumptions about their friends' political views based on what they share on social media—whether they post support for a brand or recirculate a celebrity statement—even without seeing explicitly political content. Facebook feeds can also make users assume the worst of their political opposition based on extreme examples of the other side's behavior.[18]

One of online politicos' biggest misconceptions is to assume that other people are paying attention to the same content they see. Some citizens follow news regularly and may read a newspaper, watch cable news, or share news stories online. But this is far from the norm: most Americans, when given the option, prefer sports and entertainment to news.[19] As Election Day approaches, citizens watch more news overall—but some watch obsessively. Americans who are news junkies tend to be stronger partisans and assume that others are as well. For politicians, this means it is hard to use news media to reach potential voters who are not already on their side. For news media outlets, this means their readers, listeners, and viewers comprise a minority of Americans who hold stronger views on politics. And unlike politicians trying to win over undecideds, the media have more incentives to cater to people who are already convinced—who will more readily click on their stories—than to reach those who are paying less attention.

Nationalization

Both American media coverage and consumption of news have become more nationalized over the last few decades. Because large state and local media operations became less sustainable as advertising and subscription revenues declined, in-depth reporting on state and local politics became less feasible. By choosing national outlets over local media, news audiences have reinforced this pattern: they have enhanced the business model for national coverage while further diminishing it for local coverage. To compete, local outlets also cover national politics—especially in politically competitive states. But the local angles they choose emphasize national personalities and stakes.[20]

As a result, Americans now know less about subnational politics—even the name of their state's governor—than they used to know, but they know more about national political actors and events. Because Americans have less information that they can use to differentiate their local politicians from national ones, they tend to vote increasingly along partisan lines based on their views of the president rather than the warm images they used to have of their local representatives.[21]

Political scientists have found ways to test the effects of media on the nationalization of elections. Some research has looked at Americans who live in one state but are in a different state's media market (meaning that they receive news originating in another state, usually because they live close to a state border).[22] Americans in this situation know little about their own state's candidates for governor and senator during an election year—and that makes them more likely to vote for the same party for all offices. It turns out that Americans as a whole are following the same trend: most people no longer rely on media in their own geographic area. The shift to reading, listening, and watching more news online has accelerated this pattern.

Government's Limited Oversight of the News Media

Constitutional doctrines and government policies affect the content of media coverage. The First Amendment's guarantee of a free press means that relatively few rules constrain the media. Given that Supreme Court interpretations of the First Amendment have allowed the media to publish stories about classified government programs, where the stakes are much higher than they are in political campaigns, the media can largely report on campaigns as they see fit.

The restrictions that do exist pertain mainly to broadcast radio and television, which includes the major networks (ABC, NBC, CBS, and Fox) and their affiliates but not cable television networks. The Federal Communications Commission (FCC) regulates broadcast radio and television because there is limited space on the broadcast spectrum—think of the FM radio dial, which has space only between 87.5 and 108.0 megahertz. The Supreme Court has ruled that this scarce spectrum provides a rationale for regulations on broadcasting but that newspapers cannot be subject to the same restrictions.

The FCC rule that is most relevant to political campaigns is the **right to equal time**. Stations with FCC licenses are required to provide "equal time" to all candidates for office. They cannot simply advertise on behalf of a favored candidate and ignore the others. This means that if a TV station sells time to a candidate who wants to air ads on that station, it must make the same opportunity available to all candidates for that office.

But important loopholes allow unequal time. Events such as news interviews, on-the-spot news events, and debates are exempt. Debate organizers, including representatives of the major parties and media companies, can thus exclude third-party candidates from debates without breaking the rule. The incumbent president, whether or not they are running for reelection, gets news coverage simply for doing their job.

Even when the right to equal time does apply, it does not require media outlets to broadcast significant coverage of campaigns. Television news outlets do not feel obligated to carry every gubernatorial, Senate, or House candidate debate; often, interested viewers have to watch these events online or on a public television channel.

Media regulation is much weaker in the United States than it is in other democratic countries. Because both parties and media outlets are largely unregulated, candidates have to pay for advertising and must generate coverage by drawing interested viewers. Many nations instead have strong and well-funded public media outlets and more requirements for private media companies that are covering campaigns. One consequence is that other countries tend to provide more free time for parties and candidates to speak directly to voters without the media interrupting.[23] The hands-off American approach extends to social media companies, which generally have to make their own decisions about whether to remove political messages or actors from their platforms. But with that freedom also comes a responsibility that they may not seek. For instance, social media companies had to decide on their own whether to restrict Trump's access to their platforms after his posts about the Capitol riot on January 6, 2021.

The Business of News and the Norm of Objectivity

The government's minimal restrictions on news media mean that outlets are free to base their decisions about coverage on other factors. News outlets face practical constraints of time, space, and personnel. They cannot cover every potentially newsworthy event and must make choices. Their choices are guided by both the profit motive of business and the professional norm of objectivity.

News as a Business

The economics of the news business demand that the news be profitable, first and foremost. Today, large corporations traded on public stock exchanges own many news outlets, and these firms do not have the same personal investment in the news product as the families that used to own most local newspapers once did. Corporations are not content to lose money maintaining a news operation simply for the satisfaction of creating a quality news product. Many news outlets are losing audience share, meaning that they have a reduced audience to sell to advertisers. Newspapers in particular are suffering. At one time, they generated substantial revenue from distributing advertising flyers with their print products and from running classified sections (unrelated to the news) used to sell goods or advertise jobs. When better options for classifieds became widely available online, newspapers' advertising revenue declined sharply—even among those papers that maintained the same readership.

FIGURE 8.1 Newspaper Advertising Revenue

In billions (2020 dollars)

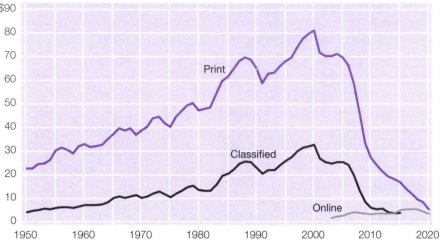

Source: Newspaper Association of America data, compiled by the Pew Research Center.

Newspapers also used to be the main platforms enabling local advertising, but now local targeting is widely available online. Most newspapers have not figured out a way to make nearly as much money from their online content as they did from their print editions (see Figure 8.1). Television outlets also make less money online, even when posting the same videos there that originally aired on TV. There are now better local advertising options available from platforms that know not only where you are but also who you are and what you like (such as Facebook) or what you are searching for at that moment (such as Google). And covering political campaigns is not cheap. The length of many American campaigns means that news outlets must commit significant resources if they want to provide continuous coverage.

One strategy that media outlets use to maintain viability in the face of these challenges is to cut their operating costs by eliminating reporting positions and other staff. Some newspapers, such as Denver's *Rocky Mountain News*, have closed outright, and others, such as the *Seattle Post-Intelligencer*, now publish only online editions. Other news outlets have closed news bureaus, reducing the number of reporters who are based in places outside of the outlet's hometown, and have reconsidered whether to send reporters along on the president's travels.[24] News outlets also have fewer staff dedicated to coverage of important state elections, which cannot deliver either local or national audiences.

A second strategy for economic success is raising revenue. News outlets, especially newspapers, increasingly charge for access to their news online. However, this strategy reduces the audience and encourages the outlets to cater their content even more to the super politically engaged. Free news outlets try to appeal to the broader public with stories that are laden with emotion, have stimulating visual images and clickable headlines, or are simply sensationalistic. This is nothing new, of course. As we discussed in Chapter 3, newspapers in the nineteenth century began to cover scandals, sports, crime, politics, and other stories in an often lurid way. But the continued rise of **infotainment**—a combination of informational and entertainment programming—is evident today. For example, nightly news broadcasts have increased their coverage of celebrities, athletes, and famous criminals and have decreased the fraction of important congressional votes that they cover.[25] It is easy to criticize the news media for this, but news consumers may also bear some responsibility. These decisions reflect careful monitoring of what the audience reads, watches, or hears. News outlets also pay close attention to what stories are shared on Facebook and Twitter, leading to a proliferation of news items in the form of funny lists, heartwarming stories, viral videos, and coverage of gaffes.

However, some news media organizations have established more highbrow outlets that are distinguished by their use of data, statistics, and background information to better explain the news. FiveThirtyEight, The Upshot, and Vox have emerged as part of this trend. These sites merge scholarly analysis from political science and other disciplines with traditional journalism and opinion columns, though much of their campaign content is focused on analyzing polling movements in real time. Most outlets may stick with funny videos, but political junkies can now consume even more polling data and analysis.

The Norm of Objectivity

Economic pressures are not the only influence on the contemporary news media. Most reporters, editors, and other news professionals subscribe to a set of norms that inform how they do their jobs. The most important norm is objectivity, but it was not always that way. The American print media were largely partisan until well into the twentieth century. Newspapers used to directly ally with political parties, which in turn helped to fund their costs of production. Some newspapers still retain "Democrat" or "Republican" in their titles, such as the *Arkansas Democrat-Gazette*, based in Little Rock, AR, and *The Republican*, in Springfield, MA.

The decline of the partisan press and the rise of objectivity came about partly because newspaper owners sought to build larger and broader audiences by producing news that would appeal to many different kinds of readers. They sent journalists to report on events firsthand by seeking out information and interviewing sources.

Journalists then began to see it as their job to report on events fairly and accurately, with appropriate attention paid to all sides of controversial issues. The norm of objectivity became codified in the guidelines of news organizations. For example, the code of the American Society of Newspaper Editors, which was founded in 1922, included a principle of "impartiality": "News reports should be free from opinion or bias of any kind." This principle was taught to aspiring journalists in newly founded journalism schools. Technology also enabled the spread of more objective journalism. The development of the telegraph in the 1830s led to the creation of **wire services** like the Associated Press, which produce content that is shared among news outlets. Wire services—named for the wires used to send messages via telegraph—allowed stories to be disseminated quickly to many outlets. A similar pattern evolved in radio and television news, where local stations chose to affiliate with national networks and reuse their news products.

An autonomous and impartial press also began to scrutinize the government and politicians more closely. Events such as the Vietnam War and the Watergate scandal weakened trust in political leaders and fueled the rise of investigative reporting. Some things that journalists knew about but did not report on— such as the extramarital affairs of Presidents Franklin Delano Roosevelt and John F. Kennedy—became fair game for later generations of journalists.

This talk of objectivity might seem dated to today's media consumers. After all, with the proliferation of cable news talk shows, is objective journalism a thing of the past? Since most reporters personally identify as liberals, conservatives are particularly likely to argue that their reporting cannot be fair. Because more negative messages about the media come from Republican politicians, conservatives are less likely to trust mainstream media, which for some further justifies only listening to conservative sources. But there is still a much larger audience for traditional news outlets, which generally strive to be ideologically neutral, than for outlets with an ideological or partisan agenda.

Reporters dedicated to appearing impartial are even sometimes criticized for "false balance"—that is, the tendency to treat statements from each candidate's campaign equally even when one side is clearly stretching the truth. This norm changed somewhat under President Trump; the *Washington Post*, for example, cataloged 30,573 false or misleading claims by Trump over his four years in office. In the eyes of reporters, this record justified a less evenhanded approach to covering Trump. That posture, in turn, temporarily raised trust in news media among Democrats.

But reporters usually seek to cover each side in debates between candidates and will try to avoid arbitrating between them or deciding who is right. This approach perhaps provides a disincentive for candidates to tell the truth, as the news media will repeat candidates' less honest statements in good faith alongside those of the opposition. Many commentators blamed the news media for helping to "normalize" Donald Trump's 2016 campaign for president (which they felt violated norms of civility) and for treating Hillary Clinton's scandals more seriously than those associated with Trump. Indeed, coverage of Clinton's use of a private email server while secretary of state and the ties between her family foundation and foreign countries exceeded coverage of any of Trump's scandals,[26] leading voters to report that they heard more about Clinton's emails than anything else related to her campaign. Meanwhile, Trump received coverage of his views on immigration and many other topics, though much of it was also negative.[27]

Despite the widespread norm of objectivity, openly ideological and partisan outlets are flourishing, as the audience growth for Fox News, MSNBC, and ideological websites suggests. While this strategy will not earn them the loyalty of the majority of news consumers—as many people are on the opposite side ideologically, and others prefer impartial news—it can earn them a niche audience that is sizable enough to produce revenue.

In sum, the rules and reality that affect the news media present something of a paradox. On the one hand, the government does relatively little to regulate the media, which gives them considerable discretion to write and publish what they wish. On the other hand, the news media face significant constraints of time and resources, even with the internet providing essentially infinite space for news. These conditions support an increasingly diverse media landscape, with most outlets continuing to observe the traditional norm of objectivity but other outlets pursuing a partisan or ideological agenda for a smaller but loyal audience. These constraints affect how the news media cover campaigns.

What Does the Media Cover, and How?

A top priority for most campaigns is to get the news media to cover their candidate and their message. This is often easier said than done. Campaigns vie with other candidates, other races, and the events of the day for the media's attention. Getting the media to communicate the campaign's message is partly a matter of skill and partly a matter of conditions and luck.

Which Races Get Covered?

In deciding which campaigns to cover, the media must allocate their limited resources while stimulating interest among their audience. The media are more likely to cover a campaign when the race is competitive because races in which one candidate cruises to easy victory rarely generate stories that the media consider newsworthy. Front-runners can campaign conservatively, never risking events where they might slip up and say something controversial. Challengers in these races, if there are any, most likely lack the resources to promote their candidacies or to draw unfavorable attention to the front-runners. If new polls are conducted and released, they show little change. In sum, nothing dramatic happens. Of course, uncompetitive races might become more competitive if voters learned about the challengers through news coverage.

The media are also more likely to cover a campaign when the office at stake has more authority. The national news media cover the presidential campaigns extensively as well as a few campaigns for governor and senator. They rarely cover campaigns for state legislature or local offices. To the extent that they cover congressional races, the national news media focus on the broader competition between Democrats and Republicans for majority control rather than on the particular candidates or issues in each race. Local media cover more state and local elections, but they also report on the presidential campaign and the battle for control of Congress.

Media outlets are more likely to cover a congressional race when more of their audience lives in the relevant congressional district and can vote in that election.[28] The media are also drawn to celebrity candidates, such as Trump and former California governor Arnold Schwarzenegger, and they are drawn to scandals, particularly if sex or money is involved. Reporters covered Anthony Weiner's long-shot bid for New York mayor in 2013 because he had resigned from Congress following the release of sexually suggestive photos he had sent to several female Twitter followers. He went on to place fifth in the Democratic primary but not before generating yet more news coverage: he admitted that—after apologizing for the earlier incidents—he had sent lurid pictures to yet another woman, this time under the pseudonym "Carlos Danger."

Which Aspects of Campaigns Get Covered?

Although newspapers typically run general profiles of candidates and campaigns, the vast majority of news is driven by events. What kinds of events do the media judge to be particularly newsworthy? We speak of their criteria for newsworthiness as **news values**.

The first and most important news value is *novelty*. The term *news* does contain the word *new*, after all. Typically, this means that the news follows what happened recently—that is, since the last edition, newscast, or online update. Candidates and their advisers know this, of course, so they organize a continuous stream of new events to gain the media's attention. Consider the events that take place before the actual campaign begins. Potential candidates coyly suggest that they might enter the race in order to generate speculation in the media. When a politician formally announces their candidacy, it is treated as news, even when it is a foregone conclusion that they will be running.

The media also value *personality*. Newsworthy stories often involve compelling people, and news audiences are presumed to be engaged by the "characters" in the campaign—whether they are good or bad. Reporters will repeatedly dwell on the biographies of candidates in an attempt to understand what they are "really like." There are stories about where the candidates grew up, whether they were popular in high school, and so on. Sometimes politicians go overboard trying to show their novel personalities: former Democratic senator from Louisiana Mary Landrieu received coverage after she assisted Louisiana State University students in keg stands at a football game (though she declined to partake herself).

Journalists even play amateur psychologists and look for evidence of candidates' personality traits in their words and deeds, especially for presidential candidates. Barack Obama was portrayed as intellectual and emotionally unflappable. John McCain was described as angry. Mitt Romney was regularly characterized as out of touch. Hillary Clinton was seen by journalists as overly guarded and insincere. Donald Trump was portrayed as a volatile playboy, and Joe Biden was seen as boring and forgetful. All of these characterizations may have some truth to them, and reporters try to document them with information from sources—although the sources are often described simply as "some" people or "observers" so that reporters do not appear to be passing judgment themselves.

Another news value in campaign coverage is *conflict*. It is easier to generate newsworthy stories when the candidates, their surrogates, the parties, interest groups, and other campaign actors are at each other's throats. (Fortunately, all of these actors often comply.) The media's emphasis on negativity is evident in how it portrays campaign advertisements: negative ads, especially ones with outlandish claims, are discussed to a far greater extent than positive ads are—even when positive ads are actually more numerous.[29] Candidates can sometimes get the media to cover negative ads simply by releasing them on YouTube without ever paying to air them on television. The media also focus on conflict within the Democratic and Republican parties, highlighting dissenters even when most party members agree.[30]

The media cover candidate debates or other joint appearances with a similar hope for conflict. When the candidates do not disagree, the event is less newsworthy, perhaps frustratingly so from the media's perspective. In February 2008, a presidential primary debate between Hillary Clinton and Barack Obama was billed as "fight night" on CNN. CNN commentator Jack Cafferty previewed the debate by saying: "Remember last week, the heated debate in South Carolina? Tonight could make that seem like a garden party." But Clinton and Obama, fearful that the South Carolina debate had been too rancorous, came out and played nice, much to the media's disappointment.

A fourth news value is *skepticism*. Today's professional journalists are trained to be dubious about the claims that politicians make, and perhaps for good reason. Thus, what candidates say is rarely taken at face value. At a minimum, the norm of objectivity encourages news outlets to engage in "he said, she said" journalism, pairing claims by one candidate with responses from the opponent. Reporters sometimes engage in fact-checking and evaluate candidates' claims in advertisements and elsewhere for their accuracy. Some news outlets have even created fact-checking websites; one prominent example is PolitiFact, which monitors politicians' statements and ranks them on a scale from "true" to "pants on fire."

Perhaps the preeminent focus of coverage across all campaigns, however, is *strategy*. This kind of campaign coverage is part of **horse race journalism**, which focuses on which candidate is ahead or behind, who is gaining or losing ground, and what the candidates are trying to do to win (i.e., their strategies), much the way the announcer at a horse race describes which horses are winning, surging, or faltering. A study of the 2016 general election found that 42 percent of presidential campaign coverage was about the horse race and only 10 percent dealt with policy issues. In coverage of the 2020 presidential election, 74 percent of Biden's coverage and 35 percent of Trump's coverage on one network was focused on the horse race. While the horse race was also a major focus of election coverage in 2008 and 2012, policy coverage was more prominent in these earlier campaigns.[31] Horse race coverage is appealing because there are many ways to determine who is ahead or behind: fundraising, endorsements, polls, the size of rallies, and so on. These indicators can be frequently updated as candidates release fundraising numbers or as media outlets field new polls, creating fresh grist for a story. Stories about undecided voters also generate horse race coverage, as these voters can be canvassed again and again to see if they have moved toward one candidate or another.

Similarly, candidate debates are scored in terms of who "won" or "lost." Television networks sometimes convene small groups of undecided voters to watch presidential debates and then interview them afterward. One experiment, however, showed that viewers' opinions of a debate were more influenced by the tone of the media's post-debate coverage than by the candidates' performance.[32] Both media pundits and voters largely judged Biden to be the winner of the two 2020 presidential debates—though that does not mean his performance earned him new votes. The 2020 debates were overshadowed by Trump's personal COVID diagnosis, which even canceled the second debate. (Mike Pence was judged the winner of the vice-presidential debate, but Trump still seemed displeased with his performance.)

Within the context of horse race coverage, the media's discussion of strategy allows them to engage in what is sometimes called **interpretive journalism**. Reporters do not simply report on what the candidates do and say—they provide further analysis and interpretation. That is, they attempt to tell their audience why the candidates are doing what they are doing and thereby reveal the candidates' underlying strategies. Trump's moves between the hospital and the White House for COVID-19 treatment gave the media an opportunity to narrate the importance of his statuesque stance, mask removal, and facial expression—all apparently designed to reassure his supporters. Journalists see their obligation as not just to narrate events but also to provide context. They draw on their perceived expertise to read between the lines and to help their audience understand what is "really going on." When Biden entered the race in 2019, reporters portrayed him as lacking support from his parties' most liberal voters and seeking to make the campaign a referendum on who was best equipped to face Trump.

Did News Values Help or Hurt Trump?

Before he announced his 2016 candidacy, Trump had toyed with running for president for decades. Oprah Winfrey asked him whether he would run in the 1980s. He ran a six-month exploratory campaign for the Reform Party's 2000 nomination, appearing at campaign events and on television programs. He almost jumped into the 2012 race and was the front-runner in several polls. Reporters initially suspected that Trump was engaged in publicity stunts to promote his television program—but he was still a good story.

When Trump eventually entered the 2016 presidential contest, he generated little support from Republican politicians or party leaders, but he did generate interest from the public. Reporters knew that interviews with Trump would generate high ratings.

Meanwhile, other candidates had to decide how to respond to Trump's sudden rise. Several candidates thought that public support for Trump would fade early, and they wanted to avoid offending him or his supporters. By the time opponents decided to take him seriously, Trump was completely dominating television news, debate performances, and polls. He came up with nicknames for his competitors for the Republican nomination, such as "little Marco" (for Marco Rubio) and "low-energy Jeb" (for Jeb Bush), eventually goading them into responding.

Reporters reacted to every Trump gaffe with more rounds of news cycle domination—and Trump knew how to generate attention with every tweet and every interview. Living by the adage that all publicity is good publicity, Trump was willing to insult and shock his way to more coverage than all of the other candidates combined. As he generated coverage, voters learned his stances on immigration and crime and heard his critiques of President Obama and the Washington establishment, giving him credit for positions shared by other candidates.

Even when reporters suspect that a candidate is not playing by the normal rules, they can rarely turn away from a spectacle. If politicians appeal to news values, they can take advantage of more coverage. Trump took this strategy to a whole new level and stimulated imitators in later state campaigns. But in retrospect, it looks like this strategy had its limits. The 2020 campaign followed nearly four years of mostly negative press coverage of Trump based on his statements and scandals in office—followed by a pandemic that dominated news in a way that even Trump could not match. By the time Trump was officially set to face off against Biden for the presidency, he was still generating a lot of attention, but most of it was very negative, cataloging how he was well behind in the polls and unable to stop the pandemic or the cratering economy. Coverage in 2020 also demonstrated reporters following news values, but it had a different result for Trump.

Is Campaign Coverage Biased?

The most frequent public criticism of campaign coverage is that it is ideologically biased. One version of this complaint singles out specific news outlets. Some of these complaints may have merit, as newspaper coverage tends to favor incumbent candidates that the newspaper supports on its editorial page.[33] Analyses that compare the word usage of Democratic and Republican members of Congress with that of news outlets also classify some outlets as more liberal and some as more conservative (that is, more closely matching the rhetoric of Democratic and Republican congresspeople, respectively).[34] But it is difficult to know whether this kind of bias simply reflects the preferences of media outlets' audiences. Any bias may be coming from the "demand side," which is based on what the audience wants, rather than the "supply side," which is based on what the news media provides. Some of the programming decisions on the more conservative Fox News and the more liberal MSNBC, for example, may be driven by the partisan biases of their audiences.

A broader complaint about bias targets all news outlets. Supporters on both sides commonly complain that "the media" as a whole favor someone other than their preferred candidate. But Republicans have long complained more about bias. President George H. W. Bush's 1992 campaign produced bumper stickers that said, "Annoy the Media: Re-Elect Bush!" Trump dramatically upped the ante on this strategy, repeatedly calling news stories he disliked "fake" and calling journalists "dishonest people" who "don't like our country." The long-term conservative challenge has reduced public confidence in the press, especially among Republicans, and has made it harder for citizens to learn facts from media coverage.[35]

Of course, it is easy to find examples of news coverage that seem more favorable to one candidate or the other, but it is difficult to prove that candidate coverage is consistently biased toward one party or ideology. Despite persistent claims, traditional news coverage is not reliably more favorable toward liberal or Democratic candidates. Although journalists tend to be more liberal than the general public, studies examining the actual content of coverage have found little evidence of consistent bias in either direction.[36] When political scientists study many elections rather than focusing on just a few, they find that news coverage is more positive toward some Republicans and some Democrats, with the tone of coverage more attributable to who is already holding office or who is gaining or losing ground in the polls.

Some news outlets, such as Fox News Channel and MSNBC, consistently favor one side's candidates, and often repeat their preferred candidates' messages.

In addition to news content, many media outlets produce editorials, commentary, and more opinionated pieces framed as "news analysis." Avowedly conservative or liberal outlets also produce and share news. Some outlets and programs focused on commentary, such as prime-time MSNBC or Fox News Channel coverage, are biased. They show up as more favorable toward one side's candidates, year after year.[37]

This is not to say that the media are not biased in other ways. News coverage tends to be more favorable to candidates who are ahead in the polls.

Reporters write stories about how the losing campaign is "in disarray" and "floundering" while they extol the strategic prowess of the winning campaign. This bias has been evident during recent presidential campaigns. In 2012, there were four negative stories about Mitt Romney for every positive story from late August to early October. Following Barack Obama's poor performance in the first presidential debate, however, coverage of Obama turned much more negative and coverage of Romney was more positive. In 2016, 77 percent of stories about Donald Trump's campaign were negative overall, but they became less negative in the final two weeks of the campaign when Trump gained ground; 64 percent of stories about Hillary Clinton were negative, but her coverage became even more negative in the final two weeks.[38]

Whatever their personal political preferences, reporters have an incentive to appear balanced while favoring dramatic coverage of the changing fortunes of each candidate. Outlets with clear liberal or conservative audiences have different incentives—to tell viewers what they want to hear— but even they tend to portray the drama of campaigns.

How Do Candidates and the News Media Interact?

Campaigns seek to influence news media coverage and to use the news media to reach potential voters. Candidates get attention by becoming the news and by getting reporters to cover them. Political consultants speak about "earned media" or "free media," meaning news coverage given to the candidates, as distinct from "paid media," or advertising. Candidates interact directly with the media in interviews, meetings with newspaper editorial boards, and press conferences. They hold public events and give speeches, and they invite reporters to attend. They issue press releases, report polling data, publish policy position papers, and announce endorsements. They also leak stories to selected reporters. Nearly everything a candidate does is designed to be picked up in the next day's newspaper, that night's television broadcast, the next hour's website update, or the next minute's tweet.

Candidates want every interaction with the news media to be on their terms. They seek to control when and where interactions take place, whom they interact with, and what they talk about. Candidates fearful of negative news coverage sometimes limit their interactions with reporters by eschewing interviews or press conferences. Campaigns sometimes take further steps to ensure that rallies and speeches lead to good media coverage—for example, by screening the attendees to guarantee that only cheering supporters, and not jeering opponents, are in the audience.

Campaigns' media strategies can help reporters do their jobs. The media want to tell their audience how day-to-day events might affect election outcomes, and campaigns strive to provide something eventful every day. The media are also always looking for a good story, preferably one with drama and conflict. The candidates are often only too happy to provide scandalous tidbits of information about each other.

But there are fundamental conflicts between the agendas of candidates and the news media. Candidates may schedule new events every day, but the content of those events is often repetitive because candidates want to present a consistent message. The audience at any given speech will not have heard it—in fact, the candidate will have just flown into their town an hour before. But the reporters who traveled with the candidate on that plane have been to dozens of towns and heard the speech dozens of times. The day-to-day routine of a campaign does not usually satisfy the media's desire for fresh story lines every day. Rallies with supporters rarely supply the sort of drama and conflict that the media want. If everybody is cheering for the candidate, nobody is arguing.

Trump's innovation in 2016—whether accidental or intended—was to constantly supply news through outlandish remarks and made-for-television events. Even his rallies were dramatic, as they provoked protests and occasional fistfights. He often went off script in freewheeling comments attacking opponents and reporters. The cost of such antics is that the stories they produce often highlight how a candidate is out of control or unprepared to hold office. But they did gain an audience: cable news networks often carried Trump's speeches live (in anticipation of the next outrage), which enabled him to spread his message more widely. Although live coverage of Trump rallies was not as overwhelming in 2020, Trump still dominated coverage over Biden.

The national party conventions are staid events that are always covered but usually have trouble generating much news. The media have long complained that live coverage of the conventions is not newsworthy. In 1996, ABC News anchor Ted Koppel actually left the Republican convention midway through the proceedings, declaring, "This convention is more of an infomercial than a news event. Nothing surprising has happened; nothing surprising is anticipated."[39] From the perspective of the parties, this is what is supposed to happen. Parties would like the media to report that conflict is limited and that the party has a consistent message—but this does not make for much of a news story. Both 2016 conventions gave the media more of what they wanted (to the detriment of the candidates). Supporters of Bernie Sanders's candidacy for the Democratic presidential nomination protested throughout the convention, with some even interrupting speeches and pledging to defect to third parties. At the Republican convention, Senator Ted Cruz refused to endorse Trump from the stage, arguing that his supporters should "vote their conscience" and provoking crowd-wide boos. The dissent distracted from the candidates' messages but made for good television. In 2020, both parties switched to virtual conventions that generated less viewership and coverage, though Trump and Pence did speak to smaller live audiences at picturesque locations and Biden spoke to supporters in their cars. Reporters covered the novelty of these conventions, but the changed format made the live events look like stunts and further emphasized the context of the deadly COVID-19 pandemic.

Perhaps the most fundamental conflict between reporters and campaign organizations is that reporters do not want to simply deliver the candidate's message. For example, although candidates spend most of their speeches talking, even if vaguely, about their policy agendas and goals, the media often talk about the horse race, especially when polls suggest that the race is becoming more competitive.[40] Even when journalists and commentators focus on what the candidates are talking about, they typically subject the candidates' messages to their own analysis.

Newsworthy events such as the COVID-19 pandemic also drive the news media's agenda and force candidates to respond accordingly. Reporters also follow up on the story lines developed by other reporters or commentators. This is the phenomenon of **pack journalism**. Reporters who cover campaigns tend to travel together, talk to each other, and read each other's stories. Because they fear missing an important story, they tend to converge on similar ideas and themes. On a day-to-day basis, even MSNBC and Fox News generally highlight the same campaign events and candidate statements.

Sometimes candidates try to ingratiate themselves with reporters—becoming part of the pack. In *Journeys with George*, a documentary about George W. Bush's 2000 presidential campaign, Bush is depicted playing games with the reporters covering him. He gives them nicknames, spends time in their section of the plane, and attempts to make friends with many of them. He even kisses the cheek of the movie's producer, who happens to be the daughter of Representative Nancy Pelosi (D-Calif.). But Bush's relations with the news media were sometimes frostier. At one campaign event, he was overheard telling his running mate Dick Cheney, "There's Adam Clymer—major league asshole—from the *New York Times*." This contradictory behavior reflects the tension in the reporter-candidate relationship: they both need to stay on good terms with one another, but they have differing goals and incentives.

The Effects of Media Coverage on Citizens

Campaigns seek to influence media coverage because they believe it will influence what the public thinks about the candidates and thus will affect the election's outcome. But the media cannot easily move public opinion, and the effects of media coverage are often not that dramatic.

Many people fear that partisan media outlets, in particular, are contributing to political polarization, but evidence on this point is mixed.[41] In experiments, some consumers do gravitate to news sources associated with their own partisan slant, but others seek information from both sides. Most MSNBC viewers watch some Fox News, though the most dedicated Fox viewers rarely watch a full MSNBC or CNN program.[42] Cable news watchers also tend to watch local news, which usually lacks an ideological or partisan slant. A study of web browsing found that ideological and partisan segregation in online media is limited in comparison with segregation in face-to-face interactions: conservative Republicans talk mostly in person to others who already share their views, but they visit a mix of liberal and conservative websites (and vice versa).[43] Most Americans have ideologically moderate or mixed media diets, with overlap between most Democrats' and Republicans' online media consumption. Yet most viewership and readership comes from a small group of partisans who repeatedly visit ideologically slanted websites, which skews the audience for online news.[44]

However, the evidence is building that Fox News has contributed to both polarization and Republican electoral gains. Researchers have long known that Fox News viewers tend to skew conservative and Republican, but that fact alone was not enough to conclude that the channel changed voters' attitudes (while also moving rightward): its viewers may have instead been attracted to the network because of their prior partisanship and ideology. Recent studies have used external factors that influence viewing, such as the geographic availability of the channel or its position on the dial (because lower numbered channels are watched more), to enable better causal inferences. They show that easier access to Fox News was associated with increased Republican voting, while MSNBC had no effect on Democratic voting, in part because of its much lower viewership.[45]

These studies are surprising because it is difficult for information presented by the media to *persuade* people to change their opinions. As news coverage of a candidate becomes more favorable, one might expect the public's view of that candidate to become more favorable as well. But this is not so common, for two reasons. First, many people do not follow politics very closely. They are unlikely to read, see, or hear much about political campaigns, and thus their opinions about the candidates, if they have any, will not change.

Second, among those who do follow politics, relatively few people are undecided about political candidates, especially at higher levels of office. Instead, these people tend to interpret information from the news media in ways that support the choice they have already made.[46] People are motivated reasoners, meaning that they are emotionally invested in a desired conclusion; they learn, recall, and interpret information in a biased fashion to make it more consistent with their prior views.

Because of this, media coverage more commonly strengthens or *reinforces* people's preexisting views. This happens not so much because people deliberately ignore contrary news. Instead, people simply interpret information in ways that confirm what they already think. Supporters of two different candidates who see a news report on the campaign will each see yet more reasons to support their favored candidate and oppose the other. Even a news report that is highly unfavorable to a particular candidate is unlikely to change the opinions of that candidate's supporters. People have an impressive ability to ignore, rationalize, or argue against information that is contrary to their views.[47] They will find reasons to dispute such a report or dismiss its importance.

Persuasion is thus more common when people do not have strong preexisting opinions and are more susceptible to new information. Primaries, especially those for lower-level offices, offer a good example of this type of situation. When voters are choosing among candidates from the same party, whether voters are Democrats or Republicans themselves does not help them make a choice. Moreover, many primary candidates are not familiar figures, and so voters may not know much about them. Under these conditions, media coverage can affect opinions. Even in recent presidential primaries, public support suddenly increased for several different flavor-of-the-month candidates following favorable media coverage associated with the sort of novel or dramatic event that attracts media attention, such as the speeches and debate performances by Democratic candidates Pete Buttigieg and Kamala Harris in 2020. That media coverage eventually gained the candidate more scrutiny, which reduced their public support.[48]

Although the media are often less effective at persuasion—or changing what people think—they are more effective at changing what people think *about*. This role is called **agenda setting**. The idea is simple: the more the media report on something, the more the public regards it as important. If the media talk a lot about health care, citizens are more likely to cite health care as an issue of concern. People who are randomly assigned in experiments to view newscasts with several stories about a given issue will believe that issue to be more important than will people who watch newscasts that include no stories about the issue.[49] The 2016 election cycle saw heightened media coverage of the candidates' positions on immigration and trade, increasing the salience of those issues among voters. In 2020, the COVID-19 pandemic dominated the news.

Related to agenda setting is a process called **priming**. The media influence, or "prime," the criteria that citizens use to judge candidates due to the degree of emphasis issues receive, even if the media are not explicitly telling the public to make judgments in this manner. For example, the more reporters discuss an ongoing war, the more the public will judge the president for their performance on the war, even if reporters do not explicitly credit or blame the president for the war. In 2016, the continuous focus on Donald Trump's negative comments about immigrants and women—in both news reports and Hillary Clinton's campaign ads—helped make voters' attitudes toward those groups a more significant factor in their voting decisions. But priming can also occur even when media reports do not mention the candidates in the context of an issue; more COVID-19 pandemic coverage, for example, may have increased viewers' association between the disease and judgments of the president.

Finally, the news media affect citizens by *informing*. News coverage of campaigns can help citizens learn relevant facts about the candidates, including candidates' biographies and issue positions. As campaigns attract more media coverage, citizens are more likely to recognize and recall the names of the candidates and to identify the issues that the candidates are discussing.[50]

None of these effects are mutually exclusive. The information conveyed in the news media could simultaneously educate people about a candidate's position on an issue (informing), make them feel that the issue is an important problem (agenda setting), and lead them to draw on that issue when deciding whom to vote for (priming). Candidates' attempts to influence news media coverage, if they are successful, might also have multiple concurrent effects.

Yet there are inherent limits to how much the media can influence opinions. Many people avoid politics. Others have well-defined viewpoints that are unlikely to change. Since the rise of cable television and the internet, Americans who do not want to watch news have been able to choose from an increasing array of nonpolitical programming. With more channels, most people can avoid the news. The result is an increasingly divided electorate, where some people pay attention to news, learn about politics, and participate in political activities, while the rest of the population tunes out most of the time.[51]

Evaluating the News Media's Role in Campaigns

How well do the news media uphold the democratic ideals of free choice, equality, and deliberation by which we might judge political campaigns? In some ways, the media support the standard of free choice because media coverage helps citizens learn who the candidates are and what they stand for—information that allows them to make informed choices when they cast their votes. But news coverage is not created with education in mind: it is designed by companies trying to maximize the attention of audiences coveted by advertisers. As a result, most campaigns receive little attention from the news media. For those that do get attention, media coverage often emphasizes what is new, dramatic, or scandalous. Unlike the candidates themselves, the news media—or at least those outlets that strive for objectivity—are not seeking to manipulate citizens into voting for particular candidates. Instead, they are seeking to build and maintain an audience. If juicy revelations surrounding a candidate's divorce emerge, then the media will report on them regardless of whether it is the most important information for citizens to learn.

We can also ask whether news media contribute to information equality. There is always the potential for information in the news media to reach a wide and diverse audience, but this rarely happens—usually only when a big story breaks and receives nonstop coverage by multiple outlets. More often, the many channels and websites available to consumers encourage segmentation, with political junkies getting their fill of campaign news and most other people watching entertainment and sports programming. This information inequality reflects and may reinforce a broader economic inequality: people with lower incomes and education levels are less likely to see political news.

A third standard is deliberation. In a large democracy, deliberation must be mediated: Americans cannot all talk to one another or to the candidates face-to-face. Thus, it is up to the media to convey information that clarifies the views of each side. The media's interest in conflict means that they will often report on the differences among the candidates. At times they play referee, intervening as if moderating a debate, investigating the claims that candidates make, and helping citizens understand what the candidates are saying and whether it is truthful. The prevalence of online misinformation raises concerns about whether traditional objective news can still dominate public knowledge, especially if voters would rather seek out and circulate positive news about their candidate and negative news about their candidate's opponent without considering the credibility of the sources they share. In 2016, one rumor that Hillary Clinton's campaign was running a pedophilia ring out of a pizza parlor actually led one man to show up and fire his rifle in the restaurant. Although these conspiracy theories can lead to disastrous results even if they are narrowly circulated, scholars have found that traditional news coverage still dominates campaign information. Larger impacts arise when candidates promote the conspiracy theories and tie a belief in them to partisanship.

There is mixed evidence that the media facilitate person-to-person deliberation among citizens. Social networks have the potential to allow millions of people to communicate and respond to one another's views. Yet partisans may often be speaking mainly to one another, with disinterested citizens opting out of the conversation. Online communities can still promote involvement in campaigns: large experiments on Facebook found that users who saw that their friends had reported voting were themselves a bit more likely to turn out to vote.[52] But there is also evidence that offering token public support for a cause on Facebook or Twitter may make one less likely to be involved in offline campaign activities.[53]

Commentators raise other ethical concerns about media coverage. Some argue that the media are too adversarial and thus too quick to criticize candidates or seize on any hint of scandal, no matter how minor.[54] Some fear that negative media coverage of campaigns has made people more cynical about politics generally.[55] Others accuse the media of trying too hard to be evenhanded, either by treating each candidate's scandals as equivalent or by reporting each side's accusations about the other even if the facts behind their claims do not warrant equal alarm. In a democracy, we also need the news media to hold candidates accountable, and many media outlets see this as one of their roles. So critical coverage of candidates may be necessary, but it is often in the eye of the beholder where accountability ends and cynicism begins.

Furthermore, blaming the media for the campaign coverage we see gets us only so far. Studies in which people are given a variety of information about candidates, including their biographies, their views on issues, their strategies, and their horse race positions, show that people gravitate to the stories about polls and strategy—precisely the kinds of topics that the news media are so often criticized for emphasizing.[56] In fact, people who pay a lot of attention to politics, and are thus likely to be regular readers of the news, are more likely to read these kinds of stories. Thus, the news media's focus on campaign strategy and the horse race may simply give consumers the information they want. This is what we would expect when news organizations need to maintain and build an audience in order to sell advertising. It is not always easy to tell how much blame media outlets and their consumers each deserve.

Conclusion

The media play important roles in communicating information about campaigns, determining the issues discussed in them, and shaping the images that voters develop of each candidate. The frenzy surrounding the video of Donald Trump's remarks on the set of *Access Hollywood* illustrates how the news media cover campaigns as well as the potential for and the limits to their influence on voters. The attention to the video reflected the news values of journalists and how the news media's agenda may diverge from candidates' agendas. Candidates cannot avoid interacting with the media because it is an important way in which they speak to the public. The episode also shows us how difficult it is for the news media to affect public opinion. When the video appeared, those paying attention to politics had already formed opinions of Trump and Hillary Clinton, and its revelation did little to change them. News coverage of political campaigns often implies that campaign events have a powerful impact on the public. But although the media do help determine the issue content of campaigns and the criteria by which candidates are judged, their effect on the political attitudes of Americans is much more limited. By Election Day 2016—and certainly by 2020—reporters, candidates, and voters had all moved on to other concerns and mostly forgotten the tapes that had initially captivated them.

Four years later, as votes were tallied in the 2020 election, Americans watched the returns on television networks and read analyses from reporters for clues on who was likely to emerge victorious. Despite Americans' frequent claims to distrust media sources, most waited for the clarity provided by all major television networks projecting Joe Biden's victory four days after Election Day. Biden supporters immediately took to the streets to celebrate.

With political news competing for attention with announcements from friends and celebrity gossip in our social media feeds, it may seem that the news media have lost control of political information. Today, viral videos of unknown origin can make news alongside traditional reporting. But reporting on major campaign events, still predominantly carried out by institutions designed in a previous era, accounts for the major narratives of contemporary campaigns. Even voters who never subscribe to a newspaper or watch television news are still affected by the practices of the organizations developed to print and broadcast news. Wherever voters receive their information, the collective judgments of news media about who and what to cover and how to present the stakes of the campaign represent a key source of voter information.

At their best, the news media can uphold the ideals we would like political campaigns to embody. Journalists can convey messages from candidates while also serving as watchdogs. News coverage can contrast the views of the parties, correct untruths, and direct attention to important issues and to the candidates' strengths and weaknesses. At the same time, the coverage also focuses on sideshows and horse race trivia while ignoring the bigger picture—a fact that must be blamed not only on the news media themselves but also on the citizens who consume news.

KEY TERMS

news media (p. 211)

sound bite (p. 212)

right to equal time (p. 216)

infotainment (p. 219)

wire services (p. 220)

news values (p. 223)

horse race journalism (p. 224)

interpretive journalism (p. 225)

pack journalism (p. 231)

agenda setting (p. 233)

priming (p. 234)

FOR DISCUSSION

1. Who is more responsible for the weaknesses of campaign coverage in the American news media: reporters or consumers?

2. If you were starting a news site about campaigns in your state, what would you cover? How would you generate an audience? Would the need to build your audience change the types of stories that you covered?

3. How should the media have covered the release of the Trump *Access Hollywood* video? Could they have ignored it? Was it a legitimate campaign issue? Should they have returned to it in 2020?

4. With Trump as a model, are any changes likely to occur in how candidates interact with the media? How much did the media change its behavior in response to Trump?

9

Presidential Campaigns

During the last weekend of the 2016 presidential election campaign, it seemed to many that Donald Trump and his running mate, Governor Mike Pence of Indiana, were engaged in a desperate attempt to transform an electoral map that had turned against them. On Friday, Trump gave a speech in Reno, Nevada, where early voting totals showed Democratic nominee Hillary Clinton with a commanding lead. Later that day, he held a rally in Denver, Colorado, where Clinton and her campaign were so confident they would win that they had pulled their television ads in early September. On Saturday, Trump campaigned in Virginia, a state where polls showed Clinton up by double digits. He also visited Minnesota, a state that has been reliably Democratic since the Great Depression. Meanwhile, Clinton seemed to be expanding her list of targeted states, visiting the traditional Republican stronghold of Arizona and keeping the pressure on in Iowa and Ohio, nonessential states where Trump's polling numbers were relatively rosy.

But there were signs that Trump's strategy was more savvy than chaotic. On Saturday, at the same time as Trump's rally in Minnesota, Pence held a major event in Wisconsin alongside then Speaker of the House Paul Ryan and GOP Senate candidate Ron Johnson. Later that Saturday and throughout Sunday and Monday, both Trump and Pence made multiple appearances in Michigan and Pennsylvania, long regarded as essential (and safe) bricks in the Democrats' "Blue Wall"—states that had gone Democratic in every presidential election from 1992 through 2012. These visits were a hot ticket locally, and they garnered tremendous regional television and newspaper coverage. The late activities of the Clinton team seemed to validate the notion that the vote in these upper Midwest states might be very

close. Clinton added last-minute stops in Michigan and Pennsylvania on Monday, the day before the election. Clinton's running mate, Tim Kaine of Virginia, spent part of Sunday stumping in Wisconsin. Clinton's campaign even had President Barack Obama and the first lady campaign in Ann Arbor and Detroit on Monday afternoon and evening. As the votes were tallied, it became clear that the Trump campaign's late flurry of activity was justified: Trump defeated Clinton by a mere 44,000 votes in Pennsylvania, 22,000 votes in Wisconsin, and 10,000 votes in Michigan. Many commentators, as well as some Democrats, argued that Clinton's campaign had blown the election by ignoring telltale signs and neglecting states that proved to be decisive.

It is far from clear, however, that personal appearances in Pennsylvania, Wisconsin, and Michigan won Trump and Pence these three states.[1] In fact, it is far from clear that Trump's campaign itinerary was more prescient than Clinton's. After all, he did spend considerable time in states that Clinton carried, such as Colorado, Nevada, New Hampshire, and Virginia. And his late-October forays into Minnesota and New Mexico did little to help his standing in either of those long-shot states. Furthermore, Clinton did not ignore the upper Midwest states that ultimately proved her undoing; between Labor Day and Election Day, she made 14 appearances in Michigan, Pennsylvania, and Wisconsin, while Kaine made 18. Still, the Democrats' decision to attempt to expand the map and the Republicans' decision to continue their

Core of the Analysis

- Presidential candidates have two goals: to secure their party's nomination and to win a majority of electoral college votes.

- Electoral rules structure the presidential nomination process, and as candidates campaign for their party's nomination, they encounter a variety of election formats in different states.

- Nominating conventions may provide significant boosts to the presidential candidates, as can events that occur later in the campaign.

- The electoral college structures the general-election campaign, and candidates target particular states in order to win a majority of electoral votes.

- Political reality—including the state of the economy—influences presidential elections.

In November 2016, Republican vice-presidential candidate Mike Pence (center) campaigned in Wisconsin with Speaker of the House Paul Ryan (second from left) and Senate candidate Ron Johnson (second from right). This last-minute trip may have increased support for the Republican ticket among key constituencies.

efforts in the upper Midwest illustrate the strategic choices that animate modern presidential campaigns. And in close elections, these strategic choices might be critical.

In the 2020 presidential election, strategic decisions about where to campaign were subordinate to the larger strategic decision about whether to hold in-person events at all, given the public health implications of staging rallies during a global pandemic. Joe Biden's campaign eschewed almost all in-person activity in favor of virtual town halls and other online events. Trump's campaign continued a robust set of public rallies—mostly outdoors—until the president was sidelined with COVID-19 himself in early October. As in 2016, the candidates made important specific strategic decisions about where and how to campaign—Biden's allocation of critical advertising resources in the previously deep-red states of Georgia and Arizona is the most obvious example. But the broader posture of the presidential campaigns toward personal appearances was the main strategic consideration. Although Trump hit the campaign trail again in late October and early November and attracted sizable crowds in battleground states, it is difficult to argue that Biden was hurt by staying mostly on the sidelines.

The statement that these strategic choices *"might* be critical" reflects skepticism about the extent to which presidential campaigns affect election outcomes.[2] This is not to say that presidential campaigns do not matter. Rather, research suggests that campaigns reinforce citizens' underlying partisan loyalties and raise the salience of other fundamental factors that affect who gets elected, such as the state of the economy.[3] But campaigns do not necessarily decide who wins; broader political and economic realities may be more significant. Put another way, just because certain campaign strategies are correlated with victory does not mean that they *cause* victory.

In this chapter, we explain how presidential campaigns act strategically to maximize the chances that their candidate will win the White House. Two institutional arrangements, in particular, affect the development of campaign strategy. First, campaigns must consider the series of statewide nominating contests—primaries and caucuses—during the first five months of every presidential election year. Second, they must reckon with the electoral college. In this system, electors cast the deciding ballots for president, and the electors are allocated among candidates largely on the basis of winner-take-all statewide popular vote outcomes. Both arrangements demonstrate how electoral rules affect campaign strategy. Maximizing a candidate's prospects for victory also means acknowledging the political reality of a given presidential election cycle. Candidates are likely to pursue different strategies depending on whether the economy is strong or weak, whether the country is at war or peace, and which party holds the White House.

We begin our exploration of presidential campaigns by examining their basic goals. We then turn to the three major stages of presidential elections—the nomination contest, the national convention, and the general election—taking care to consider the important rules and broader realities that affect strategy at each stage. We also discuss the effects of conventions and debates on public opinion. We conclude by considering how well modern presidential campaigns serve American democracy.

Goals of Presidential Campaigns

Candidates must achieve two goals in order to win the White House. The first goal is to win a party's nomination for president—that is, to amass a sufficient number of delegates to secure victory at a party's national nominating convention. Most convention delegates (roughly 80 percent) are chosen in statewide primary elections, caucuses, and county or state party conventions. Of these selection methods, primary elections are the most common.

The second goal is to win enough states in the general election to collect at least 270—a majority—of the 538 available electoral college votes and thus win the presidency. Note that the goal is *not* to win a majority of the popular vote; this is usually necessary to claim enough states to win 270 electoral votes, but not always. There have been five presidents who lost the popular vote but still won the election: John Quincy Adams (1824), Rutherford B. Hayes (1876), Benjamin Harrison (1888), George W. Bush (2000), and Trump (2016). There is even some evidence that John F. Kennedy lost the popular vote in 1960.[4]

The problem is that these two goals can be somewhat incompatible. To win the nomination, a candidate must win the votes of a plurality of partisans. But partisans, whether Republican or Democrat, might be different from the average voter in the general election. For example, primary voters, who are generally more ideologically extreme than general-election voters, incentivize candidates to move away from the political center during primary and caucus season in order to cater to ideologues and win the nomination before turning back toward the center to win the election.[5] (This is related to the median voter theorem introduced in Chapter 5. More will be said about this and the broader spatial theory of voting in Chapter 13.) Some recent candidates have sought to avoid the inconsistency of following up strident partisan appeals during the primaries with more inclusive, moderate policy appeals during the general election. George W. Bush (2000), Hillary Clinton (2008 and 2016), and Biden (2020) were careful not to embrace nomination-stage strategies that were inconsistent with their longer-term plans for the general election. But this strategy is risky, too: appealing to more centrist general-election voters can alienate hard-core partisans who play a major role in primaries and caucuses.

Winning the Nomination

Before the convention and the general-election campaign, presidential candidates have several important tasks to accomplish. We focus on two of the most important: contesting the party's primaries and caucuses and selecting a vice-presidential candidate to be their running mate.

Primaries and Caucuses

In Chapters 3 and 6, we discussed how the political parties no longer directly control the presidential nominating process. Some research shows that party officials and donors remain important gatekeepers and that their endorsements matter to voters and to the overall outcome.[6] But the days of party elites meeting behind closed doors in smoke-filled rooms to pick the nominee are long gone.[7] As a consequence, individual candidates must campaign state by state to win state-level primary elections and party caucuses. These elections determine who the state party will send to represent the state at the national party nominating convention. These representatives are called **delegates**. To win the nomination at the national party convention, a candidate has to accumulate delegates by winning an array of statewide elections, each with distinct rules, over a period of several months. This makes four different kinds of rules important: how states structure these elections, how delegates are allocated to candidates, how delegates are selected to attend the national convention, and the order in which states hold their elections.

States typically employ either caucuses or primary elections to determine who their delegates will be. **Caucuses** are relatively closed affairs in which registered partisans attend meetings at election precinct locations and vote to select delegates to the county or state party conventions. Typically, these delegates are "pledged" to support a particular presidential candidate at the next level. The actual delegates to the national convention are then selected at the state convention. To be successful in a caucus state, a candidate must have a committed group of followers and an organization that can deliver these followers to the caucus locations. The first contests of the presidential nomination process are the Iowa caucuses.[8]

More commonly, states use some form of **primary election** to choose their delegates to the national convention. The form of the primary election affects the kinds of voters who can participate. As we discussed in Chapter 2, primaries can be closed, open, or semi-closed. In closed primaries, only registered partisans can vote. That is, only registered Democrats can vote in the Democratic primary, and only registered Republicans can vote in the Republican primary. In open primaries, voters can choose the primary in which they will vote, regardless of their party, but they may vote only in one party's primary.[9] In semi-closed primaries, both unaffiliated voters and those registered as members of a party can vote in that party's primary—so, for example, registered Republicans and independents may vote in the Republican primary. Therefore, depending on the type of primary, the electorates may be more or less ideological. For instance, a socially conservative

Senator Bernie Sanders won the New Hampshire primary during the 2020 Democratic primaries. The New Hampshire primary is typically the second contest after the Iowa caucus.

candidate who appeals to the Republican base might stand a better chance in a closed-primary state than in an open-primary state in which independents and Democrats are allowed to vote. However, recent research finds minimal variation in the electorate across different types of primary systems.[10] Still, it remains the conventional wisdom among many pundits and practitioners that rules allowing independent voters to participate could help moderate candidates. The first primary of the presidential election year, in New Hampshire, is a semi-closed primary.

Most states allocate delegates in proportion to the percentage of the vote won by each candidate in the primary or caucuses. It is important to note that a candidate usually must reach a threshold—often 15 percent of the vote—before earning a proportional allocation of delegates. Candidates not reaching this threshold do not receive any delegates. Under this system, a candidate with 40 percent of the vote in a state's primary gets 40 percent of the delegates from that state. The Democratic Party requires states to use a proportionality rule for delegate allocation. In the Republican nomination process, some states have historically used a winner-take-all rule, allocating all delegates from the state to the winning candidate regardless of the vote margin. In recent election years, the Republican side has begun to phase out these winner-take-all rules, and more and more states are adopting a proportional process.

To select individual delegates, some states (such as New York) directly vote for the delegates, others (such as California) allow the candidates to select as many delegates as they are entitled to on the basis of the primary or caucus results, and still others (such as Texas) allow delegates to pledge themselves to candidates and then stand for election at the state convention. In the past, these different arrangements affected what a campaign could do to maximize the number of delegates it could obtain. But in recent years, the national parties have standardized these selection procedures so that such maneuvering is much less possible.

In addition to the delegates selected through these competitive statewide nomination contests, roughly one-fifth of delegates to the national nominating conventions achieve that status because they are officeholders or occupy certain positions within the party. These are referred to as *unpledged* delegates (by the Democrats) or *unbound* delegates (by the Republicans) and often have not pledged to support any particular candidate based on a statewide vote.[11] They are commonly free agents who must be persuaded, one by one, by the candidate and campaign. Vermont senator Bernie Sanders's 2016 campaign worked long and hard to convince unpledged delegates to ignore Hillary Clinton's edge in pledged delegates and to vote for him at the convention. In the end, however, unpledged delegates sided with Clinton. After the election, Sanders's supporters on the Unity Reform Commission—a group established by the Democratic National Committee to reform the nomination system—weakened the number and power of the unpledged delegates for 2020.[12]

State-level nomination contests occur in a sequence, with some states' primaries or caucuses held as early as February and others as late as June. The influence of the early contests—especially the Iowa caucuses and the New Hampshire and South Carolina primaries—is generally seen as disproportionate to the actual number of delegates from those states. This is because their results are seen by both the news media and citizens as conveying important information about the **viability** of the candidates, or their chances of winning the nomination.[13] Because choosing between candidates is often complex and may require more resources than some are willing or able to invest, the news media and citizens seek ways to simplify the choice, especially when many candidates are running for a party's nomination. The early races thus serve to narrow the field, as some candidates inevitably drop out after their performance in Iowa, New Hampshire, or South Carolina indicates that they have no chance of winning the nomination.

For instance, at the beginning of 2020, 13 Democrats were seeking their party's nomination; shortly after the March 17 primaries, only two remained: Biden and Sanders. Because the early contests are so important, state legislatures have an incentive to schedule their primaries and caucuses earlier in the calendar so that they will exert greater influence on the nominating process, a trend known as **front-loading**.[14] The national party organizations, aware that a system in which all states hold early primaries might propel a charismatic but still relatively unknown and flawed candidate to win the nomination, have discouraged front-loading in order to provide additional time for citizens to learn about the candidates. The Republican National Committee (RNC), for example, adopted a "preferred" calendar for 2016 with no primaries or caucuses scheduled before February 1, and it specified that states jumping to the front of the calendar must use a proportional allocation method (which minimizes the delegate totals for a "winning" candidate as compared with a winner-take-all system). The RNC's preferences were somewhat realized, although state legislatures remain the ultimate authorities on election rules and dates.

Taken together, these features of the presidential nominating process have important implications for campaign strategy. Candidates face a demanding task. They must develop a campaign organization that can compete in a rapid-fire sequence of contests with different eligible voters and different rules: the precinct caucuses in Iowa, the semi-closed primary election in New Hampshire a week later, the county caucuses in Nevada 10 days after that, the open primary election in South Carolina one or two weeks after that, and then the numerous primaries (including California, Texas, Georgia, and Virginia) that mark "Super Tuesday." It is a significant test that requires money, attention from news media, and the support of at least some people within the party organization.

Thus, the first strategic decision we discussed in Chapter 5—whether to run in the first place—entails a calculation about whether candidates can muster the resources needed to compete. Candidates must ask themselves whether they can raise the money necessary to assemble campaign organizations across the many states holding nominating contests. If they cannot, then they must answer a different question: whether they can convince enough voters in one of the early states to support them, thereby earning greater attention and ensuring that they remain relevant in subsequent contests. At this early stage of the election season, some lesser-known candidates craft issue-based or ideological appeals and hammer their message home, hoping to attract wider attention.[15] For example, in 2020 Massachusetts senator Elizabeth Warren presented an array of specific proposals designed to curb the power of Wall Street and reduce income inequality. By doing so, she hoped to appeal to progressive voters and distinguish herself from Bernie Sanders, a self-proclaimed democratic socialist. Warren generated enough support and attention early on to sustain her campaign through Super Tuesday.

National conventions used to be the setting in which the party's presidential and vice-presidential nominees were selected. Today, the nominees are almost always determined in advance of the convention through primary elections and caucuses, as was the case for Joe Biden and Kamala Harris in 2020.

For candidates who do run, subsequent decisions will depend on their level of prominence. **Front-runners**—candidates who are well-known by the electorate, are in (or very near) the lead in the polls, and have substantial campaign war chests—must decide how much time and money to spend in the early states, since some of them are small and have fewer delegates than the large states whose primaries fall on Super Tuesday and later in the calendar. Hillary Clinton's campaign in 2008 emphasized the early contests in Iowa and New Hampshire, which was a controversial strategy. She could have ignored Iowa, for example, which may have minimized the significance of an upset victory by Barack Obama or John Edwards, who both campaigned and organized tirelessly in the state. But ignoring Iowa would have raised questions about her front-runner status: Was she afraid of losing? How dominant was she really? By contrast, Biden was considered a likely nominee, if not the front-runner, in 2020; he also campaigned in the early contests in Iowa, New Hampshire, and Nevada, but he downplayed his chances and was aided by the fact that different candidates won each of those states (South Bend, Indiana, mayor Pete Buttigieg narrowly carried Iowa, while Sanders narrowly carried New Hampshire and went on to dominate in Nevada). Instead, Biden went all-in in South Carolina, and his victory there legitimized the earlier presumption that he was a formidable candidate.

Lesser-known candidates face a different strategic challenge: Which of the early contests are the most promising targets for pulling off an upset and thereby generating important publicity for the campaign? Surpassing low expectations and thereby triggering favorable media coverage generates momentum. Candidates with momentum can build on early victories to win later primaries and ultimately the nomination. Candidates who benefited from momentum include Jimmy Carter in 1976, George H. W. Bush in 1980, Gary Hart in 1984, John McCain in 2000, Howard Dean in 2004, Barack Obama in 2008, and Bernie Sanders and Ted Cruz in 2016. Only one of these candidates won the nomination, however, illustrating that early victories are usually not enough.

For all intents and purposes, a nominating contest is over when one candidate has earned a sufficient number of delegates to claim a majority at the convention. Oftentimes, the race is called by the news media, or even the candidates themselves, who update their delegate counts after every contest. Although the result is not official until the **roll-call vote** at the convention, there is pressure on the other candidates to drop out and rally behind the expected winner after the outcome begins to look clear. This was the case for the Democrats after the 2020 South Carolina primary; Biden's win there left him hundreds of pledged delegates short of the number necessary for nomination, yet Pete Buttigieg and Minnesota senator Amy Klobuchar suspended their campaigns the next morning and endorsed the former vice president. They clearly believed that they no longer had a pathway to victory and that Biden was the likely nominee.

Choosing a Running Mate

After the nominations are clinched, the presidential campaign enters the preconvention phase. An important part of this phase is the selection of the vice-presidential nominees. Even though little evidence shows that the prospective vice presidents have any direct effect on the outcome of the general election, these decisions drive media coverage before and during the convention.[16] There are at least five strategic options for the vice-presidential pick. The first is to select someone whose knowledge and expertise compensate for the shortcomings of the presidential candidate. In 2008, Obama, a first-term senator from Illinois with almost no foreign policy experience, selected Biden, a six-term senator who had served as chairman of the Foreign Relations Committee. In 2000, Texas governor George W. Bush also sought to bolster his ticket's foreign policy credentials by selecting former defense secretary Dick Cheney.[17] In 2016, Trump's selection of Pence, a former U.S. representative and a member of the Foreign Affairs Committee, was likewise seen as an effort to help him on foreign policy issues.

A second option is to choose someone who can help the candidate carry a state or region. For example, John F. Kennedy's selection of Texas senator Lyndon Johnson in 1960 probably helped win the state for the Democrats. Many believe that Hillary Clinton's choice of Tim Kaine in 2016 was made in part to lock down the state of Virginia, where Kaine had served as governor, for the Democrats. Some even thought it would help her compete in the neighboring battleground state of North Carolina. More generally, presidential nominees often select running mates from large states, like Texas, where there are more electoral votes in play.

A third option is to select someone from a political or demographic group whose support the candidate needs. In 2012, Mitt Romney was viewed unenthusiastically by conservatives because of his support for health care reform in Massachusetts and his formerly pro-choice position on abortion. To win over conservatives, he selected Wisconsin representative Paul Ryan, who had designed the House Republicans' aggressive deficit-reduction plan. Many observers believe that Trump's selection of Pence was designed to help him among Republicans who doubted the New York mogul's commitment to conservative Republican principles. And Biden's selection of Harris in 2020 was widely seen as an attempt to increase enthusiasm for the Democratic ticket among African American and female voters.

A fourth option is to select someone to heal intraparty wounds. In 1980, Ronald Reagan reached out to his chief rival from the primaries, George H. W. Bush. In 1976, Gerald Ford almost asked Reagan to be his running mate, even though the two had just come off a bruising struggle for the nomination. In 2008, many Democrats urged Obama to ask Hillary Clinton to join the ticket despite their nomination fight. In the end, however, both Ford and Obama saw more downside than upside to this strategy.

Finally, a fifth option would be to select someone who reinforces the presidential candidate's image. Although it may seem counterintuitive, the vice-presidential selection need not always be about shoring up weaknesses. In 1992, Bill Clinton asked Tennessee senator Al Gore to be his running mate. Both were young, white, and southern. But Clinton's campaign strategists saw the virtue of reinforcing their candidate's image via a new, fresh face.

Presidential candidates must also decide when to announce their choice of a running mate. Announcing several weeks before the convention maximizes the time that both the presidential and vice-presidential nominees are on the trail and ensures two media "hits" (the announcement plus the convention). In contrast, announcing the pick right before the convention helps to maximize the convention's impact. In recent years, major-party candidates have typically opted for the second strategy.

The National Conventions

The Republican and Democratic national conventions mark the formal transition from the nominating process to the general-election campaign, even though the general election is always the ultimate goal as the nominating contest unfolds. Today's system of primaries, caucuses, and national conventions is quite different from the nominating process in decades past. Until the 1970s, the political parties exercised a great deal of control over presidential nominations, and the conventions were deliberative meetings at which party officials and state delegates bargained and cut deals to arrive at a consensus choice for the nomination. But the role of political caucuses and primaries, which had been slowly building over the course of the twentieth century, became decisive following rule changes made before the 1972 election cycle. These rule changes—most notably those mandated by the Democrats' McGovern–Fraser Commission—were aimed at increasing the say of rank-and-file partisans in determining the presidential nominees. As a result, the Republican and Democratic nominees are now typically known well in advance of the national conventions, and delegate totals are easily calculated based on primary outcomes, caucus results, and the commitments of unelected delegates. Today's conventions have transformed from determinative political events into four-day public-relations spectacles during which the nominees present themselves and their policies to the American electorate.

Conventions as Showcase Events

Those running presidential campaigns consider the major parties' nominating conventions premier opportunities to define their candidates and offer compelling narratives heading into the general election. Indeed, given the opportunity to drive political story lines and target important voting groups, campaign strategists would like to control the timing and the location of the conventions.[18] Unfortunately for the candidates, the parties choose the location well in advance of the actual campaign, after a selective bidding process. Parties also set the timing in advance. Traditionally, the party that is not in power (the "out-party") holds its convention first, and sometimes there is a significant gap between the two conventions. For example, in 1992, seven weeks separated the conventions: the Democrats held theirs in mid-July and the Republicans held theirs in late August. More recently, both parties have attempted to hold their conventions as late as possible—after the Summer Olympics but before Labor Day—in order to maximize television audiences and the presumed impact of coverage on voters.

Campaign strategists have three goals at the convention: tell voters what the past four years have been about, identify how the current candidates are different, and offer a vision for the country. Most conventions thus begin with a narrative of what has happened over the past four years. Speakers at the out-party convention talk about what has gone wrong and why there is a need for change. Speakers at the incumbent party's convention talk about what has been successfully accomplished and how it occurred. These contrasting narratives are usually conveyed by well-known politicians on Monday and Tuesday nights of the convention week. Then conventions tend to focus on the contrasts between the candidates, with convention speakers describing the choice before the nation: What are the stakes and options the party faces? What would the party's candidate do, and how does that differ from how the opposing candidate would act? This is usually accomplished in the vice-presidential nominee's Wednesday speech. Last, the party and its candidate offer a vision for the future: Where is the country headed, and how will it get there? This is the goal of the presidential nominee's speech on Thursday night. The 2020 conventions followed this general form, even though both were held mostly online due to COVID-19 public health concerns and protocols.

Convention Effects

Do conventions actually affect what the public thinks of the two candidates? They certainly seem to, although the magnitude of these effects appears to have decreased in recent years. Still, each party's nominee appears to garner additional support from the public after the convention. This is commonly referred to as the **convention bump (or convention bounce)**.[19] More precisely, the convention bump is defined as the candidate's share of the two-party vote in trial-heat polls conducted one to seven days after the convention minus their share of the two-party vote in polls conducted one to seven days before the convention. Since 1972, the average convention bump has been about 5 points, as measured by polling data from Gallup and other reputable national

FIGURE 9.1 National Convention Bounces, 1972–2020

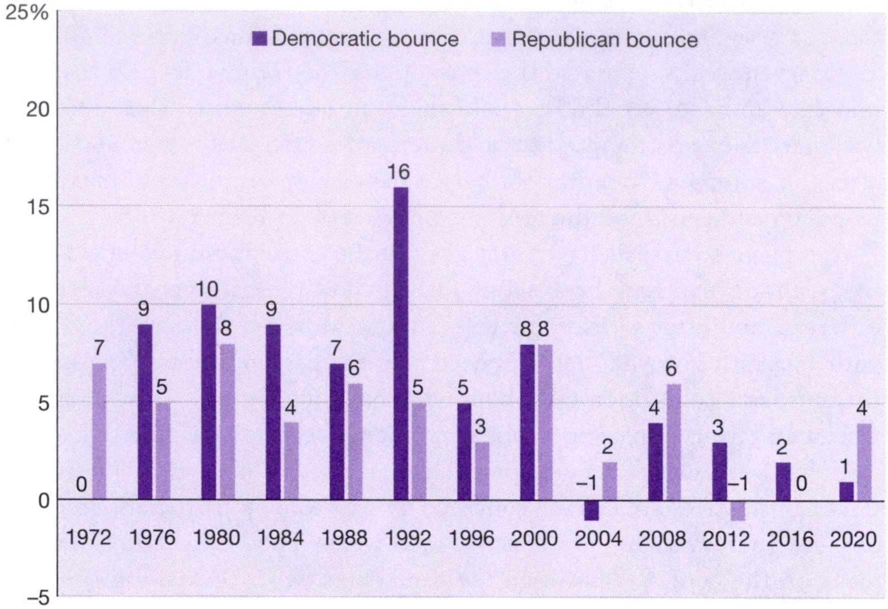

Source: Calculated by the authors using the margin between the major-party candidates' share of the two-party vote from the national polls most immediately before and after the national conventions. For 1972–2012, data are from Gallup. For 2016–20, we rely on an aggregation of the five national probability samples conducted most immediately before and then most immediately after the conventions.

surveys (see Figure 9.1). From 2008–20, it has been about 2.5 points. As we will see, conventions have tended to have larger effects than other presidential campaign events, such as the debates. Political scientists believe that convention effects are often larger for two main reasons. First, conventions occur relatively early in the general-election campaign, when there are a larger number of citizens who are undecided or only weakly committed to a candidate. There is thus a greater potential for persuasion. Later in the campaign, with fewer undecided voters, events serve mainly to reinforce preexisting opinions about the candidates. Second, conventions produce news stories that tend to be favorable to the candidate being nominated, which is what the convention hoopla is designed to do. This effect is amplified by the fact that the candidate from the opposition party is likely to campaign less vigorously during this period, knowing that it is not easy to compete with the speeches and images of the other party's convention.

Of course, not all convention bumps are equal. Bill Clinton's 1992 convention stands out as the most effective since 1972, although it was due mostly to an unusual occurrence: on the last day of the Democratic convention, Ross

Perot, who had run as an independent candidate, dropped out of the race, thus leaving his supporters, about one-third of likely voters, looking for a new candidate to support. More often, the size of the convention bump depends on how well the candidate is doing given prevailing political realities, such as the state of the economy and approval of the incumbent president.[20] Candidates who are favored by these realities but are underperforming in the polls for other reasons will tend to get a larger bump—in part because convention messages often include messages about the economy and the incumbent president. The Democratic and Republican conventions of 2020 were, of course, highly unusual. The Democratic convention in Milwaukee, Wisconsin, was almost entirely virtual, while the Republicans shifted most of their convention from Charlotte, North Carolina, to Jacksonville, Florida, because Florida permitted them to have (limited) crowds for a few speeches. Yet Biden and Trump both received small bumps in the polls, and Biden came out with a lead of approximately 6 points.

However, some political scientists believe that convention bounces—especially those associated with recent elections—are both minimal and ephemeral. Political scientists Doug Rivers and Ben Lauderdale argue that the surge in support for a candidate after a convention is mostly a function of "response bias" in polls. That is, supporters of the other candidate are less likely to agree to take a poll during this time, inflating the estimated support for the candidate whose convention just concluded. This response bias fades after 10 days or so, leaving the race roughly where it was before the convention.[21] Other political scientists point to reduced news media coverage of the conventions as well as the hyperpartisanship of today's politics, which leaves relatively fewer voters available for persuasion today compared with 20 years ago.[22] On the plus side, conventions nowadays showcase party change and diversity, allow rising stars to become known, and honor losing (but important) candidates from the nominating season. The consensus among both academics and practitioners is that conventions remain important campaign events but are rarely game changers.

The General Election

After the convention balloons have popped and the confetti has been swept up, the presidential candidates and their running mates hit the campaign trail, followed by a gaggle of reporters. At the same time, the campaigns blanket the airwaves with radio and television advertisements. But the states and media markets where the candidates travel and broadcast advertisements are not chosen at random. Moreover, candidates assiduously court some citizens more than others. Understanding contemporary presidential campaigning requires an understanding of the rules and reality that govern it. The resulting system, though often criticized, has positive as well as negative implications for democratic values.

The Electoral College

The strategic context of the general election is dominated by the institutional reality of the electoral college. According to Article II of the Constitution, each state has a number of electoral votes equal to its total number of representatives to the U.S. Congress—that is, its members in the House plus its two senators. The passage of the Twenty-Third Amendment gave the District of Columbia three electoral votes. In sum, there are 538 electors (based on 435 House members plus 100 senators plus three electors from Washington, D.C.). Most states use a winner-take-all rule in assigning electoral college votes to candidates: the candidate with the most votes in the state gets all of the state's electoral votes. This is a matter of state law, however, and Maine and Nebraska allocate two votes based on the statewide vote and then allow vote totals in the congressional districts to determine their remaining electors. As noted earlier, candidates' strategic goal is to win some combination of states whose electoral votes total at least 270.

Despite its longevity, the electoral college is controversial. One criticism involves the method used to determine each state's number of electoral votes. The formula—a state's total number of representatives plus its total number of senators—was derived to secure the support of small states in the fight over the ratification of the Constitution, and it creates a bias in favor of those smaller states. For example, Wyoming has one elector for every 195,167 residents, while California has one for every 713,637. However, some argue that the electoral college actually benefits large states because carrying large states by tiny margins creates an electoral college windfall due to the winner-take-all rule. For example, Obama won 62 percent of the electoral vote in 2012 despite getting only 51 percent of the popular vote.

Another criticism is that the electoral college benefits Republican candidates. This is a relatively recent development. From 1980–2012, neither party had a consistent electoral college advantage. But in 2016 and then again in 2020, the Republican advantage was significantly larger.[23] One reason is that the battleground states that determine the electoral college outcome tend to be more Republican than the nation as a whole. Another reason is that

Democrats often carry populous, deep-blue states like California, New York, and Illinois by large margins. In the parlance of social scientists, the relative geographic concentration of the Democratic vote means it is "inefficiently distributed."

Concerns about these issues have led to various attempts for reform. For instance, a group called National Popular Vote has called for state legislatures to commit their state's electoral votes to the candidate who receives the most popular votes nationwide. These bills would take effect only when enough states passed them to represent a majority of electoral votes—that is, sufficient votes to elect a president. As of 2021, 15 states (plus Washington, D.C.) have passed such bills into law; combined, these states are worth 195 electoral votes, or 36 percent of the electoral college and 72 percent of the 270 votes needed to give the compact the force of law.[24] The laws would in effect create a system in which the president wins by a plurality of the popular vote. There is majority support for the direct election of the president; according to a 2021 Pew Research Center poll, 55 percent of people favor direct election and 43 percent favor keeping the current system. However, opinion varies considerably by partisan affiliation; 71 percent of Democrats prefer direct election whereas 63 percent of Republicans prefer the electoral college.[25] These differences are perhaps unsurprising given the controversies over the 2000 and 2016 presidential elections, when some questioned the legitimacy of George W. Bush's and Trump's victories after both lost the popular vote. Of course, the reforms manifest in the National Popular Vote movement are also designed to circumvent the difficulties in actually amending the Constitution to replace the electoral college with another system. Still, at this point in time, National Popular Vote bills seem unlikely to pass in enough states to affect presidential elections in the near future.

Recent Trends in Electoral College Outcomes To win enough electoral votes to capture the presidency, presidential candidates must understand the partisan complexion of individual states. Some states tend to produce close presidential elections, while others are predictably Republican or Democratic. Furthermore, some states are more likely than others to swing between parties in different presidential elections. Figure 9.2 shows how states might be categorized based on presidential elections from 2000 to 2020, with states that voted the same way every time ("base states") distinguished from those that produced mixed results ("battleground states"). Despite concerns about a Republican bias to the electoral college, in purely numerical terms, the Democrats start off with a slight advantage because they dominate heavily populated states such as California, New York, New

FIGURE 9.2 Presidential Election Results, 2000–20

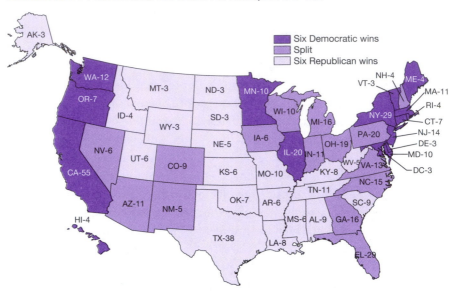

Note: 2020 electoral votes are presented after the state abbreviations.

Jersey, and Illinois. More generally, since 2000, Democratic candidates have dominated in the Northeast and on the Pacific Coast, while Republican candidates have dominated in the South and Mountain West, creating what analysts call the "Republican L."

The outcomes of recent elections have thus hinged on the results in a handful of states. As shown in Figure 9.2, 35 states (and Washington, D.C.) voted for the same party in presidential elections from 2000 to 2020, while 15 states did not: Arizona, Colorado, Florida, Georgia, Indiana, Iowa, Michigan, Nevada, New Hampshire, New Mexico, North Carolina, Ohio, Pennsylvania, Virginia, and Wisconsin. These **battleground (or swing) states** combined for 191 electoral votes in 2020, and when they have disproportionately favored a single candidate, as they did Obama in 2008, they provide that candidate with a comfortable margin of victory. Other states are sometimes considered battleground states by campaign experts even though they have consistently (but narrowly) favored one party or the other. Although knowledgeable people may differ with respect to which states they consider battleground states, the main point is that battleground states are targeted in presidential campaigns.

The decennial U.S. census can change the playing field. As mandated by the Constitution, House seats, and therefore electoral votes, are reapportioned

TABLE 9.1 Electoral Vote Change Based on the 2020 Census

Safe Democratic States	Battleground States	Safe Republican States
California (−1)	Florida (+1)	Montana (+1)
Colorado (+1)	Michigan (−1)	Texas (+2)
Illinois (−1)	N. Carolina (+1)	W. Virginia (−1)
New York (−1)	Ohio (−1)	
Oregon (+1)	Pennsylvania (−1)	
Overall (−1)	Overall (−1)	Overall (+2)

according to changes in state populations after each census. Reapportionment based on the 2020 census cost states that were safely Democratic in 2020 a net loss of one House seat, and it dealt reliably Republican states a net gain of two seats. In the 2024 elections, this will result in a loss of one electoral vote for the Democrats and a gain of two electoral votes for the Republicans (see Table 9.1). This may not help Democratic candidates in the 2024 election and beyond, but it might not hurt them very much either. In 2020, for example, Biden would have won by a healthy margin even with the post-2020 allocation of electoral votes.

Strategic Impact of the Electoral College We have emphasized how rules affect campaign strategy, and presidential campaigns offer an obvious example. In particular, the electoral college affects how and where candidates campaign. Presidential campaigns begin with a list of targeted states that they must win to reach 270 electoral votes. Whether (and how much) to campaign depends not only on how competitive a state is and whether it is critical to achieving 270 votes but also on the relative cost of campaigning in that state compared with other target states. Thus, candidates concentrate their television ads and in-person visits on the most cost-effective states and media markets on their list.[26]

Despite limitations on travel and gatherings due to the pandemic, in 2020 both the Biden and Trump campaigns focused on television advertising and visits to states thought to be critical to the election outcome. Trump spent 60 percent of his total advertising budget, an estimated $97 million, on ads in 10 media markets that his campaign deemed crucial. Biden spent approximately

TABLE 9.2 Biden/Harris and Trump/Pence Television Ad Airings: Top 10 Media Markets

Biden/Harris		Trump/Pence	
Market	Advertising (in millions of dollars)	Market	Advertising (in millions of dollars)
Phoenix, AZ	$20.62	Phoenix, AZ	$8.12
Philadelphia, PA	$14.69	Tampa, FL	$7.88
Orlando, FL	$13.17	Miami–Ft. Lauderdale, FL	$7.34
Miami–Ft. Lauderdale, FL	$11.47	Orlando, FL	$7.11
Detroit, MI	$9.62	Charlotte, NC	$6.25
Tampa, FL	$8.82	Atlanta, GA	$5.51
Charlotte, NC	$7.73	Detroit, MI	$4.81
Pittsburgh, PA	$7.35	Philadelphia, PA	$4.39
Harrisburg, PA	$6.53	Raleigh, NC	$3.63
Raleigh, NC	$6.04	Tucson, AZ	$2.80

Source: Data are from Advertising Advantage and cover television ads from September 1, 2020, through November 3, 2020.

50 percent of his total television advertising budget, an estimated $211 million, on his top 10 markets (Table 9.2). Their personal appearances were also concentrated on battleground states, with the top five most-visited states receiving nearly 70 percent of all campaign visits (Table 9.3). Furthermore, visits to nonbattleground states were typically tied to fundraising events.

In 2020, Biden and Democratic groups raised and spent more money than Trump and Republican groups did. Indeed, the data show that while Trump made more personal appearances during the campaign (77 distinct events) than Biden did (51 distinct events), Biden and the Democratic Party vastly outspent Trump and the Republicans on television advertising. This disadvantage made it imperative for Trump to deploy his resources as strategically as possible. Conversely, Biden's advantage allowed him to advertise in places normally considered out of reach for Democratic

TABLE 9.3 Biden/Harris and Trump/Pence Appearances: Top Five States

Biden/Harris		Trump/Pence	
State	Appearances	State	Appearances
Pennsylvania	22	Pennsylvania	15
Florida	12	North Carolina	14
Michigan	11	Florida	14
Ohio	8	Michigan	12
North Carolina	7	Arizona/Wisconsin	10
Total (All states)	88	Total (All states)	116

Source: For the Republican ticket, data are from the White House daily schedule. For the Democratic ticket, data are from the campaign's website, *New York Times*, *Washington Post*, and Associated Press. Notes: Candidate appearances include all events, including fundraisers, from September 1, 2020, to November 3, 2020.

candidates, such as Arizona, Georgia, and even Texas—two of which he managed to swing.

Although all presidential campaigns target battleground states, they differ in how ambitious their targeting is. Some campaigns, such as George H. W. Bush's 1988 and Hillary Clinton's 2016 campaigns, play "offense" by targeting a number of states that usually vote for the other party. Other campaigns, such as Bill Clinton's in 1996, play "defense" by looking to solidify states that voted for them last time or that look "safe" in the current election. Still other campaigns, such as Al Gore's in 2000, concentrate on a very small number of highly competitive battleground states in an attempt to create a narrow electoral college majority—a tactic referred to as "threading the needle." Finally, campaigns can employ a "mixed" strategy—emphasizing defensive campaigning at one stage of the campaign and then offensive campaigning at another stage. George W. Bush's campaign organization did this in 2000, casting a very broad net early and then narrowing it considerably when data showed progress in some states but not in others.[27] There is some evidence that Biden's campaign pursued a mixed strategy in 2020.

Political and Economic Realities

Presidential campaigns are substantially constrained not only by electoral rules but also by political reality. In any given election, a campaign is dealt a deck of cards. How the campaign plays the cards is important, but the luck of the draw has a major impact on who wins the hand. Three factors in a presidential election are particularly important: incumbency, war, and the economy. Of these, the economy is usually considered paramount.

Incumbent presidents have natural advantages. They have the advantage of experience, having run a previous presidential campaign. They have the trappings of the office of the presidency, including the pomp and circumstance and an enhanced ability to make news, communicate with the public, and shape the national agenda. They also have an easier road to the party's nomination, with typically no significant opposition. It is no surprise, then, that two-thirds of incumbent presidents who seek reelection win. Typically, they begin the campaign with a larger lead than nonincumbent candidates and hold on to a larger portion of this lead during the campaign.[28]

Ongoing wars matter in both positive and negative ways. An incumbent president up for reelection at the outset of a war will likely benefit from the public's tendency to rally behind the president in times of crisis. But it has been rare for an election to occur just as a conflict is getting underway. At the same time, it is often thought that presidents will seek to create such a crisis right before the election—sometimes referred to as an "October Surprise." This, too, is rare. Historically, wars have more often had a negative impact on the incumbent president's reelection bid. The number of American military personnel killed in action during war tends to sour voters on the war's mission, producing more negative evaluations of the president's job performance and reducing their support at the polls.[29] This was particularly consequential for the Democratic Party in both 1952 and 1968, when Presidents Harry Truman and Lyndon Johnson were presiding over the wars in Korea and Vietnam, respectively.

The economy also influences presidential elections. The candidate of the incumbent party, and especially an incumbent president, is more likely to win if the economy is growing strongly. In recent presidential elections, there has been a clear relationship between the incumbent party's share of the vote and economic indicators, such as the change in average disposable income in the year before the election. The upward sloping line of Figure 9.3 captures the trend: as economic growth increases, so does the incumbent party's share of the vote. Carter, who ran for reelection when incomes were shrinking, won only 45 percent of the two-party vote. But his

FIGURE 9.3 Election Year Income Growth

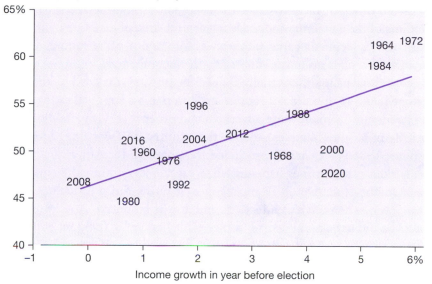

Incumbent party's share of two-party vote

Income growth in year before election

successor, Reagan, was reelected easily, thanks to the booming economy of 1984. Given this general tendency, 2020 was an outlier: Trump received just over 48 percent of the two-party vote share in 2020, significantly less than what one would predict given the preceding year's 4.5 percent growth in personal income. Perceptions of the economy in 2020, and the more general impact of the economy on the presidential vote, were undoubtedly complicated by both the pandemic and the debate about "reopening" the economy versus instituting lockdowns for public health.

Still, the impact of the economy creates strategic imperatives for the candidates. Candidates who benefit politically from the state of the economy tend to make it the central issue of their campaign. Thus, an incumbent president or incumbent party candidate will emphasize the economy during periods of economic growth. Conversely, the opposition party will emphasize the economy during an economic downturn. Candidates who are not favored by the economy need to change the subject by emphasizing other issues.[30] This dynamic was evident in the 2020 presidential campaign. Before the pandemic and the resulting recession, Trump claimed that the economy under his watch was the greatest in American history, while Biden argued that the economy under Republican control was only making the rich wealthier. After the economy cratered and then only partially recovered in 2020, Biden was able to broaden his critique of the Trump administration's handling of the issue.

Of course, the reality of the 2020 election year also included the COVID-19 pandemic itself. Did the pandemic influence the election? Clearly, it created different incentives for the candidates. Biden seized on Trump's handling of the pandemic and made it a central issue of his campaign. In that sense, the pandemic became another way for the out-party candidate to try to pin poor conditions in the country on the incumbent.

But did the pandemic actually change the results? It is hard to know. On the one hand, Trump did not receive any bump in his approval rating during the pandemic, as many state governors and other world leaders did.[31] Perhaps Trump's unwillingness to put the country on "wartime" footing in response to the coronavirus precluded the potential for Americans to rally to his side, as sometimes happens when presidents commit the country to war. On the other hand, Trump's approval rating did not decline during 2020, even as coronavirus infections and deaths mounted. And in terms of votes, he did not do any worse in places hit harder by the pandemic, suggesting that he was not being punished for pandemic deaths in the same way that presidents can be punished for casualties during war.[32] In this way, the electoral consequences of COVID-19 resembled the implications of the 1918 Spanish flu in the United States: election results in neither 1918 nor 1920 were correlated with flu deaths at the state or local levels.[33]

Thus, it may have been that the pandemic's impact was indirect, primarily through the economy, which was battered as consumer and employment options cratered due to public health–related restrictions. However, the substantial job loss and negative economic growth in the immediate wake of the coronavirus did not eliminate economic growth entirely and thereby handicap Trump's reelection bid the way one might have expected. Our sense is that the pandemic was a unique event and that perceptions of Trump's handling of the coronavirus became the *sine qua non* of the 2020 election.

The Fall Campaign

As the campaign gets underway after the national nominating conventions, candidates must make a series of strategic decisions within the context of electoral college math and broader realities. Here we discuss several important parts of that process: message development, the timing of campaign activity, the candidate debates, and voter mobilization.

Message Development As presidential candidates shift from the primary campaign to the general-election campaign, they often refine their message, particularly to emphasize how they contrast with their opponent. As we discussed in Chapter 5, campaign messages are designed to appeal to unde-cided voters or to mobilize sympathetic partisans. Typically, campaigns rely on polls and focus groups to discern which issues are salient to the public, which issue positions are most popular, and how issues can be framed to improve the campaign's chances for success. Candidates have their own ideas about political issues, of course, but no serious presidential campaign makes a move without surveying public opinion. Campaigns do not always follow the results of their polls, but they need to know how the public will likely react to the campaign's message.

As candidates decide which issues to emphasize, they are thinking not only about the broader political realities but also about any other factor that might advantage or disadvantage them. One factor is their party's political reputation. In 2020, Biden's team decided that he would do best if his mes-sage focused on issues directly affecting suburban voters and people of color, such as education and civil rights. They were confident that Ameri-cans would trust their candidate to handle these issues more effectively than Trump would. A second factor is the particular positions of "swing voters." As we discussed in Chapter 5, campaigns have an incentive to locate their issue positions close to those of the so-called median voter so that candidates can maximize their appeal to the public. In the United States, this incentive pushes candidates to the center of the political spectrum because many Americans hold fairly centrist positions on political issues.

But calculations about issue agendas and positions are fraught with diffi-culties. What if a candidate would prefer to ignore an issue that is a top pri-ority of the party's base? For example, some Democrats took up the cry to "defund the police" in 2020, but Biden was not interested in making this appeal a centerpiece of his campaign. What if a candidate's position appeals to a slim majority of voters overall but is unpopular with the base? And what if the popular position contradicts the candidate's previous position? In 2004, Democratic presidential candidate John Kerry attempted to explain how, as a U.S. senator, he had supported a bill allocating $87 billion for the troops fighting the Iraq War but then ended up opposing the funding bill that ultimately passed. He famously said, "I actually did vote for the $87 bil-lion before I voted against it." This quote was later used by the Bush cam-paign to portray Kerry as a flip-flopper.

Presidential campaigns can sometimes finesse the challenges of message development by delivering different messages via different media. In televi-sion ads and public speeches, candidates focus on broadly salient issues and popular positions. In direct mail, phone calls, and emails, candidates focus on issues and positions popular with their party's base. This is because they can use **narrow-casting**, targeting a smaller audience using these media, without the visibility that mass media entail. In 2020, for example, Biden targeted seniors in Florida "with testimonial-style advertising featuring residents of the Trump-leaning retirement community 'The Villages' discussing how the president's inability to control the virus has forced them to stay inside and away from their families."[34]

Of course, campaign plans are not enough. Despite all of the planning that goes into developing a message, life intervenes. Campaigns are particularly sensitive to the harsh judgments of the electorate, and they have up-to-the-minute feedback loops in the form of polls from all of their battleground states. By mid- to late September, they have enough information about public opinion to know whether they need to change course or not.

Front-runners usually have less need to adjust unless their lead is shrinking. The trailing candidate, however, may decide to do something different. The most common major strategic adjustment is often to "go negative." In 1988, George H. W. Bush was trailing by double digits when his campaign made a strategic decision to attack Michael Dukakis's record as governor of Massachusetts. This was deemed easier and more effective than rebuilding Bush's image. After all, Bush had been in the public eye for over two decades, while Dukakis was a newcomer and had received little scrutiny during the Democratic primaries. In August, Bush strongly criticized Dukakis's record on crime and the environment. By early September, Bush had pulled ahead strongly, and the entire dynamic of the election had changed.[35]

In general, incumbent presidents are much more likely to engage in negative campaigning than their opponents, mostly because they are well-known and people have formed opinions about the president that are difficult to change.[36] It is therefore difficult to "reset" their image or "move the dial" in a positive manner. Conversely, challengers are more of a blank slate. They tend to be new on the scene and often come to the fray with mostly positive associations born out of winning the nomination. However, these positive attitudes are typically shallow and easily changed, especially among members of the opposite party. Incumbent presidents therefore seek to define the opposition and influence voters' positive associations with that candidate by going negative. Bill Clinton, George W. Bush, and Barack Obama were much more negative in their reelection campaigns than their opponents were, not because they were dirty campaigners but because they recognized that they could drive up the negative ratings on their challengers much more easily than they could recast their own images in a more positive light.[37]

As noted in Chapter 3, neither Biden nor Trump featured many negative attacks in their 2020 advertisements. According to the Wesleyan Media Project, from September 1 through Election Day, only slightly more than 20 percent of their television ads were "attack" ads. In comparison, 57 and 63 percent of ads over this time period were "attack" ads in 2016 and 2012, respectively. The obvious explanation for the downturn in 2020 is that the peculiar circumstances of the race—held during a global pandemic that had caused over a quarter of a million deaths in the United States at the time of the election—precluded traditional negative advertising. To be sure, Biden aired television ads slamming Trump's handling of the pandemic, while Trump aired ads accusing Biden of favoring "socialist" policies, but both campaigns seemed mindful of not veering off course and thereby offending an anxious and fearful electorate. It is also likely that Biden's personal popularity was a factor in the relatively positive tone of the campaign.

By contrast, 2016 better illustrates when (and how) campaigns choose to go negative, as both Trump and Hillary Clinton did so early and often. Clinton's negativity is somewhat easy to understand and contextualize. Her favorability ratings dropped substantially during late 2015 and early 2016 because of questions about her use of a personal email server as secretary of state under President Obama. Meanwhile, Trump provided lots of fodder for Clinton by saying offensive things about women (most notably, journalist Megyn Kelly and former beauty pageant queen Alicia Machado), Latinos (Machado and U.S. District Court Judge Gonzalo Curiel), and war heroes (Arizona senator John McCain and Captain Humayun Khan). Then, in early October 2016, it was revealed that Trump had made several particularly offensive and outrageous statements about women on the set of *Access Hollywood* in 2005 (see Chapter 8). This presented Clinton with an obvious opportunity to frame the election as a choice between an experienced, steady, and knowledgeable candidate versus a "loose cannon." Still, after the election, many criticized her campaign for focusing too much on Trump and neglecting a positive message.

For Trump, the strategic thinking behind the decision to attack in 2016 is less obvious. Clinton's negative ratings were already high by the spring of 2016. Why not focus on the positive case for change (in general) and Trump (in particular)? The answer seems to be that Trump was less strategic and more instinctual than any other major-party presidential candidate in recent memory. When Clinton (or anyone else) hit him, he would hit back harder. The veracity of his claims was often questionable, but it seemed that the tone of his messaging was more important to voters than its content. In this way, he accomplished something strategically, perhaps without even knowing it—his image as a brash, fight-back, don't-care-what-elites-think-of-me "winner" was reinforced (especially among his supporters).

Timing Although the electoral college dominates decision-making about *where* campaign activity occurs, *when* that activity occurs is a separate question. Some campaigns prefer to stockpile their resources and end the campaign with a massive advertising blitz, presumably when more citizens are paying attention. In 2016, Trump's campaign—which was low on cash and actually suspended TV advertising for a time in early September—spent much of its resources in the final 10 days. His campaign strategists assumed that citizens are most affected by the last thing they see or hear and that the best strategy was to conserve money for the home stretch. Other campaigns like to spend more of their resources earlier, hoping to define the race at the beginning of the campaign. Still others expend resources during such high-profile events as the conventions and debates.

There is no conclusive evidence that any particular timing strategy is best. The relatively large size of convention bumps is consistent with the notion that it is easier to influence the public's preferences early in the campaign, when more people have yet to develop strong opinions of the candidates. Polling in presidential elections from 2004 to 2020 showed that citizens made up their minds about the candidates quite early in the campaign season—much earlier than they had in 2000. However, other evidence suggests that many citizens do not pay attention to the campaign until late in the process and that the effects of a television advertisement or candidate visit usually dissipate after only a few days.[38]

Candidate Debates Every fall campaign has its share of important events. But televised candidate debates stand out as the only potentially significant events that a campaign knows are coming. These are the most-watched events of the campaign, and underdog candidates often look to them with the hope that they will reshape a race.

The bipartisan Commission on Presidential Debates was established in 1987 to ensure that debates are a part of every presidential campaign. The commission, which sponsors the debates, varies their geographic location and format in an effort to engage as much of the public and to provide as much information as possible. After the major-party candidates accept their nominations, the commission produces a debate schedule, and the campaigns are obliged either to accept or decline their recommendations. If they decline (as Trump did for the second debate in 2020) or even suggest direct negotiations between the campaigns (as George H. W. Bush did in

In the first televised presidential debate, in 1960 (top), John F. Kennedy delivered a surprisingly strong performance against the more experienced Richard Nixon. Joe Biden was judged by many to have won the presidential debates in 2020 (bottom), but this appeared to have little impact on the vote.

1992 and George W. Bush did in 2000) they must explain their reasoning to the news media and the public. Any campaign that does not immediately accept the commission's recommendations will surely face the accusation that their candidate is dodging the debates, and so the standard in recent years has been to accept.

During the debates, campaigns have several goals. The first and most obvious goal is to "do no harm"—that is, avoid the sort of gaffe that drives subsequent news media coverage and undermines the campaign's effort to control messaging. To minimize the chances of a major mistake, presidential candidates prepare well in advance, usually for an hour or two each week during the summer and early fall and then all day for three to four days before the debate itself.[39] Campaigns run mock debates for the candidate, using stand-ins for the opposition and staging the aggressive questioning that sometimes occurs. These efforts are videotaped and then critiqued on the basis of style and substance. Campaign staff make sure that the candidates absorb voluminous briefing books on issues; candidates are then quizzed and asked to redress substantive weaknesses. In 2020, Biden devoted considerable time to debate preparation and was widely judged to have won his two encounters with Trump, who reportedly engaged in only very minimal debate prep.[40]

During the debate, candidates essentially seek to implement a miniature version of their overall campaign strategy. They emphasize issues and appeals that benefit them and avoid issues on which their opponent has the advantage. Viewers may not tune in to the debate for very long and may not be paying much attention, so candidates want to broadcast the strongest case for their candidacy. This is why candidates often seem to be answering questions besides the ones that debate moderators actually ask. When challenged, candidates tend to respond to every charge that the opposition makes. They do this because it has been shown that viewers may assume that any charge, no matter how outrageous, is true if not contradicted.

Candidates also address their answers to the television audience and not to the other candidate or the audience in the debate venue (unless the debate is held in a town hall format with actual citizens asking questions). The reaction of those in the auditorium is much less important than the reaction of those watching on television, especially the news media. Media coverage of the debates is actually more important for influencing public opinion than the debates themselves.[41] For example, immediately after the first debate of the 2000 presidential campaign, Al Gore was judged to have scored a slight victory over George W. Bush, but subsequent media coverage of several questionable claims he made during the debate, as well as mocking coverage of his colorful makeup, turned opinion around. One week after the debate, Bush was judged to have been the winner. The lesson here reinforces the main goal of debates (do no harm) but also emphasizes the need for campaigns to defend their candidate's performance in order to shape news media interpretations.

Despite all the preparation and strategizing that goes into debates, and despite the public's opinions about who did or did not win a particular debate, there are rarely large changes in public support for the candidates after a debate.[42] Simply put, most debates have little impact on the polls and on the election's outcome. Because debates occur relatively late in the campaign, most people have already made up their minds by the time the debates air. People then view the debates through partisan lenses: the vast majority of partisans believe that their candidate won. An example from the 2020 race is illustrative: according to a CNN poll conducted after the final 2020 presidential debate, 93 percent of Democrats thought Biden had won, and 73 percent of Republicans thought Trump had won.[43] Moreover, whereas during each convention one party dominates the news, debates broadcast opposing messages from both parties. In a sense, these messages cancel each other out, making it difficult for either party's candidate to get much of a boost in the polls from debates.[44] Even when debates do seem to move the electorate a point or two, as happened after the first presidential debate in 2016, when Hillary Clinton scored a clear victory over Trump in the view of voters and the news media, the effect is usually ephemeral.

Mobilizing Citizens At the end of the campaign, the candidate's staff work furiously to reach out to supporters and encourage them to vote. Complicating this effort is the rise of convenience voting, which (as noted in Chapter 2) encompasses a variety of ways in which citizens can vote without actually going to the polls on Election Day (Figure 9.4). Methods of convenience voting include in-person early voting and voting by mail (either by absentee or another form of mail ballot). In 2020, convenience voting surged as states expanded mail voting options in response to the coronavirus. Approximately 70 percent of Americans cast their presidential votes before Election Day in 2020. It is unclear whether vastly expanded mail voting is here to stay, but even if pre-pandemic voting rules return, convenience voting has become more and more prevalent. Faced with this reality, presidential campaigns must therefore ensure that supporters get mail or absentee ballot applications and information about early voting locations well in advance of the relevant deadlines.

In addition, presidential campaigns have to time their outreach appropriately. In 2020, almost 85 percent of Arizona voters voted early, as did 80 percent of Florida voters and 44 percent of Pennsylvania voters; it would

FIGURE 9.4 Convenience Voting Rates, 2004–20

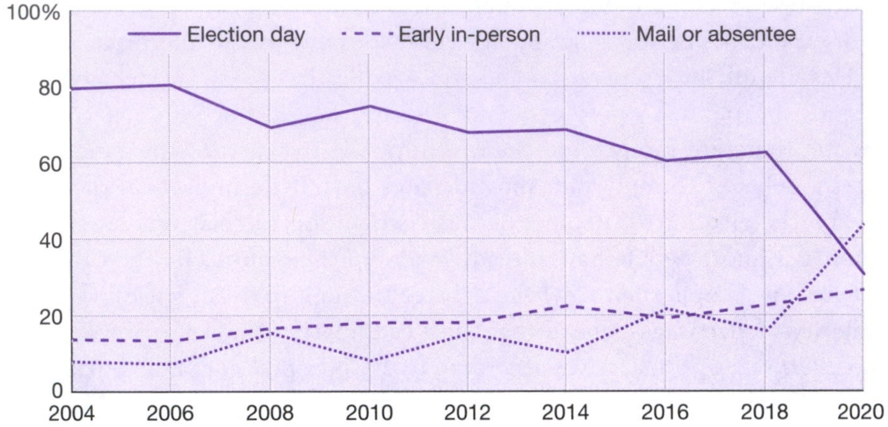

Source: U.S. Census Bureau, "Voting and Registration Supplement of the Current Population Survey, 1992–2020," April 2021, www.census.gov/topics/public-sector/voting.html (accessed 9/1/21).

thus have been foolish to wait until early November to launch an extensive persuasion or get-out-the-vote operation.[45] Campaigns must also monitor states' early voting records to see which of their targets have failed to vote (these individuals receive additional outreach) and which have voted (these individuals may be asked to contribute to or volunteer for the campaign).

One extremely important feature of the 2020 election was the partisan polarization of the vote by mode of voting. Democrats dominated mail voting while Republicans dominated Election Day voting. This development can be attributed to the Trump campaign's claim that expanding convenience voting was a Democratic plot to "steal" the election and the campaign's subsequent rejection of substantive efforts to increase Republican mail voting rates. Democrats, on the other hand, embraced mail voting and made it a centerpiece of their efforts to mobilize core constituencies. Ironically, strong partisan patterns by vote mode did not exist before 2020.[46] We will discuss convenience voting in more detail in Chapter 12.

Despite these recent declines in Election Day voting, campaigns tend to increase their activities as the race draws to a close, especially with respect to the most critical locales and groups. In an effort to drive more (and more favorable) coverage, campaigns sometimes try gimmicks to get the news media's attention. In 2000, for example, Gore vowed to campaign without sleep for the final 72 hours of the campaign. His midnight and early morning events produced large crowds and extensive media coverage.

Gore's personal efforts and the perceived success of the Democratic Party's last-minute organizational outreach prompted a comparable effort by the Republicans in 2002 and 2004. This "72-hour plan" featured extensive door-to-door campaigning and phone calls in the three days before the election, and it was credited with mobilizing the Republican base in key areas. Naturally, Democrats responded in kind. In 2008 and 2012, Obama and the Democrats flooded neighborhoods with volunteer workers and used email lists and social networking websites to greatly extend the range and scope of their outreach. In 2016, Trump and the Republicans spent fully half of their media budget on digital outreach, targeting likely GOP voters with personalized emails, texts, and Instagram and Snapchat messages. In 2020, Biden's team engaged in unprecedented outreach over the weekend immediately before the election, contacting an estimated 58 million people through calls, texts, and door-knocks.[47] Political science scholarship has confirmed that contact with a campaign does raise the likelihood that an individual will turn out to vote.[48]

Election Day and Beyond

On Election Day, citizens have to be contacted (via phone, email, or text message) and mobilized to vote (using buses, cars, walks, and so on). As the day wears on, reports from precincts allow campaign staff to know where they are "light" (getting fewer targeted votes) and "heavy" (getting all or most targeted votes). Campaign attention can be refocused accordingly. Lawyers are also employed to file motions to keep the polls open in places where candidates expect to win and where there might be "irregularities," such as too few ballots or long lines. This has become a standard tactic in recent elections, especially among Democrats, who want to ensure that lower-income precincts and precincts that serve people of color are properly equipped.

Of course, the 2020 presidential election showed that the election may not end on Election Day. Indeed, the contest dragged on until the Saturday after the election—when most major news media organizations finally called the election for Biden—and beyond, as Trump and many Republicans continued the fight until the electoral college results were certified in Washington, D.C., on January 6, 2021.

The events of 2020 do not appear to be anomalous. After the 2000 presidential election controversy, from 2004 through 2016, Democratic and Republican campaigns allocated money not only for election night parties but also for operations to influence news media reportage of close contests and for legal teams in case of recounts. Campaigns even developed plans to influence state legislatures' electoral certification efforts and to lobby presidential electors. To be sure, this preparation was ratcheted up in 2020; both the Biden and Trump teams foresaw a protracted fight ahead, given the need to certify and then count millions of mail and absentee ballots. Still, the combination of expanded convenience voting and the hyperpolarized nature of political competition suggests that post-election campaigns may become a durable feature of modern U.S. elections.

Conclusion

American presidential elections illustrate a crucial feature of elections everywhere: they depend a great deal on the rules and realities that candidates confront. For presidential candidates, the rules of the nomination process and the electoral college strongly affect strategies—the decision to run, the states to target, and so on. Candidates are also constrained by the realities of whether an incumbent is running, whether the country is at war or at peace, and whether the economy is prospering or struggling. As a result, candidates will often find it difficult to persuade the public. There are different perspectives on the degree to which these factors constrain campaign effects: some observers emphasize the limits to what electioneering can accomplish, while others emphasize the small effects that a good campaign can produce—effects that could decide a close election.

Do American presidential elections meet democratic ideals? Both the nomination and the general-election processes frequently elicit criticisms. For one, some claim that the nominating process produces unrepresentative candidates. Specifically, the complaint is that the sequence of primaries and caucuses allows small and ideologically extreme groups to exercise disproportionate influence by electing their favored candidates in states such as Iowa or New Hampshire. In this sense, the system fails with respect to the norm of equality. A cursory examination of the historical record casts doubt on this claim. Republicans John McCain, Robert Dole, George W. Bush, George H. W. Bush, and Mitt Romney and Democrats Bill Clinton, Hillary Clinton, Al Gore, John Kerry, Barack Obama, and Joe Biden hardly seem out of the mainstream. One could argue that Ronald Reagan was more conservative than the average Republican or that Michael Dukakis was more liberal than the average Democrat, but their records as governors offer many examples of pragmatism. Moreover, this is consistent with political science research demonstrating that while presidential primary electorates tend to be older and slightly more ideological than the party electorate as a whole, they are not necessarily ideologically extreme.[49]

A second complaint is that the national conventions are just public relations events. There is no deliberation about the candidates and little meaningful debate about the parties' platforms. This complaint is undoubtedly justified. It is less clear, however, that conventions themselves are simply fluff. Conventions help to unify parties after divisive primaries. They also allow the candidates to present themselves and their campaigns to a wide swath of citizens. The nominees' speeches are often rich in information about their policy agendas and goals.[50] After the conventions, citizens typically express more interest in the campaign.[51] The television networks may claim that the conventions are staged, but it may not be a bad thing to allow the parties to speak directly to the American people once every four years.

A third complaint is similar to the second: debates are uninspired and scripted. This may be true at times, although one would be hard-pressed to see the 2016 and 2020 presidential debates as "scripted." Even if many presidential debates have been tedious and predictable, they still have positive consequences. After the debates, citizens tend to be more interested in the campaign, feel more favorably about the candidates, and be more knowledgeable about the candidates in some ways.[52] However, the knowledge they've gained is not always about the candidates' issue positions. Thus, it is quite possible that debates could be reformed to become more informative or empowering. Citizens seem especially impressed by the town hall debate format, suggesting that more direct citizen involvement in the debates would be desirable. There are also those who would like to see more debates spread out over the entirety of the campaign.

A final set of complaints concerns the electoral college. As mentioned earlier, perhaps the most prominent of these is that the electoral college is not as democratic as a direct popular vote and can produce a winner who did not win the popular vote. Other complaints center on the perceived built-in biases of the electoral college—most notably, that it favors smaller states and leads candidates to focus on battleground states and ignore others. In particular, critics fear that this focus on battleground states demotivates citizens in other states when it comes time to vote on Election Day.

Defenders of the electoral college respond that discrepancies between the electoral college and popular vote are rare. They also note that battleground states are actually quite representative of the country as a whole.[53] Moreover, although voters in battleground states, particularly those with lower incomes, have relatively higher turnout rates, this is due to a surge in interest and engagement among those battleground electorates and not because those in other states are demobilized, as some electoral college critics maintain.[54]

Would a new presidential election system have comparable or even greater drawbacks? A direct national vote would have the virtue of enhancing legitimacy: a popularly elected president would automatically be able to lay claim to a mandate from the people, and we would never again have to deal with a split between the electoral college and the national vote. This is the most obvious upside to changing the system, although some might object to an executive with a claim to representing the people beyond that envisioned by the framers of the Constitution. In other respects, the virtues of a direct popular vote are more contentious. For instance, it may not stop candidates from campaigning selectively. In a national election, Democrats would be tempted to spend a lot of time mobilizing reliably Democratic constituents in major urban areas such as New York, Chicago, and Los Angeles. Republicans, meanwhile, would have incentives to concentrate on more conservative suburban areas around cities such as Dallas, Atlanta, and Phoenix. For candidates to campaign nationally, they might also have to work harder and spend more money than they currently do. This would make presidential campaigns even more arduous and expensive than they currently are—and the challenges and costs of campaigns are already criticized as discouraging potential candidates from running and allowing too much money into politics.

Of course, it is entirely possible that the presidential election system could be improved. But alternatives entail trade-offs among competing values, with any improvements creating new and even unforeseen problems. This is not an excuse for inaction; rather, it is a reminder that the words *perfection* and *democracy* rarely appear in the same sentence.

KEY TERMS

delegates (p. 245)

caucuses (p. 245)

primary election (p. 245)

viability (p. 247)

front-loading (p. 248)

front-runners (p. 249)

roll-call vote (p. 250)

convention bump/convention bounce (p. 253)

battleground (or swing) states (p. 258)

narrow-casting (p. 266)

FOR DISCUSSION

1. Why do states want to move their primary dates up in the election calendar? What is this process called? What is the effect of this process on campaigning?

2. How are the national party conventions different today compared with conventions in the 1950s?

3. How does the electoral college affect the strategies of presidential campaigns?

4. Why might a presidential candidate want to campaign relatively early in the fall? Why might a candidate want to campaign relatively late?

10

Congressional Campaigns

On election night in 2014, Cory Gardner was riding high. At just 40 years of age, he had defeated incumbent senator Mark Udall, winning one of Colorado's Senate seats and thus Republican party control of the U.S. Senate. Gardner accomplished this in part by nationalizing the election through an emphasis on Udall's connections to President Barack Obama and his support for the Affordable Care Act. During much of 2014, Obama's approval ratings were low, hovering just above 40 percent. Gardner and his supporters aired ads claiming that Udall voted with the president "99 percent of the time" in the hope that voters' disapproval of Obama would rub off on the incumbent. While Udall may have made some missteps—he ran a campaign that focused almost exclusively on reproductive rights, earning him the nickname "Senator Uterus"—the tide against Obama clearly hurt him and handed Gardner and Republicans a crucial victory.

Up for reelection six years later, Gardner would learn the hard way that what the national political tides give, they can also take away. In the summer and fall of 2020, a majority of Americans disapproved of President Donald Trump's handling of the COVID-19 pandemic. Gardner's Democratic opponent, former Colorado governor John Hickenlooper, flooded the airwaves with ads claiming that "Cory Gardner's on vacation" and that Gardner was "still silent about Donald Trump's failures on COVID."[1] Gardner countered with ads featuring Coloradans stating that "Cory Gardner got us help," but he ultimately failed to convince enough voters to support his bid for a second term. On election night in 2020, he found himself in Udall's shoes—he was an incumbent without a job.

Gardner's loss cannot be blamed entirely on Trump. In the six years since Gardner's initial election, the Colorado electorate had shifted toward the Democratic Party. Of the nearly 600,000 new voters who registered during Gardner's term in office, two-thirds were under 34 years old.[2] Having come of age during the Obama administration, these young voters leaned heavily toward the Democrats. Gardner had no control over Trump's handling of the pandemic or the shift in the electorate, but he paid the price regardless.

Udall's experience in 2014 and Gardner's experience in 2020 illustrate two trends that have characterized congressional elections in the last two decades: the nationalization of congressional campaigns and the declining dominance of incumbents. Traditionally, congressional incumbents have enjoyed large advantages over challengers due to a variety of factors, including the relative ease with which they can raise money and the personal connections they have with voters in their districts. In recent years, these advantages have eroded, making it harder for incumbents to win elections by running on their record of service to their district or state. Voters have become less concerned about what an incumbent has done for them lately and more concerned about backing their party. For example, it was common in the 1970s and 1980s for voters to split their tickets—that is, to vote for a president from one party and a senator from another. Now, split-ticket voting is virtually unheard of.

Core of the Analysis

- Congressional elections have been nationalized, weakening the incumbency advantage.
- The rules governing congressional elections and campaign finance directly shape the strategies of House and Senate candidates.
- The political fortunes of congressional candidates often hinge on factors beyond their control, such as the popularity of the president and the state of the economy.
- Potential congressional candidates are ambitious and strategic about when they run.
- Voters typically know little about congressional candidates, especially challengers.

Senator Cory Gardner (R-Colo.) benefited from the nationalization of congressional elections in 2014 but was hurt by it in 2020.

When voters perceive elected officials' partisan identification to be as important as or even more important than their performance in office, incumbents' fortunes become untethered from local factors and more tightly linked to national political tides beyond their control. A handful of elected officials have been able to buck this trend. In 2020, for example, four-term incumbent Republican senator Susan Collins was a primary target for Democrats who wanted to take back control of the Senate. Collins defied them in part by emphasizing her deep roots in Maine and the fact that her opponent, Democrat Sara Gideon, was from Rhode Island.[3] Being from out of state may not matter much in New York or California, but it matters a great deal in Maine. As a result, Collins was able to win in a state that voted for Democrat Joe Biden over Republican Donald Trump by a 9-point margin. These days, however, Collins has become the exception that proves the rule.

In this chapter, we explore the nature and effects of congressional campaigns. As with presidential campaigns, we find that the impact of congressional campaigns depends on the particular rules that govern them and the strategies candidates use. Constitutional provisions and campaign finance law are especially important. We also find that incumbents' electoral advantage has been declining in part because many are being challenged by more extreme members of their own party in primary elections. Still, incumbents win more often than not. In 2020, 97 percent of House incumbents and 90 percent of Senate incumbents who ran won reelection. Even in 2018, a year that featured a political tide against Republicans that had the potential to dislodge many of them from office, 91 percent of House incumbents and 82 percent of Senate incumbents won. This raises an important question: Are congressional elections competitive enough to meet the standards we might want for a democracy?

Rules, Reality, and Who Runs for Congress

If you decide to run for Congress, few legal obstacles stand in your way. As we discussed in Chapter 2, the Constitution requires only a minimum age (25 years to serve in the House and 35 years to serve in the Senate), U.S. citizenship for a number of years, and residency in the state that you want to represent. If you satisfy these requirements and meet state requirements for having your name appear on the ballot, such as paying a filing fee or collecting a certain number of signatures, you can run for Congress. Because the bar for running is so low, one might assume that people from all walks of life can and do run for office. If this were the case, Congress would be representative of the electorate in terms of demographics such as age, income, race, and gender. However, both those who run and those who win are quite unrepresentative of the broader electorate.

As we explained in Chapter 5, most individuals who run for office are ambitious and strategic. Congressional candidates have often held a lower political office that has provided them with experience and connections that are helpful to their campaign. Serious candidates will also enter a race only when their prospects of winning are good. However, the person with the best odds of winning an election is the **incumbent**, or the person who already occupies the office. As we discuss later in the chapter, this is especially true if the partisan composition of an incumbent's district or state favors the incumbent's party. Figure 10.1 shows the percentage of House and Senate incumbents who sought reelection and won from 1946 to 2020. Over this time period, the average percentage of House incumbents running who were reelected was 93 percent, while the average for Senate incumbents was

FIGURE 10.1   Percentage of House and Senate Incumbents Seeking Reelection Who Won, 1946–2020

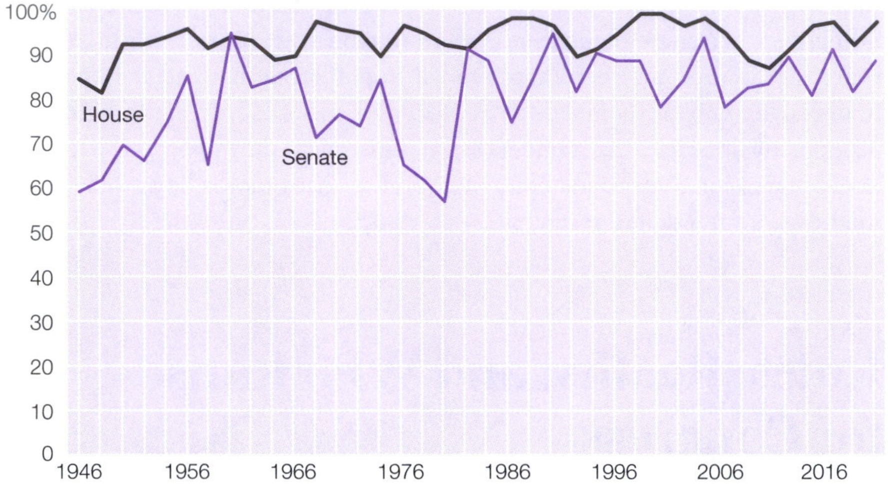

Source: Gary C. Jacobson, *The Politics of Congressional Elections*, 7th ed. (New York: Longman, 2008), 28–29. Additional data for 2008–20 collected by the authors.

80 percent. Although the incumbency advantage has been declining in recent years, challengers still face an uphill battle.

Because their odds of winning are high, incumbents will nearly always run for reelection unless extraordinary circumstances, such as poor health, prevent them from doing so. Incumbents may also step down because of scandal. For example, in 1992, 66 members of the House decided to retire after a banking scandal broke involving representatives who wrote checks from their House bank accounts without the funds to cover them.

House incumbents may also decide to retire when their districts change after redistricting, because the changes to their district require them to court new constituents to hold on to their seats. Districts can be drawn to protect incumbents of both parties, but partisan redistricting can endanger incumbents in the party that does not get to draw the new district boundaries. For example, in 2003, Texas Republicans undertook an unusual mid-decade redistricting. Their plan targeted 10 Democratic incumbents, most of whom faced the prospect of competing in the 2004 election in substantially changed districts.[4] Although many of these incumbents decided to run in their new districts and lost, one incumbent—Congressman Jim Turner, a Democrat who had served Texas's 2nd District for six years—saw the writing on the wall. Republican state legislators had moved most of Turner's former district into the 8th District and moved his home along with just

4.4 percent of his former constituents into the conservative 6th District, where he would have to compete against 10-term Republican incumbent Joe Barton.[5] In redistricting parlance this is known as "hijacking," and it involves redrawing district lines so that two incumbents have to run against each other. In this case, Turner didn't stand a chance against Barton, so he decided it was a good time to retire.

House and Senate incumbents may also retire if they feel that the country is experiencing a wave of anti-incumbent sentiment or a wave of sentiment that favors the opposing party. For example, in both the 2017–18 and the 2019–20 election cycles, more Republicans than Democrats retired in the House of Representatives because the election climate was perceived as being unfavorable to Republicans.

When incumbents decide to retire, their decisions create **open seats**, which allow for contests between nonincumbents. Open seats attract candidates who have already served in public office because they have the experience and backing necessary to run competitive campaigns. Candidates with political experience are referred to as **quality challengers**. They are strategic and recognize that their chances of winning are higher with the incumbent out of the picture. Occasionally, quality challengers will run against a vulnerable incumbent— one who is winning by smaller margins or struggling to raise money—but they prefer to wait for a seat to open. Quality challengers are often contrasted with **political amateurs** who lack political experience. Historically, political amateurs were more likely than quality challengers to compete against an incumbent because their goal was not necessarily to win: they often ran simply to bring attention to a particular issue or to raise their own profiles. Today, however, political amateurs are political activists who run to win. Their strategy is generally to contest primary elections in safe districts.[6] Thus, while quality challengers usually target competitive open seats vacated by retiring incumbents, political amateurs tend to target incumbents from their own party.

In order to mount successful campaigns, challengers need resources. They may turn to their party for these resources, but the party's support is not always guaranteed; parties typically focus their resources only on competitive contests where they have a chance of picking up or losing a seat. The clearest indication of whether a party supports a challenger is if it recruited them to run in the first place. The "**Hill committees**"—the National Republican Senatorial Committee (NRSC), Democratic Senatorial Campaign Committee (DSCC), National Republican Congressional Committee (NRCC), and Democratic Congressional Campaign Committee (DCCC)— encourage prospective candidates throughout the country to run for office. Much like scouts in sports, the parties are always looking for business and community leaders who might make successful candidates for office. These individuals are courted by party leaders and sent to workshops to learn how to run campaigns. They may also be provided with lists of potential donors. Without such support, an ambitious and strategic individual might make the rational calculation that it is better to keep their current job than to run for Congress.

In recent years, interest groups have become an important source of candidate support, especially for political amateurs who may lack the backing of their party. This trend began in 2010 when groups such as the Club for Growth supported candidates identifying with the Tea Party. The Club for Growth, which advocates for lower taxes and a free market, does not coordinate its activities with the Republican Party and operates chiefly in Republican primary elections in conservative districts. The Republican congressional campaign committees are then left to fund candidates in toss-up general-election contests. A spokesman for the Club for Growth, Andy Roth, explains, "Why spend a lot of money in the primary and then spend a lot of money again in the general, when you can operate in districts where you can spend a lot of money in the primary and spend nothing in the general?"[7] Progressive interest groups such as the Justice Democrats employ similar tactics and have supported a wave of amateur candidates challenging more moderate incumbents. A good example is Alexandria Ocasio-Cortez's stunning defeat of 10-term incumbent representative Joseph Crowley in the 2018 Democratic primary for New York's 14th District.[8]

Because winning a congressional election requires resources and connections, certain types of individuals are more likely to run. On average, those who choose to run are more educated and wealthier than most Americans. They are also overwhelmingly White and male. Successful candidates tend to work in business, the law, or politics and have large networks that can be tapped for campaign resources. For example, lawyers are particularly adept at getting elected to Congress because they are able to raise money early in the campaign season from their professional network. This allows them to build momentum and defeat their opponents in primary elections.[9] In Chapter 5, we mentioned that one reason for the dearth of women in politics is that they are not as ambitious as men. Another reason is that they are underrepresented in the professions with networks that can generate the financial resources one needs to be a viable candidate for Congress.[10] The same is true for people of color. Thus, members of Congress are unrepresentative of the nation in terms of their education, wealth, race, and gender because the people who run for office are unrepresentative of the nation.

Campaign Organization and Funding

Once candidates have decided to run for Congress, they need to put together a campaign staff. Because campaigns in the United States are candidate centered, candidates, rather than parties, are almost entirely responsible for raising money and putting together a campaign organization. This is true even if parties have recruited the candidates. The parties might provide their candidates with lists of suggested political consultants, but the candidates still must choose consultants that they feel will best help them win. And many candidates have to piece together a campaign staff as best they can using only their own devices.

Congressional campaign organizations range widely from bare-bones operations run by unpaid volunteers to big organizations run by paid professional consultants. A well-funded congressional campaign typically has a campaign manager who oversees the day-to-day operations of the campaign and helps develop strategy. There may also be a separate campaign strategist. Other staff deal with press relations, issue and opposition research, fundraising, accounting, and grassroots organizing. The best-funded candidates, including many House and Senate incumbents, may also hire consultants to conduct polls, develop radio and television advertisements, create direct mail pieces, and operate phone banks.

The size and shape of congressional campaign organizations depend almost entirely on how much money the campaigns can raise. In the 2019–20 election cycle, the average House incumbent raised $2.7 million, while the average House challenger raised $418,000; the average Senate incumbent raised $28.7 million, while the average Senate challenger raised $5.3 million.[11] Congressional candidates differ greatly in how much they raise and spend, however. For instance, in 2020, incumbent senator James Risch (R-Idaho) easily won reelection after spending just $3 million. In contrast, Jon Ossoff, a Democratic Senate candidate in Georgia, spent $149 million to narrowly defeat an incumbent in a race that included a runoff election.[12]

The funding sources for congressional candidates are different from those for presidential candidates. First, unlike presidential candidates, congressional candidates are not eligible for public financing (although, as we discussed in Chapter 4, few presidential candidates now take public funding). Congressional candidates must raise money from individuals and political action committees (PACs). Compared with presidential candidates, congressional candidates rely

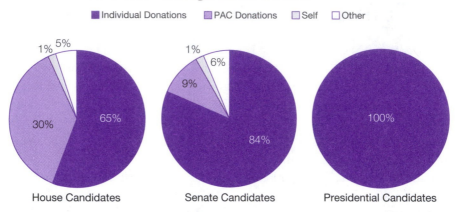

FIGURE 10.2 Comparison of House, Senate, and Presidential Candidate Funding Sources in 2020

■ Individual Donations   ▨ PAC Donations   ☐ Self   ☐ Other

House Candidates

Senate Candidates

Presidential Candidates

Note: Pie charts depict percentage of funds raised from each source during the general-election campaign.
Source: OpenSecrets.org.

more on PAC contributions and less on individual contributions. Figure 10.2 shows that House candidates in 2020 raised 65 percent of their funds from individual contributions and 30 percent of their funds from PACs. The comparable figures for Senate candidates were 84 percent and 9 percent, respectively. In contrast, presidential candidates Joe Biden and Donald Trump relied almost exclusively on individual contributions. Because PACs are limited to a contribution of $5,000 per candidate for each election cycle, total PAC contributions are a drop in the bucket for presidential campaigns but a more significant amount for congressional candidates.

Despite these differences, congressional candidates, like presidential candidates, raise most of their funds from individuals. But these individual contributions do not necessarily come from the candidates' own districts or states. For example, the median House incumbent in 2020 received two-thirds of their individual contributions from outside their district. Congressional leaders can receive especially large amounts of nonresident funding because they have name recognition. In 2020, 93 percent of then Senate majority leader Mitch McConnell's (R-Ky.) contributions came from people outside Kentucky.[13] In addition, candidates can attract large amounts of out-of-state funding when a race is competitive or highly consequential, such as the 2020 races for Georgia's two Senate seats that determined party control of the chamber. In those races, 88 percent of then senator Kelly Loeffler's (R-Ga.) funds came from nonresidents. Citizens who contribute to out-of-district (or out-of-state) candidates appear to be chiefly motivated by partisanship, seeking to increase their party's power in Congress.

Beyond individual and PAC contributions, House and Senate candidates may self-finance most or part of their campaigns. In 2020, for example, 34 House and Senate candidates wrote themselves checks of $1 million or more.[14] Self-financed candidates do not always win, but they can give their opponents a run for their money.

Candidates may also rely on spending by outside groups unaffiliated with the parties that campaign on their behalf, such as the super PACs and 501(c)4s discussed in Chapter 4. In 2020, these groups spent almost $2.3 billion in House and Senate races combined, which amounted to approximately 60 percent of the amount that all House and Senate candidates spent on the election.[15] Like candidates, outside groups are strategic, which means they target races in which their money is likely to make a difference. For example, with control of the Senate at stake in 2020, outside groups focused their contributions on the closest races, spending $245 million alone in the Senate race in Georgia between Jon Ossoff and David Perdue.[16] This number is staggering—it is more than 2.5 times the amount that outside groups have ever spent on a single race. This level of spending was facilitated by two 2010 federal court rulings, *Citizens United v. Federal Election Commission* and *SpeechNow v. Federal Election Commission*, which gave a green light to individuals and corporations to form super PACs and spend unlimited amounts in campaigns.

The Nomination Process

Like all candidates who run for a partisan office in the United States, congressional candidates must first compete for their party's nomination in a primary election. It is not uncommon for congressional primaries to be uncontested. Such primaries usually feature a popular incumbent whose seniority, power, and connections discourage would-be challengers. The number of competitive primaries has been increasing in the last decade, however, with a notable rise in primaries in which a more ideologically extreme candidate takes on a comparatively moderate incumbent.[17] While such races might receive more attention from the media and pundits, they are rarely competitive. In 2020, just eight House incumbents, or 2.1 percent, lost their primary.[18]

Open-seat primaries occur when a party's incumbent has retired or when the party that is out of power must choose a candidate to challenge the incumbent in the general election. These are typically the most competitive primaries and the most likely to attract quality challengers. In such contests, the party normally remains neutral and lets the voters decide who the party should back in the general election. From time to time, however, party leaders back an open-seat primary candidate who they believe has a good chance of winning the general election. There is some evidence that a party is more likely to do this in years when the political tides are in its favor. In 2010, for example, approximately 22 percent of Republican primary candidates came through the NRCC's "Young Guns" recruitment program, while in 2018, 24 percent of Democratic primary candidates had participated in the DCCC's "Red to Blue" program.[19] These numbers are high, however. Typically, the number of candidates recruited through these programs is closer to 10 percent for both parties. Parties rarely get involved in congressional primaries because they prefer to save their limited resources for the general election.

Just like candidates in presidential primaries, candidates in House and Senate primaries must compete for votes from an electorate that is more ideologically extreme than the general-election electorate. Candidates can respond by trying to convince voters in the general-election campaign that they are more moderate, or they can choose to "stay the course" by maintaining the ideological positions that they had in the primary. If the general election is competitive, they might attempt the former strategy—emphasizing ideological issues in the primary election and then focusing on nonideological issues in the general election. General-election talking points might include personal character or valence issues upon which most people agree, such as ensuring that children have good schools and increasing the number of available jobs. However, candidates must be careful not to change their agendas or positions too dramatically, or else they might be criticized for flip-flopping.

Instead of moderating their positions, candidates may also decide to stay the course as they move from the primary to the general election. They might adopt this strategy because their district is safe or because they are worried about upsetting donors who supported them in the primary and who they are hoping to tap again for the general election.[20] Candidates might also make the calculation that voters who identify with their party will care less about their extremism than they will about winning, meaning that they will support their party's candidate irrespective of that candidate's ideological positioning. Indeed, research suggests that members of Congress are becoming increasingly polarized in part because voters refuse to punish their party's more extreme general-election candidates by not voting for them.[21]

Democratic senator Joe Manchin of West Virginia provides a good example of how a candidate may try to appeal to primary voters without necessarily

Representative Lauren Boebert, who ran as a "no-compromise conservative," defeated a five-term incumbent in the Republican primary and her Democratic opponent in the general election.

turning off general-election voters. West Virginia is solidly Republican, and Manchin's politics therefore reflect a balancing act. On abortion, he identifies as pro-life and has voted to ban abortion after 20 weeks of gestation, but he has signaled that he does not want the Supreme Court to overturn *Roe v. Wade*, the 1973 case that established a constitutional right to abortion. Similarly, Manchin supported some aspects of President Trump's agenda, like a wall at the U.S.-Mexico border, but he also supported key Democratic achievements like the Affordable Care Act, President Obama's signature health care reform. In 2018, this strategy helped Manchin win reelection in a state that had voted for Trump for president over Hillary Clinton by a stunning 68-to-26 percent margin just two years earlier.

On the other hand, Colorado representative Lauren Boebert illustrates how extreme candidates can win in the general election without moderating their tone at all. In 2020, Boebert defeated a more moderate incumbent in the Republican primary for Colorado's 3rd District. Boebert, owner of Shooters Grill in Rifle, Colorado, ran as a Washington outsider and a gun rights activist who encouraged her food servers to openly carry guns while on the job. Given that Boebert's district is somewhat competitive, one might have expected her to moderate her tone in the general election. Instead, she doubled down. She reopened her restaurant, which had been shut down because of the COVID-19 pandemic, in defiance of public health directives. She held in-person rallies during the pandemic with her Glock pistol strapped to her thigh, claiming that she would take on the "socialist ideology" being spread in Washington, D.C., by people such as Ocasio-Cortez. Boebert's strategy to campaign as a "no-compromise conservative" ultimately worked in part because Republican voters backed her even if she made them uncomfortable. Judi Lichliter, a registered Republican, said that she would vote for Boebert "[b]ecause she is a Republican and on the Republican ticket. . . . But I am not supportive of her as an individual. I think it's very sad that we would be sending her to Washington."[22]

The General Election

Once candidates have secured their party's nomination, they must quickly turn their attention to the general-election campaign. Some candidates who were uncontested in the primary or did not have any serious challengers may even start their general-election campaign earlier if they have the resources to do so. Incumbents typically have these resources, so challengers face a particularly difficult path: while they are battling for the nomination, the incumbent has already started appealing to the general-election electorate.

Voters often know far less about House and Senate candidates than they do about candidates for president. For example, only one in five Americans can name both of their state's U.S. senators, and only a third know the name of their congressional representative.[23] Thus, many citizens vote for congressional candidates without knowing their names, let alone anything substantive about them. Congressional candidates and their political consultants are well aware of voters' lack of knowledge. Challengers, in particular, are aware that people rarely vote for someone they do not know. Thus, many congressional candidates spend their entire campaign simply introducing themselves to voters. They do this by communicating with potential supporters and working to ensure that supporters turn out on Election Day.

Developing a Campaign Message

As we discussed in Chapter 5, knowing the electorate is key to winning an election. Candidates need to know who their supporters are and where they live. They also need to know who the persuadable voters are in their district or state and how to get their message to these voters. The next step is to craft a campaign message that resonates with groups of voters who are important for a candidate's victory.

One of the most important determinants of a congressional candidate's campaign message is whether the candidate is an incumbent or a challenger. Incumbents tend to focus on their experience in public office and what they have achieved for their district or state.[24] Challengers, on the other hand, are more likely to try to contrast themselves with their opponents in terms of issue positions and personal characteristics. They are also more likely to go negative and attack. One of the most common criticisms that challengers lob at incumbents is that they have become "Washington insiders" who have lost touch with their constituents back home.[25] For example, Democrat Amy McGrath, who challenged then Senate majority leader Mitch McConnell for one of Kentucky's Senate seats in 2020, ran ads that repeatedly criticized McConnell for meeting for less than one minute with coal miners who had traveled more than 10 hours to see him. McConnell, who is depicted as a "swamp turtle" in the animated ad, says, "Well, they should feel lucky to see me." It is unclear if the claims in McGrath's ad are true—two of the coal miners who participated in the meeting disavowed the ad—but both its tone and theme are typical for a congressional challenger.

Gender is also an important determinant of campaign messages in congressional campaigns. Voters perceive male and female candidates as being stronger or weaker on certain issues. Candidates are aware of this and try to use these perceptions to their advantage. For example, women are perceived as "owning" topics such as health care and education, while voters perceive men as being stronger on foreign policy, defense, and the economy. As a result, male and female candidates are more likely to discuss the issues that their gender "owns."[26] In addition, candidates find it beneficial to counter gender stereotypes about personality traits. As a result, female candidates will often emphasize traits associated with men, such as toughness, while men will emphasize traits typically associated with women, such as compassion and empathy. For example, in her biographical ad "Doors," MJ Hegar, a Texas Democrat who ran in a heavily Republican congressional district in 2018, emphasized her experiences as a helicopter pilot in Afghanistan and her battle to get Congress to allow women to fight in ground combat. Some research has found, however, that female candidates are punished for being too masculine, especially by voters from the opposing party.[27] This may be why Hegar's ad also showed her caring for her children.

Unlike presidential candidates, whose messages are focused almost exclusively on national politics, congressional candidates have historically faced the challenge of crafting campaign messages that address both local and national issues. The conventional wisdom used to be that local issues should predominate—a sentiment best captured by former Speaker of the House Thomas "Tip" O'Neill's famous assertion that "All politics is local." Yet studies of congressional campaign messages have found that national issues have become more prevalent than local issues over time.[28] This trend has been driven by several factors. First, over the last few decades, the national parties have developed professional messaging strategies to help them prepare for elections. Part of this strategy involves forcing their members to vote the party line on certain key votes,[29] which has made it harder for individual members to craft their own messages or take issue positions distinct from the party. The result is that there is less and less variation in campaign messages among candidates from the same party. In addition, after the 2010 election, Congress banned the use of "earmarks" that allowed individual lawmakers to slip funding for local projects, such as bridges and flood levees, into federal legislation. Before the ban, incumbents were incentivized to focus on local issues because they could take credit for earmarked projects in their campaigns. Now, that incentive has been removed, further nationalizing campaigns.[30]

Communicating the Message

Once candidates have determined what they want to say to voters, they communicate that message in several ways. Like presidential candidates, congressional candidates rely on a combination of digital, radio, and television advertisements as well as direct mail, but the extent to which they rely on each of these is different. For example, presidential and Senate candidates spend a higher percentage of their advertising budget on television than on digital platforms, and the reverse is true for candidates in House elections.[31] House candidates rely the least on television ads because they are expensive, and they typically have less money to spend per voter than Senate and presidential candidates do. In fact, many House races feature no television advertising whatsoever.

Another problem for House and Senate candidates is that television advertisements are purchased in predefined media markets. Large media markets often serve more than one congressional district, which means that a House candidate who purchases television ads may be paying for people in neighboring districts to see those ads. Media markets do not necessarily respect state borders either. If one state has a competitive Senate race, voters in neighboring states that share media markets with the competitive state may see ads for races in which they cannot vote. For example, New Jersey has no television media markets of its own. Its northern half lies in the New York City market and its southern half sits in the Philadelphia market. Thus, congressional candidates in New Jersey must purchase airtime in one or both of these extremely expensive media markets if they want to run television ads. For these reasons, congressional candidates rely more on digital and radio advertisements, billboards, and yard signs.

Congressional candidates, especially House candidates, can also rely more than presidential candidates can on communicating with citizens directly. Presidential candidates have no personal contact with most Americans; the population is simply too large. Citizens "experience" presidential candidates mainly as talking heads on their television screens. In contrast, House candidates can have direct, unmediated contact with a larger portion of their constituency. They attend parades, sporting events, or any type of event where large numbers of potential voters gather. This kind of contact is intended to increase name recognition and to make a favorable impression, not to convey substantive information about policy agendas or proposals.

House challengers rely heavily on personal contacts to get their name out. It is not unheard of for House challengers to literally walk across their district to meet voters and generate publicity. For example, in preparation for the 2018 election, Ian Golden, a Democratic candidate for New York's 23rd District, embarked on a walking tour as part of his primary campaign.[32] This was no small feat: the district is 450 miles long. Though such tactics might seem gimmicky, they are often one of the few means by which an underfunded challenger can generate name recognition. Apart from House candidates running in the seven states that have only one representative, meaning that the state and congressional district have identical boundaries, Senate candidates usually have a much larger territory to cover than House candidates do. As a result, it is often more practical for senators to rely on ads than on personal contact with voters.

Congressional candidates also differ from presidential candidates in how much they rely on earned media. **Earned media (or free media)** is the publicity that candidates get by engaging in promotional activities. For example, candidates frequently hold press conferences or give speeches in the hope that that these events will be covered by the local media. Candidate appearances such as Golden's walking tour have the same goal. Earned media is essential for congressional candidates, who typically have fewer financial resources than presidential candidates but need to make sure that voters see and hear them.

Mobilizing Voters

Congressional candidates use the same basic tactics that presidential candidates use to get their supporters to the polls on Election Day, including mailers, phone calls, and neighborhood canvassing. The main differences are the size and sophistication of their mobilization drives. Presidential candidates have vast resources at their disposal that enable them to develop extensive field organizations. In presidential election years, congressional candidates benefit from the presidential campaigns' mobilization efforts because most voters who go to the polls to cast a ballot for the president usually cast a ballot for candidates in other races at the same time. In midterm election years, however, congressional candidates must turn out voters themselves, assisted by other organizations such as state and national party committees and interest groups. Despite those efforts, congressional campaigns rarely generate the kind of interest that presidential campaigns do. As a result, voter turnout in midterm elections is lower than turnout in presidential elections.

The Role of the Parties and the Hill Committees

Political parties can play a significant role in congressional campaigns. The Hill committees defined earlier in this chapter focus exclusively on electing party members to Congress. They accomplish this by targeting the handful of House and Senate races that are closely contested in each election cycle and ignoring the rest. Their first priority is to protect incumbents who are in jeopardy of losing their seats. For example, the DCCC has an effort called "Frontline" that seeks to protect the most vulnerable incumbent Democrats. As of this writing, it had announced that in the 2021–22 election cycle, the Frontline program would focus on protecting 32 incumbents.[33] The second priority of Hill committees is to defend the seats of members of the party who are leaving office. Finally, when national political and economic conditions favor one party, that party may also try to flip vulnerable seats that have been controlled by the other party. In 2018, for example, the DCCC launched a "March into '18" campaign that targeted 20 vulnerable Republicans (and it won 12 of those seats).

The Hill committees do not rigidly adhere to campaign plans. In response to campaign events, they may redirect resources to crucial races. They typically begin the election season with a longer list of competitive races and whittle that number down as the campaigns evolve and it becomes clear which ones will be the most fiercely contested. They may decide that some races are not worth their involvement. In the races where they are involved, the committees can make direct contributions, coordinate expenditures with the candidate, or make independent expenditures without a candidate's involvement. **Coordinated expenditures** involve collaboration between the committee and the candidate or a representative of the candidate. They are usually spent on services that are given to a candidate directly or performed by a political consultant on a candidate's behalf. Such services might include the purchase of airtime on television and radio, direct mail, polling, or the organization of fundraising events. Campaign finance law treats coordinated expenditures the same way it treats direct contributions to a candidate, which means that they are subject to strict limits.

As a result, the Hill committees usually rely on **independent expenditures** to fund their campaign efforts. As discussed in Chapter 4, these expenditures cannot be limited but must be made without consulting or coordinating with a candidate. This allows the committees to spend large sums of money on a race. In 2020, for example, the NRCC and DCCC spent heavily in New Mexico's 2nd District. The NRCC spent $4.4 million to support its candidate, Yvette Herrell, while the DCCC spent $3.5 million to defend its incumbent, Representative Xochitl Torres Small. To put this amount of money in perspective, consider that Herrell herself spent just $2.9 million while Torres Small spent $8.5 million. While Torres Small faced an uphill battle to hold onto her seat in a district that favored President Trump in the 2020 election, the NRCC's independent expenditures helped compensate for Herrell's inability to keep up with Torres Small's fundraising.

Whereas the Hill committees tend to help candidates purchase campaign communications and provide technical expertise, state and local party committees more often help candidates with grassroots activities, such as voter registration and mobilization drives designed to get voters to the polls. In addition, they organize phone banks and neighborhood canvassing campaigns to knock on doors and provide voters with campaign literature.

The Incumbency Advantage

For decades, a defining feature of congressional elections was the large electoral advantage that incumbents enjoyed over challengers. Figure 10.3 shows how the **incumbency advantage**, which is defined as the vote share earned by an incumbent compared with what a nonincumbent would have earned, has changed since the 1950s. The incumbency advantage grew from the 1950s to the 1980s, reaching a high of just under 10 percentage points in

FIGURE 10.3 The Rise and Fall of the Incumbency Advantage, 1954–2020

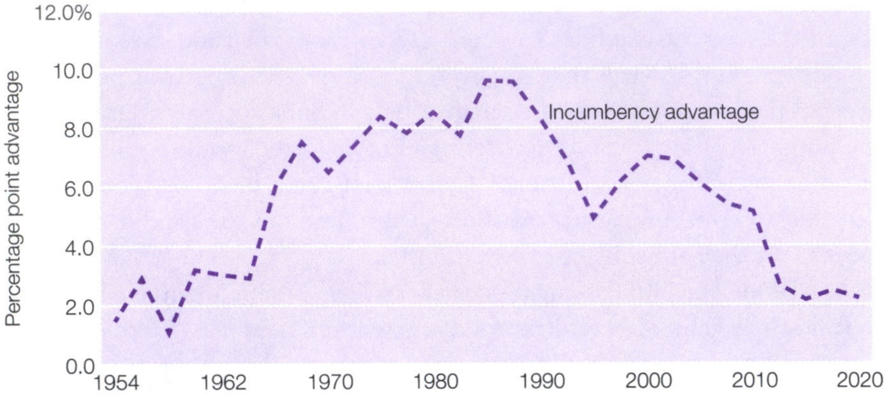

Source: Courtesy of Gary Jacobson and Jamie Carson.

1986. It then began to slowly decline. In 2020, its value was just 2.2 percentage points.[34] What explains this pattern over time? Did the factors that gave rise to the incumbency advantage disappear, or did other factors emerge that overwhelmed them?

The source of the incumbency advantage has been the subject of much scholarly debate for several decades. One group has argued that incumbents simply got better at raising money and "scaring off" high quality challengers who found it difficult to compete for donations.[35] Contributors like to back winners, and they know that challengers are more likely to lose.[36] Only challengers in competitive races or candidates in open-seat races can typically raise anything close to what incumbents raise. Similarly, parties and interest groups funnel resources to candidates who have a greater chance of winning. As a result, in 2020 the average House incumbent raised more than six times what the average challenger raised. The average Senate incumbent raised more than five times as much as the average challenger.[37] Quality challengers fare better than the average challenger, but they typically cannot match incumbents dollar for dollar. Because incumbents got better at discouraging quality challengers by raising large amounts of money, they faced less and less serious competition at the ballot box.

Other scholars argue that the incumbency advantage increased because incumbents became better at developing the **personal vote**, which is that portion of an elected official's vote share that can be attributed to their relationship with constituents. Citizens see incumbents in the news and around the district or state attending events and making speeches. Incumbents can also make use of certain perquisites of office to get publicity. For example, the **franking privilege** allows members of Congress to send mail to constituents without postage. Although it cannot be used for campaigning purposes, it can be used to send out newsletters and other informational mailings. Members of Congress also employ staff for **casework**, which typically involves helping constituents deal with government bureaucracies.[38] Whenever a staff member solves a constituent's problem, that constituent is likely to view the congressperson who helped out more favorably.

Today, incumbents still have an easier time raising money than challengers do and enjoy the many perquisites of their office—so why has the incumbency advantage declined since the 1980s? The chief reason is that party loyalty was quite low in the 1980s and has grown dramatically since then. Voters now care more about an incumbent's party than how the incumbent has served the district. This means that districts' partisan composition has become more predictive of general-election outcomes.[39] It has become harder and harder for moderates of one party to get reelected in districts that favor the opposing party. This development also reflects the growing nationalization of congressional elections—whereby congressional elections are influenced less by local factors, such as the personal vote accrued by an incumbent, and more by national political factors, like the popularity of the president.

Although the incumbency advantage has declined, it still exists. Nevertheless, despite the advantages that incumbents have, they rarely act as if they are confident about winning. Even incumbents who represent districts with a partisan composition that favors them worry about losing their elections. This creates a paradox in congressional elections: many incumbents are "running scared" even though incumbents rarely lose.[40] Why? For one, incumbents do occasionally lose—especially when they are vulnerable because of personal scandals or a national political climate that is not favorable to their party. They also lose in primaries to challengers from their own party. Moreover, the cost of losing is high. When incumbents lose elections, they also lose their jobs and the political power and reputation that they have amassed. Losses might even mean the end of their political careers. Thus, despite their advantages, incumbents in campaigns often behave as if they are fighting for their political lives. This is one reason they are constantly raising money: amassing a huge war chest helps scare off serious competitors. They want to avoid sending any signal that they may be vulnerable.

The Competitiveness of Congressional Races

Competitive congressional elections have become rarer since the 1950s. This may seem counterintuitive given how narrowly divided control of Congress has become during that time. Since 1990, for instance, partisan control of the House has switched four times, while partisan control of the Senate has switched six times. Such volatility is unusual in American history. Even so, the competitiveness of individual congressional races is relatively low. A simple measure of competitiveness is the number of House seats won by less than 10 percent of the vote (Figure 10.4).

Electoral competitiveness declined from 1952 through the late 1980s, likely because of the growing incumbency advantage discussed earlier. Indeed, electoral competitiveness decreased only in House elections that featured an incumbent. It did not decrease in open-seat House races. For the last three decades, the average competitiveness of House races has remained relatively low but with considerable volatility. Certain years clearly stand out for high levels of competition: 1992, 1994, 2010, 2018, and 2020. In 1992, there was the previously mentioned scandal in which House incumbents overdrew their House bank accounts. In 1994, 2010, and 2018, the national political climate produced conditions very favorable to one party, which gave that party's candidates a good opportunity to defeat the other party's incumbents. In 2020, many

FIGURE 10.4 Number of House Elections Won by 10 Points or Less, 1952–2020

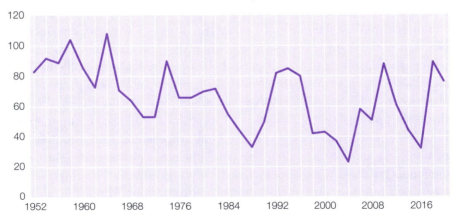

Source: Authors' data.

Democrats who were swept into office on the blue tide of 2018—especially those who won in traditionally Republican districts—found themselves fighting to hold onto their seats, which kept levels of competition high.

Nevertheless, the relatively low level of competition in congressional races raises at least three concerns about the American electoral system. First, uncompetitive elections can undermine democratic accountability. In a representative democracy, the main way to ensure that politicians respond to citizens is to hold frequent elections; if the public is unhappy with a politician, voters can replace that person. But if representatives know that their reelection is virtually guaranteed, they respond less to citizens and rely more on their own views or on those of interest groups and lobbyists. Second, competitive elections force candidates to spend money on communicating with and mobilizing voters, and they encourage the media to cover politicians. As a result, voters in competitive districts are much more likely to know who their representatives are and something about what they stand for.[41] Third, uncompetitive elections can prevent the demographics of Congress from changing to reflect the electorate. This is a major problem for women and people of color, both of whom are underrepresented in Congress. Relatedly, the demographics of a state or district can change during an incumbent's tenure. If so, then incumbents may lose touch with constituents. Without competitive elections, incumbents have less incentive to bring their views into line with those of a changing electorate. This is only a problem, however, if the ideology of an incumbent's electorate becomes more moderate or shifts toward the opposing party. If a district becomes more ideologically extreme, democratic accountability can happen in a primary election if a more extreme candidate challenges an incumbent.

At the same time, some argue that low competition may not be a serious problem. It may be less important whether party control of a congressional district changes regularly than whether party control of Congress as a whole changes regularly, which it clearly does. In addition, some researchers argue that voters who are on the losing side of a hard-fought race are less likely to trust or be satisfied with their representatives.[42] Finally, even if incumbents almost always win the general election, they must fight for their party's nomination in the primaries. Direct primaries were adopted precisely because they would introduce contested elections into jurisdictions dominated by a single party. And primaries do appear to provide some accountability for incumbents.[43] Critics point out, however, that some states have closed primaries, meaning that only registered members of the party can vote in them. Moreover, most primaries are not competitive, and many House incumbents do not face any primary opposition. In 2020, just 54 percent of Democratic and Republican House primaries were contested.[44]

Observers have proposed several reforms that might improve the competitiveness of congressional elections, including term limits, public financing, and redistricting. In a 2016 Quinnipiac poll, 82 percent of Americans embraced term limits, which require incumbents to leave office after having served a certain number of terms.[45] The Supreme Court, however, has ruled that term limits are unconstitutional for federal officeholders, so term limits could be adopted only through a constitutional amendment.

Public financing for congressional candidates would entail providing all candidates with a minimum amount of money to help get their campaigns off the ground. As we noted in Chapter 4, public financing does appear to increase competitiveness. But it is not clear whether Congress or most Americans would support public funding. Critics of public financing have noted that it can create "false" competitiveness since some districts really are decidedly Republican or Democratic. Subsidizing candidates of the minority party in such districts seems unnecessary and even wasteful.

A third kind of reform involves redistricting. Proposed reforms include taking the redistricting process out of the hands of state legislatures and giving it to independent commissions. There is some evidence that independent commissions create more competitive House districts.[46] States can also adopt guidelines that promote competition—for example, by requiring that competitive districts be created whenever possible. But these guidelines can actually conflict with other priorities, such as the imperative to create majority-minority districts under the Voting Rights Act. In 2000, Arizonans adopted a proposition that established an independent redistricting commission as well as a list of criteria for redistricting that included competitiveness. However, the redistricting commission found that once Native American and Latino districts had been drawn to comply with the Voting Rights Act, few Democrats were left in the state to spread around in the interest of creating competitive districts.[47] As a result, the districts created by the new commission were no more competitive than the districts that had been drawn by the state legislature in the past.[48]

Conclusion

The congressional scholar David Mayhew has described members of Congress as being "single-minded seekers of reelection."[49] Although this statement may be somewhat unfair to public servants who are motivated by other purposes, members of Congress do want to be reelected and spend a great deal of time pursuing reelection. The two-year House election cycle means that House members are campaigning virtually all of the time, while senators have time to focus on governing before turning their attention to the next election. However, even those senators who are not up for reelection may campaign on behalf of other senators in their party who are running. Thus, elections are always central for members of Congress.

Because of this "permanent campaign," the lines between campaigning and governing have become blurred. Members of Congress have changed the rules and procedures of Congress to aid them in pursuing reelection. For instance, prior to the institution of electronic voting in 1973, many votes taken in the House and Senate were anonymous. Since then, it has become common to demand a recorded vote, which makes all votes public. This has both made the legislative process more transparent and forced members of Congress to think of every vote as a potential campaign issue.[50] This can undermine the collegiality of Congress and contribute to gridlock.

Ultimately, focusing on electoral goals can make it difficult for party members to work together. At the same time, focusing on electoral goals is what keeps representatives "running scared" and in contact with their constituents—even if they are likely to win their next race. This is an important trade-off inherent in the permanent campaign: it may improve the quality of representation even as it hurts the quality of governance.

KEY TERMS

incumbent (p. 281)

open seat (p. 283)

quality challengers (p. 283)

political amateurs (p. 283)

Hill committees (p. 283)

earned media (or free media) (p. 293)

coordinated expenditures (p. 295)

independent expenditures (p. 295)

incumbency advantage (p. 295)

personal vote (p. 296)

franking privilege (p. 297)

casework (p. 297)

FOR DISCUSSION

1. What kinds of people make successful congressional candidates?
2. What roles do the parties play in congressional campaigns?
3. What explains the declining incumbency advantage in recent years?
4. How has the growing strength of the partisan vote affected congressional elections?

11

State and Local Campaigns

On the evening of November 5, 2019, most Americans who were paying close attention to politics were probably focused on the two dozen candidates who were competing for the Democratic nomination to take on President Donald Trump, who was himself in the middle of an impeachment inquiry, in 2020. But several states were holding important elections that night, and Kentucky was one of them. Incumbent Republican governor Matt Bevin was in a tight race with Democratic challenger Andy Beshear, the state's attorney general. Bevin's tenure as governor had been fraught with controversy, punctuated by an extended teachers' strike in protest of a Bevin-backed bill that would have reduced teachers' pension benefits. In response, Bevin called the teachers "selfish" and "thugs" and suggested that children were at risk of being sexually assaulted because they could not go to school and had to stay home alone during the strike. Beshear ran on a platform that, among other things, promised pay raises for teachers. He even picked a high school assistant principal as his running mate.[1]

The race between Bevin and Beshear was expensive and went down to the wire. The two candidates spent over $20 million combined.[2] On November 5, Beshear won by less than a percentage point, with a margin of only about 5,000 votes out of the 1.4 million cast. It was a major upset in a state that Trump had won by almost 30 percentage points in 2016. Beshear moved quickly to reshape the state's education policy. On his first day in office, he fired the state education board's 11 members, all of whom had been appointed by Bevin.

About 250 miles away on that same night, Zachary Baiel was attempting to become the next mayor of West Lafayette, Indiana. It was a long shot at best. Baiel's opponent, Democratic incumbent John Dennis, was running for his fourth term, and as of late October, Baiel had raised exactly $0. His campaign relied on door hangers he had photocopied at the public library and on his own personal door-to-door canvassing.[3] It made for a good underdog story, but like many underdogs, Baiel didn't win. On election night, he won 724 votes, while Dennis won 2,274.

Our focus in this chapter is on state and local races—that is, elections other than those that occur at the federal level. Although these elections receive far less attention than federal elections do, they make up most of the elections that take place in the United States. The winners have important power over where we can live, how we can act in public places and in our homes, and what our children will learn in school. During the COVID-19 pandemic, it was primarily state and local leaders who determined whether to close certain businesses and other institutions, impose mask mandates, require people to stay at home except for essential travel, and take other steps to reduce the transmission of the novel coronavirus. Even small differences in state and local election outcomes can generate important changes in policy, as Beshear's narrow victory illustrates. Indeed, Beshear's approach to the pandemic, which included restrictions on mass gatherings and in-person dining

Core of the Analysis

- State and local political offices and election laws often differ from their federal counterparts, and these differences affect campaign strategies.

- National political realities shape both candidate strategy and the outcomes of state and local races.

- State and local campaigns are increasingly adopting the techniques of national campaigns and are thereby becoming more expensive and professionalized.

- At the same time, many state and local campaigns attract scant media attention and require little fundraising, thereby necessitating very different campaign strategies and tactics.

- The rules of state and local elections, combined with their low visibility, affect the extent to which different groups of voters are effectively represented and can hold state and local officeholders accountable for their decisions.

In 2019, Democrat Andy Beshear eked out a victory against incumbent Kentucky governor, Republican Matt Bevin. What state and local factors may have contributed to Beshear's win in a state that Trump won by 30 points three years prior?

in restaurants as well as mask mandates for public schools, diverged significantly from what many Republican governors did and thus what Bevin would likely have done had a few thousand votes gone the other way. In short, state and local governments are a consequential part of America's governing structure.

State and local elections involve a wide array of offices, but an easy way to think about them is in terms of the three traditional branches of government. At the state and local levels, voters select members of the executive branch (such as governors, lieutenant governors, attorneys general, mayors), members of the legislature (state senates and houses, city councils), and often members of the judiciary (judges and justices). In addition, Americans elect a variety of other officials, including auditors, road and highway commissioners, surveyors, assessors, and coroners. Because there are so many states and localities with governments—the 50 states, over 3,000 counties, over 19,000 cities or municipalities, and nearly 14,000 school districts—the number of elections is vast.[4] In addition, many states and localities afford citizens the opportunity to vote on public policies (an opportunity that does not exist at the federal level) via ballot propositions, initiatives, and referenda. Citizens can also vote on whether to recall politicians from office and hold new elections to replace them. In 2020, almost 300 officials were targeted with recall efforts (although only 34 were successful).[5]

The "state and local" category is very broad, as the contrast between the Kentucky governor's election and the West Lafayette mayoral election reveals. Within this category, races vary dramatically in their resources and thus in the visibility of the campaigns themselves. Expensive statewide races, such as those for governor, are essentially analogous to U.S. Senate races. They have features similar to campaigns for federal office: professional consultants, pollsters, television and radio advertising, and so on. But many other races—in fact, most state and local races—have little if any of these features. They are often run on shoestring budgets. Family and friends replace paid consultants. Door hangers replace television advertisements. If one imagines a spectrum of campaigns running from those relying on lawn signs to those relying on television advertising to get out their message, most state and local races are closer to the lawn sign end of the spectrum.

In recent years, however, state and local elections have become both more professionalized and more nationalized. As money spent on state and local races has increased over time, some of these races have come to resemble more expensive campaigns. In part, outside groups are driving this trend; they have found that influencing these kinds of elections can be an effective way to shape policy. State party organizations also encourage their candidates to professionalize their campaigns to boost their chances of winning.

Even as candidates are able to muster more resources for their campaigns, state and local elections are becoming more and more linked to forces outside candidates' control—forces that seem far away from state capitals and local communities. Voting in state and local elections is increasingly tied to the national standing of the political parties and its most visible leaders, especially the president. It may seem strange that people's feelings about the president would shape the success of the president's party in local or state races, but this is often true in these elections, much as it is true in congressional elections.

Despite these trends, a large number of state and local campaigns remain uncompetitive, even relative to congressional elections. Incumbents frequently run unopposed. The news media's attention is usually elsewhere. Citizens turn out to vote in lower numbers and have little information to use in making their choices. And, just as with congressional districts, local districts can be drawn so that only one party has a realistic chance of winning. Under these circumstances, highly organized parties, activists, and interest groups can influence campaigns and election outcomes in ways that may not coincide with the preferences of most citizens in a district.

Zachary Baiel ran as an independent candidate for mayor of West Lafayette, Indiana, in 2019. Image © Nikos Frazier—USA TODAY NETWORK

Thus, state and local races—the ones that most affect many aspects of citizens' daily lives—are often the ones that live up to ideals of political campaigns the least. This is particularly unfortunate because state and local elections have the potential to promote citizen participation far more than national elections do. Not only does the sheer number of local and state elections offer citizens a multitude of opportunities to participate, but people also seem to be more comfortable getting involved in elections closer to home.[6] When citizens do participate, such elections move closer to the ideal.

We begin this chapter by discussing how local and state electoral rules affect these elections. We also consider how state and local elections depend on the prevailing political and economic winds—the reality that candidates must confront, such as a weak economy or an unpopular party. We discuss the broader impact of rules and reality on the incumbency advantage that is prevalent in state and local races and that influences how competitive these races are.

We then describe how both rules and reality lead to differences among federal, state, and local campaign strategies, and we also consider how these strategies are becoming more similar thanks to the increasing professionalization of state and local campaigns. We look at campaigns for state courts and ballot initiatives. We also discuss how the uncompetitive features of state and local campaigns have historically advantaged, and continue to advantage, organized interests of various kinds, especially political parties. The concluding section considers the paradox of local elections and its implications for democratic ideals.

Rules and Reality in Local Elections

Local elections typically operate under a very different set of rules than state and federal elections do, and they may also occur in a different context, or reality. Local electoral rules may differ from the electoral rules at other levels of government in three important ways: the use of nonpartisan ballots, at-large elections, and off-cycle elections. In addition, the reality of local elections is shaped in large part by the small scale and limited power of local governments and by the fact that the media largely ignore local elections.

Nonpartisan Elections

The use of nonpartisan ballots reflects a particular philosophy of governance that is associated with the turn-of-the-last-century Progressive movement (see Chapter 3). At that time, party machines governed many localities, especially large cities. Progressives thought that this system facilitated corruption, and they promoted reforms that stripped power from parties. One of these reforms was the institution of nonpartisan elections—that is, elections in which candidates are listed on the ballot without any party affiliations. This change curtailed party machines' ability to choose candidates and help them get elected to office (although, as we discuss later, this has not made parties irrelevant in contemporary city politics). The reform was also intended to promote the election of city officials more concerned with the practical challenges of policy making than with partisan politics. Today, over 75 percent of city council and mayoral elections are nonpartisan—differentiating them from the vast majority of state races and all federal races.

Studies of the nonpartisan ballot have shown, however, that it tends to decrease voter turnout. Voting may become more costly for some citizens if they cannot use partisanship as a simple rule for figuring out how to vote. Nonpartisan elections also appear to increase voters' reliance on another simple rule: incumbency. Without party labels, voters appear to gravitate toward the more familiar candidates, which only helps incumbents win reelection.[7]

At-Large Elections

A second way local elections differ is in the types of constituencies represented by elected officeholders. Recall from Chapter 2 that districts for the U.S. House of Representatives each elect a single representative, which makes them single-member districts. Many state legislatures also feature single-member districts. City council elections, by contrast, use a variety of methods of representation. Less than 20 percent of cities use districts (sometimes called *wards*) exclusively, although district elections are more common in the largest metropolitan areas, such as Los Angeles. Just over 20 percent use a mixed system, with some members elected from districts or wards and other members elected "at large." All voters in a city can vote for candidates for the at-large seats. The majority of cities, however, use at-large elections exclusively; this is particularly true among small and medium-sized cities (that is, those with populations of less than 200,000).[8] When mayors are elected by voters, they are always elected in at-large elections. The decision to use wards or districts as opposed to at-large elections can have important consequences for who gets elected. At-large elections disadvantage candidates of color if the local electorate is mostly composed of White voters who are more likely to support White candidates. Ward or district elections, on the other hand, can help candidates of color if ward boundaries are drawn to encompass neighborhoods in which people of color make up a large fraction of voters and provide a natural base of support for these candidates.[9]

Off-Cycle Elections

Local elections are often held off-cycle, meaning that they are not held concurrently with state or federal elections—another change instituted as part of Progressives' broader attempts to reform city governments. For example, like the mayoral race in West Lafayette, more than half of city council elections across the country are held at different times than state and national elections.[10] At the local level, off-cycle elections have at least two important consequences. First, they have significantly lower turnout. One study of 340 mayoral elections from 1996–2011 found that turnout in off-cycle mayoral elections is 27 percentage points lower than turnout in mayoral elections held concurrently with a presidential election and 15 percentage points lower than turnout in elections that coincide with midterm elections.[11] Second, off-cycle elections reduce the incumbency advantage in mayoral elections, perhaps because the smaller electorate in off-cycle elections is composed of politically engaged voters who know more about the candidates and rely less on simple cues like incumbency.[12]

Many cities hold off-cycle elections in an attempt to insulate local candidates from the events and issues that may be prominent in elections for higher levels of office. There is certainly evidence that voters judge local candidates based on how they handle issues specific to their community, such as the quality of the roads.[13] For example, one study of how voters in Houston, Texas, responded to deaths and damage caused by Tropical Storm Allison in 2001 found that those who disapproved of how Houston's mayor handled the crisis were less likely to vote for him in the next election.[14] At the same time, contentious battles over local governments' responses to the COVID-19 pandemic—including mask mandates and other measures— show how national issues and debates affect local politics and elections.

The Reality of Small-Scale Democracy

Just like federal officeholders and candidates, candidates and officeholders in local communities confront important aspects of reality that constrain their campaigns. First, many local jurisdictions are small, and they bring in lower revenues and provide fewer services than larger jurisdictions do. For example, cities with fewer than 100,000 people rarely offer services beyond water, sewage, police, fire, parks, and street repair. This limits the formal powers of elected officials and their ability to target services toward important constituencies, especially compared with federal officials who can target programs to seniors, farmers, and many other different groups and try to leverage those programs to build support in an election.[15]

Another reality of local elections is that they get very little news coverage, especially if the contest is taking place in a large media market.[16] Because media markets often span large geographic areas encompassing multiple municipal, county, congressional, and even state boundaries, the media in larger markets tend to focus on higher-level races that interest a broader segment of their viewers. In fact, research has found that local elections typically account for less than 5 percent of campaign-related television news stories, even in midterm years when there is no presidential contest to steal the spotlight.[17] This trend has gotten even worse as local television stations have been acquired by national conglomerates that emphasize national politics at the expense of local politics.[18] Local elections also feature less prominently in local newspapers, whose financial challenges and shrinking staffs translate into fewer resources for coverage of local government.[19]

A third reality is that incumbents accrue significant advantages. Compared with challengers, incumbents are better positioned to have personal contact with voters. They are more likely to get endorsements from prominent leaders and media outlets, and they are better able to raise money. Thus, research on local elections has found incumbency advantages for offices like mayor that are larger than those for the U.S. House. For example, in mayoral elections from 1988 to 2016, incumbents were 33 percent more likely than nonincumbents to win.[20] John Dennis's easy victory in West Lafayette—with 76 percent of the vote—illustrates this incumbency advantage. The power of incumbency means that many local elections are not very competitive.

A final reality confronting local candidates is the power of partisanship. Although the issues in local politics can seem far removed from the partisan debates in Washington, D.C., voters still tend to vote for the candidate of the party they favor. Indeed, the correlation between voting for president and voting for local offices has increased over time, suggesting that local elections, similar to congressional elections, are now more nationalized.[21] To be sure, the nonpartisan ballot and the incumbency advantage mean that partisanship in local elections is still not as powerful as it is in federal elections, and there is more split-ticket voting in local elections.[22] Nevertheless, liberal cities tend to elect Democratic mayors and conservative cities tend to elect Republican mayors. Candidates for office have to face the reality of whether they match a community's political and ideological complexion closely enough to win.

Rules and Reality in State Elections

Certain rules distinguish state elections from both local and federal elections. Many states use term limits, which have implications for both aspiring officeholders and incumbents. Variations in state laws concerning how long state legislatures are in session and how much state legislators get paid have consequences for how professionalized state legislatures are, which in turn affects state legislative elections. State elected officials also confront distinct political realities that arise from variations in the strength of state party organizations.

In other respects, however, state elections face the same realities that affect local and federal elections. One is the possibility of coattail effects, whereby the outcomes at higher levels of office affect the outcomes of state elections. Another is the incumbency advantage. Third, and perhaps most important, are the national forces beyond state candidates' control that may affect their chances of winning. The importance of national forces has grown in recent years as gubernatorial and state legislative elections have become more closely connected to the standing of the national parties and national political figures, such as the president.

Term Limits

Many state elections are affected by a rule that members of Congress never confront: term limits. As we noted in Chapter 2, most states limit the number of terms that a governor can serve, and a substantial minority limit the terms of state legislators as well. The most common limit for governor, following the restrictions on presidents, is two consecutive terms. Statewide offices therefore see more turnover than either the U.S. House or Senate, where incumbents can accrue some advantage from their years of service, as we discussed in Chapter 10. Term limits can change the calculus of both aspiring and current officeholders. Aspiring officeholders know that they will be able to run for an open seat on a regular basis. Current officeholders know that their tenure is short-lived, and they may therefore be even more inclined to position themselves to run for higher levels of office once, or even before, their term has expired.

The natural conclusion, then, would be that term limits make elections more competitive by weakening incumbents' advantages and increasing the number of open-seat races. However, the real story is more complicated. Although term limits have been instrumental in reducing the number of incumbents running in elections, this does not necessarily make elections as a whole more competitive.[23] Instead, what often happens is that first-term officeholders run for reelection without a serious challenger; serious challengers would rather wait until the incumbent leaves office at the end of the term limit than mount a long-shot challenge. Moreover, several factors often combine to make it difficult for more than one serious challenger to compete for a newly open seat. In legislative elections, districts may be dominated by one party due to underlying demographics or prior redistricting. Leaders in the dominant party may work to promote one favored candidate and thereby avoid a hotly contested primary. As a consequence, term limits do not consistently result in closer races.

Legislative Professionalism

Another category of rules concerns the **professionalism** of state legislatures. The U.S. Congress is perhaps the most salient model of a professional legislature: seats in Congress are full-time jobs that come with a substantial salary and staff support. Being a senator or representative in the national legislature is essentially a profession, like being a doctor or lawyer. But this model is hardly universal. State legislatures are often far less professional. Depending on state law, they may meet for only a few months every other year, as in North Dakota and Texas. Legislators in some states receive only small salaries. In fact, New Mexico state legislators receive no salary, only reimbursement for expenses. State legislatures also vary widely in the number of staff they employ. New York's professionalized state legislature has almost 3,000 staff members, but Vermont's has fewer than 100.[24] Legislatures that are not as professionalized are sometimes called **citizen legislatures**.[25] Four state legislatures—Montana, North Dakota, South Dakota, and Wyoming—might be characterized in this way. On the other end, about 25 percent of state legislatures are highly professionalized, with the rest falling somewhere in between.[26]

The professionalism of the legislature has a two-edged effect on the incumbency advantage. On the one hand, the more professionalized the legislature, the likelier its incumbents are to attract challengers. This is not surprising: jobs in a professionalized legislature are particularly attractive. But even though they face challengers more often, incumbents in professional legislatures are *less* vulnerable because they have more resources at their disposal. Like members of Congress, they can claim credit for significant legislative accomplishments and serve their constituents' needs via casework. They can use the perquisites of their office to raise more money than incumbents in citizen legislatures can. This helps explain why incumbents in professionalized legislatures are reelected at higher rates.[27]

State and Local Party Organizational Strength

State and local party organizations across the country vary dramatically in terms of their strength, with Republicans generally being stronger organizationally than Democrats.[28] They act as service organizations that supplement candidates' campaigns with important resources, such as financial support, polling services, media consulting, and voter mobilization programs. They also connect candidates with party-allied interest groups. Candidates running where their party organization is strong will have considerably more help than those running where their party organization is weak.

What determines a state or local party's organizational strength? First, urban, educated communities tend to foster better-developed party organizations.[29] Such areas tend to be dense in local organizations that create social capital, which parties can tap. There is also evidence that parties are stronger in more competitive jurisdictions because that is where they are needed most.[30] Finally, most state parties consist of an alliance of official party organizations, unofficial party organizations led by individual party leaders, and various interest groups—all of which must coordinate on candidates to support for office.[31] To the extent that there is fighting within a party or between a party and its interest group allies, the party will face additional challenges. An example of such a fight would be the attempts by progressive activists and leaders, many of whom were aligned with Senator Bernie Sanders in the 2016 and 2020 presidential primaries, to promote progressive candidates in Democratic primaries for state and local offices. These efforts frequently led to fights and acrimony between progressives and more moderate leaders and candidates in the Democratic Party.

Coattail Effects

The presence of higher-profile candidates on the ballot, such as candidates for president, can help candidates for state and local office. This is particularly true in places where state and local elections occur alongside more-visible federal elections. Only five states—Kentucky, Louisiana, Mississippi, New Jersey, and Virginia—hold their gubernatorial elections off-cycle, just as many municipalities across the nation do, so that they do not compete with any federal elections.

What happens when candidates for more-visible offices are on the ballot? They may create a **coattail effect**: candidates for less-visible offices will "ride the coattails" of a popular candidate of the same party who is on the ballot and thereby do better at the polls. For example, for every additional 10 points of vote share that go to a party's gubernatorial candidate, 1–2 points of vote share go to that party's candidates for other statewide offices, such as attorney general.[32]

Coattails may matter most for challengers and open-seat candidates, who do not have the advantages of incumbency. Coattails also matter more in the seven states where voters can cast a "straight-ticket" vote by pulling a single lever or punching a single button to select all the Democrats or all the Republicans on the ballot.[33]

FIGURE 11.1 Percentage of General-Election Candidates in 2020 State Legislative Races with No Major-Party Opposition

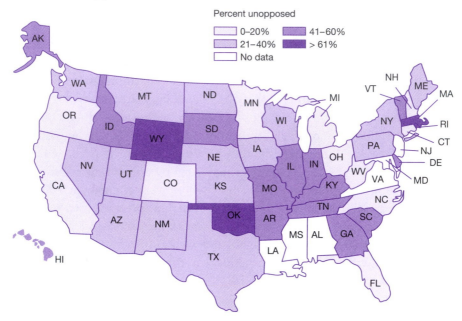

Source: Percentages calculated by the author.

Incumbency Advantage

While the advantages that accrue to incumbents are visible in state elections, they are more relevant for state legislators than for governors. The incumbency advantage for governors has shrunk, much like it has for members of Congress.[34] This reflects the nationalization of state elections, a topic that we will turn to next. Incumbent state legislators retain certain advantages because they often face little competition at all. Many state legislative elections, including both primary and general elections, are not even contested—meaning that one candidate runs unopposed. There has been a striking decline in contested primaries for state legislative elections: from 1910 to 1938, 50 percent of primaries were contested, but from 1992 to 2016, fewer than 20 percent were.[35] In general-election state legislative races in 2020, 35 percent of major-party candidates faced no major-party opposition. In many states, that fraction was even higher (see Figure 11.1).[36] By contrast, in the 2020 U.S. Senate and House general election, this was true of only 3 percent of seats.[37] This lack of competitiveness tends to help incumbents. It is especially rare for incumbents to face challengers who have raised as much money as they have, or even anything close to it. In an effort to provide funding to lesser-known challengers, a few states have adopted clean elections laws—that is, full public funding for statewide and legislative elections (see Chapter 4). Public funding is associated with a greater likelihood that an incumbent will face a challenger, but this effect is quite small; public funding alone is no panacea for uncompetitive state legislative elections.[38]

National Factors

Elections for state offices, like those for the presidency or Congress, are strongly affected by national factors, not just by conditions in a particular state or community. This has become even truer over time, just as it has in congressional elections. To be sure, we do not mean to suggest that individual states have no unique circumstances or trends; one can often see clear differences in the dynamics of federal and state elections. For example, in the American South, the gradual shift from one-party rule by the Democrats to a strong tendency to support Republicans occurred much more quickly at the federal level than it did at the state level.[39]

It was once true that conservative Democrats in state and local races could win over southerners who otherwise supported Republicans for president. But now voters rarely split their tickets in this fashion. Statewide elections thus tend to produce leaders who match the partisanship of the state, and fewer states have "split outcomes," such as when the state elects a governor from one party but favors the presidential candidate of the other party.[40] This means that a state's overall partisanship affects election outcomes more than the unique characteristics of candidates for statewide office do.

Growing party loyalty in state elections helps to make these elections more nationalized. For example, voting in gubernatorial elections is increasingly correlated with voting in presidential elections—that is, people tend to vote for the same party's candidate at both levels of office.[41] Moreover, state and local candidates in the president's party often do better when the president is more popular. In fact, this is true regardless of whether a presidential election is occurring when local candidates are on the ballot. Just as the president's party loses seats in Congress when the president is unpopular, it loses seats in, and sometimes control of, state legislatures.[42] The 2010 midterm illustrates this point: the Democrats not only lost seats in Congress but also lost control of six governorships and nearly 700 state legislative seats (including control of 21 different legislative chambers). Another national factor that affects state elections is the economy. State leaders are judged not only on the economy in their state but also on national economic performance, even though there is almost nothing they can do to affect the national economy.[43]

Another factor that may increase nationalization is the news media's declining attention to state races, which parallels the decline in attention to local races. The number of staff at local newspapers—including the number of reporters who cover state politics—has dropped significantly.[44] Unsurprisingly, the number of voters who can correctly recall the name of their governor has also fallen.[45] The consequences of getting at least some local news coverage about state politics are visible in a study of television news. This research takes advantage of the fact that media markets can include portions of more than one state, meaning that some people who live in that market will see news about politicians from a different state. For example, the Philadelphia media market includes not just the Philadelphia area but also southern New Jersey. Compared to people in an out-of-state market, like residents of southern New Jersey, people who live in an in-state market see more news coverage of their governor and are less likely to vote in a purely partisan fashion. For example, they are about 4–5 percentage points more likely to split their ticket in the presidential and gubernatorial races. This seems to be the consequence of getting more information about incumbent governors and gubernatorial elections.[46]

Campaign Strategies Big and Small

As the stories at the beginning of this chapter make clear, it is not easy to generalize about the strategies of state and local campaigns. At a minimum, of course, almost every candidate for any level of office wants the same thing: to win enough votes to win the election. Certain features of state and local governments, however, shape candidates' strategies for achieving that goal. In particular, the size of a jurisdiction, the powers of the office, the rules that govern election to that office, and the growing nationalization of state and local politics all interact to shape a candidate's strategy.

One important feature is the size of a jurisdiction. In cities and districts with fewer people, candidates rely heavily on personal connections for campaigning. This is why many local and state campaigns are nearly invisible. Candidates raise little money. Their campaign organizations are composed of a few friends and family. They take no polls, air no ads, and rely on relatively

Many state and local races are less visible to voters, who may know little about the candidates in downticket races (those below president and Congress). For example, voters in this Texas county were called on to elect a county commissioner and several judges.

cheap forms of communication, such as Zachary Baiel's door hangers, social media, billboards, and the occasional radio ad. In more populated places, personal connections and groups still matter, but candidates must use mass advertising on television and radio to reach more voters. This means raising larger sums of money, hiring consultants, and the like. A statewide campaign for governor, like the 2019 Kentucky race, is essentially a presidential campaign run on a smaller scale.

Candidate strategy depends on the powers of the office as well. For example, mayors of small towns mainly oversee services such as fire and police protection, water, and sewage. Governors and state legislators oversee a wider range of policy areas that involve more explicitly ideological debates, including economic policy, Medicaid funding, state educational curricula, and so on. As a result, candidates for mayor in a small town are more likely to emphasize their managerial skills, while candidates for governor may express a larger vision for the state that involves taking liberal or conservative positions.[47] Candidates in larger jurisdictions, such as a state, also need to appeal to different groups in order to build a winning coalition. They may emphasize issues important to key constituent groups—for example, by defending the Second Amendment to appeal to gun owners. A small-town mayor may find such targeted appeals less necessary.

Candidate strategy should also vary based on the rules that govern the election. City council races are a good example. In cities with single-member districts, residential segregation may mean that many districts include a large majority of one racial or ethnic group. In turn, this means that candidates must appeal to voters from the dominant group in their district. Washington, D.C., for instance, has eight members elected from wards and five members, including the chair, elected at large. City council wards tend to be majority White or Black and to elect White or Black city council members, respectively. Candidates for at-large seats may not need to appeal to smaller racial or ethnic groups, however: a winning coalition can be built from the dominant or majority racial or ethnic group within the city. This is why at-large systems can disadvantage candidates from minority racial and ethnic groups.

Nationalization has implications for candidate strategy as well: it tends to make strategies in state and local races similar to those in federal races. Voting patterns in state and local races show that partisanship and ideology shape how citizens vote and who wins. Thus, states and localities that lean Democratic are more likely to elect Democrats, with a similar result for Republican localities and candidates.[48] This will be increasingly true as politics continues to nationalize. One implication of this trend is its effect on who runs for office in the first place. In some predominantly Democratic cities, there may be only Democratic candidates for mayor. Nationalization also has implications for the messages that candidates choose. In a more nationalized political environment, federal debates about issues such as immigration, education, and COVID-19 filter down to states and communities, and state and local candidates debate the very issues that routinely divide candidates for Congress and the White House. Data show that state political parties increasingly talk about the same national issues in their platforms, and governors' annual "State of the State" addresses increasingly talk about the same issues as the president's State of the Union address.[49] National politics can thus overshadow the distinctive political complexion and concerns of communities around the country.

The Push toward Professionalization

Even as state and local campaigns are, on average, less professionalized than federal campaigns, they have increasingly come to resemble them—with more spending, television advertising, and consultants than in the past. State parties are also driving professionalization. They conduct polls and hire consultants to help formulate strategy that the party's candidates can then implement. Many political consultants focus their practice within a given state and advertise their detailed knowledge of the local terrain. To some extent, the push toward professionalization is simply an arms race: once one side raises enough money to hire consultants and air television advertising, the other side will try to do the same. The push to professionalization is perhaps most evident in two types of campaigns: those for ballot initiatives and referenda and those for state judicial offices.

Ballot Initiatives

Ballot initiatives and **referenda** are proposals placed on the ballot that allow citizens to change law and public policy. Their forms vary, but in most cases, initiatives involve citizens or interest groups drafting legislation and getting it put on the ballot. These are called *direct initiatives*. In the case of referenda, the legislature refers a piece of legislation to the people to approve or reject it. The most common type of referendum is a proposed amendment to the state constitution. Ballot initiatives and referenda are sometimes called "direct democracy" because they are voted on directly by citizens rather than by elected representatives. Twenty-four states and the District of Columbia allow ballot initiatives, and 26 states allow referenda. Each state has its own criteria for how initiatives and referenda get on the ballot.[50] The number of initiatives or referenda varies by year. In 2020, 129 ballot measures addressing a wide range of topics were put to voters across the country. For example, voters in six states chose to decriminalize marijuana use or to allow its use for medical purposes. A number of initiatives and amendments had to do with election procedures. In California, voters passed a measure extending voting rights to people convicted of felonies who are now on parole. In Massachusetts, voters defeated a measure that would have enabled ranked-choice voting for statewide and congressional elections. There were also initiatives related to affirmative action, the use of psychedelic mushrooms, and the reintroduction of wolves, among other issues.[51]

Although direct democracy empowers citizens in some respects, many ballot initiatives are hardly the results of grassroots organizing. Instead, interest groups and wealthy individuals work to place their proposals on the ballot and then spend money to promote them. A highly controversial ballot measure in a large state will ultimately cost supporters and opponents many millions of dollars. For example, in California in 2020, the campaigns for and against categorizing app-based drivers as independent contractors—a measure favored by companies such as Uber and Lyft—spent about $225 million. Little can be done to limit the amounts spent in ballot initiative campaigns. Supreme Court precedent forbids limits on donations to committees formed to support or oppose initiatives; it also forbids bans on corporate spending in ballot initiative campaigns. The logic is that initiatives, unlike candidates, cannot be corrupted by money, and thus there is no compelling interest that would allow restrictions on speech.[52]

With so much money involved, the task of getting a measure on the ballot and promoting it now involves a wide array of campaign professionals. There are law firms who craft the wording of the initiative, consulting firms who specialize in gathering the signatures needed to get the initiative on the ballot, media firms who produce radio and television ads promoting or denouncing the initiative, pollsters who monitor public opinion about the initiative, and direct-mail firms who design and send letters to citizens about the initiative. Consultants often relish the opportunity to work on these campaigns, which offer them greater latitude to shape the campaign message than they might have working with an actual candidate. As one consultant said, "With ballot issues you build your own candidate."[53]

There is evidence that ballot initiative campaigns can influence the outcomes of votes on these measures. In one study from the 2008 election in Oregon (which we discussed in Chapter 7), a subset of voters was randomly assigned to receive ballot guides from a political action committee that took positions on 12 different initiatives. Receiving a guide (as opposed to not receiving a guide) shifted people's voting patterns by anywhere from 3 to 6 points. For two initiatives, the effects were large enough to potentially change the outcome.[54]

Of course, not all initiative campaigns will have such an impact. In particular, these campaigns must deal with the general tendency of some voters to vote "no" on initiatives—a sort of "status quo bias" that leads many initiatives to fare worse at the ballot box than they initially did in the polls.[55] This bias may also make it harder for the side favoring an initiative to win, even when it spends more money than the initiative's opponents do. For example, out of the 13 initiatives on the ballot in California in 2020, the side that spent more money won nine times. In the other four cases, the majority voted "no" even though the "yes" side spent more money, potentially illustrating the status quo bias at work.[56]

Judicial Elections

Judicial elections are quite common in U.S. states. Only eight states do not elect any judges.[57] There are three basic types of judicial elections. Partisan elections pit opposing candidates identified with political parties against each other. Nonpartisan elections also feature opposing candidates, but they run without party labels (although political parties may endorse them). **Retention elections** are referenda on sitting judges in which voters decide whether they should remain on the bench. Typically, judges in a retention system are appointed for a period of years by the governor and are subject to a retention election after that period is over. Judges are normally retained, but occasionally they are removed if they have made an unpopular ruling. For example, in 2010, three justices from the Iowa Supreme Court lost their retention elections after the court ruled in favor of gay marriage. Only three other judges had suffered this fate in the 48-year history of judicial elections in Iowa.

Campaigns for judicial offices were once staid affairs that featured little electioneering, but they have come to resemble campaigns for executive and legislative offices. Judicial campaigns are costly: the total amount of money raised by state supreme court candidates across the country jumped from $11.5 million in the 1989–90 election cycle to almost $67.6 million a decade later (see Figure 11.2).[58] Candidate fundraising has not hit that peak since, but spending by both political parties and outside groups has increased since 2000. In 2016, for example, parties and interest groups accounted for 41 percent of the total spending in state supreme court campaigns.[59] One consequence of this spending is an increasing number of television advertisements. For example, in midterm elections, the number of ad spots in state supreme court campaigns increased from 24,762 in 2002 to 40,314 in 2018. In presidential election years, the number increased from 44,741 in 2004 to 71,571 in 2016.[60] The ads are frequently hard-hitting, accusing judges of sleeping during trials, "putting criminals on the street," and the like. There are fewer ads in judicial races for lower courts, but there are still concerted campaigns to elect local judges. In the 2018 election in Harris County, Texas—where Houston is located—Democrats unseated more than 50 incumbent Republican judges. Among the newly elected Democratic judges were 17 African American women whom the party supported as part of a "Black Girl Magic" ad campaign.[61]

One reason for the existence and increased expense of state judicial elections is that political actors see value in holding these elections and in spending money to influence them. Conservative politicians—who must deal with a legal system in which many leading lawyers and law professors

FIGURE 11.2 Contributions to State Supreme Court Candidates, 1990–2018 Election Cycles

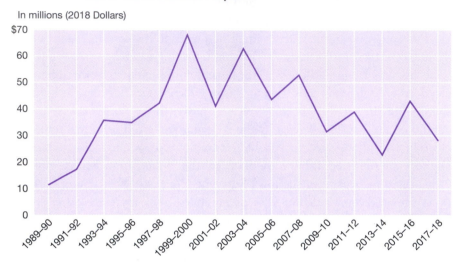

Source: Brennan Center for Justice.

are liberal—have pushed for judicial elections knowing that the less-liberal average electorate might put more conservative judges on the bench.[62]

Interest groups also participate in judicial elections to help elect judges more sympathetic to their position. For example, starting in the 1990s, business groups increasingly came into conflict with trial lawyers, consumer groups, and labor unions over tort reform. Tort reform typically entails limits to the awards that plaintiffs can win from corporations and businesses for, say, an allegedly faulty product. Business groups favored these reforms, but trial lawyers and consumer groups did not. This conflict spilled over into the judicial arena because appellate and state court justices often heard tort cases on appeal and could adjust the amount of money awarded to plaintiffs. For interest groups, it can even be cheaper to influence judicial elections than to elect a favorable majority in the state legislature or a sympathetic governor. As one Ohio union official put it, "We figured out a long time ago that it's easier to elect seven judges than to elect 132 legislators."[63]

Needless to say, such sentiments do nothing to allay the fear that expensive campaigns compromise judges' integrity. A case in point involved West Virginia supreme court justice Brent Benjamin. In 2004, Benjamin defeated incumbent justice Warren McGraw with the help of Don Blankenship, the CEO of a West Virginia mining company, Massey Energy. Before the campaign, Massey Energy had been sued by Harman Mining Company for breach of contract, and a jury ruled that Massey owed $50 million. Blankenship then spent $3 million in an attempt to defeat McGraw, establishing a group called "And for the Sake of the Kids" that aired ads accusing McGraw of "voting to let a child rapist out of prison." Three years after Benjamin won the judgeship, West Virginia's supreme court heard Massey Energy's appeal of the earlier $50 million verdict. Benjamin provided the swing vote in a 3–2 decision that overturned the verdict. Later, the U.S. Supreme Court threw out the West Virginia court's decision, arguing that Benjamin faced a conflict of interest so extreme that Harman Mining's due process rights may have been violated.[64]

Even retention elections, which were originally created to help insulate judges from political pressures, create their own unintended consequences. As the 2010 Iowa judicial races showed, retention elections have become weaponized for partisan goals. Research has found that judges in retention election systems are actually very sensitive to public opinion, suggesting that they are well aware that an unpopular decision could lead to a successful campaign to throw them out.[65]

Accountability and Representation in State and Local Politics

The entry of interest groups into state judicial elections exemplifies a broader feature of many state and local campaigns. With less visible campaigning and media coverage, dedicated activists, including motivated groups of voters, party organizations, and interest groups, can powerfully affect these races without attracting much attention or even competition. For them, it takes fewer resources to get a larger benefit: greater influence over state and local races than might be possible in more-visible federal races. As a consequence, elected officials may better represent the views of activists than the views of voters as a whole.

The rules of local elections, especially their timing, also contribute to this distortion in representation. Parties and activists have long sought to manipulate the timing of elections to maximize their electoral or policy goals.[66] Holding elections off-cycle has a particularly notable effect because these elections draw a lower turnout, which in turn empowers habitual voters, who tend to be older, as well as interest groups whose members are likely to vote.[67]

One example that illustrates the importance of off-cycle elections has to do with teacher pay. In school districts with off-cycle elections, teachers are typically paid more than teachers in districts with on-cycle elections. That is, in the former type of district, teachers' unions are more likely to get their desired outcome: larger paychecks. This may result from the ability of teachers and their allies to have influence in low-turnout elections. It may also result from the fact that older voters, most of whom do not have school-age children, may be paying less attention to school board elections and educational issues, thus allowing the voices of teachers to have more weight. The risk is that these policies do not represent what most voters want. Indeed, school board elections conducted off-cycle appear to elect board members whose views are further from those of their constituents.[68]

Local electoral rules that lead to lower levels of turnout also create biases in terms of which groups are represented in government. The people who vote and are otherwise active in local politics tend to be Whiter, wealthier, and more conservative than those who do not regularly partici-pate.[69] The representation of people of color suffers as a consequence. In low-turnout elections, candidates of color are more likely to lose mayoral elections and elections for city council; consequently, the spending priori-ties of local governments are often out of step with the views of constitu-ents of color.[70] The same is true for housing policy. When cities consider building affordable housing, which would disproportionately benefit poor people and people of color, those projects are often derailed or curtailed by local residents who tend to be Whiter and wealthier than voters as a whole.[71]

A partial remedy for these representational inequalities would be shift-ing local elections from off-cycle to on-cycle. Local elections held on the same date as presidential elections produce higher turnout as well as an electorate that is more representative in terms of race, class, ideology, and party. This in turn leads to better representation for people of color as well as people with lower incomes.[72]

A challenge related to representational inequality has to do with account-ability. State and local elections are often uncompetitive and attract little news coverage, so voters do not get much information about what incum-bent officials are doing or what their challengers would do differently. Thus, voters are not always able to hold state and local leaders accountable for their decisions in office.

As a result, evidence is mixed on the question of whether local leaders are held sufficiently accountable for things like the local economy, the perfor-mance of schools, and the crime rate. A similar finding emerges in state legis-latures: there is little evidence that voters sanction their state representatives for casting unpopular votes or being ideologically out of step overall. This lack of accountability is worsened when there is little media coverage of state politics.[73] Thus, state legislative elections provide another opportunity for motivated citizens and activists to assert their influence.[74]

The Paradox of State and Local Elections

The invisibility of many state and local campaigns gives rise to a paradox. State and local leaders are in some sense "closest" to citizens: they are intimately involved with the communities they represent, and their decisions affect virtually every aspect of life there—from whether schools get new textbooks to whether potholes get filled. Despite their potential significance, state and local elections engage many fewer voters than federal and especially presidential elections do. With little spending by the candidates and little attention from the media, voters are unfamiliar with the candidates and do not learn much during the campaigns. Reforms like the nonpartisan ballot and off-cycle elections make things even worse. As a consequence, turnout in many state and local elections has not followed the trend of increasing turnout that has characterized presidential elections. Instead, state and local turnout has stagnated or even declined.[75]

This state of affairs has important implications for the democratic values that we can use to evaluate campaigns. When state and local elections are uncompetitive, and even uncontested, it is not clear that they meet the standard of free choice, which requires that citizens can choose between at least two candidates, or the standard of deliberation, which requires that citizens have adequate information about the candidates. This lack of competitiveness stems from various factors. One is the incumbency advantage, as we have noted. Another is the fact that many localities are not politically diverse and so tend not to have competitive general elections. Any lack of competitiveness can also stem from actions taken by leaders, parties, and interest groups. When one party dominates a city's politics, it often tries to perpetuate its reign via strategies that render elections less competitive and reduce turnout.[76]

These shortcomings are connected to concerns about another value: political equality. The rules that govern state and especially local elections appear to put a disproportionate burden on people of color and people with lower incomes. In particular, off-cycle elections appear to create an electorate that is unrepresentative in terms of race, ethnicity, and social class. In turn, this means that voters who generally are not part of this electorate are not well represented in local offices. They are less able to elect candidates who share their demographics or views.

It is clear, however, that remedying these problems may raise other concerns. The kinds of campaigns and elections that see higher levels of competitiveness and voter engagement are also those that are more expensive, more partisan, and often nastier. State judicial elections illustrate this trade-off. We have described the concerns that many observers have with electing judges and the politicization of even nonpartisan retention elections. But at the same time, expensive judicial elections, including retention elections, tend to increase voter turnout and reduce the advantages of incumbent judges.[77]

Moreover, competitive judicial elections may improve the deliberative quality of elections by giving voters what they want: information about what judges believe and how they are likely to rule. In one 2008 survey, large majorities of respondents thought that judicial candidates should be allowed to attack their opponents and express their views on controversial issues. This may reflect a very reasonable desire to have a judiciary that is not out of step with the electorate. As a result, citizens do not necessarily react negatively to contested judicial elections. In one careful study of the 2006 Kentucky judicial elections, which included interviews with respondents before and after the campaign, the majority of respondents did not come to view the Kentucky courts as less legitimate because of the campaign.[78]

In short, any solution to the paradox of state and local elections requires significant trade-offs. There are clear benefits to more competitive elections, including higher turnout and better representation of different groups in the electorate and in political office. But it is hard to get those benefits without tolerating aspects of campaigns and elections that frequently make us uncomfortable. Hotly contested elections tend to be more professionalized and more expensive. This can make for mean and rowdy campaigns, while the money flowing into them raises additional concerns about the possibility of corruption. There is no easy way to make state and local elections more engaging to voters without dealing with potential downsides.

Conclusion

State and local elections may often seem like small potatoes. The candidates are typically little known, and the campaigns are often unsophisticated. But they have considerable strategic importance. For ambitious people, state and local offices can be important for incubating political careers. Presidents Barack Obama and Jimmy Carter began their careers as state legislators. Other presidents began their careers in elected office as governors, including Ronald Reagan, Bill Clinton, and George W. Bush.

State and local politics are especially important for candidates from groups that have traditionally been underrepresented in political office, such as women and people of color. Potential candidates from these groups face significant barriers if they want to start their political careers at higher levels of office, such as Congress. Success is more likely within state and local politics, where the barriers are lower and where candidates can gain the experience, visibility, and viability needed to seek higher office.

State and local politics are also important to political parties and interest groups. Decision-making at these levels affects a variety of policies that parties and groups care about, including taxation, schools, prisons, roads, and health care. Because most state and local elections are rarely covered by the news media and thus largely invisible to voters, party and interest group activists can work behind the scenes. As a result, the outcomes—who gets elected, which policies are passed—may reflect their goals more than the average voter's.

KEY TERMS

professionalism (p. 312)	ballot initiatives (p. 319)
citizen legislatures (p. 312)	referenda (p. 319)
coattail effect (p. 313)	retention elections (p. 321)

FOR DISCUSSION

1. What is legislative professionalism and how does it affect the advantages of incumbents in state legislatures?

2. How do the strategies employed in state and local campaigns typically differ from those in federal campaigns?

3. Why do many state and local races give political party organizations and interest groups a particular opportunity to influence elections?

4. What are the possible advantages and disadvantages of having state and local elections become more competitive?

12

Voter Participation

A few days before the 2018 midterm elections, one of the authors of this text-book was having a conversation with an operative from U.S. senator Ted Cruz's campaign. Cruz, who had unsuccessfully sought the 2016 Republican presidential nomination, was in an unexpectedly close contest with Democratic challenger Robert "Beto" O'Rourke, a congressman from El Paso, for Texas's junior seat in the U.S. Senate. O'Rourke had become a true phenomenon: over the course of his campaign, he visited all 254 counties in the state, raised $80 million from donors across the country, and used social media and livestreaming to connect directly with voters. Polls showed a tight race, and early voting numbers from the Lone Star State indicated an exceptionally heavy turnout in urban areas where Democrats have an advantage, such as Houston, Dallas–Fort Worth, San Antonio, and Austin.

The political scientist asked the operative whether he was concerned about Cruz's chances in an election with very high turnout. In the 2014 midterm elections, when Cruz won his Senate seat, 4.7 million Texans cast ballots. Surely Cruz would be concerned if turnout in 2018 approached the 8 million voters that some analysts were now projecting. No, the operative said: the Cruz team was actually hoping that turnout would top 8 million. He argued that O'Rourke's voters, many of whom genuinely supported O'Rourke and many of whom simply wanted to register their opposition to President Donald Trump, were so motivated that their participation was all but guaranteed. Rather, the real question was whether Republicans in Texas's exurban and rural counties would show up to support Cruz, a polarizing figure who was unpopular in the Senate. Cruz campaign officials believed that they could be in trouble if turnout hit the 7.5 to 8 million range, but anything north of

8 million would mean that their voters had come through. In the latter scenario, Cruz would win by a couple of percentage points. In the end, close to 8.4 million votes were cast, and Cruz was reelected by a margin of 2.6 percentage points.

This story illustrates several themes in this chapter. First, voters are fired up. Turnout in presidential elections has been increasing since 2000, and turnout in the 2018 midterm election broke records around the country. In Texas, for example, 2018 turnout was 18 percentage points higher than turnout in the 2014 midterm. Usually, high levels of turnout are a sign of a healthy democracy, but that may not be the case in the United States. Majorities of both parties agree that voters in the two parties cannot come to terms on basic facts and describe supporters of the other party as closed-minded. A majority of Republicans say that Democrats are unpatriotic.[1] This growing dislike and distrust between partisans may be motivating citizens to vote, in turn generating record high turnout.

This story also illustrates the baseless nature of a widely believed conventional wisdom: that Democratic candidates benefit from high turnout. As Senator Bernie Sanders claimed during his run for the Democratic nomination for president in 2016, "Democrats win when turnout is high. . . . Republicans win when the voter turnout is low."[2] O'Rourke learned the hard way in 2018 that this is simply not the case. Marginal voters—those who are on the fence about voting—tend to be less interested in and knowledgeable about politics than habitual voters. When an election brings them to the polls, they "blow with the political wind," voting for whichever candidate is benefiting from

Core of the Analysis

- The rules that govern elections determine who is eligible to vote and how easy it is for an individual to participate.

- Because of its rules, the United States has lower voter turnout than other developed democracies.

- Citizens' participation depends on three factors: ability, motivation, and opportunity.

- These factors create participatory distortions when they encourage some groups of people to participate more than others.

- Mobilization by political campaigns and high-stakes elections encourage people to participate.

current conditions.[3] Thus, a low-turnout midterm election can benefit Democrats, just as the 2006 midterm did. And a high-turnout election can benefit Republican candidates, such as Ted Cruz, just as it did in 2018.

Finally, the story about Cruz and O'Rourke illustrates a hard truth for reformers: people vote when they are engaged in an election and believe that the stakes of voting are high. Lowering the costs associated with voting—for example, by making registration easier or by extending the voting period—rarely results in substantial gains in turnout. In some cases, these reforms simply make it easier for people who were already planning to vote to cast a ballot, and they bring few new voters to the polls. In short, turnout in Texas jumped by 18 percentage points between the 2014 and 2018 midterms not because it was easier for Texans to vote but because they thought the 2018 election mattered more.

This chapter will delve into what motivates people to participate in politics. Many factors can explain why people choose to participate. Some of the factors are characteristics of individual voters themselves. Do they typically follow politics? How many years of schooling do they have? Other factors, however, pertain to their environment. Has their pastor or minister encouraged their congregation to vote? Have campaign volunteers knocked on their door? Have their unions contacted them about participating in canvassing drives? As we will discuss later in this chapter, the most effective way to get people to vote is to ask them to do so. If that request never comes, a potential voter is more likely to decide that they have better things to do than vote on Election Day.

What Is Electoral Participation?

Political participation during the electoral season can take many forms. The most common form of participation is voting, but participation encompasses other activities as well, such as trying to persuade a friend or coworker to vote for a particular candidate or writing a check to a candidate's campaign committee. **Electoral participation** refers to the range of activities through which individuals attempt to affect the outcome of an election, including both partisan activities, which favor a particular candidate, and nonpartisan activities, such as participation in voter registration drives.

Forms of electoral participation vary along two key dimensions: how often they can be performed and what personal resources are required to participate. For example, citizens have only one vote, but they can volunteer and

Despite a high-turnout election in 2018, Democrat Robert "Beto" O'Rourke, who traveled to all 254 Texas counties, lost to incumbent Republican senator Ted Cruz.

donate as frequently as they like, especially if they have resources such as free time and money. This means that certain individuals can have an impact on the electoral process far beyond a single vote, which can create **participatory inequalities**. A participatory inequality occurs when one group of people has a greater impact on the political process than another group of people.[4] For example, older people, who vote at higher rates than young people do, are more concerned about issues such as Social Security and Medicare, while younger people care more about issues such as college tuition and environmental degradation. Because older people vote more, however, elected officials pay more attention to their political agenda.[5]

Trends in Participation in the United States

Voter participation broke records in the 2020 presidential election: a stunning 67 percent of eligible voters mailed in a ballot or went to a polling station,[6] the highest rate of voting since 1900. Figure 12.1 shows how unusual such high levels of voting have been in the last 50 years. While voting rates typically hovered just above 60 percent in the 1950s and 1960s, they declined between 1972 and 2000 (with the exception of 1992, when the three-way presidential race featuring candidates George H. W. Bush, Bill Clinton, and

FIGURE 12.1 Electoral Participation in Presidential Elections, 1952–2020

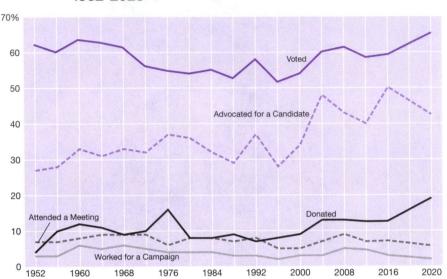

Sources: Turnout rates based on voting eligible population. All turnout data are from Michael P. McDonald, "Voter Turnout," United States Elections Project, www.electproject.org/home/voter-turnout (accessed 9/10/21). The nonvoting activities data are from the American National Election Study Cumulative File and the 2020 Times Series Study.

Ross Perot piqued voters' interest). Starting in 2004, voting rates began to rebound to their midcentury levels. In 2020, they surpassed them.

Figure 12.1 reveals that while the turnout rate was high in 2020, other forms of electoral participation were down. Compared to 2016, people were less likely to try to persuade other people to vote for a particular candidate, to attend a meeting, or to work for a campaign. The decline in these forms of participation was almost certainly driven by the COVID-19 pandemic and people's fear of interacting with strangers. Interestingly, however, 19 percent of Americans reported donating to a campaign, the highest level ever. It is possible that some were compensating for not helping out candidates in other ways, but this number could be indicative of higher levels of interest and engagement that may continue in future election years.

Levels of electoral participation in the United States decrease sharply in midterm years. Turnout typically hovers around 40 percent, or 10 to 20 points lower than turnout in presidential election years (see Figure 12.2). All other forms of participation are less prevalent in midterm election years as well. The 2014 midterm election, with a 36 percent turnout, featured the lowest

FIGURE 12.2 Voter Participation in Midterm Elections, 1962–2018

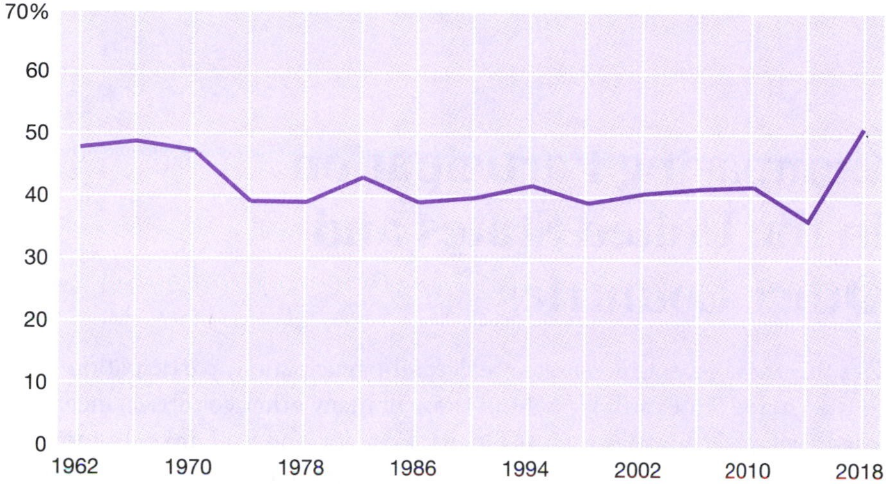

Source: Michael P. McDonald, "Voter Turnout," United States Elections Project, www.electproject.org/home
/voter-turnout (accessed 9/10/21).

turnout of any midterm since 1942. Surprisingly, the 2018 midterm had the highest level of participation since then: nearly 50 percent of eligible voters cast a ballot in what was perceived as a referendum on the Trump presidency. As we discussed in Chapter 10, congressional elections have become nationalized, and 2018 may be the best example yet of this phenomenon. One way to measure nationalization is to examine how well a person's feeling about the president predicts the way they vote in congressional elections. In 2018, the correlation between presidential approval and vote choice was the highest it had ever been.[7]

Turnout in midterm elections did not exhibit the same dip between 1960 and 1996 that we saw in presidential election years, in part because people who vote in midterm elections are typically habitual voters—people who vote in most elections. People who vote in presidential elections include both habitual voters and those who are mobilized by the campaigns or motivated by the excitement and media coverage generated by the election. In fact, the decline in presidential election voter turnout between 1960 and 1996 could be attributed to unexciting elections: they were uncompetitive, and candidates and parties invested less in **get-out-the-vote (GOTV) efforts**.[8] Both factors have changed in recent presidential elections. Not only have voters been more interested in the elections, but candidates and parties have also invested more in GOTV efforts. This investment appears to have produced results, as we will see later in this chapter.

Comparing Participation in the United States and Other Countries

Despite these recent increases in electoral participation, participation rates in the United States still lag behind those of many other countries, including less-developed countries such as Ghana, Ecuador, and Sri Lanka. In terms of voter turnout rates, the United States ranks 23rd out of the 72 countries that held presidential elections between 2010 and 2020 (see Figure 12.3).[9] Turnout rates in American midterm elections are even lower relative to those in other countries' parliamentary elections. If we compare the turnout in the most recent parliamentary elections of the 52 countries that held such elections between 2007 and 2018, the record-setting turnout we saw in the United States' 2018 midterm ranks a dismal 47th.[10]

This difference between the United States and many other democracies does not mean that Americans are less politically engaged. Americans actually report a stronger attachment to their party than citizens of other countries do. Americans are also more likely to believe that voting matters.[11] Instead, many of the rules that govern elections in America depress participation. For one, the United States does not make voting compulsory as 26 other countries do, including Argentina, Australia, Brazil, Singapore, and Turkey.[12] Compulsory voting is estimated to increase turnout by 10 to 15 percentage points.[13] A second consideration is that Election Day in the United States occurs on a workday, while in many other countries it occurs on a weekend or public holiday. Even though American employers are required by law to allow their employees to vote during work hours without docking their pay, employees may be hesitant to ask for the time off. It is important to note, however, that holding elections on "rest days" instead of workdays appears to have only a small effect on turnout.[14] Another factor that depresses turnout is that voting is a two-step process in most of the United States; in every state except North Dakota, voters must register before they are allowed to vote. Twenty states and the District of Columbia have made the process of voting easier by allowing voters to register on the

FIGURE 12.3 Comparing Turnout in Presidential Elections, 2010–20

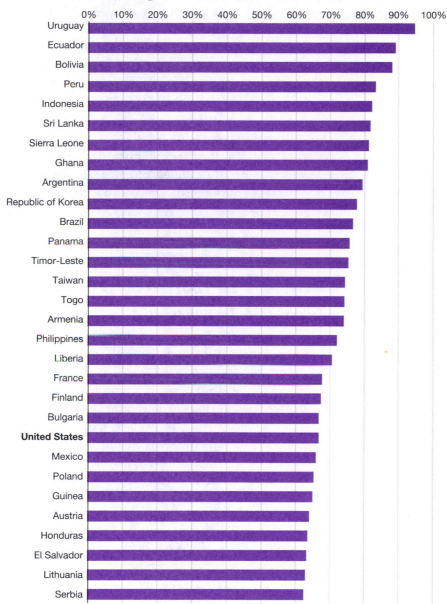

Source: Institute for Democracy and Electoral Assistance, Voter Turnout Database.
Note: Turnout calculated based on voting-age population to make comparison across countries possible.
Only the top 30 countries with the highest turnout rates are shown.

day they vote. As we mentioned in Chapter 2, this is referred to as same-day registration, and states who have adopted it have seen their turnout rates increase by approximately 5 percent. If a state does not have same-day registration, voters must register in advance of the election. In addition, a growing number of states are adopting "use it or lose it" voting laws: if voters do not vote in a certain number of consecutive elections, they are removed from the voter rolls. (Usually, they can retain their eligibility if they respond to a notice sent in the mail.) In most Western democracies, however, citizens are automatically registered to vote. For example, in Canada, when a person turns 18 or becomes a citizen, they are automatically added to the voter rolls and remain on the voter rolls regardless of how many times they move. The fact that U.S. citizens are responsible for registering adds a significant cost to voting.

Why Do People Participate in Campaigns and Elections?

People who regularly participate in campaigns and elections possess a greater *ability*, *motivation*, and *opportunity* to participate than those who do not. This section discusses factors that influence electoral participation in terms of these three characteristics, paying close attention to the forms of participation affected. As mentioned earlier, forms of electoral participation vary along a number of different dimensions, including how often they can be performed and whether they are performed with others. As a result, we cannot expect any given factor to affect every form of participation in the same way. Research has confirmed, however, that each of the following individual and contextual factors has an effect on participation *ceteris paribus*, meaning all other things being held equal. Within each subsection, the factors are discussed in order of the size of their impact on electoral participation.

Ability

An individual's ability to participate in campaigns and elections depends a great deal on their education and income. Although it might seem obvious why this is the case, researchers have struggled to pin down what exactly accounts for the relationships between these factors and rates of participation.

Education Besides political interest, which we will discuss later, a person's level of formal education is the strongest predictor of how likely they are to participate in politics overall—especially for forms of participation that are more time intensive and that require interacting with others.[15] The importance of education for participation has been well documented, but it is difficult to determine why it matters so much. The traditional view is that education provides Americans with the skills and resources necessary to participate in politics.[16] For example, primary and secondary education helps students understand how their democratic system functions and encourages them to discuss current events. It also exposes them to the norm that voting is an important civic duty.[17] These are the functions of high school civics classes, for example. Primary and secondary education also increases students' reading, writing, and speaking skills, all of which we associate with electoral participation.[18] By contrast, some recent studies have shown that attending college has only muted effects on participation because people who attend college are often already politically engaged.[19] Thus, even college coursework that focuses on political science or other social sciences has only a small impact on one's likelihood of voting.[20]

Does this mean that a formal education is the only way to learn the skills necessary for electoral participation? Absolutely not. Workplaces, churches, and other institutions provide opportunities to organize events, put together presentations, and develop other skills that are useful in politics. For example, churches have long fostered political activism in Black communities by teaching civic skills. This is one reason Black churches provided the organizational backbone of the civil rights movement. At the same time, educational attainment increases the chances that an individual will be able to get the kind of job that teaches civic skills. For example, teachers and lawyers are more likely than blue-collar workers to acquire civic skills on the job.[21]

Income Income is another resource that enables individuals to participate in politics, although it matters much less than education as a predictor of most forms of electoral participation. The one exception, unsurprisingly, is that income is the strongest predictor of whether and how much individuals contribute to a political cause. What is surprising is that those with higher incomes are more likely to engage in every form of participation—even in protests, which are sometimes considered a "weapon of the weak."[22] What is it about having a higher income that enables wealthier people to participate more than people with less money? This answer is obvious for making a political contribution but less so for other forms of participation. It is not that people with higher incomes have more free time. Careers that provide higher incomes, like those in medicine or law, typically provide very little free time. Instead, it appears that people with low incomes must put more of their time and energy into simply trying to get by, an effort that squeezes out room for political participation of any kind. Participation increases as income increases for those on the lowest end of the income spectrum, but once people achieve a comfortable standard of living, research has found that increases in their income no longer increase their participation rates. When people feel they no longer must live from hand to mouth, they are better able to focus on other things, including politics.[23]

Motivation: Individual-Level Factors

People who participate in an election not only possess the resources to do so but also are motivated to get involved. Motivations can be loosely grouped into two categories: those that are individual, such as a general interest in politics, and those that are generated by the environment in which individuals live, such as a phone call from a campaign. The main individual-level factors that push people to venture into politics are their general interest in the topic, their knowledge about politics, their level of commitment to a party, and a sense that they stand to gain from getting involved.

Political Interest   The single most important individual-level factor affecting whether a person participates in campaigns and elections is **political interest**, which is simply a person's reported level of interest in government and public affairs. Interest matters the most in determining a person's willingness to discuss an election with others, but it is also a strong predictor of whether one decides to cast a ballot or engages in forms of participation that require a time commitment, such as attending a rally. It matters much less for donating to a candidate.

Although certain events can increase a person's political interest temporarily, political interest is a relatively stable characteristic that one either has or does not have.[24] Because it is stable over a person's lifetime, one must look to preadult factors to explain its origins. Parents can certainly pass their passion for politics on to their children, and formal education plays a role. Another source of political interest may be personality. Basic personality traits can affect how people think and act politically. For example, people who are open to new experiences—that is, who are naturally curious and interested in learning—are significantly more likely to be interested in politics than people who are more conservative in their approach to life.[25] Recent research also suggests that genes may play a role in developing one's political interest.[26]

Participating in campaigns can bring people together, creating solidary benefits. Here, supporters of Donald Trump work together to assemble yard signs for the Trump campaign.

Political Knowledge   People vary substantially in how much they know about politics. Political knowledge can take a variety of forms, including facts about how the political process works, familiarity with elected officials, and awareness of the current issues of the day. As a predictor of political participation, its effects are on par with formal education. It is a powerful predictor of voting and whether a person is inclined to discuss politics, but it also matters for engaging in more time-intensive campaign activities. Interestingly, it has no effect on donating. In general, people who are politically interested, better educated, wealthy, and White tend to have higher levels of political knowledge than those who are not. In addition, men often perform better on tests of political knowledge than women do, but this gap can be reduced by asking questions on political topics that are more relevant to women.[27]

Partisan Strength   Partisan strength captures the degree to which people identify with a party. As we discussed in Chapter 6, Americans typically identify with one of the two major parties or remain unaffiliated and refer to themselves as "independent." Independents are considered to be the weakest in partisan strength. Partisan strength affects electoral participation because the more strongly people identify with a party, the more invested they are in its success. Overall, partisan strength's effect on participation is less than that of education, political interest, and political knowledge but roughly similar to that of income. It matters the most for voting, but it also affects whether a person donates and discusses campaigns. Unlike political interest, partisan strength does not vary according to education, income, or gender. Partisan strength typically increases as people get older and is associated with particular personality traits. For example, people who are highly extroverted or sociable are more likely to be partisans.[28]

In recent years, political scientists have observed the emergence of negative partisanship—that is, disliking the opposing party more than liking one's own—among Americans.[29] Negative partisanship feeds on anger and can motivate people to vote, although research has found that it has less of an impact on turnout than does positive partisanship, or the enthusiasm that people feel for candidates from their own party.[30] Still, the emergence of negative partisanship may be part of the reason why extreme candidates who win their party's primary spur voters from the opposing party to turn out in the general election.[31] Anger that the opposing party has nominated, for instance, a "socialist" or a "religious zealot" drives voters to the polls.

Self-Interest   People participate in politics because they derive some benefit from doing so. They may receive **material benefits**, or something tangible in exchange for participating. For instance, individuals may be paid to collect petition signatures to help get a candidate's name on the ballot. Individuals also participate in order to receive **solidary benefits**, which are the intangible rewards that come from being part of a collective effort, such as friendship with fellow volunteers or status in the community. In addition, individuals may participate in order to receive **purposive benefits**, which are associated with satisfaction for having advanced an issue or ideological position or for having fulfilled a duty. Ultimately, participating in a political campaign or election could bring all of these benefits: participants may benefit tangibly from getting paid for their work, enjoy the camaraderie among those working for the campaign, and feel good for having helped a worthy candidate.

Motivation: Contextual Factors

Although individuals' own particular qualities or characteristics affect their willingness to participate in politics, the broader environment in which people live has an enormous effect on their choice to participate. We consider two types of contextual effects: those related to campaign activities and those related to an individual's social network. The former have an especially large effect on the decision to participate,[32] but the social pressure that people feel to get involved when their peers are doing so is another important contextual factor. Little research exists on how environmental factors affect different forms of participation, so here we discuss their effect on participation in general.

Mobilization   The most important contextual factor promoting electoral participation is mobilization. **Mobilization** refers to the range of activities that candidates, parties, activists, and interest groups engage in to encourage people to participate. These activities usually occur during a campaign, but groups can mobilize people at other times and for reasons besides electing a candidate. For instance, they can encourage citizens to support certain legislation by writing letters to their members of Congress or to show up at a town hall meeting to oppose an action of their city council. To be sure, the goal of actors who try to mobilize others is not simply to increase civic participation; it is to use that participation to achieve certain ends, such as the election of a candidate or the defeat of a ballot initiative. Thus, groups target their mobilization efforts at people who share their goals.

Individuals and groups seeking to mobilize others do so directly and indirectly. They mobilize directly when they contact citizens and encourage them to act. They mobilize indirectly by reaching people through their social networks, including workplaces, churches, schools, labor unions, neighborhood associations, and large national organizations such as the National Rifle Association or the AARP. During a campaign, for example, candidates seek the endorsements of community groups and national organizations in the hope that these endorsements will encourage group members to vote for them. This saves candidates some effort, not only because the groups assume some of the costs of communicating with their members but also because group members are more likely to trust recommendations from group leaders than direct appeals from candidates themselves.

Mobilization efforts work because people respond when someone asks them to get involved. This may be because people are flattered by the request, like the idea of being involved in a collective effort, or find it difficult to say no and then feel they must follow through once they have committed. Groups seeking to mobilize members of a community are likely to focus their attention on individuals who are already active in that community. Active people have two qualities that mobilizers appreciate. First, they are easy to reach because they belong to a variety of organizations. Second, they are more likely to be influential when they do participate because they have a large social network and greater status in their community. Similarly, mobilization efforts are likely to target people with more education and higher incomes because they are more likely to participate in the first place.

As we noted earlier, at least some of the decline in turnout in presidential elections between 1960 and 1996 occurred because campaigns abandoned traditional mobilization activities, such as neighborhood canvassing. Instead, they turned to television advertising to communicate with voters.[33] Television advertisements, however, are not particularly effective mobilization tools. For example, eligible voters in media markets that witness a slew of presidential advertisements are no more likely to vote than people who live in markets that see no such advertisements.[34] It does not make much difference whether the ads are predominantly positive (promoting a candidate) or negative (attacking a candidate). Although some commentators worry that negative advertising drives down turnout because citizens' distaste for attacks makes them feel alienated from politics, the sum of the evidence suggests that negative advertising does not affect turnout in any consistent fashion.[35]

What are the most effective mobilization strategies? Research to date has found that the specific messages used in mobilization activities do not matter a great deal. For example, reminding citizens that voting is their civic duty seems to be no more or less effective than reminding them that the election

TABLE 12.1 Effectiveness and Cost-per-Voter of Various Campaign Activities

Rank	Campaign activity	Effectiveness	Approximate cost per vote
1	Door-to-door canvassing	1 per 15 contacted	$31
2	Phone calls made by volunteers	1 per 35 contacted	$35
3	Phone calls made by telemarketers	1 per 125 contacted	$63
4	Nonpartisan direct mail	1 per 273 reached	$91
5	Direct mail from campaigns	No significant effect	—
6	Emails	No significant effect	—
7	Leaving campaign materials on doors	No significant effect	—
8	Robocalls	No significant effect	—

Note: Cost-per-vote is not calculated for tactics that are not proven to raise turnout.
Source: Donald P. Green and Alan S. Gerber, *Get Out the Vote: How to Increase Voter Turnout*, 4th ed. (Washington, DC: Brookings Institution Press, 2019), 128.

will be close and "every vote counts." In general, how voters are contacted is much more important than message content. Table 12.1 shows the results of a meta-analysis that reviewed the effectiveness and approximate cost of various campaigning techniques.[36] A meta-analysis systematically assesses a body of research—in this case, hundreds of randomized field experiments examining the effects of mobilization tactics—to summarize its findings. The studies included in this meta-analysis used voter files to create treatment groups and then used the files again to confirm that the individuals in the experiments actually voted. This is important because many people will report to researchers that they have voted even when they have not.

As the table shows and as we noted in Chapter 5, the most effective way to get a person to vote is to have someone talk to them face-to-face. Campaigns that contact eligible voters this way can expect to turn out one additional voter for every 15 contacted. That single individual may even encourage a housemate to vote, creating what is called a "spillover effect."[37] Phone calls made by volunteers are also quite effective, turning out one additional voter for every 35 people who speak to a volunteer. Phone calls made by telemarketers are much less effective (one for every 125 contacted), as is direct mail sent out by governmental entities or nonpartisan groups (one for every 273 reached). The results of the meta-analysis, however, suggest that direct mail, emails, leaflets, and robocalls all have no significant effect on voter turnout. The final column of Table 12.1 shows the cost of turning out each additional vote. It reveals that because canvassing is so effective, it is the cheapest form of mobilization even though it is labor intensive.

Other forms of contacting voters may also be effective but have not been studied as extensively (and so were not included in the meta-analysis just discussed). For example, a 2006 study found that text messaging increased turnout by 3.1 percentage points. A handful of later studies, including a large experiment conducted by Rock the Vote during the 2012 presidential campaign, found a much smaller effect, suggesting that the novelty of text messages has worn off. Texts can still boost turnout, but the effect is quite small: approximately 0.5 percent.[38]

The messenger also matters when it comes to mobilization tactics. As Table 12.1 indicates, direct mail sent by candidates does not turn out voters, but reminders sent by governmental organizations and nonpartisan groups do. One randomized experiment assessed the effectiveness of sending a series of GOTV messages via Facebook to college students who had friended the author of the study. The study found that the messages increased student turnout by 8 percentage points,[39] suggesting that using social networks to mobilize voters may be very successful.

The effects of campaign mobilization depend on people's underlying capacity and motivation to participate. As a result, it can be easier to mobilize citizens who are already likely to vote than to motivate those who are less likely.[40] This is because likely voters are easier to reach and tend to be more responsive to campaign messages than marginal voters. The bottom line, unfortunately, is that campaign mobilization may actually exacerbate existing participatory inequalities by making voting even more convenient for people who are already likely to vote.[41]

Starting in the 1998 midterm elections, the Democratic Party and its affiliated interest groups began to shift their resources from advertising to voter outreach. The success enjoyed by the Democrats in the 1998 and 2000 elections inspired the Republican Party to focus more of its resources on voter outreach as well. As a result, 2004 saw unprecedented mobilization efforts by both parties—efforts that actually built on some of the mobilization research we have described. This heightened focus on mobilization continued through 2018, translating into high turnout rates. The 2020 election was something of an anomaly since it featured high turnout even though the COVID-19 pandemic complicated campaign mobilization efforts. The turnout almost certainly had to do with the intense feelings inspired by President Trump on both sides of the aisle as well as the fact that many states made it easier to vote by mail. Once campaigns can return to traditional methods of mobilization, turnout may climb even higher.

Social Network   Family, friends, classmates, coworkers, and neighbors constitute a person's **social network**, and all can affect an individual's decision to participate in politics. A growing body of literature suggests that voting is a social behavior and even contagious.[42] For example, researchers have found that people living with a person who is contacted by a GOTV campaign are significantly more likely to vote themselves, particularly if they are young.[43] Another study—a massive experiment involving 61 million Facebook users—found that simply being told that close friends have voted increases the chances that individuals will seek out polling place information and vote.[44] And even though there is not much difference in the effects of various mobilization messages, threatening to reveal a person's voting history to neighbors or to publish a list of voters in the local paper can be effective.[45] All of these studies demonstrate that a person's social network and the social pressure it generates are major factors in political participation.

One of the most important elements of a person's social network is their family.[46] Parents can help to inculcate political interest and efficacy in their children. Some of this happens through mimicry. When children come of

The family is an important influence on whether individuals participate in elections and politics in general. Children often follow the models provided by their parents' political participation.

age politically, they may vote in part because they watched their parents vote. Besides acting as role models for their children, parents may also deliberately try to instill political interest in their children. One important way they do this is simply by talking about politics. Conversations at the dinner table help communicate parents' interest in politics to their children, who will then be more likely to become interested in politics themselves. Parents who adhere to the convention of not discussing politics at the dinner table might be decreasing the chances that their children will be interested in politics.[47]

Schools are also an important part of one's social network, as we noted when discussing the role of formal education. Taking part in certain types of high school activities, particularly those that emphasize student government and community service, make young people more interested in politics and more likely to participate as adults. High school activities that emphasize public performance, such as debate and drama, also appear to promote political participation, though participating in sports teams does not have the same effect.[48] The effects of nonathletic high school activities are evident irrespective of students' family income or the education level of their parents.[49] This suggests that cutting these activities from high school curricula, as many

school districts across the nation are doing, may have troublesome consequences for the future political participation of younger generations. Families
and schools are particularly important because they open up avenues for
children to think about politics at a time when there is no formal way for them
to participate. They cannot vote until they are 18, for example, and they generally lack other opportunities to participate meaningfully in political life.[50] It
is no wonder that a survey of ninth graders found that they did not believe
politics would affect them until they were older.[51]

People's level of attachment to their communities also affects whether
they vote. In particular, people who feel that they belong to a community
are likely to feel empowered and participate. By contrast, those who feel
alienated or marginalized may withdraw politically. For example, the turnout gaps between White people and various communities of color are smaller
in counties where the communities of color constitute a larger portion of the
population.[52] Studies have also shown that Democrats and Republicans living in "enemy territory"—that is, communities dominated by the opposing
party—are less likely to participate and discuss politics than their counterparts living in friendlier areas.[53] Even young people living in areas with a
significantly older population are less likely to vote than young people living
among a younger population.

Finally, different **generational cohorts**—people who came of age politically
at about the same time—have distinctive patterns of electoral participation
that arise from the norms of behavior and the levels of civic and political
engagement that were pervasive when they came of age. For example, people
who grew up during the Great Depression and World War II were part of what
has been called the Greatest Generation, the most civically and politically
active generation of the twentieth century—one that stayed politically involved
throughout their lives. In contrast, Baby Boomers—those born between 1946
and 1964—have been less engaged in civic life and politics even though many
of them came of age in the 1960s and witnessed the civil rights movement and
protests against the Vietnam War firsthand. Subsequent generations—those
sometimes referred to as "Generation X," "Generation Y," "Millennials," and
"Generation Z"—have continued the trend and are even less interested in politics than Baby Boomers are.[54]

Why have later generations been less politically engaged than the "long
civic generation" of the 1930s and '40s? One factor is technological change,
beginning with the rapid arrival of television. Television offers people alternative ways to spend their leisure time that often compete with other activities,
such as volunteering for a local organization or participating in politics. One
study estimates that every additional hour of television viewing per day is

associated with a 10 percent reduction in civic activism.[55] The arrival and penetration of the internet, mobile phones, video games, and social media may be having a similar effect. Today, young people spend more than 30 hours per week on their devices.[56]

Opportunity

Even if people have the ability and motivation to participate, they may still fail to do so if they lack the opportunity. They might not be eligible to participate, or the costs of participating—that is, the associated challenges and time—may be too steep. As we discussed in Chapter 2, one must be an American citizen of at least 18 years of age to vote. These requirements for voting are far less stringent than they were in earlier periods of history, when women, African Americans, and other groups were barred from voting. The primary groups excluded today include the country's 74 million children and its 13 million permanent residents who work, live, and pay taxes in the United States but are not citizens. As we discussed in Chapter 2, 6 million people who have been convicted of felonies cannot vote, either. People in these groups can engage in nonvoting forms of participation, but research suggests that they are much less likely to do so than those who are eligible to vote.[57] For eligible Americans, the costs of voting depend on the costs entailed in each step: registering to vote and casting a ballot.

Voter Registration   In most states, people who are not registered cannot vote. As we discussed earlier in this chapter, it is unusual for a developed democracy to make citizens responsible for registering, which adds an additional cost to voting. This extra burden, however, is no accident. Voter registration was enacted by Progressive-era reformers in the early twentieth century (see Chapter 3) as part of a broader effort to challenge the political machines, whose power derived from their ability to mobilize immigrants and the urban working poor. The Progressives believed—often with good reason—that these machines were corrupt and that the methods by which they achieved high rates of turnout among their supporters were corrupt as well. They also believed that party bosses manipulated the vote choices of uneducated and illiterate people. Voter registration was intended to help prevent fraud by requiring citizens to appear periodically before local officials to verify their eligibility.

As we discussed in Chapter 2, both the timing of registration and the magnitude of registration requirements affect the cost of voting. Because it is easier to remember to register when Election Day is near, the earlier a person must register, the more difficult the process becomes. At present, no state has a registration closing date more than 31 days before an election. Furthermore, if a person must travel to a distant location to register, that also imposes a cost.

The National Voter Registration Act of 1993, also known as the **Motor Voter Act**, requires states to allow people to register to vote when they are applying for a driver's license or public assistance programs, such as food stamps, or to allow Election Day registration. As a result, the costs of registering are now lower than they have been at any point since registration laws were first enacted. However, the Motor Voter Act did not significantly increase turnout in presidential or midterm elections, raising the question of whether further weakening registration laws would actually increase turnout.[58] As we discussed in Chapter 2, same-day registration and automatic voter registration appear to have small but significant effects on turnout when states implement them.

Voting   Other costs are associated with actually casting a ballot. About 85 percent of the people who are registered typically vote in presidential elections. What prevents the remaining 15 percent from getting to the polls? One possibility is that they do not know where their polling place is. Some states mail citizens polling place information or sample ballots, which are especially helpful in boosting turnout among less-educated people and young people.[59]

As we discussed in Chapter 2, many states have tried to boost turnout by experimenting with ways of making the act of voting easier. **Convenience voting** refers to methods of voting that do not involve actually casting a ballot at a polling place on Election Day. Convenience voting measures include allowing people to vote absentee, providing mail ballots upon request, and giving people the option of voting in person before Election Day. Convenience voting is designed to make voting less costly and to increase turnout, but whether it actually accomplishes these goals has been debated. There is some evidence that sending mail ballots to all residents, as California, Colorado, Hawaii, Nevada, Oregon, Utah, Vermont, and Washington have done, increases turnout, but the benefits appear to be small and to wear off over time.[60] Recent research has found that allowing people to register on the day they vote boosts turnout, but allowing people to vote early actually depresses turnout unless it is combined with same-day registration. This surprising finding may be explained by the fact that early voting makes it harder for campaigns to mobilize voters in a systematic fashion.[61] In general, same-day registration encourages participation by people of color and young people, which reduces some participatory inequalities.[62]

In 2016, California lawmakers passed the Voter's Choice Act (VCA), which allows counties to provide voters with a wide variety of choices about when and where to vote. Participating counties eliminate traditional polling places and instead send ballots to voters in the mail; voters can then return their ballots via mail, in a ballot drop box, or at a handful of vote centers. Voters can also choose to cast their ballots in person at one of those vote centers before Election Day instead of using their mail ballot. The lawmakers who passed the law hoped that it would increase turnout in the counties that adopted it, and early assessments suggest that the VCA's comprehensive approach to convenience voting has achieved this goal.[63] In the 2018 midterm election, the first five counties that adopted the VCA saw their turnout rise by approximately 5 percentage points relative to the previous election, while turnout in non-VCA counties increased by only 2 points.

Electoral Competitiveness   Thus far, our discussion of opportunity has focused on voting, but there are many other ways to participate politically, especially in campaigns. One factor that affects the opportunity to engage in these other forms of participation is the competitiveness of the election. When elections are close, candidates, parties, and interest groups have incentives not only to encourage voters to participate but also to create more opportunities for participation. For example, a person who lives in a battleground state during a presidential election has ample opportunity to attend candidate events, help canvass neighborhoods, and call friends because presidential candidates set up campaign organizations in these states specifically to create such opportunities.

Group Differences in Electoral Participation

The factors that encourage electoral participation reinforce one another. For example, people with more education are likely to have higher incomes and jobs that allow them to develop the confidence and skills that facilitate electoral participation. Their education and jobs also embed them in social networks that are more likely to mobilize them. In addition, their education and income make it more likely that they can access the internet and learn about opportunities to participate in campaigns. Understanding how these factors work together illuminates why certain groups in America are more likely to participate and why others are not, creating participatory inequalities. Here we discuss such inequalities as they appear in presidential elections, but they are typically even more extreme in midterm elections.

FIGURE 12.4 Self-Reported Voting in the 2020 Presidential Election

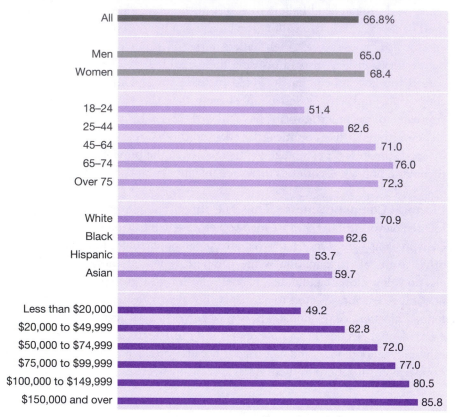

Source: "Voting and Registration in the Election of November 2020," U.S. Census Bureau, April 2021, www.census.gov/data/tables/time-series/demo/voting-and-registration/p20-585.html (accessed 9/24/21).

Figure 12.4 illustrates group differences in electoral participation. It is important to note, however, that this figure is based on self-reported voting behavior. Although researchers have long observed that reported political participation in surveys is higher than actual participation, recent research has demonstrated that older, educated, wealthy, and politically engaged people are the most likely to misrepresent their behavior because they feel the most pressure to vote in the first place.[64] As a result, the differences in reported voting across income and, to a lesser extent, age are very likely exaggerated. Race is unrelated to overreporting, but men are significantly more likely than women to report that they have voted when they have not. Unfortunately, it is difficult to validate a person's reported voting behavior, so political scientists working with surveys often must take respondents' word at face value.

Here we describe some of the more important group differences in electoral participation and draw on the discussion in the previous section to explain them. In the final section, we consider whether these differences matter for election outcomes and government policies.

Income

An especially large disparity in voter turnout exists between people with high and low incomes. In 2020, for example, the reported turnout among citizens making more than $75,000 per year was almost 30 percentage points higher than turnout among those making less than $20,000 (77 versus 49 percent). From a certain perspective, this inequality makes little sense. Low-income earners should be less satisfied with the political institutions and policies that make it so difficult for them to get ahead, and thus they should participate more. Meanwhile, high-income earners should be content with the status quo since they have benefited from it. Yet this is clearly not the case for the reasons we have discussed: wealthier people typically have more education and professional careers that provide them with politically useful skills. They are also embedded in large social networks that encourage their participation, and they can be easily reached by groups and individuals who want to mobilize them.[65]

Age

As discussed earlier, young people are less likely to participate than older people. In 2020, 51 percent of people ages 18 to 24 reported voting compared with 76 percent of people 65 and older. What explains this lower rate of participation among the young? First, research finds that young people are just as likely as older Americans to say that they *intend* to vote, but they are less likely to follow through.[66] This suggests that young people have a harder time surmounting the costs associated with voting. For instance, younger people move around a lot, and with each move, they must reregister to vote.[67] Their mobility also makes them more difficult to mobilize because they are harder to track. Young people are also undergoing many other transitions—leaving school, getting married, starting new jobs, having children—that in the short term may depress participation because of the physical and psychological commitments they entail.[68] Of these, the first two—leaving school[69] and getting married[70]—appear to depress turnout the most. As people settle into their jobs and marriages over time and as their children become less dependent on them, the costs associated with political participation decrease. Independent of such life transition effects, however,

Young people are much less likely than older Americans to vote. In recent years, there has been a push to mobilize young voters. Here, voters in Austin, Texas, line up to vote in 2020.

aging has a strong positive effect on political participation. Although scholars are still debating why this is the case, many believe that it can be explained by pure learning—that is, as one ages, one becomes more knowledgeable about the political system and how to engage with it. An accumulation of life experience also seems to spur engagement.[71]

Race and Ethnicity

Certain groups of people in the United States have become more likely to participate in politics over time, demonstrating that participatory inequalities are not immutable. Before the adoption of the 1965 Voting Rights Act, African American turnout was understandably low due to discriminatory laws that effectively disenfranchised Black Americans, especially in the South. The Voting Rights Act empowered the federal government to take over voter registration in southern states to ensure that African Americans could vote. This legislation quickly yielded results. Within 20 years, the gaps in registration rates between Black and White people in the South—which had been 50 percentage points or higher in Mississippi, North Carolina, and Alabama—dropped to less than 10 points.

Today, African Americans and White Americans report voting at virtually the same rates in presidential elections. Their reported voting rates were identical in 2008, and African American voter turnout actually surpassed White voter turnout in 2012 (66 versus 62 percent). In both 2016 and 2020, however, a turnout gap reemerged. In 2016, the White voter turnout rate was 4 percentage points higher than Black voter turnout (63 versus 59 percent), and in 2020 it was 8 percentage points higher (71 versus 63 percent). There is evidence that Barack Obama's candidacy in 2008 and 2012 created social pressure for some Black people to say they had voted when they had not.[72] If this is true, their 6 percent decrease in reported voting from 2012 to 2016 is less cause for concern. In 2020, both White and Black people were more likely to report voting than ever before, but White people were much more likely. Future research will tell us if this record turnout among White people was due to campaign mobilization, enthusiasm for the candidates, or increased social pressure to report voting.

Turnout gaps aside, it should be noted that the electoral participation rates of Black people are especially remarkable because of their lower average income and education levels. Part of the explanation for Black electoral activism is the mobilization that occurs in Black churches. Another part may be the Democratic Party's heavy mobilization efforts in Black communities. The party has learned that it cannot assume that Black people will turn out to vote even though they might be a "natural" constituency; they need to be heavily courted.[73] More recently, research has suggested that the Black Lives Matter movement and protests over police brutality have spurred African American turnout.[74]

Latinos and Asian Americans participate at lower rates than Black and White people do despite being the fastest-growing racial and ethnic groups in the country. However, ethnicity does not account for their participation rates. For Latinos, lower levels of education and income explain their lower participation. For Asian Americans, those born abroad are less likely to vote than those whose families have been in the United States for several generations. In addition, political participation varies among Asian Americans based on national origin. For example, in 2016, Filipino and Vietnamese Americans were more likely to vote than members of other Asian origin groups.[75]

Gender

Women were excluded from voting in most American states until the ratification of the Nineteenth Amendment in 1920. Today, women vote at a slightly higher rate than men, again demonstrating that participatory inequalities can be erased. In 2020, 68 percent of women reported voting compared with 65 percent of men. The gap is especially large between unmarried men and women: in 2020, only 53 percent of unmarried men reported voting compared with 61 percent of unmarried women.[76] There are few disparities between men and women in terms of whether they attend political meetings or work for campaigns, but men are more likely than women to report donating and discussing politics and to actually run for elected office. Men typically have higher salaries than women do, which explains why they would donate more. The difference in engagement in political discussions may arise because men also report more interest in politics and appear to be more comfortable with the kinds of heated exchanges that political discussions often entail.[77] Another factor may be the perception that politics is a "man's world." When women do hold high-profile offices, young women and girls become more interested in politics.[78] Thus, having few women in office may create a vicious cycle whereby young girls do not develop as great an interest in politics and do not run for office themselves, perpetuating the underrepresentation of women in elected positions. See Chapters 5 and 10 for a more detailed discussion of some of the factors that lead women not to run for office.

The Intersection of Race and Gender

All of the categories we have discussed overlap. An individual can be a young White male with a low income or an older Hispanic female with a high income, for example. What do we know about political participation at the intersection of categories? Unfortunately, surprisingly little because scholars tend to study these demographics in isolation. In other words, they tend to study only race or only gender without considering how the two overlap.

However, one group that has received significant attention from scholars is Black women. Black women's participation rates are not easily explained by traditional theories of political participation, which link higher rates of participation to having more resources.[79] Black women have historically voted at much higher rates than Black men and have engaged in other forms of political participation at higher rates than White women.[80] For example, in the 2018 midterm election, Black women were 19 percentage points more likely to vote than Black men and voted at a similar rate to White women.[81] Understanding what gets African American women to the polls may help people and groups who hope to boost participation rates in general. Researchers studying this puzzle have found that Black women have a particularly strong sense of linked fate—that is, the sense that their fate depends on the fate of their racial group.[82] Black women also seem to be especially mobilized in areas with high concentrations of African Americans.[83] While there is still more to learn, both of these findings suggest that psychological factors related to community explain why Black women are more likely to engage in politics than their male counterparts are.

Are Voters Representative of Nonvoters?

Would politics in America be dramatically different if everyone voted? The first question to consider is whether the same candidates would be elected. The second question is whether, once elected, those candidates would advance the same kinds of policies that elected officials pursue now, assuming that they are responsive to the preferences of voters. If the answer to one or both of these questions is "no," then it is evidence of a participatory inequality.

As we argued earlier in this chapter, research has demonstrated that increases in turnout do not consistently favor Republican or Democratic candidates, which suggests that nonvoters are not significantly different from voters in terms of their party preferences. This is the case even though studies have found that nonvoters are slightly more sympathetic than voters on average to the Democratic Party.[84] How do we square these two findings? First, the research suggesting that nonvoters may lean Democratic also finds that this bias has varied across states and years. Second, even if all nonvoters got registered and voted, not much would change because few elections are close enough for high turnout to make a difference.[85]

While higher turnout is unlikely to change election outcomes (except in the closest elections), it might affect policy if new voters have significantly different preferences than voters do. After all, studies have found that elected officials are more responsive to the preferences of voters than to the wishes of nonvoters.[86] What would happen if a large number of nonvoters suddenly decided to vote? Would it change the policies advocated by their elected officials?

Although an early study on the topic concluded that, in terms of issue preferences, "voters are virtually a carbon copy of the citizen population," evidence has been mounting that this is not always the case: it depends on the policy.[87] Figure 12.5 shows that, in 2020, the differences between voters and nonvoters were relatively small on issues such as gun control, abortion, immigration, and policing, but they were larger with respect to health care and the use of the U.S. military. For instance, 73 percent of nonvoters support expanding Medicare to cover everyone, while only 58 percent of voters

FIGURE 12.5 Policy Preferences of Voters and Nonvoters in 2020

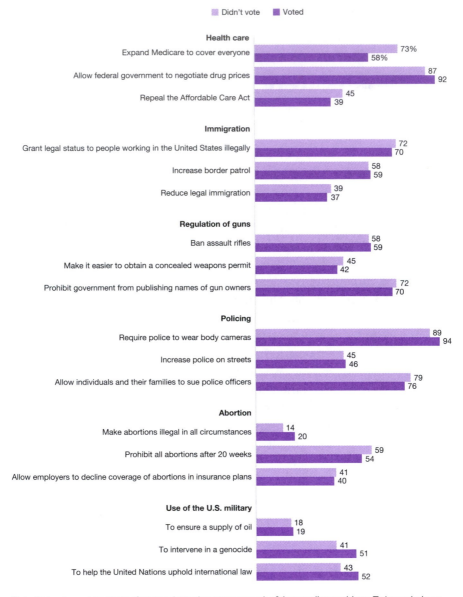

Note: Data show percentage of respondents that support each of these policy positions. To be coded as a voter, respondents had to report being registered and report voting, and they had their votes validated. Nonvoters reported not being registered, not voting, or had no registration record.
Source: Cooperative Election Study Common Content, 2020.

do. Nonvoters also appear to favor using the military less: whereas a majority of voters supports using the U.S. military to intervene in a genocide or to help the United Nations uphold international law, approximately 40 percent of nonvoters do. These differences are not surprising given that nonvoters are less likely to have health insurance. They are also younger, less educated, and more racially and ethnically diverse, which aligns with the demographic groups who are more likely to serve or to know someone who serves in the military. Therefore, nonvoters and their family and friends are more likely to risk bodily injury when the military sends forces overseas.

Conclusion

Political participation comes in a wide array of forms. Turnout in elections—as the most obvious and, in some ways, least demanding form of participation—captures the most attention. Turnout in the United States is low compared with turnout in other countries, and it actually declined from 1960 to 1996. In recent elections, however, turnout has increased, due in part to the mobilization efforts of campaigns and voters' stronger sense that elections matter.

Of course, one might ask why anyone participates in politics at all. Some would argue that the costs of electoral participation outweigh its benefits.[88] After all, the likelihood that a citizen's vote will decide the outcome of an election is infinitesimal. Part of the story is that citizens may value participation in politics for other reasons. Citizens receive a variety of nontangible benefits from participation that make it enjoyable—such as a sense of satisfaction from fulfilling their civic duty or from helping a cause or candidate they believe in.

What affects the participation of those citizens who do involve themselves in campaigns and elections? We have suggested that ability, motivation, and opportunity are important factors. Ability is related to formal education, financial resources, free time, and the civic skills acquired at work and through involvement in community groups. The motivation to participate stems from an interest in politics and the encouragement that one receives from one's social network and from candidates, parties, and groups who engage in mobilization. The role of social networks suggests that participation is, in a sense, contagious. Parents who care about politics and vote are more likely to have children who are politically engaged than are parents who do not care or vote. People who are politically active encourage other people in their social networks to participate. The role of mobilization also demonstrates that campaigns themselves can affect people's decisions to vote or participate in elections in other ways. In fact, even mobilization efforts are contagious: when campaigners knock on a door and remind the person who answers the door to vote, it makes other eligible voters in that household more likely to vote.[89]

Finally, having the ability and motivation to participate is not enough if one does not have the opportunity. In the case of voting, one has the opportunity to participate if one is eligible to vote and has registered. For other forms of participation, opportunities to participate are more likely to arise when elections are closely contested. Thus, citizens living in competitive jurisdictions will find themselves with ample opportunity to participate, while those living in noncompetitive jurisdictions will find that they have fewer opportunities to flex their democratic muscles.

As we first noted in Chapter 2, political participation is intrinsic to many conceptions of what "good" elections look like. One such conception promotes the ideal of political equality. Egalitarians lament participatory inequalities because they can produce electoral outcomes and policies that are not representative of what the general population wants. Yet studies that have examined such questions argue that if all nonvoters participated, only some electoral outcomes and policies would change. The reason only some would change is that an election must be close for the participation of nonvoters to make a difference, and close elections are becoming rarer in the United States. Beyond election outcomes, growing evidence suggests that government is more responsive to those who participate than to those who do not. Thus, the way that members of Congress vote appears to reflect the preferences of voters more than the preferences of nonvoters and the preferences of wealthier people more than the preferences of those with less money.[90]

Such findings raise important concerns about the quality of American democracy. At the same time, however, we must think critically about whether participatory equality is the most important ideal for elections and how it should be balanced with other ideals. Those who support imposing restrictions on voter registration claim that they would prevent voter fraud and corruption and mitigate the degree to which political parties can manipulate the electoral process. Moreover, some argue that it is more important for citizens to vote in an informed manner than for all citizens to vote. In this view, it is actually worse if more people participate but do not know much about the candidates or the issues facing the country. Needless to say, these debates cannot be resolved easily, but as we try to understand them, it is useful to recognize that increasing electoral participation entails trade-offs between competing values.

KEY TERMS

electoral participation (p. 330)

participatory inequalities (p. 331)

get-out-the-vote (GOTV) efforts (p. 333)

political interest (p. 338)

material benefits (p. 340)

solidary benefits (p. 340)

purposive benefits (p. 340)

mobilization (p. 341)

social network (p. 344)

generational cohorts (p. 346)

Motor Voter Act (p. 348)

convenience voting (p. 348)

FOR DISCUSSION

1. How much does it matter for the quality of democracy if certain groups of citizens participate more in the political process than others?
2. How can voting be made more convenient for young people?
3. Are you interested in politics? If so, who or what encouraged your interest?
4. Do you benefit from participating in politics? How?
5. Looking ahead to 2024, what new techniques do you think candidates will use to mobilize citizens?

13

Voter Choice

In their evaluations of the 2020 presidential race, many analysts blamed President Donald Trump's defeat on his "erratic behavior and failure on coronavirus."[1] A consensus among pundits and practitioners emerged that Trump's campaign had never figured out how to maintain the president's image as a strong and decisive leader while bending to the realities of the pandemic. A campaign that had planned to focus its reelection messaging on a resurgent economy was instead often perplexed by questions such as whether the president should wear a mask during a speech at the Ypsilanti, Michigan, Ford plant. The shoot-from-the-hip, take-no-prisoners style that had served Trump so well in 2016 seemed out of place to many as a global pandemic raged and death tolls rose across the United States.

These same observers concluded that Joe Biden's campaign was greatly advantaged by this turn of events. The spread of the coronavirus and its toll on the economy turned what might have been a choice between Biden and Trump into a referendum on President Trump's record and leadership. Following the first wave of hospitalizations in the United States, Biden did not leave his Delaware house for 71 days. And when he finally ventured out for a Memorial Day visit to a veterans park, his aides were unanimous in recommending that he wear a mask. Indeed, Biden's large black mask—mocked by Trump on Twitter—became a symbol of his campaign: a cloth representation of his caution and deliberation, his steady leadership style, and his adherence to scientific recommendations and advice.

In short, most analysts argued that the election was largely about Trump and that Trump lost because he and his campaign could not figure out an appropriate national response to COVID-19. To a slightly lesser degree,

Biden won the election by simply positioning himself as a reliable alternative to the president who was more attuned to the challenges presented by the raging virus. According to exit polls, 17 percent of voters said that the coronavirus was the most important issue influencing their vote. Biden won these voters by a margin of 81 percent to 15 percent.

However, the narrative that Biden won because his campaign was able to make the election a referendum on Trump and the pandemic seems overly simplistic. When asked which issue was the most important to their vote decision, 35 percent of voters said the economy. Trump carried these voters by a margin of 83 percent to 17 percent. Another 20 percent chose racial equality, and these voters preferred Biden 92 percent to 7 percent. Eleven percent chose crime and safety, with Trump winning these voters 71 percent to 27 percent. And 11 percent chose health care, with Biden preferred in this segment 62 percent to 37 percent.[2] All of these issues were on voters' minds because of outside factors: a public health crisis, an economy thrown into disarray, and a social justice movement that tapped into much broader social and historical problems. As we discussed in Chapter 9, these factors are largely outside either candidate's control but still powerfully affect presidential election outcomes.

Although Biden was ultimately helped by Trump's stumbles in dealing with these emergent issues, the mere fact that these issues arose did not necessarily doom the president's reelection campaign. Election forecasts from

Core of the Analysis

- Many Americans are not especially attentive to election campaigns and tend to rely on simple strategies for deciding among candidates.

- Individuals tend to develop a psychological attachment to a political party, and this attachment colors opinions about political issues and candidates.

- Appraisals of national conditions are often important factors for presidential vote choice.

- Campaigns can affect voters' decisions, but mainly when voters do not have preexisting views and when one candidate outspends another by a wide margin.

- Campaigns are more likely to activate the partisan predispositions of voters than they are to persuade voters.

What was responsible for Joe Biden's win in 2020? Was it a deadly pandemic, an economic crisis, and a volatile incumbent—or a winning campaign message?

August 2020—before the fall campaign got underway—support the idea that the Trump and Biden campaigns had only a limited role in reshaping voters' fundamental perceptions of the state of the country. Political scientists offered predictive models of the final vote tally based on an understanding of how voters incorporate factors such as the state of the economy and presidential approval into their choices, and these models estimated that Trump would receive 237 electoral votes, on average. This forecast was close: Trump ultimately received 232 electoral votes. To be sure, election forecasting models are not always this accurate. In 2000, for example, the models predicted that Democratic candidate Al Gore would receive about 56 percent of the two-party vote, when in fact he received just over 50 percent. And in 2016, statistical analyses relying on polling data alone predicted that Democratic candidate Hillary Clinton's chances of winning the election against Trump (not just the popular vote) were between 70 percent and 99 percent.[3] Still, voters' ambivalent mood about the country drove a close national vote in 2020, and political science models relying on economic measures and presidential approval effectively predicted this final vote—even though they did not take the general election campaign into account.

That vote totals in presidential elections are predictable, even months before Election Day, flies in the face of many media accounts of presidential campaigns. These accounts often portray the outcome as uncertain, creating a dramatic narrative in which crucial voters are on the fence and every twist and turn of the campaign—even a single misstatement in a debate—could make the difference between winning and losing. More to the point, the predictability of presidential elections calls into question the importance of the campaign itself. If the campaign matters, how can presidential elections be forecast with such accuracy so far in advance? Do Americans cast their votes based largely on broader political and economic realities and not on campaign messages and events?

In this chapter, we focus on voters and their decisions about which candidates to support. We begin by exploring the reasons behind voting decisions. Our starting point is a fact we have highlighted throughout this book: many Americans do not follow politics very closely. Consequently, their voting decisions are not based on a wealth of information about the candidates. Instead, American voters are more likely to rely on shortcuts and rules of thumb when deciding, and they tend to vote for the party that is aligned with the social groups to which they belong. Perhaps more importantly, they develop an attachment to the party itself that guides their decisions in elections for all levels of office. Additionally, voters—particularly those who don't pay attention to politics and do not have strong partisan attachments—tend to take stock of the performance of the incumbent party and reward or punish it accordingly. Thus, voting decisions often depend on long-standing social and political identities or evaluations of conditions that the candidates themselves cannot change.

Does this mean, then, that political campaigns are irrelevant? Not at all. Campaigns remind people of their underlying attachments, thereby leading them to vote for the party or candidate they are predisposed to support. But, as we discussed in Chapter 5, it is less common for campaigns to actually persuade voters—or change their minds. Even so, under the right conditions, campaigns can move enough voters to shift the outcome of an election. In this chapter, we discuss several of those conditions, such as how familiar the candidates are to citizens and the balance of resources among the competing candidates. We conclude by considering whether Americans' voting decisions are in line with the democratic ideals set out in Chapter 1.

What Influences Vote Choice

By and large, Americans do not spend a great deal of time following politics. This is true even in presidential elections—when politics seems extraordinarily salient. In surveys conducted in every presidential election from 1952 to 2020, fewer than half of Americans said that they were "very interested in the current campaign" (Figure 13.1). This has two implications. First, as we have discussed, campaigns may have difficulty attracting the attention of potential voters, some of whom might prefer watching football, reality television, or anything else. This is one reason why many scholars are skeptical about campaigns' ability to persuade voters and shape election outcomes. Second, Americans may not have a detailed understanding of the party platforms or the positions of the candidates running for office. Their choices in elections may therefore depend on more limited information, especially factors that enable them to make choices relatively quickly and easily. In the following sections, we consider five such factors: party identification, social groups, the performance of incumbents, policy issues, and candidate traits.

Party Identification

Perhaps the most important factor that influences voting in the United States is the identification that voters have with political parties themselves. This idea of a psychological attachment to a political party is called **party identification**. The concept was developed by scholars at the University of Michigan drawing on nationally representative surveys conducted during the 1952 and 1956 elections.[4]

Party identification does not mean identification with a particular political ideology or particular opinions. For example, to identify as a Democrat is not the same as identifying as a liberal. Nor can party identification be equated with how someone is registered to vote or even how they vote at the ballot box, although it is highly correlated with each. Instead, party identification is like other social identities. People feel that they are a member of a group ("I am a Democrat" or "I am a Republican") and tend to feel positively about that group. So people cheer when their "team" wins (and the other loses).

Where does party identification come from? Oftentimes, it is learned relatively early in life, primarily from those who are closest to us for the most extended periods of time. Thus, people's parents have traditionally been the dominant influence on their party identification, although this tendency may

FIGURE 13.1 How Interested Are Americans in Political Campaigns?

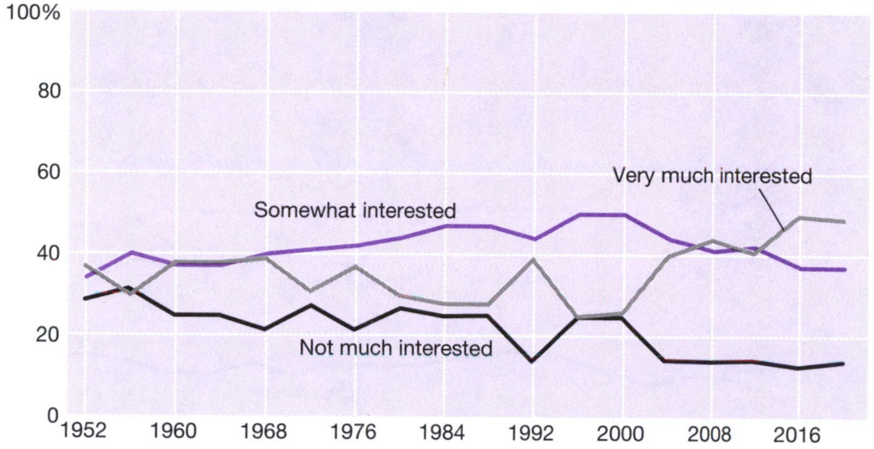

Source: Data are from the American National Election Studies Cumulative Files, 1952–2020.

be weakening somewhat.[5] Besides parents, other people and institutions—such as friends, schools, and churches—can also shape party identification.

The prevailing political context when one comes of age also matters: people who enter young adulthood with a popular president in office will be more likely to identify with the president's party than will people who come of age under an unpopular president.[6] For example, young people who came of age when Republican Ronald Reagan was president are still more likely to be Republicans than those who came of age under the unpopular and scandal-ridden Republican Richard Nixon.[7] Regardless of its sources, party identification is typically formed by young adulthood. Because it is learned so early, it is a durable attitude. People tend not to change much, even as they grow up, learn more, and see their circumstances evolve. In short, with party identification, where people end up depends in large part on where they start.

Of course, this discussion raises an important question: Does everyone develop a party identification? What about those people who identify as "independent"? To assess the true number of political independents, it is important to consider how party identification is typically measured. In a survey, respondents will be asked a question such as: "Generally speaking, do you consider yourself a Republican, a Democrat, or an independent?" If respondents identify as a Republican or Democrat, they are then asked, "Would you call yourself a strong or a not very strong Republican/Democrat?" Respondents who say they are "independent" or express no preference are then asked, "Do you think of yourself as closer to the

FIGURE 13.2 Trends in Party Identification, 1952–2020

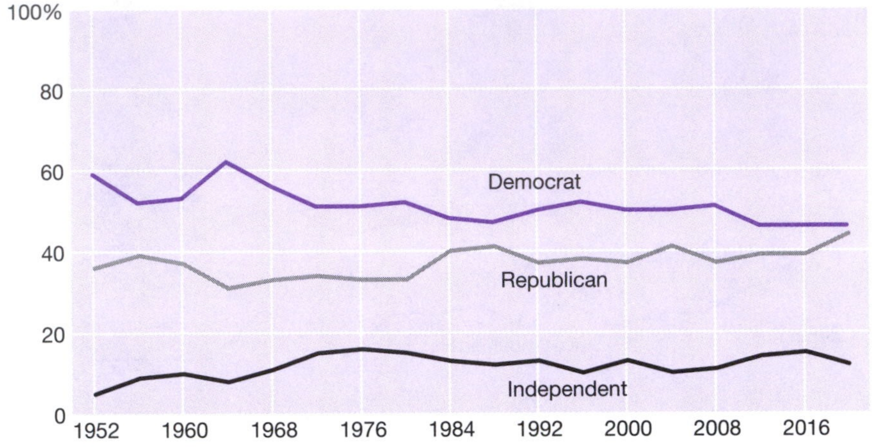

Note: Data for Democrats and Republicans include voters who identify as "leaning" toward one party.
Source: Data are from the American National Election Studies Cumulative Files, 1952–2020.

Republican or Democratic Party?" These questions measure the direction and intensity of party identification and are used to create a seven-point scale: 1. Strong Democrat; 2. Weak Democrat; 3. Leans Democrat; 4. Independent; 5. Leans Republican; 6. Weak Republican; 7. Strong Republican.

As measured by the first in this series of questions, the percentage of independents (those who do not call themselves Republicans or Democrats) is rising—from 23 percent of Americans in 1952 to 33 percent in 2020. But nearly all political independents think of themselves as closer to one party. Only 12 percent do not "lean" toward a party and could be considered "pure" independents. As Figure 13.2 shows, this percentage has been relatively stable since the mid 1980s. Moreover, independents who lean toward a party are almost as likely to support that party's candidates as are those voters who call themselves Republicans or Democrats.[8]

For those who study elections, party identification matters for three reasons. First, it functions as a filter or screen through which information must pass. In other words, people tend to accept information that comes from the party they identify with, or from sources closely identified with that party, and to discount information coming from sources on the other side.[9] This is why, as we noted in Chapter 9, partisans routinely think that their party's presidential nominee won every general election debate.

Second, as we noted in Chapter 12, party identification also motivates people to vote; stronger partisans are more likely to vote than weak and leaning partisans, who in turn are more likely to vote than independents.

FIGURE 13.3 Partisan Loyalty in Presidential Voting, 1980–2020

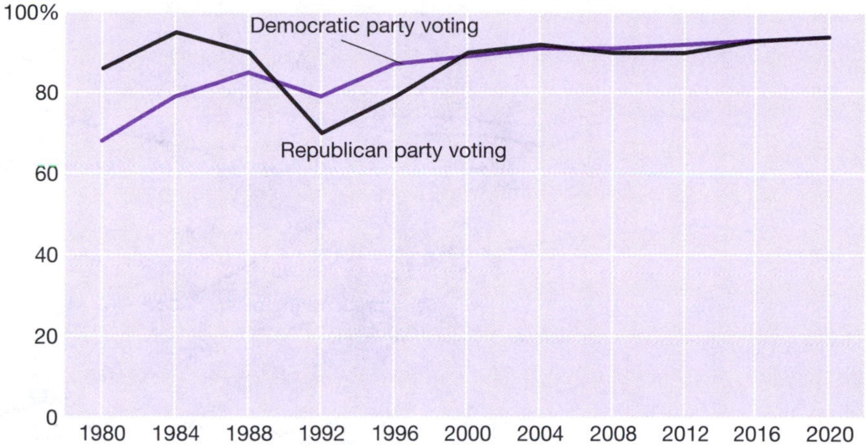

Source: Data are from the American National Election Studies Cumulative Files, 1952–2020.

Finally, and perhaps most important, party identification is a powerful predictor of how citizens vote. In presidential elections, as shown in Figure 13.3, approximately 90 percent of Democrats and Republicans vote for their respective party's nominee. Many races at other levels of office, such as those for the U.S. House and Senate, also see high levels of party loyalty. In fact, partisan loyalty in voting has been increasing over time across almost all races.[10]

One reason for the growing power of party identification is the development of **negative partisanship** (or, relatedly, **affective partisanship**), which refers to the fact that voters who identify with one party are increasingly inclined to view the other party—its candidates and adherents—in an unfavorable light. Figure 13.4 shows how ratings by partisans of the other party have declined over time.

To be sure, party loyalty is not an absolute. From time to time, partisans defect and vote for a candidate of the opposite party—for example, because that candidate is a talented incumbent who has no credible challenger. But defections are the exception rather than the rule. According to the American National Election Studies, only 11 percent of voters split their presidential and congressional ballots in 2020 (7 percent voted for Biden for president and for a Republican for Congress, while 4 percent voted for Trump for president and for a Democrat for Congress). Because of this, campaigns typically try to reinforce partisan loyalties among their followers and to persuade independents to vote for their candidate.

Furthermore, party identification matters for elections at all levels of government. Party identification can provide voters with actionable

FIGURE 13.4 Ratings of Parties by Partisans, 1980–2020

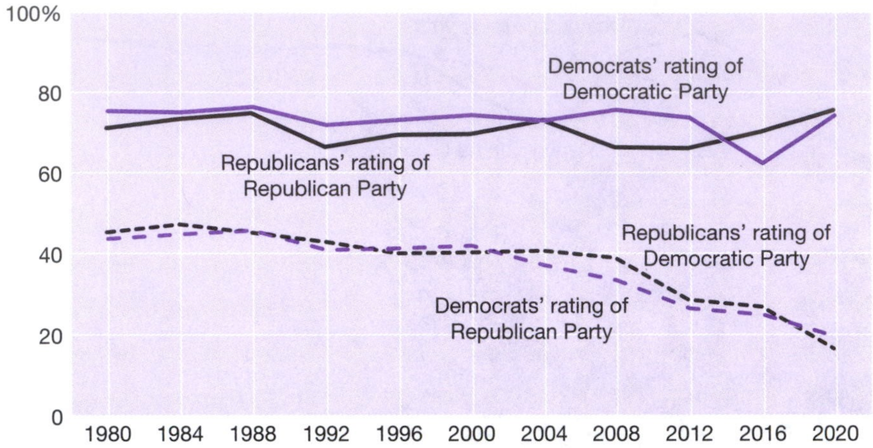

Note: "Feeling thermometer" questions ask survey respondents to use a 0–100 scale to rate how favorably they view a person. Ratings between 50 degrees and 100 degrees mean that the respondent feels favorable and warm toward the person. Ratings between 0 degrees and 50 degrees mean that they don't feel favorable toward the person. Ratings at the 50-degree mark mean that they don't feel particularly warm or cold toward the person.
Source: Data are from the American National Election Studies Cumulative Files, 1952–2020.

information for contests in which they are not particularly well informed about the candidates. Thus, party identification can be a useful shortcut for political decision-making in low-profile elections. Indeed, as noted earlier, today we often see party driving vote choice in down-ballot races, such as state legislative elections and even county or city-level contests.

Social Groups

While party identification is the dominant factor explaining vote choice in America, vote choice is often deeply affected by social group identities as well. In fact, these identities often shape partisanship and other political attitudes. Moreover, social group identity's importance for vote choice is an enduring feature of American elections. Studies of campaign effects in the 1940s and 1950s revealed a crucial fact about voters' political attitudes: they depended on the **social groups** to which voters belonged.[11] For example, Catholic voters tended to have similar partisan leanings and political views, as did Latino voters, union voters, African American voters, white-collar voters, and so on. In other words, voters were aligned with political parties because of class background, ethnicity, religion, or some other group affiliation.

To some degree, groups have long-standing attachments to one party or the other because of their historical experiences and issue priorities. Groups' partisan affiliations also reflect the relative attention that parties pay to the distinct interests of different groups: the party that best serves the interests of a group may attract the enduring loyalty of its members. Once these attachments develop, partisanship becomes the proximate cause of group members' voting behavior, but group members would not necessarily have had these partisan identities without their social group connection.

Group attachments can be quite powerful. For example, in every election since the passage of the Voting Rights Act of 1965—a law championed by Lyndon Johnson, a Democrat—about 90 percent of African Americans have voted for Democratic candidates for president. In 2020, 87 percent of Black voters voted for Biden. Similarly, the Republican Party's promotion of socially conservative policies, such as laws limiting abortion, has garnered the support of most evangelical Christians. In 2020, 76 percent of White born-again or evangelical Christians voted for Trump. Figure 13.5 shows how various social groups for president voted in 2020. These numbers shift from election to election, but many of the basic demographic contours of the vote have been in place since the 1960s.

Of course, voters who identify with a social group will not always automatically vote for the political party aligned with that group. They may need some sort of "reminder"—one that essentially says: "People like you should vote for this candidate." Research has found that the degree to which Americans vote according to their social group identities often depends on their having regular contact and conversation with other members of their social group.[12] Communication with fellow church, workplace, school, and community members often exposes potential voters to more politically interested and engaged voters—so-called **opinion leaders**. As an election nears, these individuals talk about the election in ways that rekindle long-standing allegiances. In the 1948 presidential election, for example, some wavering Democrats came to support the Democratic nominee, Harry Truman, when opinion leaders within Catholic churches and labor unions explained how Truman was for the "little guy" while his opponent Thomas Dewey was just another business-friendly fat cat.[13]

For voters who do not always pay much attention to politics, social group identities serve as a relatively easy way to reach a decision. It does not take much information to align one's vote with the preferences of one's social group, and this information may come without any effort on the part of the voter, perhaps just a brief conversation with a coworker or friend. And because people often trust coworkers and friends more than, say, political candidates, they will view their opinions as particularly credible. Explanations of voting that emphasize the importance of social groups implicitly

FIGURE 13.5 2020 Presidential Vote by Social Groups

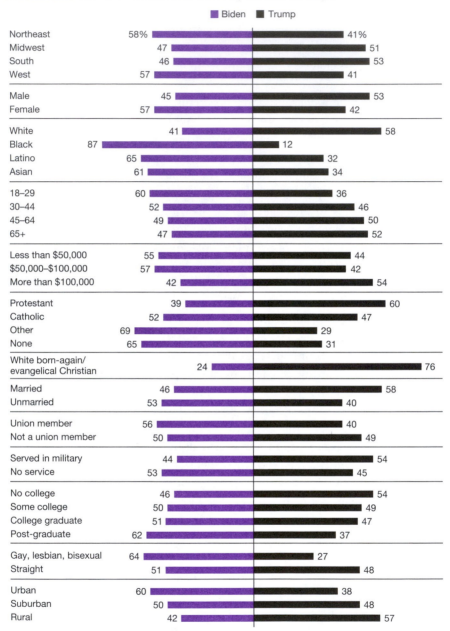

Source: 2020 National Election Pool exit poll, conducted by Edison Research ($N=15{,}590$ respondents).

suggest that campaigns have minimal effects on voters, except insofar as they supply information that helps voters connect their social group identities to their vote choices.

Incumbent Performance

A third factor in many voters' decisions is the performance of the incumbent party or officeholder. An especially important criterion in evaluating this performance is the state of the economy. Historically, when the economy is growing, voters have tended to reward the incumbent party.[14] For example, incumbent presidents have been more likely to be reelected when the country is prosperous. But when the economy is growing slowly or not at all, voters have tended to punish the incumbent president or, if that person is not running, the nominee of the incumbent party. As we discussed in Chapters 9 and 10, macroeconomic variables, such as changes in the average income of Americans, have in the past predicted presidential and even congressional election outcomes. This lends credence to the idea that economic performance is a factor when voters go to the polls. In recent times, however, partisan polarization and the proliferation of alternative news sources have complicated the relationship between the economy and voting. Recent research indicates that voters can be motivated by their partisan leanings to find economic information that fits with their preexisting beliefs about the superiority of their party's policies and performance (or, conversely, the inferiority of the other party's).[15] Still, it remains likely that the party in power and its candidates are better off when the economy is growing and unemployment is low.

How do voters use their perceptions about the economy to decide how to vote? For starters, voters rely on their evaluations of how the economy has performed in the past rather than how it might perform in the future. Using past performance to decide between candidates is called **retrospective voting**, and it is often encapsulated by a single question: "Are we better off now than when the incumbent took office?" While basing one's voting decisions on the answer to this question may appear simpleminded, it is plausible that past performance predicts future performance.[16] In this way, retrospective voting provides an efficient shortcut for citizens looking to make choices about future leadership.

Research also indicates that voters rely more on their assessments of the national economy (**sociotropic voting**) than on assessments of their own financial situation (**pocketbook voting**).[17] Moreover, when voters assess the economy, they focus most on recent changes—especially changes in the election year itself.[18] Even if a president has presided over three years of a weak economy, if the economy shows strong growth in the fourth year, the incumbent or the candidate from the incumbent's party is likely to be rewarded by the electorate.

Once again, however, it is important to remember that voters' evaluations of the economy are biased by their party identification. When a Democrat is president, Democrats evaluate the economy more positively than Republicans do. Republicans exhibit this same tendency when a Republican is president. And even if partisans do pick up on more objective information about the economy, this does not mean that negative economic assessments will cause them to defect from their party's candidates. In 2016, for instance, nearly 57 percent of Democrats said that the economy was either "bad" or "very bad" under the incumbent Democratic administration, but 72 percent of them still voted for the Democratic presidential candidate, Hillary Clinton. Ultimately, because partisans tend to judge the performance of their own officeholders more generously, it is independent voters whose vote choice is most influenced by the incumbent party's handling of the economy.

Policy Issues

In a typical campaign, candidates spend a great deal of time talking about issues related to government policy, such as the regulation of environmental pollution or the future solvency of Social Security and Medicare. When voters make choices, do they factor these sorts of issue positions into their decisions?

In Chapter 5, we introduced the median voter theorem, which posits that candidates take issue positions that are close to the hypothetical median voter whose support is necessary to win the election. The median voter theorem assumes that voters make choices in a particular way: they evaluate the candidates' ideologies or their positions on issues and then choose the candidate who, on average, has positions most similar to their own. This strategy is called **proximity voting**—voters choose the candidates whose views are closest or most proximate to theirs.

Does proximity voting actually happen? Is voting really about "the issues"? In general, no. The strategy of proximity voting takes more time and effort, which voters do not often invest, than the other simple decision-making shortcuts that we have described. To vote based on policy issues, voters first need to have opinions about those issues. But they often do not pay enough attention to politics to form opinions in the first place, especially about complex public policies. Even if they do have opinions, they may not pay enough attention to the campaign to discern where the candidates stand and which candidate is most proximate to them. Moreover, candidates do not always make their views clear. As we discussed in Chapter 5, candidates may have an incentive to be ambiguous.

One prominent study estimated that less than half of the electorate has the requisite opinions on issues and sufficient knowledge of candidates' views to engage in issue voting.[19] When issue voting does occur, it is usually limited to particular groups of voters within the broader electorate. These groups, called *issue publics*, consist of voters who are more likely to have strong opinions about a particular issue, to learn where the candidates stand on this issue, and to vote for a candidate only if that candidate agrees with them. Senior citizens, who are especially attentive to protecting their current Medicare benefits, are a good example of an issue public. However, attention to policy seems to be the exception and not the rule. Furthermore, there is some evidence that rather than voting based on their own policy opinions, voters are more likely simply to adopt the policy positions of the candidates they already support based on party identification.[20]

Candidate Traits

Do voters respond differently to certain kinds of candidates? With respect to gender, recent studies show that while voters say they are willing to vote for female candidates, many people's assumptions about what it means to be a woman and what it means to be an elected leader still do not line up. This can put female candidates at a disadvantage when they step into the political sphere. The traits most people associate with politicians—for example, competence, ambition, aggressiveness, confidence, and toughness—are considered masculine behavior. Studies have found that, as a result, men are often assumed to be viable candidates while women must work to be taken seriously.[21] Another issue is that "likability," an important trait for candidates, may be more difficult for women to cultivate because of the trade-off between exuding strength (necessary to overcome gender stereotypes) and appearing likable. The experiences of female presidential and vice-presidential candidates such as Amy Klobuchar, Kamala Harris, Sarah Palin, and Hillary Clinton demonstrate the difficulty of walking this tightrope.

With respect to race, studies indicate that White voters may oppose Black candidates for different reasons. Overt racism may depress support for African American candidates if some portion of White voters refuses to support Black candidates based on their skin color alone. However, White opposition to African American candidates may also arise from racial stereotypes. For example, White people perceive Black candidates as less competent and more liberal than their White counterparts.[22] Thus, some White voters may be willing to vote for an African American candidate in theory, but their propensity to attribute negative stereotypes to that candidate on the basis of their race makes it unlikely that the candidate will win their votes in reality.[23] Interestingly, some research has found that White voters who are more self-aware of racial stereotypes might actually be more receptive to Black candidates than to White candidates.[24]

The success of both female and Black candidates in recent election cycles raises an important caveat to the general discussion of candidate traits: in modern American elections, the partisan identities of voters still drive vote choice and typically overwhelm the significance of candidates' demographic characteristics. Candidates matter—but only for a relatively small subset of the electorate.

Still, candidates spend a great deal of time promoting not only their views but also their biographies and personal qualities. Is there evidence that some voters draw on their perceptions of candidates' personal qualities, such as appearance or personality, when making decisions in an election? This would seem to be a simple strategy that would not demand much time or effort from voters. They could merely get an impression of the candidates as people, perhaps from television advertising or candidate debates, and then use this impression to select the candidate that seems to be the stronger leader, more honest, better looking, and so on. Indeed, conventional accounts of presidential campaigns often draw attention to personal qualities. In 1960, Democratic candidate John F. Kennedy was considered youthful and energetic, but perhaps a bit inexperienced. His Republican opponent, Richard Nixon, was considered experienced and knowledgeable, but not especially trustworthy. In 2008, Barack Obama was considered youthful, intelligent, and inexperienced, while John McCain's image as a maverick unafraid to buck the system contrasted with concerns about his age and temperament. In 2016, Hillary Clinton was considered experienced and knowledgeable, but not very honest. Donald Trump, on the other hand, was viewed as eager to shake things up, but not very knowledgeable. Trump maintained this image in 2020, while Joe Biden cultivated the impression that he was steady, experienced, and empathetic.

But do such qualities matter? There is some evidence that they do. For example, better-looking candidates appear to get more votes than less-attractive opponents do.[25] Similarly, the more positively people assess a candidate's personality—attributing traits to them such as honesty or capacity for leadership—the more likely they are to vote for the candidate.[26] However, partisanship (once again) affects these judgments.[27] Candidates also suffer

Like political scientists, campaign consultants recognize party identification as a strong influence on vote choice. Campaign strategists look at the partisan composition of the district as a starting point in determining whose votes they can count on and whose they can hope to win through persuasion.

when scandals, especially those involving allegations of official corruption, cast doubt on their character (though they often survive).[28] In advance of the 2016 presidential campaign, for example, the investigation into Hillary Clinton's use of a private email server during her time as secretary of state—and especially news media coverage of Clinton's response to the investigation— caused her favorability ratings to plummet from 66 percent favorable in late 2014 to 42 percent by summer 2015.[29] In addition to individual personalities, perceptions of the parties also seem to influence how voters see candidates' characteristics; certain traits are more likely to be "owned" by Democratic candidates (for example, empathy) and others are more likely to be "owned" by Republican candidates (such as leadership). Even in the face of partisan polarization, Democrats who are able to establish themselves as strong leaders and Republicans who project caring appear to do relatively better at attracting independents and even some partisans from the other side.[30]

At the same time, other evidence suggests that a candidate's appearance and personality may matter very little and may be dependent on the nature of the race. For instance, one study demonstrated that attractive candidates tend to run in races where they have a better chance of winning.[31] Thus, if attractive candidates get more votes than less-attractive candidates do, it is unclear whether this is because of attractiveness or because these races are simply easier to win. The same logic may extend to other candidate attributes, such as their personalities. A candidate's appearance or personality will typically matter most when voters have little other information to draw on, such as in smaller races that feature unfamiliar candidates and attract little media coverage. In races where voters have much more information—such as a presidential race—it is less clear that people's evaluations of the candidates' personalities actually decide their vote. In such races, people may have a preferred candidate for other reasons—especially because of party identification—and thus evaluate their party's candidate more favorably. Such biases are not absolute, however. In 2016, many Republicans rated Hillary Clinton as more knowledgeable, and many Democrats rated Donald Trump as more likely to "say what he means." Nevertheless, close to 90 percent of both Democrats and Republicans voted for their party's nominee despite any misgivings.

When Campaigns Matter

Although campaign consultants and political scientists share many beliefs about vote choice, they disagree over a key question: how much campaigns can affect voters' attitudes toward the candidates. Campaign consultants believe that their activities—television and radio advertisements, phone calls, direct mail, the internet, social media, and person-to-person contact— help persuade voters and thus win elections. Political scientists are more skeptical but nevertheless acknowledge that campaigns can sometimes change voters' minds and even affect election outcomes. The crucial task is to identify *when* campaigns are likely to matter. In this section we are particularly concerned with **persuasion**—a concept we introduced in Chapter 5 that means, in this context, convincing undecided voters to support a particular candidate or convincing the other party's supporters to defect.

Campaigns have their largest persuasive effects when two conditions are met. First, campaigns matter more when the candidates are relatively unfamiliar to voters. When candidates are not well known, voters are less likely to have opinions about them. Although party identification is likely to affect their initial assessments, they will still be more susceptible to persuasive appeals from the candidates because they will not already have strongly held opinions about them.

Second, with a few notable exceptions, campaigns matter more when one side is able to dominate by virtue of more or better resources.[32] That is to say, voters are more likely to be persuaded when one side can campaign more heavily than the other side can, typically when it has more money and thus a more extensive campaign organization, a larger presence on television and other media, and a better-developed infrastructure for contacting and mobilizing voters. In local races, for example, a better-funded candidate can totally eclipse a relatively impoverished opponent. When opposing campaigns are more equally balanced in terms of resources, it is difficult for either campaign to get an edge. Advertisements by one side can be matched by competing advertisements from the other side. The respective efforts of the two sides thus tend to cancel each other out. In light of these two conditions, we can evaluate how much of an impact campaigns at different levels of office will likely have.

Presidential Elections

Campaign effects tend to be most obvious and influential in the nomination phase of presidential elections. At this stage, candidates for the nomination vary greatly in their resources. Some are heavyweights: politicians with national visibility and the campaign war chests, media attention, and party endorsements to show for it. In the 2020 Democratic presidential primaries, Joe Biden fit this description. Other candidates, however, struggle for visibility and can rarely raise as much money or attract the same level of attention as heavyweight candidates can. In the run-up to the 2020 Democratic primaries, this described candidates such as New Jersey senator Cory Booker and former secretary of housing and urban development Julián Castro. Disparities in campaign resources help the heavyweights dominate the field, pulling voters to their side.

Candidates in presidential primaries are also much less well known than the eventual nominees will be. Although some may be national figures, as Biden and Trump were in 2020, many others are familiar only to the voters of the state or district that they represent as members of Congress or as governor. Thus, voters do not have well-formed opinions about many primary candidates, leaving more potential for the campaign to influence these opinions.

Furthermore, voters cannot rely on their party identification to make decisions because all of the candidates in a party primary share the same party identification. As we discussed in Chapter 9, the primary campaign often matters in this fashion: a candidate's victories in the early caucuses and primaries signal to voters that the candidate is viable. This creates a bandwagon effect as voters gravitate toward successful candidates who they believe will be able to compete effectively in the general election. Joe Biden began the 2020 nomination season polling at 28 percent support among Democratic primary voters, while his closest competitor, Vermont senator Bernie Sanders, had the support of 19 percent. After Sanders's victory in the Nevada caucuses on February 22, support for Biden fell to 17 percent while support for Sanders rose to 29 percent. But then Biden won the South Carolina primary on February 29. By March 11, 17 days after the Nevada election and 11 days after the South Carolina contest, support for Biden had reached 53 percent while support for Sanders was at 35 percent. Granted, several candidates dropped out over this time period, but this swing was much larger than the swings typically seen in presidential general election campaigns. Primary candidates know that by campaigning effectively in early primaries and caucuses, they can build the momentum necessary to contest the nomination.

But while campaign effects are common in the nomination contests, they are less noticeable as presidential campaigns move toward the fall. In fact, despite the vast amounts of money that presidential candidates spend, presidential general election campaigns are less likely to decide election outcomes than campaigns at other levels of office are. By the time the party conventions are over and the general election campaign has begun, the Democratic and Republican nominees are already relatively well known. They have been campaigning for months, if not years. At the national party conventions, the parties spend several days promoting their nominees for a large television audience. Moreover, when incumbent presidents run for reelection, voters have had five or six years to get to know them, at least from the time their first campaign for president began.

Competing major-party presidential campaigns also tend to be roughly equal in terms of resources—including not only money but also motivation, information, and expertise. Though in recent years presidential campaigns have not always been on level ground in terms of money—Hillary Clinton and Joe Biden both outspent Donald Trump in 2016 and 2020, respectively—highly motivated, ideological outside groups tend to help less-well-heeled candidates make up the dollar gap. Beyond money, it is obvious that the campaigns of the two major parties have equal motivation. The presidential election is, in the words of Republican media consultant Stuart Stevens, "the big enchilada." Both parties try hard to win. It is only slightly less obvious that the campaigns are working with equal information. Both the Democratic and Republican presidential campaigns have ready access to information about voters' preferences via polling and focus groups. Opposition research arms both campaigns with data on rival candidates' relevant issue positions and backgrounds. And experts work with the candidates and their teams on issue positions and policy papers.

Taken together, these equalities lead to the possibility that presidential general election campaigns will fight to a draw. The winner will be determined not by the campaign but by the broader conditions in the country, especially the economy. Of course, even if this is true as a general rule, there are moments when the campaign itself appears crucial. It is possible, even in presidential campaigns, for one side to get a financial advantage over the other. In the 2020 presidential race, Joe Biden outspent Donald Trump on advertising in Arizona, Pennsylvania, Michigan, and Wisconsin during the last two months of the campaign, which may have helped Biden's cause in those key states.[33] In 2000, George W. Bush outspent Al Gore in battleground states late in the campaign, and the resulting advantage in advertising may have cost Gore four points off the final vote margin—a large number in states such as Florida, where the race was close.[34] In 2008, when Barack Obama bypassed public funding and outspent John McCain by an enormous margin, Obama did better in most areas of the country than did his Democratic counterpart in 2004, John Kerry. More importantly, Obama did particularly well the more he outspent McCain. Obama's largest campaign spending advantages were in Florida ($28 million), Virginia ($16.3 million), Indiana ($11.4 million), and North Carolina ($7.2 million); even though these states had voted Republican in 2004 by 5, 8, 21, and 12 points, respectively, all four went for Obama in 2008. In general, however, a presidential candidate needs a fairly substantial advantage over an opponent to shift voters in their direction, and, even then, this shift will likely be small.[35] This is why presidential election outcomes are not usually decided by the campaign. One study of presidential campaigns from 1948 to 2000 found that only five of the 14 elections appeared to have been decided by the campaign.[36]

Nonpresidential Elections

Campaigns for offices below the presidential level—for U.S. House and Senate and for state and local offices—are more likely to influence voters relative to presidential general election campaigns. Again, familiarity with the candidates and resource disparities are reasons why. As we discussed in Chapters 10 and 11, citizens know little about their representatives at lower levels of office. They often do not even know the names of their congressional representatives, to say nothing of their representatives in the state legislature, their state's attorney general, and so on. Thus, voters' views about these people can be changed by vigorous campaigning. We often see this dynamic in U.S. House elections, particularly in the campaigns of candidates who are challenging incumbents. Campaign activity matters more for challengers because so few voters know them. Challengers with more money to spend become better known than less-well-funded challengers do over the course of the campaign.[37]

This fact makes campaign resource disparities all the more important. And, indeed, resource disparities are common in congressional, state, and local elections. One reason incumbents have dominated these elections in the past is because challengers did not raise enough money to compete with them. This has been less true in recent years,[38] as increased polarization nationally has driven increased funding for challengers locally. In congressional elections from 2000 to 2020, no challenger who raised less than $100,000 won. By contrast, roughly one-third of those who raised at least $1 million won.[39] Campaign spending is arguably even more vital for challengers in elections for state legislative seats, state supreme court posts, and city council.[40] In these elections, which attract relatively little media coverage, voters are not likely to see, hear, or read anything about challengers unless it comes from their campaigns. Thus, campaigns can be crucial to the outcomes of such elections, even if the dollar amounts spent on them are minuscule compared with what is spent in higher-profile races. That said, other factors—including party identification, the economy, and national tides—are still extremely important for understanding vote choice.

How Campaigns Matter

The preceding discussion focused on the conditions under which campaigns can persuade voters. But how do campaigns actually affect voters' choices? Three types of effects are important: persuasion, reinforcement, and priming.

Persuasion

As we have discussed, campaigns are more likely to persuade voters when voters are unfamiliar with the candidates and when one side can outspend the other. But this observation only scratches the surface when it comes to analyzing how campaigns persuade. Although resource disparities are important, much of campaigning is not simply about spending more than the opponent: it is about crafting specific messages intended to persuade voters. This is what campaign consultants focus on, using polling data, focus groups, and their own experiences to design advertisements, write speeches, and produce other kinds of media. Campaigning also involves choosing the appropriate time to air those messages so that they will have the maximum possible impact on voters. Unfortunately, we do not know very much about what kinds of persuasion strategies consistently work. Campaign consultants sometimes rely on results from polls or focus groups, but often they rely on guesswork and interpretations of past elections. Free from the daunting prospect of a looming election, social scientists tend to put little stock in such evidence when they evaluate persuasion strategies, but more rigorous data are usually difficult to come by.

One aspect of persuasive messaging that has been studied extensively is tone—that is, whether the messages promote a candidate (positive campaigning), attack that candidate's opponent (negative campaigning), or offer some combination of the two (contrast campaigning). Campaign consultants tend to place great faith in the power of negativity. One Democratic consultant put it this way: "The big question in most campaigns . . . is whose negative campaign is better. If it's negative, it works. If it's positive, save it for your tombstone."[41] But is negativity really that powerful?

There is some evidence that negative advertising is more memorable than positive advertising. This is because negative information typically stands out in people's daily lives, which generally consist of positive interactions.[42] For example, a couple arguing in a quiet restaurant is much more memorable than a couple enjoying their meal and conversing pleasantly. But there is much less evidence that negative campaigning actually helps the candidate who goes on the attack. On the whole, negative campaigning makes voters feel less favorable toward the candidate being attacked, which is the goal. However, it also makes voters feel less favorable toward the attacker, and this backlash may be stronger than the effect on voters' views of the attacked candidate.[43] Negative advertising is thus a risky strategy at best.

Besides tone, another important aspect of messaging is issue content. In fact, a strategy that campaigns often employ to attempt to persuade voters is to focus on **wedge issues**. Campaigns use these issues to try to convince voters in the opposite party to defect and vote for the other side. The legality of marijuana is one such wedge issue. An overwhelming percentage of Democrats support decriminalizing marijuana possession, and many Republicans also support this policy, often on grounds of personal freedom.[44] In 2016, Democrats attempted to get so-called "pot initiatives" on the ballot in many states, and several Democratic congressional candidates in states where marijuana ended up on the ballot directed digital, phone, and mail communications at "libertarian" Republican voters on the issue. These candidates hoped to draw a favorable contrast with their Republican opponents, who supported government regulation of marijuana and criminal sentencing for small-time users, and ultimately to attract support from some Republican voters. Wedge issues are intended to take advantage of **cross pressures** within voters—that is, the fact that voters sometimes hold ideologically conflicting issue opinions (as in the case of a Republican who supports decriminalizing marijuana). Voters who experience such cross pressures are more susceptible than non-cross-pressured voters to persuasion during a presidential campaign.[45] At the same time, given that most partisans vote loyally for their party's candidates, wedge issue strategies may not be as effective as the strategies that parties pursue to solidify their ranks.

Another aspect of persuasion is timing: When can persuasive campaigning most effectively be deployed? Typically, campaigns increase their volume of advertising and other activities as the election draws closer, believing that this is when most voters begin to focus on the choice ahead of them. If so, the most important information is that which voters encounter immediately prior to casting their ballots. For example, in 2016, Donald Trump's campaign sent out last-minute emails and text messages that focused on FBI director James Comey's October 28 announcement that he was reopening his investigation into Hillary Clinton's use of a private email server. The Trump camp believed this message reinforced the argument that Clinton was not honest, and they have suggested (off the record) that it might have helped put Trump over the top. More to the point, the message was effective because it went out just as voters were tuning into the campaign so they could make their final vote choice.

Other practitioners and consultants believe that campaigns should move early—before the race and its candidates are defined and the cacophony of competing messages reaches a crescendo. Available evidence suggests that early campaigning can move voters but may not have lasting effects. A study of Rick Perry's 2006 Texas gubernatorial campaign found that early television ads significantly improved Perry's standing in the polls, but this effect faded within a week of the ads' airing.[46] Comparable analyses of other campaigns in 2006, 2012, and 2016 found a similarly rapid rate of "decay," suggesting again that campaign activities tend to have an immediate but short-lived impact.[47] Does this mean that early campaigning is always fruitless? Not necessarily. Candidate images and issue priorities are often established well before the last month of the campaign. Moreover, given the substantial and increasing fraction of voters who cast their ballots before Election Day, unleashing one's campaign in the waning days of October may be too late.

Reinforcement

Because we have emphasized the challenges that campaigns face in persuading voters, it may seem as if campaigns matter only if they change people's attitudes. But campaigns are also important when they reinforce attitudes. **Reinforcement** occurs when a campaign solidifies voters' preferences. Reinforcement is particularly likely to occur when most voters are already predisposed to support one party because of social group identities or identification with that party. For example, a voter may tend to vote Republican but not know much about or feel strongly committed to a particular Republican candidate. In practice, then, reinforcement consists of making voters more comfortable with the candidate they already lean toward or prefer—or perhaps making them less comfortable with the alternative. Campaign activity can potentially increase a voter's level of commitment. Sometimes this is referred to as "rallying the base."

Although reinforcement is an important effect of campaigns, it is difficult to measure and thus somewhat underappreciated. Preelection polls that simply ask voters whether they plan to vote Democratic or Republican will not capture how strongly voters feel or how certain they are of their choice. With further questioning, it might become clear that many voters express a degree of uncertainty early on in a campaign—an uncertainty that disappears by late in the campaign, when voters have become devotees of their party's candidate and opponents of the other side's candidate. Of course, there is nothing automatic about reinforcement. A campaign might fail to rally its base. Such campaigns will naturally face long odds.

Priming

Campaigns not only influence vote choice but also influence *why* people vote the way they do. That is, campaigns affect the criteria that voters use in choosing a candidate, a process known as **priming** (Chapter 8). In any given election year, candidates know that they have some biographical details, personal experiences, and issue positions that give them an advantage and some that do not. Campaigns will work to focus attention on issues that benefit them as well as issues that disadvantage their opponents, and this strategy may help them win. Thus, campaigns are not simply about persuasion but about controlling the agenda and defining what the election is about.

Understanding priming helps answer an interesting question about elections, presidential elections in particular: How can elections be so predictable and yet the polls fluctuate so much? We discussed in Chapter 9 (and alluded to at the outset of this chapter) how presidential elections can be forecast with considerable accuracy based on factors such as presidential approval and the state of the economy. And yet, during presidential campaigns, there can be notable swings in the polls—for example, in 2008, John McCain took the lead after the Republican National Convention, only to lose it two weeks later and never recover it for the rest of the campaign. Priming offers one explanation for why poll numbers eventually converge on the forecast. As the election goes on, campaign activities tend to focus voters' attention on fundamental factors like the economy.[48] As these issues become more important to voters' decisions, the polls move in the direction of the candidate favored by these factors—as, for example, an incumbent president would be favored if the economy were growing robustly. Of course, if the challenger to that incumbent president successfully changes the subject so that voters focus on some other issue, the incumbent may lose. A systematic study of presidential elections since 1952 shows the importance of priming: when candidates who benefit from the state of the economy and other conditions emphasize these factors in their campaigns, they are more likely to win than are similarly situated candidates who focus on some other issue.[49]

The 2020 election illustrates the importance of priming. Trump spent much of the campaign talking about the "greatest economy ever" and warning voters that Biden's policies would extend the economic shutdown and dampen any prospective recovery with burdensome taxes and regulations. Trump's campaign wanted to prime voters to focus on the economy and to view the pandemic (and Trump's reelection bid) through the lens of economic policies. In contrast, Biden spent much of the campaign priming voters to view the election as a referendum on Trump and his handling of the coronavirus pandemic. When Biden spoke of the economy, it was largely within the context of the pandemic, promising to "build back better."

Conclusion

The decisions Americans make about political candidates—and the campaign's role in influencing those decisions—are frequently the subject of concern. Commentators speculate about whether Americans make decisions that are well informed based on their specific knowledge of the candidates and their own views about issues. This concern speaks to the standard of *deliberation* that we introduced in the first chapter. Typically, that standard is applied to how candidates are campaigning or how the media covers campaigns. But the same standard could be applied to citizens. For one, healthy deliberation implies that citizens are themselves paying attention, willing to learn, and willing to contribute to the national conversation that happens in and around elections. Moreover, if the news media and candidates are expected to provide detailed information to voters but voters simply are not paying attention, then perhaps the voters bear as much or more responsibility as the quality of media coverage or campaign messages.

This perspective may give voters far less credit than they deserve. We have emphasized throughout this chapter that voters often rely on simple decision rules that do not require detailed information. For example, Americans often rely on long-standing psychological attachments to one of the two major political parties. They also draw on appraisals of the country's condition to evaluate incumbent performance. These strategies may be simple, even simplistic, but they may also be good shortcuts. What does it mean to say that something is a good shortcut? The question is whether voters who choose a Democratic or Republican candidate based on party identification would be likely to choose that same candidate if they had received and digested reams of information about everyone running. In other words, did the shortcut get voters to the same place that they would have reached had they devoted considerable time and energy to researching the alternatives? In many cases, the answer is probably yes. Some research has demonstrated that voting based on issue proximity calculations often gets citizens to the same vote choice they would have made had they relied solely on their partisanship. This is why social identities and party identification in particular may be reliable shortcuts. If so, then we might be slightly less concerned if voters do not follow the campaign closely.

A second concern raised about voters' behavior in elections concerns the impact of the campaign itself. Commentators sometimes worry that voters—particularly those who are not paying close attention to the campaign—could be unduly affected by clever television advertisements or other kinds of campaign appeals. This speaks to the standard of *free choice*. If campaigns can influence voters by airing ads with exaggerated attacks on the opponent that play on voters' fears, or ads that contain misleading information or even outright falsehoods, then perhaps voters' choices are not quite free but are instead being manipulated by the candidates.

By and large, such fears seem unfounded. Campaigns can be important for the voting process. They reinforce the views of partisans and occasionally persuade some voters who are on the fence. But their effects appear to stop well short of manipulation. Indeed, political reality—objective factors and conditions—significantly constrains the degree to which campaigns can influence voters. Campaigns are hard-pressed to overcome political reality and voters' partisan habits, particularly when the efforts of one candidate are countered and offset by the efforts of the other. This is especially true for presidential election campaigns. The result is that presidents presiding over peaceful and prosperous times typically win (for example, Ronald Reagan in 1984 and Bill Clinton in 1996), and those presiding over violent times or economic recessions typically lose (for example, Jimmy Carter in 1980 and George H. W. Bush in 1992). Only when voters know little about the candidates or when they cannot rely on shortcuts like party identification do campaigns seem to be more influential—and even then only when one candidate can outspend the other.

We are not suggesting that campaigns do not matter at all. For one, they might be important even if they do not persuade many voters. They provide information, mobilize voters, and force candidates to articulate policy positions that become the basis for subsequent accountability. Furthermore, in some cases, they do persuade enough voters to affect the outcome. The 2020 presidential election might be such a case, given that Biden's victory rested on only 42,844 votes in three states (Arizona, Georgia, and Wisconsin). Thus, the campaign can be the difference between winning and losing—certainly at lower levels of office and perhaps even in presidential elections from time to time.

The 2020 election also shows that the campaign itself may not end even after the votes are counted and the winner declared. Indeed, one might wonder if the lesson of 2020 is that our entire electoral system is broken and that American democracy itself has been damaged beyond repair. When the legitimacy of an election is called into question, citizens are right to be concerned.

But we do not believe the problems facing this country are the fault of the electoral process. Aside from a pandemic that affected how candidates campaigned and the methods by which ballots were cast, the 2020 presidential election was not that unusual. The candidates campaigned on common themes, and partisan identification predicted how most people voted. What was unusual was what happened after the election: the losing candidate refused to accept his defeat, undermining the legitimacy of the electoral process by claiming that the election was rigged.

If this was the fault of the electoral process, it would suggest that some type of election reform—for example, requiring all voters to provide identification or increasing the transparency of the ballot counting process—might have improved the election's perceived legitimacy. But it is hard to imagine any reforms that would have prevented Trump and his followers from questioning the election's outcome. If individuals believe that *any* process that does not elect their candidate is illegitimate, the process itself is not to blame. The fault lies with political leaders who sow the seeds of distrust. The solution is not to change the electoral system but for political leaders to graciously accept defeat and to encourage their followers to do the same. After all, in a democracy, there is always the next election.

KEY TERMS

party identification (p. 364)

negative partisanship (p. 367)

affective partisanship (p. 367)

social groups (p. 368)

opinion leaders (p. 369)

retrospective voting (p. 371)

sociotropic voting (p. 371)

pocketbook voting (p. 371)

proximity voting (p. 372)

persuasion (p. 376)

wedge issues (p. 381)

cross pressures (p. 382)

reinforcement (p. 383)

priming (p. 383)

FOR DISCUSSION

1. What is party identification and how does it influence the behavior of voters? What is "negative partisanship"?

2. Why do scholars believe that most voters do not engage in issue voting?

3. Identify and briefly describe three ways in which campaigns might "matter" for voters.

4. Why is it that political scientists are particularly skeptical about the ability of presidential campaigns to determine election outcomes?

5. Do you think the 2020 presidential election confirms the findings in this chapter or contradicts them?

Glossary

501(c) organizations—Organizations that are exempt from federal taxation and may be able to engage in political activity, subject to certain restrictions

527 organizations—Officially designated political organizations under the tax code that are required to disclose their contributors to the Internal Revenue Service; came to the fore in 2004, the first election after the Bipartisan Campaign Reform Act's ban on soft money for parties

absentee voting—The process by which citizens who cannot vote in person on Election Day request that ballots be mailed to their homes and then vote by mailing those ballots to election officials

affective partisanship—Identifying as a Republican or Democrat based on one's dislike of the other party

agenda setting—The news media's ability to influence the issues that the public regards as important by selecting which stories to cover

analytics—In the context of American elections, the use of sophisticated statistical models to identify politically meaningful patterns within large sets of voter data

at-large elections—Geographic units that elect multiple members as their representatives

attack ads—Advertisements in which supporters of one candidate question the character, ethics, and/or integrity of their candidate's opponent

Australian ballot—A method of voting by secret ballot, widely adopted in the United States in the early part of the 1900s, that made it impossible for casual observers or party workers to determine for whom a citizen had cast a vote

automatic voter registration—A system of voter registration in which state government agencies register people to vote unless they choose to opt out

ballot initiative campaigns—Campaigns surrounding specific propositions put directly to voters for their approval. Since there are no candidates in these campaigns, interest groups are the main actors influencing voters.

ballot initiatives—Measures that affect laws or public policy and that are proposed by interested citizens and then voted on by citizens in elections

battleground (or swing) states—States that are competitive between the major party candidates and whose outcome may decide the presidential election

big data—In the context of American elections, large data sets containing extensive information on individual voters

Bipartisan Campaign Reform Act (BCRA)—2002 law that prohibited soft money spending by national, state, and local parties; limited soft money spending by outside groups; and increased individual contribution limits

blanket (or jungle) primary—Election in which all candidates for an office are listed on the ballot, and anyone registered to vote in that election may vote for any one candidate; typically, the top two vote-getters advance to a runoff election

Buckley v. Valeo—1976 Supreme Court decision overturning the Federal Election Campaign Act's limits on spending by federal candidates as a violation of the First Amendment

campaign agenda—The issue areas discussed during a campaign

campaign strategy—A campaign's understanding of how its candidate is going to win the election, who will vote for the candidate, and why

campaign—An organized effort to persuade and mobilize voters to support or oppose a party or candidate

casework—The work performed by members of Congress or their staff to help constituents deal with government bureaucracies

caucuses—Relatively closed affairs in which registered partisans attend meetings at election precinct locations and vote to select delegates to the county or state party conventions

citizen legislatures—Legislatures in which serving as a legislator is a part-time position that comes with relatively little salary or staff support

Citizens United v. Federal Election Commission—2010 Supreme Court decision holding that under the First Amendment, corporate funding of independent political broadcasts in candidate elections cannot be limited

civil service—Government jobs or positions in which employment and promotions are based on professional qualifications and performance

clean elections system—A system of campaign finance whereby candidates who raise a minimum amount of private donations qualify for public funding from the government; once candidates accept public funding, they cannot spend any more money raised from private donors

closed primary—Election for a party's nominee in which only those registered as party members can vote

coattail effect—When a popular high-profile candidate is on the ballot, lesser-known candidates in that candidate's party benefit from that candidate's appeal to voters—they "ride the coattails" of the high-profile candidate

communities of interest—Redistricting principle that districts should attempt to keep together citizens in areas that share a political history or set of interests

constituencies—Subsets of the American public for whom interest groups or candidates claim to speak, such as ethnic or religious groups

contrast advertisements—Advertisements in which supporters of a candidate seek to favorably compare their candidate's record and positions to their opponent's record and positions

control group—In an experiment, a randomly assigned group composed of

participants who do not receive the experimental treatment

convenience voting—Methods of voting that do not involve actually casting a ballot at a polling place on Election Day, such as absentee, early, or mail voting conducted before Election Day

convention bump/convention bounce—Increased support for a candidate resulting from the party's national convention

coordinated expenditures—Money that political parties spend to help cover a candidate's campaign costs in a federal election. Such expenditures are limited by law.

cross pressures—Two or more beliefs, identities, or issue positions that pull a voter in different partisan directions

delegates—People chosen to vote for a party's presidential nominee at the national convention

Democratic Party—Political party from 1828 to the present, associated with Andrew Jackson, representing interests suspicious of an entrenched commercial class; the first party to embrace mass democratic participation

Democratic-Republican Party—Political party from 1796 to 1824, associated with Thomas Jefferson, representing a more limited view of federal governing power, preferring state and local governing authority; support was strongest in the southern and western states

Duverger's Law—Single-member, simple plurality election systems tend to produce two major political parties

early voting—In-person voting that takes place before Election Day

earned media (or free media)—The publicity that candidates get by engaging in promotional activities

election—The selection of persons to hold public office by means of a vote

electoral participation—The range of activities through which individuals attempt to affect the outcome of an election

era of pre-democratic campaigns—Time between the ratification of the U.S. Constitution in 1788 and the widespread expansion of elected public offices in the 1820s

express advocacy—Specifically advocating the election or defeat of a candidate

Federal Election Campaign Act (FECA)—1971 law, substantially amended in 1974, that set limits on contributions to federal campaigns, provided for public funding of presidential election campaigns, mandated contribution disclosure and finance report filings, established the Federal Election Commission to oversee finance laws, and set limits on candidate spending; the last of these provisions was overturned by the Supreme Court

Federal Election Commission (FEC)—The regulatory agency that enforces the laws governing federal elections

Federalist Party—Political party from 1796 to 1828, associated with Alexander Hamilton, representing a more expansive view of federal governing power, especially with respect to regulating commercial interests; support was strongest in the northeastern and mid-Atlantic states

field experiments—A form of research in which subjects (in the case of campaigns, voters) are randomly assigned into treatment and control groups, treatment groups receive a particular stimulus, and outcomes are compared between the two groups; an important new way for campaigns to test outreach and persuasion

focus group—A form of qualitative research in which a group of people is asked about their perceptions, opinions, beliefs, and attitudes toward a product, service, concept, advertisement, idea, or packaging; questions are asked in an interactive group setting where participants are free to talk with other group members. In campaigns, small groups of persuadable voters are interviewed in depth to gather additional data and test specific issue positions.

framing—Choosing the language used to define issues of importance during a campaign; the news media's ability to influence what the public thinks is at stake in a debate by categorizing issues into one of many possible interpretations

franking privilege—The ability of members of Congress to send mail to constituents without postage

front-loading—Moving statewide nominating contests earlier in the calendar to increase their influence

front-porch campaign—Tactic whereby a candidate stays at home and allows their campaign team to arrange for select meetings with news media outlets

front-runners—Candidates perceived to have the money, experience, and popular support to win

generational cohorts—Groups of people who came of age politically at about the same time

gerrymandering—Drawing district lines to maximize some political interest

get-out-the-vote (GOTV) efforts—The efforts of candidates, parties, and interest groups to get citizens to vote

hard money—Money raised in accordance with campaign finance laws

Hill committees—A term used to refer to the four major party campaign committees involved in congressional elections

horse race journalism—News reporting that focuses on which candidates are becoming more or less likely to win an election as well as what each candidate is doing to improve their standing in the polls

incumbency advantage—The vote share earned by an incumbent compared to what a nonincumbent would have earned if they had run

incumbent—The candidate in an election who already occupies the office

independent candidates—Persons running for office who are not affiliated with any particular political party

independent expenditure committees—Political action committees that can raise unlimited donations from various sources and then spend money to advocate for or against candidates

independent expenditures—Campaign communication by an independent group that engages in express advocacy; party expenditures made without consulting or coordinating with a candidate

infotainment—Media content that provides a combination of information and entertainment, such as comedy news programs or coverage of celebrities

interest group—A collection of people with the shared goal of influencing public policy that does not run its own candidates for office

interpretive journalism—News reporting that includes analysis of the reasons why events happen and the likely effects that the events will have

issue advocacy—Advocating a position on a political issue without explicitly advocating for the election or defeat of a candidate

issue ownership—The concept that political parties have differential credibility on certain issues and that their candidates try to win elections by convincing voters that issues they "own" are the most important ones in a given election

literacy tests—Questions that purported to measure citizens' ability to read and understand English but really were used to prevent Black people from voting in southern states; literacy tests were suspended by federal legislation, beginning with the Voting Rights Act (1965)

magic words—Words that make an advertisement subject to campaign finance laws and regulations

majority-minority districts—Districts in which racial or ethnic minorities form a majority of the population

malapportionment—Any significant differences in the number of citizens across districts

material benefits—Rewards or payments received in exchange for political participation

median voter theorem—In a majority election, if voter policy preferences can be represented as points along a single dimension, and if all voters vote for the candidate who commits to a policy position closest to their own preference, and if there are only two candidates, then a candidate maximizes their votes by committing to the policy position preferred by the median voter

message—Information repeated by a candidate or surrogates during a campaign that communicates who the candidate is and why voters should cast their ballots for them

microtargeting—To direct tailored advertisements, political messages, and the like toward people based on detailed information about them, such as their demographic, attitudinal, or consumer characteristics; this detailed information is sometimes estimated from statistical models

mobilization—The range of activities that candidates, parties, activists, and interest groups engage in to encourage people to participate

Motor Voter Act—A federal law requiring states to allow people to register to vote when they are applying for a driver's license and public assistance programs or to allow Election Day registration

narrow-casting—Targeting a message to a small audience using email, direct mail, and telephone calls

negative campaigning—Campaign messages that consist of criticism leveled by one candidate against another during a campaign

negative partisanship—Forming candidate preferences and other political views favorable toward the Republicans or Democrats based on one's hostility towards the other party

news media—Regular communicators of information designed to reach large audiences

news values—The criteria reporters and editors use to determine what is newsworthy, such as how recently an event occurred and whether it was unexpected

one person, one vote—The principle that each person's vote should have equal weight in determining representation

open primary—Election for the parties' nominees in which registrants are allowed to vote in any primary they choose (but only in one)

open seat—An election in which no incumbent is running

opinion leaders—Individuals who follow politics and help inform other members of their group about issues and candidates

pack journalism—The tendency of reporters to read and discuss each other's stories and converge on a similar narrative about the campaign

participatory inequalities—Inequalities that occur when certain groups of citizens have a greater impact on the political process than other groups

partisan gerrymandering—A method of redrawing legislative district boundaries in which one political party draws district lines in an attempt to maximize the number of seats it will win

party identification—A citizen's allegiance to one of the political parties, including both party preference and level of commitment

party-as-organization—The institutions, professionals, and activists that administer party affairs, including the official bodies that raise funds and create the rules for the party

party-in-government—The members of a party who hold public office

party-in-the-electorate—The group of citizens who identify with a political party or regularly support candidates from one party

permanent campaign—The notion that candidates never stop campaigning because of the constant need to raise money for the next election cycle

personal vote—The portion of an elected official's vote share that can be attributed to their relationship with constituents

persuadable (swing) votes—The number of voters in a given election who are not committed to supporting a particular candidate; usually estimated by the percentage point difference between the maximum and minimum vote for a major party's candidates across recent elections

persuasion—Convincing undecided voters to support a particular candidate or convincing the other party's supporters to defect

plurality rule—A way of determining who wins elections in which the candidate with the most votes wins (even if they do not get a majority of the votes)

pocketbook voting—Choosing between candidates based on how one's personal finances have fared under the incumbent

political action committees (PACs)—Private groups organized to elect political candidates

political amateurs—Candidates with no political experience

political interest—A person's ongoing interest in politics

political machines—Party organizations that mobilized lower-status citizens to win office and then used government to reward party workers and bestow services and benefits to their constituents

political party—A group of people with the shared interest of electing public officials under a common label

poll taxes—Fee requirements for voting that were typically used to keep Black people from voting in southern states; outlawed by the Voting Rights Act of 1965

positive campaigning—Campaign messages in which candidates make an affirmative case for their election based on their background, experience, record, or issue positions

primary election—Election in which voters select the candidate that will run for a party in the general election

priming—The ability of the news media and candidates themselves to influence the criteria that citizens use to make judgments about candidates by selecting which stories to cover or issues to focus on

probability sample—Some number of individuals from a certain population randomly selected and asked a set of questions; key is that every individual in the population of interest has a known probability of being selected

professionalism—A quality of legislatures that captures how much work legislators perform and the status they receive. In a more professionalized legislature, serving as a legislator is a full-time job with a substantial salary and staff support.

Progressive (or "Bull Moose") Party—Political party from 1912 to 1914, associated with Theodore Roosevelt, representing disaffected Republicans who favored greater power and democratic prerogatives for the "little man" and regulation of major industries

proportional representation—System of legislative representation in which seats are allocated based on the percentage of the vote won by each party

proximity voting—Choosing a candidate based on how close the candidate's views are to one's own views across a range of relevant issues

public funding—Campaign funds provided by the government

purposive benefits—The satisfaction one derives from having advanced an issue or ideological position or from having fulfilled a duty

quality challengers—Candidates with the experience and backing necessary to run a competitive campaign

ranked-choice voting—A system of voting in which voters rank their top candidates in order; if no one candidate is the top choice of a majority of voters, then the winner is determined by using the information in voters' rankings to identify the candidate with the most support among the majority

reapportionment—Process of determining the number of U.S. House representatives allotted to each state after the decennial census count

Reconstruction—Era immediately after the Civil War in which policies were enacted to protect the freedoms and rights of Black citizens. Reconstruction policies were particularly important in the southern states, where Union troops were stationed to enforce these policies. The Reconstruction era ended at different times for different states, but many believe that the Compromise of 1877 effectively ended Reconstruction.

redistricting—Drawing new state legislative and U.S. House district lines after the decennial census count

referenda—Measures that affect laws or public policy that allow citizens to vote on a statute already passed by state legislatures

reinforcement—The notion that news consumers interpret information as giving added strength or support to their existing views; the process of solidifying voters' support for a candidate

Republican Party—Political party from 1860 to the present, originally associated with Abraham Lincoln and representing interests opposed to slavery and favoring the continuation of the Union

retail politics—Face-to-face communication about political positions and arguments between candidates and voters

retention elections—Judicial elections in which voters decide whether a sitting judge should continue in that position; these elections do not feature a competition between the sitting judge and an opponent

retrospective voting—Choosing between candidates according to broad appraisals of whether things have improved or gotten worse under the incumbent

right to equal time—A Federal Communications Commission rule that requires most radio and television broadcasters to treat candidates equally when selling or giving away airtime

roll-call vote—At a party convention, the aggregation of state-by-state votes of delegates

same-day (or Election Day) registration—System in which eligible citizens may register to vote as late as Election Day itself

semi-closed primary—Election for a party's nominee in which party registrants and those unaffiliated with any party are allowed to vote

single-member districts—Geographic units that elect only one person to represent the entire unit

social groups—Associations of people who share a class background, ethnicity, religion, or some other affiliation; perceived social group membership may affect political attitudes

social network—The people with whom one communicates and interacts, such as family, friends, classmates, coworkers, and neighbors

sociotropic voting—Choosing between candidates based one's assessment of national economic conditions under the incumbent

soft money—Money raised outside the limits normally established by campaign finance laws

solidary benefits—Intangible rewards for political participation that come from being part of a collective effort

sorting—The phenomenon in which people's partisan preferences have become more closely aligned with their political views

sound bite—A short segment of sound or video used in a news report as an excerpt of an event or interview

strategic voting—In an election with more than two candidates, voting for a candidate other than one's first choice in order to prevent an undesirable outcome

super PACs—PACs that can collect unlimited amounts of donations as a consequence of a 2010 Supreme Court decision, *Citizens United v. FEC*; super PACs are required to disclose their donors

survey research—A research method involving the use of questionnaires and/or statistical surveys to gather data about people and their thoughts and behaviors

term limits—Legal restrictions on the maximum time a person can hold a specific office

Tillman Act—1907 law banning corporate contributions to political campaigns

treatment group—In an experiment, a group that receives a message or advertisement or some other "treatment"

viability—A candidate's ability to win a nomination

vote targets—Estimates of how many votes a candidate will need to win the election; based on calculations of how many people will vote in a particular election, what percentage of the vote will be needed to win, how many votes can be counted on, and how many votes are persuadable

vote-by-mail—When jurisdictions conduct elections using ballots that are automatically mailed to voters

voter identification (voter ID) calls—Calls, usually via telephone, to every person on the voter list to ask about the candidates and issues in the upcoming election

voter identification laws—Laws that require registered voters to show some sort of government-issued identification before they are allowed to vote

Voting Rights Act of 1965 (VRA)—Congressional legislation designed to end discriminatory practices disenfranchising Black people, especially in the South

wedge issues—Political issues intended to persuade voters to abandon the party they traditionally support and support the opposite party

Whig Party—Political party from 1832 to 1852 that rose in response to the Democratic Party in the 1830s, representing voters concerned by Andrew Jackson's expansive view of the presidency and his attacks on commercial interests

White primary—Primary elections held in the South that allowed only White voters to participate

wholesale politics—Mass communication about political positions and arguments from candidates directed to voters

wire service—A news agency that collects and distributes news stories to many outlets

Endnotes

Chapter 1

1. Frances E. Lee, *Insecure Majorities: Congress and the Perpetual Campaign* (Chicago: University of Chicago Press, 2016).

2. Jennifer L. Lawless and Richard L. Fox, "Why Are Women Still Not Running for Public Office?" *Brookings Institution Issues in Governance Studies*, no. 16 (May 2008): 1–20, www .brookings.edu/wp-content/uploads/2016/06/05_women_lawless_fox.pdf (accessed 7/6/21).

3. John R. Petrocik, "Issue Ownership in Presidential Elections, with a 1980 Case Study," *American Journal of Political Science* 40, no. 3 (August 1996): 825–50, https://doi.org/10 .2307/2111797.

4. Erika Franklin Fowler, Michael M. Franz, and Travis N. Ridout, *Political Advertising in the United States* (Boulder, CO: Westview Press, 2016). 54–55.

5. Danny Hayes, "The Dynamics of Agenda Convergence and the Paradox of Competitiveness in Presidential Campaigns," *Political Research Quarterly* 63, no. 3 (September 2010): 594–611, https://doi.org/10.1177/1065912909331426.

6. Jesse Yoder, Cassandra Handan-Nader, Andrew Myers, Tobias Nowacki, Daniel M. Thompson, Jennifer A. Wu, Chenoa Yorgason, and Andrew B. Hall, "How Did Absentee Voting Affect the 2020 U.S. Election?" SIEPR Working Paper No. 21-011, Stanford University, March 2021, https://siepr.stanford.edu/sites/default/files/publications/21-011 .pdf (accessed 7/7/21).

7. "2020 primary election competitiveness in state and federal government," Ballotpedia, March 3, 2021, https://ballotpedia.org/2020_primary_election_competitiveness_in_state _and_federal_government (accessed 7/6/21).

8. Robert A. Dahl, *A Preface to Democratic Theory* (Chicago: University of Chicago Press, 1956).

9. Chris Cillizza, "Three Quarters of Republicans Believe a Lie about the 2020 Election," CNN, February 4, 2021, www.cnn.com/2021/02/04/politics/2020-election-donald-trump -voter-fraud/index.html (accessed 4/26/21).

10. Makini Brice and Tim Reid, "Texas may not limit ballot drop boxes for U.S. election: appeals court," Reuters, October 23, 2020, www.reuters.com/article/us-usa-election-texas /texas-may-not-limit-ballot-drop-boxes-for-u-s-election-appeals-court-idUSKBN2782UH (accessed 8/10/21).

11. Katherine Fung, "Texas Governor Announces Counties Can Only Have One Ballot Drop-Off Location, Forcing Harris County, Other Large Dem Counties to Remove Drop Boxes," *Newsweek*, October 1, 2020, www.newsweek.com/texas-governor-announces -counties-can-only-have-one-ballot-drop-off-location-forcing-harris-1535747 (accessed 4/26/21).

12. Barry C. Burden, David T. Canon, Kenneth R. Mayer, and Donald P. Moynihan, "Election Laws, Mobilization, and Turnout: The Unanticipated Consequences of Election Reform," *American Journal of Political Science* 58, no. 1 (January 2014): 95–109, https://doi .org/10.1111/ajps.12063.

13. "Debunking the Voter Fraud Myth," Brennan Center for Justice, January 31, 2017, www.brennancenter.org/sites/default/files/analysis/Briefing_Memo_Debunking_Voter _Fraud_Myth.pdf; Lorraine Minnite, *Election Day Registration: A Study of Voter Fraud Allegations and Findings on Voter Roll Security* (New York: Dēmos, 2007), www .brennancenter.org/sites/default/files/analysis/edr_fraud.pdf (accessed 7/6/21).

14. Dahl, *A Preface to Democratic Theory.*

15. Ronald Dworkin, *Sovereign Virtue: The Theory and Practice of Equality* (Cambridge, MA: Harvard University Press, 2002).

16. Dennis F. Thompson, "Electoral Simultaneity: Expressing Equal Respect," *Journal of Social Issues* 64, no. 3 (September 2008): 487–501, https://doi.org/10.1111/j.1540-4560 .2008.00574.x.

17. Igor Bobic, "Some Californians Regret Voting Early," HuffPost, March 2, 2020, www .huffpost.com/entry/super-tuesday-california_n_5e5d0b8fc5b6beedb4eea987 (accessed 4/26/21).

18. Tara Subramaniam and Holmes Lybrand, "10 False or Misleading Claims Biden and Trump Make about Each Other," CNN, September 29, 2020, www.cnn.com/2020/09/29 /politics/biden-trump-attacks-debate-fact-check/index.html (accessed 4/26/21).

19. Glenn Thrush and Matt Stevens, "5 Policy Issues Where Trump and Biden Diverged at Final Debate," *New York Times*, January 7, 2021, www.nytimes.com/2020/10/23/us/politics /trump-biden-health-care-immigration.html (accessed 4/26/21).

20. Thomas E. Patterson, "A Tale of Two Elections: CBS and Fox News' Portrayal of the 2020 Presidential Campaign," Shorenstein Center on Media, Politics, and Public Policy, Harvard Kennedy School, December 17, 2020, https://shorensteincenter.org/patterson-2020 -election-coverage (accessed 3/31/21).

21. Shanto Iyengar, Helmut Norpoth, and Kyu S. Hahn, "Consumer Demand for Election News: The Horserace Sells," *Journal of Politics* 66, no. 1 (February 2004): 157–75, https:// doi.org/10.1046/j.1468-2508.2004.00146.x.

22. 424 U.S. 1 (1976).

23. Bruce I. Buchanan, "Mediated Electoral Democracy: Campaigns, Incentives, and Reform," in *Mediated Politics: Communication in the Future of Democracy*, eds. W. Lance Bennett and Robert M. Entman (New York: Cambridge University Press, 2001), 366.

Chapter 2

1. This anecdote comes from Ryan Lizza, "Making It: How Chicago Shaped Obama," *New Yorker*, July 21, 2008, www.newyorker.com/magazine/2008/07/21/making-it (accessed 7/6/21).

2. *Smith v. Allwright*, 321 U.S. 649 (1944).

3. Desmond Ang, "Do 40-Year-Old Facts Still Matter? Long-Run Effects of Federal Oversight Under the Voting Rights Act," *American Economic Journal: Applied Economics* 11, no. 3 (July 2019): 1–53, https://doi.org/10.1257/app.20170572.

4. "Felon Voting Rights," National Conference of State Legislatures, June 28, 2021, www .ncsl.org/research/elections-and-campaigns/felon-voting-rights.aspx (accessed 7/6/21).

5. Marc Meredith and Michael Morse, "Discretionary Disenfranchisement: The Case of Legal Financial Obligations," *Journal of Legal Studies* 46, no. 2 (June 2017): 309–38.

6. *California Democratic Party v. Jones*, 530 U.S. 567 (2000).

7. "Automatic Voter Registration," National Conference of State Legislatures, February 8, 2021, www.ncsl.org/research/elections-and-campaigns/automatic-voter-registration.aspx (accessed 5/29/21).

8. "Same Day Voter Registration," National Conference of State Legislatures, May 7, 2021, www.ncsl.org/research/elections-and-campaigns/same-day-registration.aspx (accessed 5/28/21). These states do not include Montana or North Carolina, which allow same-day registration only during the early voting period, not on Election Day itself.

9. "Voter Identification Requirements," National Conference of State Legislatures, July 6, 2021, www.ncsl.org/research/elections-and-campaigns/voter-id.aspx (accessed 7/6/21).

10. Eric McGhee and Mindy Romero, "Registration Effects of Automatic Voter Registration in the United States," 2019, https://cpb-us-w2.wpmucdn.com/web.sas.upenn.edu/dist/7/538/files/2019/07/avr_multistate_esra.pdf (accessed 5/29/21); Sean McElwee, Brian Schaffner, and Jesse Rhodes, *Automatic Voter Registration in Oregon* (New York: Dēmos, 2017), www.demos.org/sites/default/files/publications/AVR%20in%20Oregon%20FINAL.pdf (accessed 7/7/21).

11. This estimate is from Jan E. Leighley and Jonathan Nagler, *Who Votes Now? Demographics, Issues, Inequality, and Turnout in the United States* (Princeton, NJ: Princeton University Press, 2014). See also Michael J. Hanmer, *Discount Voting: Voter Registration Reforms and Their Effects* (Cambridge: Cambridge University Press. 2009). For a detailed study of Wisconsin's rollout of same-day registration in the 1970s, see Jacob R. Neiheisel and Barry C. Burden, "The Impact of Election Day Registration on Voter Turnout and Election Outcomes," *American Politics Research* 40, no. 4 (July 2012): 636–64, https://doi.org/10.1177/1532673X11432470.

12. Justin Grimmer and Jesse Yoder, "The Durable Differential Deterrent Effects of Strict Photo Identification Laws," *Political Science Research and Methods* (2021), 1–17, https://doi.org/10.1017/psrm.2020.57

13. Phoebe Henninger, Marc Meredith, and Michael Morse, "Who Votes Without Identification? Using Individual-Level Administrative Data to Measure the Burden of Strict Voter Identification Laws," *Journal of Empirical Legal Studies* 18, no. 2 (June 2021): 256–86, https://doi.org/10.1111/jels.12283.

14. Robert S. Erikson and Lorraine C. Minnite, "Modeling Problems in the Voter Identification–Voter Turnout Debate," *Election Law Journal* 8, no. 2 (2009): 85–101, https://doi.org/10.1089/elj.2008.0017; Bernard L. Fraga, *The Turnout Gap: Race, Ethnicity, and Political Inequality in a Diversifying America* (Cambridge: Cambridge University Press, 2018); Enrico Cantoni and Vincent Pons, "Strict ID Laws Don't Stop Voters: Evidence from a U.S. Nationwide Panel, 2008–2018," *Quarterly Journal of Economics* (2021): qjab019, https://doi.org/10.1093/qje/qjab019.

15. Nicholas A. Valentino and Fabian G. Neuner, "Why the Sky Didn't Fall: Mobilizing Anger in Reaction to Voter ID Laws," *Political Psychology* 38, no. 2 (April 2017): 331–50. https://doi.org/10.1111/pops.12332.

16. Jacob R. Neiheisel and Rich Horner, "Voter Identification Requirements and Aggregate Turnout in the U.S.: How Campaigns Offset the Costs of Turning Out When Voting Is Made More Difficult," *Election Law Journal* 18, no. 3 (2019): 227–42; Cantoni and Pons, "Strict ID Laws."

17. Daniel R. Biggers, "Can the Backlash Against Voter ID Laws Activate Minority Voters? Experimental Evidence Examining Voter Mobilization Through Psychological Reactance," *Political Behavior* (2019), https://doi.org/10.1007/s11109-019-09587-0.

18. Daniel J. Hopkins, Marc Meredith, Michael Morse, Sarah Smith, and Jesse Yoder, "Voting But for the Law: Evidence from Virginia on Photo Identification Requirements," *Journal of Empirical Legal Studies* 14, no. 1 (March 2017): 79–128, https://doi.org/10.1111/jels.12142.

19. "2012 Obama Campaign Legacy Report," https://time.com/wp-content/uploads/2015/02/legacy-report.pdf (accessed 5/29/21).

20. McGhee and Romero, "Registration Effects"; McElwee, Schaffner, and Rhodes, "AVR in Oregon."

21. R. Michael Alvarez, Stephen Ansolabehere, and Catherine H. Wilson, "Election Day Registration in the United States: How One-Step Voting Can Change the Composition of the American Electorate," Caltech/MIT Voting Technology Project Working Paper No. 5, November 30, 2008, http://vote.caltech.edu/working-papers/5 (accessed 9/20/17); Stephen Knack and James White, "Election-Day Registration and Turnout Inequality," *Political Behavior* 22, no. 1 (March 2000): 29–44; Leighley and Nagler, *Who Votes Now?*

22. Devin McCarthy, "Partisanship vs. Principle: Understanding Public Opinion on Same-Day Registration," *Public Opinion Quarterly* 83, no. 3 (Fall 2019): 568–83, https://doi.org/10.1093/poq/nfz027; Daniel Biggers, "Does Partisan Self-Interest Dictate Support for Election Reform? Experimental Evidence on the Willingness of Citizens to Alter the Costs of Voting for Electoral Gain," *Political Behavior* 41 (2019): 1025–46, https://doi.org/10.1007/s11109-018-9481-5.

23. Neiheisel and Burden, "The Impact of Election Day Registration."

24. Marc Meredith and Michael Morse, "Why Letting Ex-Felons Vote Probably Won't Swing Florida," *Vox*, November 2, 2018, www.vox.com/the-big-idea/2018/11/2/18049510/felon-voting-rights-amendment-4-florida (accessed 1/2/19).

25. Jack Citrin, Eric Schickler, and John Sides, "What If Everyone Voted? Simulating the Impact of Increased Turnout in Senate Elections," *American Journal of Political Science* 47, no. 1 (January 2003): 75–90, https://doi.org/10.2307/3186094.

26. Adam J. Berinsky, "The Perverse Consequences of Electoral Reform in the United States," *American Politics Research* 33, no. 4 (July 2005): 471–91, https://doi.org/10.1177/1532673X04269419.

27. See, for example, Matt A. Barreto, Stephen A. Nuño, and Gabriel R. Sanchez, "The Disproportionate Impact of Voter-ID Requirements on the Electorate—New Evidence from Indiana," *PS: Political Science and Politics* 42, no. 1 (January 2009): 111–16, https://doi.org/10.1017/S1049096509090283.

28. Jesse H. Rhodes, *Ballot Blocked: The Political Erosion of the Voting Rights Act* (Palo Alto, CA: Stanford University Press, 2017).

29. 570 U.S. 529 (2013).

30. Christopher S. Elmendorf and Douglas M. Spencer, "Administering Section 2 of the Voting Rights Act After *Shelby County*," *Columbia Law Review* 115, no. 8 (2015): 2143–218.

31. Catalina Feder and Michael G. Miller, "Voter Purges After *Shelby*," *American Politics Research* 48, no. 6 (November 2020): 687–92, https://doi.org/10.1177/1532673X20916426.

32. Gregory A. Huber, Marc Meredith, Michael Morse, and Katie Steele, "The Racial Burden of Voter List Maintenance Errors: Evidence from Wisconsin's Supplemental Movers Poll Books," *Science Advances* 7, no. 8 (February 2021): eabe4498, https://doi.org/10.1126/sciadv.abe4498.

33. Kyle Raze, "Voting Rights and the Resilience of Black Turnout," Working Paper, University of Oregon, February 7, 2021, https://kyleraze.com/files/shelby_county_voting.pdf (accessed 6/1/21).

34. An extensive list of studies that find little evidence of voter fraud is maintained by the Brennan Center for Justice at New York University School of Law: www.brennancenter.org/our-work/research-reports/resources-voter-fraud-claims (accessed 5/30/21). For example, see Sharad Goel, Marc Meredith, Michael Morse, David Rothschild, and Houshmand Shirani-Mehr, "One Person, One Vote: Estimating the Prevalence of Double Voting in U.S. Presidential Elections," *American Political Science Review* 114, no. 2 (2020): 456–69, https://doi.org/10.1017/S000305541900087X.

35. "State Laws Governing Early Voting," National Conference of State Legislatures, June 11, 2021, www.ncsl.org/research/elections-and-campaigns/early-voting-in-state-elections.aspx (accessed 7/6/21).

36. Leighley and Nagler, *Who Votes Now?*

37. Leighley and Nagler, *Who Votes Now?*; Paul Gronke, Eva Galanes-Rosenbaum, Peter A. Miller, and Daniel Toffey, "Convenience Voting," *Annual Review of Political Science* 11 (June 2008): 437–55; Barry C. Burden, David T. Canon, Kenneth R. Mayer, and Donald P. Moynihan, "Election Laws, Mobilization, and Turnout: The Unanticipated Consequences of Election Reform," *American Journal of Political Science* 58, no. 1 (January 2014): 95–109, https://doi.org/10.1111/ajps.12063.

38. Steven L. Taylor, Matthew S. Shugart, Arend Lijphart, and Bernard Grofman, *A Different Democracy: American Government in a Thirty-One-Country Perspective* (New Haven: Yale University Press, 2014), 148.

39. Paul Gronke and Peter Miller, "Voting by Mail and Turnout in Oregon: Revisiting Southwell and Burchett," *American Politics Research* 40, no. 6 (November 2012): 976–97, https://doi.org/10.1177/1532673X12457809; Alan S. Gerber, Gregory A. Huber, and Seth J. Hill, "Identifying the Effect of All-Mail Elections on Turnout: Staggered Reform in the Evergreen State," *Political Science Research and Methods* 1, no. 1 (2013): 91–116, https://doi.org/10.1017/psrm.2013.5; Gronke, Galanes-Rosenbaum, Miller, and Toffey, "Convenience Voting."

40. Daniel M. Thompson, Jennifer A. Wu, Jesse Yoder, and Andrew B. Hall, "Universal Vote-by-Mail Has No Impact on Partisan Turnout or Vote Share," *Proceedings of the National Academy of Sciences* 117, no. 25 (2020): 14052–56, https://doi.org/10.1073/pnas.2007249117.

41. Gronke, Galanes-Rosenbaum, Miller, and Toffey, "Convenience Voting," 445.

42. Thompson, Wu, Yoder, and Hall, "Universal Vote-by-Mail"; Gronke, Galanes-Rosenbaum, Miller, and Toffey, "Convenience Voting."

43. U.S. Census Bureau, "Voting and Registration in the Election of November 2020," April 2021, Table 14, www.census.gov/data/tables/time-series/demo/voting-and-registration/p20-585.html (accessed 5/31/21). See also Jay Lee, "Huge 2020 Spikes in Alternative Voting Methods," Early Voting Information Center, April 29, 2021, https://evic.reed.edu/commentary/alternative-voting-2020 (accessed 5/31/21).

44. See "Changes to absentee/mail-in voting procedures in response to the coronavirus (COVID-19) pandemic, 2020," Ballotpedia, https://ballotpedia.org/Changes_to_absentee/mail-in_voting_procedures_in_response_to_the_coronavirus_(COVID-19)_pandemic,_2020 (accessed 5/31/21).

45. Joshua David Clinton, John S. Lapinski, Sarah Lentz, and Stephen Pettigrew, "Trumped by Trump? Public Support for Vote by Mail Voting in Response to the COVID-19 Pandemic," Social Science Research Network, June 16, 2020, https://doi.org/10.2139/ssrn.3630334.

46. Karlyn Bowman and Samantha Goldstein, "Voice on the Vote," Democracy Fund Voter Study Group, May 2021, www.voterstudygroup.org/publication/voices-on-the-vote (accessed 6/1/21).

47. Hope Yen, Jeff Amy, and Michael Balsamo, "AP Fact Check: Trump's Made-up Claims of Fake Georgia Votes," Associated Press, January 3, 2021, https://apnews.com/article/ap-fact-check-donald-trump-georgia-elections-atlanta-c23d10e5299e14daee6109885f7dafa9 (accessed 6/1/21).

48. Jennifer Wu, Chenoa Yorgason, Hanna Folsz, Sandy Handan-Nader, Andrew Myers, Toby Nowacki, Daniel M. Thompson, Jesse Yoder, and Andrew B. Hall, "Are Dead People Voting by Mail? Evidence from Washington State Administrative Records," Working Paper, Stanford University Democracy and Polarization Lab, October 27, 2020, https://stanforddpl.org/papers/wu_et_al_2020_dead_voting/ (accessed 6/1/21).

49. Andrew Prokop, "Pennsylvania's Naked Ballot Problem, Explained," *Vox*, September 28, 2020, www.vox.com/21452393/naked-ballots-pennsylvania-secrecy-envelope (accessed 6/1/21).

50. Michaela Winberg, "Good Job, Philly: Only 1% of City Mail Ballots Were 'Naked,'" *BillyPenn*, November 11, 2020, https://billypenn.com/2020/11/11/philly-naked-ballots -pennsylvania-mail-votes-november-election (accessed 6/1/21); Teresa Boeckel, "Naked Ballots, Other Errors Disqualified Hundreds of Votes in York, Lebanon, and Franklin Cos.," *York Daily Record*, November 17, 2020, www.ydr.com/story/news/politics/2020/11/17/naked -ballots-and-other-errors-disqualified-votes-central-pa/6279641002 (accessed 6/1/21).

51. Miles Parks, "States Expand Internet Voting Experiments Amid Pandemic, Raising Security Fears," NPR, April 28, 2020, www.npr.org/2020/04/28/844581667/states-expand -internet-voting-experiments-amid-pandemic-raising-security-fears (accessed 7/7/21); "Securing the Vote," National Academies of Sciences, Engineering and Medicine, 2018, www.nap.edu/resource/25120/interactive (accessed 6/1/21).

52. Stephen Pettigrew, "The Downstream Consequences of Long Waits: How Lines at the Precinct Depress Future Turnout," *Electoral Studies* 71 (June 2021): 102188, https://doi.org /10.1016/j.electstud.2020.102188.

53. Stephen Pettigrew, "The Racial Gap in Wait Times: Why Minority Precincts Are Underserved by Local Election Officials," *Political Science Quarterly* 132, no. 3 (Fall 2017): 527–47, https://doi.org/10.1002/polq.12657.

54. Bowman and Goldstein, "Voice on the Vote."

55. Jesse Yoder, Sandy Handan-Nader, Andrew Myers, Toby Nowacki, Daniel M. Thompson, Jennifer Wu, Chenoa Yorgason, and Andrew B. Hall, "How Did Absentee Voting Affect the 2020 U.S. Election?" Working Paper, Stanford University Democracy and Polarization Lab, March 11, 2021, https://stanforddpl.org/papers/yoder_et_al_2020_turnout (accessed 6/1/21).

56. August Heckscher, *Woodrow Wilson: A Biography* (New York: Scribner, 1991).

57. See www.sos.state.tx.us/elections/candidates/guide/newparty2018.shtml (accessed 8/3/17).

58. *U.S. Term Limits, Inc. v. Thornton*, 514 U.S. 779 (1995).

59. For more information, see "States with Gubernatorial Term Limits," Ballotpedia, http://ballotpedia.org/States_with_gubernatorial_term_limits (accessed 6/1/21).

60. "The Term Limited States," National Conference of State Legislatures, November 12, 2020, www.ncsl.org/research/about-state-legislatures/chart-of-term-limits-states.aspx (accessed 6/1/21).

61. Thad Kousser, *Term Limits and the Dismantling of State Legislative Professionalism* (New York: Cambridge University Press, 2005).

62. "Senate Legislative Process," U.S. Senate, www.senate.gov/legislative/common/briefing /Senate_legislative_process.htm (accessed 9/20/17).

63. Cyra Master, "*60 Minutes*: Fundraising Demands Turning Lawmakers into Telemarketers," *The Hill*, April 24, 2016, https://thehill.com/blogs/blog-briefing-room/news/277462 -60-minutes-fundraising-demands-turning-lawmakers-into (accessed 7/6/21).

64. Randolph T. Stevenson and Lynn Vavreck, "Does Campaign Length Matter? Testing for Cross-National Effects," *British Journal of Political Science* 30, no. 2 (April 2000): 217–35, https://doi.org/10.1017/S0007123400000107.

65. John Sides, Lynn Vavreck, and Chris Warshaw, "The Effect of Television Advertising in United States Elections," *American Political Science Review*, forthcoming.

66. For additional detail on how this is done, see Brian J. Gaines and Jeffery A. Jenkins, "Apportionment Matters: Fair Representation in the U.S. House and Electoral College,"

Perspectives on Politics 7, no. 4 (December 2009): 849–57, https://doi.org/10.1017 /S1537592709991848.

67. Stephen Ansolabehere and James M. Snyder, Jr., *The End of Inequality: One Person, One Vote and the Transformation of American Politics* (New York: W. W. Norton, 2008).

68. 369 U.S. 186 (1962).

69. 372 U.S. 368 (1963).

70. *Wesberry v. Sanders*, 376 U.S. 1 (1964); *Reynolds v. Sims*, 377 U.S. 533 (1964).

71. See *Cox v. Larios*, 542 U.S. 947 (2004).

72. *Evenwel v. Abbott*, 136 S. Ct. 1120 (2016).

73. Drew DeSilver, "Supreme Court Could Reshape Voting Districts, with Big Impact on Hispanics," Pew Research Center, December 10, 2015, www.pewresearch.org/fact-tank /2015/12/10/supreme-court-could-reshape-voting-districts-with-big-impact-on-hispanics (accessed 9/20/17).

74. Ansolabehere and Snyder, *The End of Inequality*, 187–88.

75. *Gomillion v. Lightfoot*, 364 U.S. 339 (1960).

76. 478 U.S. 30 (1986).

77. See T. Alexander Aleinikoff and Samuel Issacharoff, "Race and Redistricting: Drawing Constitutional Lines after *Shaw v. Reno*," *Michigan Law Review* 92, no. 3 (1993): 588–651.

78. Alexa Ura and Jim Malewitz, "Federal Court Invalidates Part of Texas Congressional Map," *Texas Tribune*, August 15, 2017, www.texastribune.org/2017/08/15/federal-court -invalidates-part-texas-congressional-map (accessed 8/24/17).

79. Michael Peress and Yangzi Zhao, "How Many Seats in Congress Is Control of Redistrict- ing Worth?" *Legislative Studies Quarterly* 45, no. 3 (July 2020): 433–68, https://doi.org/10 .1111/lsq.12268.

80. Jowei Chen and David Cottrell, "Evaluating Partisan Gains from Congressional Gerrymandering: Using Computer Simulations to Estimate the Effect of Gerrymandering in the U.S. House," *Electoral Studies* 44 (December 2016): 329–40, https://doi.org/10.1016/j .electstud.2016.06.014.

81. This GOP advantage is noted in Peress and Zhao, "How Many Seats in Congress"; Chen and Cottrell, "Evaluating Partisan Gains"; Nicholas Stephanopoulos and Eric McGhee, "Partisan Gerrymandering and the Efficiency Gap," *University of Chicago Law Review* 82 (2015): 831–900; and Anthony J. McGann, Charles Anthony Smith, Michael Latner, and Alex Keena, *Gerrymandering in America: The House of Representatives, the Supreme Court, and the Future of Popular Sovereignty* (New York: Cambridge University Press, 2016).

82. 509 U.S. 630 (1993).

83. Those decisions were *Shaw v. Hunt*, 517 U.S. 899 (1996), *Hunt v. Cromartie*, 526 U.S. 541 (1999), and *Easley v. Cromartie*, 532 U.S. 234 (2001); the latter is sometimes also called *Hunt v. Cromartie* (2001).

84. The North Carolina case is *Cooper v. Harris*, 581 U.S. ___ (2017). The Alabama case is *Alabama Black Legislative Caucus v. Alabama*, 575 U.S. ___ (2015). The Virginia case is *Bethune-Hill v. Virginia State Board of Elections*, 580 U.S. ___ (2017).

85. *Gaffney v. Cummings*, 412 U.S. 735 (1973).

86. See Nathaniel Persily, "The Place of Competition in American Election Law," in *The Marketplace of Democracy: Electoral Competition and American Politics*, eds. Michael P. McDonald and John Samples (Washington, DC: Brookings Institution Press, 2006), 171–95.

87. *Davis v. Bandemer*, 478 U.S. 109 (1986); *Vieth v. Jubelirer*, 541 U.S. 267 (2004); Jowei Chen, "The Impact of Political Geography on Wisconsin Redistricting: An Analysis of

Wisconsin's Act 43 Assembly Districting Plan," *Election Law Journal* 16, no. 4 (2017): 1–10, https://doi.org/10.1089/elj.2017.0455; *Gill v. Whitford*, 585 U.S. ___ (2018).

88. *Rucho v. Common Cause*, 588 U.S. ___ (2019).

89. Thomas L. Brunell, "Rethinking Redistricting: How Drawing Uncompetitive Districts Eliminates Gerrymanders, Enhances Representation, and Improves Attitudes toward Congress," *PS: Political Science and Politics* 39, no. 1 (January 2006): 77–85, https://doi.org/10.1017/S1049096506060173.

90. Nicholas O. Stephanopoulos and Christopher Warshaw, "The Impact of Partisan Gerrymandering on Political Parties," *Legislative Studies Quarterly* 45, no. 4 (November 2020): 609–43, https://doi.org/10.1111/lsq.12276.

91. Keena Lipsitz, *Competitive Elections and the American Voter* (Philadelphia: University of Pennsylvania Press, 2011).

92. "Redistricting Commissions: State Legislative Plans," National Conference of State Legislatures, June 21, 2021, www.ncsl.org/research/redistricting/2009-redistricting-commissions-table.aspx (accessed 7/6/21).

93. *Arizona State Legislature v. Arizona Independent Redistricting Commission*, 576 U.S. 787 (2015).

94. Jamie L. Carson, Michael H. Crespin, and Ryan D. Williamson, "Reevaluating the Effects of Redistricting on Electoral Competition, 1972–2012," *State Politics and Policy Quarterly* 14, no. 2 (2014): 165–77, https://doi.org/10.1177/1532440013520245; Barry Edwards, Michael Crespin, Ryan D. Williamson, and Maxwell Palmer, "Institutional Control of Redistricting and the Geography of Representation," *Journal of Politics* 79, no. 2 (April 2017): 722–26, https://doi.org/10.1086/690633.

95. Nolan McCarty, Keith T. Poole, and Howard Rosenthal, "Does Gerrymandering Cause Polarization?" *American Journal of Political Science* 53, no. 3 (July 2009): 666–80, https://doi.org/10.1111/j.1540-5907.2009.00393.x.

96. James G. Gimpel and Laurel Harbridge-Yong, "Conflicting Goals of Redistricting: Do Districts That Maximize Competition Reckon with Communities of Interest?" *Election Law Journal* 19, no. 4 (2020): 451–71, https://doi.org/10.1089/elj.2019.0576.

97. Jowei Chen and Jonathan Rodden, "Unintentional Gerrymandering: Political Geography and Electoral Bias in Legislatures," *Legislative Studies Quarterly* 8 (2013): 239–60, https://doi.org/10.1561/100.00012033.

98. André Blais, "Turnout in Elections," in *The Oxford Handbook of Political Behavior*, eds. Russell J. Dalton and Hans-Dieter Klingemann (Oxford: Oxford University Press, 2007), 621–35.

99. Todd Donovan, Caroline Tolbert, and Kellen Gracey, "Self-Reported Understanding of Ranked-Choice Voting," *Social Science Quarterly* 100, no. 5 (August 2019): 1768–76, https://doi.org/10.1111/ssqu.12651.

100. Craig M. Burnett and Vladimir Kogan, "Ballot (and Voter) 'Exhaustion' Under Instant Runoff Voting: An Examination of Four Ranked-Choice Elections," *Electoral Studies* 37 (March 2015): 41–49, https://doi.org/10.1016/j.electstud.2014.11.006.

Chapter 3

1. Reid Wilson, "Why 2016 Will Be the Most Negative Campaign in History," *Morning Consult*, May 23, 2016, https://morningconsult.com/2016/05/23/2016-will-negative-campaign-history (accessed 6/5/17). Reprinted with permission.

2. Alan Rappaport, "Donald Trump's Latest Jab at Hillary Clinton: 'No Stamina,'" *New York Times*, August 16, 2016, www.nytimes.com/2016/08/17/us/politics/donald-trump-hillary-clinton-stamina.html (accessed 9/26/17).

3. Jeremy Diamond, "Trump Escalates Attacks on Clinton's Character," CNN, August 5, 2016, www.cnn.com/2016/08/05/politics/donald-trump-hillary-clinton-unhinged-lock-her-up/index.html (accessed 9/26/17).

4. Amy Chozick, "Hillary Clinton Calls Many Trump Backers 'Deplorables,' and G.O.P. Pounces," *New York Times*, September 10, 2016, www.nytimes.com/2016/09/11/us/politics/hillary-clinton-basket-of-deplorables.html (accessed 9/26/17).

5. Philip Elliott, "Hillary Clinton Tears into Donald Trump on Foreign Policy, Temperament," *Time*, June 2, 2016, http://time.com/4355791/hillary-clinton-donald-trump-temperament (accessed 9/26/17).

6. "Political Ads in 2020: Fast and Furious," Wesleyan Media Project, March 23, 2021, https://mediaproject.wesleyan.edu/2020-summary-032321 (accessed 6/7/21).

7. These examples come from Paul F. Boller, Jr., *Presidential Campaigns* (New York: Oxford University Press, 1984).

8. Boller, *Presidential Campaigns*.

9. Edward J. Larson, *A Magnificent Catastrophe: The Tumultuous Election of 1800, America's First Presidential Campaign* (New York: Free Press, 2007), 93.

10. Doris Kearns Goodwin, *Team of Rivals: The Political Genius of Abraham Lincoln* (New York: Simon & Schuster, 2006); Stephen Oates, *With Malice toward None: A Life of Abraham Lincoln* (New York: Harper Perennial, 2011).

11. Boller, *Presidential Campaigns*, 134.

12. Adam Sanchez, "The Other '68: Black Power During Reconstruction," The Zinn Education Project, August 14, 2018, www.zinnedproject.org/if-we-knew-our-history/black-power-during-reconstruction (accessed 7/6/21).

13. Rebekah Barker and Billy Corriher, "Honoring Reconstruction's Legacy: The Freedom to Vote," *Facing South*, September 13, 2018, www.facingsouth.org/2018/09/honoring-reconstructions-legacy-freedom-vote (accessed 7/6/21).

14. Luke Keele, William Cubbison, and Ismail White, "Suppressing Black Votes: A Historical Case of Voting Restrictions in Louisiana," *American Political Science Review* 115, no. 2 (May 2021): 694–700, https://doi.org/10.1017/S0003055421000034.

15. Boller, *Presidential Campaigns*, 173.

16. The amount of money raised and spent by the McKinley campaign is a matter of some controversy, with estimates ranging from $3.35 million to $16.5 million. The former figure is cited most often and is used in the most comprehensive account of campaign spending in the U.S. (Herbert Alexander, *Financing Elections: Money, Politics, and Political Reform* [Washington, DC: CQ Press, 1976]). It is, however, most likely an underestimation of McKinley's actual spending. For an excellent account of the controversy, see D. Aaron Chandler, "A Short Note on the Expenditures of the McKinley Campaign of 1896," *Presidential Studies Quarterly* 28, no. 1 (Winter 1998): 88–91. Surrogate figures come from H. Wayne Morgan, *From Hayes to McKinley: National Party Politics, 1877–1896* (Syracuse, NY: Syracuse University Press, 1969).

17. Vanessa M. Perez, "America's First Voter Identification Laws: The Effects of Personal Registration and Declining Political Party Competition on Presidential Election Turnout, 1880–1916," *Electoral Studies* 69 (February 2021): 102263, https://doi.org/10.1016/j.electstud.2020.102263.

18. Christina Wolbrecht and J. Kevin Corder, *A Century of Votes for Women: American Elections Since Suffrage* (New York: Cambridge University Press, 2020), 80.

19. Wolbrecht and Corder, *A Century of Votes*, 66.

20. According to Nielsen, which monitors broadcast and cable television consumption and thereby helps establish advertising rates, there are 212 media markets in the United States.

They vary in geographic size and population, with New York City being the largest and Glendive, Montana, being the smallest.

21. These data are from American National Election Studies, www.electionstudies.org /nesguide/toptable/tab2a_2.htm (accessed 7/15/21).

22. For data on how these developments played out in the 2020 presidential election, see William H. Frey, "Exit Polls Show Both Familiar and New Voting Blocs Sealed Biden's Win," Brookings, November 12, 2020, www.brookings.edu/research/2020-exit-polls-show-a -scrambling-of-democrats-and-republicans-traditional-bases (accessed 6/7/21).

23. Eitan Hersh, *Hacking the Electorate: How Campaigns Perceive Voters* (New York: Cambridge University Press, 2015); Sasha Issenberg, *The Victory Lab: The Secret Science of Winning Campaigns* (New York: Crown Publishing, 2013); Jon Gertner, "The Very, Very Personal Is the Political," *New York Times Magazine*, February 15, 2004, www.nytimes.com /2004/02/15/magazine/15VOTERS.html (accessed 9/26/17).

24. Hersh, *Hacking the Electorate.* See also Eitan D. Hersh and Brian F. Schaffner, "Targeted Campaign Appeals and the Value of Ambiguity," *The Journal of Politics* 75, no. 2 (April 2013): 520–34, https://doi.org/10.1017/S0022381613000182.

25. Issenberg, *The Victory Lab.*

26. Jonathan M. Ladd, *Why Americans Hate the Media and How It Matters* (Princeton, NJ: Princeton University Press, 2011).

27. Mark Jurkowitz, Amy Mitchell, Elisa Shearer, and Mason Walker, "U.S. Media Polariza-tion and the 2020 Election: A Nation Divided," Pew Research Center, January 24, 2020, www.journalism.org/2020/01/24/u-s-media-polarization-and-the-2020-election-a-nation -divided (accessed 6/6/20).

28. Shanto Iyengar and Kyu S. Hahn, "Red Media, Blue Media: Evidence of Ideological Selectivity in Media Use," *Journal of Communication* 59, no. 1 (March 2009): 19–39, https://doi .org/10.1111/j.1460-2466.2008.01402.x; Taeku Lee and Christian Hosam, "Fake News is Real: The Significance and Sources of Disbelief in Mainstream Media in Trump's America," *Sociological Forum* 35, no. S1 (September 2020): 996–1018, https://doi.org/10.1111/socf.12603.

29. Corwin D. Smidt, "Polarization and the Decline of the American Floating Voter," *American Journal of Political Science* 61, no. 2 (April 2017): 365–81, https://doi.org/10.1111 /ajps.12218; Bill Bishop, *The Big Sort: Why the Clustering of Like-Minded Americans Is Tearing Us Apart* (New York: Mariner Books, 2009).

30. Costas Panagopoulos, *Bases Loaded: How U.S. Presidential Campaigns Are Changing and Why It Matters* (New York: Oxford University Press, 2020). But see Seth Hill, Daniel J. Hopkins, and Gregory Huber, "And Not by Turnout Alone: Measuring the Sources of Electoral Change, 2012 to 2016," Social Science Research Network, October 21, 2020, https://doi.org/10.2139/ssrn.3716305.

31. Current population figures can be found at www.census.gov/quickfacts/fact/table/US /RHI725219. The projections are available at www.census.gov/content/dam/Census/library /publications/2020/demo/p25-1144.pdf (accessed 7/6/21).

32. Barbara A. Bardes and Robert W. Oldendick, *Public Opinion: Measuring the American Mind* (New York: Rowman and Littlefield, 2016).

33. See "In U.S., Decline of Christianity Continues at Rapid Pace," Pew Research Center, October 17, 2019, www.pewforum.org/2019/10/17/in-u-s-decline-of-christianity-continues -at-rapid-pace; "Why America's 'Nones' Don't Identify with a Religion," Pew Research Center, August 8, 2018, www.pewresearch.org/fact-tank/2018/08/08/why-americas-nones -dont-identify-with-a-religion (accessed 6/7/21).

34. See Nathaniel Rakich and Julia Wolfe, "White Voters without a Degree Remained Staunchly Republican in 2018," FiveThirtyEight, December 11, 2018, https://fivethirtyeight

.com/features/white-voters-without-a-degree-remained-staunchly-republican-in-2018 (accessed 6/7/21).

35. Rachel Caulfeld, "How Did the Presidential Campaign Get to Be So Long?" The Conversation, July 30, 2019, https://theconversation.com/how-did-the-presidential-campaign-get-to-be-so-long-119571 (accessed 6/5/21).

36. Caulfeld, "How Did."

37. Tom Murse, "When the Race for President Begins," ThoughtCo., December 10, 2020, www.thoughtco.com/when-the-race-for-president-begins-3367552 (accessed 6/5/21).

38. Arthur H. Miller, Martin P. Wattenberg, and Oksana Malanchuk, "Schematic Assessments of Presidential Candidates," *American Political Science Review* 80, no. 2 (June 1986): 521–40, https://doi.org/10.2307/1958272; Kim L. Fridkin and Patrick J. Kenney, "The Role of Candidate Traits in Campaigns," *The Journal of Politics* 73, no. 1 (January 2011): 61–73.

39. For example, see Hersh and Schaffner, "Targeted Campaign Appeals." Also see Michael Tomz and Robert P. Van Houweling, "The Electoral Implications of Candidate Ambiguity," *American Political Science Review* 103, no. 1 (February 2009): 83–98, https://doi.org/10.1017/S0003055409090066. For a broader overview, see R. Michael Alvarez, *Information and Elections* (Ann Arbor: University of Michigan Press, 1997).

40. Emmett H. Buell and Lee Sigelman, *Attack Politics: Negativity in Presidential Campaigns since 1960*, 2nd ed. (Lawrence: University of Kansas Press, 2009).

Chapter 4

1. The presidential data is compiled by the Center for Responsive Politics (OpenSecrets .org). See "Elections Overview," OpenSecrets.org, www.opensecrets.org/elections-overview?cycle=2020 and www.opensecrets.org/elections-overview?cycle=2016 (accessed 7/19/21). The House and Senate data for 1980–2018 were compiled by the Campaign Finance Institute: www.cfinst.org/pdf/federal/HistoricalTables/CFI_Federal-CF_18_Table2-02.xlsx (accessed 7/20/21). The 2020 data are from "Elections Overview," OpenSecrets.org, www.opensecrets.org/elections-overview?cycle=2020&display=A&type=G (accessed 7/20/21).

2. Harrison's fundraising total is here: "South Carolina Senate 2020 Race," OpenSecrets.org, www.opensecrets.org/races/summary?cycle=2020&id=SCS2 (accessed 7/20/21). On his out-of-state donors, see Lucia Geng, "From South Carolina to Maine, Out-of-State Donors Give Big in Senate Races," OpenSecrets.org, www.opensecrets.org/news/2020/10/senate-races-outstate-donors (accessed 7/20/21).

3. See the breakdown at "Expenditures," OpenSecrets.org, www.opensecrets.org/campaign-expenditures (accessed 7/20/21).

4. These figures are in 2018 dollars and include all fundraising by the Democratic and Republican national committees and by their respective campaign committees for the House of Representatives and the Senate.

5. The estimated cost of the election was $14.4 billion; see "Cost of Election, OpenSecrets .org, www.opensecrets.org/elections-overview/cost-of-election (accessed 7/20/21). For the estimated money spent on pizza delivery, see S. Lock, "Consumer Spending on Pizza Delivery in the U.S., 2004–2020," Statista, April 26, 2021, www.statista.com/statistics/259168/pizza-delivery-consumer-spending-in-the-us (accessed 7/20/21).

6. Stephen Ansolabehere, John M. de Figueiredo, and James M. Snyder, Jr., "Why Is There So Little Money in U.S. Politics?" *Journal of Economic Perspectives* 17, no. 1 (Winter 2003): 105–30, https://doi.org/10.1257/089533003321164976.

7. Stephen Ansolabehere, Erik C. Snowberg, and James M. Snyder, Jr., "Unrepresentative Information: The Case of Newspaper Reporting on Campaign Finance," *Public Opinion Quarterly* 69, no. 2 (Summer 2005): 213–31, https://doi.org/10.1093/poq/nfi022.

8. "Where the Money Came From," OpenSecrets.org, www.opensecrets.org/elections-overview /where-the-money-came-from (accessed 7/20/21).

9. *McCutcheon v. Federal Election Commission*, 572 U.S. 185 (2014).

10. National Conference of State Legislatures. 2021. "State Limits on Contributions to Candidates." http://www.ncsl.org/Portals/1/Documents/Elections/Contribution_Limits _to_Candidates_2020_2021.pdf (accessed 11/4/2021).

11. "Soft Money Backgrounder," OpenSecrets.org, www.opensecrets.org/parties/softsource .php (accessed 9/9/17). In nominal dollars, the amount was $457 million, which was approximately $718 million in 2021 dollars.

12. David B. Magleby, *Dictum without Data: The Myth of Issue Advocacy and Party Building* (Provo, UT: Center for the Study of Elections and Democracy, 2000).

13. "Political Parties: Overview," OpenSecrets.org, www.opensecrets.org/parties/index.php (accessed 9/10/17).

14. Derek Willis, "The Special Powers of Super PACs, and Not Just for Federal Elections," *New York Times*, December 8, 2014, www.nytimes.com/2014/12/09/upshot/the-special -powers-of-super-pacs-and-not-just-for-federal-elections.html (accessed 1/4/15).

15. "527s: Advocacy Group Spending," OpenSecrets.org, www.opensecrets.org/527s/index .php (accessed 7/21/21).

16. "Social Welfare Organizations," Internal Revenue Service, September 7, 2021, www.irs .gov/Charities-&-Non-Profits/Other-Non-Profits/Social-Welfare-Organizations (accessed 9/8/21).

17. Michael Luo and Stephanie Strom, "Donor Names Remain Secret as Rules Shift," *New York Times*, September 20, 2010, www.nytimes.com/2010/09/21/us/politics/21money.html (accessed 1/4/15).

18. 424 U.S. 1 (1976).

19. See "Gubernatorial Public Financing," New Jersey Election Law Enforcement Commission, November 2020, www.elec.state.nj.us/download/gubernatorial/GubPublicFinPP _112020.pdf (accessed 7/21/21).

20. "Public Financing of Campaigns: Overview," National Conference of State Legislatures, February 8, 2019, www.ncsl.org/research/elections-and-campaigns/public-financing-of -campaigns-overview.aspx (accessed 7/21/21).

21. "How Clean Funding Works," Arizona Citizens Clean Elections Commission, www .azcleanelections.gov/en/run-for-office/how-clean-funding-works (accessed 7/21/21).

22. "Democracy Voucher Program," City of Seattle, www.seattle.gov/democracyvoucher /about-the-program; KING 5 Staff, "Democracy Vouchers: Seattle Voters Will Soon Have $100 Sitting in Their Mailbox," February 16, 2021, www.king5.com/article/news/local /democracy-vouchers-seattle/281-efe5599c-1046-4f12-a794-1c9df7e5dd32 (accessed 7/21/21).

23. Christina Holtz-Bacha and Lynda Lee Kaid, "Political Advertising in International Comparison," in *The Sage Handbook of Political Advertising*, ed. Lynda Lee Kaid and Christina Holtz-Bacha (Thousand Oaks, CA: Sage, 2006), 3–13.

24. Matea Gold and Colby Itkowitz, "Justice Department Ramps up Scrutiny of Candidates and Independent Groups," *Washington Post*, February 27, 2015, www.washingtonpost.com /politics/justice-department-ramps-up-scrutiny-of-candidates-and-independent-groups /2015/02/27/f28409d8-be8e-11e4-8668-4e7ba8439ca6_story.html (accessed 9/8/21); Paul Blumenthal, "2016 Candidates Thumb Their Noses at Campaign Finance Rules," *HuffPost*, March 18, 2015, www.huffpost.com/entry/2016-election-campaign-finance_n_6886908 (accessed 9/8/21); Matea Gold, "It's Bold, But Legal: How Campaigns and Their Super PAC Backers Work Together," *Washington Post*, July 6, 2015, www.washingtonpost.com/politics

/here-are-the-secret-ways-super-pacs-and-campaigns-can-work-together/2015/07/06
/bda78210-1539-11e5-89f3-61410da94eb1_story.html (accessed 9/8/21).

25. *Citizens United v. Federal Election Commission*, 558 U.S. 310 (2010).

26. Travis N. Ridout, Erika Franklin Fowler, and Michael M. Franz, "Spending Fast and Furious: Political Advertising in 2020," *Forum* 18, no. 4 (2021): 465–92, https://doi.org/10.1515/for-2020-2109.

27. Michael M. Franz, "Interest Groups in Electoral Politics: 2012 in Context," *Forum* 10, no. 4 (2013): 62–79, https://doi.org/10.1515/forum-2013-0007.

28. Ansolabehere et al., "Why Is There So Little Money in U.S. Politics?"; Michael J. Barber, Brandice Canes-Wrone, and Sharece Thrower, "Ideologically Sophisticated Donors: Which Candidates Do Individual Contributors Finance?" *American Journal of Political Science* 61, no. 2 (April 2017): 271–88, https://doi.org/10.1111/ajps.12275.

29. Diana C. Mutz, "Effects of Horse-Race Coverage on Campaign Coffers: Strategic Contributing in Presidential Primaries," *Journal of Politics* 57, no. 4 (November 1995): 1015–42, https://doi.org/10.2307/2960400.

30. Paul S. Herrnson and Ronald A. Faucheux, *The Good Fight: How Political Candidates Struggle to Win Elections without Losing their Souls* (Washington, DC: Campaigns and Elections Magazine, 2001).

31. Ryan Grim and Sabrina Siddiqui, "Call Time for Congress Shows How Fundraising Dominates Bleak Work Life," *HuffPost*, January 8, 2013, www.huffingtonpost.com/2013/01/08/call-time-congressional-fundraising_n_2427291.html (accessed 1/4/2015).

32. "Donald Trump (R)—WINNER," OpenSecrets.org, www.opensecrets.org/pres16/candidate?id=N00023864 (accessed 9/8/21) and "Hillary Clinton (D)," OpenSecrets.org, www.opensecrets.org/pres16/candidate?id=N00000019 (accessed 9/8/17).

33. Patrick Ruffini, "Can You Buy a Presidential Election?" FiveThirtyEight, June 3, 2020, https://fivethirtyeight.com/features/can-you-buy-a-presidential-election (accessed 7/21/21).

34. See Jennifer A. Steen, *Self-Financed Candidates in Congressional Elections* (Ann Arbor: University of Michigan Press, 2006).

35. Jennifer A. Heerwig and Katie M. Gordon, "Buying a Voice: Gendered Contribution Careers among Affluent Political Donors to Federal Elections, 1980–2008," *Sociological Forum* 33, no. 3 (September 2018): 805–25, https://doi.org/10.1111/socf.12444; Jacob M. Grumbach and Alexander Sahn, "Race and Representation in Campaign Finance," *American Political Science Review* 114, no. 1 (February 2020): 206–21, https://doi.org/10.1017/S0003055419000637; Jacob M. Grumbach, Alexander Sahn, and Sarah Staszak, "Gender, Race, and Intersectionality in Campaign Finance," *Political Behavior* (2020), https://doi.org/10.1007/s11109-020-09619-0.

36. David Broockman and Neil Malhotra, "What Do Partisan Donors Want?" *Public Opinion Quarterly* 84, no. 1 (Spring 2020): 104–18, https://doi.org/10.1093/poq/nfaa001.

37. For evidence that candidates respond to the policy preferences of national donors, see Brandice Canes-Wrone and Kenneth M Miller, "Out-of-District Donors and Representation in the US House," *Legislative Studies Quarterly* (2021), https://doi.org/10.1111/lsq.12336.

38. See Michael M. Franz, *Choices and Changes: Interest Groups in the Electoral Process* (Philadelphia: Temple University Press, 2008).

39. Michael M. Franz, Erika Franklin Fowler, and Travis N. Ridout, "Loose Cannons or Loyal Foot Soldiers? Toward a More Complex Theory of Interest Group Advertising Strategies," *American Journal of Political Science* 60, no. 3 (July 2016): 738–51, https://doi.org/10.1111/ajps.12241.

40. Kenneth M. Miller, "The Divided Labor of Attack Advertising in Congressional Campaigns," *Journal of Politics* 81, no. 3 (July 2019): 805–19, https://doi.org/10.1086/703133.

41. "Independent Ads: The National Security Political Action Committee 'Willie Horton',"
www.insidepolitics.org/ps111/independentads.html (accessed 7/22/21).

42. Douglas M. Spencer and Alexander G. Theodoridis, "'Appearance of Corruption':
Linking Public Opinion and Campaign Finance Reform," *Election Law Journal* 19, no. 4
(December 2020): 510–23, http://doi.org/10.1089/elj.2019.0590.

43. Danielle M. Thomsen, "Dropout Decisions in U.S. House Elections" (working paper,
University of California, Irvine, 2020), https://daniellethomsen.files.wordpress.com/2020
/05/thomsen_dropouts.pdf (accessed 7/22/21).

44. Jennifer L. Lawless and Richard L. Fox, *Men Rule: The Continued Under-Representation
of Women in U.S. Politics* (Washington, DC: Women & Politics Institute, School of Public
Affairs, American University, 2012), www.american.edu/spa/wpi/upload/2012-Men-Rule
-Report-final-web.pdf (accessed 9/9/17).

45. Richard L. Hasen, *Plutocrats United: Campaign Money, the Supreme Court, and the
Distortion of American Elections* (New Haven, CT: Yale University Press, 2016).

46. Adam Bonica, Nolan McCarty, Keith T. Poole, and Howard Rosenthal, "Why Hasn't
Democracy Slowed Rising Inequality?" *Journal of Economic Perspectives* 27, no. 3 (Summer
2013): 103–24, https://doi.org/10.1257/jep.27.3.103.

47. Nicholas Confessore, Sarah Cohen, and Karen Yourish, "Small Pool of Rich Donors
Dominates Election Giving," *New York Times*, August 1, 2015, www.nytimes.com/2015/08
/02/us/small-pool-of-rich-donors-dominates-election-giving.html (accessed 10/26/17).

48. "Business-Labor-Ideology Split in PAC & Individual Donations to Candidates, Parties,
Super PACs and Outside Spending Groups," OpenSecrets.org, www.opensecrets.org
/bigpicture/blio.php (accessed 7/22/21).

49. Matea Gold, "One Single Donation to Crossroads GPS in 2012: $22,500,000," *Washing-
ton Post*, November 15, 2013, www.washingtonpost.com/blogs/the-fix/wp/2013/11/15/one
-single-donation-to-crossroads-gps-in-2012-22500000 (accessed 1/4/15). These figures are
in nominal dollars.

50. "Joint Fundraising Committees," OpenSecrets.org, www.opensecrets.org/jfc (accessed
7/22/21).

51. Karl Evers-Hillstrom, "Who's Funding the Virtual Republican National Convention?"
OpenSecrets.org, August 20, 2020, www.opensecrets.org/news/2020/08/virtual-republican
-national-convention (accessed 7/22/21).

52. Chelsea Bailey, "At Rally, Parkland Shooting Survivors Rail against Gun Laws, NRA,
and Trump," *NBC News*, February 17, 2018, www.nbcnews.com/news/us-news/rally
-parkland-shooting-survivors-rail-against-gun-laws-nra-trump-n849076 (accessed 4/24/19).

53. Lynda W. Powell, *The Influence of Campaign Contributions in State Legislatures* (Ann
Arbor: University of Michigan Press, 2012).

54. Morgan L. W. Hazelton, Jacob M. Montgomery, and Brendan Nyhan, "Does Public
Financing Affect Judicial Behavior? Evidence from the North Carolina Supreme Court,"
American Politics Research 44, no. 4 (July 2016): 587–617, https://doi.org/10.1177
/1532673X15599839.

55. Common Cause, "Bipartisan Fair Elections Now Act Reaches Majority of Majority in U.S.
House," press release, February 4, 2010, www.commondreams.org/newswire/2010/02/04
/bipartisan-fair-elections-now-act-reaches-majority-majority-us-house (accessed 10/31/17).

56. See, for example, Steven Sprick Schuster, "Does Campaign Spending Affect Election
Outcomes? New Evidence from Transaction-Level Disbursement Data," *Journal of Politics*
82, no. 4 (October 2020): 1502–15, https://doi.org/10.1086/708646.

57. Raymond J. La Raja and Brian F. Schaffner, "The Effects of Campaign Finance Spending
Bans on Electoral Outcomes: Evidence from the States about the Potential Impact of *Citizens*

United v. FEC," *Electoral Studies* 33, no. 1 (March 2014): 102–14, https://doi.org/10.1016/j
.electstud.2013.08.002; Thomas Stratmann and Francisco J. Aparicio-Castillo, "Competition
Policy for Elections: Do Campaign Contribution Limits Matter?" *Public Choice* 127, no. 1–2
(2006): 177–206, https://doi.org/10.1007/s11127-006-1252-x.

58. Peter L. Francia and Paul S. Herrnson, "The Impact of Public Finance Laws on Fundraising in State Legislative Elections," *American Politics Research* 31, no. 5 (September 2003):
520–39, https://doi.org/10.1177/1532673X03256784; Powell, *The Influence of Campaign
Contributions*; Michael G. Miller, *Subsidizing Democracy: How Public Funding Changes
Elections and How It Can Work in the Future* (Ithaca, NY: Cornell University Press, 2013).

59. Kenneth R. Mayer and John M. Wood, "The Impact of Public Financing on Electoral
Competitiveness: Evidence from Wisconsin, 1964–1990," *Legislative Studies Quarterly* 20, no. 1
(February 1995): 69–88, https://doi.org/10.2307/440150; Patrick D. Donnay and Graham
P. Ramsden, "Public Financing of Legislative Elections: Lessons from Minnesota," *Legislative
Studies Quarterly* 20, no. 3 (August 1995): 351–64, https://doi.org/10.2307/440225; Neil
Malhotra, "The Impact of Public Financing on Electoral Competition: Evidence from Arizona
and Maine," *State Politics and Policy Quarterly* 8, no. 3 (2008): 263–81, https://doi.org/10.1177
/153244000800800303.

60. Richard L. Hall and Frank W. Wayman, "Buying Time: Moneyed Interests and the
Mobilization of Bias in Congressional Committees," *American Political Science Review* 84,
no. 3 (1990): 797–820, https://doi.org/10.2307/1962767. See also Amy Melissa McKay,
"Buying Amendments? Lobbyists' Campaign Contributions and Microlegislation in the
Creation of the Affordable Care Act," *Legislative Studies Quarterly* 45, no. 2 (May 2020):
327–60, https://doi.org/10.1111/lsq.12266.

61. Joshua L. Kalla and David E. Broockman, "Campaign Contributions Facilitate Access to
Congressional Officials: A Randomized Field Experiment," *American Journal of Political
Science* 60, no. 3 (July 2016): 545–58, https://doi.org/10.1111/ajps.12180.

62. David M. Primo and Jeffrey D. Milyo, *Campaign Finance and American Democracy: What
the Public Really Thinks and Why It Matters* (Chicago: University of Chicago Press, 2020), 8.

63. For example, see John J. Coleman and Paul F. Manna, "Congressional Campaign Spending
and the Quality of Democracy," *Journal of Politics* 62, no. 3 (August 2000): 757–89, https://doi
.org/10.1111/0022-3816.00032.

64. See https://slideplayer.com/slide/3532615/ (accessed 10/11/21).

65. Emily Swanson and Julie Bykowicz, "AP-NORC Poll: Americans Not Fans of Public
Financing," *AP News*, December 8, 2015, www.apnews.com/1a0f52ec099d4e82a0f6ed168f
9756c9 (accessed 9/9/17). See also the 2015–16 data reported in Primo and Milyo,
Campaign Finance, 106–08.

66. Echelon Insights (@EchelonInsights), "The concept of public campaign financing $ is
deeply unpopular to voters. 67% of voters strongly/somewhat oppose the idea in general,
and 69% strongly/somewhat oppose it," Twitter, March 24, 2021, https://twitter.com
/EchelonInsights/status/1374755869322321924 (accessed 7/22/21).

67. Jeffrey M. Jones, "Campaign Financing Appears to Be Non-Issue for Voters," *Gallup*,
October 30, 2008, www.gallup.com/poll/111652/Campaign-Financing-Appears-NonIssue
-Voters.aspx (accessed 1/4/15).

68. Primo and Milyo, *Campaign Finance*, chapter 8.

69. Seth J. Hill and Gregory A. Huber, "Representativeness and Motivations of the Contemporary Donorate: Results from Merged Survey and Administrative Records," *Political
Behavior* 39, no. 1 (2017): 3–29, https://doi.org/10.1007/s11109-016-9343-y.

70. Jordan Kujala, "Donors, Primary Elections, and Polarization in the United States,"
American Journal of Political Science 64, no. 3 (July 2020): 587–602, https://doi.org/10.1111
/ajps.12477.

71. Raymond L. La Raja and Brian F. Schaffner, *Campaign Finance and Political Polarization: When Purists Prevail* (Ann Arbor: University of Michigan Press, 2015); Michael J. Barber, "Ideological Donors, Contribution Limits, and the Polarization of American Legislatures," *Journal of Politics* 78, no. 1 (January 2016): 296–310, https://doi.org/10.1086/683453.

72. Andrew Hall, "How the Public Funding of Elections Increases Candidate Polarization" (working paper, Department of Government, Harvard University, August 13, 2014), www .andrewbenjaminhall.com/Hall_publicfunding.pdf (accessed 9/8/21).

73. Seth E. Masket and Michael G. Miller, "Does Public Election Funding Create More Extreme Legislators? Evidence from Arizona and Maine," *State Politics and Policy Quarterly* 15, no. 1 (March 2015): 24–40, https://doi.org/10.1177/1532440014563682.

Chapter 5

1. Jonathan Allen and Amie Parnes, *Lucky: How Joe Biden Barely Won the Presidency* (New York: Crown Publishing, 2021).

2. Joel Bradshaw, "Campaign Strategy," in *Campaigns and Elections American Style: Transforming American Politics*, 2nd ed., ed. James A. Thurber and Candice J. Nelson (Boulder, CO: Westview Press, 2004), 38–40.

3. Costas Panagopoulos, *Bases Loaded: How U.S. Presidential Campaigns Are Changing and Why It Matters* (New York: Oxford University Press, 2020). See also Daniel J. Galvin, "Party Domination and Base Mobilization: Donald Trump and Republican Party Building in a Polarized Era," *The Forum* 18, no. 2: 135–68, https://doi.org/10.1515/for-2020-2003.

4. In some states, voters register with a political party. In these states, party affiliation is largely (though not entirely) estimated based on party registration. In other states, especially in the South, voters do not register by party. In these states, party affiliation is estimated based on whether one typically votes in the Republican or Democratic primaries along with demographic and other data.

5. For further explanation, see Sasha Issenberg, "How Obama's Team Used Big Data to Rally Voters," *MIT Technology Review*, December 19, 2012, www.technologyreview.com/2012/12 /19/114510/how-obamas-team-used-big-data-to-rally-voters (accessed 8/25/21).

6. Polls are not the only way to ascertain which voters are susceptible to which messages. For example, the 2012 Obama campaign conducted experiments to help develop more effective models of which voters were actually persuadable. See Sasha Issenberg, *Victory Lab: The Secret Science of Winning Campaigns* (New York: Broadway Books, 2012). Also see Issenberg, "Obama's Team." Despite the sophistication of the modeling and causal estimation strategies, there is mixed evidence with respect to the efficacy of these persuasion scores. See John Sides and Lynn Vavreck, "Obama's Not-So-Big Data," *Pacific Standard*, June 14, 2017, https://psmag .com/social-justice/obamas-big-data-inconclusive-results-political-campaigns-72687 (accessed 8/25/21).

7. Cherie D. Maestas et al., "When to Risk It? Institutions, Ambitions, and the Decision to Run for the U.S. House," *American Political Science Review* 100, no. 2 (May 2006): 195–208, https://doi.org/10.1017/S0003055406062101.

8. The Institute of Politics, John F. Kennedy School of Government, Harvard University, *Campaign for President: The Managers Look at 2008* (New York: Rowman & Littlefield, 2009), 22.

9. Institute of Politics, *Campaign*, 29.

10. See Adam Bonica, "Why Are There So Many Lawyers in Congress?" *Legislative Studies Quarterly* 45, no. 2 (2020): 253–89, https://doi.org/10.1111/lsq.12265. Bonica points out that a main reason for the prevalence of attorneys as candidates and officeholders is that they have access to money, either personally or through their professional networks.

11. Although the fear of "being primaried" may be increasing, the actual number of primary challenges does not appear to be on the upswing. See Robert G. Boatright, *Getting Primaried: The Changing Politics of Congressional Primary Challenges* (Ann Arbor: University of Michigan Press, 2013). Data from state legislative primary elections confirm this point for 2016–20. See Douglas Kronaizl, "79.6% of Incumbents Faced No Primary Challenges This Year, Highest Rate Since 2014," Ballotpedia, September 4, 2020, https://news.ballotpedia .org/2020/09/04/79-6-of-incumbents-faced-no-primary-challenges-this-year-highest-rate -since-2014 (accessed 8/25/21).

12. Gary C. Jacobson and Samuel Kernell, *Strategy and Choice in Congressional Elections* (New Haven, CT: Yale University Press, 1983).

13. There do appear to be some differences by party, as Republican primaries are more likely to include inexperienced candidates. See Raymond J. La Raja and Jonathan Rauch, "How Inexperienced Candidates and Primary Challenges Are Making Republicans the Protest Party," Brookings, June 29, 2020, www.brookings.edu/blog/fixgov/2020/06/29/how -inexperienced-candidates-and-primary-challenges-are-making-republicans-the-protest -party (accessed 8/25/21).

14. See La Raja and Rauch, "Inexperienced Candidates."

15. Jennifer L. Lawless and Richard L. Fox, *Women, Men & U.S. Politics: 10 Big Questions* (New York: W. W. Norton, 2017).

16. Rebecca J. Kreitzer and Tracy L. Osborn, "The Emergence and Activities of Women's Recruiting Groups in the U.S.," *Politics, Groups, and Identities* 7, no. 4 (2019): 842–52, https://doi.org/10.1080/21565503.2018.1531772.

17. Eric Gonzalez Juenke, "Ignorance Is Bias: The Effect of Latino Losers on Models of Latino Representation," *American Journal of Political Science* 58, no. 3 (July 2014): 593–603, https://doi.org/10.1111/ajps.12092.

18. See Keith Reeves, *Voting Hopes or Fears? White Voters, Black Candidates, and Racial Politics in America* (New York: Oxford University Press, 1997).

19. Kristofer A. Frederick and Judson L. Jeffries, "A Study in African American Candidates for High-Profile Statewide Office," *Journal of Black Studies* 39, no. 5 (May 2009): 689–718, https://doi.org/10.1177/0021934707299641.

20. John R. Petrocik, "Issue Ownership in Presidential Elections, with a 1980 Case Study," *American Journal of Political Science* 40, no. 3 (August 1996): 825–50, https://doi.org/10 .2307/2111797.

21. See Patrick Egan, *Partisan Priorities: How Issue Ownership Drives and Distorts American Politics* (New York: Cambridge University Press, 2013). Egan also argues that party ownership of an issue does not necessarily mean that the party produces better public policy on that issue.

22. John Sides, "The Origins of Campaign Agendas," *British Journal of Political Science* 36, no. 3 (2006): 407–36, https://doi.org/10.1017/S0007123406000226.

23. There is a burgeoning literature on how gender affects candidate agendas. See Maura McDonald, Rachel Porter, and Sarah A. Treul, "Running as a Woman? Candidate Presentation in the 2018 Midterms," *Political Research Quarterly* 73, no. 4 (December 2020): 967–87, https://doi.org/10.1177/1065912920915787.

24. Anthony Downs, *An Economic Theory of Democracy* (New York: Harper & Row, 1957); Harold Hotelling, "Stability in Competition," *Economic Journal* 39, no. 153 (March 1929): 41–57, https://doi.org/10.2307/2224214.

25. Andrew B. Hall and Daniel M. Thompson, "Who Punishes Extremist Nominees? Candidate Ideology and Turning Out the Base in US Elections," *American Political Science Review* 112, no. 3 (2018): 509–24, https://doi.org/10.1017/S0003055418000023.

26. Jonathan Rauch and Raymond J. La Raja, "Re-Engineering Politicians: How Activist Groups Choose Our Candidates—Long Before We Vote," Brookings, December 7, 2017, www.brookings.edu/research/re-engineering-politicians-how-activist-groups-choose-our -politicians-long-before-we-vote (accessed 8/25/21).

27. For example, see Eitan D. Hersh and Brian F. Schaffner, "Targeted Campaign Appeals and the Value of Ambiguity," *The Journal of Politics* 75, no. 2 (April 2013): 520–34, https://doi.org/10.1017/S0022381613000182. Also see Michael Tomz and Robert P. Van Houweling, "The Electoral Implications of Candidate Ambiguity," *American Political Science Review* 103, no. 1 (February 2009): 83–98, https://doi.org/10.1017/S0003055409090066. For a broader overview, see R. Michael Alvarez, *Information and Elections* (Ann Arbor: University of Michigan Press, 1997).

28. John G. Geer, *In Defense of Negativity: Attack Ads in Presidential Campaigns* (Chicago: University of Chicago Press, 2006), 23.

29. Stergios Skaperdas and Bernard Grofman, "Modeling Negative Campaigning," *American Political Science Review* 89, no. 1 (1995): 49–61, https://doi.org/10.2307/2083074; John Theilmann and Allen Wilhite, "Campaign Tactics and the Decision to Attack," *Journal of Politics* 60, no. 4 (November 1998): 1050–62, https://doi.org/10.2307/2647730.

30. Kim Fridkin and Patrick Kenney, *Taking Aim at Attack Advertising: Understanding the Impact of Negative Campaigning in U.S. Senate Races* (New York: Oxford University Press, 2019). See also Travis N. Ridout and Glen R. Smith, "Free Advertising: How the Media Amplify Campaign Messages," *Political Research Quarterly* 61, no. 4 (December 2008): 598–608, https://doi.org/10.1177/1065912908314202.

31. Geer, *In Defense*; Emmett H. Buell, Jr., and Lee Sigelman, *Attack Politics: Negativity in Presidential Campaigns since 1960*, 2nd ed. (Lawrence: University Press of Kansas, 2009).

32. Swift Boat Veterans for Truth (SBVT) was angry at Kerry for his testimony before a U.S. Senate committee on April 22, 1971, when he spoke on behalf of the group Vietnam Veterans Against the War. The SBVT ads asserted that Kerry was "unfit to serve" as president based upon his alleged "willful distortion of the conduct" of Americans who served in Vietnam and his alleged "withholding and/or distortion of material facts" as to his own conduct during that war.

33. Conor M. Dowling and Amber Wichowsky, "Attacks without Consequence? Candidates, Parties, Groups, and the Changing Face of Negative Advertising," *American Journal of Political Science* 59, no. 1 (2015): 19–36, https://doi.org/10.1111/ajps.12094.

34. See Fridkin and Kenney, *Taking Aim*.

35. Exit polls from Edison Research show that Trump carried independents, 46 percent to 42 percent, over Hillary Clinton. Subsequent research from Pew questions this finding; see Pew Research Center, "An Examination of the 2016 Electorate, Based on Validated Voters," August 9, 2018, www.pewresearch.org/politics/2018/08/09/an-examination-of-the-2016 -electorate-based-on-validated-voters (accessed 8/25/21).

36. Daron R. Shaw, *The Race to 270: The Electoral College and the Campaign Strategies of 2000 and 2004* (Chicago: University of Chicago Press, 2006). See also Mitchell Lovett and Michael Peress, "Targeting Political Advertising on Television," *Quarterly Journal of Political Science* 10, no. 3 (2015): 391–432, https://doi.org/10.1561/100.00014107.

37. Taofang Huang and Daron Shaw, "Beyond the Battlegrounds? Electoral College Strategies in the 2008 Presidential Election," *Journal of Political Marketing* 8, no. 4 (2009): 272–91, https://doi.org/10.1080/15377850903263771.

38. For an overview, see Joshua P. Darr, "Abandoning the Ground Game? Field Organization in the 2016 Election," *Presidential Studies Quarterly* 50, no. 1 (2009): 163–75, https://doi .org/10.1111/psq.12612.

39. Donald P. Green and Alan S. Gerber, *Get Out the Vote! How to Increase Voter Turnout*, 4th ed. (Washington, DC: Brookings Institution Press, 2019).

40. Brian Bennett and Tessa Berenson, "An Election Day Upset Hangs on Donald Trump's Formidable Ground Game," *Time*, November 2, 2020, https://time.com/5906581/donald -trump-campaign-ground-game (accessed 8/25/21).

41. Quoted in Philip Bump, "How Hillary Clinton's 'Happy Volunteer' Strategy Works," *Washington Post*, September 22, 2016, www.washingtonpost.com/news/the-fix/wp/2016/09 /22/how-hillary-clintons-happy-volunteer-strategy-works (accessed 8/25/21).

42. Theodore H. White, *The Making of the President 1960* (New York: Atheneum, 1961).

43. Joe McGinniss, *The Selling of the President: The Classic Account of the Packaging of a Candidate* (New York: Simon & Schuster, 1969).

44. Stephen K. Medvic, *Political Consultants in U.S. Congressional Elections* (Columbus: Ohio State University Press, 2001).

Chapter 6

1. Mark Z. Barabak, "Key Democrats Support Biden in Attempt to Derail Sanders," *Los Angeles Times*, March 2, 2020, https://enewspaper.latimes.com/infinity/article_share.aspx ?guid=221be678-6ab1-417e-8a46-c4bdc4ce0ea8.

2. Marty Cohen et al., *The Party Decides: Presidential Nominations before and after Reform* (Chicago: University of Chicago Press, 2008). The authors of the book discussed Trump and the popularity of their theory in 2016 in Steve Kolowich, "The Life of 'The Party Decides'," *Chronicle of Higher Education*, May 16, 2016, www.chronicle.com/article/the-life-of-the -party-decides (accessed 9/14/21).

3. Marty Cohen et al., "Party Versus Faction in the Reformed Presidential Nominating System," *PS: Political Science & Politics* 49, no. 4 (2016): 701–08, https://doi.org/10.1017/S104909651 6001682.

4. Hans J. G. Hassel, *The Party's Primary: Control of Congressional Nominations* (New York: Cambridge University Press, 2018).

5. V. O. Key, Jr., *Politics, Parties, and Pressure Groups*, 3rd ed. (New York: Thomas Y. Crowell, 1952).

6. Paul S. Herrnson, "The Roles of Party Organizations, Party-Connected Committees, and Party Allies in Elections," *Journal of Politics* 71, no. 4 (October 2009): 1207–24, https://doi .org/10.1017/s0022381609990065.

7. Gregory Koger, Seth Masket, and Hans Noel, "Partisan Webs: Information Exchange and Party Networks," *British Journal of Political Science* 39, no. 3 (2009): 633–53, https://doi.org /10.1017/S0007123409000659.

8. John H. Aldrich, *Why Parties? The Origin and Transformation of Political Parties in America* (Chicago: University of Chicago Press, 1995).

9. Kathleen Bawn et al., "A Theory of Political Parties: Groups, Policy Demands and Nomina- tions in American Politics," *Perspectives on Politics* 10, no. 3 (2012): 571–97, https://doi.org /10.1017/S1537592712001624.

10. Matt Grossmann and David A. Hopkins, *Asymmetric Politics: Ideological Republicans and Group Interest Democrats* (New York: Oxford University Press, 2016).

11. According to aggregated Gallup polls, Nader voters preferred Gore to Bush by a margin of more than two to one.

12. Jacob R. Brown and Ryan D. Enos, "The Measurement of Partisan Sorting for 180 Million Voters," *Nature Human Behaviour* 5, no. 8 (August 2021): 998–1008, https://doi.org /10.1038/s41562-021-01066-z.

13. Steven J. Rosenstone and John Mark Hansen, *Mobilization, Participation, and Democracy in America* (New York: Macmillan, 1993).

14. Donald P. Green and Alan S. Gerber, *Get Out the Vote! How to Increase Voter Turnout*, 2nd ed. (Washington, DC: Brookings Institution Press, 2008).

15. Andrew B. Hall, *Who Wants to Run? How the Devaluing of Political Office Drives Polarization* (Chicago: University of Chicago Press, 2019).

16. David Doherty, Conor M. Dowling, and Michael G. Miller, "Do Local Party Chairs Think Women and Minority Candidates Can Win?" *Journal of Politics* 81, no. 4 (October 2019): 1282–97, https://doi.org/10.1086/704698.

17. Gary C. Jacobson and Jamie L. Carson, *The Politics of Congressional Elections*, 10th ed. (Lanham, MD: Rowman & Littlefield, 2020).

18. Samara Klar and Yanna Krupnikov, *Independent Politics: How American Disdain for Parties Leads to Political Inaction* (New York: Cambridge University Press, 2016).

19. Carlee Beth Hawkins and Brian Nosek, "Motivated Independence? Implicit Party Identity Predicts Political Judgments Among Self-Proclaimed Independents," *Personality and Social Psychology Bulletin* 38, no. 11 (November 2012): 1437–52, https://doi.org/10.1177/0146167212452313.

20. Aaron C. Weinschenk, "Partisanship and Voting Behavior: An Update," *Presidential Studies Quarterly* 43, no. 3 (September 2013): 607–17, https://doi.org/10.1111/psq.12048.

21. Aldrich, *Why Parties?*

22. Rebecca S. Hatch, "Party Organizational Strength and Technological Capacity," *Party Politics* 22, no. 2 (March 2016): 191–202, https://doi.org/10.1177/1354068815605673.

23. Cohen et al., *The Party Decides*.

24. Jeff Manza and Clem Brooks, *Social Cleavages and Political Change: Voter Alignments and U.S. Party Coalitions* (New York: Oxford University Press, 1999).

25. Edward G. Carmines and James A. Stimson, *Issue Evolution: Race and the Transformation of American Politics* (Princeton, NJ: Princeton University Press, 1989).

26. Ian Haney López, *Dog Whistle Politics: How Coded Racial Appeals Have Reinvented Racism and Wrecked the Middle Class* (New York: Oxford University Press, 2015).

27. Geoffrey C. Layman, Thomas M. Carsey, and Juliana Menasce Horowitz, "Party Polarization in American Politics: Characteristics, Causes, and Consequences," *Annual Review of Political Science* 9, no. 1 (June 2006): 83–110, https://doi.org/10.1146/annurev.polisci.9.070204.105138.

28. Alan I. Abramowitz and Steven Webster, "The Rise of Negative Partisanship and the Nationalization of U.S. Elections in the 21st Century," *Electoral Studies* 41, no. 1 (March 2016): 12–22, https://doi.org/10.1016/j.electstud.2015.11.001.

29. Dan Burns, "U.S. Consumer Sentiment Slips but Shows Massive Partisan Divide," Reuters, January 15, 2021, www.reuters.com/article/us-usa-economy-sentiment/u-s-consumer-sentiment-slips-but-shows-massive-partisan-divide-idUSKBN29K1WK (accessed 9/14/21).

30. Danielle M. Thomsen, *Opting Out of Congress: Partisan Polarization and the Decline of Moderate Candidates* (New York: Cambridge University Press, 2017).

31. Richard R. Lau and David P. Redlawsk, "Advantages and Disadvantages of Cognitive Heuristics in Political Decision Making," *American Journal of Political Science* 45, no. 4 (October 2001): 951–71, https://doi.org/10.2307/2669334.

32. Gabriel S. Lenz, "Learning and Opinion Change, Not Priming: Reconsidering the Priming Hypothesis," *American Journal of Political Science* 53, no. 4 (October 2009): 821–37, https://doi.org/10.1111/j.1540-5907.2009.00403.x.

33. Keena Lipsitz, "Democratic Theory and Political Campaigns," *Journal of Political Philosophy* 12, no. 2 (2004): 163–89, https://doi.org/10.1111/j.1467-9760.2004.00196.x.

Chapter 7

1. See Theda Skocpol, Caroline Tervo, and Kirsten Walters, "Social Justice Campaigns and Democratic Party Gains: How Georgia's Partisan Reformers Overtook North Carolina's Moral Advocates" (working paper, Harvard University, July 2021), https://scholar.harvard.edu/files/thedaskocpol/files/skocpol-tervo_-walters_nc_ga_july_2021_appendix_a_only.pdf. We also rely on this investigation for this chapter's introductory narrative comparing Georgia and North Carolina.

2. Jack L. Walker, Jr., *Mobilizing Interest Groups in America: Patrons, Professions, and Social Movements* (Ann Arbor: University of Michigan Press, 1991).

3. "Data (in constant 2016 dollars)," Campaign Finance Institute, 2016, http://www.cfinst.org/data.aspx (accessed 11/1/17).

4. Michael M. Franz, Erika Franklin Fowler, and Travis N. Ridout, "Accessing Information about Interest Group Advertising Content," *Interest Groups and Advocacy* 9 (2020): 373–83, https://doi.org/10.1057/s41309-020-00083-z.

5. Paul Frymer, *Uneasy Alliances: Race and Party Competition in America* (Princeton, NJ: Princeton University Press, 1999).

6. Arthur Lupia, "Shortcuts versus Encyclopedias: Information and Voting Behavior in California Insurance Reform Elections," *American Political Science Review* 88, no. 1 (March 1994): 63–76, https://doi.org/10.2307/2944882.

7. Thomas Stratmann, "The Effectiveness of Money in Ballot Measure Campaigns," *Southern California Law Review* 78, no. 4 (May 2005): 1041–64; Joshua J. Dyck and Shanna Pearson-Merkowitz, "Ballot Initiatives and Status Quo Bias," *State Politics and Policy* Quarterly 19, no. 2 (June 2019): 180–207, https://doi.org/10.1177/1532440018815067.

8. Lee Drutman, *The Business of America Is Lobbying: How Corporations Became Politicized and Politics Became More Corporate* (New York: Oxford University Press, 2015).

9. Michael M. Franz, *Choices and Changes: Interest Groups in the Electoral Process* (Philadelphia: Temple University Press, 2008).

10. Dino P. Christenson and Corwin D. Smidt, "Following the Money: Super PACs and the 2012 Presidential Nomination," *Presidential Studies Quarterly* 44, no. 3 (September 2014): 410–30, https://doi.org/10.1111/psq.12130.

11. David Lynn Painter, "Collateral Damage: Involvement and the Effects of Negative Super PAC Advertising," *American Behavioral Scientist* 58, no. 4 (April 2014): 510–23, https://doi.org/10.1177/0002764213506210.

12. Travis N. Ridout, Erika Franklin Fowler, and Michael M. Franz, "Spending Fast and Furious: Political Advertising in 2020," *The Forum* 18, no. 4 (2021): 465–92, https://doi.org/10.1515/for-2020-2109.

13. Nicholas Confessore, "Big Money to Fight Big Donors," *New York Times*, September 7, 2014, A1.

14. Todd Rogers and Joel Middleton, "Are Ballot Initiative Outcomes Influenced by the Campaigns of Independent Groups? A Precinct-Randomized Field Experiment Showing That They Are," *Political Behavior* 37, no. 3 (2015): 567–93, https://doi.org/10.1007/s11109-014-9282-4.

15. Michael M. Franz, Erika Franklin Fowler, and Travis N. Ridout, "Loose Cannons or Loyal Foot Soldiers? Toward a More Complex Theory of Interest Group Advertising Strategies," *American Journal of Political Science* 60, no. 3 (July 2016): 738–51, https://doi.org/10.1111/ajps.12241.

16. Kay Lehman Schlozman, Henry E. Brady, and Sidney Verba, *Unequal and Unrepresented: Political Inequality and the People's Voice in the New Gilded Age* (Princeton, NJ: Princeton University Press, 2018).

17. Katharine Q. Seelye, "Clinton and the Lobbyists," *New York Times*, August 6, 2007, https://thecaucus.blogs.nytimes.com/2007/08/06/clinton-and-the-lobbyists (accessed 10/28/17).

Chapter 8

1. The video is available at "Transcript: Donald Trump's Taped Comments about Women," *New York Times*, October 8, 2016, www.nytimes.com/2016/10/08/us/donald-trump-tape -transcript.html (accessed 9/14/17).

2. The media coverage of all of these events is reviewed in Michael Kruse and Taylor Gee, "The 37 Fatal Gaffes That Didn't Kill Donald Trump," *Politico*, September 25, 2016, www .politico.com/magazine/story/2016/09/trump-biggest-fatal-gaffes-mistakes-offensive -214289 (accessed 11/1/17).

3. The data derive from the Newspaper Association of America (now called News Media Alliance) and are available via "Newspapers Fact Sheet," Pew Research Center, June 29, 2021, www.journalism.org/fact-sheet/newspapers (accessed 9/27/21).

4. Danny Hayes and Jennifer Lawless, "The Decline of Local News and Its Effects: New Evidence from Longitudinal Data," *Journal of Politics* 80, no. 1 (January 2018): 332–36, https://doi.org/10.1086/694105.

5. 2019 RTDNA survey of Syracuse University Newhouse School of Public Communications.

6. Knight Foundation, *The State of the Industry*, https://bit.ly/3ocLBDp.

7. These figures are based on ratings for ABC, NBC, CBS, and Fox and their affiliates. All viewership numbers are available from "Network News Fact Sheet," Pew Research Center, July 13, 2021, www.pewresearch.org/journalism/fact-sheet/network-news (accessed 9/27/21).

8. Stephen J. Farnsworth and S. Robert Lichter, *The Nightly News Nightmare: Media Coverage of U.S. Presidential Elections: 1988–2008* (Lanham, MD: Rowman & Littlefield, 2010).

9. These figures are based on Arbitron ratings. Listenership numbers are available from "Public Broadcasting Fact Sheet," Pew Research Center, June 29, 2021, www.pewresearch .org/journalism/fact-sheet/public-broadcasting (accessed 9/27/21).

10. Pew Research Center, "Audio and Podcasting Fact Sheet," June 29, 2021, https://www .pewresearch.org/journalism/fact-sheet/audio-and-podcasting/ (accessed 1/5/22).

11. "Digital News Fact Sheet," Pew Research Center, July 27, 2021, www.pewresearch.org /journalism/fact-sheet/digital-news (accessed 10/28/21).

12. Robert W. McChesney and John Nichols, *The Death and Life of American Journalism: The Media Revolution Will Begin the World Again* (New York: Nation Books, 2010).

13. Yochai Benkler, Robert Faris, and Hal Roberts, *Network Propaganda: Manipulation, Disinformation, and Radicalization in American Politics* (New York: Oxford University Press, 2018).

14. Andrew M. Guess, Brendan Nyhan, and Jason Reifler, "Exposure to Untrustworthy Websites in the 2016 US Election," *Nature Human Behaviour* 4 (2020): 472–80, https://doi .org/10.1038/s41562-020-0833-x.

15. Amy Mitchell et al., "1. Pathways to News," Pew Research Center, July 7, 2016, www .journalism.org/2016/07/07/pathways-to-news (accessed 11/1/17).

16. Matthew Hindman, *The Myth of Digital Democracy* (Princeton, NJ: Princeton University Press, 2008).

17. Mason Walker and Katerina Eva Matsa, "News Consumption Across Social Media in 2021," Pew Research Center, September 20, 2021, www.pewresearch.org/journalism/2021/09/20/news-consumption-across-social-media-in-2021 (accessed 10/28/21).

18. Jaimie E. Settle, *Frenemies: How Social Media Polarizes America* (New York: Cambridge University Press, 2018).

19. Markus Prior, *Post-Broadcast Democracy: How Media Choice Increases Inequality in Political Involvement and Polarizes Elections* (New York: Cambridge University Press, 2007).

20. Kerri Militia and John Barry Ryan, "Battleground States and Local Coverage of American Presidential Campaigns," *Political Research Quarterly* 72, no. 1 (March 2019): 104–16, https://doi.org/10.1177/1065912918781752.

21. Daniel Hopkins, *The Increasingly United States: How and Why American Political Behavior Nationalized* (Chicago: University of Chicago Press, 2018).

22. Daniel J. Moskowitz, "Local News, Information, and the Nationalization of U.S. Elections," *American Political Science Review* 115, no. 1 (2021): 114–29, https://doi.org/10.1017/S0003055420000829.

23. Shanto Iyengar, *Media Politics: A Citizen's Guide*, 4th ed. (New York: W. W. Norton, 2019).

24. Brian Stelter, "When the President Travels, It's Cheaper for Reporters to Stay Home," *New York Times*, May 23, 2010, www.nytimes.com/2010/05/24/business/media/24press.html (accessed 5/22/14).

25. James T. Hamilton, *All the News That's Fit to Sell: How the Market Transforms Information into News* (Princeton, NJ: Princeton University Press, 2003).

26. Thomas E. Patterson, "News Coverage of the 2016 General Election: How the Press Failed the Voters," Harvard Kennedy School Shorenstein Center on Media, Politics and Public Policy, December 7, 2016, https://shorensteincenter.org/news-coverage-2016-general-election (accessed 11/1/17).

27. Letitia Bode et al., *Words That Matter: How the News and Social Media Shaped the 2016 Presidential Campaign* (Washington, DC: Brookings Institution Press, 2020).

28. James M. Snyder, Jr., and David Strömberg, "Press Coverage and Political Accountability," *Journal of Political Economy* 118, no. 2 (April 2010): 355–408, https://doi.org/10.1086/652903.

29. Travis N. Ridout and Glen R. Smith, "Free Advertising: How the Media Amplify Campaign Messages," *Political Research Quarterly* 61, no. 4 (December 2008): 598–608.

30. Tim Groeling, *When Politicians Attack: Party Cohesion in the Media* (New York: Cambridge University Press, 2010).

31. Thomas E. Patterson, "A Tale of Two Elections: CBS and Fox News' Portrayal of the 2020 Presidential Campaign," Harvard Kennedy School Shorenstein Center on Media, Politics and Public Policy, December 17, 2020, https://shorensteincenter.org/patterson-2020-election-coverage (accessed 10/28/21).

32. Michael I. Norton and George R. Goethals, "Spin (and Pitch) Doctors: Campaign Strategies in Televised Political Debates," *Political Behavior* 26, no. 3 (2004): 227–48, https://doi.org/10.1023/B:POBE.0000043454.25971.6a.

33. Kim Fridkin Kahn and Patrick J. Kenney, "The Slant of the News: How Editorial Endorsements Influence Campaign Coverage and Citizens' Views of Candidates," *American Political Science Review* 96, no. 2 (2002): 381–94, https://doi.org/10.1017/S0003055402000230.

34. Matthew Gentzkow and Jesse M. Shapiro, "What Drives Media Slant? Evidence from U.S. Daily Newspapers," *Econometrica* 78, no. 1 (January 2010): 35–71, https://doi.org/10.3982/ECTA7195.

35. Jonathan M. Ladd, *Why Americans Hate the Media and How It Matters* (Princeton, NJ: Princeton University Press, 2012).

36. David H. Weaver et al., *The American Journalist in the 21st Century: U.S. News People at the Dawn of a New Millennium* (New York: Routledge, 2006); Dave D'Alessio and Mike Allen, "Media Bias in Presidential Elections: A Meta-Analysis," *Journal of Communication* 50, no. 4 (December 2000): 133–56, https://doi.org/10.1111/j.1460-2466.2000.tb02866.x.

37. William P. Eveland, Jr., and Dhavan V. Shah, "The Impact of Individual and Interpersonal Factors on Perceived News Media Bias," *Political Psychology* 24, no. 1 (March 2003): 101–17, https://doi.org/10.1111/0162-895X.00318.

38. Patterson, "News Coverage of the 2016 General Election"; and "Winning the Media Campaign 2012," Pew Research Center, November 2, 2012, www.journalism.org/2012/11/02/winning-media-campaign-2012 (accessed 11/1/17).

39. *Nightline*. 1996. Transcript, August 13.

40. Danny Hayes, "The Dynamics of Agenda Convergence and the Paradox of Competitiveness in Presidential Campaigns," *Political Research Quarterly* 63, no. 3 (September 2010): 594–611, https://doi.org/10.1177/1065912909331426.

41. Markus Prior, "Media and Political Polarization," *Annual Review of Political Science* 16 (May 2013): 101–27, https://doi.org/10.1146/annurev-polisci-100711-135242.

42. Natalie Jomini Stroud, *Niche News: The Politics of News Choice* (New York: Oxford University Press, 2011).

43. Matthew Gentzkow and Jesse M. Shapiro, "Ideological Segregation Online and Offline," *Quarterly Journal of Economics* 126, no. 4: 1799–839.

44. Andrew M. Guess, "(Almost) Everything in Moderation: New Evidence on Americans' Online Media Diets," *American Journal of Political Science* 65, no. 4 (October 2021): 1007–22, https://doi.org/10.1111/ajps.12589.

45. Stefano DellaVigna and Ethan Kaplan. 2007. "The Fox News Effect: Media Bias and Voting." *Quarterly Journal of Economics* 122, 3: 1187–234; Gregory J. Martin and Ali Yurukoglu. 2017. "Bias in Cable News: Persuasion and Polarization." *American Economic Review* 107, 9: 2565–99.

46. David O. Sears and Richard Kosterman. 1994. "Political Persuasion," in *Persuasion: Psychological Insights and Perspectives*, eds. Sharon Shavitt and Timothy C. Brock. Boston: Allyn & Bacon, pp. 251–78.

47. Michael F. Meffert, Sungeun Chung, Amber J. Joiner, Leah Waks, and Jennifer Garst. 2006. "The Effects of Negativity and Motivated Information Processing during a Political Campaign." *Journal of Communication* 56, 1: 27–35.

48. John Sides and Lynn Vavreck, *The Gamble: Choice and Chance in the 2012 Presidential Election* (Princeton, NJ: Princeton University Press, 2015).

49. Shanto Iyengar and Donald R. Kinder, *News That Matters: Television and American Opinion* (Chicago: Chicago University Press, 1987).

50. Kim Fridkin Kahn and Patrick J. Kenney, *The Spectacle of U.S. Senate Campaigns* (Princeton, NJ: Princeton University Press, 1999).

51. Prior, *Post-Broadcast Democracy*.

52. Robert M. Bond et al., "A 61-Million-Person Experiment in Social Influence and Political Mobilization," *Nature* 489 (2012): 295–98, https://doi.org/10.1038/nature11421.

53. Kirk Kristofferson, Katherine White, and John Peloza, "The Nature of Slacktivism: How the Social Observability of an Initial Act of Token Support Affects Subsequent Prosocial Action," *Journal of Consumer Research* 40, no. 6 (April 2014): 1149–66, https://doi.org/10.1086/674137.

54. Thomas E. Patterson, *Out of Order* (New York: Knopf, 1993).

55. Joseph N. Cappella and Kathleen Hall Jamieson, "News Frames, Political Cynicism, and Media Cynicism," *Annals of the American Academy of Political and Social Science* 546, no. 1 (July 1996): 71–84, https://doi.org/10.1177/0002716296546001007.

56. Shanto Iyengar, Helmut Norpoth, and Kyu S. Hahn, "Consumer Demand for Election News: The Horse Race Sells," *Journal of Politics* 66, no. 1 (February 2004): 157–75, https://doi.org/10.1046/j.1468-2508.2004.00146.x.

Chapter 9

1. There is some evidence that Trump's rallies produced a short-lived bump in the polls and helped with fundraising. Other recent candidates, however, have seen a null effect associated with their rallies. See James A. Snyder, Jr., and Hasin Yousaf, "Making Rallies Great Again: The Effects of Presidential Campaign Rallies on Voter Behavior, 2008–2016" (working paper, National Bureau of Economic Research no. 28043, October 2020), https://doi.org/10.3386/w28043.

2. John Sides, Michael Tesler, and Lynn Vavreck, *Identity Crisis: The 2016 Campaign and the Battle for the Meaning of America* (Princeton, NJ: Princeton University Press, 2018).

3. Robert S. Erikson and Christopher Wlezien, *The Timeline of Presidential Elections: How Campaigns Do (and Do Not) Matter* (Chicago: University of Chicago Press, 2012); Lynn Vavreck, *The Message Matters: The Economy and Presidential Campaigns* (Princeton, NJ: Princeton University Press, 2010).

4. Brian J. Gaines, "Popular Myths about Popular Vote–Electoral College Splits," *PS: Political Science and Politics* 34, no. 1 (2001): 71–75, https://doi.org/10.1017/S1049096501000105.

5. James Adams and Samuel Merrill, III, "Candidate and Party Strategies in Two-Stage Elections Beginning with a Primary," *American Journal of Political Science* 52, no. 2 (April 2008): 344–59, https://doi.org/10.1111/j.1540-5907.2008.00316.x. See also David W. Brady, Hahrie Han, and Jeremy C. Pope, "Primary Elections and Candidate Ideology: Out of Step with the Primary Electorate?" *Legislative Studies Quarterly* 32, no. 1 (February 2007): 79–105, https://doi.org/10.3162/036298007X201994.

6. Most notably, Cohen and colleagues contend that higher-level party officials and donors remain the dominant forces in the selection of candidates. Their analysis features a case study of George W. Bush's rise in 1999, based on the preferences of the Republican Party's power brokers. See Marty Cohen et al., *The Party Decides: Presidential Nominations before and after Reform* (Chicago: University of Chicago Press, 2008).

7. See Sean A. Cain, "Polls and Elections: Leviathan's Reach? The Impact of Political Consultants on the Outcomes of the 2012 Republican Primaries and Caucuses," *Presidential Studies Quarterly* 45, no. 1 (2015): 132–56, https://doi.org/10.1111/psq.12174.

8. For a description of caucus processes and a defense of Iowa's "first in the nation" status, see David P. Redlawsk, Caroline J. Tolbert, and Todd Donovan, *Why Iowa? How Causes and Sequential Elections Improve the Presidential Nominating Process* (Chicago: University of Chicago Press, 2010).

9. In fact, most open-primary states do not have voters register by party.

10. John Sides et al., "On the Representativeness of Primary Electorates," *British Journal of Political Science* 50, no. 2 (2020): 677–85, https://doi.org/10.1017/S000712341700062X.

11. In the past, unpledged delegates have been called "superdelegates" by the Democrats. In addition, "at-large delegates" have been synonymous with unbound or unpledged delegates in the past, but now at-large delegates are sometimes constrained to support particular candidates based on the vote of their home state.

12. For a comprehensive look at how the national parties control the nominating convention (and influence the selection process), see Caitlin E. Jewitt, *The Primary Rules: Parties, Voters, and Presidential Nominations* (Ann Arbor: University of Michigan Press, 2019).

13. John H. Aldrich, *Before the Convention: Strategies and Choices in Presidential Nomination Campaigns* (Chicago: University of Chicago Press, 1980); Larry M. Bartels, *Presidential Primaries and the Dynamics of Public Choice* (Princeton, NJ: Princeton University Press, 1988); Stephen M. Utych and Cindy D. Kam, "Viability, Information Seeking, and Vote Choice," *Journal of Politics* 76, no. 1 (January 2014): 152–66. https://doi.org/10.1017/S0022381613001126.

14. William G. Mayer and Andrew E. Busch, *The Front-Loading Problem in Presidential Nominations* (Washington, DC: Brookings Institution Press, 2004).

15. Richard Ben Cramer, *What It Takes: The Way to the White House* (New York: Vintage Publishing, 1993).

16. Christopher J. Devine and Kyle C. Kopko, *Do Running Mates Matter? The Influence of Vice Presidential Candidates in Presidential Elections* (Topeka: Kansas University Press, 2020).

17. Lee Sigelman and Paul J. Wahlbeck, "The 'Veepstakes': Strategic Choice in Presidential Running Mate Selection," *American Political Science Review* 91, no. 4 (1997): 855–64, https://doi.org/10.2307/2952169.

18. Matthew D. Atkinson et al., "(Where) Do Campaigns Matter? The Impact of National Party Convention Location," *The Journal of Politics* 76, no. 4 (2014): 1045–58, https://doi.org/10.1017/S0022381614000413.

19. See Erikson and Wlezien, *Timeline.*

20. Thomas M. Holbrook, *Do Campaigns Matter?* (Thousand Oaks, CA: Sage Publications, 1996).

21. Benjamin Lauderdale and Douglas Rivers, "Beware the Phantom Swings: Why Dramatic Bounces in the Polls Aren't Always What They Seem," *YouGov*, November 1, 2016, https://today.yougov.com/news/2016/11/01/beware-phantom-swings-why-dramatic-swings-in-the-p (accessed 8/25/21). See also Andrew Gelman et al., "The Mythical Swing Voter," *Quarterly Journal of Political Science* 11, no. 1 (2016): 103–30, http://dx.doi.org/10.1561/100.00015031.

22. See the discussion citing Thomas Holbrook and Gerhard Peters in Willie James Inman, "Convention Polling 'Bounces' Aren't What They Used to Be," Newsy, August 17, 2020, www.newsy.com/stories/experts-say-post-convention-bounce-lower-than-decades-past (accessed 8/25/21).

23. On the electoral college advantage in 1980–2016, see Robert S. Erikson, Karl Sigman, and Linan Yao, "Electoral College Bias and the 2020 Presidential Election," *Proceedings of the National Academy of Sciences* 117, no. 45 (2020): 27940–44, https://doi.org/10.1073/pnas.2013581117. On the Republican advantage in 2020, see Ian Millhiser, "The Enormous Advantage that the Electoral College Gives Republicans, in One Chart," Vox, January 11, 2021, www.vox.com/2021/1/11/22224700/electoral-college-joe-biden-donald-trump-bias-four-points-one-chart (accessed 9/1/21) and Geoffrey Skelley, "Even Though Biden Won, Republicans Enjoyed the Largest Electoral College Edge in 70 Years. Will That Last?" FiveThirtyEight, January 19, 2021, https://fivethirtyeight.com/features/even-though-biden-won-republicans-enjoyed-the-largest-electoral-college-edge-in-70-years-will-that-last (accessed 9/1/21).

24. There is also the matter of the constitutionality of this agreement. Article I, Section 10, Clause 3 of the Constitution forbids states from "enter[ing] into any Agreement or Compact with another State."

25. For poll results, see Bradley Jones, "Majority of Americans Continue to Favor Moving Away from Electoral College," Pew Research Center, January 27, 2021, www.pewresearch.org/fact-tank/2021/01/27/majority-of-americans-continue-to-favor-moving-away-from-electoral-college (accessed 9/1/21).

26. Daron R. Shaw, *The Race to 270: The Electoral College and the Campaign Strategies of 2000 and 2004* (Chicago: University of Chicago Press, 2006).

27. Shaw, *The Race to 270*.

28. David R. Mayhew, "Incumbency Advantage in U.S. Presidential Elections: The Historical Record," *Political Science Quarterly* 123, no. 2 (2008): 201–28, https://doi.org/10.1002/j.1538 -165X.2008.tb00622.x; James E. Campbell, *The American Campaign: U.S. Presidential Campaigns and the National Vote* (College Station, TX: Texas A&M University Press, 2000).

29. Douglas A. Hibbs, Jr., "Bread and Peace Voting in U.S. Presidential Elections," *Public Choice* 104 (2000): 149–80, https://doi.org/10.1023/A:1005292312412.

30. Lynn Vavreck, *The Message Matters: The Economy and Presidential Campaigns* (Princeton, NJ: Princeton University Press, 2009).

31. See John Sides, Chris Tausanovitch, and Lynn Vavreck, *The Bitter End: The 2020 Presidential Campaign and the Challenge to American Democracy* (Princeton, NJ: Princeton University Press, 2022).

32. Seth Masket, "How Much Did COVID-19 Affect the 2020 Election?" FiveThirtyEight, January 27, 2021, https://fivethirtyeight.com/features/how-much-did-covid-19-affect-the -2020-election (accessed 9/1/21).

33. Christopher H. Achen and Larry M. Bartels, *Democracy for Realists: Why Elections Do Not Produce Responsive Government* (Princeton, NJ: Princeton University Press, 2016).

34. Marianna Sotomayor and Mike Memoli, "Florida Offers Key Test of Biden Team's Pandemic Campaign Plan," NBC News, September 15, 2020, www.nbcnews.com/politics /2020-election/florida-offers-key-test-biden-team-s-pandemic-campaign-plan-n1240109 (accessed 9/1/21).

35. As noted in Chapter 2, in early September of 1988, an independent conservative group aired an advertisement emphasizing Dukakis's role (as Massachusetts governor) in a statewide prison furlough program. The ad showed an image of a Black man, Willie Horton, who escaped while on furlough and subsequently raped and killed a White woman. The ad's appeal to racial fears has made it notorious in American political history as the exemplar of "dog whistle" politics. The Bush campaign disavowed the ad and argued that it had no prior knowledge of its airing.

36. Emmett H. Buell, Jr., and Lee Sigelman, *Attack Politics: Negativity in Presidential Campaigns Since 1960* (Topeka: University Press of Kansas, 2008). See also Shaw, *The Race to 270*. We should also point out that presidential campaigns do not adhere to the general strategic dictum articulated in Chapter 5, which argues that incumbents should not attack (and thereby bring attention to) the opposition. This assumes that the opposing candidate will be ignored by most voters unless the incumbent pays attention to them. This is obviously not the case in a presidential race, in which the opponent is going to be known by all. Under these circumstances, an incumbent's campaign *needs* to define the opposition.

37. For a comparison of 2020 with 2012 and 2016, see Wesleyan Media Project, "Political Ads in 2020: Fast and Furious," March 23, 2021, https://mediaproject.wesleyan.edu/2020 -summary-032321 (accessed 9/1/21). For discussions of incumbents' incentives to "go negative," see Buell and Sigelman, *Attack Politics*.

38. Alan S. Gerber et al., "How Large and Long-Lasting Are the Persuasive Effects of Televised Campaign Ads? Results from a Randomized Field Experiment," *American Political Science Review* 105, no. 1 (February 2011): 135–50, https://doi.org/10.1017/S000305541000047X; Daron R. Shaw and James G. Gimpel, "What If We Randomized the Governor's Schedule? Evidence on Campaign Appearance Effects from a Texas Field Experiment," *Political Communication* 29, no. 2 (2012): 137–59, https://doi.org/10.1080/10584609.2012.671231.

39. See Kathleen Hall Jamieson and David S. Birdsell, *Presidential Debates: The Challenge of Creating an Informed Electorate* (New York: Oxford University Press, 1990).

40. CNN's "instant polls" showed Biden winning the first debate, 60 percent to 28 percent, and the final debate, 53 percent to 39 percent. See Jennifer Agiesta, "CNN Poll: Biden Wins Final Presidential Debate," CNN, October 23, 2020, www.cnn.com/2020/10/22/politics /cnn-poll-final-presidential-debate/index.html (accessed 9/1/21).

41. Kim L. Fridkin et al., "Spinning Debates: The Impact of the News Media's Coverage of the Final 2004 Presidential Debate," *The International Journal of Press/Politics* 13, no. 1 (January 2008): 29–51, https://doi.org/10.1177/1940161207312677; see also Richard Johnston, Michael G. Hagen, and Kathleen Hall Jamieson, *The 2000 Presidential Election and the Foundations of Party Politics* (New York: Cambridge University Press, 2004).

42. Mitchell S. McKinney and Benjamin R. Warner, "Do Presidential Debates Matter? Examining a Decade of Campaign Debate Effects," *Argumentation and Advocacy*, 49, no. 4 (2013): 238–58, https://doi.org/10.1080/00028533.2013.11821800. See also Erikson and Wlezien, *Timeline*.

43. SSRS, "CNN October 22, 2020 Debate Reaction Poll (Poll 14)," CNN, October 22, 2020, http://cdn.cnn.com/cnn/2020/images/10/23/october.22.debate.reaction.poll.pdf (accessed 9/1/21).

44. Thomas Holbrook, *Do Campaigns Matter?* (Beverly Hills, CA: Sage Publishing, 1996).

45. Estimates based on AP VoteCast/Fox News Voter Analysis surveys.

46. Daniel M. Thompson et al., "Universal Vote-by-Mail Has No Impact on Partisan Turnout or Vote Share," *Proceedings of the National Academy of Sciences* 117, no. 25 (2020): 14052–56, https://doi.org/10.1073/pnas.2007249117.

47. Charlotte Alter, "Inside Joe Biden Campaign's Plan to Get Out the Vote Online," *Time*, November 2, 2020, https://time.com/5906237/inside-joe-biden-campaigns-plan-to-get-out -the-vote-online (accessed 9/1/21).

48. Donald P. Green and Alan S. Gerber, *Get Out the Vote! How to Increase Voter Turnout*, 4th ed. (Washington, DC: Brookings Institution Press, 2019).

49. See Sides et al., "Representativeness"; John G. Geer, "Assessing the Representativeness of Electorates in Presidential Primaries," *American Journal of Political Science* 32, no. 4 (November 1988): 929–45, https://doi.org/10.2307/2111195.

50. Marion Just, Tami Buhr, and Ann Crigler, "Shifting the Balance: Journalist versus Candidate Communication in the 1996 Presidential Campaign," in *Campaign Reform: Insights and Evidence*, ed. Larry M. Bartels and Lynn Vavreck (Ann Arbor: University of Michigan Press, 2000).

51. For data from the 2000 campaign, see Johnston, Hagen, and Jamieson, *The 2000 Presidential Election*.

52. Larry M. Bartels, "Campaign Quality: Standards for Evaluation, Benchmarks for Reform," in *Campaign Reform: Insights and Evidence*, ed. Larry M. Bartels and Lynn Vavreck (Ann Arbor: University of Michigan Press, 2000); Thomas M. Holbrook, "Political Learning from Presidential Debates," *Political Behavior* 21, no. 1 (March 1999): 67–89, https://doi.org /10.1023/A:1023348513570.

53. Darshan J. Goux and David A. Hopkins, "The Empirical Implications of Electoral College Reform," *American Politics Research* 36, no. 6 (November 2008): 857–79, https://doi .org/10.1177/1532673X08324213.

54. James G. Gimpel, Karen M. Kaufmann, and Shanna Pearson-Merkowitz, "Battleground States versus Blackout States: The Behavioral Implications of Modern Presidential Campaigns," *Journal of Politics* 69, no. 3 (August 2007): 786–97, https://doi.org/10.1111/j.1468 -2508.2007.00575.x; Keena Lipsitz, "The Consequences of Battleground and 'Spectator' State Residency for Political Participation," *Political Behavior* 31, no. 2 (2009): 187–209, https://doi .org/10.1007/s11109-008-9068-7.

Chapter 10

1. Jesse Paul, "Health Care, the Environment, Coronavirus: How the Pandemic Has Become a Top Election-Year Issue in Colorado," *The Colorado Sun*, September 16, 2020, https://coloradosun.com/2020/09/16/coronavirus-campaign-issue-colorado-2020-election (accessed 10/28/21).

2. Sandra Fish and John Frank, "5 Numbers that Show Why 2020 Was Never Going to Be an Easy Year for Cory Gardner in Colorado," *The Colorado Sun*, October 28, 2020, https://coloradosun.com/2020/10/28/2014-election-cory-gardner-2020-colorado (accessed 10/28/21).

3. Mark D. Brewer, "The Political Survival of Susan Collins," Brookings, December 22, 2020, www.brookings.edu/blog/fixgov/2020/12/22/the-political-survival-of-susan-collins (accessed 10/28/21).

4. Steve Bickerstaff, *Lines in the Sand: Congressional Redistricting in Texas and the Downfall of Tom DeLay* (Austin: University of Texas Press, 2007).

5. Seth McKee and Daron Shaw, "Redistricting in Texas: Institutionalizing Republican Ascendancy," in *Redistricting in the New Millennium*, ed. Peter F. Galderisi (Lanham, MD: Lexington Books, 2005), 298.

6. Jonathan Rausch and Raymond La Raja, "Re-engineering politicians: How activist groups choose our candidates—long before we vote," Brookings, December 7, 2017, www.brookings.edu/research/re-engineering-politicians-how-activist-groups-choose-our-politicians-long-before-we-vote (accessed 7/14/21).

7. Rausch and La Raja, "Re-engineering Politicians."

8. Emily Cochrane, "Justice Democrats Helped Make Ocasio-Cortez. They're Already Eying Their Next Targets," *New York Times*, February 23, 2019, www.nytimes.com/2019/02/23/us/politics/justice-democrats-ocasio-cortez.html (accessed 11/1/21).

9. Nicholas Carnes and Meredith L. Sadin, "The 'Mill Worker's Son' Heuristic: How Voters Perceive Politicians from Working-Class Families—and How They Really Behave in Office," *The Journal of Politics* 77, no. 1 (January 2015): 285–98, https://doi.org/10.1086/678530; Adam Bonica, "Why Are There So Many Lawyers in Congress?" *Legislative Studies Quarterly* 45, no. 2 (May 2020): 253–89, https://doi.org/10.1111/lsq.12265.

10. Danielle M. Thomsen and Aaron S. King, "Women's Representation and the Gendered Pipeline to Power," *American Political Science Review* 114, no. 4 (November 2020): 989–1000, https://doi.org/10.1017/S0003055420000404.

11. "Incumbent Advantage," OpenSecrets.org, April 1, 2021, www.opensecrets.org/elections-overview/incumbent-advantage (accessed 7/14/21).

12. "Fundraising Totals: Who Raised the Most?" OpenSecrets.org, April 1, 2021, www.opensecrets.org/elections-overview/fundraising-totals?cycle=2020&type=C2&view=topraise (accessed 7/14/21).

13. "In-State vs. Out-of-State," OpenSecrets.org, March 22, 2021, www.opensecrets.org/elections-overview/in-state-vs-out-of-state (accessed 7/14/21).

14. "Top Self-Funding Candidates," OpenSecrets.org, April 1, 2021, www.opensecrets.org/elections-overview/top-self-funders (accessed 7/15/21).

15. "2020 Outside Spending, by Race," OpenSecrets.org, January 7, 2021, www.opensecrets.org/outsidespending/summ.php?cycle=2020&disp=R&pty=N&type=A (accessed 7/15/21); "Elections Overview," OpenSecrets.org, April 1, 2021, www.opensecrets.org/elections-overview (accessed 7/15/21).

16. "2020 Outside Spending, by Race."

17. Caitlin Jewitt and Sarah Treul, "Ideological Primaries and Their Influence in Congress," in *Routledge Handbook of Primary Elections*, ed. Robert G. Boatright (New York: Routledge, 2018).

18. Nathaniel Rakich, "Ed Markey Won, But It's Still Been a Rough Year for Incumbents," FiveThirtyEight, September 2, 2020, https://fivethirtyeight.com/features/ed-markey-won -but-its-still-been-a-rough-year-for-incumbents (accessed 10/28/21).

19. Austin Bussing, Maura McDonald, and Sarah Treul, "Making the Right Bet," in *Routledge Handbook of Primary Elections*, ed. Robert G. Boatright (New York: Routledge, 2018).

20. Jordan Kujala, "Donors, Primary Elections, and Polarization in the United States," *American Journal of Political Science* 64, no. 3 (July 2020): 587–602, https://doi.org/10.1111 /ajps.12477.

21. Benjamin Highton and Walter J. Stone, "Reconciling Candidate Extremism and Spatial Voting," *Legislative Studies Quarterly* 46, no. 2 (May 2021): 585–613, https://doi.org/10 .1111/lsq.12289.

22. Caitlyn Kim, "The Lauren Boebert-Diane Mitsch Bush Race in Colorado's 3rd District Appears to Be Cast out of Larger Presidential Politics," Colorado Public Radio, October 29, 2020, www.cpr.org/2020/10/29/lauren-boebert-diane-mitsch-bush-colorado-cd3-race -presidential-politics (accessed 10/28/21).

23. *Edward M. Kennedy Institute Civics Survey*, version 1 (2017), Edward M. Kennedy Institute for the United States Senate; *Gallup News Service Poll: Values and Beliefs*, version 2 (2013), Roper Center for Public Opinion Research.

24. James N. Druckman, Martin J. Kifer, and Michael Parkin, "Campaign Communications in U.S. Congressional Elections," *American Political Science Review* 103, no. 3 (2009): 343–66, https://doi.org/10.1017/S0003055409990037.

25. Gary C. Jacobson and Jamie L. Carson, *The Politics of Congressional Elections*, 10th ed. (New York: Rowman & Littlefield, 2020).

26. Kim L. Fridkin and Patrick J. Kenney, *The Changing Face of Representation: The Gender of U.S. Senators and Constituent Communications* (Ann Arbor: University of Michigan Press, 2014).

27. Nichole M. Bauer, "Untangling the Relationship between Partisanship, Gender Stereo-types, and Support for Female Candidates," *Journal of Women, Politics & Policy* 39, no. 1 (2018): 1–25, https://doi.org/10.1080/1554477X.2016.1268875.

28. Stephen Ansolabehere, James M. Snyder, Jr., and Charles Stewart III, "Candidate Position-ing in U.S. House Elections," *American Journal of Political Science* 45, no. 1 (January 2001): 136–59, https://doi.org/10.2307/2669364; Barry C. Burden, "Candidate Positioning in U.S. Congressional Elections," *British Journal of Political Science* 34, no. 2 (April 2004): 211–27.

29. Frances E. Lee, *Insecure Majorities: Congress and the Perpetual Campaign* (Chicago: University of Chicago Press, 2016).

30. Jamie L. Carson, Jason M. Roberts, and Rachel Porter, "Congress and the Nationaliza-tion of Congressional Elections," in *New Directions in Congressional Politics*, ed. Jamie L. Carson and Michael S. Lynch (New York: Routledge, 2020), 87–105.

31. Erika Franklin Fowler et al., "Political Advertising Online and Offline," *American Political Science Review* 115, no. 1 (2021): 130–49, https://doi.org/10.1017/S0003055420000696.

32. Cody Carlson, "Local Congressional Candidate Walking across NY 23rd District," WENY News, September 27, 2017, www.weny.com/story/36462799/local-congressional -candidate-walking-across-ny-23rd-district (accessed 10/25/17).

33. "DCCC Announces Members of 2021–2022 Frontline Program," DCCC, March 1, 2021, https://dccc.org/dccc-announces-members-of-2021-2022-frontline-program (accessed 10/28/21).

34. Jacobson and Carson, *Politics of Congressional Elections*, 61.

35. Steven D. Levitt and Catherine D. Wolfram, "Decomposing the Sources of Incumbency Advantage in the U.S. House," *Legislative Studies Quarterly* 22, no. 1 (1997): 45–60, https://doi

.org/10.2307/440290; Gary W. Cox and Jonathan N. Katz, "Why Did the Incumbency Advantage in U.S. House Elections Grow?" *American Journal of Political Science* 40, no. 2 (1996): 478–97, https://doi.org/10.2307/2111633.

36. Jacobson and Carson, *Politics of Congressional Elections*.

37. "Incumbent Advantage."

38. Morris P. Fiorina, *Congress: Keystone of the Washington Establishment* (New Haven, CT: Yale University Press, 1977).

39. Jacobson and Carson, *Politics of Congressional Elections*, 64.

40. Anthony King, *Running Scared: Why America's Politicians Campaign Too Much and Govern Too Little* (New York: Free Press, 1997).

41. Keena Lipsitz, *Competitive Elections and the American Voter* (Philadelphia: University of Pennsylvania Press, 2016).

42. See for example Thomas L. Brunell and Justin Buchler, "Ideological Representation and Competitive Congressional Elections," *Electoral Studies* 28, no. 3 (September 2009): 448–57, https://doi.org/10.1016/j.electstud.2009.05.003.

43. Shigeo Hirano and James M. Snyder, Jr., "Primary Elections and the Quality of Elected Officials," *Quarterly Journal of Political Science* 9, no. 4 (2014): 473–500, https://doi.org/10.1561/100.00013096.

44. "2020 Primary Election Competitiveness in State and Federal Government," Ballotpedia, August 13, 2021, https://ballotpedia.org/2020_primary_election_competitiveness_in_state_and_federal_government (accessed 9/3/21).

45. Philip Bump, "What Problem Is Steyer's Term Limit Proposal Trying to Fix?" *Washington Post*, January 13, 2020, www.washingtonpost.com/politics/2020/01/13/what-problem-is-steyers-term-limit-proposal-hoping-fix (accessed 11/10/21).

46. Jamie L. Carson and Michael H. Crespin, "The Effect of State Redistricting Methods on Electoral Competition in United States House of Representatives Races," *State Politics & Policy Quarterly* 4, no. 4 (December 2004): 455–69, https://doi.org/10.1177/153244000400400406.

47. Michael P. McDonald, "Redistricting and Competitive Districts," in *The Marketplace of Democracy: Electoral Competition and American Politics*, ed. Michael P. McDonald and John Samples (Washington, DC: Brookings Institution Press, 2006), 222–44; Michael McDonald, "Legislative Redistricting," in *Democracy in the States: Experiments in Election Reform*, ed. Bruce E. Cain, Todd Donovan, and Caroline J. Tolbert (Washington, DC: Brookings Institution Press, 2008), 147–60.

48. McDonald, "Legislative Redistricting," 150.

49. David R. Mayhew, *Congress: The Electoral Connection*, 2nd ed. (New Haven, CT: Yale University Press, 2004).

50. David Brady and Morris Fiorina, "Congress in the Era of the Permanent Campaign," in *The Permanent Campaign and Its Future*, ed. Norman J. Ornstein and Thomas E. Mann (Washington, DC: American Enterprise Institute, 2000), 141.

Chapter 11

1. Alexia Fernández Campbell, "How the Teachers Strike Gave Democrats a Win in Deep Red Kentucky," Vox, November 6, 2019, www.vox.com/identities/2019/11/6/20951459/kentucky-democrat-beshear-bevin-teachers (accessed 10/28/21).

2. See www.followthemoney.org/show-me?s=KY&y=2019&c-r-ot=G&gro=c-t-id (accessed 8/31/21).

3. Dave Bangert, "'Pain' or Civic Hero? Sizing Up the Man Who Would be West Lafayette Mayor," *Journal & Courier*, October 26, 2019, www.jconline.com/story/news/2019/10/26/pain -civic-hero-sizing-up-man-who-would-west-lafayette-mayor/4007254002 (accessed 10/28/21).

4. John P. Pelissero, "The Political Environment of Cities in the Twenty-First Century," in *Cities, Politics, and Policy: A Comparative Analysis*, ed. John P. Pelissero (Washington, DC: CQ Press, 2003), 10.

5. "Ballotpedia's 2020 Recall Analysis," Ballotpedia, July 27, 2021, https://ballotpedia.org /Ballotpedia%27s_2020_Recall_Analysis (accessed 8/31/21).

6. Andrea McAtee and Jennifer Wolak, "Why People Decide to Participate in State Politics," *Political Research Quarterly* 64, no. 1 (March 2011): 45–58, https://doi.org/10.1177/10659 12909343581.

7. Brian F. Schaffner, Matthew Streb, and Gerald Wright, "Teams without Uniforms: The Nonpartisan Ballot in State and Local Elections," *Political Research Quarterly* 54, no. 1 (March 2001): 7–30, https://doi.org/10.2307/449205.

8. Timothy B. Krebs and John P. Pelissero, "City Councils," in *Cities, Politics, and Policy: A Comparative Analysis*, ed. John P. Pelissero (Washington, DC: CQ Press, 2005), 172.

9. Jessica Trounstine and Melody E. Valdini, "The Context Matters: The Effects of Single-Member versus At-Large Districts on City Council Diversity," *American Journal of Political Science* 52, no. 3 (July 2008): 554–69, https://doi.org/10.1111/j.1540-5907.2008.00329.x; Carolyn Abott and Asya Magazinnik, "At-Large Elections and Minority Representation in Local Government," *American Journal of Political Science* 64, no. 3 (July 2020): 717–33, https://doi.org/10.1111/ajps.12512.

10. Krebs and Pelissero, "City Councils," 170.

11. Thomas M. Holbrook and Aaron C. Weinschenk, "Campaigns, Mobilization, and Turnout in Mayoral Elections," *Political Research Quarterly* 67, no. 1 (March 2014): 42–55, https://doi.org/10.1177/1065912913494018. See also Melissa Marschall and John Lappie, "Turnout in Local Elections: Is Timing Really Everything?" *Election Law Journal* 17, no. 3 (September 2018): 221–33, https://doi.org/10.1089/elj.2017.0462.

12. Justin de Benedictis-Kessner, "Off-Cycle and Out of Office: Election Timing and the Incumbency Advantage," *Journal of Politics* 80, no. 1 (January 2018): 119–32, https://doi.org /10.1086/694396.

13. Chris Warshaw, "Local Elections and Representation in the United States," *Annual Review of Political Science* 22 (May 2019): 461–79, https://doi.org/10.1146/annurev-polisci -050317-071108.

14. Kevin Arceneaux and Robert M. Stein, "Who Is Held Responsible When Disaster Strikes? The Attribution of Responsibility for a Natural Disaster in an Urban Election," *Journal of Urban Affairs* 28, no. 1 (January 2006): 43–53, https://doi.org/10.1111/j.0735-2166.2006.00258.x.

15. J. Eric Oliver, with Shang E. Ha and Zachary Callen, *Local Elections and the Politics of Small-Scale Democracy* (Princeton, NJ: Princeton University Press, 2012).

16. Scott L. Althaus and Todd C. Trautman, "The Impact of Television Market Size on Voter Turnout in American Elections," *American Politics Research* 36, no. 6 (November 2008): 824–56, https://doi.org/10.1177/1532673X08317767.

17. Erika Franklin Fowler et al., "Does Local News Measure Up?" *Stanford Law & Policy Review* 18, no. 2 (May 2007): 411; Martin Kaplan, Kenneth Goldstein, and Matthew Hale, "Local TV News Coverage of the 2002 General Election," Norman Lear Center, https:// learcenter.org/wp-content/uploads/2014/10/LCLNAReport2.pdf (accessed 6/13/17).

18. Gregory J. Martin and Joshua McCrain, "Local News and National Politics," *American Political Science Review* 113, no. 2 (2019): 372–84, https://doi.org/10.1017/S000305541 8000965.

19. Danny Hayes and Jennifer L. Lawless, *News Hole: The Demise of Local Journalism and Political Engagement* (New York: Cambridge University Press, 2021).

20. This estimate is from Warshaw, "Local Elections." See also Jessica Trounstine, "Evidence of a Local Incumbency Advantage," *Legislative Studies Quarterly* 36, no. 2 (May 2011): 255–80, https://doi.org/10.1111/j.1939-9162.2011.00013.x; and Jens Hainmueller, Andrew B. Hall, and James M. Snyder, Jr., "Assessing the External Validity of Election RD Estimates: An Investigation of the Incumbency Advantage," *Journal of Politics* 77, no. 3 (July 2015): 707–20, https://doi.org/10.1086/681238.

21. Warshaw, "Local Elections."

22. Shiro Kuriwaki, "Ticket Splitting in a Nationalized Era" (working paper, October 31, 2020), https://doi.org/10.31235/osf.io/bvgz3.

23. Seth E. Masket and Jeffrey B. Lewis, "A Return to Normalcy? Revisiting the Effects of Term Limits on Competitiveness and Spending in California Assembly Elections," *State Politics and Policy Quarterly* 7, no. 1 (Spring 2007): 20–38, https://doi.org/10.1177/153244000700700102; Scot Schraufnagel and Karen Halperin, "Term Limits, Electoral Competition, and Representational Diversity: The Case of Florida," *State Politics and Policy Quarterly* 6, no. 4 (December 2006): 448–62, https://doi.org/10.1177/153244000600600405.

24. These numbers are from a 2015 legislative staff census. "Size of State Legislative Staff," National Conference of State Legislatures, May 18, 2021, www.ncsl.org/research/about-state-legislatures/staff-change-chart-1979-1988-1996-2003-2009.aspx (accessed 12/6/18).

25. City councils also vary in their level of professionalization, although there have been fewer studies of how professionalization affects campaign strategies in local elections.

26. "Full- and Part-Time Legislatures," National Conference of State Legislatures, July 28, 2021, www.ncsl.org/research/about-state-legislatures/full-and-part-time-legislatures.aspx#average (accessed 9/2/21).

27. John M. Carey, Richard G. Niemi, and Lynda W. Powell, "Incumbency and the Probability of Reelection in State Legislative Elections," *Journal of Politics* 62, no. 3 (August 2000): 671–700, https://doi.org/10.1111/0022-3816.00029; Robert E. Hogan, "Challenger Emergence, Incumbent Success, and Electoral Accountability in State Legislative Elections," *Journal of Politics* 66, no. 4 (November 2004): 1283–303, https://doi.org/10.1111/j.0022-3816.2004.00300.x.

28. Thomas M. Holbrook and Raymond J. La Raja, "Parties and Elections," in *Politics in the American States: A Comparative Analysis*, 10th ed., ed. Virginia Gray, Russell L. Hanson, and Thad Kousser (Washington, DC: CQ Press, 2013), 73.

29. Douglas D. Roscoe and Shannon Jenkins, *Local Party Organizations in the 21st Century* (Albany, NY: SUNY Press, 2015), 69.

30. Roscoe and Jenkins, *Local Party Organizations*, 69; James L. Gibson et al., "Assessing Party Organizational Strength," *American Journal of Political Science* 27, no. 2 (May 1983): 216, https://doi.org/10.2307/2111015.

31. Seth E. Masket, *No Middle Ground: How Informal Party Organizations Control Nominations and Polarize Legislatures* (Ann Arbor: University of Michigan Press, 2009).

32. Marc Meredith, "Exploiting Friends-and-Neighbors to Estimate Coattail Effects," *American Political Science Review* 107, no. 4 (2013): 742–65, https://doi.org/10.1017/S0003055413000439.

33. "Straight Ticket Voting," National Conference of State Legislatures, June 25, 2021, www.ncsl.org/research/elections-and-campaigns/straight-ticket-voting.aspx (accessed 6/25/21).

34. Joel Sievert and Seth C. McKee, "Nationalization in U.S. Senate and Gubernatorial Elections," *American Politics Research* 47, no. 5 (September 2019): 1055–80, https://doi.org/10.1177/1532673X18792694.

35. The number from 1910 to 1938 is from Stephen Ansolabehere et al., "The Decline of Competition in U.S. Primary Elections," in *The Marketplace of Democracy: Electoral Competition and American Politics*, ed. Michael P. McDonald and John Samples (Washington, DC: Brookings Institution Press, 2006). Calculated from Table 4.1, 87. The number from 1992 to 2016 is from Steve Rogers, "Accountability in American Legislatures" (unpublished manuscript), PDF. www.dropbox.com/s/sicyhgw2pavke0n/AAL%20-%20Chapter%202%20-%20Challenger.pdf?dl=0.

36. "Major Party Candidates with Major Party Competition in the 2020 State Legislative Elections," Ballotpedia, January 22, 2021, https://ballotpedia.org/Major_party_candidates_with_major_party_competition_in_the_November_2020_state_legislative_elections (accessed 9/3/21).

37. "2020 Election Analysis: Uncontested Races by State," Ballotpedia, December 16, 2020, https://ballotpedia.org/2020_election_analysis:_Uncontested_races_by_state (accessed 9/3/21).

38. Rogers, "Accountability."

39. Charles S. Bullock III, "Introduction: Southern Politics in the Twenty-first Century," in *The New Politics of the Old South: An Introduction to Southern Politics*, 4th ed., ed. Charles S. Bullock III and Mark J. Rozell (Lanham, MD: Rowman & Littlefield, 2010), 1–26.

40. Sievert and McKee, "Nationalization."

41. Daniel J. Hopkins, *The Increasingly United States: How and Why American Political Behavior Nationalized* (Chicago: University of Chicago Press, 2018); Sievert and McKee, "Nationalization"; Warshaw, "Local Elections."

42. Steven Rogers, "National Forces in State Legislative Elections," *ANNALS of the American Academy of Political and Social Science* 667, no. 1 (September 2016): 207–25.

43. James D. King and Jeffrey E. Cohen, "What Determines a Governor's Popularity?" *State Politics and Policy Quarterly* 5, no. 3 (September 2005): 225–47, https://doi.org/10.1177/153244000500500302.

44. Mason Walker, "U.S. Newsroom Employment Has Fallen 26% Since 2008," Pew Research Center, July 13, 2021, www.pewresearch.org/fact-tank/2021/07/13/u-s-newsroom-employment-has-fallen-26-since-2008 (accessed 10/31/21); Katerina Eva Matsa and Jan Lauren Boyles, "America's Shifting Statehouse Press," Pew Research Center, July 10, 2014, www.pewresearch.org/journalism/2014/07/10/americas-shifting-statehouse-press (accessed 10/31/21).

45. Hopkins, *Increasingly United States*, 68.

46. Daniel J. Moskowitz, "Local News, Information, and the Nationalization of U.S. Elections," *American Political Science Review* 115, no. 1 (2021): 114–29, https://doi.org/10.1017/S0003055420000829.

47. Oliver, Ha, and Callen, *Local Elections*, 33.

48. Warshaw, "Local Elections."

49. Hopkins, *Increasingly United States*, 153–59; Joseph L. Sutherland, "Three Essays on the Study of Nationalization with Automated Content Analysis" (doctoral dissertation, Columbia University, 2020), https://doi.org/10.7916/d8-wf0x-6k97.

50. "States with Initiative or Referendum," Ballotpedia, https://ballotpedia.org/States_with_initiative_or_referendum (accessed 10/31/21).

51. See "2020 Ballot Measures," Ballotpedia, https://ballotpedia.org/2020_ballot_measures (accessed 10/31/21).

52. Richard L. Hasen, "Rethinking the Unconstitutionality of Contribution and Expenditure Limits in Ballot Measure Campaigns," *Southern California Law Review* 78, no. 4 (2005): 885–926.

53. Quoted in Dennis W. Johnson, *No Place for Amateurs: How Political Consultants Are Reshaping American Democracy*, 2nd ed. (New York: Routledge, 2007), 201.

54. Todd Rogers and Joel A. Middleton, "Are Ballot Initiative Outcomes Influenced by the Campaigns of Independent Groups? A Precinct-Randomized Field Experiment Showing That They Are," *Political Behavior* 37, no. 3 (September 2015): 567–93, https://doi.org/10 .1007/s11109-014-9282-4.

55. See, for example, Soren T. Anderson, Ioana Marinescu, and Boris Shor, "Can Pigou at the Polls Stop Us Melting the Poles?" (working paper, National Bureau of Economic Research no. 26146, August 2019), https://doi.org/10.3386/w26146.

56. See "California 2010 Ballot Propositions," Ballotpedia, https://ballotpedia.org/California _2020_ballot_propositions (accessed 10/31/21).

57. See "Judicial Election Methods by State," Ballotpedia, https://ballotpedia.org/Judicial _election_methods_by_state (accessed 10/31/21).

58. James J. Sample et al., *The New Politics of Judicial Elections 2000–2009: Decade of Change* (New York: Brennan Center for Justice, 2010), www.brennancenter.org/our-work/research -reports/new-politics-judicial-elections-2000-2009-decade-change (accessed 9/4/21); Douglas Keith and Patrick Berry, *The Politics of Judicial Elections, 2017–18* (New York: Brennan Center for Justice, 2019), www.brennancenter.org/our-work/research-reports/politics-judicial -elections-2017-18 (accessed 9/4/21).

59. Alicia Bannon, Cathleen Lisk, and Peter Hardin, *Who Pays for Judicial Races?* (New York: Brennan Center for Justice, 2017), www.brennancenter.org/sites/default/files/publications /Politics_of_Judicial_Elections_Final.pdf (accessed 12/7/18).

60. The 2002, 2004 and 2016 figures are from Bannon, Lisk, and Hardin, *Who Pays*. The 2018 figures were calculated by the authors from the 2018 Wesleyan Media Project television advertising dataset.

61. Deanna Paul, "In Texas, 17 New Judges Bring 'Black Girl Magic' to Courthouses," *Washington Post*, January 2, 2019, www.washingtonpost.com/nation/2019/01/02/texas-new -judges-bring-black-girl-magic-courthouses (accessed 10/31/21).

62. Adam Bonica and Maya Sen, *The Judicial Tug of War: How Lawyers, Politicians, and Ideological Incentives Shape the American Judiciary* (New York: Cambridge University Press, 2020).

63. Quoted in Sample et al., *The New Politics*, 9.

64. *Caperton v. A. T. Massey Coal Co.*, 129 S. Ct. 2252 (2009).

65. Brandice Canes-Wrone, Tom S. Clark, and Jee-Kwang Park, "Judicial Independence and Retention Elections," *Journal of Law, Economics, and Organization* 28, no. 2 (June 2012): 211–34, https://doi.org/10.1093/jleo/ewq009.

66. Sarah F. Anzia, "Partisan Power Play: The Origins of Local Election Timing as an American Political Institution," *Studies in American Political Development* 26, no. 1 (2012): 24–49, https://doi.org/10.1017/S0898588X11000149.

67. Sarah F. Anzia, "Election Timing and the Electoral Influence of Interest Groups," *Journal of Politics* 73, no. 2 (April 2011): 412–27, https://doi.org/10.1017/S0022381611000028; Vladimir Kogan, Stéphane Lavertu, and Zachary Peskowitz, "Election Timing, Electorate Composition, and Policy Outcomes: Evidence from School Districts," *American Journal of Political Science* 62, no. 3 (July 2018): 637–51, https://doi.org/10.1111/ajps.12359.

68. Michael T. Hartney and Sam D. Hayes, "Off-Cycle and Out of Sync: How Election Timing Influences Political Representation," *State Politics and Policy Quarterly* (2021): 1–20, https://doi.org/10.1017/spq.2020.6.

69. Brian F. Schaffner, Jesse H. Rhodes, and Raymond L. La Raja, *Hometown Inequality: Race, Class, and Representation in American Local Politics* (New York: Cambridge University Press, 2020).

70. Zoltan Hajnal, *America's Uneven Democracy: Race, Turnout, and Representation in City Politics* (New York: Cambridge University Press, 2010).

71. Katherine Levine Einstein, David M. Glick, and Maxwell Palmer, *Neighborhood Defenders* (New York: Cambridge University Press, 2019).

72. Zoltan L. Hajnal, Vladimir Kogan, and George Markarian, "Who Votes: City Election Timing and Voter Composition," *American Political Science Review* (2021): 1–10, https://doi.org/10.1017/S0003055421000915; Schaffner, Rhodes, and La Raja, *Hometown Inequality.*

73. Steven Rogers, "Electoral Accountability for State Legislative Roll Calls and Ideological Representation," *American Political Science Review* 111, no. 3 (2017): 555–71, https://doi.org/10.1017/S0003055417000156.

74. Seth Masket, *No Middle Ground: How Informal Party Organizations Control Nominations and Polarize Legislatures* (Ann Arbor: University of Michigan Press, 2011).

75. Hopkins, *Increasingly United States.*

76. Jessica Trounstine, *Political Monopolies in American Cities: The Rise and Fall of Bosses and Reformers* (Chicago: University of Chicago Press, 2008), chap. 5.

77. David Hughes, "New-Style Campaigns in State Supreme Court Retention Elections," *State Politics and Policy Quarterly* 19, no. 2 (2019): 127–54, https://doi.org/10.1177/1532440018807256; Melissa Gann Hall and Chris W. Bonneau, "Mobilizing Interest: The Effects of Money on Citizen Participation in State Supreme Court Elections," *American Journal of Political Science* 52, no. 3 (July 2008): 457–70, https://doi.org/10.1111/j.1540-5907.2008.00323.x.

78. James L. Gibson, *Electing Judges: The Surprising Effects of Campaigning on Judicial Legitimacy* (Chicago: University of Chicago Press, 2012).

Chapter 12

1. "Partisan Antipathy: More Intense, More Personal," Pew Research Center, October 10, 2019, www.pewresearch.org/politics/2019/10/10/partisan-antipathy-more-intense-more-personal (accessed 11/19/21).

2. Lori Robertson, "Sanders' Shaky Turnout Claim," FactCheck.org, June 6, 2016, www.factcheck.org/2016/06/sanders-shaky-turnout-claim (accessed 11/10/21).

3. Daron R. Shaw and John R, Petrocik, *The Turnout Myth: Voting Rates and Partisan Outcomes in American National Elections* (New York: Oxford University Press, 2020), 213.

4. Kay Lehman Schlozman, Sidney Verba, and Henry E. Brady, *The Unheavenly Chorus: Unequal Political Voice and the Broken Promise of American Democracy* (Princeton, NJ: Princeton University Press, 2012).

5. Andrea Louise Campbell, *How Policies Make Citizens: Senior Political Activism and the American Welfare State* (Princeton, NJ: Princeton University Press, 2003).

6. It is important to calculate the voter turnout rate based on those who are eligible to vote as opposed to those of voting age. Many adults in the United States are not citizens and some cannot vote because they are in prison or have been convicted of a felony. For example, if the 2020 turnout rate had been calculated based on the voting-age population, it would have been just 62 percent.

7. Gary C. Jacobson, "Extreme Referendum: Donald Trump and the 2018 Midterm Elections," *Political Science Quarterly* 134, no. 1 (2019): 9–38, https://doi.org/10.1002/polq.12866.

8. Donald P. Green and Jennifer K. Smith, "Professionalization of Campaigns and the Secret History of Collective Action Problems," *Journal of Theoretical Politics* 15, no. 3 (July 2003): 321–39, https://doi.org/10.1177/0951692803015003005.

9. This analysis was based on data obtained from the International Institute for Democracy and Electoral Assistance. Only the most recent presidential election since 2010 was used for each country. Countries with populations smaller than 1 million or that were considered to be "not free" in the year of the election by Freedom House were excluded from the analysis.

10. Only the most recent parliamentary election from 2007 to 2018 that was not held at the same time as a presidential election was used for each country.

11. Jeffrey A. Karp, "Electoral Systems, Party Mobilisation and Political Engagement," *Australian Journal of Political Science* 47, no. 1 (2012): 71–89, https://doi.org/10.1080/10361146.2011.643165.

12. "Voter Turnout Database," International Institute for Democracy and Electoral Assistance, www.idea.int/data-tools/data/voter-turnout (accessed 10/15/21).

13. André Blais, "Turnout in Elections," in *Oxford Handbook of Political Behavior*, ed. Russell J. Dalton and Hans-Dieter Klingemann (Oxford: Oxford University Press, 2007), 621–35.

14. Blais, "Turnout," 627.

15. Sidney Verba, Kay Lehman Schlozman, and Henry E. Brady, *Voice and Equality: Civic Voluntarism in American Politics* (Cambridge, MA: Harvard University Press, 1995), 358.

16. Verba, Schlozman, and Brady, *Voice and Equality*.

17. Eric R. Hansen and Andrew Tyner, "Educational Attainment and Social Norms of Voting," *Political Behavior* 43, no. 2 (June 2021): 711–35, https://doi.org/10.1007/s11109-019-09571-8.

18. D. Sunshine Hillygus, "The Missing Link: Exploring the Relationship between Higher Education and Political Engagement," *Political Behavior* 27, no. 1 (March 2005): 25–47, https://doi.org/10.1007/s11109-005-3075-8.

19. Cindy D. Kam and Carl L. Palmer, "Reconsidering the Effects of Education on Political Participation," *Journal of Politics* 70, no. 3 (July 2008): 612–31, https://doi.org/10.1017/S0022381608080651; Steven Tenn, "The Effect of Education on Voter Turnout," *Political Analysis* 15, no. 4 (Autumn 2007): 446–64, https://doi.org/10.1093/pan/mpm012; Adam J. Berinsky and Gabriel S. Lenz, "Education and Political Participation: Exploring the Causal Link," *Political Behavior* 33, no. 3 (September 2011): 357–73, https://doi.org/10.1007/s11109-010-9134-9.

20. Hillygus, "The Missing Link."

21. Verba, Schlozman, and Brady, *Voice and Equality*, 314–16.

22. James C. Scott, *Weapons of the Weak: Everyday Forms of Peasant Resistance* (New Haven, CT: Yale University Press, 1985).

23. Raymond E. Wolfinger and Steven J. Rosenstone, *Who Votes?* (New Haven, CT: Yale University Press, 1980), 23–26.

24. Markus Prior, *Hooked: How Politics Captures People's Interest* (New York: Cambridge University Press, 2019).

25. Jeffery J. Mondak and Karen D. Halperin, "A Framework for the Study of Personality and Political Behaviour," *British Journal of Political Science* 38, no. 2 (April 2008): 335–62, https://doi.org/10.1017/S0007123408000173.

26. Aaron C. Weinschenk et al., "New Evidence on the Link between Genes, Psychological Traits, and Political Engagement," *Politics and the Life Sciences* 38, no. 1 (Spring 2019): 1–13, https://doi.org/10.1017/pls.2019.3.

27. Jennifer Jerit and Jason Barabas, "Revisiting the Gender Gap in Political Knowledge," *Political Behavior* 39, no. 4 (December 2017): 817–38, https://doi.org/10.1007/s11109-016

-9380-6; Dietlind Stolle and Elisabeth Gidengil, "What Do Women Really Know? A Gendered Analysis of Varieties of Political Knowledge," *Perspectives on Politics* 8, no. 1 (2010): 93–109, https://doi.org/10.1017/S1537592709992684.

28. Bert N. Bakker, David Nicolas Hopmann, and Mikael Persson, "Personality Traits and Party Identification over Time," *European Journal of Political Research* 54, no. 2 (May 2015): 197–215, https://doi.org/10.1111/1475-6765.12070; Alan S. Gerber et al., "Personality and the Strength and Direction of Partisan Identification," *Political Behavior* 34, no. 4 (December 2012): 653–88, https://doi.org/10.1007/s11109-011-9178-5.

29. Alan I. Abramowitz and Steven W. Webster, "Negative Partisanship: Why Americans Dislike Parties But Behave Like Rabid Partisans," *Political Psychology* 39, no. S1 (February 2018): 119–35, https://doi.org/10.1111/pops.12479.

30. Alexa Bankert, "Negative and Positive Partisanship in the 2016 U.S. Presidential Elections," *Political Behavior* 43 (December 2021): 1467–85, https://doi.org/10.1007/s11109-020-09599-1.

31. Andrew B. Hall and Daniel M. Thompson, "Who Punishes Extremist Nominees? Candidate Ideology and Turning Out the Base in U.S. Elections," *American Political Science Review* 112, no. 3 (August 2018): 509–24, https://doi.org/10.1017/S0003055418000023.

32. Ryan D. Enos and Anthony Fowler, "Aggregate Effects of Large-Scale Campaigns on Voter Turnout," *Political Science Research and Methods* 6, no. 4 (October 2018): 733–51, https://doi.org/10.1017/psrm.2016.21; Steven J. Rosenstone and John Mark Hansen, *Mobilization, Participation, and Democracy in America* (New York: Macmillan, 1993).

33. Rosenstone and Hansen, *Mobilization*.

34. Jonathan S. Krasno and Donald P. Green, "Do Televised Presidential Ads Increase Voter Turnout? Evidence from a Natural Experiment," *Journal of Politics* 70, no. 1 (January 2008): 245–61, https://doi.org/10.1017/S0022381607080176.

35. Richard R. Lau, Lee Sigelman, and Ivy Brown Rovner, "The Effects of Negative Political Campaigns: A Meta-Analytic Reassessment," *Journal of Politics* 69, no. 4 (November 2007): 1176–209, https://doi.org/10.1111/j.1468-2508.2007.00618.x.

36. Donald P. Green and Alan S. Gerber, *Get Out the Vote: How to Increase Voter Turnout*, 4th ed. (Washington, DC: Brookings Institution Press, 2019), 128.

37. Green and Gerber, *Get Out the Vote*.

38. Green and Gerber, *Get Out the Vote*, 84.

39. Holly Teresi and Melissa R. Michelson, "Wired to Mobilize: The Effect of Social Networking Messages on Voter Turnout," *The Social Science Journal* 52, no. 2 (2015): 195–204, https://doi.org/10.1016/j.soscij.2014.09.004.

40. Ryan D. Enos, Anthony Fowler, and Lynn Vavreck, "Increasing Inequality: The Effect of GOTV Mobilization on the Composition of the Electorate," *Journal of Politics* 76, no. 1 (January 2014): 273–88, https://doi.org/10.1017/S0022381613001308.

41. Kevin Arceneaux and David W. Nickerson, "Who Is Mobilized to Vote? A Re-Analysis of 11 Randomized Field Experiments," *American Journal of Political Science* 53, no. 1 (January 2009): 1–16, https://doi.org/10.1111/j.1540-5907.2008.00354.x.

42. Meredith Rolfe, *Voter Turnout: A Social Theory of Political Participation* (Cambridge, UK: Cambridge University Press, 2012).

43. David W. Nickerson, "Is Voting Contagious? Evidence from Two Field Experiments," *American Political Science Review* 102, no. 1 (February 2008): 49–57, https://doi.org/10.1017/S0003055408080039; Edward Fieldhouse and David Cutts, "The Companion Effect: Household and Local Context and the Turnout of Young People," *Journal of Politics* 74, no. 3 (July 2012): 856–69, https://doi.org/10.1017/S0022381612000345.

44. Robert M. Bond et al., "A 61-Million-Person Experiment in Social Influence and Political Mobilization," *Nature* 489, no. 7415 (2012): 295–98, https://doi.org/10.1038/nature11421.

45. Alan S. Gerber, Donald P. Green, and Christopher W. Larimer, "Social Pressure and Voter Turnout: Evidence from a Large-Scale Field Experiment," *American Political Science Review* 102, no. 1 (February 2008): 33–48, https://doi.org/10.1017/S000305540808009X; Costas Panagopoulos, "Affect, Social Pressure and Prosocial Motivation: Field Experimental Evidence of the Mobilizing Effects of Pride, Shame and Publicizing Voting Behavior," *Political Behavior* 32, no. 3 (September 2010): 369–86, https://doi.org/10.1007/s11109-010-9114-0.

46. M. Kent Jennings, Laura Stoker, and Jake Bowers, "Politics across Generations: Family Transmission Reexamined," *Journal of Politics* 71, no. 3 (July 2009): 782–99, https://doi.org/10.1017/S0022381609090719.

47. Verba, Schlozman, and Brady, *Voice and Equality*; Molly W. Andolina et al., "Habits from Home, Lessons from School: Influences on Youth Civic Development," *PS: Political Science and Politics* 36, no. 2 (April 2003): 275–80, https://doi.org/10.1017/S104909650300221X; Hugh McIntosh, Daniel Hart, and James Youniss, "The Influence of Family Political Discussion on Youth Civic Development: Which Parent Qualities Matter?" *PS: Political Science and Politics* 40, no. 3 (July 2007): 495–99, https://doi.org/10.1017/S1049096507070758.

48. Daniel A. McFarland and Reuben J. Thomas, "Bowling Young: How Youth Voluntary Associations Influence Adult Political Participation," *American Sociological Review* 71, no. 3 (June 2006): 401–25, https://doi.org/10.1177/000312240607100303; Jacquelynne S. Eccles and Bonnie L. Barber, "Student Council, Volunteering, Basketball, or Marching Band: What Kind of Extracurricular Involvement Matters?" *Journal of Adolescent Research* 14, no. 1 (January 1999): 10–43, https://doi.org/10.1177/0743558499141003; Paul Allen Beck and M. Kent Jennings, "Pathways to Participation," *American Political Science Review* 76, no. 1 (March 1982): 94–108, https://doi.org/10.1017/S000305540018606X.

49. McFarland and Thomas, "Bowling Young."

50. Virginia Sapiro, "Not Your Parents' Political Socialization: Introduction for a New Generation," *Annual Review of Political Science* 7 (June 2004): 1–23, https://doi.org/10.1146/annurev.polisci.7.012003.104840.

51. James G. Gimpel, J. Celeste Lay, and Jason E. Shuknecht, *Cultivating Democracy: Civic Environments and Political Socialization in America* (Washington, DC: Brookings Institution Press, 2003).

52. Bernard L. Fraga, *The Turnout Gap: Race, Ethnicity, and Political Inequality in a Diversifying America* (New York: Cambridge University Press, 2018).

53. James G. Gimpel, Joshua J. Dyck, and Daron R. Shaw, "Registrants, Voters and Turnout Variability across Neighborhoods," *Political Behavior* 26, no. 4 (December 2004): 343–75, https://doi.org/10.1007/s11109-004-0900-4; Robert Huckfeldt and John Sprague, *Citizens, Politics, and Social Communication: Information and Influence in an Election Campaign* (New York: Cambridge University Press, 1995).

54. Richard Fry, "Millenials Approach Baby Boomers as America's Largest Generation in the Electorate," Pew Research Center, April 23, 2018, www.pewresearch.org/fact-tank/2018/04/03/millennials-approach-baby-boomers-as-largest-generation-in-u-s-electorate (accessed 9/17/21).

55. Robert D. Putnam, *Bowling Alone: The Collapse and Revival of American Community* (New York: Simon & Schuster, 2000), 228.

56. Victoria J. Rideout, Ulla G. Foehr, and *Generation M2: Media in the Lives of 8- to 18-Year-Olds* (Menlo Park, CA: Kaiser Family Foundation, 2010), 2, www.kff.org/entmedia/upload/8010.pdf (accessed 7/17/17).

57. For a discussion of felon and ex-felon participation, see Jeff Manza and Christopher Uggen, *Locked Out: Felon Disenfranchisement and American Democracy* (New York: Oxford University Press, 2008), chaps. 5 and 7. For a discussion of youth political participation, see Cliff Zukin et al., *A New Engagement? Political Participation, Civic Life, and the Changing American Citizen* (New York: Oxford University Press, 2006).

58. Benjamin Highton, "Voter Registration and Turnout in the United States," *Perspectives on Politics* 2, no. 3 (September 2004): 507–15, https://doi.org/10.1017/S1537592704040307.

59. Raymond E. Wolfinger, Benjamin Highton, and Megan Mullin, "How Postregistration Laws Affect the Turnout of Citizens Registered to Vote," *State Politics & Policy Quarterly* 5, no. 1 (Spring 2005): 1–23, https://doi.org/10.1177/153244000500500101.

60. Paul Gronke, Eva Galanes-Rosenbaum, and Peter A. Miller, "Early Voting and Turnout," *PS: Political Science and Politics* 40, no. 4 (October 2007): 639–45, https://doi.org/10.1017/S1049096507071028.

61. Barry C. Burden et al., "Election Laws, Mobilization, and Turnout: The Unanticipated Consequences of Election Reform," *American Journal of Political Science* 58, no. 1 (January 2014): 95–109, https://doi.org/10.1111/ajps.12063.

62. R. Michael Alvarez, Stephen Ansolabehere, and Catherine H. Wilson, "Election Day Registration in the United States: How One-Step Voting Can Change the Composition of the American Electorate" (working paper, Caltech/MIT Voting Technology Project no. 5, November 30, 2008), http://vote.caltech.edu/working-papers/5 (accessed 9/20/17).

63. Eric McGhee et al., "How Did the Voter's Choice Act Affect Turnout in 2018?" *California Journal of Politics and Policy* 12, no. 1 (2020), https://doi.org/10.5070/P2cjpp1150410.

64. Stephen Ansolabehere and Eitan Hersh, "Validation: What Big Data Reveal about Survey Misreporting and the Real Electorate," *Political Analysis* 20, no. 4 (Autumn 2012): 437–59, https://doi.org/10.1093/pan/mps023.

65. Verba, Schlozman, and Brady, *Voice and Equality.*

66. John B. Holbein and D. Sunshine Hillygus, *Making Young Voters: Converting Civic Attitudes into Civic Action* (New York: Cambridge University Press, 2020).

67. Benjamin Highton, "Residential Mobility, Community Mobility, and Electoral Participation," *Political Behavior* 22, no. 2 (June 2000): 109–20, https://doi.org/10.1023/A:1006651130422; M. Margaret Conway, *Political Participation in the United States*, 3rd ed. (Washington, DC: CQ Press, 2000).

68. John M. Strate et al., "Life Span Civic Development and Voting Participation," *American Political Science Review* 83, no. 2 (June 1989): 443–64, https://doi.org/10.2307/1962399; Philip E. Converse and Richard Niemi, "Non-Voting among Young Adults in the United States," in *Political Parties and Political Behavior*, 2nd ed., ed. William J. Crotty, Donald M. Freeman, and Douglas S. Gatlin (Boston: Allyn & Bacon, 1971).

69. Benjamin Highton and Raymond E. Wolfinger, "The First Seven Years of the Political Life Cycle," *American Journal of Political Science* 45, no. 1 (January 2001): 202–9, https://doi.org/10.2307/2669367.

70. Laura Stoker and M. Kent Jennings, "Life-Cycle Transitions and Political Participation: The Case of Marriage," *American Political Science Review* 89, no. 2 (1995): 421–33.

71. M. Kent Jennings and Laura Stoker, "The Persistence of the Past: The Class of 1965 Turns Fifty," (paper presented at the Annual Meeting of the Midwest Political Science Association, Chicago, IL, April 1999); Rosenstone and Hansen, *Mobilization.*

72. Seth C. McKee, M. V. Hood III, and David Hill, "Achieving Validation: Barack Obama and Black Turnout in 2008," *State Politics & Policy Quarterly* 12, no. 1 (March 2012): 3–22, https://doi.org/10.1177/1532440011433591; Bernard L. Fraga, "Candidates or Districts? Reevaluating the Role of Race in Voter Turnout," *American Journal of Political Science* 60, no. 1 (January 2016): 97–122, https://doi.org/10.1111/ajps.12172; for an opposing view, see Ansolabehere and Hersh, "Validation."

73. Tasha S. Philpot, Daron R. Shaw, and Ernest B. McGowen, "Winning the Race: Black Voter Turnout in the 2008 Presidential Election," *Public Opinion Quarterly* 73, no. 5 (2009): 995–1022, https://doi.org/10.1093/poq/nfp083.

74. Daniel Q. Gillion, *The Loud Minority: Why Protests Matter in American Democracy* (Princeton, NJ: Princeton University Press, 2020).

75. Natalie Masuoka, Kumar Ramanathan, and Jane Junn, "New Asian American Voters: Political Incorporation and Participation in 2016," *Political Research Quarterly* 72, no. 4 (December 2019): 991–1003, https://doi.org/10.1177/1065912919843342.

76. "Table 9. Reported Voting and Registration, by Marital Status, Age, and Sex: November 2020," U.S. Census Bureau, April 2021, www.census.gov/data/tables/time-series/demo/voting-and-registration/p20-585.html (accessed 9/24/21).

77. Sidney Verba, Nancy Burns, and Kay Lehman Schlozman, "Knowing and Caring about Politics: Gender and Political Engagement," *Journal of Politics* 59, no. 4 (November 1997): 1051–72, https://doi.org/10.2307/2998592; Stacy G. Ulbig and Carolyn L. Funk, "Conflict Avoidance and Political Participation," *Political Behavior* 21, no. 3 (September 1999): 265–82, https://doi.org/10.1023/A:1022087617514.

78. David E. Campbell and Christina Wolbrecht, "See Jane Run: Women Politicians as Role Models for Adolescents," *Journal of Politics* 68, no. 2 (2006): 233–47, https://doi.org/10.1111/j.1468-2508.2006.00402.x. See also Lonna Rae Atkeson, "Not All Cues Are Created Equal: The Conditional Impact of Female Candidates on Political Engagement," *Journal of Politics* 65, no. 4 (November 2003): 1040–61, https://doi.org/10.1111/1468-2508.t01-1-00124.

79. Henry E. Brady, Sidney Verba, and Kay Lehman Schlozman, "Beyond SES: A Resource Model of Political Participation," *American Political Science Review* 89, no. 2 (June 1995): 271–94, https://doi.org/10.2307/2082425.

80. Evelyn M. Simien, *Black Feminist Voices in Politics* (Albany, NY: SUNY Press, 2006).

81. Vladimir E. Medenica and Matthew Fowler, "The Intersectional Effects of Diverse Elections on Validated Turnout in the 2018 Midterm Elections," *Political Research Quarterly* 73, no. 4 (December 2020): 988–1003, https://doi.org/10.1177/1065912920945781.

82. Nadia E. Brown, "Political Participation of Women of Color: An Intersectional Analysis," *Journal of Women, Politics & Policy* 35, no. 4 (2014): 315–48, https://doi.org/10.1080/1554477X.2014.955406.

83. Katelyn E. Stauffer and Bernard L. Fraga, "Contextualizing the Gender Gap in Voter Turnout," *Politics, Groups, and Identities* (2021): 1–8, https://doi.org/10.1080/21565503.2021.1893195.

84. Jack Citrin, Eric Schickler, and John Sides, "What If Everyone Voted? Simulating the Impact of Increased Turnout in Senate Elections," *American Journal of Political Science* 47, no. 1 (January 2003): 75–90, https://doi.org/10.1111/1540-5907.00006.

85. Citrin, Schickler, and Sides, "What If Everyone Voted?"

86. John D. Griffin and Brian Newman, "Are Voters Better Represented?" *Journal of Politics* 67, no. 4 (November 2005): 1206–27, https://doi.org/10.1111/j.1468-2508.2005.00357.x.

87. Wolfinger and Rosenstone, *Who Votes?*, 109.

88. Andrew Gelman, Gary King, and W. John Boscardin, "Estimating the Probability of Events That Have Never Occurred: When Is Your Vote Decisive?" *Journal of the American Statistical Association* 93, no. 441 (March 1998): 1–9; Donald P. Green and Ian Shapiro, *Pathologies of Rational Choice Theory: A Critique of Applications in Political Science* (New Haven, CT: Yale University Press, 1994), chap. 4; John A. Ferejohn and Morris P. Fiorina, "The Paradox of Not Voting: A Decision Theoretic Analysis," *American Political Science Review* 68, no. 2 (June 1974): 525–36, https://doi.org/10.1017/S0003055400117368; William H. Riker and Peter C. Ordeshook, "A Theory of the Calculus of Voting," *American Political Science Review* 62, no. 1 (March 1968): 25–42, https://doi.org/10.2307/1953324; Anthony Downs, *An Economic Theory of Democracy* (New York: Harper & Row, 1957).

89. Nickerson, "Is Voting Contagious?"

90. Griffin and Newman, "Are Voters Better Represented?"; Larry Bartels, *Unequal Democracy: The Political Economy of the New Gilded Age* (Princeton, NJ: Princeton University Press, 2010).

Chapter 13

1. See Ashley Parker et al., "How Trump's Erratic Behavior and Failure on Coronavirus Doomed His Reelection," *Washington Post*, November 7, 2020, www.washingtonpost.com /elections/interactive/2020/trump-pandemic-coronavirus-election (accessed 11/30/21).

2. All data are from 2020 exit polls conducted by Edison Research.

3. FiveThirtyEight.com pegged Clinton's probability of election at about 0.70 right before the election, while The Upshot had it at about 0.99.

4. Angus Campbell et al., *The American Voter* (Chicago: University of Chicago Press, 1960).

5. Christopher Ojeda and Peter K. Hatemi, "Accounting for the Child in the Transmission of Party Identification," *American Sociological Review* 80, no. 6 (December 2015): 1150–74, https://doi.org/10.1177/0003122415606101.

6. See, for example, data referenced in Amanda Cox, "How Birth Year Influences Political Views," *New York Times*, July 7, 2014, www.nytimes.com/interactive/2014/07/08/upshot /how-the-year-you-were-born-influences-your-politics.html (accessed 11/30/21).

7. Scott Keeter, Juliana Menasce Horowitz, and Alec Tyson, "Gen Dems: The Party's Advantage among Young Voters Widens," Pew Research Center, April 28, 2008, www.pewresearch .org/2008/04/28/gen-dems-the-partys-advantage-among-young-voters-widens (accessed 11/30/17).

8. John R. Petrocik, "Measuring Party Support: Leaners are not Independents," *Electoral Studies* 28, no. 4 (December 2009): 562–72, https://doi.org/10.1016/j.electstud.2009.05 .022. See also Bruce E. Keith et al., *The Myth of the Independent Voter* (Berkeley: University of California Press, 1992).

9. Philip E. Converse, "Information Flow and the Stability of Partisan Attitudes," *Public Opinion Quarterly* 26, no. 4 (Winter 1962): 578–99, https://doi.org/10.1086/267129; Diana C. Mutz, "Cross-Cutting Social Networks: Testing Democratic Theory in Practice," *American Political Science Review* 96, no. 1 (March 2002): 111–26.

10. Gary C. Jacobson, "Donald Trump and the Parties: Impeachment, Pandemic, Protest, and Electoral Politics in 2020," *Electoral Studies* 50, no. 4 (December 2020): 762–95, https://doi.org /10.1111/psq.12682. See also Larry M. Bartels, "Partisanship and Voting Behavior, 1952–1996," *American Journal of Political Science* 44, no. 1 (January 2000): 35–50, https://doi.org/10.2307 /2669291.

11. Bernard R. Berelson, Paul F. Lazarsfeld, and William N. McPhee, *Voting: A Study of Opinion Formation in a Presidential Campaign* (Chicago: University of Chicago Press, 1954); Paul F. Lazarsfeld, Bernard Berelson, and Hazel Gaudet, *The People's Choice: How the Voter Makes Up His Mind in a Presidential Campaign* (New York: Columbia University Press, 1948). Also see Steven E. Finkel, "Reexamining the 'Minimal Effects' Model in Recent Presidential Campaigns," *Journal of Politics* 55, no. 1 (February 1993): 1–21, https://doi.org /10.2307/2132225.

12. See Allison P. Anoll, "What Makes a Good Neighbor? Race, Place, and Norms of Political Participation," *American Political Science Review* 112, no. 3 (August 2018): 494–508, https://doi .org/10.1017/S0003055418000175. See also Ismail K. White and Cheryl N. Laird, *Steadfast Democrats: How Social Forces Shape Black Political Behavior* (Princeton, NJ: Princeton University Press, 2020).

13. David McCullough, *Truman* (New York: Simon & Schuster, 1993).

14. See for example Ray C. Fair, "The Effect of Economic Events on Votes for President," *Review of Economics and Statistics* 60, no. 2 (April 1978): 159–73, https://doi.org/10.2307

/1924969; Michael S. Lewis-Beck and Tom W. Rice, *Forecasting Elections* (Washington, DC: CQ Press, 1992); Edward R. Tufte, *Political Control of the Economy* (Princeton, NJ: Princeton University Press, 1978).

15. Christopher R. Ellis and Joseph Daniel Ura, "Polarization and the Decline of Economic Voting in American National Elections," *Social Science Quarterly* 102, no. 1 (January 2021): 83–89, https://doi.org/10.1111/ssqu.12881.

16. Morris P. Fiorina, *Retrospective Voting in American National Elections* (New Haven, CT: Yale University Press, 1981).

17. Donald R. Kinder and D. Roderick Kiewiet, "Sociotropic Politics: The American Case," *British Journal of Political Science* 11, no. 2 (April 1981): 129–61, https://doi.org/10.1017 /S0007123400002544. For a more recent study based on Swedish data, see Andrew J. Healy, Mikael Persson, and Erik Snowberg, "Digging into the Pocketbook: Evidence on Economic Voting from Income Registry Data Matched to a Voter Survey," *American Political Science Review* 111, no. 4 (November 2017): 771–85, https://doi.org/10.1017 /S0003055417000314.

18. Christopher H. Achen and Larry M. Bartels, *Democracy for Realists: Why Elections Do Not Produce Responsive Government* (Princeton, NJ: Princeton University Press, 2017). See also Larry M. Bartels, *Unequal Democracy: The Political Economy of the New Gilded Age* (Princeton, NJ: Princeton University Press, 2008). For a differing point of view, see Christopher Wlezien and Robert S. Erikson, "Temporal Horizons and Presidential Election Forecasts," *American Politics Research* 24, no. 4 (October 1996): 492–505, https://doi.org/10.1177/1532673X 9602400406.

19. Michael S. Lewis-Beck et al., *The American Voter Revisited* (Ann Arbor: University of Michigan Press, 2008), chap. 8.

20. Gabriel S. Lenz, "Learning and Opinion Change, Not Priming: Reconsidering the Priming Hypothesis," *American Journal of Political Science* 53, no. 4 (October 2009): 821–37, https://doi.org/10.1111/j.1540-5907.2009.00403.x.

21. Tessa M. Ditonto, Allison J. Hamilton, and David P. Redlawsk, "Gender Stereotypes, Information Search, and Voting Behavior in Political Campaigns," *Political Behavior* 36, no. 2 (June 2014): 335–58, https://doi.org/10.1007/s11109-013-9232-6.

22. Carol K. Sigelman et al., "Black Candidates, White Voters: Understanding Racial Bias in Political Perceptions," *American Journal of Political Science* 39, no. 1 (February 1995): 243–65, https://doi.org/10.2307/2111765; Monika L. McDermott, "Race and Gender Cues in Low-Information Elections," *Political Research Quarterly* 51, no. 4 (December 1998): 895–918, https://doi.org/10.1177/106591299805100403; Jack Citrin, Donald Phillip Green, and David O. Sears, "White Reactions to Black Candidates: When Does Race Matter?" *Public Opinion Quarterly* 32, no. 4 (Spring 1990): 588–606, https://doi.org/10.1086 /269185.

23. David O. Sears et al., "Is It Really Racism?: The Origins of White Americans' Opposition to Race-Targeted Policies," *Public Opinion Quarterly* 61, no. 1 (May 1997): 16–53, https://doi .org/10.1086/297785.

24. Benjamin Highton, "White Voters and African American Candidates for Congress," *Political Behavior* 26, no. 1 (March 2004): 1–25, https://doi.org/10.1023/B:POBE.0000022341 .98720.9e.

25. Sebastian Jäckle et al., "A Catwalk to Congress? Appearance-Based Effects in the Elections to the U.S. House of Representatives 2016," *American Politics Research* 48, no. 4 (July 2020): 427–41, https://doi.org/10.1177/1532673X19875710. Also see Christopher Y. Olivola, Dustin Tingley, and Alexander Todorov, "Republican Voters Prefer Candidates Who Have Conservative-Looking Faces: New Evidence from Exit Polls," *Political Psychology* 39, no. 5 (October 2018): 1157–71, https://doi.org/10.1111/pops.12489.

26. Chappell Lawson et al., "Looking Like a Winner: Candidate Appearance and Electoral Success in New Democracies," *World Politics* 62, no. 4 (October 2010): 561–93, https://doi .org/10.1017/S0043887110000195; Donald R. Kinder et al., "Presidential Prototypes," *Political Behavior* 2, no. 4 (December 1980): 315–37, https://doi.org/10.1007/BF00990172.

27. Danny Hayes, "Candidate Qualities through a Partisan Lens: A Theory of Trait Ownership," *American Journal of Political Science* 49, no. 4 (October 2005): 908–23, https://doi.org /10.1111/j.1540-5907.2005.00163.x.

28. Scott J. Basinger, "Scandals and Congressional Elections in the Post-Watergate Era," *Political Research Quarterly* 66, no. 2 (June 2013): 385–98, https://doi.org/10.1177/1065912912451144; Tim Fackler and Tse-min Lin, "Political Corruption and Presidential Elections, 1929–1992," *Journal of Politics* 57, no. 4 (November 1995): 971–93, https://doi.org/10.2307/2960398; Daron R. Shaw, "A Study of Presidential Campaign Event Effects from 1952 to 1992," *Journal of Politics* 61, no. 2 (May 1999): 387–422, https://doi.org/10.2307/2647509.

29. Other specific negative trait perceptions have been damaging to particular candidates in presidential elections. See Gabriel S. Lenz, *Follow the Leader? How Voters Respond to Politicians' Policies and Performance* (Chicago: University of Chicago Press, 2012).

30. Hayes, "Candidate Qualities."

31. Matthew D. Atkinson, Ryan D. Enos, and Seth J. Hill, "Candidate Faces and Election Outcomes: Is the Face–Vote Correlation Caused by Candidate Selection?" *Quarterly Journal of Political Science* 4, no. 3 (2009): 229–49, https://doi.org/10.1561/100.00008062.

32. Chris W. Bonneau and Damon M. Cann, "Campaign Spending, Diminishing Marginal Returns, and Financial Restrictions in Judicial Elections," *Journal of Politics* 73, no. 4 (October 2011): 1267–80, https://doi.org/10.1017/S0022381611000934.

33. For evidence that net ad effects can influence localized results, see John Sides, Lynn Vavreck, and Christopher Warshaw, "The Effect of Television Advertising in U.S. Elections," *American Political Science Review* (2021), https://doi.org/10.1017/S000305542100112X.

34. Richard Johnston, Michael G. Hagen, and Kathleen Hall Jamieson, *The 2000 Presidential Election and the Foundations of Party Politics* (Cambridge, UK: Cambridge University Press, 2004).

35. Daron R. Shaw, *The Race to 270: The Electoral College and the Campaign Strategies of 2000 and 2004* (Chicago: University of Chicago Press, 2006).

36. James E. Campbell, "When Have Presidential Campaigns Decided Election Outcomes?" *American Politics Research* 29, no. 5 (September 2001): 437–60, https://doi.org/10.1177 /1532673X01029005002.

37. Gary C. Jacobson, "Measuring Campaign Spending Effects in U.S. House Elections," in *Capturing Campaign Effects*, ed. Henry E. Brady and Richard Johnston (Ann Arbor: University of Michigan Press, 2006): 199–220; Laurel Elms and Paul M. Sniderman, "Informational Rhythms of Incumbent Dominated Congressional Elections," in *Capturing Campaign Effects*, ed. Brady and Johnston, 221–41.

38. Gary C. Jacobson, "It's Nothing Personal: The Decline of the Incumbency Advantage in US House Elections," *Journal of Politics* 77, no. 3 (July 2015): 861–73, https://doi.org/10.1086 /681670.

39. Gary C. Jacobson and Jamie L. Carson, *The Politics of Congressional Elections*, 9th ed. (New York: Rowman and Littlefield, 2015). Amounts are in 2014 dollars and thus adjusted for inflation. Updated through 2020 by reference to spending data from www.fec.gov.

40. Anthony Gierzynski and David Breaux, "Legislative Elections and the Importance of Money," *Legislative Studies Quarterly* 21, no. 3 (August 1996): 337–57, https://doi.org/10.2307 /440248; Chris W. Bonneau, "The Effects of Campaign Spending in State Supreme Court Elections," *Political Research Quarterly* 60, no. 3 (September 2007): 489–99, https://doi.org/10

.1177/1065912907305680; Timothy B. Krebs, "The Determinants of Candidates' Vote Share and the Advantages of Incumbency in City Council Elections," *American Journal of Political Science* 42, no. 3 (July 1998): 921–35, https://doi.org/10.2307/2991735.

41. Quoted in Richard R. Lau et al., "The Effects of Negative Political Advertisements: A Meta-Analytic Assessment," *American Political Science Review* 93, no. 4 (December 1999): 852, https://doi.org/10.2307/2586117.

42. Susan Fiske and Shelley Taylor, *Social Cognition: From Brains to Culture*, 3rd ed. (New York: Sage, 2017).

43. Richard R. Lau, Lee Sigelman, and Ivy Brown Rovner, "The Effects of Negative Political Campaigns: A Meta-Analytic Reassessment," *Journal of Politics* 69, no. 4 (November 2007): 1176–1209, https://doi.org/10.1111/j.1468-2508.2007.00618.x.

44. Andrew Daniller, "Two-Thirds of Americans Support Marijuana Legalization," Pew Research Center, November 14, 2019, www.pewresearch.org/fact-tank/2019/11/14/americans-support-marijuana-legalization (accessed 11/30/21).

45. D. Sunshine Hillygus and Todd G. Shields, *The Persuadable Voter: Strategic Candidates and Wedge Issues in Political Campaigns* (Princeton, NJ: Princeton University Press, 2007).

46. Alan S. Gerber et al., "How Large and Long-Lasting Are the Persuasive Effects of Televised Campaign Ads? Results from a Randomized Field Experiment," *American Political Science Review* 105, no. 1 (February 2011): 135–50, https://doi.org/10.1017/S000305541000047X.

47. Seth J. Hill et al., "The Duration of Advertising Effects in Political Campaigns" (paper presentation, Annual Meeting of the American Political Science Association, Chicago, IL, August 18, 2008). Also see John Sides and Lynn Vavreck, *The Gamble: Choice and Chance in the 2012 Presidential Election* (Princeton, NJ: Princeton University Press, 2013) and John Sides, Michael Tesler, and Lynn Vavreck, *Identity Crisis: The 2016 Presidential Campaign and the Battle for the Meaning of America* (Princeton, NJ: Princeton University Press, 2016).

48. Andrew Gelman and Gary King, "Why Are American Presidential Election Polls So Variable When Votes Are So Predictable?" *British Journal of Political Science* 23, no. 4 (October 1993): 409–51, https://doi.org/10.1017/S0007123400006682; Thomas M. Holbrook, *Do Campaigns Matter?* (Thousand Oaks, CA: Sage, 1996).

49. Lynn Vavreck, *The Message Matters: The Economy and Presidential Campaigns* (Princeton, NJ: Princeton University Press, 2009).

Credits

Chapter 1: **p. 5** AP Photo/Andrew Harnik, Pool; **p. 13** Mark Makela/Getty Images

Chapter 2: **p. 28** Mario Tama/Getty Images; **p. 29** Library of Congress; **p. 46** Gretchen Ertl/Reuters/Alamy

Chapter 3: **p. 62** Reid Wilson, "Why 2016 Will Be the Most Negative Campaign in History." *Morning Consult*, May 23, 2016, https://morningconsult.com/2016/05/23/2016-will -negative-campaign-history/. Reprinted with permission; **p. 70** Sarin Images/GRANGER—All rights reserved; **p. 71** GRANGER—All rights reserved; **p. 72** Library of Congress

Chapter 4: **p. 114** Mark Reinstein/Alamy Stock Photo; **p. 118** Drew Angerer/Getty Images

Chapter 5: **p. 139** C-Span/ZUMA Wire/Alamy Live News; **p. 151** Geopix/Alamy Stock Photo; **p. 158 (left)** AP Photo/Andrew Harnik; **p. 158 (right)** Chip Somodevilla/Getty Images

Chapter 6: **p. 166 (a)** Fox News/ZUMA Wire/Alamy Live News; **p. 166 (b)** Pictorial Press Ltd/Alamy Stock Photo; **p. 166 (c)** REUTERS/Kevin Lamarque/Alamy Stock Photo; **p. 166 (d)** C-Span/ZUMA Wire/Alamy Live News; **p. 183** Christopher Dolan/The Times & Tribune via AP Photo

Chapter 7: **p. 188** Melina Mara/The Washington Post via Getty Images; **p. 202** Daniel Acker/ Bloomberg via Getty Images

Chapter 8: **p. 228 (top)** © Fox News/ZUMA Wire/Alamy; **p. 228 (bottom)** Msnbc/ZUMA Wire/Alamy Live News

Chapter 9: **p. 242** © Pat A. Robinson; **p. 246** Matthew Healey/UPI/Alamy Live News; **p. 249** REUTERS/Kevin Lamarque/Alamy Stock Photo; **p. 269 (top)** Corbis via Getty Images; **p. 269 (bottom)** Kevin Dietsch/Pool via CNP/MediaPunch/Alamy Stock Photo

Chapter 10: **p. 280** Shutterstock; **p. 289** Patrick Cavan Brown/Alamy Stock Photo

Chapter 11: **p. 304** Reuters/Alamy Stock Photo; **p. 306** © Nikos Frazier—USA TODAY NETWORK; **p. 317** Dan Tian/Xinhua/Alamy Live News

Chapter 12: **p. 331** Gary Miller/Getty Images; **p. 339** REUTERS/Al Drago/Alamy Stock Photo; **p. 345** Imagespace/Alamy Live News/Alamy Stock Photo; **p. 352** Bob Daemmrich /Alamy Live News

Chapter 13: **p. 362** Pavlo Conchar/SOPA Images/LightRocket via Getty Images; **p. 375** Anthony Kwan/Bloomberg via Getty Images

Index